Lecture Notes in Computer Science 16470

Founding Editors

Gerhard Goos
Juris Hartmanis

Editorial Board Members

Elisa Bertino, *Purdue University, West Lafayette, IN, USA*
Wen Gao, *Peking University, Beijing, China*
Bernhard Steffen, *TU Dortmund University, Dortmund, Germany*
Moti Yung, *Columbia University, New York, NY, USA*

The series Lecture Notes in Computer Science (LNCS), including its subseries Lecture Notes in Artificial Intelligence (LNAI) and Lecture Notes in Bioinformatics (LNBI), has established itself as a medium for the publication of new developments in computer science and information technology research, teaching, and education.

LNCS enjoys close cooperation with the computer science R & D community, the series counts many renowned academics among its volume editors and paper authors, and collaborates with prestigious societies. Its mission is to serve this international community by providing an invaluable service, mainly focused on the publication of conference and workshop proceedings and postproceedings. LNCS commenced publication in 1973.

Maurice H. ter Beek · Stefania Gnesi ·
Anne E. Haxthausen · Laura Semini
Editors

Journeys Between Formal Methods and the Railway Industry

Essays Dedicated to Alessandro Fantechi
on the Occasion of His 70th Birthday

Editors
Maurice H. ter Beek
CNR-ISTI
Pisa, Italy

Stefania Gnesi
CNR-ISTI
Pisa, Italy

Anne E. Haxthausen
Technical University of Denmark
Lyngby, Denmark

Laura Semini
University of Pisa
Pisa, Italy

ISSN 0302-9743   ISSN 1611-3349 (electronic)
Lecture Notes in Computer Science
ISBN 978-3-032-12483-8   ISBN 978-3-032-12484-5 (eBook)
https://doi.org/10.1007/978-3-032-12484-5

© The Editor(s) (if applicable) and The Author(s), under exclusive license
to Springer Nature Switzerland AG 2026

This work is subject to copyright. All rights are solely and exclusively licensed by the Publisher, whether the whole or part of the material is concerned, specifically the rights of translation, reprinting, reuse of illustrations, recitation, broadcasting, reproduction on microfilms or in any other physical way, and transmission or information storage and retrieval, electronic adaptation, computer software, or by similar or dissimilar methodology now known or hereafter developed.
The use of general descriptive names, registered names, trademarks, service marks, etc. in this publication does not imply, even in the absence of a specific statement, that such names are exempt from the relevant protective laws and regulations and therefore free for general use.
The publisher, the authors and the editors are safe to assume that the advice and information in this book are believed to be true and accurate at the date of publication. Neither the publisher nor the authors or the editors give a warranty, expressed or implied, with respect to the material contained herein or for any errors or omissions that may have been made. The publisher remains neutral with regard to jurisdictional claims in published maps and institutional affiliations.

The cover illustration is the work of Eleonora Fantechi, Italy. Used with permission. It is based on a draft illustration by Alessandro Fantechi, Italy. Used without his permission because this Festschrift volume is a surprise for him.

This Springer imprint is published by the registered company Springer Nature Switzerland AG
The registered company address is: Gewerbestrasse 11, 6330 Cham, Switzerland

If disposing of this product, please recycle the paper.

Alessandro Fantechi – Summer 2025

Preface

This Festschrift contains 18 contributions by collaborators, colleagues and friends of Alessandro Fantechi to celebrate his 70th birthday.

Following a foreword that serves as a homage to Alessandro (Sandro for friends) and personal recollections from Alessandro's brother, these 18 contributions are grouped into three sections that reflect Alessandro's research, namely *journeys between formal methods and the railway industry*.

Each research contribution was carefully reviewed by two readers. We would like to thank these colleagues, all contributors to this Festschrift, listed below, for their assistance.

The Festschrift was presented to Alessandro on November 28, 2025, during an afternoon colloquium held in Pisa, Italy, succeeding the 6th International Conference on Reliability, Safety, and Security of Railway Systems (RSSRail 2025). We would like to thank the Scuola Normale Superiore (SNS), and in particular Fosca Giannotti, for hosting the Festschrift colloquium celebrating Alessandro, who's a former student of the SNS.

The cover illustration is the work of Eleonora Fantechi, used with her permission. It is based on a draft illustration by Alessandro Fantechi, used without his permission because this Festschrift volume was a surprise for him. The photograph of the honoree above was taken by Stefania Gnesi, used with permission.

Finally, we would like to thank Springer for agreeing to publish this Festschrift and we acknowledge the support from Easy-Chair in assisting us in managing the complete process from submissions to this volume.

November 2025

Maurice H. ter Beek
Stefania Gnesi
Anne E. Haxthausen
Laura Semini

Reviewers

Davide Basile	CNR–ISTI, Pisa, Italy
Maurice H. ter Beek	CNR–ISTI, Pisa, Italy
Cinzia Bernardeschi	University of Pisa, Italy
Antonia Bertolino	Gran Sasso Science Institute, L'Aquila, Italy
Giovanna Broccia	CNR–ISTI, Pisa, Italy
Antonio Bucchiarone	University of L'Aquila, Italy
Laura Carnevali	University of Florence, Italy
Vincenzo Ciancia	CNR–ISTI, Pisa, Italy
Alessandro Cimatti	FBK, Trento, Italy
Simon Collart Dutilleul	Gustave Eiffel University, Lille, France
Rocco De Nicola	CNR–IIT, Pisa, Italy, and Gran Sasso Science Institute, L'Aquila, Italy
Felicita Di Giandomenico	CNR–ISTI, Pisa, Italy
Alessio Ferrari	University College Dublin, Ireland, and CNR–ISTI, Pisa, Italy
Francesco Flammini	University of Florence, Italy, and University of Applied Sciences and Arts of Southern Switzerland, Lugano, Switzerland
Stefania Gnesi	CNR–ISTI, Pisa, Italy
Gloria Gori	University of Florence, Italy
Anne E. Haxthausen	Technical University of Denmark, Lyngby, Denmark
Paola Inverardi	Gran Sasso Science Institute, L'Aquila, Italy
Cosimo Laneve	University of Bologna, Italy
Diego Latella	formerly with CNR–ISTI, Pisa, Italy
Thierry Lecomte	CLEARSY, Aix-en-Provence, France
Michael Leuschel	Heinrich Heine University Düsseldorf, Germany
Christophe Limbrée	Infrabel, Brussels, Belgium
Gianluca Mandò	Hitachi Rail GTS, Florence, Italy
Tiziana Margaria	University of Limerick, Ireland
Mieke Massink	CNR–ISTI, Pisa, Italy
Radu Mateescu	Université Grenoble Alpes and Inria, Grenoble, France
Franco Mazzanti	CNR–ISTI, Pisa, Italy
Jan Peleska	University of Bremen, Germany
Alfonso Pierantonio	University of L'Aquila, Italy
Matteo Rossi	Polytechnic University of Milan, Italy
Laura Semini	University of Pisa, Italy

x   Reviewers

Giorgio Oronzo Spagnolo   CNR–ISTI, Pisa, Italy
Enrico Vicario   University of Florence, Italy
Valeria Vittorini   University of Naples Federico II, Italy

Foreword

Maurice H. ter Beek[1] , Stefania Gnesi[1] , Anne E. Haxthausen[2] ,
and Laura Semini[3]

[1] Formal Methods and Tools lab, CNR–ISTI, Pisa, Italy
`{maurice.terbeek,stefania.gnesi}@isti.cnr.it`
[2] Technical University of Denmark, Lyngby, Denmark
`aeha@dtu.dk`
[3] University of Pisa, Pisa, Italy
`laura.semini@unipi.it`

Sandro's research journey has reliably pursued a clear and coherent goal: rigorous modeling and analysis of challenging safety-critical systems, particularly in the railway domain, through the systematic development and application of formal methods and tools throughout the entire system's life cycle.

A significant portion of his work has been devoted to the application of formal methods for the formal verification of system properties by means of model checking. In this regard, his contributions to the railway sector have played a particularly prominent role, advancing the field both in theory and in practice.

Although verification has been a central focus of his research, Sandro has also shown a strong commitment to validation activities. He has proposed and evaluated approaches for both testing and runtime monitoring, always with a keen eye on their practical applicability in industrial settings. His work, especially in the context of safety-critical systems, stands out for its balance between scientific rigor and real-world relevance.

This Festschrift volume is a tribute to Sandro's scientific journey between formal methods and railway industry—marked by intellectual depth, methodological precision, and a constant drive to bridge academic research with practical challenges. It also reflects the respect and admiration of the many colleagues who have had the pleasure of working with him, learning from his insights, and sharing his passion for safety-critical (railway) systems.

Sandro has a unique talent for identifying what really matters in research, combined with a clear vision of how to achieve it. His ideas are truly innovative, frequently ahead of their time, and have often led to high-impact results.

But Sandro is more than a great researcher. He is a remarkable person: caring, generous, insightful and always a joy to be around. He is a wonderful colleague and friend. The four of us have had the privilege of collaborating with him for many years, and it has been a true pleasure to share not only a professional journey, but also a personal friendship. For this, we are deeply grateful. Working with him has been not only productive, but also personally rewarding.

Sandro, thank you for so many years of outstanding collaboration and friendship. Our warmest congratulations on your birthday and our very best wishes for a happy, healthy, and fulfilling journey ahead–may it always run on the right track!

Personal Recollections

Riccardo Fantechi[1,2]

[1] INFN Sezione di Pisa, Pisa, Italy
[2] CERN, Geneva, Switzerland
riccardo.fantechi@cern.ch

For this Festschrift for Alessandro, I would like to add some personal recollections. The title of this volume is "Journeys Between Formal Methods and the Railway Industry". I am not at all an expert on formal methods (my work as an experimental particle physicist many times is everything but formal $\cdots$), but I can offer a comment about Alessandro as a railway enthusiast, like myself: with a rough estimation, he and I have each travelled by train for a total distance of at least one one-way trip Earth–Moon.

I want then to outline the roots of both Alessandro's works in the Railway Industry and in Formal Methods.

In the sixties, it was very common for kids to have an electric train setup of some dimension. Following a gift from our grandfather, we started to develop our game setup with the support of our father who, with his ingenuity, prepared a removable plane with rails and a box with a transformer and a rectifier to power our locomotives. The plane usually stayed hidden in the closet and was deployed on our beds on rainy Sundays for some hours of playing.

Later, in early adolescence, with Alessandro's "leadership", we started to identify and classify with a "phenomenological approach" the coding of the various wagons (and in particular freight ones), visiting the freight yard in Florence or looking out of the windows during our frequent train journeys.

A little bit later, we started to play with electronics, again with the early trigger and support by our father. We built radios, amplifiers and other objects. In the early seventies we discovered digital electronics and built and debugged a digital frequency meter. Alessandro was more interested than me in digital logic and I can remember a lot of paper sheets with logic schematics, Karnaugh maps, truth tables and so on. The choice of the Computer Science faculty followed naturally.

I hope that these personal recollections will please Alessandro (he always says that I remember the past better than him) and I join the community saying: *Happy birthday Sandro!*

Contents

Railway Industry

Journeys

A Scientist Steadily Advancing Along the Tracks

Antonia Bertolino[1]([⊠]) , Rocco De Nicola[1,2]([⊠]) , and Paola Inverardi[1]([⊠])

[1] Gran Sasso Science Institute, L'Aquila, Italy
`antonia.bertolino@gssi.it` , `paola.inverardi@gssi.it`
[2] IIT—CNR, Pisa, Italy
`rocco.denicola@gssi.it`

Abstract. Three colleagues and friends retrace some stages of the long and prolific scientific career of Alessandro Fantechi.

Keywords: Ada · Formal Methods · Railway Systems · Temporal Logic · Validation

1 Introduction

All three of us have had the privilege of collaborating with Alessandro (or Sandro as we call him) during our professional careers. More than this, we are honored to count him among our friends and are happy to celebrate his seventieth birthday.

Fig. 1. Our mental image[1] of Sandro advancing science.

© The Author(s), under exclusive license to Springer Nature Switzerland AG 2026
M. H. ter Beek et al. (Eds.): Fantechi Festschrift, LNCS 16470, pp. 3–12, 2026.
https://doi.org/10.1007/978-3-032-12484-5_1

On this occasion, we briefly retrace some stages of his long and productive scientific career. Given his big passion for trains, which he largely manifests in his work, and in personal life as well, when thinking back to his scientific career, we naturally picture Sandro steadily advancing along the railway tracks: AI[1] helped us to visualize our mental image as in Fig. 1.

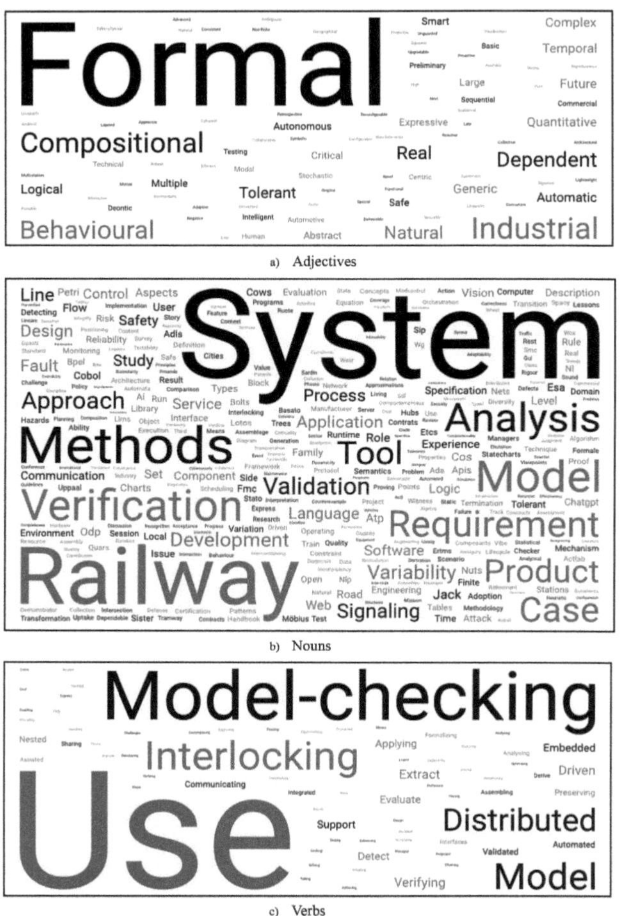

a) Adjectives

b) Nouns

c) Verbs

Fig. 2. Word clouds[2] of adjectives, nouns and verbs of Sandro's papers.

In the past decades, Sandro's research path has reliably taken a well-determined direction: the rigorous development of large critical systems, especially in the railways domain, through the application of formal methods all along

---

[1] For the image creation we used Gemini Nano Banana at https://gemini.google/it/ overview/image-generation/.

the life cycle [16, 21]. He has worked on the phase of requirements elicitation and analysis, on the definition of the software architecture, on the verification and validation stage, including model-checking and testing methods, and on facilitating the practical adoption of formal methods in industrial applications through his many collaborations with small and large companies.

From the titles of his publications, we derived three separate word clouds[2] for the adjectives, nouns, and verbs he used most frequently: these are shown in Fig. 2 a, b, and c, respectively. Among the adjectives, "formal" is the one clearly standing out; but also "compositional" and "industrial" are evidenced, to testify his continuous aim of making formal approaches applicable by devising compositional approaches. Among the names, "system" and "railway" are the most used in his titles, and we would have been surprised if this had not been the case. It is interesting to list the other emerging terms, more or less with same size: Analysis, Methods, Requirement, Model, Verification, Validation, Tool. As we anticipated, this clearly shows how the work of Sandro has embraced all steps of the life cycle. Finally, in the word cloud of verbs, we see a big "Use" to testify his firm intent of achieving results that can be used in practice; and of course the term "model-checking" predominates over others: Sandro is a renowned expert in model-checking approaches. Significant is also the emergence of "Interlocking", with reference to railway signalling systems on which he published extensively.

The long research journey of Sandro "along the tracks" has figuratively stopped at many "stations". In the following we recall briefly some of his contributions to the stations at which also our research paths have stopped.

2   Starting the Journey with Lady Lovelace

Sandro took his first steps in research with some of us during the first national project Informatica [22], led by Angelo Raffaele Meo. Ugo Montanari was leading the Computer Industry section of the project and Norma Lijtmaer was heading the sub-project Campus Net (CNet), in which the Pisa community was involved. Being part of the project was a great experience for all of us. At that time, in the early eighties, the entire Italian computer science community was involved in the project, allowing us, as young researchers, to interact and work with people from different backgrounds and education.

One core element of the CNet project was the use of the Ada language, which had just been released by the U.S. Department of Defense (DoD). The language was named in honor of Lady Ada Lovelace, Fig. 3, known as the first programmer for her work with the Analytical Engine, proposed by Charles Babbage as a first attempt of general-purpose computer.

Sandro was already involved in the use of Ada, in a European project PAPS (Portable Ada Programming System - 1981–82) [17] where he investigated the interrelationships among (M)APSE programs, the (K)APSE and the Ada run-time support. The Ada supporting environment was one of the first examples of the use of layered architectures to enable program portability.

---

[2] The world clouds have been created with WordArt from https://wordart.com/.

Together with Sandro and Norma Lijtmaer, the third author explored the use of Ada to model Local Computer Network Communication [20] aiming at exploiting the high level characteristics of the language to support what we can today imagine as a first attempt to use Ada as an Architectural Description Language (ADL).

Fig. 3. Ada Lovelace (Wikipedia, The Free Encyclopedia).

Sandro's journey with Ada continued, intersecting with formal methods and concurrency models. Together with colleagues—including Paola and under the supervision of Ugo Montanari—Sandro worked on the development of an execution environment for the Ada language based on its formal dynamic semantics. The approach was based on translating in Prolog the two-step semantics provided for Ada and based on the SMoLCS model, developed by Egidio Astesiano's group in Genova [1] to model the concurrent aspects of programming languages. The paper [18] was presented in the first European software engineering conference and represents a sort of summa of the research directions that shaped Sandro's career: formal methods, concurrency and software engineering.

These works represent the first station of Sandro's *track* record, many others followed.

3   The Formal Methods Station

A large part of Sandro's work has focused on the application of formal methods to the verification of system properties. The second author of this short contribution shares some responsibility for this work — including, perhaps, the application of formal methods to railway systems. Here, we will touch only on the beginnings of Sandro's journey with formal methods. Otherwise, we would have had to take on the role of the editors of this book, who surely have a chapter dedicated to all of Sandro's activities and certainly formal methods applied to railway systems have a major role. In fact, one of the first interactions Rocco and Sandro had (they were sharing a room at IEI - CNR in Pisa) was about the response Rocco had to write to an invited talk at the IFIP World Congress in 1986. The invited paper was on Petri Nets and Rocco wanted to advocate the use of Process Algebras for system specification as an alternative to Petri Nets. Well, a running example of the paper by Genrich [23] was about modelling two trains (A, B) moving on a circular track with six sections (see Fig. 4) while avoiding them to crash. After discussing with Sandro, the response paper [11] contained three specifications in CCS [24] of the train system at three different levels of abstraction. The remaining task was to prove either that the three systems were equivalent or that they satisfied a given logical specification.

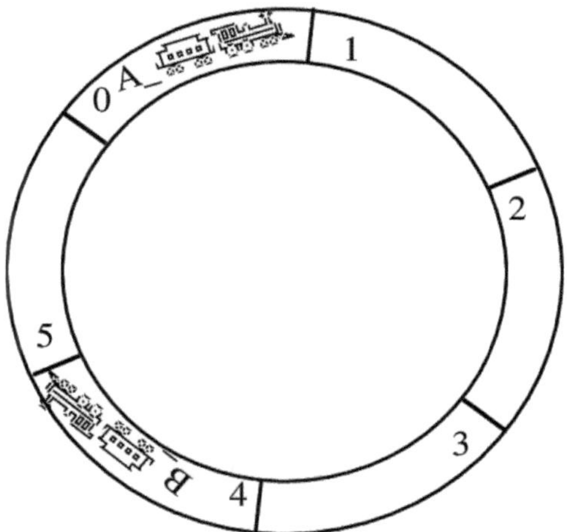

Fig. 4. A Circular Railway with 6 sections.

Shortly after this discussion, the second author, together with Frits Vaandrager from CWI Amsterdam, proposed ACTL, a temporal logic inspired by CTL [9]. ACTL is a temporal logic based on actions rather than on states and is interpreted over labelled transition systems, while CTL was interpreted over Kripke structures. It was proved that ACTL has essentially the same expressive power as CTL, making it sufficiently expressive to describe safety and liveness properties of reactive systems.

This was the start of a fruitful collaboration between the second author with Sandro, Stefania Gnesi, and a talented student, Gioia Ristori, who left us too early and whom we still miss. We worked on using ACTL to prove properties of systems and developed JACK (an acronym for Just Another Concurrency Kit), a workbench integrating a set of verification tools for concurrent system specifications, supported by a graphical interface that offered facilities for using these tools separately or in combination. In [12], JACK was used to formally specify the hardware components of a buffer system and to verify the correctness of the specification with respect to some safety requirements expressed in ACTL. In another work [13], we began considering Sandro's first love—railway systems—and analyzed a level crossing where a road intersects a railway line.

The tools we had been using were mainly those developed by others, so we started thinking about developing our own. We began working on a model checker for ACTL and found an effective integration approach. The integration was realized by means of two translation functions: one from the action-based branching time logic ACTL to CTL, another from transition-labelled to state-labelled structures. The correctness of the integration was guaranteed by proving that the two translation functions, when coupled, preserve satisfiability of logical formulae. These results were presented in [14], where the key example was exactly the train system shown in Fig. 4 which was taken from that work.

One issue with that model checker for ACTL was that, due to the two translations of models and formulae, it turned out to be difficult to provide counterexamples when the specified property was not satisfied. Recognizing this limitation, Sandro and the others, with new collaborators joining the effort, started working on developing a"direct" model checker for ACTL. They developed SAM [15], a symbolic model checker for ACTL that relies on implicit representations of Labelled Transition Systems (LTSs), the semantic domain for ACTL formulae, and uses symbolic manipulation algorithms. This direct approach enabled the generation of proper counterexamples.

Their work on model-checking tools and their application to system specification and verification have continued to evolve, with further enhancements including research on identifying ACTL formulae that admit linear counterexamples—particularly valuable for providing diagnostic information when verification fails. This research continues to this day, with Sandro remaining an active advocate for the use of formal methods in both industry and academia as evidenced by one of his most recent papers [7].

4   The Validation Station

Although Sandro's research has primarily focused on verification, he has also devoted large attention to validation activities, by proposing and evaluating approaches for both testing and monitoring, which are the main research interests of the first author. With Sandro, Antonia had a short but fruitful scientific collaboration in the area of Software Product Line (SPL) Engineering, and in particular in the context of the ITEA project CAFÈ in the first half of the 2000s, which was led in CNR by Stefania Gnesi. Over the years, and still today, Sandro has devoted a considerable interest to the specification of variability in SPLs, not surprisingly given the high industrial relevance of the topic. The project CAFÈ was titled "From Concept to Application in System Family Engineering", which well reflects Sandro's attitude. Together with Stefania, Giuseppe Lami and Alessandro Maccari, Sandro contributed to the project with PLUC, a notation for specifying SPL requirements [3], which extended the well-known structure of Cockburn's Use Cases [10] with more elements for expressing the variation points and the optional parts typical in SPLs. Then, in [2] our team showed how a PLUC use case effectively supports *i)* the derivation of compliant product instances called PUCs; and *ii)* the generation of test scenarios, both at family and product level, by taking into account the specified variabilities and commonalities.

Sandro has produced several other works in validation, consistently driven by concern for practical applicability in industrial contexts, particularly in systems with safety-critical requirements. An interesting line of work in testing is reported, among others, in [4–6]. The work was conducted as part of a long-term collaboration with General Electric Transportation Systems (GETS) in Florence, and was customized to their specific situation, constrained by severe safety regulations on the one side, and strict industrial policies on the other. The approach proposed by Sandro and co-authors departs from more traditional model-based testing papers, in which a set of test cases is first derived from a system model according to some method and is then executed on the final implemented system. Instead, they develop and evaluate a simulation-based testing methodology, in which an early validation of the system is achieved by simulating the execution of the test cases on a model that is reverse-engineered from the actual system documentation. They employ an original model extraction procedure generating a Simulink model that mimics the behaviour of the production target system, as ruled by the actual control tables used by GETS. As the authors report, the proposed approach could not avoid the final costly stage of executing the validation tests on the target. However, thanks to their method, GETS could early detect errors in the control tables or inaccuracies in the test suites. Moreover, the extracted model could introduce a form of redundancy with diversity in the validation process, and supported the application of formal verification techniques. As reported in [5], for the extracted model they developed an iterative verification process implementing slicing and CEGAR-like techniques, suitable for addressing the high complexity of the railway domain.

More recently, Sandro has also focused on the evaluation of the software reliability of complex systems [8, 19]. With co-authors, he proposed a compositional evaluation of reliability that allows the derivation of reliability curves for highly complex systems, by progressively decomposing them into independent subsystems. Then they also introduced the idea of a cost-effective predictive maintenance policy that is triggered by the reliability monitor.

Sandro's contribution to software validation constitutes a fine example of a solid, well-grounded approach to research: in all his papers at this station, he adopts a realistic perspective, acknowledging what can be achieved given practical constraints, while never sacrificing rigor and formality.

5   Concluding ... or Continuing the Journey?

As we have retraced some of the many stations along Sandro's research journey, a clear picture emerges: that of a scientist who has consistently pursued rigor and practical applicability with equal determination. His work has spanned the entire lifecycle of critical systems development, from requirement elicitation to validation, always keeping formal methods at the core of his approach. The railway metaphor we have used throughout this tribute is not merely coincidental. Just as trains reliably follow their tracks, guided by precise signaling systems and safety mechanisms, Sandro's research has followed a well-defined path: the rigorous development of dependable systems through formal methods. And just as railway systems require both theoretical understanding and practical engineering, his work has successfully bridged the gap between academic research and industrial application. Looking at the evolution of his contributions – from the early days of Ada, process algebras, and temporal logics, through the development of verification tools like JACK and SAM, to the more recent work on testing methodologies and reliability evaluation – we see a trajectory that has consistently addressed the needs of the formal methods community and of the practitioners who build safety-critical systems. What strikes us most about Sandro's career is not just the breadth of his technical contributions but also his ability to build lasting collaborations. The work we have described here has involved numerous colleagues and students over the decades, creating a network of researchers who continue to advance the field of formal methods.

Today, as formal methods continue to gain recognition as essential tools for developing trustworthy systems, especially in domains like autonomous vehicles, cyber-physical systems, and AI-based applications, Sandro's advocacy for their adoption becomes even more relevant. His recent work [7] on whether every computer scientist needs to know formal methods reflects his continued commitment to making these techniques accessible and demonstrating their practical value.

As we celebrate Sandro's seventieth birthday, we recognize that this is certainly not a conclusion, but rather a switch, like a train changing track while still progressing, along a journey that continues. The tracks extend forward and we are confident that Sandro will continue to advance science with the same rigor, passion, and dedication that have characterized his career so far. The railway systems he loves so much continue to evolve, presenting new challenges that will undoubtedly benefit from his expertise. Likewise, the formal methods community will continue to benefit from his contributions.

Dear Sandro, thank you for the journey we have shared with you, your friendship, and for showing how to advance science steadily along the tracks. We look forward to seeing you at many more stations!

References

1. Astesiano, E., Reggio, G.: The SMoLCS approach to the formal semantics of programming languages - a tutorial introduction. In: Habermann, A.N., Montanari, U. (eds.) Software Development and Ada, CRAI Workshop on Software Factories and Ada. Lecture Notes in Computer Science, vol. 275, pp. 81–116. Springer (1986)
2. Bertolino, A., Fantechi, A., Gnesi, S., Lami, G.: Product line use cases: scenario-based specification and testing of requirements. In: Käköla, T., Duenas, J.C. (eds.) Software Product Lines, pp. 425–445. Springer (2006). https://doi.org/10.1007/978-3-540-33253-4_11
3. Bertolino, A., Fantechi, A., Gnesi, S., Lami, G., Maccari, A.: Use case description of requirements for product lines. In: International Workshop on Requirements Engineering for Product Lines (REPL'02), pp. 12–18. IEEE (2002)
4. Bonacchi, A., Fantechi, A.: Validation of interlocking systems by testing their models. In: 2014 9th International Conference on the Quality of Information and Communications Technology, pp. 226–229. IEEE (2014)
5. Bonacchi, A., Fantechi, A., Bacherini, S., Tempestini, M.: Validation process for railway interlocking systems. Sci. Comput. Program. **128**, 2–21 (2016)
6. Bonacchi, A., Fantechi, A., Bacherini, S., Tempestini, M., Cipriani, L.: Validation of railway interlocking systems by formal verification, a case study. In: Revised Selected Papers of the SEFM 2013 Collocated Workshops on Software Engineering and Formal Methods vol. 8368, pp. 237–252. Springer-Verlag (2013). https://doi.org/10.1007/978-3-319-05032-4_18
7. Broy, M., et al.: Does every computer scientist need to know formal methods? Formal Aspects Comput. **37(1), 6: 1–6**, 17 (2025). https://doi.org/10.1145/3670795
8. Carnevali, L., Ciani, L., Fantechi, A., Papini, M.: A novel layered approach to evaluate reliability of complex systems. In: In: 2019 IEEE 5th International forum on Research and Technology for Society and Industry (RTSI), pp. 291–295. IEEE (2019)
9. Clarke, E.M., Emerson, E.A.: Design and synthesis of synchronization skeletons using branching-time temporal logic. In: Kozen, D. (ed.) Logics of Programs, Workshop, Yorktown Heights, New York, USA, May 1981. Lecture Notes in Computer Science, vol. 131, pp. 52–71. Springer (1981). https://doi.org/10.1007/BFB0025774
10. Cockburn, A., Cockburn, L.: Writing effective use cases. Pearson Education India (2008)
11. De Nicola, R.: Net theory and application - response. In: Kugler, H. (ed.) Information Processing 86, Proceedings of the IFIP 10th World Computer Congress, Dublin, Ireland, September 1-5, 1986, pp. 833–836. North-Holland/IFIP (1986)
12. De Nicola, R., Fantechi, A., Gnesi, S., Larosa, S., Ristori, G.: Verifying hardware components within JACK. In: Camurati, P., Eveking, H. (eds.) Correct Hardware Design and Verification Methods - CHARME '95. Lecture Notes in Computer Science, vol. 987, pp. 246–260. Springer (1995). https://doi.org/10.1007/3-540-60385-9_15
13. De Nicola, R., Fantechi, A., Gnesi, S., Ristori, G.: An action based framework for verifying logical and behavioural properties of concurrent systems. In: Larsen, K.G., Skou, A. (eds.) Computer Aided Verification, 3rd International Workshop, CAV '91. Lecture Notes in Computer Science, vol. 575, pp. 37–47. Springer (1991), https://doi.org/10.1007/3-540-55179-4_5
14. De Nicola, R., Fantechi, A., Gnesi, S., Ristori, G.: An action-based framework for verifying logical and behavioural properties of concurrent systems. Com-

put. Networks ISDN Syst. **25**(7), 761–778 (1993). https://doi.org/10.1016/0169-7552(93)90047-8

15. Fantechi, A., Gnesi, S., Mazzanti, F., Pugliese, R., Tronci, E.: A symbolic model checker for ACTL. In: Hutter, D., Stephan, W., Traverso, P., Ullmann, M. (eds.) Applied Formal Methods — FM-Trends 98, pp. 228–242. Springer (1999). https://doi.org/10.1007/3-540-48257-1_14

16. Fantechi, A.: Formal techniques for a data-driven certification of advanced railway signalling systems. In: International Workshop on Automated Verification of Critical Systems, pp. 231–245. Springer (2016)

17. Fantechi, A., Gallo, F.: Portable Ada programming system: a proposed run-time architecture. In: Fisher, G.A. (ed.) Proceedings of the AdaTEC Conference on Ada, 1982, pp. 48–56. ACM (1982). https://doi.org/10.1145/3304133.3304140

18. Fantechi, A., Gnesi, S., Inverardi, P., Montanari, U.: An executon environment for the formal definiton of Ada. In: Nichols, H.K., Simpson, D. (eds.) ESEC '87, 1st European Software Engineering Conference. Lecture Notes in Computer Science, vol. 289, pp. 327–335. Springer (1987). https://doi.org/10.1007/BFb0022125

19. Fantechi, A., Gori, G., Papini, M.: Software rejuvenation and runtime reliability monitoring. In: 2022 IEEE International Symposium on Software Reliability Engineering Workshops (ISSREW), pp. 162–169. IEEE (2022)

20. Fantechi, A., Inverardi, P., Lijtmaer, N.: Using high level languages for local computer network communication: a case study in Ada. Softw. Pract. Exp. **16**(8), 701–717 (1986)

21. Ferrari, A., Fantechi, A., Gnesi, S., Magnani, G.: Model-based development and formal methods in the railway industry. IEEE Softw. **30**(3), 28–34 (2013)

22. Gadducci, F.: Ugo Montanari and friends. In: Degano, P., De Nicola, R., Meseguer, J. (eds.) Concurrency, Graphs and Models. Lecture Notes in Computer Science, vol. 5065, pp. 743–746. Springer (2008). https://doi.org/10.1007/978-3-540-68679-8_45

23. Genrich, H.J.: Net theory and application (invited paper). In: Kugler, H. (ed.) Information Processing 86, Proceedings of the IFIP 10th World Computer Congress, Dublin, Ireland, September 1-5, 1986, pp. 823–832. North-Holland/IFIP (1986)

24. Milner, R.: A Calculus of Communicating Systems, Lecture Notes in Computer Science. Springer **92** (1980) https://doi.org/10.1007/3-540-10235-3

A Train to the OPERA

Roberto Cavada[1], Alessandro Cimatti[1] , Giuseppe Scaglione[2],
Angelo Susi[1(✉)] , and Matteo Tessi[2]

[1] Fondazione Bruno Kessler, Digital Industry Center, Trento, Italy
`{cavada,cimatti,susi}@fbk.eu`
[2] Rete Ferroviaria Italiana, Rome, Italy
`{g.scaglione,m.tessi}@rfi.it`

Abstract. Interlocking systems carry out the critical function of routing of trains throughout a station. In this paper, we discuss the research underlying the program to migrate the Italian Railway Network from legacy relay-based to software-based interlocking.

The long-term program tackles many challenges: dealing with legacy, relay-based intelockings; providing a solution amenable for domain experts; developing a unique, highly configurable framework for large-scale deployment.

The overarching ecosystem, called OPERA, relies on the adoption of controlled natural languages, model-based technologies, and formal verification. OPERA integrates five tools: AIDA, for interlocking procedures specification and code generation; TOSCA, for test case specification and generation; CARMEN, for formal verification; LUCIA, for the formalization of guideline documents; NORMA, for the specification and verification of relay-based interlocking.

Keywords: Railways Interlocking · Model-based Design · Automated Testing · Formal verification

1 Introduction

Most of the Italian railway stations are controlled by electromechanical Interlocking systems (*IxL*) based on relay technologies introduced in the '60s. Such systems suffer from a number of drawbacks. First, they are hard to modify and extend, and to adapt to changing railway standard. Second, the technology is expensive and potentially prone to physical faults. The designs are the result of both redundancies and optimizations, and are hence non-trivial to understand. Finally, relay *IxL* are based on legacy technology, that requires knowledge that is disappearing, superseded by more modern software-based control.

This paper is dedicated to Alessandro Fantechi, a pioneer in the application of formal methods to railways, who was working on model checking when we did not even know it existed. Your works have been a great inspiration.

© The Author(s), under exclusive license to Springer Nature Switzerland AG 2026
M. H. ter Beek et al. (Eds.): Fantechi Festschrift, LNCS 16470, pp. 13–30, 2026.
https://doi.org/10.1007/978-3-032-12484-5_2

In this paper, we describe a long term research program, started in 2017 by the Italian Railway Network company (RFI) together with Fondazione Bruno Kessler, to support the migration of current legacy relay-based *IxL* technology to modern, software based interlocking.

This initiative faced multiple challenges. The first is to provide a solution amenable for domain experts, so that the more advanced techniques blend with the traditional development process based on substantial background information and railways lingo. The second is to develop a highly configurable framework for large-scale deployment of new-generation control for more than 1500 stations. Finally, we must retain traceability with respect to the legacy, relay-based intelockings, a key difficulty being the semantic reconciliation of the computational models of relay circuits and software-based control systems.

In the rest of this paper, we present OPERA, an overarching framework designed to address the above challenges. In Sect. 2 we discuss the OPERA vision, the supported process and the high level structure of the integrated toolchain. In Sect. 3 we discuss LUCIA, a tool for the formalization of provisions and the extraction of test scenarios. In Sect. 4 we present NORMA, a tool for the formal modeling and analysis of relay circuits. In Sect. 5 we describe the representation and compilation of interlocking procedures in AIDA. In Sect. 6 we present the formal verification approach implemented in CARMEN. In Sect. 7 we discuss the approach to test case modeling and generation implemented in TOSCA. Section 8 reports relevant related works on requirements formalisation and system verification. In Sect. 9 we draw some conclusions and outline the directions for future work.

2   The OPERA Vision

OPERA is a long-term research and development programme, started in 2017, with the objective of specifying and implementing a methodology and related ecosystem of supporting tools covering all phases of the software engineering process for *IxL* systems. Specifically, the primary objective of the program is to tackle the challenges illustrated in the introduction, and to support railway experts covering different roles in the design and development process with a comprehensive methodology and tool ecosystem for the specification and verification of *IxL* systems.

This effort has been supported by a series of projects funded by Rete Ferroviaria Italiana. The activities were carried out with teams maintaining a close connection with domain experts, enabling continuous feedback on design and implementation choices throughout the process. The early adoption of the methodology and supporting tools also paved the way for new and unexpected research lines.

2.1   The OPERA Principles

OPERA is a model-based, tool-supported methodology for specifying, implementing, and verifying interlocking systems for the Italian Railway Network. Its aim is to ensure product standardisation, smooth specification of requirements, and automated code generation and verification of the system. It also supports a systematic strategy for migrating legacy relay systems to computer-based systems.

OPERA is based on some distinguishing features. First, it pervasively adopts Controlled Natural Language (CNL) to support railway experts, with a deep knowledge of regulations and provisions, in specifying interlocking procedures and test scenarios using their own language. The CNL is designed to be very close to the jargon used by domain experts while remaining unambiguous. Interestingly, the importance of Natural Language Processing in the railway domain is well established in the literature [17], touching different aspects of the development process, such as the extraction and representation of relevant properties or requirements contained in the domain documents, or the formalisation of the relevant documents into unambiguous languages to allow automated implementation and verification of the systems. Second, it relies on model-based design techniques to automatically generate SysML, documentation, formal models, test vectors and executable C/Python code from the CNL specifications, whilst ensuring full traceability between the artifacts at different abstraction layers. Third, the adopted process cleanly separates the general design principles and the concrete products, so that the resulting logic is generic, specified at the level of railway procedures rather than on a single specific railway plant. Finally, OPERA provides solutions to harmonize the current, legacy solutions with the newly developed ones. The approach includes, for example, the digitalisation of the schematics of relay circuits and the formalization of uncontrolled natural language provisions, in order to automate the extraction of test scenarios and properties.

2.2   The OPERA Process

OPERA proposes a methodology that aims at covering all phases of the design, development, verification, and testing of IxL systems. The approach intends to support the formalisation of railway regulations and relay schematics, the modelling of the specifications of the system, the automatic derivation of the control system, and the specification of the properties to be verified and of the test scenarios for the IxL system.

Figure 1 gives a high-level overview of the different parts of the methodology, processes, and supporting tools. The entire process can be summarized in four main steps. The formalisation of input documents related to the IxL system, including natural language specifications, topological and signalling data about railroad tracks and stations, is performed by experts. This is followed by the automated modelling of requirements, code generation, and code verification. Additionally, automated extraction and formalisation of legacy relay logics, represented as schematics, are carried out. Finally, the artefacts produced by these activities are utilised in analysis steps such as testing, simulation, and cross-validation.

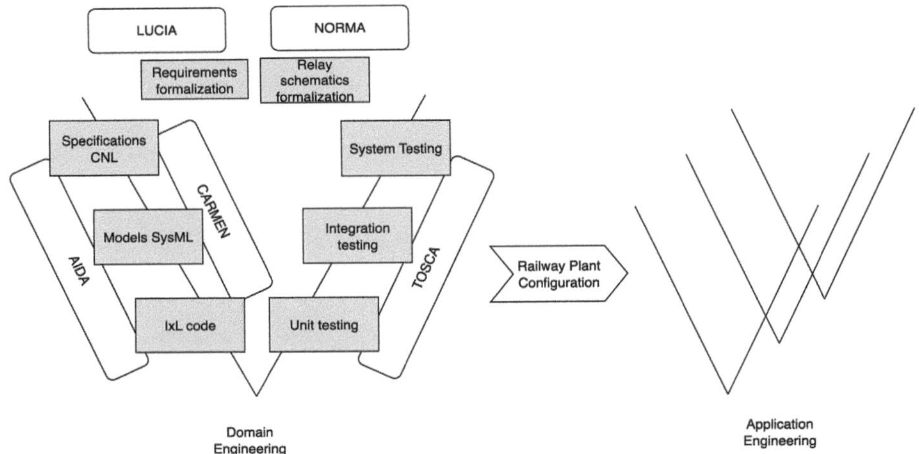

Fig. 1. The OPERA methodology and tools.

Given the parameterized nature of the *IxL* procedures, we adopted a double V model (W-model) [24], consisting of two phases: (1) Domain Engineering (Fig. 1, left) and (2) Application Engineering (right). During the Domain Engineering phase, the features of the domain are analyzed to identify the points of variability (e.g. the station topology, the possible train routes). Then, from the resulting requirements a generic logic is defined and implemented, producing parameterized artifacts that can be instantiated into specific applications through the definition of configurations. The testing activities during Domain Engineering (right side of the first "V") are carried out by applying component testing to the developed components, their integration, and to the platform. In the Application Engineering part, the specification, development and testing processes is followed multiple times, for each given Railway Plant Configuration: one Application Engineering "V" is followed for each instantiation of the generic system designed in the first "V".

2.3 The OPERA Toolset

The OPERA process is supported by an ecosystem made of five integrated tools (LUCIA, NORMA, AIDA, CARMEN and TOSCA), also outlined in Fig. 1, that implement the following features.

- LUCIA aims at the representation of provisions in CNL and their analysis to extract *IxL* specifications and related test scenarios.
- NORMA deals with the modeling and analysis of relay circuits. The NORMA front end allows the user to graphically represent and navigate relay schematics. NORMA implements various syntactic checks and the transformation of relay circuits into formal models. These are analayzed with model checking

techniques to collect sets of covering behaviors. Moreover, it supports the generation of test cases and the extraction of properties from circuits [2,6].

– AIDA supports the specification of interlocking procedures in a controlled natural language (CNL), and the related syntactic consistency checks, transformation from CNL to SysML specifications, generation of executable code in Python and C. It also supports the simulation and debugging environment [3].

– TOSCA supports the CNL specification of abstract test cases and instantiation in concrete test cases for given a specific configuration. TOSCA has an integrated test harness, to support the execution of test cases, and is able to automatically generate test reports. It also supports the automatic generation of test cases for coverage objectives [14].

In the following sections we give an overview of the different phases of the methodology and of the functionalities of the supporting tools.

3   LUCIA: IxL Provisions in CNL

Several works focused on the formalisation of requirements to obtain an unambiguous representation, in various critical areas such as control systems and cybersecurity in railways [9,19]. Our methodology adopts Controlled Natural Language to support the representation of the requirements, the specifications of the *IxL* system and its verification and testing phases.

Our work focuses on the requirements for the *IxL* systems that are extracted from railway domain documents, such as railway regulations, provisions, and diagrams describing the structure of a railway station. These documents are written in free natural language, which is inherently ambiguous and is heavily based on implicit knowledge held by railway experts. The methodology aims to translate this knowledge expressed in natural language and railway jargon into documents in a Controlled Natural Language (CNL).

The formalisation process is supported by the tool LUCIA. This tool enables railway experts to define the formalised set of provisions and regulations in CNL. This CNL is expressed in the same jargon but in a formal and unambiguous manner. The primary objective is to create a set of documents that can be completely understood by domain experts while also being automatically processed by algorithms to check various properties, such as avoiding contradictory specifications or ensuring completeness in the definition of regulations. Additionally, the formalisation supports the automatic or semi-automatic extraction of test scenarios, to be analysed and executed via the TOSCA tool. The goal is to define test suites that cover all the requirements contained within the formalised provisions and regulations. This aspect is particularly relevant for experts who are currently manually specifying set of test cases that aim at producing the same coverage. Moreover, LUCIA has also the objective of deriving properties to be formally verified on the *IxL* system via the CARMEN tool.

4   NORMA: Formalization of Relay IxL Systems

4.1   Relay-Based Interlocking

In traditional electromechanical *IxL*, an operator activates a route for a train entering or exiting the station, and the relay logic checks all the safety conditions, commands the required field devices like points and signals to the expected positions and aspects, and logically locks them to prevent all conflicting routes from being activated at the same time. As the train goes through the route, the freed track sections are unlocked to allow for safe activation of the other conflicting routes.

At the core of such interlocking systems are Relays, electromechanical components made by a coil, a magnetic core and one or more contacts. Each contact can be initially open or closed depending on relay configuration. When the coil is traversed by sufficient current, the core magnetizes and the state of all the contacts gets inverted: open contacts close, and closed contacts open. This new state is preserved until the current flow is interrupted, or until the next activation of the coil, depending on the type of the relay.

Relay-based *IxL* logics are composed relays, buttons, levers, switches, resistances, lamps, diodes, transformers, and other components electrically connected by wires to form circuits. Each circuit is associated with an interface composed of inputs and outputs. Inputs from the environment include field devices (e.g. track occupation signals) and operator devices (e.g. buttons or levers). Outputs to the environment to command the field devices (like the lamp of a signal or the motor of a switch) or to the operator (like a bulb that represents a signal light on the control panel). A circuit interface also includes the magnetic connections of relays, as inputs [outputs, resp.] from [to] the coils [contacts] of the other circuits.

A collection of circuits is concretely represented by relay diagrams whose symbols and syntax vary depending on the country where the *IxL* is installed. In Italy (Fig. 2) a component is a combination of one symbol, one or more electrical terminals and optional specifiers that specialize the behaviour of the component. Some types of components have an associated name and/or parameters (like the voltage for a generator). The combination of symbols, specifiers and parameters leads to more than 5000 components types which can be instantiated in a circuit. For example, there exist dozens of relay types which can be delayed or not (when activating, deactivating, or both), polarized or not, single or double coil, stabilized or not, etc. Furthermore, the circuits can be operating either with direct or alternate current, and discrete information (e.g. the maximum allowed train speed in a track segment) are encoded by means of frequency or amplitude modulation. There are a few more interesting characteristics of these domain-specific diagrams. (1) The diagrams are a logical representation of the circuits, as a relay coil and its contacts are positioned in the diagram according to their logical function (in contrast to their physical placement). The magnetic connections between coils and contacts are represented by naming conventions. (2) Units are a practical mechanism for reusing parts of a diagram. A unit is a set of circuits associated with a name and represents a generic functionality. Other circuits can refer to the components contained in a unit by using the same component names along with the unit name as namespace. For example, in Fig. 2, all contacts 'H' belong to the unit 'UGB92'.

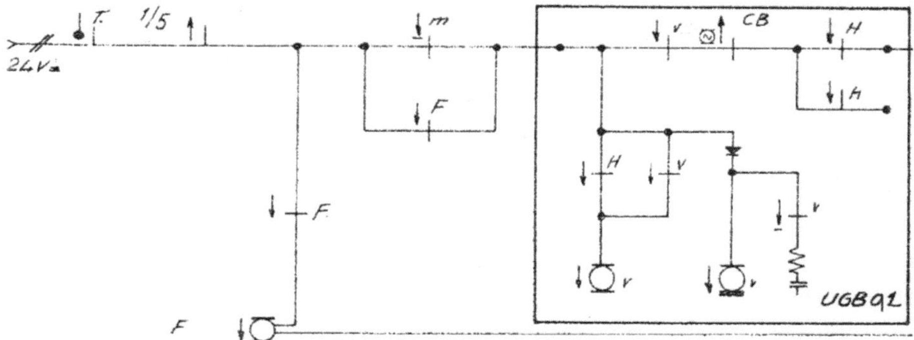

Fig. 2. Extract of diagram from Italian legacy relay logic.

4.2   Overview of NORMA

NORMA [2, 4] is a tool to formally model and analyze legacy *IxL* systems represented by relay circuit diagrams. In the scope of OPERA, the goal of NORMA is to support the understanding of the properties of the legacy *IxL* logics encoded as relay circuits.

The workflow is organized according to modeling, traceability and analysis. Modeling supports the modeler in the digitalization of circuit diagrams. The modeler can overlay the model of the circuits on the original diagram image, by selecting components from a palette, positioning them in the diagram, and connecting the component terminals by electrical wires. The modeling is supported by checkers that verify syntactic and semantic rules and report to the user any violations (e.g. dangling ports). Relay circuits can be abstracted by modeling *Stub* circuits interfaces and can specify behaviour of the corresponding signals. Stubs allows for partial modeling of circuits and for constraining the behaviour of the environment. Navigation and visualization functionalities allow the user inspect, search and highlight regions of the circuits. An ongoing activity is development of a (semi)automated digitalization process based on the use of AI-based techniques for detection and classification [27].

NORMA implements a semantic analysis based on model checking of user properties to help the understanding of the behaviour of the *IxL*, to validate the models against the expected behaviours, and to generate test cases.

NORMA supports traceability links between the created models and artifacts with the original diagrams and other regulatory documents. This allows for the use of coverage criteria of produced tests wrt the requirements of the *IxL*. The traceability between the circuits modeled in NORMA and the corresponding fragments in the AIDA logics are under development. The theoretical foundation is based on the identification of common abstractions that allow to harmonize the computational models of relays and cycle-based control [5,7,8]. The aim is to allow for automatic conversion of the tests and properties produced by NORMA into the corresponding tests for TOSCA and properties for CARMEN [6].

4.3   From Relay Circuits to SMV Models

Model checking relay circuits is a nontrivial task. NORMA implements a conversion from the representation resulting from the modeling activity into the SMV language processed by the nuXmv model checker. Before translating the network into SMV models, combinational loops due to the magnetic connections are found and removed by introducing delays. Then, a compiler transforms the internal model of the relay circuits into a formal model, by traversing the internal representation and substituting each component with a corresponding formal component taken from a SMV library of timed automata with real-valued variables.

The SMV library contains currently 41 modules to model parametric component types. Many components types in the palette of NORMA are modeled by a single SMV module thanks to the use of parameters that condition the internal behaviour. The electrical interface between SMV components follows the paradigm of Kirchhoff networks, so that each electrical connection of a terminal results in a pair of electrical variables representing, respectively, the current and the voltage at the terminal [12]. Then, the compiler composes the networks according to the electrical and magnetic logical connections, and injects and connects the stubs modeled by the user. The result of the compilation is an SMV model whose size is directly related to the size of the modeled circuits.

A subsequent simplification process is carried out by identifying equivalent signals and functionally dependent signals. In particular, when the properties of interest contain only references to discrete modes and the state of the relays, a large number of electrical variables can be eliminated. This step often results in dramatic reductions of the size of the generated SMV model.

5   AIDA: IxL Specification and Implementation

A second step in the process of formalization is the extraction and formalization of the Functional Requirements Specification (FRS) of the *IxL* system that is supported by the tool AIDA [3]. This document consists of a set of sheets, each one containing the definition of the structure and behavior of a Class of Logic. Each class describes elements of a railway system that are relevant for the *IxL*, such as the safety logics of physical devices (e.g. Railroad Switch, Train Track, different kinds of Signals), or the safety logics of higher level entities (e.g. Train Itinerary, Section Block). The specification of the FRS is currently performed by domain experts carrying out three main activities:

- Analysis of railway documents to identify relevant aspects and concepts.
- Describing the collection of classes using the CNL, a language closely related to the jargon of the domain, specifying the structure and behaviour of each class in a textual form.
- Definition of traceability links between the formalised railway documents originated from LUCIA and the resulting FRS.

One of the key aspects is guiding railway experts through every step of the process, particularly in specifying the FRS. To achieve this, a set of CNL patterns has been defined, analyzing specification documents produced by experts in previous projects. Each document describing a class comprises two main sections: one for defining the attributes of the class, and the other for describing its behaviour in terms of the states and transitions of the Finite State Machine (FSM).

The attributes of a class define the interface and the internal state of each class. The interface defines the inputs coming from the field devices and from the operator, the outputs for sending actuations to the field devices and information to the user interface, and the internal messages ("automatic commands") exchanged with the other classes. The internal attributes are configuration parameters, configured relations to other class instances, and variables. Functions are also supported in the form of macro definitions.

The FSM is described in CNL by the definition of the initial transitions and the description of each state along with the specification of all transitions exiting that state. Each transition in the FSM is described by a set of guards as triggering conditions, a set of effects that specifies the actions the class performs when taking that transition, and a priority.

An example of a transition is:

```
conditions: verify that the control Position is not equal to Normal
            verify that cdb is free and not locked
            verify that the timer TOWait is expired
...
effects: assign to control Position the value Normal
         activate the timer TOWait
```

Guards are expressed in terms of manual and automatic commands received by the FSM, and of the internal state (including visible state of linked instances and functional macros). Effects include state assignments (including accessible state of linked class instances), automatic commands, and invocation of procedural macros.

The approach supported by AIDA is based on three levels of abstraction, as shown in Fig. 3. The CNL specifications are automatically transformed into a SysML model, namely a Block Definition Diagram and a State Machine Diagram for each class of the logic. AIDA processes the SysML model and generates executable code and documentation. Python code is suitable for the debugging the logic, while the MISRA-C code is used for testing and for the deployment phase. Both the Python and C code and the associated schedulers are *generic*, i.e. they are suitable for any possible station compatible with the logic type. To instantiate and execute the logic of a specific station, a station *configuration* must be loaded at runtime in order to instantiate all required class instances, configure their parameters and link the related instances.

Finally, AIDA provides a runtime environment, a debugger and an execution environment with scripting capabilities to support testing of both the C and Python implementations.

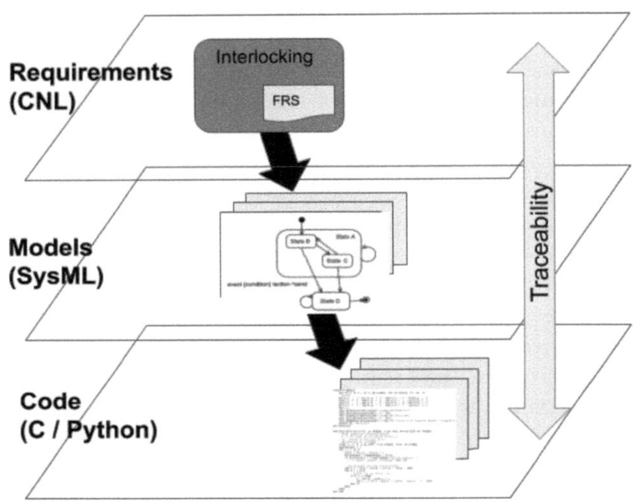

Fig. 3. The three levels development process in AIDA.

6   CARMEN: Formal Verification of IxL

Several works deal with the formalization and verification of properties of railways systems, e.g. [13,20–22,25]. The approach supported in CARMEN aims at verifying three different aspects of the specification and implementation of *IxL* systems:

Verification of Structural Properties of Components (SysML Level) supports local checks on the SysML state machines generated by the CNL translation. These checks verify structural properties independent of the application domain, such as the absence of deadlock states in state machines, mutual exclusion among transition guards, and the absence of unreachable states or transitions (due to tautological or contradictory guard combinations).

Verification of Properties of Abstract IxL Logic tackles the correctness of the interlocking logic independently of any specific configuration. Formally, it can be seen as a parametric verification problem, where each class of Logic corresponds to a different process type [10,11]

Verification of Properties of Generated C Code (Specific Station/Configuration)
checks the correctness of the automatically generated implementation of the *IxL*
logic for a specific station with respect to user-specified properties.

7   TOSCA: Testing the IxL

The test specification and execution process are guided by a methodology and
supported by the tool TOSCA [14] that enables testers to write test suites based
on the Railway *IxL* Regulations. These test suites contain abstract test scenarios
for the generic *IxL* system, avoiding specific entities of a particular railway plant.
Experts can specify test cases using a controlled natural language tailored to represent assumptions, assertions, and verification statements, which are common
components of test cases.

Abstract test cases can be instantiated for a specific plant configuration,
resulting in a set of concrete test cases that consider the actual entities of that
configuration. The concrete test cases are expressed in the same controlled natural language as that used for the abstract test cases.

For each abstract test case, TOSCA provides the tester with two options:
select a specific instantiation, such as a particular route, signal, or track circuit,
or generate all possible concrete and executable test cases that can be instantiated for the plant under test. The three main components characterizing a test
case are:

- *Assumption Statements*: Defines pre-conditions, in terms of boolean predicates, that must hold for the test execution to continue. Failure of the assumption means that the necessary pre-conditions for the test are not satisfied, and
  hence the outcome of the test is unknown.
- *Input Statements*: Defines input to the system in the form of railway operator
  commands or changes in the state of one or more entities within the railway
  plant.
- *Assertion Statements*: Defines boolean predicates similar to assumptions; in
  this case their failure results in a failure of the test (so indicating a deviation
  from the expected outcome defined by the domain expert).

Test cases in TOSCA are organised into test suites. A test suite is a set of
semantically related test cases that are defined within the same test file.

7.1   Abstract and Concrete Test Cases

Abstract test cases allow domain experts to define test cases independently of the
plant configuration. This enables the specification of test cases applicable to a
generic plant within the railway system. In abstract test cases, the various plant
elements are represented as abstract symbols (variables) rather than references to
actual instances in a specific plant. The TOSCA language provides a mechanism
for defining these variables and their subsequent use in test statements. Figure 4

```
Test case: "route activation"
Author: "RFI"

let mainRoute be a Route in the Station

initial state: PAD
step:
  assume that mainRoute is in the state Idle
step after 10 cycles:
  manual command Activation to mainRoute
step within 100 cycles:
  verify that mainRoute is in the state signalManuvered
```

Fig. 4. An example of an abstract test case whose objective is that of activating a route in a station.

shows an example of abstract test case. The structure of the test case follows the typical test case template with assumptions (the keyword `assume`), test inputs (the keyword `manual command`) and assertions (the keyword `verify`). The test is simply assuming that a route (called *mainRoute*) is initially not activated (in state *Idle*), an activation command is fired by an operator and after a given number of cycles of the logic the test checks if the *mainRoute* has been activated (so if it is in a state called *signalManuvered*). The TOSCA frontend supports type checking, type proposals, and other related checks to facilitate the editing of test cases by railway domain experts.

```
Test case: "route activation"
Author: "RFI"
Station: "Pesaro"

initial state: PAD
step:
  assume that Route "01-08D" of Pesaro is in the state Idle
step after 10 cycles:
  manual command Activation to Route "01-08D" of Pesaro
step within 100 cycles:
  verify that Route "01-08D" of Pesaro is in the state signalManuvered
```

Fig. 5. A concrete test case that is an instantiation of the abstract test case in Fig. 4 to a specific Railway Plant (Pesaro) and mainRoute (Route "01-08D").

Concrete test cases, on the other hand, allow for the definition of test cases for a specific plant so they refer to the entities that are described in the plant configuration. Unlike abstract test cases, concrete test cases do not involve abstract variables to refer to railway elements. Instead, they directly refer to the names of the entities in the specific railway plant for which the test case is being written.

Figure 5 illustrates a TOSCA concrete test case resulting from the instantiation of the abstract test case in Fig. 4 on the Station of Pesaro. In this case the variable *mainRoute* is instantiated into the specific *Route "01-08D"* in Pesaro.

7.2   Instantiation and Execution of Test Scenarios

TOSCA enables experts to complete the testing process by converting abstract test cases into concrete ones once a specific railway plant configuration is provided. In fact, the configuration contains the description of all the entities that are relevant to the *IxL* system of the specific railway plant. The instantiated test cases can be executed on the *IxL* system of the railway plant thanks to a test harness composed by two elements, gray in Fig. 6: the *Testing Agent*, which interprets the test case instructions and sends commands to the *IxL* and stimuli to the simulator to influence the status of the physical entities in the (simulated) railway plant, and the *Railway Plant Simulator*, which receives the stimuli from the *Testing Agent*, the commands from the *IxL* and reports the current status of the plant to the *IxL* system. In general, the two components of the test harness are responsible for managing the evolution of the actual *IxL* system.

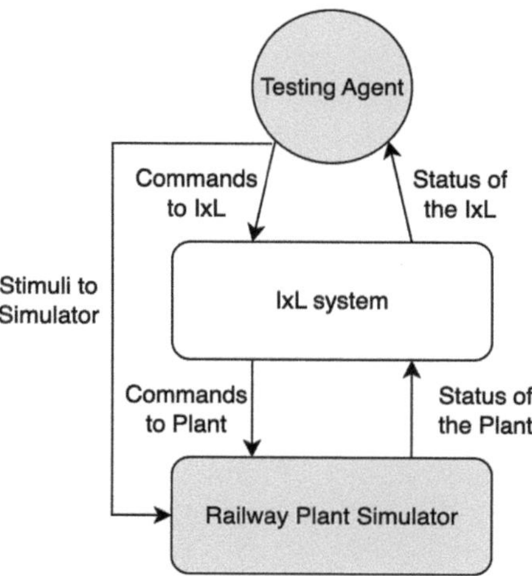

Fig. 6. The test harness for the *IxL* system composed by the *Testing Agent* and the *Railway Plant Simulator*.

The Test Agent reads the test case instructions and coordinates the evolution of the *IxL* system and the simulator during the test. The plant simulator interacts directly with the *IxL* Classes by providing inputs that match the outputs produced by the classes. For instance, if an *IxL* class controlling a railroad switch commands a change of direction for the formation of a route, the simulator captures the *IxL* output, simulates the physical change of the switch direction, and returns the appropriate values to the *IxL*. This setup enables a closed-loop execution, where all inputs to the *IxL* are defined and controllable, so ensuring the full reproducibility of the test cases.

8   Related Works

Several works in the literature focused on the different aspects of the development methodologies and supporting tools for critical systems and for specifically railway applications. Here we report on related works that inspired the development of our methodology focusing on the aspects related to the formalisation of the requirements and the verification and testing of the systems.

Use of Natural Language in Requirements Formalisation. A crucial aspect of designing critical systems is establishing an unambiguous set of requirements. This can be achieved by formalising the requirements to support clear and unambiguous semantics. The FRETISH methodology, and the related tool FRET, proposes a structured natural language that incorporates features recognized in the practice of several projects in NASA applications [19]. The underlying semantics of the language is determined by the types of four fields in which the requirements are expressed: scope, condition, timing, and response. Each combination of field types defines a requirement template with Real-Time Graphical Interval Logic (RTGIL) semantics. Other efforts have also been made in the same direction in the critical area of control systems and security for railway applications as described, for example, in [9] where AI and natural language techniques are used to formalize railway cybersecurity requirements.

System Verification and Testing. A large investigation on the use of formal methods is presented in [16]. A set of 328 relevant primary studies is identified, and the information is extracted about their demographics, the characteristics of formal methods used and railway-specific aspects. This study is a basis for future studies on the application of formal techniques and on their evaluation in context of the railway domain. In [18] a formal modeling approach for the control of railway switches within the ETCS-L3 framework is described. Specifically, it focuses on the control logic of railway switches, capturing the behavior of the point control subsystem and leveraging various modeling approaches such as SysML for the system representation, Stochastic Activity Networks, to model behaviors, and Event-B to support the verification of properties. The switch control models address various operational scenarios, including normal operations, failure modes, and recovery procedures. Results show that formal methods can significantly improve the robustness of railway switch systems, thereby contributing to safer and more efficient railway networks. The work [15] proposes a safety strategy which uses functional specification of the existing train normative documents, Subset 26 and Subset 125, in the case of low traffic railway lines. A methodological objective is to enrich the existing autonomous train protection level, providing a global software framework from the specification to a formally proved Event-B model that can be used in a certified framework to produce executable code. The methodology aims at considering new requirements for these railways using a model-based approach that generates new specific proof obligations in the Event-B model of a system graphically specified using SysML/KAOS for modelling requirements and an extension of SysML to represent High Level Architectures (HLA), called HLA/SysML. A study on the application of ERTMS to design of the railway control systems is presented [23]. ERTMS is quite difficult to implement and deploy. The specification, expressed in the form of thematic SUBSETS, gives a direction but leaves a great deal of freedom to manufacturers. The work described as some of the formal verification and validation methods, including formal modelling, automatic proof and model-checking, that are being used today to improve the confidence level of actual deployments.

Formalization and validation of Legacy or Relay Schemes. The application of Formal techniques to relay systems described in [1] has the objective of monitoring the legacy relay-based RIS to improve their safety during their execution. The strategy is to describe the system safety properties using logic and then implement it in an industrial tool, the CLEARSY Safety Platform (CSSP), which in turn is responsible for monitoring the system components to ensure its correct functioning and raise flags when an unsafe state is found.

9   Conclusions and Future Work

In this paper we described OPERA, an overarching framework for the development and verification of interlocking systems. OPERA is based on the following key concepts. First, it adopts controlled natural language to support domain experts in precisely modeling high-level properties, interlocking procedures and testing scenarios. Second, it leverages a W-model, separating domain engineering and application engineering, to provide means for the large-scale deployment of a single solution on many different configurations. Model based design techniques are used to help the domain expert in writing high-quality textual descriptions, and to automatically generate both abstract test scenarios, concrete test cases, properties and code. Finally, it supports extended verification capabilities including simulation and formal verification to prove properties at different levels of abstraction.

In the future, we plan to work along the following directions. On the one side, we will work on the formalization of a large body of regulation documents and of relay-based circuits schematics. On the formal verification side, additional efforts are needed to increase the automation of the engines, to make the techniques more directly available to the domain experts, and to integrate the produced artifacts into the certification process [26].

Upcoming activities are related to the possibility of using various forms of generative AI to complement the work of the domain experts. On the one side, we aim at reasoning on railway documents by way of LLMs, to automatically extract formalised provisions and relevant properties, or to automatically generate test scenarios. On the other side, we will investigate AI-based techniques to extract digital representations of the legacy relay schematics [27].

Acknowledgments. We would like to thank the research programs promoted by Rete Ferroviaria Italiana, and the many colleagues who contributed to this research program: Arturo Amendola, Alessandro Arenella, Anna Becchi, Leonardo Collizzolli, Luca Cristoforetti, Alberto Griggio, Shaker Khandaker, Fitsum Kifetew, Pietro Lechthaler, Christian Lidström, Davide Prandi, Gianluca Redondi, Sergio Repetto, Mirko Sessa, Dylan Trenti.

References

1. de Almeida Pereira, D.I., Jamain, F., Lecomte, T.: Formal analysis and monitoring of legacy safety-critical interlocking systems with the use of certified industrial tools. In: Haxthausen, A.E., Serwe, W. (eds.) 29th International Conference on Formal Methods for Industrial Critical Systems, FMICS 2024. LNCS, Proceedings, Milan, Italy, 9–11 September 2024, vol. 14952, pp. 182–198. Springer, Cham (2024). https://doi.org/10.1007/978-3-031-68150-9_11
2. Amendola, A., et al.: NORMA: a tool for the analysis of relay-based railway interlocking systems (2022). https://doi.org/10.1007/978-3-030-99524-9_7
3. Amendola, A., et al.: A model-based approach to the design, verification and deployment of railway interlocking system. In: Margaria, T., Steffen, B. (eds.) ISoLA 2020. LNCS, vol. 12478, pp. 240–254. Springer, Cham (2020). https://doi.org/10.1007/978-3-030-61467-6_16
4. Becchi, A., Cimatti, A.: Abstraction modulo stability for reverse engineering. In: CAV 2022. LNCS, vol. 13371, pp. 469–489. Springer, Cham (2022). https://doi.org/10.1007/978-3-031-13185-1_23
5. Becchi, A., Cimatti, A.: Abstraction modulo stability. Formal Meth. Syst. Des. **66**(2), 134–169 (2025)
6. Becchi, A., Cimatti, A., Scaglione, G.: Testing the migration from analog to software-based railway interlocking systems. In: CAV 2024. LNCS, vol. 14682, pp. 219–232. Springer, Cham (2024). https://doi.org/10.1007/978-3-031-65630-9_11
7. Becchi, A., Cimatti, A., Zaffanella, E.: Reverse engineering with p-stable abstractions. In: OVERLAY@GandALF. CEUR Workshop Proceedings, vol. 2987, pp. 91–95. CEUR-WS.org (2021)
8. Becchi, A., Cimatti, A., Zaffanella, E.: P-stable abstractions of hybrid systems. Softw. Syst. Model. **23**(2), 403–426 (2024)
9. ter Beek, M.H., Fantechi, A., Gnesi, S., Lenzini, G., Petrocchi, M.: Can AI help with the formalization of railway cybersecurity requirements? In: Margaria, T., Steffen, B. (eds.) 12th International Symposium on Leveraging Applications of Formal Methods, Verification and Validation. REoCAS, Colloquium in Honor of Rocco De Nicola, ISoLA 2024. LNCS, Proceedings, Part I, Crete, Greece, 27–31 October 2024, vol. 15219, pp. 186–203. Springer, Cham (2024). https://doi.org/10.1007/978-3-031-73709-1_12
10. Cavada, R., et al.: Automated parameterized verification of a railway protection system with Dafny. In: CAV 2025. LNCS, vol. 15934, pp. 364–376. Springer, Cham (2025). https://doi.org/10.1007/978-3-031-98685-7_17
11. Cavada, R., et al.: Formal analysis of a railway signaling block designed in AIDA. In: ter Beek, M.H., Collart-Dutilleul, S., Lecomte, T. (eds.) Reliability, Safety, and Security of Railway Systems. Modelling, Analysis, Verification, and Certification, pp. 303–312. Springer, Cham (2026). https://doi.org/10.1007/978-3-032-10762-6_23

12. Cavada, R., Cimatti, A., Mover, S., Sessa, M., Cadavero, G., Scaglione, G.: Analysis of relay interlocking systems via SMT-based model checking of switched multi-domain Kirchhoff networks. In: Bjørner, N., Gurfinkel, A. (eds.) 2018 Formal Methods in Computer Aided Design, FMCAD 2018, Austin, TX, USA, 30 October–2 November 2018, pp. 1–9. IEEE (2018). https://doi.org/10.23919/FMCAD.2018.8603007

13. Cimatti, A., Griggio, A., Redondi, G.: Verification of SMT systems with quantifiers. In: ATVA 2022. LNCS, vol. 13505, pp. 154–170. Springer, Cham (2022). https://doi.org/10.1007/978-3-031-19992-9_10

14. Cimatti, A., et al.: Model-based testing of railway interlocking systems. In: Margaria, T., Steffen, B. (eds.) 12th International Symposium on Leveraging Applications of Formal Methods, Verification and Validation. Application Areas, ISoLA 2024. LNCS, Proceedings, Part V, Crete, Greece, 27–31 October 2024, vol. 15223, pp. 112–126. Springer, Cham (2024). https://doi.org/10.1007/978-3-031-75390-9_8

15. Dutilleul, S.C., Bon, P., Laleau, R.: Securing automatic small railway vehicles using automatic train protection. In: Margaria, T., Steffen, B. (eds.) 12th International Symposium on Leveraging Applications of Formal Methods, Verification and Validation. Application Areas, ISoLA 2024. LNCS, Proceedings, Part V, Crete, Greece, 27–31 October 2024, vol. 15223, pp. 159–173. Springer, Cham (2024). https://doi.org/10.1007/978-3-031-75390-9_11

16. Ferrari, A., ter Beek, M.H.: Formal methods in railways: a systematic mapping study. ACM Comput. Surv. **55**(4), 69:1–69:37 (2023). https://doi.org/10.1145/3520480

17. Ferrari, A., et al.: Detecting requirements defects with NLP patterns: an industrial experience in the railway domain. Empir. Softw. Eng. **23**(6), 3684–3733 (2018). https://doi.org/10.1007/s10664-018-9596-7

18. Flammini, F., et al.: Railway switch control modeling in European train control system level 3. In: Margaria, T., Steffen, B. (eds.) 12th International Symposium ON Leveraging Applications of Formal Methods, Verification and Validation. Application Areas, ISoLA 2024. LNCS, Proceedings, Part V, Crete, Greece, 27–31 October 2024, vol. 15223, pp. 174–189. Springer, Cham (2024). https://doi.org/10.1007/978-3-031-75390-9_12

19. Giannakopoulou, D., Pressburger, T., Mavridou, A., Schumann, J.: Automated formalization of structured natural language requirements. Inf. Softw. Technol. **137**, 106590 (2021). https://doi.org/10.1016/J.INFSOF.2021.106590

20. Haxthausen, A.E., Fantechi, A., Gori, G., Mikkelsen, Ó.K., Petersen, S.A.: Automated compositional verification of interlocking systems. In: Milius, B., Collart-Dutilleul, S., Lecomte, T. (eds.) Reliability, Safety, and Security of Railway Systems. Modelling, Analysis, Verification, and Certification, pp. 146–164. Springer, Cham (2023). https://doi.org/10.1007/978-3-031-43366-5_9

21. Haxthausen, A.E., Peleska, J., Pinger, R.: Applied bounded model checking for interlocking system designs. In: Counsell, S., Núñez, M. (eds.) Softw. Eng. Formal Meth., pp. 205–220. Springer, Cham (2014)

22. Haxthausen, A.E., Fantechi, A.: Compositional verification of railway interlocking systems. Formal Aspects Comput. **35**(1), 4:1–4:46 (2023). https://doi.org/10.1145/3549736

23. Lecomte, T.: Formal validation and ERTMS simulation. In: Margaria, T., Steffen, B. (eds.) Leveraging Applications of Formal Methods, Verification and Validation. Application Areas - 12th International Symposium, ISoLA 2024. LNCS, Proceed-

ings, Part V, Crete, Greece, 27–31 October 2024, vol. 15223, pp. 142–158. Springer, Cham (2024). https://doi.org/10.1007/978-3-031-75390-9_10
24. Li, J., Li, Q., Li, J.: The w-model for testing software product lines. In: ISCSCT 2008, pp. 690–693. IEEE Computer Society (2008)
25. Limbrée, C., Haxthausen, A.E., Gori, G., Fantechi, A.: Formal verification of railway interlockings: a compositional approach based on a library of pre-verified components. In: Margaria, T., Steffen, B. (eds.) 12th International Symposium on Leveraging Applications of Formal Methods, Verification and Validation. Application Areas, ISoLA 2024. LNCS, Proceedings, Part V, Crete, Greece, 27–31 October 2024, vol. 15223, pp. 127–141. Springer, Cham (2024). https://doi.org/10.1007/978-3-031-75390-9_9
26. Sindoni, G., et al.: A theorem prover based approach for sat-based model checking certification. In: CADE. LNCS, vol. 15943, pp. 449–467. Springer, Heidelberg (2025)
27. Stefenon, S.F., Cristoforetti, M., Cimatti, A.: Automatic digitalization of railway interlocking systems engineering drawings based on hybrid machine learning methods. Exp. Syst. Appl. **281**, 127532 (2025). https://doi.org/10.1016/J.ESWA.2025.127532

Formal Methods for Railway Systems: A Survey of Research and Technology Transfer Projects

Davide Basile[1], Maurice H. ter Beek[1], Giovanna Broccia[1],
Stefania Gnesi[1], Franco Mazzanti[1], Giorgio Oronzo Spagnolo[1],
Stefano Bacherini[3], Carlo Becheri[3], Daniele Grasso[4], Gianluca Magnani[3],
Matteo Tempestini[3], Niccolò Zingoni[3], and Alessio Ferrari[1,2]

[1] Formal Methods and Tools Lab, CNR–ISTI, Pisa, Italy
`{davide.basile,maurice.terbeek,giovanna.broccia,stefania.gnesi,`
`franco.mazzanti,spagnolo}@isti.cnr.it, alessio.ferrari@ucd.ie`
[2] School of Computer Science, University College Dublin, Dublin, Ireland
[3] Alstom Ferroviaria S.p.A., Firenze, Italy
`{stefano.bacherini,carlo.becheri,gianluca.magnani,matteo.tempestini,`
`niccolo.zingoni}@alstomgroup.com`
[4] Digitense S.r.l., Firenze, Italy
`danielegrasso@digitense.it`

Abstract. This paper offers a retrospective on collaborative projects that involved Alessandro Fantechi and the authors over the past two decades, from the shared perspective of the Formal Methods and Tools (FMT) lab of the Italian National Research Council (CNR) and former collaborators at General Electric (GE) Transportation and Alstom. The focus is on research and technology transfer efforts in the field of formal methods for railway systems, where Alessandro Fantechi's contributions have been central to the development and application of formal specification, model-based verification, and tool-supported analysis. Joint work in projects such as ASTRail, 4SECURail, and TRACE-IT, as well as in industrial collaborations with Alstom and GE Transportation Systems illustrates the sustained impact of these activities on both academic research and industrial practice. This contribution reflects on the evolution of these efforts, the formal methods adopted, and the outcomes achieved in terms of methodologies, tools, and integration into safety-critical development processes. It also highlights the collaborative environment fostered across institutions and organizations, which has been instrumental in advancing the use of formal methods in the railway domain.

Keywords: Formal Methods · Railways · Model-based Development

© The Author(s), under exclusive license to Springer Nature Switzerland AG 2026
M. H. ter Beek et al. (Eds.): Fantechi Festschrift, LNCS 16470, pp. 31–54, 2026.
https://doi.org/10.1007/978-3-032-12484-5_3

1   Introduction

Alessandro Fantechi is well recognized as one of the foremost experts on the application of formal methods (FMs) and tools to railway systems [31,51–53, 55]. He is the most cited researcher in Scopus when searching for publications on "formal method" and "railway". He is member of the steering committee of the dedicated conference series RSSRail on *Reliability, Safety, and Security of Railway Systems: Modelling, Analysis, Verification, and Certification.*

Alessandro is an authority in the field of FMs [40] and member of the board of the ERCIM Working Group on Formal Methods for Industrial Critical Systems (FMICS), which organises a dedicated annual conference for three decades now.[1]

Alessandro's involvement in the railway industry is also witnessed by the numerous collaborations he has had with the main companies in this sector, such as Ansaldo Ferroviaria, Alstom Ferroviaria, General Electric (GE) Transportation Systems, SIRTI s.p.a., and others. Alessandro Fantechi is also a member of the Strategic Technological Steering Committee (STSC) of DITECFER S.c.ar.l (an acronym for "District for Railway Technologies, High Speed, Network, Safety & Security"), whose objective is to promote collaboration, innovation, research and development among its members to make them more competitive and support integrated internationalization in foreign markets.

Arguably the first applications of FMs and tools to railway designs in which Alessandro was involved concern two exemplary cases. In both cases, a CCS dialect is used to model the example, ACTL—an action-based extension of CTL [48,49]—is used to specify the logical properties to be verified, and EMC— the first model checker developed by E.M. Clarke et al. [43,44]—is used to perform the formal verification. In [46], a road crossing a railway is modeled and both safety ("it never happens that both a car and a train are able to cross") and liveness ("whenever a train (a car) approaches, it eventually crosses") properties are model checked. In [47], a circular railway, divided into six track sections, with two trains is modeled and the property "it never happens that both trains are running on the same track section" is model checked.

In the context of industrial collaborations, which have characterized Alessandro's career, one of his first experiences of applying FMs and tools to railway systems concerns the formal verification of a computer-based interlocking system provided by the Italian railway company Ansaldo Trasporti. The system was modeled in CCS and a number of safety properties expressed in ACTL were verified using the ACTL model checker AMC developed at CNR [6,36]. This experience was followed a few years later by related experiences on the specification and validation of fault-tolerance mechanisms for safety-critical systems, among which a railway interlocking system, inside the EU project GUARDS [35], and by a number of other national and international projects dedicated to the railway domain, discussed in more detail in the remainder of this paper.

---

[1] https://fmics.inria.fr/.

Outline In Sect. 2, we discuss some of Alessandro Fantechi's aforementioned collaborations with the Railway industry. In Sect. 3, we describe the regional project TRACE-IT. In Sects. 4 and 5, we describe the EU H2020 projects ASTRail and 4SECURail, financed under the Shift2Rail initiative. In Sect. 6, we describe the regional project STINGRAY. In Sect. 7, we describe the NextGenerationEU project MOST (National Center for Sustainable Mobility), Spoke 4: Rail Transportation, financed under the Italian National Recovery and Resilience Plan (PNRR). Section 8 provides a summary of contributions and lessons learned, while Sect. 9 concludes the paper.

2   GE and Alstom Collaborations

Alessandro Fantechi has collaborated extensively with railway signaling manufacturers, including General Electric (GE) Transportation Systems and Alstom Ferroviaria (now part of Alstom), on projects involving FMs, model-based development, and requirements analysis in safety-critical railway systems. These collaborations span interlocking systems, automatic train protection (ATP) systems, and the detection of defects in requirements documents. The projects emphasize the adoption of formal modeling and verification techniques, such as SDL (Specification and Description Language), Statecharts, model-based testing, abstract interpretation, and natural language processing (NLP) for requirements quality assurance.

Early work with industry explored modeling choices for complex interlockings, contrasting "geographical" vs. "functional" Statechart decomposition and its impact on understandability and reuse [10]. In parallel, a component-oriented SDL specification—explicitly based on an interlocking model from GE—was validated using MSC-driven techniques and coverage criteria [9]. A companion experience report describes the overall adoption path of FMs in a signaling manufacturer, detailing drivers like European standards and process constraints [8]. Foundational background on distributed interlocking modeling and the role of FMs is reported in [11]. A broader experience report in [8] detailed the adoption of FMs at GE, including SDL-based modeling of interlocking systems. External factors like European regulations (e.g., EN 50128) and university collaborations drove the choice of notations and tools, leading to internal acceptance.

A later collaboration with GE's Safety & Validation group engineered a *model-extraction* pipeline from delivered interlocking logic: the extracted model is (1) executed against planned test suites to accelerate fault finding and reduce target testing cost, and (2) formally verified with an iterative process combining slicing and CEGAR-like refinement to tame complexity [38]. A short, practice-oriented precursor shows how exercising the extracted model enables order-of-magnitude faster feedback than on-target tests [37].

The Metrô Rio ATP case study in [61] applied Simulink/Stateflow for on-board equipment development. A two-phase verification approach (model-based testing and abstract interpretation) ensured functional correctness and runtime error freedom, with formal verification as a side activity. Results showed reduced bugs and verification costs. Reference [62] reported restructuring unit-level verification at GE from code-based to model-based testing plus abstract interpretation, achieving 70% cost reduction and improved bug detection on two case studies. Complementing this, a set of guidelines codified modeling rules aimed at *qualified code generation* in the railway domain, explicitly contextualized at GE and their ATP products [57]. In [58], lessons from adopting formal model-based design at GE were reviewed. Challenges included defining a safe subset of Simulink/Stateflow, ensuring code-model conformance via back-to-back testing, and integrating with EN 50128 processes. Incremental refinements across projects enhanced safety and cost-effectiveness. A final magazine publication summarizing all these experiences was published in IEEE Software [59].

Recent work addressed requirements quality in the railway domain using NLP techniques. With Rosadini et al. [72] and Ferrari et al. [60], Fantechi applied NLP patterns with the GATE tool to detect defects in 1866 requirements from a railway signaling manufacturer (likely GE/Alstom context). Patterns identified vagueness, optionality, and other issues, complemented by the SREE tool for ambiguity detection. The study highlighted discrepancies between manual and NLP-based analysis, suggesting hybrid approaches for industrial use. Although not strictly FM studies, these works focus on preparatory activities in requirements, which are needed for later translation into formal logic expression, an area that is seeing an increasing interest thanks to recent developments in Large Language Models (LLMs) [66].

Across two decades, these collaborations demonstrate how FMs and model-based techniques were concretely *embedded in industrial practice*:

- For **interlockings**, the pathway led from exploratory modeling choices and SDL validation with GE artefacts [9,10] to *scalable validation processes* that extract models from logic and leverage testing and model checking [37,38].
- For **ATPs**, the emphasis was on *process integration*: safe modeling subsets, evidence of model–code conformance, and certification-friendly workflows [57, 58], supported by a published product case [61].
- For **requirements**, the Alstom collaboration shows the feasibility and limits of NLP-based defect detection at scale, and how results feed back into both tools and company practices [60].

3   TRACE-IT

TRACE-IT (Train Control Enhancement via Information Technology) was a 4-year project started in 2011, funded by the Tuscany Region. It was coordinated by ECM (now Caterpillar) with the participation of CNR and the University of Florence. The project's objective was the development of an ATP system and an Automatic Train Control (ATC) system based on ERTMS/ETCS levels 2 and 3, and an innovative Communication Based Train Control System (CBTC).

The involvement of CNR–ISTI in the project centered around the development of a demonstrator of the ATC system integrating the ECM components with a custom Automatic Train Supervision (ARS) system based on a specific railway layout selected as case study (cf. Fig. 1).

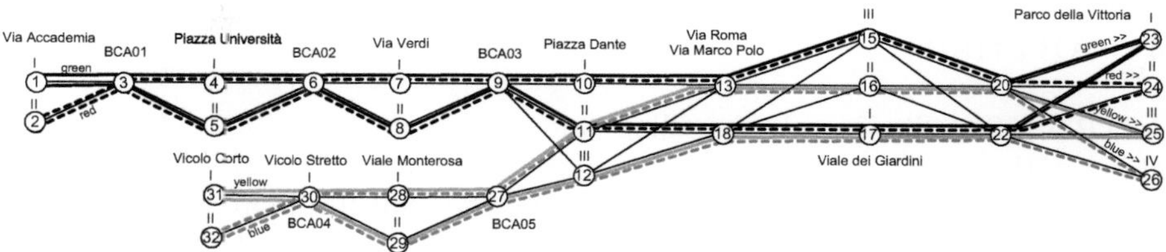

Fig. 1. The railway layout user for the case study (from [71]).

The case study used for the demonstrator was supposed to model a CBTC-based metro system, in which 8 trains have the mission to safely and continuously loop in the system. The developed ATS system was not concerned with modeling specific timetables at the various stations, but focused on the more challenging problem of defining a strategy for avoiding deadlocks in the system and on formally proving its correctness [70]. The formal proof was achieved by modeling the layout and the strategy with the UMC tool, and using the UMC on-the-fly model-checking features to prove the absence of (partial) deadlocks (i.e., it never happens that a train is no longer able to continue its mission).

The strict collaboration between academia and the industrial partner has been very productive for increasing the awareness of CNR–ISTI concerning railway-related topics, and for increasing the awareness of the industrial partner towards advanced methods of system modeling, analysis and verification.

From the point of view of CNR–ISTI, the selected case study has been the starting point for further studies on formal methods diversity. After the project, in fact, at CNR–ISTI, we performed the experiment of modeling and verifying the same TRACE-IT case study using nine other different formal methods approaches [68,69] (SPIN, NuSMV, mCRL2, CPN, FDR4, CADP, TLA+, ProB, and UPPAAL). This complex experiment has been useful for better understanding the position of our UMC tool in the context of the state of the art of formal modeling and verification, and for gaining valuable knowledge of the advantages and difficulties of the various frameworks. This acquired knowledge proved to be very useful in enriching the CNR's participation in other projects.

The TRACE-IT project also produced other outputs focused on CBTC. Specifically, in [65], a global model for CBTC systems was developed by combining semi-formal modeling with product line engineering, based on a comprehensive market analysis. The methodology enabled the derivation of novel CBTC products and system requirements for individual components. Scenario-based requirements elicitation, supported by rapid prototyping, was employed, with requirements written in constrained natural language (CNL) and evaluated using NLP techniques to enhance quality. The approach aimed toward formal requirements representation and was applied to derive a novel CBTC architecture and a prototype tool showcased in collaboration with ECM, the company involved in the project, demonstrating practical implementation.

4 ASTRail

ASTRail (SAtellite-based Signalling and Automation SysTems on Railways along with Formal Method and Moving Block validation) [74] was a 2-year project funded by the European Union under the Shift2Rail initiative, started in 2017 and coordinated by ISMB, with the participation of SIRTI S.p.A., Ardanuy Ingenieria, ENAC, UNIFE, and CNR–ISTI. The involvement of CNR–ISTI centered on review and assessment of the main formal modeling and verification languages and tools used in the railway domain, with the aim of evaluating the actual applicability of the most promising ones to a moving block signaling system model provided by an industrial partner. This has been achieved in four steps:

1. A survey on the state of art on the use of FMs in Railways;
2. Experimentations of an extensive set of FM tools and systematic evaluation;
3. A trial application of a moving block system with a short list of tools;
4. A final validation of the designs of the moving block and the ATO system.

The first two steps involved a detailed study of the state-of-the-art, by scrutinizing the existing literature, performing surveys, observing recent projects, and carrying out a set of experimentations with a list of 14 candidate methods and tools to get first-hand experience concerning their usability, availability and efficacy (cf. Fig. 2). These studies have been published in [7,28,56,63,64].

The last two steps have been performed by developing and modeling the system requirements starting from descriptions in the form of UML statecharts. A short list of frameworks (Simulink, UMC, and ProB) has been used to get a feeling of three different kinds of approaches: fully industrial (Simulink), experimental academic (UMC), and mature academic (ProB). The moving block system was also formalized and analyzed using UPPAAL and the original Simulink design, and the results have been published in [12,15,16].

The result of the survey and classification of the state-of-the-art in the application of FMs in the railway sector has been very successful and has been cited and referred to by many studies on the use of FMs.

The first-hand modeling with the final three selected frameworks has allowed us to experience directly the actual importance of standard (framework-independent) notations like UML, and the importance of simulation and animation, at different levels of abstraction, to achieve a deep understanding of the system behavior. The formal verification of the systems has proved useful to get a more complete picture of the system under development, but at a much higher cost and requiring particularly well-trained personnel.

As the modeled systems are just academic case studies and not parts of any real industrial product, the impact of the formal experimentation on the actual software development process of the industrial partner has not gone beyond an increased awareness of the potentialities of FMs.

5   4SECURail

4SECURail (Formal methods and CSIRT for the railway sector) [4,73] was a 2-year project funded by the European Union under the Shift2Rail initiative, started in 2019 and coordinated by Ardanuy Ingegneria S.A. The project had two completely independent objectives, involving different and non-interacting teams. A first activity, led by Hit Rail B.V. with the collaboration of UIC and Tree Technology, was targeted at the design and delivery of a prototype of "Computer Security Incident Response Team" (CSIRT). A second activity, led by CNR–ISTI with the collaboration of SIRTI (later MerMec STE) and Fit Consulting, had as objective the setup of a FMs Demonstrator for the evaluation, in terms of costs, benefits and required learning curve, of the impact of the use of FMs for the rigorous specification of the components of railway signaling infrastructures.

At the European level, the importance of a set of rigorous railway standards like UNISIG, ERTMS, and EULYNX to guide the development of a common european railway infrastructure is well recognized. Railway standards are however written in natural language, often with the support of UML-like statechart images to highlight the main state transition concepts of the protocols, and this leaves spaces to potential ambiguities, incompleteness, and inconsistencies. It is therefore of high interest to evaluate how the introduction of FMs might be of help in the strengthening of the standards, and at what cost.

It is important to observe that the focus of CNR's activity, in which Alessandro Fantechi was involved, was the evaluation of the introduction of FMs from the point of view of the infrastructure managers, interested in the definition of high-quality standards, and only secondarily to the point of view of the system providers, potentially interested in the rigorous development of commercial products conforming to the standards or, more specifically, conforming to some custom developed system requirements specification.

In more detail, the "FMs Demonstrator" activity started with the definition of the tools and methodologies to be used, as described in [1,14]. UML/SysML was selected as the starting point notation for the construction of an operational model of the system under specification. Indeed UML fragments often appear inside the standard documents, and UML has been often used as a starting point for formal analysis [14,41,45,50,67]. For this reason, UML/SYSML may play the role of a bridge between for the formal and industrial world.

The tool UMC[2] was selected for initial fast prototyping of the systems and for their formal analysis. UMC is an open-access, open-source, UML-based model checker developed at CNR–ISTI that had already been used in other railway related projects. The developed UML models were translated also in the formal

---

[2] http://fmt.isti.cnr.it/kandisti/.

Category	Name	SPIN	Simulink	nuXmv	ProB	AtelierB	UPPAAL	SCADE	FDR4	CPN Tools	CADP	mCRL2	SAL	TLA+	UMC
Development Functionalities	Specification/ Modeling	TEXT	GRA	TEXTIN	TEXT	TEXT	GRA	GRA	TEXTIN	GRA	TEXTIN	TEXT	TEXTIN	TEXT	TEXT
	Code Generation	NO	YES	NO	NO	YES	NO	YES	NO	NO	YES	NO	NO	NO	NO
	Document / Report Generation	PARTIAL	YES	NO	PARTIAL	PARTIAL	PARTIAL	YES	PARTIAL	PARTIAL	PARTIAL	PARTIAL	NO	NO	PARTIAL
	Requirements Traceability	NO	YES	NO	NO	NO	NO	YES	NO	NO	NO	NO	NO	NO	NO
	Model refinement	NO	YES	NO	YES	YES	NO	YES	YES	NO	NO	NO	NO	NO	NO
Verification Functionalities	Simulation	TEX	GRA	TEX	MIX	NO	GRA	GRA	TEX	GRA	TEX	TEX	TEX	NO	TEX
	Supported problem size	LARGE	LIMITED	LARGE	MEDIUM	MEDIUM	MEDIUM	LIMITED	LARGE	LIMITED	LARGE	MEDIUM	LARGE	MEDIUM	MEDIUM
	Formal Verification	MC-L	MC-I	MC-L,MC-B	MC-L,MC-B, TP, RF	TP, RF	MC-L	MC-I	RF	MC-B	MC-B	MC-B	MC-L, TP	MC-L, TP	MC-B
	Model-based Testing	NO	YES	NO	YES	NO	NO	YES	NO	NO	YES	NO	YES	NO	NO
	Time related properties	NO	YES	YES	NO	NO	YES	YES	YES	YES	NO	YES	YES	NO	NO
	Probability properties	NO	NO	NO	NO	NO	YES	NO	NO	NO	NO	NO	NO	NO	NO
Language Expressiveness	Nondeterminism	INT	EXT	INT,EXT	INT,EXT	INT,EXT	INT	EXT	INT,EXT	INT	INT,EXT	INT,EXT	INT,EXT	INT	INT
	Concurrency	ASYNCH	NO	SYNCH	NO	NO	SYNCH	SYNCH	ASYNCH	ASYNCH	ASYNCH	ASYNCH	ASYNCH, SYNCH	ASYNCH	ASYNCH, SYNCH
	Temporal Aspects	NO	YES	NO	NO	NO	YES	YES	YES	YES	NO	NO	YES	NO	NO
	Probability	NO	NO	NO	NO	NO	YES	NO	NO	NO	NO	NO	NO	NO	NO
	Language Modularity	HIGH	HIGH	MEDIUM	LOW	LOW	MEDIUM	HIGH	HIGH	HIGH	HIGH	LOW	MEDIUM	MEDIUM	HIGH
	Supported Data Structures	BASIC	COMPLEX	BASIC	COMPLEX	COMPLEX	COMPLEX	COMPLEX	COMPLEX	COMPLEX	COMPLEX	COMPLEX	COMPLEX	COMPLEX	COMPLEX
Tool Flexibility	Backward Compatibility	LIKELY	LIKELY	LIKELY	LIKELY	MODERATE	LIKELY	LIKELY	MODERATE	LIKELY	LIKELY	LIKELY	MODERATE	MODERATE	MODERATE
	Standard Input Format	YES	PARTIAL	YES	YES	YES	PARTIAL	PARTIAL	YES	PARTIAL	YES	YES	YES	YES	YES
	Import/Export	MEDIUM	LOW	MEDIUM	HIGH	MEDIUM	LOW	LOW	MEDIUM	MEDIUM	HIGH	HIGH	MEDIUM	LOW	LOW
	Modularity of the Tool	LOW	HIGH	LOW	LOW	MEDIUM	LOW	HIGH	LOW	LOW	LOW	LOW	LOW	LOW	LOW
	Team Support	NO	NO	NO	NO	YES	NO	NO	NO	NO	NO	NO	NO	NO	NO
Maturity	Industrial Diffusion	MEDIUM	HIGH	MEDIUM	RAILWAY	RAILWAY	MEDIUM	RAILWAY	LOW	MEDIUM	MEDIUM	LOW	LOW	MEDIUM	NO
	Stage of Development	YES	YES	YES	YES	YES	YES	YES	YES	YES	YES	YES	YES	YES	NO
Usability	Customer Support	PARTIAL	YES	PARTIAL	YES	YES	YES	YES	PARTIAL	PARTIAL	PARTIAL	PARTIAL	PARTIAL	PARTIAL	PARTIAL
	Graphical User Interface	LIMITED	YES	NO	PARTIAL	PARTIAL	PARTIAL	YES	LIMITED	PARTIAL	LIMITED	LIMITED	NO	LIMITED	PARTIAL
	Easy to Use	MEDIUM	BASIC	MEDIUM	MEDIUM	ADVANCED	MEDIUM	BASIC	MEDIUM	MEDIUM	ADVANCED	ADVANCED	ADVANCED	ADVANCED	MEDIUM
	Quality of Documentation	GOOD	EXCELLENT	GOOD	GOOD	EXCELLENT	GOOD	EXCELLENT	EXCELLENT	GOOD	GOOD	GOOD	GOOD	GOOD	LIMITED
Company Constraints	Cost	FREE	PAY	MIX	FREE	FREE	MIX	PAY	MIX	FREE	MIX	FREE	FREE	FREE	FREE
	Supported Platforms	Windows, Linux, macOS	Windows, Linux, macOS	Windows, Linux, macOS	Windows, Linux, macOS	Windows, Linux, macOS	Windows, Linux, macOS	Windows	Windows, Linux, macOS	Windows	Windows, Linux, macOS	Windows, Linux, macOS	Windows, Linux, macOS	Windows, Linux, macOS	Windows, Linux, macOS
	Complexity of License Management	EASY	ADEQUATE	EASY	EASY	EASY	MODERATE	ADEQUATE	MODERATE	EASY	MODERATE	EASY	EASY	EASY	EASY
	Easy to Install	YES	YES	YES	YES	YES	YES	YES	YES	YES	PARTIAL	YES	YES	YES	YES
Railway specific Criteria	CENELEC Certification	NO	PARTIAL	NO	NO	NO	NO	YES	NO	NO	NO	NO	NO	NO	NO
	Integration into the CENELEC Process	MEDIUM	YES	MEDIUM	YES	YES	MEDIUM	YES	MEDIUM	MEDIUM	MEDIUM	LOW	LOW	LOW	LOW
		SPIN	Simulink	nuXmv	ProB	AtelierB	UPPAAL	SCADE	FDR4	CPN Tools	CADP	mCRL2	SAL	TLA+	UMC

Fig. 2. The ASTRail tool evaluation table (from [7]).

notations used by ProB and CADP/LNT to achieve a more complete and mature analysis of the systems. A partial effort has also been made on the use of the same UML models as a starting point for an industrial model-based framework (Sparx EA) to experiment a possible point of view from the developer side [2,25,26].

The overall impact of the formal modeling approach confirmed (cf. [2,3]) the actual usefulness of FMs for the identification of inconsistencies, missing points, and ambiguities in initial natural language requirements, has allowed to gain deeper insights on the intended system evolutions, and has allowed the generation or more robust specification documents [33] (cf. Fig. 3).

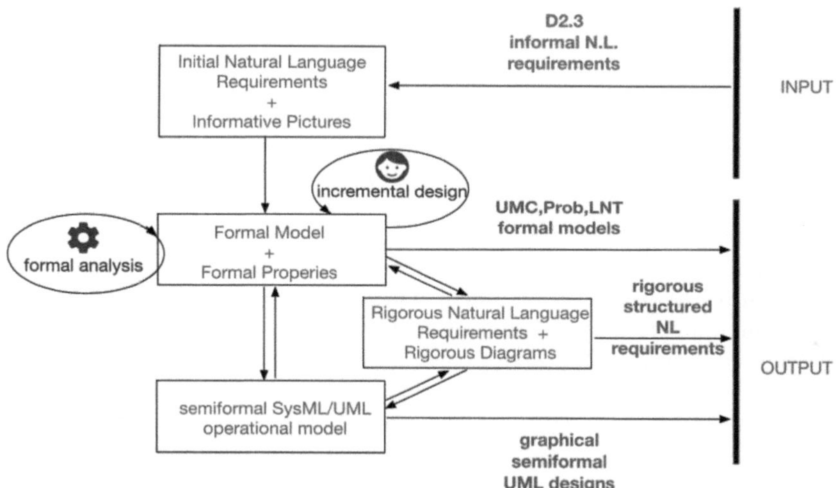

Fig. 3. The 4SECURail formal modelling process (from [4]).

The cost/benefit analysis [5,32] provided a rare insight on the economic impact of the introduction of FMs in the process of system requirements definition, both in terms of investments (CAPEX) and operational costs (OPEX) and confirmed the economic advantages of the approach.

The formal modeling experiment was conducted on a fragment of the so-called RBC/RBC handover protocols, following a case study selected by SIRTI [3] based on the standards UNISIG SUB-039 and SUB-098, and all the generated UMC, Prob, and LNT models have been made publicly available [26,67].

Another output in which Alessandro Fantechi has been involved, was to use the tool UPPAAL to model and analyze the case study of the 4SECURail project [24]. This work involved an M.Sc. student at the University of Florence, trained in FMs in a postgraduate course at the University of Florence, taught by Alessandro Fantechi. The output of this analysis has been used as input to the cost and benefit analysis phase, as well as uncovering issues in the standards UNISIG SUB-039 and SUB-098, thereby showcasing the efficacy of the application of FMs to a railway industrial project.

From the academic point of view the project was quite successful. Its results were presented in several venues, stimulating the implementation of several ideas for improving the UMC verification framework, and raising many points worthwhile of further studies. Among the points that would need further investigation, it is worth mentioning a reasonably clear and tool-supported formal semantics for simple UML/SYSML designs, the relation between abstract requirements, system requirements, and operational models, the possible integration of model-driven frameworks with formal verification frameworks, and the construction of bridges among different verification frameworks to enable the exploitation of their diversity to achieve a more complete and user friendly analysis of a system.

6   STINGRAY

STINGRAY (SmarT station INtelliGent RAilwaY was a 2-year project, started in 2018, funded by the Tuscany Region. It was coordinated by ECM with the participation of CNR and the University of Florence. STINGRAY addressed the role of the railway station, traditionally seen as a meeting point for a city, to enhance its importance and integration into the smart city of the future.

Although railway stations are a central hub of the city, a primary point of aggregation in the urban environment, they traditionally have a private energy distribution and communication system. The main reasons for this are to ensure uninterrupted power supply and security, but this isolation has two main drawbacks. First, it prohibits integration with "smart cities", in which, ideally, information between different transport systems (i.e., bike sharing, car sharing, urban transport) is synergically exploited. Second, the station system fails to benefit from modern energy-saving techniques.

To this aim, the design and development of a station communication infrastructure was studied, integrating powerline and wireless technologies (cf. Fig. 4). Powerlines are utilized to enable a more efficient management of machinery and energetic resources. The concrete goals of the project were:

1. To realise a LAN over the station plants using power line and wireless technologies;
2. To allow control and monitoring of station equipment via Supervisory Control And Data Acquisition (SCADA), in particular railroad switch heaters;
3. To create value-added services for both customers and railway staff, such as connectivity, monitoring fault prediction service (FPS), video surveillance, environmental surveying and integration and access to so-called smart city infomobility services, in particular the energy management service (EMS);
4. To optimize existing strategies for managing energy consumption within the station, to avoid wasting energy.

The case studies of STINGRAY provided by the industrial partners from the railway domain concerned station lighting and the heating of the railroad switches in ice conditions.

Railroad switch heaters assure correct working of switches in case of ice and snow through a central control unit in charge of managing policies of energy consumption while satisfying reliability constraints. Although apparently a rather focused system, with restricted functionalities, it represents very well the peculiarities of a cyber-physical system: physical components (the heater), cyber components (the heating policies and the related coordinator), stochastic aspects (failure events and weather forecasts), and logical/physical dependencies. The adopted policy of energy consumption was an on/off strategy based on temperature thresholds (both for turning off and on the energy).

In [13], Fantechi et al. addressed the railroad switch heaters case study. It was modeled and analyzed with stochastic activity networks (SAN) and Möbius on the one hand and with stochastic hybrid automata (SHA) and UPPAAL SMC on the other hand, followed by a comparison of the two methodologies.

The system was initially modeled and analyzed in [17–19,23] using Möbius and SAN. It was assumed that heaters have different priorities in accessing the energy resources, and the energy consumption policy was tuned to adapt both to the different priorities of the heaters and to the different periods of the day. The model was equipped with a logical part, representing the energy consumption policy, and a physical part, modeling temperature behavior and weather.

In [22], the same system was modeled and analyzed with UPPAAL SMC and SHA. Temporal logic was used instead of Markov reward models to capture the measures of interest, namely energy consumption and probability of failure. The logic of the energy policy was verified in [21] against the progress of interactions, to prevent deadlocks in communications between the different components.

The two formalizations were compared in [23] to highlight the pros and cons of each approach. Lastly, in [20], the methodology was generalized to automatically map an automata-based model, representing a qualitatively verified energy consumption policy, to a stochastic Petri net dialect. This enabled the inclusion of stochastic behavior (e.g., weather conditions) for quantitative evaluation.

At the end of the project, the design of future smart station lighting management applications was addressed, with the aim of reducing station illumination whenever (time) and wherever (space) possible while guaranteeing minimum illumination levels as required by legislation. A station platform's (ceiling) lights (LEDs) are equipped with a data acquisition module called MADILL. A C-MAD unit collects the messages from each MADILL and it is equipped with brightness sensors and commands to switch (groups of) lights on, off, or dim them.

In [30], the authors considered user-experience related requirements such as *"passengers should always be able to rely on an illuminated pathway when getting on or off a train, from the main entrance, to the platform"*, to avoid passengers transiting or waiting in non-illuminated areas, with the associated risks (e.g., theft or injury), or *"there should be an illumination level greater than x on platforms where a train is about to arrive, even if the train is late"*. Such requirements are inherently spatial or spatio-temporal, as they deal with the possibly complex reachability relations and pathways of a train station.

The authors described how to tackle these requirements in an experiment aimed at identifying poorly illuminated platform areas of the Pistoia railway station by the application of spatial model-checking techniques and the VoxLogicA model-checking tool [34]. Provided with concrete images and given a threshold on the illumination value, VoxLogicA managed to compute both areas that are and parts of the platforms that are not sufficiently illuminated.

The application of formal methods and tools to the STINGRAY case studies described above contributed successfully to the project's third and fourth goals.

7   MOST Spoke 4

Spoke 4 "Rail Transportation" of the Sustainable Mobility National Research Center (MOST) concerns a project, started in 2022, which received funding from the European Union NextGenerationEU framework through the Italian National Recovery and Resilience Plan (PNRR).

The initiative aims to promote sustainable and digital innovation in mobility and transportation systems through strategic collaborations between academia and industry, and Spoke 4 focuses on the development of advanced methodologies and tools for enhancing the efficiency, safety, and resilience of railway systems.

In Spoke 4, CNR–ISTI coordinates WP3 (Digitization of railway transport) and task T3.1 (Learning formal models for predictive maintenance), and participates in task T1.3 (Resilient and sustainable railway infrastructure) of WP1 (Increase of capacity of railway transport) coordinated by Alessandro Fantechi.

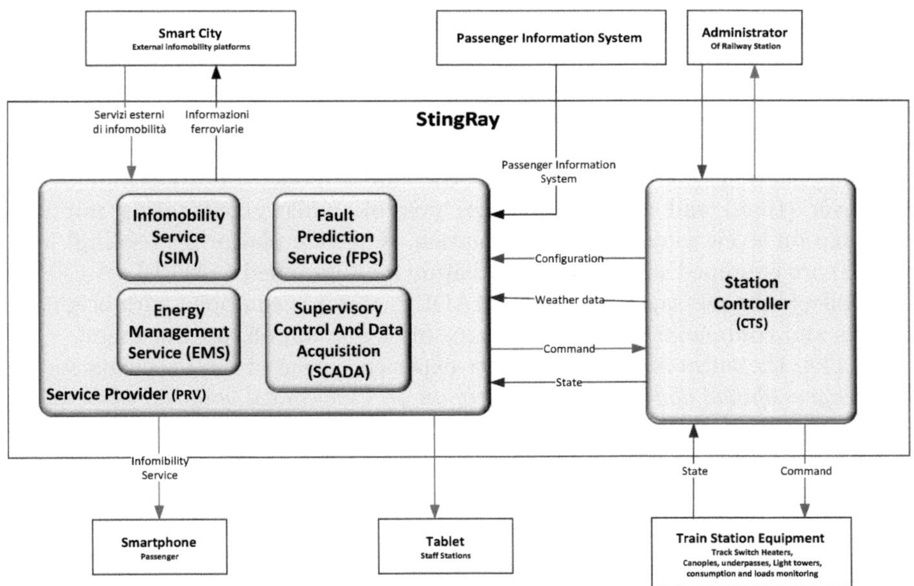

Fig. 4. The STINGRAY architecture.

In this section, we focus on the participation in task T3.1, in which CNR–ISTI actively explored predictive maintenance strategies through the integration of formal methods, machine-learning techniques, and human-centred design practices. The activities were carried out in close collaboration with a consortium of academic and industrial partners, including the University of Florence (with Alessandro Fantechi as the referent), the University of Naples Federico II, Trenord, and Lutech. As part of these activities, CNR–ISTI led two parallel yet complementary lines: (1) the development of data-driven approaches for anticipating failures in railway subsystems such as the Traction Control Unit (TCU), and (2) the design of an interactive dashboard that aggregates predictive insights from multiple data-driven approaches and facilitates decision-making for different classes of users (maintenance and engineering personnel).

The development of data-driven approaches for predicting railway maintenance needs progressed from classical statistical forecasting models to supervised machine-learning algorithms. In [54], an analysis of time-series forecasting methods applied to diagnostic event logs was conducted. Classical models including but not limited to Autoregressive Integrated Moving Average (ARIMA) and Seasonal ARIMA (SARIMA) were tested on a dataset provided by Trenord. The dataset originates from Trenord's fleet, where an on-board diagnostic platform continuously collects data from each train and transmits it to a wayside system for storage and analysis. The performance of these models was evaluated against a Random Walk baseline, using Root Mean Square Error (RMSE) as the evaluation metric. Results were promising, particularly concerning ARIMA and SARIMA algorithms. These models provided useful baselines and helped uncover temporal properties of the data, but their predictive accuracy proved highly dependent on the characteristics of each train and limited in capturing heterogeneous and non-linear patterns across fleets.

Building on these insights, we explored the adoption of supervised machine-learning methods for predictive maintenance. These methods offer greater flexibility in modeling complex, non-linear, and multivariate relationships in railway diagnostic data. To this end, time-series diagnostic logs were reformulated into a supervised learning problem through a sliding-window approach, where fixed sequences of past observations were used to predict future events. Several families of models were evaluated: tree-based ensembles (Random Forests, Gradient Boosting, and XGBoost), support vector machines, and neural networks (ANNs, LSTMs, and Temporal Convolutional Networks). Among these, XGBoost consistently provided the best trade-off between recall and precision, a crucial balance in predictive maintenance where false negatives (i.e., missed failure predictions) must be minimized for safety reasons. At the same time, limitations were identified, notably the risk of performance degradation when failure patterns evolve or sensor drift introduces non-stationarity, underscoring the need for periodic model retraining and recalibration.

Parallel to algorithmic development, CNR–ISTI employed requirements engineering and user-centred design methodologies to ensure that the predictive maintenance dashboard was aligned with the operational workflows and stakeholder needs of Trenord. The dashboard is meant to be integrated into Trenord's existing maintenance platform and to present the outcomes of different predictive approaches developed within the project: machine-learning algorithms implemented by Lutech, fault-tree analysis developed at the University of Florence by Alessandro Fantechi et al. [42], and clustering and filtering techniques contributed by the University of Naples. The platform supports both fleet-level and train-specific views, allowing maintenance personnel to access detailed information on individual predictions, while engineering personnel is provided with dedicated pages offering in-depth analyses across all three methodologies.

The development of the dashboard followed an iterative, user-centred process articulated in four phases: requirements elicitation, prototyping, interactive mock-ups, and final specification. Through meetings, focus groups, and task observations, CNR–ISTI gathered explicit and implicit knowledge of Trenord's workflows, building a clear picture of user goals and challenges. Early low-fidelity mock-ups were then used to stimulate discussion and refine requirements, before evolving into interactive prototypes that combined manual design with AI-assisted mock-up generation [39]. These prototypes were reviewed and refined in successive iterations, ensuring alignment with stakeholder expectations. The process culminated in a consolidated requirements document, serving as a shared reference for all partners and providing the foundation for the further implementation and integration of the dashboard into Trenord's diagnostic platform.

8   Summary: Achievements and Limitations

This survey has summarized over two decades of studies that were either led by or involved Alessandro Fantechi. Table 1 highlights contributions and references (cf. also [27, 31]). The overall trajectory that emerges is one of steady maturation: from early feasibility studies and targeted formal verifications, through the consolidation of methods and tools, to demonstrators and processes that increasingly satisfy the constraints of certification-oriented, safety-critical development. Across projects on interlocking and ATP functions, on standard- and requirement-level modeling, and on station-level innovation, the repeated pattern was to start from industrially understandable notations and artefacts, to formalize incrementally where risk and ambiguity were highest, and to close the loop with empirical evidence about costs and benefits.

8.1   Achievements

A central outcome of these efforts has been the improvement of specification and standard quality. By grounding models in UML/SysML fragments and constrained natural language, and then subjecting them to model checking, animation, model-based testing, and abstract interpretation, the teams repeatedly exposed ambiguities, omissions, and inconsistencies that would otherwise have propagated to design and verification phases. In the 4SECURail experience, for example, the formalization of the RBC/RBC handover (from UNISIG artifacts)

Table 1. Summary of Projects and Collaborations Involving Alessandro Fantechi

Project	Topic	Outcome	Publications
Early Work	Formal Verification of Railway Systems	- Formal models of railway crossing and circular railway using CCS and ACTL. - Verified safety and liveness properties with EMC and AMC model checkers. - Validated fault-tolerance mechanisms for interlocking systems in the GUARDS project.	[6,35,36,46,47]
GE/Alstom Collaborations	Interlocking and ATP Systems, Requirements Analysis	- Validated SDL/Statechart models for interlockings with GE artifacts. - Scalable model-extraction pipeline for fault finding and verification. - Metrô Rio ATP case study with Simulink/ Stateflow, reducing bugs and costs. - 70% cost reduction in unit-level verification via model-based testing and abstract interpretation. - NLP-based requirements defect detection with GATE/SREE tools.	[8–11,37,38,57–62,66,72]
TRACE-IT	ATP, ATC, CBTC	- ATC demonstrator with deadlock-free CBTC strategy using UMC. - Formal methods diversity study with 9 frameworks. - CBTC global model with product line engineering and NLP-based requirements. - Prototype tool for CBTC architecture.	[65,68–70]
ASTRail	Formal Methods for Moving Block Signaling	- Comprehensive survey and evaluation of 14 FMs tools. - Trial application of Simulink, UMC, and ProB to moving block systems. - Increased industry awareness of FMs potential.	[7,12,15,16,28,56,63,64]
4SECURail	Formal Methods for RBC/RBC Handover Protocols	- FMs demonstrator identifying ambiguities in UNISIG standards. - Publicly available UMC, ProB, and LNT models. - Cost-benefit analysis showing economic advantages. - Limited direct impact on standards due to absent infrastructure managers.	[1–3,5,14,24–26,32,33]
STINGRAY	Smart Station Infrastructure (Energy Management)	- Prototypes for SCADA control of railroad switch heaters and EMS. - Comparative analysis of SAN/Möbius and SHA/UPPAAL SMC. - Generalized methodology for mapping automata to stochastic Petri nets. - Spatial model checking future smart station lighting management.	[13,17–23,30]
MOST Spoke 4	Predictive Maintenance, Digitization	- Data-driven real-time failure prediction for TCU using ARIMA, SARIMA, and ML (XGBoost), as well as by data-driven synthesis of stochastic fault tree models. - User-centered dashboard design for Trenord's maintenance platform. - Iterative requirements elicitation and AI-assisted prototyping.	[39,42,54]

clarified subtle protocol corner cases and yielded actionable feedback for stakeholders. Similar effects were observed in ASTRail, where a structured comparison of tools against a moving-block design made explicit the trade-offs among analysis depth, usability, and integration potential. These results did not remain at the toy example level: even when the case studies were not product components, they were selected and parameterized to reflect realistic signaling scenarios so that the insights would transfer to practice.

Equally important has been the consolidation of repeatable engineering practices. Over time, the collaborations distilled safe modeling subsets, modeling guidelines for code generation, and practical back-to-back verification strategies that link models to code and test oracles. Combining techniques—model checking to reason about global safety and liveness, model-based testing to exercise behavior at scale and to drive regression, abstract interpretation to enforce runtime error freedom—proved more effective than relying on any single approach. This methodological pluralism, backed by tool diversity and portable artefacts, reduced lock-in and created a robust basis for technology transfer and education.

The human capital dimension deserves explicit emphasis. The projects created concrete training pathways for students and early-career researchers, many of whom moved into industry or continued to collaborate on subsequent initiatives. This injection of *nuova linfa* into the CNR and partner organizations strengthened the European FM-for-rail community at large, building shared vocabularies, data sets, and habits of collaboration across academia, suppliers, and—when involved—standardization bodies. The pedagogical impact fed back into project execution: teams with mixed profiles (researchers, developers, assessors) were better able to negotiate the trade-offs between exploratory research and compliance-driven engineering.

8.2   Limitations

An honest appraisal of technology transfer also reveals structural frictions that cannot be glossed over. The most impactful studies are invariably those closest to real systems, yet working with real artefacts is constrained by confidentiality, the limited time windows typical of funded projects, and the academic and project pressure to produce publishable results early. These forces can limit scope, reduce reproducibility, and sometimes bias the selection of problems away from the most mission-critical ones. Integration with industrial development environments poses additional challenges: researchers and developers often operate with different stacks, expectations, and acceptance criteria, and the evidence required for certification demands stability, traceability, and process discipline that go beyond the lifecycle of a research prototype. Finally, the cost of industrial-grade verification frameworks—licensing, qualification, and toolchain customization— remains a significant barrier for academia and for many collaborative projects, constraining continuity, student training at scale, and open reproducibility.

Within this landscape, the project-specific contributions highlight both utility and limits. TRACE-IT delivered an ATS demonstrator and a formal deadlock analysis on a realistic CBTC-inspired layout, offering concrete strategies for avoiding system deadlocks and a proof-of-concept pipeline that can be adapted to similar metro contexts; confidentiality and the non-product status of the demonstrator, however, curtailed direct uptake into supplier processes. ASTRail produced a widely cited survey and a rigorous tool evaluation against moving-block requirements, giving decision-makers evidence-based guidance for selecting FM workflows; its academic case focus, by construction, limited deep embedding into OEM toolchains. 4SECURail showcased how formalization can strengthen standards, from early UML/SysML operational models through translations to multiple verification back ends, while coupling these steps to a cost-benefit analysis that articulated where FM activities return the most value; the absence of infrastructure managers as primary drivers, however, reduced the leverage on standardization timelines. STINGRAY, operating at station level, advanced the integration of SCADA and energy-management requirements and demonstrated how FM-informed design can clarify interfaces and operating constraints in heterogeneous environments; the diversity of station technologies slowed convergence on common tooling and limited generalization.

Beyond immediate artefacts and demonstrators, these collaborations opened new and durable lines of research. One such line concerns the semantics of practically useful, standards-friendly fragments of UML/SysML so that models can be verified without abandoning notations familiar to stakeholders. Another concerns end-to-end traceability from controlled natural language requirements to analyzable models and, ultimately, to test oracles and evidence packages suitable for CENELEC processes. A third line, motivated by the realities of industrial artefacts, investigates scalable model extraction and hybrid verification that combines static analysis, model checking, and runtime monitoring, while preserving arguments acceptable to assessors. Each of these lines has already yielded methods and tools that subsequent projects have reused and extended.

9　Conclusions and Outlook

This survey has retraced more than two decades of research and technology transfer on formal methods for railway systems carried out around the FMT laboratory at CNR–ISTI and in close collaboration with industrial partners, under the scientific leadership and vision of Alessandro Fantechi. Looking forward, the experiences surveyed here suggest a concrete and realistic outlook. The most sustainable path to impact begins with shared notations and controlled language, formalizes incrementally around high-risk behaviour, and engineers traceability and certification evidence from day one. Tool diversity should be embraced and orchestrated rather than minimized, with open artefacts and automation to keep pipelines maintainable as personnel and tools evolve. Crucially, budgets and planning must prioritize people as much as tools: effective transfer requires mixed teams with protected time for joint engineering, training, and maintenance of reproducible assets. On the ecosystem side, there is a clear need for affordable, open verification stacks, qualified subsets, and shared benchmarks that lower the activation energy for academia, SMEs, and standardization bodies. If these conditions are met, formal methods can continue to advance both as a scientific discipline and as a practical instrument for building and assuring the next generation of signaling and control systems.

There is increasing evidence for the successful application of formal methods in industry [29], not limited to the safety-critical domain including railways and other transportation sectors. The body of work reviewed in this paper confirms that formal methods can deliver concrete benefits—clearer standards and specifications, richer verification evidence, and better informed engineering decisions—provided that they are introduced with sensitivity to industrial realities and supported by the right mix of methods, tools, and people. The collaborations with GE Transportation, Alstom, and the broader consortium of

European projects demonstrate that such a balance is achievable. The challenge, and the opportunity, is to scale these practices in a way that preserves scientific rigor while maximizing practical value for a sector where safety, reliability, and interoperability remain paramount.

Acknowledgments. The authors would like to thank Alessandro Fantechi for endless journeys involving formal methods and railways. After he left CNR in November 1992, he has always been associated with the CNR and also after he became professor at the University of Florence in 1995, he has continued to frequently take the train to Pisa to collaborate with the Formal Methods and Tools (FMT) lab, of which Alessandro has been a member from its foundation, more than two decades ago. The fact that FMT is internationally renowned for its expertise on the application of formal methods in the railway industry, is for a large part due to Alessandro.

The authors acknowledge the use of OpenAI ChatGPT and Grok for the revision of the phrasing and language of this manuscript.

Part of this work was carried out within the MUR PRIN 2022 PNRR P2022A492B project ADVENTURE (ADVancEd iNtegraTed evalUation of Railway systEms) and the MOST − Sustainable Mobility National Research Center and received funding from the European Union Next-GenerationEU (PIANO NAZIONALE DI RIPRESA E RESILIENZA (PNRR) − MISSIONE 4, COMPONENTE 2, INVESTIMENTO 1.4 − D.D. 1033 17/06/2022, CN00000023. This manuscript reflects only the authors' views and opinions, neither the European Union nor the European Commission can be considered responsible for them.

Disclosure of Interests. The authors have no competing interests to declare that are relevant to the content of this article.

References

1. 4SECURail project Deliverable D2.1: Specification of formal development demonstrator (2020). https://projects.shift2rail.org/download.aspx?id=560cdd44-83e7-4f5d-879e-d8dcdf2e2b1b

2. 4SECURail project Deliverable D2.2: Formal development Demonstrator prototype, 1st Release (2020). https://projects.shift2rail.org/download.aspx?id=1761f4fa-c701-4321-b40c-3e67146ed482

3. 4SECURail project Deliverable D2.3: Case study requirements and specification (2020). https://projects.shift2rail.org/download.aspx?id=6917d0da-122f-41cb-8194-5f3e5029516b

4. 4SECURail project Deliverable D2.5: Formal development demonstrator prototype, final release (2020). https://projects.shift2rail.org/download.aspx?id=eae0e50c-90fa-4408-b53c-f714e9dd2581

5. 4SECURail project Deliverable D2.6: Specification of cost/benefit analysis and learning curves, final release (2020). https://projects.shift2rail.org/download.aspx?id=ef729ed0-19d6-4378-aeb1-c74ced3edf50

6. Anselmi, A., et al.: An experience in formal verification of safety properties of a railway signalling control system. In: Rabe, G. (ed.) Proceedings of the 14th International Conference on Computer Safety, Reliability and Security, SAFE-COMP'95, pp. 474–488. Springer, Cham (1995). https://doi.org/10.1007/978-1-4471-3054-3_33

7. ASTRail project Deliverable D4.1: Report on Analysis and on Ranking of Formal Methods (2020). https://projects.shift2rail.org/download.aspx?id=dadd80d0-cf35-48d6-a1b7-b2a7545e37d6. Accessed Sep 2025
8. Bacherini, S., Fantechi, A., Tempestini, M., Zingoni, N.: A story about formal methods adoption by a railway signaling manufacturer. In: Misra, J., Nipkow, T., Sekerinski, E. (eds.) FM 2006. LNCS, vol. 4085, pp. 179–189. Springer, Heidelberg (2006). https://doi.org/10.1007/11813040_13
9. Banci, M., Becucci, M., Fantechi, A., Spinicci, E.: Validation coverage for a component-based SDL model of a railway signaling system. Electron. Notes Theor. Comput. **116**, 99–111 (2005). https://doi.org/10.1016/j.entcs.2004.02.083
10. Banci, M., Fantechi, A.: Geographical versus functional modelling by statecharts of interlocking systems. Electron. Notes Theor. Comput. **133**, 3–19 (2005). https://doi.org/10.1016/j.entcs.2004.08.055
11. Banci, M., Fantechi, A., Gnesi, S.: The role of formal methods in developing a distributed railway interlocking system. In: Proceedings of the 5th Symposium on Formal Methods for Automation and Safety in Railway and Automotive Systems, FORMS/FORMAT'04 (2004). https://iris.cnr.it/retrieve/32e02f77-2695-45de-9d94-cbea4e8a19ff/prod_120519-doc_125296.pdf
12. Basile, D., ter Beek, M.H., Ciancia, V.: Statistical model checking of a moving block railway signalling scenario with UPPAAL SMC. In: Margaria, T., Steffen, B. (eds.) ISoLA 2018. LNCS, vol. 11245, pp. 372–391. Springer, Cham (2018). https://doi.org/10.1007/978-3-030-03421-4_24
13. Basile, D., ter Beek, M.H., Di Giandomenico, F., Fantechi, A., Gnesi, S., Spagnolo, G.O.: 30 years of simulation-based quantitative analysis tools: a comparison experiment between Möbius and Uppaal SMC. In: Margaria, T., Steffen, B. (eds.) Proceedings of the 9th International Symposium on Leveraging Applications of Formal Methods, Verification and Validation: Verification (ISoLA'20). LNCS, vol. 12476, pp. 368–384. Springer, Germany (2020). https://doi.org/10.1007/978-3-030-61362-4_21
14. Basile, D., et al.: Designing a demonstrator of formal methods for railways infrastructure managers. In: Margaria, T., Steffen, B. (eds.) ISoLA 2020. LNCS, vol. 12478, pp. 467–485. Springer, Cham (2020). https://doi.org/10.1007/978-3-030-61467-6_30 managers. In: Margaria, T., Steffen, B. (eds.) ISoLA 2020. LNCS, vol. 12478, pp. 467–485. Springer, Cham (2020). https://doi.org/10.1007/978-3-030-61467-6_30
15. Basile, D., ter Beek, M.H., Ferrari, A., Legay, A.: Modelling and analysing ERTMS L3 moving block railway signalling with simulink and UPPAAL SMC. In: Larsen, K.G., Willemse, T. (eds.) FMICS 2019. LNCS, vol. 11687, pp. 1–21. Springer, Cham (2019). https://doi.org/10.1007/978-3-030-27008-7_1
16. Basile, D., ter Beek, M.H., Ferrari, A., Legay, A.: Exploring the ERTMS/ETCS full moving block specification: an experience with formal methods. Int. J. Softw. Tools Technol. Transf. **24**(3), 351–370 (2022). https://doi.org/10.1007/S10009-022-00653-3
17. Basile, D., Chiaradonna, S., Di Giandomenico, F., Gnesi, S.: A stochastic model-based approach to analyse reliable energy-saving rail road switch heating systems. J. Rail Transp. Plan. Manag. **6**(2), 163–181 (2016). https://doi.org/10.1016/j.jrtpm.2016.03.003
18. Basile, D., Chiaradonna, S., Di Giandomenico, F., Gnesi, S., Mazzanti, F.: Stochastic model-based analysis of energy consumption in a rail road switch heating system. In: Fantechi, A., Pelliccione, P. (eds.) SERENE 2015. LNCS, vol. 9274, pp. 82–98. Springer, Cham (2015). https://doi.org/10.1007/978-3-319-23129-7_7

19. Basile, D., Di Giandomenico, F., Gnesi, S.: Tuning energy consumption strategies in the railway domain: a model-based approach. In: Margaria, T., Steffen, B. (eds.) Proceedings of the 7th International Symposium on Leveraging Applications of Formal Methods, Verification and Validation: Discussion, Dissemination, Applications, ISoLA'16. LNCS, vol. 9953, pp. 315–330. Springer (2016). https://doi.org/10.1007/978-3-319-47169-3_23

20. Basile, D., Di Giandomenico, F., Gnesi, S.: A refinement approach to analyse critical cyber-physical systems. In: Cerone, A., Roveri, M. (eds.) Revised Selected Papers of the SEFM 2017 Collocated Workshops: DataMod, FAACS, MSE, CoSim-CPS, and FOCLASA. LNCS, vol. 10729, pp. 267–283. Springer, Cham (2017). https://doi.org/10.1007/978-3-319-74781-1_19

21. Basile, D., Di Giandomenico, F., Gnesi, S.: Enhancing models correctness through formal verification: a case study from the railway domain. In: Pires, L.F., Hammoudi, S., Selic, B. (eds.) Proceedings of the 5th International Conference on Model-Driven Engineering and Software Development, MODELSWARD 2017, pp. 679–686. SciTePress (2017). https://doi.org/10.5220/0006291106790686

22. Basile, D., Di Giandomenico, F., Gnesi, S.: Statistical model checking of an energy-saving cyber-physical system in the railway domain. In: Proceedings of the 32nd Symposium on Applied Computing, SAC'17, pp. 1356–1363. ACM (2017). https://doi.org/10.1145/3019612.3019824

23. Basile, D., Di Giandomenico, F., Gnesi, S.: On quantitative assessment of reliability and energy consumption indicators in railway systems. In: Kharchenko, V., Kondratenko, Y., Kacprzyk, J. (eds.) Green IT Engineering: Social, Business and Industrial Applications, SSDC, vol. 171, pp. 423–447. Springer, Cham (2019). https://doi.org/10.1007/978-3-030-00253-4_18

24. Basile, D., Fantechi, A., Rosadi, I.: Formal analysis of the UNISIG safety application intermediate sub-layer: applying formal methods to railway standard interfaces. In: Lluch Lafuente, A., Mavridou, A. (eds.) Proceedings of the 26th International Conference on Formal Methods for Industrial Critical Systems, FMICS 2021. LNCS, vol. 12863, pp. 174–190. Springer, Cham (2021). https://doi.org/10.1007/978-3-030-85248-1_11

25. Basile, D., Mazzanti, F.: Comparing model checking and model-based simulation. In: ter Beek, M.H., Collart-Dutilleul, S., Lecomte, T. (eds.) Proceedings of the 6th International Conference on Reliability, Safety, and Security of Railway Systems: Modelling, Analysis, Verification, and Certification, RSSRail 2025. LNCS, vol. 16236, pp. 135–155. Springer, Cham (2025). https://doi.org/10.1007/978-3-032-10762-6_12

26. Basile, D., Mazzanti, F., Ferrari, A.: Experimenting with formal verification and model-based development in railways: the case of UMC and Sparx enterprise architect. In: Cimatti, A., Titolo, L. (eds.) Proceedings of the 28th International Conference on Formal Methods for Industrial Critical Systems, FMICS 2023. LNCS, vol. 14290, pp. 1–21. Springer, Cham (2023). https://doi.org/10.1007/978-3-031-43681-9_1

27. ter Beek, M.H.: Models for formal methods and tools: the case of railway systems. Softw. Syst. Model. 24(6), 1935–1954 (2025). https://doi.org/10.1007/s10270-025-01276-3

28. ter Beek, M.H., et al.: Adopting formal methods in an industrial setting: the railways case. In: ter Beek, M.H., McIver, A., Oliveira, J.N. (eds.) FM 2019. LNCS, vol. 11800, pp. 762–772. Springer, Cham (2019). https://doi.org/10.1007/978-3-030-30942-8_46

29. ter Beek, M.H., et al.: Formal methods in industry. Formal Aspects Comput. **37**(1), 7:1–7:38 (2025). https://doi.org/10.1145/3689374

30. ter Beek, M.H., Ciancia, V., Latella, D., Massink, M., Spagnolo, G.O.: Spatial model checking for smart stations. In: Lluch Lafuente, A., Mavridou, A. (eds.) FMICS 2021. LNCS, vol. 12863, pp. 39–47. Springer, Cham (2021). https://doi.org/10.1007/978-3-030-85248-1_3

31. ter Beek, M.H., Fantechi, A., Gnesi, S.: Formal methods for industrial critical systems: 30 years of railway applications. In: Hinchey, M., Steffen, B. (eds.) The Combined Power of Research, Education, and Dissemination. LNCS, vol. 15240, pp. 327–344. Springer, Cham (2025). https://doi.org/10.1007/978-3-031-73887-6_21

32. Belli, D., et al.: The 4SECURail case study on rigorous standard interface specifications. In: Cimatti, A., Titolo, L. (eds.) Proceedings of the 28th International Conference on Formal Methods for Industrial Critical Systems, FMICS 2023. LNCS, vol. 14290, pp. 22–39. Springer, Cham (2023). https://doi.org/10.1007/978-3-031-43681-9_2

33. Belli, D., Mazzanti, F.: A case study in formal analysis of system requirements. In: Masci, P., Bernardeschi, C., Graziani, P., Koddenbrock, M., Palmieri, M. (eds.) Revised Selected Papers of the SEFM 2022 Collocated Workshops: AI4EA, F-IDE, CoSim-CPS, CIFMA. LNCS, vol. 13765, pp. 164–173. Springer, Cham (2022). https://doi.org/10.1007/978-3-031-26236-4_14

34. Belmonte, G., Ciancia, V., Latella, D., Massink, M.: VoxLogicA: a spatial model checker for declarative image analysis. In: Vojnar, T., Zhang, L. (eds.) TACAS 2019. LNCS, vol. 11427, pp. 281–298. Springer, Cham (2019). https://doi.org/10.1007/978-3-030-17462-0_16

35. Bernardeschi, C., Fantechi, A., Gnesi, S.: Formal validation of fault-tolerance mechanisms inside GUARDS. Reliab. Eng. Syst. Safety **71**(3), 261–270 (2001). https://doi.org/10.1016/S0951-8320(00)00078-8

36. Bernardeschi, C., Fantechi, A., Gnesi, S., Larosa, S., Mongardi, G., Romano, D.: A formal verification environment for railway signaling system design. Formal Meth. Syst. Des. **12**(2), 139–161 (1998). https://doi.org/10.1023/A:1008645826258

37. Bonacchi, A., Fantechi, A.: validation of interlocking systems by testing their models. In: Proceedings of the 9th International Conference on the Quality of Information and Communications Technology, QUATIC 2014, pp. 226–229. IEEE (2014). https://doi.org/10.1109/QUATIC.2014.37

38. Bonacchi, A., Fantechi, A., Bacherini, S., Tempestini, M.: Validation process for railway interlocking systems. Sci. Comput. Program. **128**, 2–21 (2016). https://doi.org/10.1016/j.scico.2016.04.004

39. Broccia, G., Borselli, A., Cefaloni, M.R., Delcorno, F., Ferrari, A.: An experience report on leveraging LLMs for GUI generation: automating coding to prioritise creativity. In: Proceedings of the 12th International Workshop on Creativity in Requirements Engineering, CreaRE 2025, co-located with the 31st International Conference on Requirements Engineering: Foundation for Software Quality, REFSQ 2025, vol. 3964. CEUR Workshop Proceedings (2025). https://ceur-ws.org/Vol-3959/CreaRE-paper2.pdf

40. Broy, M., et al.: Does every computer scientist need to know formal methods? Formal Aspects Comput. **37**(1), 6:1–6:17 (2025). https://doi.org/10.1145/3670795

41. Broy, M., Cengarle, M.V.: UML formal semantics: lessons learned. Softw. Syst. Model. **10**(4), 441–446 (2011). https://doi.org/10.1007/s10270-011-0207-y

42. Carnevali, L., et al.: Data-driven synthesis of stochastic fault trees for proactive maintenance of railway vehicles. In: Remke, A., Steffen, B. (eds.) Proceedings of the

30th International Conference on Formal Methods for Industrial Critical Systems (FMICS'25). LNCS, vol. 16040, pp. 162–181. Springer, Heidelberg (2025). https://doi.org/10.1007/978-3-032-00942-5_9

43. Clarke, E.M., Emerson, E.A., Sistla, A.P.: Automatic verification of finite state concurrent systems using temporal logic specifications: a practical approach. In: Conference Record of the 10th Annual ACM Symposium on Principles of Programming Languages, POPL 1983, pp. 117–126. ACM (1983). https://doi.org/10.1145/567067.567080

44. Clarke, E.M., Emerson, E.A., Sistla, A.P.: Automatic verification of finite-state concurrent systems using temporal logic specifications. ACM Trans. Program. Lang. Syst. **8**(2), 244–263 (1986). https://doi.org/10.1145/5397.5399

45. Cook, S.: Looking back at UML. Softw. Syst. Model. **11**(4), 471–480 (2012). https://doi.org/10.1007/s10270-012-0256-x

46. De Nicola, R., Fantechi, A., Gnesi, S., Ristori, G.: An action based framework for verifying logical and behavioural properties of concurrent systems. In: Larsen, K.G., Skou, A. (eds.) Proceedings of the 3rd International Workshop on Computer Aided Verification (CAV'91). LNCS, vol. 575, pp. 37–47. Springer, Cham (1991). https://doi.org/10.1007/3-540-55179-4_5

47. De Nicola, R., Fantechi, A., Gnesi, S., Ristori, G.: An action-based framework for verifying logical and behavioural properties of concurrent systems. Comput. Netw. ISDN Syst. **25**(7), 761–778 (1993). https://doi.org/10.1016/0169-7552(93)90047-8

48. De Nicola, R., Vaandrager, F.W.: Three logics for branching bisimulation: extended abstract. In: Proceedings of the 4th Annual Symposium on Logic in Computer Science, LICS 1989, pp. 118–129. IEEE (1990).https://doi.org/10.1109/LICS.1990.113739

49. De Nicola, R., Vaandrager, F.W.: Three logics for branching bisimulation. J. ACM **42**(2), 458–487 (1995). https://doi.org/10.1145/201019.201032

50. Derezińska, A., Szczykulski, M.: Interpretation problems in code generation from UML state machines: a comparative study. In: Kwater, T., Zuberek, W.M., Ciarkowski, A., Kruk, M., Pekala, R., Twaróg, B. (eds.) Proceedings of the 2nd Scientific Conference on Computing in Science and Technology, CSI 2011. Monographs in Applied Informatics, pp. 36–50. Warsaw University of Life Sciences (2012), https://repo.pw.edu.pl/docstore/download/WEiTI-1e8d2c48-b87c-476f-94d6-cc9df9319050/ADerSzczy.pdf

51. Fantechi, A.: The role of formal methods in software development for railway applications, chap. 12. In: Flammini, F. (ed.) Railway Safety, Reliability, and Security: Technologies and Systems Engineering, pp. 282–297. IGI Global (2012). https://doi.org/10.4018/978-1-4666-1643-1.ch012

52. Fantechi, A.: Twenty-five years of formal methods and railways: what next? In: Counsell, S., Núñez, M. (eds.) SEFM 2013. LNCS, vol. 8368, pp. 167–183. Springer, Cham (2014). https://doi.org/10.1007/978-3-319-05032-4_13

53. Fantechi, A., Fokkink, W., Morzenti, A.: Some trends in formal methods applications to railway signaling, chap. 4. In: Gnesi, S., Margaria, T. (eds.) Formal Methods for Industrial Critical Systems: A Survey of Applications, pp. 61–84. Wiley (2013). https://doi.org/10.1002/9781118459898.ch4

54. Ferdous, R., Spagnolo, G., Borselli, A., Rota, L., Ferrari, A.: Identifying maintenance needs with machine learning: a case study in railways. In: Proceedings of the 11th International Workshop on Artificial Intelligence and Requirements Engineering, AIRE 2024 of the 32nd International Requirements Engineering Conference (RE'24), pp. 22–25. IEEE (2024). https://doi.org/10.1109/REW61692.2024.00008

55. Ferrari, A., ter Beek, M.H.: Formal methods in railways: a systematic mapping study. ACM Comput. Surv. **55**(4), 69:1–69:37 (2023). https://doi.org/10.1145/3520480

56. Ferrari, A., et al.: Survey on formal methods and tools in railways: the ASTRail Approach. In: Collart-Dutilleul, S., Lecomte, T., Romanovsky, A. (eds.) RSSRail 2019. LNCS, vol. 11495, pp. 226–241. Springer, Cham (2019). https://doi.org/10.1007/978-3-030-18744-6_15

57. Ferrari, A., Fantechi, A., Bacherini, S., Zingoni, N.: Modeling guidelines for code generation in the railway signaling context. In: Proceedings of the 1st NASA Formal Methods Symposium, NFM 2009, pp. 166–170. NASA Technical Reports Server, NASA (2009). https://ntrs.nasa.gov/api/citations/20100024476/downloads/20100024476.pdf

58. Ferrari, A., Fantechi, A., Gnesi, S.: Lessons learnt from the adoption of formal model-based development. In: Goodloe, A.E., Person, S. (eds.) NFM 2012. LNCS, vol. 7226, pp. 24–38. Springer, Heidelberg (2012). https://doi.org/10.1007/978-3-642-28891-3_5

59. Ferrari, A., Fantechi, A., Gnesi, S., Magnani, G.: Model-based development and formal methods in the railway industry. IEEE Softw. **30**(3), 28–34 (2013). https://doi.org/10.1109/MS.2013.44

60. Ferrari, A., et al.: Detecting requirements defects with NLP patterns: an industrial experience in the railway domain. Empir. Softw. Eng. **23**(6), 3684–3733 (2018). https://doi.org/10.1007/s10664-018-9596-7

61. Ferrari, A., Grasso, D., Magnani, G., Fantechi, A., Tempestini, M.: The Metrô Rio case study. Sci. Comput. Program. **78**(8), 951–970 (2013). https://doi.org/10.1016/j.scico.2012.04.003

62. Ferrari, A., Magnani, G., Grasso, D., Fantechi, A., Tempestini, M.: Adoption of model-based testing and abstract interpretation by a railway signalling manufacturer. Int. J. Embed. Real-Time Commun. Syst. **2**(2), 42–61 (2011). https://doi.org/10.4018/jertcs.2011040103

63. Ferrari, A., Mazzanti, F., Basile, D., ter Beek, M.H.: Systematic evaluation and usability analysis of formal methods tools for railway signaling system design. IEEE Trans. Softw. Eng. **48**(11), 4675–4691 (2022). https://doi.org/10.1109/TSE.2021.3124677

64. Ferrari, A., Mazzanti, F., Basile, D., ter Beek, M.H., Fantechi, A.: Comparing formal tools for system design: a judgment study. In: Proceedings of the 42nd International Conference on Software Engineering, ICSE 2020, pp. 62–74. ACM (2020). https://doi.org/10.1145/3377811.3380373

65. Ferrari, A., Spagnolo, G.O., Martelli, G., Menabeni, S.: From commercial documents to system requirements: an approach for the engineering of novel CBTC solutions. Int. J. Softw. Tools Technol. Transf **16**(6), 647–667 (2014). https://doi.org/10.1007/s10009-013-0298-6

66. Ferrari, A., Spoletini, P.: Formal requirements engineering and large language models: a two-way roadmap. Inf. Softw. Technol. **181**, 107697 (2025). https://doi.org/10.1016/j.infsof.2025.107697

67. Mazzanti, F., Belli, D.: The 4SECURail formal methods demonstrator. In: Collart-Dutilleul, S., Haxthausen, A.E., Lecomte, T. (eds.) Proceedings of the 4th International Conference on Reliability, Safety, and Security of Railway Systems: Modelling, Analysis, Verification, and Certification, RSSRail 2022. LNCS, vol. 13294, pp. 149–165. Springer, Cham (2022). https://doi.org/10.1007/978-3-031-05814-1_11

68. Mazzanti, F., Ferrari, A.: Ten diverse formal models for a CBTC automatic train supervision system. In: Gallagher, J.P., van Glabbeek, R., Serwe, W. (eds.) Proceedings of the 3rd Workshop on Models for Formal Analysis of Real Systems and the 6th International Workshop on Verification and Program Transformation, MARS/VPT 2018. EPTCS, vol. 268, pp. 104–149 (2018). https://doi.org/10.4204/EPTCS.268.4
69. Mazzanti, F., Ferrari, A., Spagnolo, G.O.: Towards formal methods diversity in railways: an experience report with seven frameworks. Int. J. Softw. Tools Technol. Transf. **20**(3), 263–288 (2018). https://doi.org/10.1007/s10009-018-0488-3
70. Mazzanti, F., Ferrari, A., Spagnolo, G.O.: Experiments in formal modelling of a deadlock avoidance algorithm for a CBTC system. In: Margaria, T., Steffen, B. (eds.) ISoLA 2016. LNCS, vol. 9953, pp. 297–314. Springer, Cham (2016). https://doi.org/10.1007/978-3-319-47169-3_22
71. Mazzanti, F., Spagnolo, G.O., Della Longa, S., Ferrari, A.: Deadlock avoidance in train scheduling: a model checking approach. In: Lang, F., Flammini, F. (eds.) Proceedings of the 19th International Conference on Formal Methods for Industrial Critical Systems, FMICS 2014. LNCS, vol. 8718, pp. 109–123. Springer, Cham (2014). https://doi.org/10.1007/978-3-319-10702-8_8
72. Rosadini, B., et al.: Using NLP to detect requirements defects: an industrial experience in the railway domain. In: Grünbacher, P., Perini, A. (eds.) Proceedings of the 23rd International Working Conference on Requirements Engineering: Foundation for Software Quality, REFSQ 2017. LNCS, vol. 10153, pp. 344–360. Springer, Cham (2017). https://doi.org/10.1007/978-3-319-54045-0_24
73. Shift2Rail: 4SECURail project site. https://projects.shift2rail.org/s2r_ip2_n.aspx?p=s2r_4securail. Accessed Sept 2025
74. Shift2Rail: ASTRail project site. https://projects.shift2rail.org/s2r_ip2_n.aspx?p=S2R_ASTRAIL. Accessed Sept 2025

The Successful Use of the B Method in Industrial Development of Critical Systems: Standards Compliance and Certification in CBTC

Dalay Almeida[✉][iD] and Thierry Lecomte[iD]

CLEARSY, Aix-en-Provence, France
{dalay.almeida,thierry.lecomte}@CLEARSY.com

Abstract. The B Method has become one of the most successful formal approaches for the development of safety-critical railway software. Initially received with skepticism due to perceived costs and complexity, its industrial relevance was firmly established through milestones such as the use of the B language for the verification of SACEM and the application of the full B Method in the METEOR metro project in Paris. More recently, its widespread adoption in Communication-Based Train Control (CBTC) systems has reinforced its role in the railway industry. Its success is closely linked to the method's ability to support compliance with industrial standards, in particular EN 50128, by contributing to verification, validation, proof, testing, and maintenance activities. This paper examines the factors that have enabled the successful industrial application of the B Method, offering an experience-based account of how it is applied to meet certification requirements in CBTC development. While respecting industrial confidentiality, the discussion is illustrated with simplified examples that highlight key aspects of the methodology and its alignment with safety standards.

Keywords: B Method · CBTC · Certification · Formal Methods

1 Introduction

The industrial adoption of Formal Methods was a matter of debate throughout the late 20th century. Concerns about their cost and complexity were frequently used as arguments against their use, and for many years the benefits of Formal Methods were regarded with skepticism [13]. This perception began to shift when Formal Methods started to demonstrate concrete successes in industry. The B language and the B Method [1], for instance, achieved two remarkable milestones in the 1990s: the use of the B specification language for the verification of the SACEM [12] railway control system, and the adoption of the full B Method, including refinement and proof, in the development of the METEOR [6] metro

© The Author(s), under exclusive license to Springer Nature Switzerland AG 2026
M. H. ter Beek et al. (Eds.): Fantechi Festschrift, LNCS 16470, pp. 55–68, 2026.
https://doi.org/10.1007/978-3-032-12484-5_4

line in Paris. By proving system safety without increasing production costs, these projects established an important precedent that paved the way for the industrial use of Formal Methods.

During the first two decades of the 21st century, the Communication-Based Train Control (CBTC) industry has embraced the B Method as a key tool in the development of safety-critical software [7]. Today, companies such as Alstom and Siemens, which together account for a significant share of the global metro market, are among the main industrial actors employing the B Method in their CBTC development processes [8,15,17]. From the academic perspective, the B Method has also become the most widely used modeling language in railway-related research [11], which underlines its relevance both in industry and academia.

Several factors explain the success of the B Method over the past decades. Compliance with standards and norms, together with the availability of supporting tools, training material, and accumulated expertise, have played a decisive role. In the most recent versions of the EN 50128 standard [9], which defines process requirements and applicable techniques for the development of programmable electronic systems in the railway domain, the use of Formal Methods is not only highly recommended for the highest level of safety (SIL3 and SIL4), but it is also explicitly recognized. The standard's appendix even dedicates a specific section to the B Method, further reinforcing its industrial credibility.

In this paper, we provide an experience-based perspective on the methodologies that involve the use of the B Method for the development of CBTC systems. We discuss the characteristics that explain its industrial success and explain how its development strategies are aligned with the requirements of standards and regulations, aiming at the production of safe and certifiable systems.This paper focuses on the methodologies enforced by industrial railway norms, and explains how the B Method is applied to fulfill their goals. In this context, the B Method proves successful in many key aspects by providing effective support in system testing and proof, verification, validation, and maintenance activities. The industrial use of the B Method in all these stages, as well as an adapted version of the development cycle, are discussed in this paper. The perspective adopted here is that of an experience report: rather than presenting purely theoretical considerations, the paper reflects on concrete practices observed in industrial contexts and highlights how they contribute to the certification process.

It is worth noting that, due to confidentiality constraints and the sensitive nature of industrial projects, we do not include material directly extracted from real CBTC developments. Instead, the paper relies on illustrative examples specifically created for this work. These examples are simplified but representative, serving to highlight the main features of the methodologies without disclosing sensitive or proprietary information. This approach allows us to convey the principles of the industrial use of the B Method while respecting industrial confidentiality.

The remainder of this paper is organized as follows. Section 2 introduces the B Method and its industrial context, followed by Sect. 3, which outlines the development cycle according to the EN 50128 railway software standard. Section 4 forms the core of the paper, detailing how the B Method is applied across the different lifecycle phases, from component design and implementation to testing, verification, data verification, maintenance, and validation. Finally, Sect. 5 concludes the paper by summarizing the main outcomes and discussing perspectives for future applications and research directions.

2   The B Method

The B Method [1] was introduced in the late 80's to correctly design safe software. It is a formal method to develop software mathematically proved to comply with its specification. It relies on a mathematical model of the software, containing both what the software is expected to do and its algorithm. The software model is decomposed into smaller models in order to manage the complexity ("divide and conquer"). The model is proved: the algorithm doesn't contradict its specification. The software code is generated from the implementation model. Code is readable, very close to the model and is easily checked. The final software application is made of parts developed with B and parts not developed formally.

This modelling approach is slightly specific but comes along many other interesting features. The "specification before code" motto imposes a top-to-bottom approach (or by decomposition). Software developers are encouraged to specify first, from natural language requirements. It does not prevent reuse of existing software but avoids asking the dangerous question "what do I get if I gather all these software components together?" The target software is cyclic and mono-threaded. No interrupt should modify the state variables. Full integer arithmetic is supported (non-trivial floating-point arithmetic is practically not provable) as well as Boolean predicates and equations (and arrays of integers and Booleans). The models are text-based. The same mathematical language (B) is used for the specification model and the implementation model, based on the set theory and predicate logic. The model contains (Fig. 1) both the software properties (the static aspect) and its behaviour (the dynamic aspect). A proved model means that the specification is consistent (no contradiction) and the implementation complies with its specification. A minima, the software is proved to be programming error-free.

Promoted and supported by RATP , B and Atelier B [14] have been successfully applied to the industry of transportation, through metros automatic pilots installed worldwide. Paris Meteor line 14 driverless metro is one of the main reference applications with over 110,000 lines of B models, translated into 86,000 lines of Ada. No bugs were detected after the proof was completed, neither at the functional validation, at the integration validation, and at the on-site testing, nor since the beginning of the metro line operation (October 1998). Today, all metro lines in Paris are going to be automated with B-based CBTCs.

For years, Alstom Transportation Systems and Siemens Transportation Systems have been the two main industrial players in the development of safety-critical B software. To date, the biggest B software is an XML compiler enabling

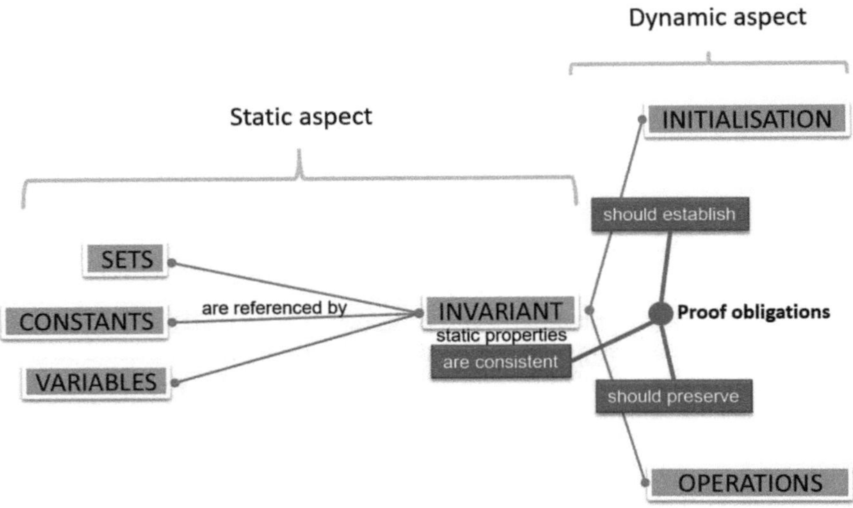

Fig. 1. The relations between the B modelling elements.

the execution of safety critical embedded applications by an interpreter, used to validate system-level design and interfaces. The B models generate more than 300,000 lines of Ada code, for this SIL4 T3-compliant (EN50128) program. The method is not limited to 300,000-lines of software code and has not met any bottleneck until now. Therefore, the method is likely to scale up to larger, non-threaded software. At the other end of the scale, with platform screen doors (PSD) or remote inputs/outputs controllers, less demanding in terms of computation, smaller applications are generated for both programmable logic controllers (PLC) and PIC32 microcontrollers, with a maximum of 64 KB in memory per software. SIL3 and SIL4 controllers, in charge of opening and closing platform screen doors have been (or will be) installed in Paris (L1, L4, L13), Stockholm (Citybanan) and Sao Paulo (L2, L3, L15 Monorail). Finally, for formal data validation, B machines generated from instanciated data models and analysed by the ProB model checker [19] contain up to 10,000,000 lines of textual model.

3   Development Cycle According to the Norms

In order to not only certify a CBTC system but also to ensure confidence in its correctness, it is essential to follow the most rigorous development practices established in the industry. In this context, railway standards provide a set of procedures that guide the development of safety-critical software. Among them, EN 50128 defines requirements and acceptable practices for the development of programmable electronic systems, describing alternative lifecycle models to structure the software process into well-defined phases and activities.

One of the proposed lifecycle models, referred to as "Development Lifecycle 2" in the EN 50128, follows a V-shaped structure, illustrated in Fig. 2. The descending branch of the V covers activities such as system and software requirements definition, architectural design, planning of verification and validation, modeling, and finally the implementation phase. The ascending branch addresses the complementary activities of component and integration testing, system validation, assessment, and ultimately the maintenance phase. Each phase is associated with specific objectives and deliverables that must be satisfied in order to achieve compliance with the standard and to build trust in the final product.

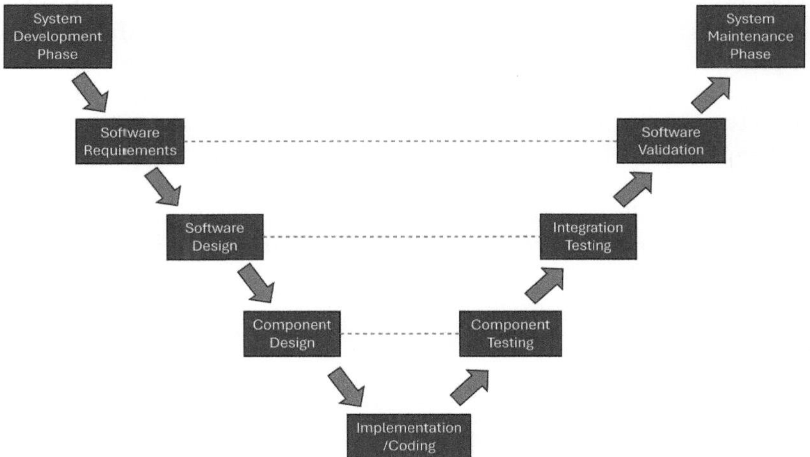

Fig. 2. Development process according to the EN 50128.

In this paper, we focus on the impact of applying the B Method within this lifecycle to meet the requirements of the standards. Not all phases are analyzed in detail, but the general structure of the development lifecycle is presented here as a foundation for the subsequent discussion.

4   The Development Cycle with the B Method

Before analyzing how the development lifecycle is impacted by the use of the B Method, it is important to understand how the method is applied in the industrial context of CBTC systems. A CBTC system is typically divided into major domains such as the trackside and the onboard system, each of which is further decomposed into subsystems. For example, the onboard system includes elements such as the driver interface and the odometry.

A fundamental distinction is systematically applied to every subsystem: the separation between safety-critical functions and functional (non-safety) functions. Safety-critical functions are those whose behavior is essential to maintaining system safety, since any error in their execution could lead to dangerous or costly consequences. Examples include train speed supervision, emergency braking logic, or interlocking consistency checks. Functional functions, in contrast, are useful to the system but do not directly affect its safe operation. Errors in these functions do not compromise safety, even though they may reduce system usability or efficiency. Examples include the driver's graphical interface, logging and diagnostic tools, or system configuration options.

This distinction has a direct impact on the way the development lifecycle is conducted. For safety-critical functions, typically associated with SIL3 and SIL4, the use of rigorous techniques such as the B Method is highly recommended by standards like EN 50128. In these cases, the development process relies on formal specification, proof, and model-based verification as key activities. In contrast, functional functions are developed through a different process, which generally does not rely on the B Method and usually employs less formal, industry-standard engineering practices. As a result, the lifecycle is effectively split into two parallel tracks: one dedicated to the safety-critical part of the system, where Formal Methods play a central role, and another dedicated to the non-safety part, where traditional approaches are applied.

This duality is illustrated in Fig. 3, which depicts the V-shaped lifecycle with two distinct development processes. The figure highlights how the B Method is integrated only in the safety-critical branch, while the functional branch follows a conventional engineering cycle.

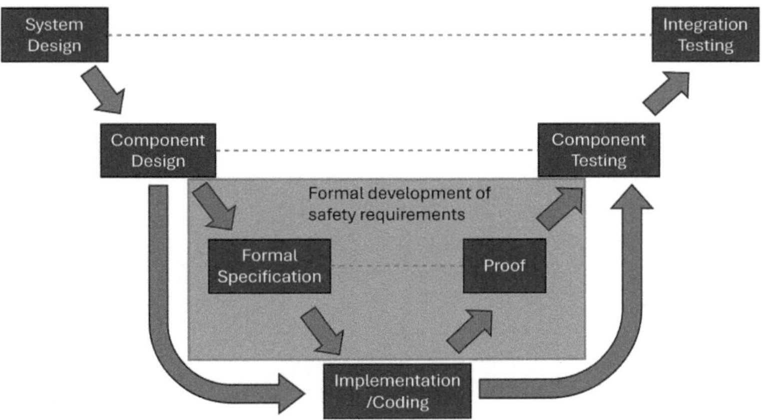

Fig. 3. Development process using the B Method.

4.1 Component Design

The component requirements document describes all expected behaviours and constraints for a component. In a development process that uses a formal method, this document is partitioned into safety and functional functions. Safety-related requirements, which are usually subject to higher Safety Integrity Levels (SIL3 and SIL4), are identified during requirements allocation and are designated for formalisation with the B Method, in alignment with the guidance of EN 50128 regarding the specification of software safety functions and the assignment of software safety integrity levels. Functional requirements remain in the same document but are not modelled with B and proceed through the standard, less formal engineering stream.

Flagging safety-critical items in the requirements document fulfils two important purposes. First, it makes the allocation explicit and auditable, supporting traceability and satisfying the expectations of certification bodies, as emphasized by EN 50128. Second, it clearly defines the scope of formal modelling: each B abstract machine corresponds directly to the subset of requirements that must be mathematically guaranteed. The textual requirements therefore remain the reference for stakeholders and reviewers, while the B Method provides formal semantics and proof obligations for the safety functions, ensuring rigorous development in accordance with high SIL levels.

The relationship between the requirements document and the formal models is maintained through explicit traceability links. Each B abstract machine is connected to the specific requirement statements it formalises, which aligns with EN 50128 by ensuring that requirements can be traced to the corresponding design elements that fulfil them. Conversely, each safety requirement is associated with the machine elements that implement or guarantee it. The refinement process further reinforces this alignment with the standard by establishing a direct and provable connection between design specifications and their implementation. Through refinement proofs, the behaviour described at higher levels of abstraction is guaranteed to be preserved in the implementation, providing formal evidence that the code satisfies both the design and the original requirements. This traceability and refinement link reduces the effort of code-level verification for safety functions and supports compliance with certification expectations.

Because only safety-critical requirements are modelled in B, the development lifecycle splits into two complementary tracks. The safety track, driven by formal modelling, refinement and proof, leads to proved implementation machines and subsequently to code generation or verified manual coding. The functional track follows the conventional design, implementation and test flow. This dual-track arrangement explains why the V-shaped lifecycle is represented with two distinct, parallel processes in this work.

4.2   Implementation

Once the component requirements have been documented and, in the case of safety-critical functions, formally modelled, the development process splits into two distinct strategies. Functional parts of the system, which are not associated with high SIL levels, proceed directly from textual design to coding in conventional programming languages such as C++ or Ada. Safety-critical parts, in contrast, follow the formal development path: they are refined step by step within the B Method until a provably correct implementation model is obtained. This approach aligns with the recommendations of EN 50128, which strongly encourages the use of formal methods for software associated with the highest Safety Integrity Levels, ensuring that the implementation systematically preserves the formally specified safety properties.

Refinement is the key element of this formal track. Each refinement step must ensure that the behaviour of the model is preserved, so that operations, initialisation, invariants and typing constraints remain consistent between abstract and concrete levels. In practice, this usually involves one or multiple intermediate refinements. Although refinement requires experience to handle interactive proofs efficiently, industrial projects have shown that the learning curve is manageable because the refinement strategies are well-established and easily learned through practice.

Once the refinement reaches the level of an implementation machine, code can be produced. If the machine is restricted to the B0 subset, there are tools that can automatically generate source code in the target language. Atelier B, for example, provides such functionality and is often used for prototyping or internal verification. In operational projects, however, companies usually rely on certified proprietary or adapted code generators tailored to their own development environments and certification processes.

Regardless of whether the code is manually written or automatically generated, both the functional and the safety-related implementations converge at the testing stage, which is discussed in the following section.

4.3 Testing and Proof

According to EN 50128, testers should be independent from the designers and developers in order to provide an unbiased evaluation of the system and its compliance with requirements. In CBTC development, testing can be divided into two main phases: component testing and integration testing. Component testing focuses on the behavior of individual components, analysing how their inputs produce outputs. In this phase, interfaces with other components are simulated to allow a thorough examination of input-output relationships. Integration testing, on the other hand, evaluates how the system performs as a whole. At this level, the behavior of a single component is relevant primarily in terms of its contribution to the overall system, and isolated component behavior becomes less critical.

Because B Method abstract machines are used to model components, the formal specification primarily impacts component-level testing: the properties of safety-critical functions can be formally proved, providing a solid foundation for verification and testing activities. According to EN 50128, formal proof is a highly recommended activity for functions associated with high Safety Integrity Levels (SIL3 and SIL4), complementing traditional testing and increasing confidence in system correctness. While integration testing can also benefit from these formal proofs, the impact is less direct at the system level.

It is important to emphasize that formally proved functions are not exempt from testing. Two key considerations make testing essential even after formal proof. First, redundancy is valuable: textual requirements may be interpreted differently by designers, developers, and testers. These different perspectives often trigger fruitful discussions, improving the understanding and robustness of the system. Second, testing provides documented evidence that the proved system behaves as expected in practice. Industrial experience, dating back to projects such as METEOR in the 1990s, shows that formally proved functions rarely fail during testing.

In the ascending phase of the V-model, testing and proof activities are performed in parallel. Although the proof phase adds complexity, its benefits can offset testing costs by reducing the likelihood of errors. Unlike the use of formal methods in the descending phase, proof at this stage requires a high degree of expertise. Multiple strategies exist for discharging proof obligations, and the chosen technique significantly affects efficiency. Experts can leverage interactive tactics in Atelier B that are more efficient in terms of memory and execution time than the tool's fully automatic prover at its highest strength levels.

Integration testing benefits indirectly from formally proved components, as these components are more likely to behave correctly. Nevertheless, at the system level, proof plays a less visible role. Regardless, testing remains essential in both component and integration phases, ensuring that the system meets requirements and behaves as expected, even when formal proofs have been applied.

4.4 Verification

Verification is the process of assessing whether each development artifact satisfies its corresponding requirements, ensuring completeness, correctness, and consistency. According to EN 50128, verification activities span all lifecycle stages and artifacts, providing documented evidence that the system design and implementation meet the specified requirements. In CBTC development, the B Method contributes by producing formal models that serve as precise references for verification, supporting traceability from requirements to design and implementation.

Code verification entails analyzing whether all requirements defined in the system design are correctly implemented, and providing justification when they are not. This process typically involves one or more experienced verifiers who compare the produced code against the requirements and draw conclusions. Traceability is essential at this stage, as verification is performed exhaustively to cover all safety requirements. Verification reports are reviewed and discussed among multiple stakeholders, and verifiers may contact developers or designers to clarify ambiguities or understand proposed solutions.

In a formal development cycle using the B Method, verification follows a dual approach. Functional code, which is not formally specified, is verified using standard industrial practices, primarily through functional testing, and may additionally include manual analysis against requirements in specific cases. Safety-related code, however, can be verified directly against the formal specification. This is possible because the code is a proved refinement of the abstract machines:

every requirement and function defined in the abstract machines and refinement steps is guaranteed to be present in the final code. Consequently, if a requirement is satisfied in the formal specification, it is also satisfied in the implementation.

This approach provides a significant benefit: the formal specification closely mirrors the semantics of the requirements and design documentation. The set-theoretic and logical foundations of the B Method allow system behaviour to be expressed in a form similar to natural-language requirements. For example, a requirement stating

```
(train_speed > section_speed_limit) => overspeed_alarm = TRUE
```

can be formally specified in the B Method in the same logical terms. From the verifier's perspective, this formal expression is much closer to the textual requirement than the equivalent code implementation. By grounding verification in the formal specification, proof results provide additional assurance, complementing and supporting the traditional documentation-based verification process.

4.5   Data Verification

An additional stage described in the standards is the development of application data and algorithms, which is necessary to configure each installation according to the specific requirements of a given application. A system configured by this data allows the customization of an already approved software. This development approach must include verification and validation activities to ensure that the data are complete, correct, and consistent with each other and with the system itself.

A typical example of such data is the information describing the structure of the railway network, including the positions of tracks, balises, signals, stations, and switches. This information is a critical input for CBTC systems, as it is used by trains for localisation and operational decision-making. Therefore, the accuracy, completeness, and consistency of this data must be verified. Moreover, validation activities are performed to ensure that the configuration of the data complies with the system's safety constraints and operational requirements, thus guaranteeing safe system operation.

A concrete example of application data is the location and configuration of balises along a track section. Each balise transmits specific information to the train, such as its precise position and identity within the signaling system. Verifying this data manually is possible, but complex installations with many balises require a more systematic and auditable approach, as recommended for high SIL levels.

To address this, formal methods are increasingly used in industry. In this context, the B Method provides a mathematical framework to define the data precisely. Sets and functions can be used to represent relationships among track elements, while logical expressions capture constraints such as positional dependencies. Using a tool like the ProB modelchecker, all combinations of related data can be systematically checked to ensure they satisfy the specified requirements.

In industrial projects, tools such as the CLEARSY Data Solver are employed for data verification; this tool leverages ProB as a backend to automate the checking of complex configurations, ensuring that application data conform to all specified constraints. This approach supports traceability, repeatable verification, and auditability, all explicitly emphasized in EN 50128 for critical data preparation.

The result of this formal verification is a comprehensive report showing which data meet the requirements and which require correction. Teams can then adjust the system configuration, fix errors in the data, or propose modifications to the system itself, ensuring that the CBTC operates safely and reliably. Furthermore, EN 50128 explicitly recommends the use of formal proof techniques for the correctness of safety-critical application data at SIL3 and SIL4. By applying formal verification and model checking to critical data, industrial projects not only comply with best practices but also significantly reduce the risk of configuration errors impacting system safety, while providing documented evidence for certification purposes.

4.6   Maintenance

The final stage of the development lifecycle is maintenance, where it is essential to ensure that the system continues to perform as required, preserving its integrity and dependability while implementing corrections, enhancements, or adaptations. According to EN 50128, maintenance must be performed with at least the same level of expertise, tools, documentation, planning, and configuration management as in the initial development, with mitigation actions proportionate to identified risks. A formal development approach must therefore provide mechanisms to modify the system and reprove it efficiently, ensuring that the methodology remains practical and cost-effective.

The B Method provides such a solution. When proving a system using the Atelier B tool, the strategies applied to discharge each proof obligation are stored in dedicated project files. During maintenance, these stored strategies can be reused to guide the reproving of abstract, refinement, and implementation machines. As a result, parts of the system unaffected by modifications can often be reproved automatically with minimal effort. Obligations not fully covered by the stored strategies can then be discharged either by the automatic prover, a combination of the automatic prover with stored strategies, or interactively by an expert using Atelier B's interactive prover. This ability to systematically and efficiently reprove the system ensures that risk mitigation is applied consistently, in line with EN 50128 requirements.

This approach significantly reduces the effort required to maintain formally specified systems, even eliminating the need to redo proofs entirely for unaffected parts of the system. Consequently, maintenance becomes more straightforward and cost-efficient, ensuring that the formal development method remains a viable and sustainable approach throughout the system's lifecycle.

4.7 Validation

The validation process assesses whether the development processes and their outputs comply with the defined Safety Integrity Level (SIL) and ultimately ensure that the delivered system fulfils its intended purpose. This activity is essential for certification and is performed independently of the development team.

Although the B Method is not applied directly during validation, its impact is indirect but significant. Over more than three decades of industrial application, systems developed with the B Method and supported by the safety-certified tool Atelier B have consistently passed validation and certification audits, including in CBTC projects. This sustained acceptance by certification bodies highlights the maturity and reliability of the method, demonstrating its compatibility with the highest safety requirements and its strong relevance for the railway industry.

5   Conclusion and Perspectives

This paper has provided an experience-based account of the application of the B Method in the development of CBTC systems, highlighting how formal methods support compliance with industrial safety standards such as EN 50128. By focusing on the certification-relevant aspects of the development lifecycle, including requirements specification, formal modelling, refinement, implementation, testing, verification, and maintenance, we have illustrated the practical benefits of formal specification and proof in ensuring the correctness and safety of critical railway functions. In particular, the industrial use of the B Method demonstrates its acceptance as a reliable approach for developing safety-critical railway software. Our experience highlights how formal specification and proof align with the expectations of safety standards, providing precise traceability, strengthening verification activities, and facilitating sustainable maintenance practices.

It is worth noting that EN 50128 [9] is being replaced by a newer standard, EN 50716 [10]. The new standard maintains and refines the core principles of EN 50128 (including traceability, formal methods usage, verification, validation, and maintenance) while expanding the scope to better integrate with other RAMS standards and to accommodate evolving technologies. Because the approach presented in this paper already aligns closely with EN 50128, its methods are also well-positioned to comply with EN 50716, thereby ensuring continuity of applicability and relevance in future certification regimes.

Beyond the CBTC domain, our industrial experience extends to other safety-critical railway systems. Notably, the design and deployment of platform screen doors around the world has leveraged the B Method and the CLEARSY Safety Platform (CSSP) to achieve high SIL levels [16, 17]. These systems, although not CBTC, illustrate the versatility of formal methods in industrial railway applications, combining rigorous formal proofs with practical, deployable solutions.

In parallel, our academic research explores novel approaches that are not yet applied industrially but show strong potential. One line of work proposes the implementation of relay-based Railway Interlocking Systems, common in many French installations [20], using formal B-based models while preserving the behavior of the legacy system [5,18]. A proof of concept investigates the use of AI to automate the transformation of relay-based models into formal specifications [3], a step that could dramatically reduce manual effort in migrating legacy systems. Another research effort focuses on monitoring legacy interlocking systems where replacement is not feasible [4], using the CSSP to detect deviations from expected behavior in real-time. Building on these experiences, we are developing a similar approach for CBTC systems, aiming to continuously monitor and generate alerts when safety requirements are not met [2]. This is particularly relevant for SIL4 systems, where incidents are most often caused by hardware failures or human errors.

Looking forward, the combination of industrial deployment and academic research points to a continuum of opportunities for formal methods in railway systems. The lessons learned from CBTC, interlocking, and platform screen doors provide a foundation for extending rigorous verification, validation, and monitoring techniques across increasingly complex and heterogeneous railway networks. The integration of AI-based automation in formal modelling, combined with real-time monitoring platforms such as CSSP, represents a promising avenue to further enhance safety, reduce certification effort, and enable predictive maintenance strategies. These perspectives suggest that formal methods, long established in critical railway software, will continue to play a central role in the evolution of safe and reliable railway operations.

References

1. Abrial, J.R., Lee, M., Neilson, D., Scharbach, P., Sørensen, I.: The B-method. In: International Symposium of VDM Europe, pp. 398–405. Springer (1991)
2. Almeida, D.: Use of certified industrial tools for formal analysis and monitoring of communications-based train control systems. In: Proceedings of the 6th International Conference on Reliability, Safety, and Security of Railway Systems (RSSRail 2025). Lecture Notes in Computer Science. Springer (2025) accepted for publication
3. Almeida, D., Glemarec, L.: From relay-based railway interlocking circuits to formal specification: An AI-driven approach. In: Proceedings of the 6th International Conference on Reliability, Safety, and Security of Railway Systems (RSSRail 2025). Lecture Notes in Computer Science. Springer (2025) accepted for publication
4. Almeida, D., Jamain, F., Lecomte, T.: Formal analysis and monitoring of legacy safety-critical interlocking systems with the use of certified industrial tools. In: International Conference on Formal Methods for Industrial Critical Systems, pp. 182–198. Springer (2024)
5. de Almeida Pereira, D.I., Deharbe, D., Perin, M., Bon, P.: B-specification of relay-based railway interlocking systems based on the propositional logic of the system state evolution. In: International Conference on Reliability, Safety, and Security of Railway Systems, pp. 242–258. Springer (2019)
6. Behm, P., Benoit, P., Faivre, A., Meynadier, J.M.: Meteor,: A successful application of b in a large project. In: International Symposium on Formal Methods, pp. 369–387. Springer (1999)

7. Butler, M., Körner, P., Krings, S., Lecomte, T., Leuschel, M., Mejia, L.F., Voisin, L.: The first twenty-five years of industrial use of the b-method. In: International Conference on Formal Methods for Industrial Critical Systems, pp. 189–209. Springer (2020)

8. Dolle, D.: The b method at siemens. Formal Methods Applied to Complex Systems: Implementation of the B Method, pp. 83–127 (2014)

9. EN 50128:2011 Railway applications - Communication, signalling and processing systems - Software for railway control and protection systems (2011), standard

10. EN 50716:2023 Railway Applications - Requirements for Software Development (2023), standard

11. Ferrari, A., ter Beek, M.H.: Formal methods in railways: a systematic mapping study. ACM Comput. Surv. **55**(4), 1–37 (2022)

12. Guiho, G., Hennebert, C.: Sacem software validation. In: [1990] Proceedings. 12th International Conference on Software Engineering, pp. 186–191. IEEE (1990)

13. Hall, A.: Seven myths of formal methods. IEEE Softw. **7**(5), 11–19 (2002)

14. Lecomte, T.: Atelier b. Formal Methods Applied to Complex Systems: Implementation of the B Method pp. 35–46 (2014)

15. Lecomte, T.: Industrial applications for modeling with the b method. Formal Methods Appl. Complex Syst. Impl. B Method, 129–150 (2014)

16. Lecomte, T., Deharbe, D., Fournier, P., Oliveira, M.: The clearsy safety platform: 5 years of research, development and deployment. Sci. Comput. Program. **199**, 102524 (2020)

17. Lecomte, T., Déharbe, D., Prun, É., Mottin, E.: Applying a formal method in industry: a 25-year trajectory. In: Brazilian Symposium on Formal Methods, pp. 70–87. Springer (2017)

18. Lecomte, T., Lavaud, B., Sabatier, D., Burdy, L.: A safety flasher developed with the clearsy safety platform. In: International Conference on Formal Methods for Industrial Critical Systems, pp. 210–227. Springer (2020)

19. Leuschel, M., Butler, M.: Prob: a model checker for b. In: International Symposium of Formal Methods Europe, pp. 855–874. Springer (2003)

20. Theeg, G., Vlasenko, S.: Railway signalling & interlocking: international compendium. PMC Media House (2019)

Quantitative Dependability Evaluation of Train Control Systems: Selected Case Studies

Laura Carnevali[1], Silvano Chiaradonna[2], Felicita Di Giandomenico[2],
Gloria Gori[1(✉)], Marco Papini[1], and Enrico Vicario[1]

[1] Department of Information Engineering, University of Florence, Florence, Italy
{laura.carnevali,gloria.gori,marco.papini,enrico.vicario}@unifi.it
[2] Institute of Information Science and Technologies (ISTI), CNR, Pisa, Italy
{silvano.chiaradonna,felicita.digiandomenico}@isti.cnr.it

Abstract. Groundbreaking technological innovations for train distancing and localization have the potential to radically boost dependability of Train Control Systems (TCSs), while actually posing notable challenges on dependability evaluation due to the uncertainty introduced on TCS vital parameters such as train position and speed. This paper focuses on applications of stochastic modeling and analysis for dependability evaluation of TCSs in presence of uncertainty, summarizing four representative case studies developed by the authors in previous publications. Without intent of completeness, this paper aims at showing the potential of quantitative evaluation methods in: i) representing and analyzing the variability of TCS parameters; ii) determining appropriate trade-offs between contrasting but equally relevant dependability-related attributes; iii) providing added value in synthesizing stochastic parameters from observed data; and, iv) supporting the definition of compositional solution methods for the analysis of complex TCSs. Along with a fairly extensive literature, this paper demonstrates the relevance and topicality of dependability evaluation of TCSs with uncertainty on vital parameters.

Keywords: Train control systems · dependability · stochastic modeling · quantitative evaluation · case studies

1 Introduction

Train Control System (TCS) generally indicates any system that controls a relevant function related to train movement and line operation, such that a failure of the system can impact regular service and/or performance, availability, capacity, and safety of the railway operation. In most cases, modern railways are controlled by real-time computer-based TCSs, featuring embedded, cyber-physical, distributed, and heterogeneous architectures, which are increasingly large and

© The Author(s), under exclusive license to Springer Nature Switzerland AG 2026

M. H. ter Beek et al. (Eds.): Fantechi Festschrift, LNCS 16470, pp. 69–91, 2026.
https://doi.org/10.1007/978-3-032-12484-5_5

complex. Based on their main functions, TCSs can be roughly classified into: i) train movement and distancing control (e.g., Automatic Train Control); ii) automatic driving (Automatic Train Operation); iii) collision avoidance in a station or junction (e.g., Input and eXit Locking); iv) scheduling and optimization of railway traffic (Automatic Train Supervision). In addition, ancillary systems contribute to fulfilling TCS operations, such as the Switch Heater Control Subsystem (in charge of keeping the railroad switches free from snow and ice) and the Integrated Power Supply (in charge of assuring a continued power supply to critical railway functions).

Recently, relevant technological innovations [19,20,27] for the improvement of *dependability* of TCSs, such as advanced distancing [31] and satellite positioning [4], have come at a significant cost in terms of assessment of dependability-related attributes, due to the *uncertainty* introduced in vital parameters to be accounted for in the analysis. Advanced solution techniques for quantitative evaluation of stochastic models can largely support the assessment of dependability of TCSs, by enabling the derivation of quantitative estimates of dependability-related attributes under uncertainty [23]. In fact, dependability assessment studies through model-based approaches, especially when performed at early stages of the system development to support design choices and promptly detect potential weaknesses, typically have to cope with inaccurate, sometimes even unknown, information on a subset of the model parameters [40]. To address this problem and assess the impact of uncertainty on the analyzed measure/attribute, *sensitivity analysis* is typically performed, where a range of values for critical model parameters can be considered instead of a single, potentially inaccurate value. Sensitivity analysis is also a powerful means to assess the adaptivity level of a system in operational contexts differing in aspects impacting dependability properties, as well as to identify suitable trade-offs between conflicting attributes (such as safety and availability).

Thus, the analysis is conducted considering variations for quantities modeling either *i*) aspects intrinsically connected with technologies the system is equipped with, or *ii*) external phenomena impacting the dependability-related indicators under evaluation. In the context of TCSs, measures of train position, speed, and acceleration, as well as measures related to delay and loss of communication messages, are among the model parameters within the first group [23]. Indicators related to weather forecasts (e.g., temperature or humidity in future time intervals) and occurrence rate of accidental faults and attacks are instead among those within the second group [16,23].

There has been growing interest in applying model-based analysis in the railway context, to cope with dependability assessment in the presence of uncertainty in system aspects. The pioneer work presented in [43] evaluates the impact of uncertainty on the train-ground communication of the European Train Control System (ETCS) [19,20], an Automatic Train Protection (ATP) system developed in the framework of the European Rail Traffic Management System (ERTMS) with the aim of not exceeding the safe speed and train-to-train distance by continuously supervising the train. In particular, the approach exploits Deterministic and Stochastic Petri Nets (DSPNs) [29] to model the process of failure and recovery of the train-ground communication as well as the exchange of location information and movement authority, and then performs rare-event simulation of the DSPN by TimeNET [42]. The obtained experimental results provide the train stopping probability due to packet delays and losses, showing that reliability and availability of the communication channel significantly affect the track utilization.

Since the seminal work [43], several papers and projects have addressed quantitative evaluation of dependability of TCSs that exploit the above-mentioned technological innovations, such as the works presented in [3,5,24,25,38,39], the Capacity4Rail FP7 project [7], the ASTRail [2] and PERFORMINGRAIL [33] H2020 Shift2Rail (S2R) Joint Undertaking (JU) projects [37], and various currently ongoing Europe's Rail (EU-Rail) projects [22]. In this context, the survey recently presented in [10], notably co-authored by Alessandro Fantechi, provides a systematic literature review of academic and industrial efforts made to investigate quantitative evaluation through model-based analysis of dependability-related attributes of TCSs, under uncertainty on vital parameters.

In line with works reported in [10], in the following, we summarize selected case studies developed by the authors in previous publications, concerning quantitative dependability evaluation in the context of TCSs. Specifically, the focus is on the following dependability-related attributes: energy efficiency-availability trade-off of anti-icing systems for railroad switches (Sect. 2), reliability and availability of integrated power supply systems (Sect. 3), predictive maintenance strategies for legacy vehicles (Sect. 4), and performability of the ERTMS/ETCS with moving block signaling (Sect. 5). Finally, we draw our conclusions (Sect. 6).

2 The Railroad Switches Anti-Icing System Case Study

Railroad switches are mechanical installations enabling trains to be guided from one track to another. They are a critical part of the safe, reliable railway operations, since the correct routing of trains strongly depends on the proper operation of such switches. In fact, in the presence of malfunctions, train derailments or train collisions could occur, with expected catastrophic consequences for passengers. During the winter months, snow and ice accumulated on the track can prevent switches from properly aligning and locking into place.

Therefore, nowadays switches are equipped with an anti-icing system, commonly consisting of electric heaters installed in their vicinity, automatically operated by an ICT control system responsible for maintaining the temperature around the switches above freezing. Since energy saving is increasingly pursued in application domains (including the railway sector) for environmental and financial reasons, useful contributions to progress towards more sustainable railway systems include the definition of both advanced control policies of the anti-icing system and analysis frameworks to assess Key Performance Indicators representative of both energy consumption and dependability properties.

At a rather abstract level (details are in [15]), the heater control system has a hierarchical, distributed organization, with several coordinating components

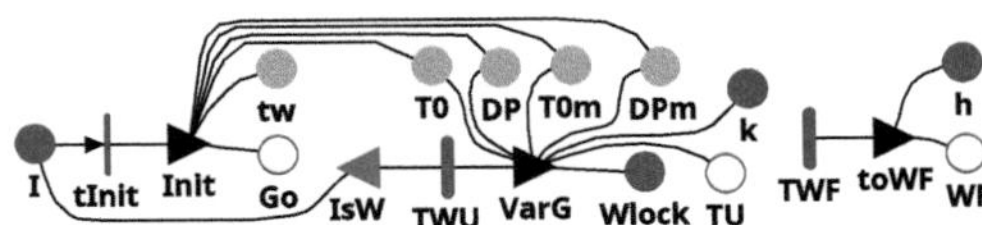

Fig. 1. SAN template model *TM_W* for global weather conditions and weather data collection.

(which depend on the size of the railway station), each controlling a set of heaters located close to the switch through a rather simple local logic. Traditionally, heaters are operated on an on/off basis [41], i.e., they are turned on as soon as the temperature falls below a defined threshold and work at full power until the temperature rises again above the threshold.

The authors belonging to the SEDC Lab at CNR in Pisa have been working for almost a decade in this area, developing increasingly sophisticated and effective energy management policies on one side, and an increasingly accurate evaluation framework able to assess dependability-energy consumption trade-offs in realistic scenarios (mainly, from the weather and failure events perspective). A selected list of papers in this research line is [14–16]. The final goal of the study is to provide actionable insights to effectively guide future anti-icing policy decisions in railroad switch heater systems, able to optimize energy usage and operational reliability while complying with the requirements of regulatory bodies and other influential authorities.

2.1 The Framework for Assessing Dependability of Anti-Icing Systems

The developed assessment framework follows a stochastic modeling approach and relies on the SAN formalism [36] to define three atomic template models that represent, respectively: i) the global weather conditions; ii) the hierarchical control regulating the switch on/off of the heaters, and the weather conditions local to each switch; and iii) for each switch, the sequence of randomly chosen time intervals during which the heating control system is active (thus, turning on or off the heater), with periods where it is not active (and the heater is always off), to take into account the actual train movements requiring the switches.

The overall system model is then obtained by generating and composing automatically one instance of the global weather model, with one instance of the other two models for each local switch controller, exploiting the features of the Mobius tool environment [17].

As an example of developed models, Fig. 1 represents the global weather conditions. In particular, the activity (transition) *tInit* is completed at time 0, performing the code of the gate Init that generates all the random weather values to initialize the places representing temperatures (*T0* and *T0m*) and dew points (*DP* and *DPm*), and the activities *TWU* and *TWF* represent the time between two consecutive weather changes and collections of weather data, respectively. More details can be found in [12].

Regarding the weather data, they are assumed to be gathered from both weather forecast stations (mainly, temperature and dew point) and sensors deployed within the railway infrastructure (the temperature near each switch). The weather conditions and their evolution have been described by a stochastic process composed of a $(n+2)$-tuple of random variables:

$$\left(T(W_k), T^d(W_k), T_{11}(W_k), \ldots, T_{1n_1}(W_k), \right.$$
$$\left. \ldots, T_{m1}(W_k), \ldots, T_{mn_m}(W_k)\right).$$

where W_k represents the time instances at which the weather conditions change, $T(t)$ and $T^d(t)$ represent the temperature and the dew point at time t, respectively, and $T_{ij}(t)$ is the temperature at time t with respect to the position of the railroad switch RS_{ij} the temperature sensor is attached to.

Then, a variety of weather patterns can be represented by different combinations of values for the four key parameters: μ_T, which is the temperature assigned to $T(0)$; σ_T, which represents how much $T(t)$ varies from its expected value; μ_Δ, which represents the expected spread between $T(t)$ and $T^d(t)$; σ_d, which represents the variation of $T^d(t)$ from the expected value. For example, weather patterns characterized by a high risk of switch freezing are mainly those with $\mu_T \leq 0$ and low values for μ_Δ.

To account for the real usage of switches (when the anti-icing system is needed), the train schedules are considered by presenting different patterns of scheduled static times and by introducing the parameter α. The latter represents the percentage of time during which the heater control is active within the analysis time interval $[0, t]$. Through these patterns, it is possible to represent a variety of different scenarios, such as a few long periods of active control alternating with short periods of inactive control, or many short periods of active control alternating with short periods of inactive control. Through the parameter α, it is possible to consider different percentages of active control for the same pattern; when it reaches 100%, the control is always active. Formally, for each railroad switch RS_{ij}, the time schedule at which trains are expected to arrive at RS_{ij} is defined by a sequence of deterministic instants from which the width of the kth scheduled active control interval, during which the heating control system is active, can be derived. The developed formalization also includes a random variable that represents how much the deterministic scheduled interval is lengthened due to the delay of the trains. Moreover, the propagation of train delays is also accounted for in the analysis by building a topology of interactions.

Finally, energy management policies have been developed, both in the presence and in the absence (because of a failure) of a communication channel that connects global and local controllers. In particular, the case of a failed channel has been explored, and different logics have been implemented that aim to compensate for the unavailability of rich meteorological information gathered by the coordinator (e.g., by keeping memory of the last dew point value received and using it directly, or resorting to a forecasted value). Note that errors introduced by imperfect forecasts, as well as measurement errors incurred by sensors, have been accounted for in the analysis.

2.2 Examples of Analysis Results

In the following, we provide two examples of analysis results obtained from the application of the developed analysis framework, shown in Figs. 2a and 2b.

In the evaluation, eight different weather scenarios (with a starting temperature equal to $-15°$C, and expected spread and variances equal to $1°$C or $10°$C) were analyzed. This variety of weather conditions well addresses the uncertainty in the values of the parameters that together represent the weather profile, which are expected to have a high impact on the assessed measure. The communication channel is considered failed, with a fixed failure rate $c = 0.5\,\text{day}^{-1}$ (i.e., a failure every two days on average).

Figure 2a shows the minimum energy consumption μ_E incurred by each policy to maintain the unavailability level of the railroad switches not higher than a fixed threshold ($\bar{u} = 285$ minutes in the example). It is determined by analyzing, for each policy (indicated in the legend), the best combination of its individual parameters that minimizes the intervals the switch heaters are on, without exceeding the unavailability threshold. Also, the policy $P_{\text{pre,mpre}}$ performs worse than $P_{\varepsilon,\text{m}\varepsilon}$ in almost all scenarios considered, due to a forecast error greater than 3, except for scenario $(-15, 1, 1, 1)$.

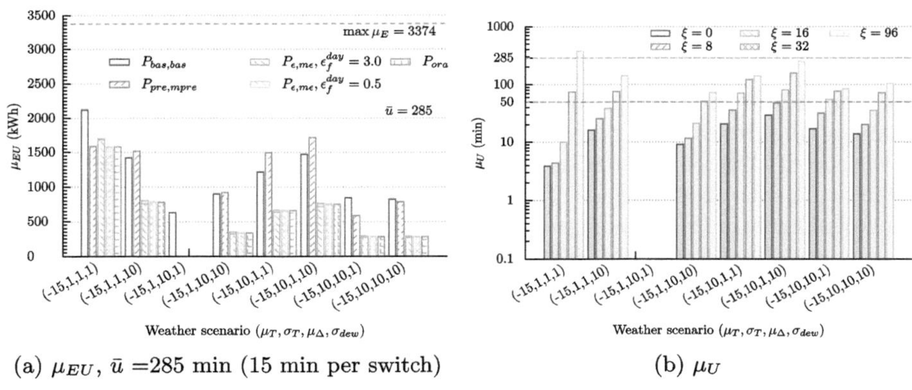

(a) μ_{EU}, $\bar{u} =$285 min (15 min per switch)   (b) μ_U

Fig. 2. Minimum energy consumption μ_{EU} (optimal cost) when $\bar{u} = 285$ minutes (a) for the different policies, forecast errors, and weather scenarios; and unavailability μ_U (in log scale) (b) for the policy $P_{\varepsilon,\text{m}\varepsilon}$, with different weather scenarios and ξ values, and positive forecast error $+\varepsilon_{\text{f}}^{day} = 3$.

In Fig. 2b, the maximum values for the average unavailability μ_U (expressed in minutes) are shown for the policy $P_{\varepsilon,\text{m}\varepsilon}$, with forecast error in one day $+\varepsilon_{\text{f}}^{day} = 3$ (the value obtained for negative error $-\varepsilon_{\text{f}}^{day} = -3$, is always 0). Different weather scenarios and values for the parameters characterizing this policy are considered (namely, the maximum number of control actions for which the dew point data are used during the channel failure, ξ, and the forecast error in one day, $\varepsilon_{\text{f}}^{day}$).

Also confirmed by the results relative to energy consumption, it can be noted that the parameter ξ has a great impact on both μ_E and the maximum value of μ_U. Moreover, the parameter ε_f^{day} has an increasing impact on μ_E as ξ increases, but still small, while it has a significant impact on μ_U, varying from a few units with $(-15, 1, 1, 1)$ and $\xi = 0$, to a few hundreds for $(-15, 1, 1, 1)$ and $\xi = 96$. Indeed, Fig. 2b allows us to identify the largest value of ξ such that μ_E is minimum and $\mu_U \leq \bar{u}$, whatever the error ε_f^{day}: e.g., $\xi = 8$ for the scenario $(-15, 10, 1, 10)$ and $\bar{u} = 50$, or $\xi = 96$ for each scenario except $(-15, 1, 1, 1)$ when $(\bar{u} = 285)$.

Although limited to two specific examples, the results discussed demonstrate the usefulness of the developed analysis framework and suggest its powerful use for the assessment of energy consumption and dependability indicators (under specific weather scenario, train schedule, and failure events) to: i) make a choice among the available heating policies; and ii) tune values for policy parameters resulting in the most effective behaviour.

3   The IPS System Case Study

Ensuring a continuous and stable power supply in railways is paramount, particularly for the execution of energy-dependent critical operations such as train movement and signaling protocols. To properly satisfy the requested uptime capacity, Integrated Power Supply (IPS) systems are typically employed to minimize disruptions and maintain operational integrity, ensuring that trains can run efficiently and safely under a wide range of conditions.

Schematically, the considered IPS system is connected to an Alternating Current (AC) source and includes transformer(s), rectifier(s), batteries, and inverter(s) as components, which altogether work to supply electrical power to (AC or Direct Current (DC)) loads when requested. It works in two modalities: a *normal* operation mode, when the AC source is functioning properly so clean and reliable electricity is supplied to loads; and a *critical* operation mode, when the AC source is interrupted and the IPS utilizes its built-in battery to maintain power for supported loads, continuing to draw from the battery until the AC input is restored or the battery is depleted.

When employed in critical railway contexts, reliable IPS are needed; therefore, their designs are developed employing some degree of redundancy to manage and mitigate unforeseen fault events effectively. By incorporating redundant components and proper control policies to manage the employed redundancy, potential disruptions and hazardous situations can be minimized.

Redundant IPS configurations differ in the internal components they select for replication. In our studies, four configurations have been progressively considered, as illustrated in Fig. 3, ranging from the full monolithic replication of the SR architecture to full component-level replication of the CR and IR architectures.

To assist designers in assessing the ability of the devised IPS architecture to ensure continuous operation despite unexpected challenges, stochastic model-based analysis is an excellent evaluation method. It is applicable since the early

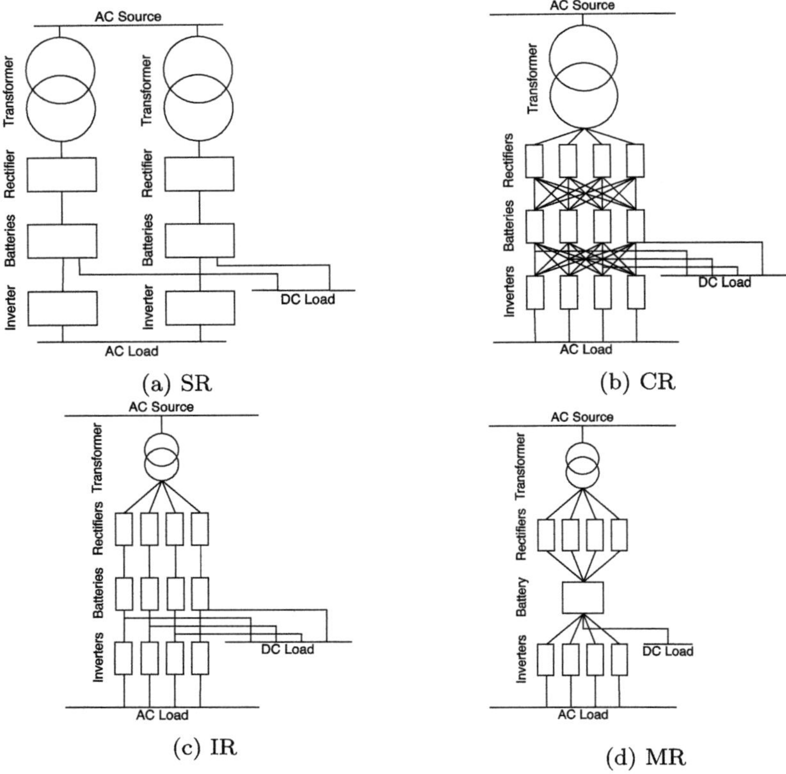

Fig. 3. Logical architectures of IPS under investigation: SR in a $1 + 1$ configuration with primary and hot standby IPS unit; CR in $n + m$ configuration for each component (excluding the transformer), with $n = 3$ and $m = 1$ primary and hot standby units, respectively; IRs is close to CR but each unit is connected only to the corresponding unit of the next layer; while MR is close to IR, but with only one large shared battery.

stage of system design, thus providing prompt and useful feedback, both in comparing alternative fault-tolerant organizations and in tuning the degree of the redundancy involved.

In this context, a first study ([30]) has been conducted to quantify measures representative of the reliability (MTTF) and availability (MTBF) of two IPS configurations related to the Italian railway system. They are the currently adopted one and its planned evolution, corresponding to the SR, and CR, architectures in Fig. 3. Then, an extension of this analysis framework to cover more IPS configurations, showing the generalization of the approach (all four depicted in Fig. 3), and more realistic operational scenarios, has been proposed in [13].

In the following, we briefly summarize the developed analysis framework and present a few results to exemplify how it can be used in practice.

3.1   The Framework for Assessing Dependability of IPS Systems

Markovian stochastic models [40] have been defined to evaluate and compare the SR, CR, IR and MR architectures in terms of the considered dependability attributes, namely: the IPS Mean Time to Failure (MTTF); the IPS steady-state availability A_∞, defined as the limit of the probability that the IPS will be operational at a specific time, as time tends to infinity; the expected time between two consecutive failures MTBF; and the percentage of improvement in MTBF of the X architecture with respect to the Y architecture. In addition to these basic ones, the framework allows for defining and assessing other dependability-related indicators, such as those considered in the next subsection.

The IPS fails when there are no redundant hot spare units left to replace the failed primary units, necessary to cover the loads. Reasonable assumptions have been made to keep the complexity of the derived models manageable without significantly impairing the accuracy of the analysis results. They mainly pertain to: i) the failure model of individual components, including the AC source; ii) the recovery time of individual failed components; iii) the discharge time of individual battery modules.

In [30], separate models have been developed for the two IPS operational modes (that is, IPS-N for the *normal* mode, and IPS-C for the *critical* mode), subsequently extended to consider their alternation.

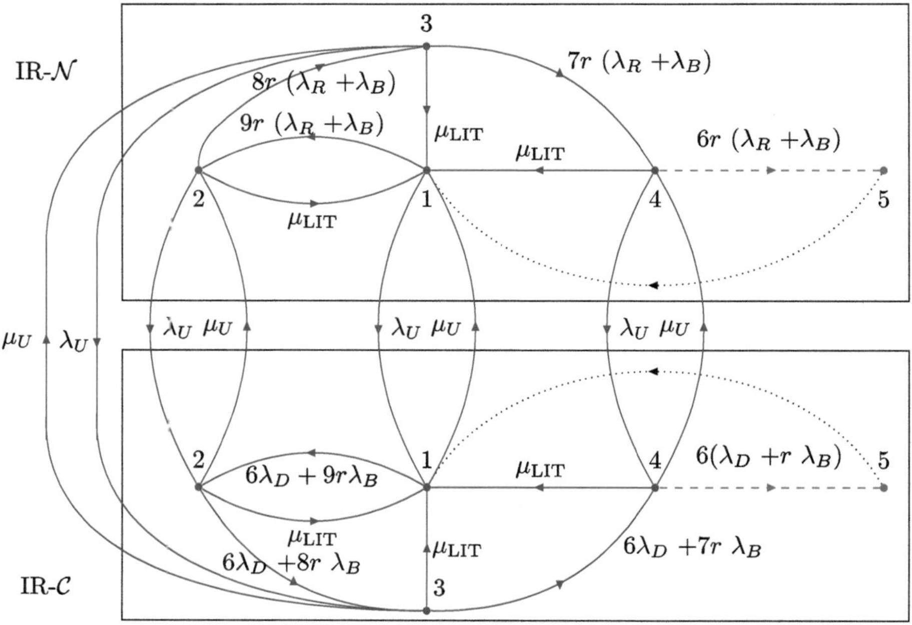

Fig. 4. Reliability and availability (including black dotted arcs) models of IR (DC loads) with ($n=6$) and ($m=3$).

Each IPS architecture model is a Continuous Time Markov Chain (CTMC) obtained by joining the IPS-N and IPS-C submodels through state transitions representing the failure and recovery of the utility providing the AC source. IPS-N and IPS-C models in turn includes: a reliability model, with absorbing states representing the IPS failure, and an availability model, with all states positive recurrent [40]. In the availability model, each failed component is always recovered, whereas in the reliability model, each failed component is only recovered if it does not cause the IPS failure, when the model enters an absorbing state. As an example of the models developed, the CTMC relative to the architecture IR is shown in Fig. 4.

Models related to DC loads (where inverters are not considered) have been explicitly defined for each considered architecture, while guidance on incorporating AC loads has been presented only in text format due to its relative simplicity. Details about the models can be found in [13,30].

3.2   Examples of Analysis Results

In the following, we provide two examples of analysis results obtained from the application of the developed analysis framework. As original contribution to the analyses already performed in previous published studies, here we focus on assessing the unavailability of the system load $U_\infty = 1 - A_\infty$ for both DC and AC loads (Fig. 5).

Specifically, the metric U_∞ is analyzed at variations of the following vital model parameters to account for the uncertainty in their values: the failure rate of the AC source (λ_U) in Fig. 5a for two different values of its recovery rate μ_U ($0.5\mathrm{h}^{-1}$ and $2\mathrm{h}^{-1}$), and the failure rate multiplicative factor r (used in the analysis of the modular architectures CR, IR and MR) in Fig. 5b.

Let U_∞^U be the steady-state unavailability of the AC source, which depends only on λ_U and μ_U, defined as: $U_\infty^U = \mu_U/(\mu_U + \lambda_U)$. The metric U_∞^U represents the unavailability of the system load in absence of IPS. Thus, to evaluate the impact of each proposed IPS architecture with respect to the worst scenario (when IPS is not considered), also the metric U_∞^U is depicted in Fig. 5.

The impact of the different IPS architectures on U_∞^U is shown in Fig. 5a, in the two extreme cases of μ_U values. As expected, all the architectures consistently show lower unavailability of the system load for $2\mathrm{h}^{-1}$. The plots for IR e CR overlap.

The MR architecture behaves better than the worst case of U_∞^U, but even its better behavior (obtained for $2\mathrm{h}^{-1}$) is worse than the best case of U_∞^U. This result depends on the impact of the failure rate of each battery module of MR, which in the analysis is set to $11.76 \times 10^{-6}\mathrm{h}^{-1}$.

Similar considerations apply to the results shown in Fig. 5b where the varying parameter is the multiplicative factor r, with an additional interesting comment. It can be noted that there is a threshold of r that, when exceeded, nullifies the initial advantages of the IPS based on modular redundant configurations to the point that the resulting load unavailability is worse than in the absence of IPS.

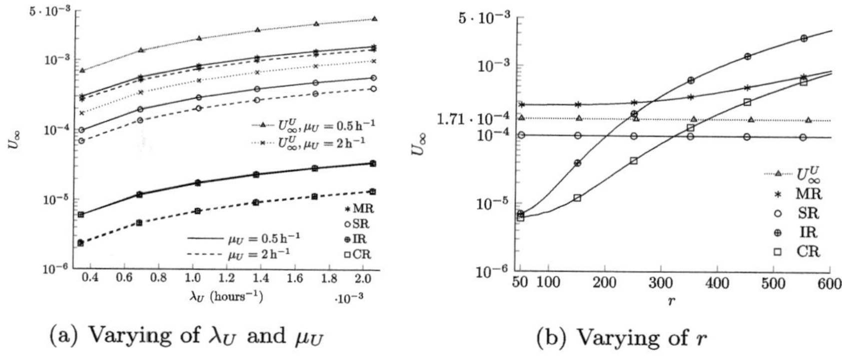

(a) Varying of λ_U and μ_U (b) Varying of r

Fig. 5. U_∞ of DC load and U_∞^U (log scale) at varying the failure rate of the AC source λ_U (a) and at varying of r (b).

Although restricted to two specific scenarios, the results discussed demonstrate the applicability of the developed analysis framework and suggest its use to support the selection of the most appropriate IPS architecture for given failure values, as well as to tune specific architecture parameters to achieve a behaviour that satisfies the desired dependability requirements.

4   Predictive Maintenance for Legacy Vehicles

Designing effective maintenance strategies for complex cyber-physical systems – particularly in the transportation domain – represents a major challenge at the intersection of reliability engineering and operational economics. The railway sector offers a prominent example of this issue, showing a marked disparity in maintenance capabilities across different generations of rolling stock. Modern high-speed trains are equipped with advanced sensor networks that enable comprehensive condition monitoring and predictive maintenance (PdM). In contrast, a significant portion of the active fleet consists of older vehicles that still rely on conventional time-based maintenance schedules. While these legacy systems often include basic diagnostic functions for fault detection and reporting, they lack predictive capabilities – despite being more prone to failures and requiring more frequent corrective interventions [6,18].

This technological gap creates a compelling opportunity for innovation. Older vehicles are typically equipped with diagnostic sensors (e.g., vibration, temperature, electrical current, and mechanical stress), which are primarily used to help maintenance engineers or drivers detect anomalies and trigger alerts. However, the data collected by these sensors contain valuable patterns and trends that, if properly analyzed, could provide early indicators of impending failures [18]. The key challenge lies in developing methodologies that exploit this existing diagnostic infrastructure for predictive purposes, without requiring costly upgrades to the sensor network. Moreover, when fault-to-failure propagations (i.e., errors that evolve until a component fails) and failure-to-fault propagations (i.e., component failures acting as external faults for other components) can be characterized probabilistically, quantitative evaluation of stochastic failure logic models enables the derivation of reliability and dependability metrics [28, 34]. Such metrics not only support the early validation of design choices but also foster the development of predictive analytics for proactive fault management [35].

The authors belonging to the STlab at DINFO – University of Florence have been working in this area, developing several tools for the reliability analysis on one side, and an evaluation framework able to support the scheduling of maintenance interventions. In particular, in [11] the main goal was to provide actionable insights to effectively guide future maintenance policy decisions in legacy railway fleets, able to both reduce the cost of maintenance interventions and increase the overall operational availability.

4.1 The Workflow to Schedule Maintenance Interventions

The developed workflow leverages the estimation of the reliability curve of the monitored system through the adoption of a layered hierarchical reliability model. In particular, two layers have been adopted: the first one, leveraging stochastic Fault Tree Analysis (FTA), is used to evaluate the subsystem-level reliability curves; the second one, leveraging Reliability Block Diagrams (RBD), allows to evaluate the system-level reliability curve.

To evaluate the subsystem-level reliability curves, the workflow is composed of the following steps.

Step 1: Data Preprocessing Raw diagnostic data on trains are collected on a central server using multiple data acquisition boards on each train. A subset of diagnostic alarms is then selected based on their relevance to known failure modes, reducing noise and focusing on indicators with diagnostic significance. We focused on the alarms concerning the failure of main Traction Control Unit system. These alarms, which are also shown to the driver on the Driver Machine Interface (DMI), may trigger a manual maintenance request. We decided to filter data by train, by coach and by causing system.

Step 2: Cross-Referencing Diagnostic Data with Maintenance Logs We processed maintenance logs containing the following information: 1) data of the request; 2) train and coach identifiers; 3) system identifier and issue; 4) closure date. We used the maintenance logs to split raw data in temporal sequences going from the end of a corrective maintenance intervention to the raise of the first following request to identify correlations between specific alarms and detect alarm sequences that lead to a system failure.

Step 3: Derivation of Fault Trees We defined the fault tree shown in Fig. 6 on the basis of the list of alarms and electrical system schematics. In the figure, the top-level event in the "AZ" box represents the system-level failure. The connections leading down from AZ represent the different potential causes or contributing factors. These are due to failures of the following subsystem:

1) IT – Traction Inverter; 2) CA – Step-down Chopper; 3) CF – Braking Chopper; 4) TCU – Train Control Unit board; 5) GS – Inverter Static Group. Each of these lower-level subsystems (IT, CA, CF, TCU, GS) has further basic failure events represented by the numbered nodes (F1, F2, F3, ..., F10). The tree-like structure with AND gates models the fact that multiple lower-level failures would need to occur in order to ultimately lead to the top-level AZ failure. In the traction system, no redundant components are inherently present since the redundancy is effectively implemented at the train composition level.

Step 4: Association of Alarms with Failure Events The railway operator provided a list with the identifier, description and severity of each alarm. We considered the high severity alarms and linked them to specific subsystems failures. The alarms were subdivided in 2 groups: the ones visible to the driver, and the ones visible only to the maintainers. In this step the help of the railway operator is crucial.

Step 5: Extraction of Failure-to-Fault Time Series In this step, the diagnostic data is partitioned into separate files, one for each coach. For each maintenance record associated with a specific coach, we identified the first occurrence of each selected alarm type A_x and computed the time difference Δt_x between the alarm and the preceding maintenance event. To extract this time series, we used data from 23 coaches across 5 trains.

Step 6: Estimation of Probability Distributions The inter-event times Δt_x were modeled using an exponential distribution.

As expected, not every alarm A_x occurs between each pair of maintenance events. In such cases, the alarm is said to be *right-censored*: we only know that the event did not occur within the observation window, but not whether or when it might occur after. To correctly account for this censoring, we extended the maximum likelihood estimate function to take into account censored events. This approach correctly incorporates both observed and censored times, resulting in a statistically sound estimation of the exponential distribution parameters while accounting for the inherent uncertainty in parameter estimation arising from limited sample sizes and censored observations.

Step 7: Evaluation Using FaultFlow We implemented the model in the Fault-Flow framework [8] to compute the time-to-failure CDF for the full AZ system and for the subsystems IT, CA, CF, TCU board, GS.

To evaluate the system-level reliability curve, the workflow starts with the analysis of the following constraints on the number of coaches for each train and on the redundancy structure:

- Each train is composed by coaches and their number is between 3 and 6;
- The composition of a train is static, i.e., the coaches composing it cannot be added, removed or swapped;
- A coach is correctly contributing to the overall traction if all its subsystems IT, CA, CF and TCU are correctly operating;

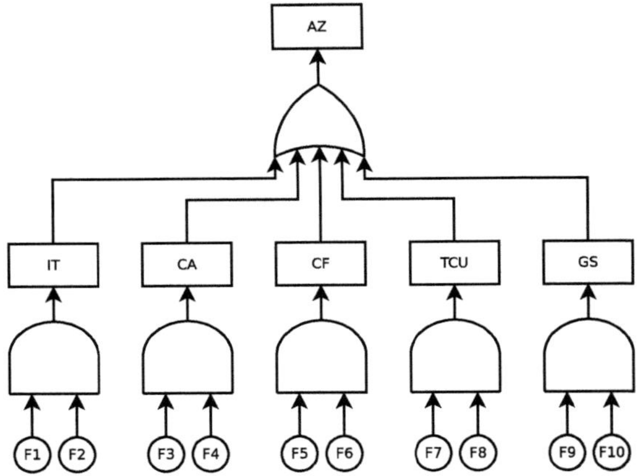

Fig. 6. High level system fault tree with main components.

- The train-level traction system is correctly working if at least $n/2$ (rounded up) out of n coaches are correctly contributing to the overall traction;
- The train-level traction system is correctly energized if both the following conditions are true: 1) at least $n/2$ (rounded up) out of n GS subsystems are correctly operating; 2) for each pair of two adjacent GSs, at least one of them is correctly operating.

To capture these constraints, we defined four RBD models, one for each train configuration, and analyzed them using a custom tool that supports the evaluation of reliability curves and leverages the librbd library [9].

4.2   Examples of Analysis Results

In the following, we provide three examples of analysis results obtained from the application of the developed analysis workflow.

The FaultFlow tool allowed us to compute and analyse both the Birnbaum and the Fussell-Vesely importance measures for each fault, shown respectively in Figs. 7a and 7b. The Birnbaum importance measure highlights the relative influence of individual components on the system's failure probability. Not all alarms contribute equally to the overall unreliability: in particular, faults F3 and F4 – associated with CA – are the most frequent and impactful. The Fussell-Vesely importance measure quantifies the probability that a given fault contributes to a system failure. Again, faults F3 and F4 dominate the ranking, confirming their critical role. This consistency across importance measures reinforced the need to prioritize these components in maintenance planning.

The FaultFlow tool allowed us to compute both the coach-level and subsystem level cumulative distribution function (CDF), i.e., the unreliability function. Figure 8 shows the CDF of the coach's traction system. As observed, after approximately $300\,h$, the probability of experiencing at least one critical alarm

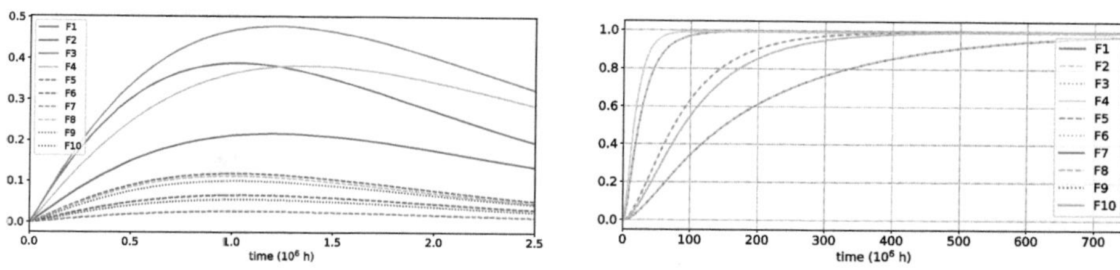

(a) Birnbaum importance measure.   (b) Fussell-Vesely importance measure.

Fig. 7. Birnbaum (a) and Fussell-Vesely (b) importance measures.

reaches 0.7. This indicates a significant degradation in reliability within the first operational window.

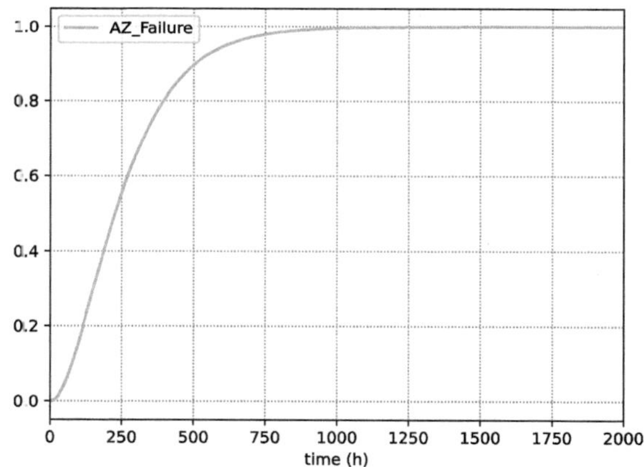

Fig. 8. Unreliability of coach evaluated using FaultFlow.

Finally, the train-level reliability evaluation performed through the librbd library allowed us to analyse the reliability curve of a train with a different number of coaches. Figure 9 shows the computed reliability for the different train configurations with $x \in [3, 6]$ coaches. We noticed that a train with 3 coaches is the most reliable as the reliability curve in this case is the highest one. This result, albeit apparently counter-intuitive since the failure of a single coach is tolerated, is due to the fact that with this configuration we have fewer combinations of possible failures.

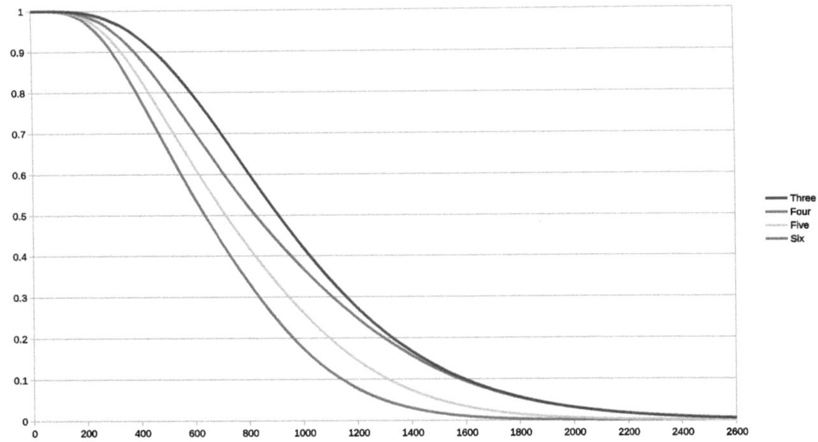

Fig. 9. Reliability analysis of trains with 3, 4, 5 or 6 coaches.

5   The ERTMS/ETCS-L3 Case Study

The ERTMS [19, 20] is a European standard developed to improve performance, reliability, safety, cross-border interoperability, and maintenance costs of rail transport. It relies on the ETCS, an automatic train protection system which continuously supervises the train not to exceed the safe speed and distance. Specifically, the on-board European Vital Computer (EVC) of each train periodically sends a Position Report (PR) and the results of the integrity check to a track-side Radio Block Centre (RBC), which sends back a Movement Authority (MA) specifying the maximum allowed advancement and speed, as well as possible temporary speed restrictions. Notably, whenever a train reaches the allowed advancement position defined by the most recent MA, its EVC activates an emergency brake, guaranteeing safe distancing from the foregoing train.

In the ERTMS/ETCS Level 3 (ERTMS/ETCS-L3) [21], the RBC computes the maximum allowed advancement of each train based on the minimum safe rear-end of the foregoing train (*moving-block signalling*), exploiting the Global System for Mobile Communications-Railway (GSM-R) [1] for a continuous bidirectional communication between the EVCs and the RBC. According to this, the ERTMS/ETCS-L3 considerably reduces headways between trains, in principle to the braking distance, provided that the GSM-R is highly available [43]. Thus, assessment of the ERTMS/ETCS-L3 performability requires evaluation of emergency stops caused by consecutive message losses. The approach presented in [5] addresses this challenge through a compositional model-based approach.

In the following, we summarize the framework developed in [5] to assess the performability of the ERTMS/ETCS-L3, and we recall the main analysis results.

5.1   Framework for Assessing the ERTMS/ETCS-L3 Performability

In the ERTMS/ETCS/L3 scenario where an RBC communicates with a pair of trains, an end-to-end message consists of: i) a PR sent by the foregoing train to the RBC and ii) the corresponding MA sent by the RBC to the chasing train. The GSM-R incurs transient failures which may cause the loss of end-to-end messages (impairing transmission of PRs or MAs), due to three different causes: i) burst noise, ii) connection losses (requiring repetition of connection trials after a timeout), or iii) handovers between neighboring radio stations (occurring periodically given the regular distance between radio stations). The analysis of a flat stochastic model of this scenario is not feasible, due to the complexity of behaviors resulting from multiple concurrent timers with general distributions (i.e., including non-exponential distributions with possibly bounded supports) and overlapping activity intervals (i.e., overlappimg time intervals during which two or more timers are active). Moreover, approximation of general distributions having firmly bounded support, e.g., using phase-type distributions, would reduce the accuracy of results. Furthermore, stochastic simulation would suffer the presence of rare events and the different order of magnitude of durations.

The approach proposed in [5] models the ERTMS/ETCS-L3 scenario through the Stochastic Time Petri Net (STPN) [32] of Fig. 10. STPNs are a formal model of concurrent timed systems with stochastic durations and discrete probabilistic choices. In particular, the stochastic durations of the STPN model of Fig. 10 fit the ERTMS/ETCS specification, using (possibly piecewise) uniform distributions or deterministic values. The STPN consists of three submodels:

- a submodel representing communication failures due to handovers, consisting of a periodic process with general jitter and initial deterministic offset;
- a submodel keeping memory of which among the last M end-to-end messages have been lost due to handovers, consisting of M places that act as watch variables ($M = 4$ in te STPN model of Fig. 10);
- a submodel representing the elaboration, generation, and transmission of end-to-end messages between an RBC and a pair of consecutive trains (i.e., the generation and transmission of PRs, followed by the computation and transmission of MAs), consisting of a periodic process with no initial offset.

The submodel that represents the generation and transmission of end-to-end messages also accounts for the event (modeled by transition **failure**) that, among the last M end-to-end messages, those that are not lost due to handovers are lost due to burst noise or connection losses, causing an emergency braking (without conditioning on the fact that no emergency braking occurred before). In particular, the probability of such event is the weight of transition **failure**, and it is computed from the probability that burst noise or connection losses impair a given number of consecutive end-to-end messages. In turn, the latter quantities are separately computed through an analytic derivation.

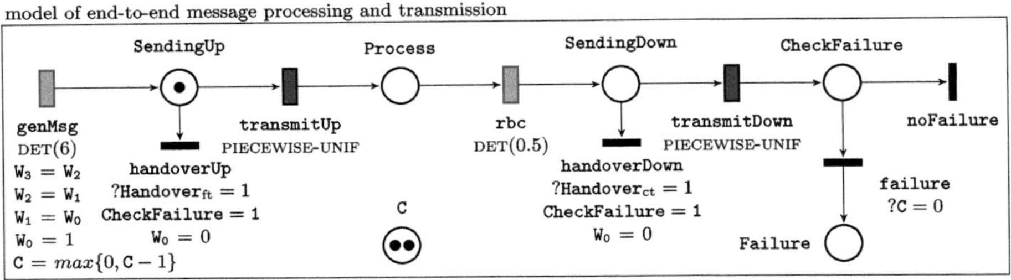

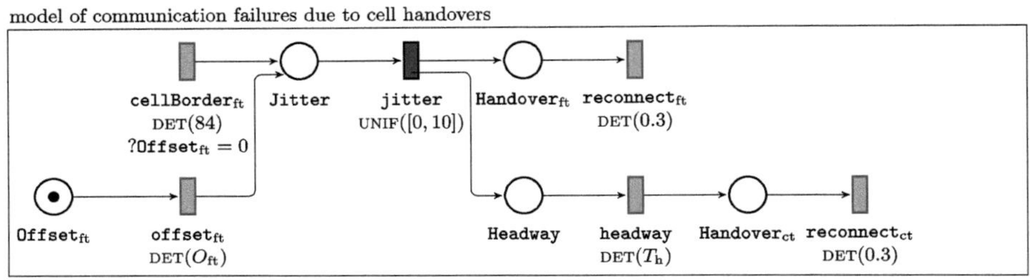

Fig. 10. The ERTMS/ETCS-L3 case study: STPN model developed in [5].

5.2 Examples of Analysis Results

The model of Fig. 10 is solved by regenerative transient analysis based on the method of stochastic state classes [26], using the SIRIO library of the ORIS tool [32], computing an upper bound on the first-passage time distribution of a spurious emergency braking as the instantaneous expected value of the reward **Failure** with stop condition **Failure==1**. The analysis incurs medium complexity mainly due to the value of M, the number of concurrent transitions with general distribution or deterministic value, and the length of behaviors between consecutive regenerations (i.e., states where the future evolution depends only on the current state and not on the past history). Since the system behavior is recurrent over the hyper-period of periodic message releases and periodic arrivals at cell borders, the upper-bound on the probability that a spurious emergency stop occurs within a hyper-period is used as the parameter of a geometric distribution, yielding an upper bound $\tilde{\beta}(M,t)$ on the first-passage probability that M consecutive losses occur within a time interval $[0,t]$ of arbitrary duration.

The compositional solution method proposed in [5] provides a sensitivity analysis with respect to the number M of consecutive tolerated losses and the headway distance T_h between trains, thus addressing the uncertainty in the values of these parameters. Figure 11 plots $\tilde{\beta}(M,t)$ for increasing values of M and T_h. Specifically, $\tilde{\beta}(M,t)$ significantly decreases by one order of magnitude as T_h increases by 6 s, which corresponds to an increase of M by 1, being at time

$t \sim 1\,\mathrm{h}$ in the order of $4.3 \cdot 10^{-1}$, $1.5 \cdot 10^{-2}$, and $6.9 \cdot 10^{-4}$ for $T_\mathrm{h} = 60\,\mathrm{s}$ ($M = 2$), $T_\mathrm{h} = 66\,\mathrm{s}$ ($M = 3$), and $T_\mathrm{h} = 72\,\mathrm{s}$ ($M = 4$), respectively. These experimental results could be used to select the delay T_h so as to achieve a trade-off between the utilization of the railway line and the probability that a train is stopped within $1\,\mathrm{h}$. in turn, the delay T_h corresponds to a headway distance, which determines the maximum number M of consecutive tolerated losses. Overall, these results prove that the headway distance must be significantly larger than the braking distance to effectively limit the expected number of spurious emergency stops.

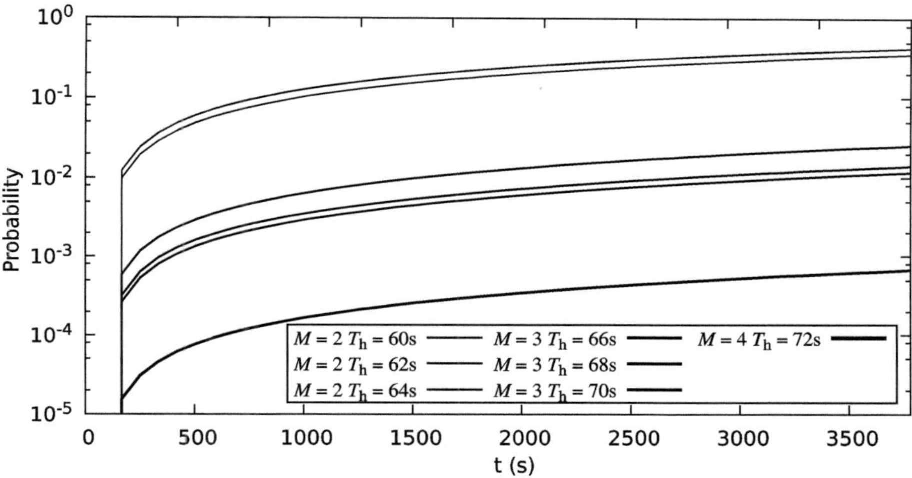

Fig. 11. The ERTMS/ETCS-L3 case study: first-passage time distribution of a spurious emergency braking computed in [5] for different values of the number M of consecutive tolerated losses and of the headway distance T_h between trains.

6   Conclusions

This paper focused on stochastic modeling and analysis methods to assess various dependability-related measures of selected TCSs, under the uncertainty of model parameters having a relevant impact on the assessed measures. Specifically, four representative case studies, developed by the authors and fully documented in previous publications, have been briefly summarized in terms of the defined modeling framework and examples of the analysis results they allow to obtain.

The intent was to highlight the suitability of stochastic modelling and analysis approaches in addressing a variety of needs in quantitative dependability assessments of TCSs, mainly: i) the variations of parameter values, as necessary in the presence of uncertainty of exact values, or to assess the adaptability of the analyzed system to different contexts subject to different requirements/conditions; ii) the ability to determine appropriate trade-offs between contrasting but equally relevant requirements imposed to the system, such as availability and energy consumption; iii) the added value of synthesizing stochastic parameters from observed data and casting them into a stochastic model, whose analysis can then provide information on system-level dependability-related attributes; and, iv) the capability to make the evaluation of complex systems viable through compositional solution methods that decompose the system model into submodels and then leverage their separate analysis to evaluate system-level properties.

Indeed, the relevance and utility of quantitative model-based analysis for assessing dependability indicators in TCSs is well-established in the literature, as recently evidenced by the systematic review presented in [10]. The surveyed literature underscores the growing importance of rigorous dependability evaluation for TCSs equipped with emerging technologies that introduce uncertainty into critical system parameters. As also shown by the selected case studies summarised herein, such approaches yield actionable insights for decision-support systems with different aims, including e.g., control policy synthesis, system architecture design, and maintenance planning–enabling stakeholders to achieve appropriate tradeoffs between contrasting dependability-related attributes.

Acknowledgement. We dedicate this paper to Alessandro Fantechi, whom we deeply admire for his invaluable contributions to the field, particularly his pioneering work on the industrial applications of Formal Methods, on software certification in accordance with safety standards, and on the railway signalling domain. We are sincerely grateful to Alessandro for so many years of enjoyable, inspiring, and fruitful collaboration.

References

1. GSM-R Interfaces: Class 1 Requirements
2. ASTRail. http://www.astrail.eu
3. Basile, D., ter Beek, M.H., Ferrari, A., Legay, A.: Exploring the ERTMS/ETCS full moving block specification: an experience with formal methods. Inter. J. Softw. Tools Technol. Trans. **24**(3), 351–370 (2022). https://doi.org/10.1007/s10009-022-00653-3
4. Beugin, J., Marais, J.: Simulation-based evaluation of dependability and safety properties of satellite technologies for railway localization. Trans. Res. Part C: Emerging Technol. **22**, 42–57 (2012)
5. Biagi, M., Carnevali, L., Paolieri, M., Vicario, E.: Performability evaluation of the ERTMS/ETCS – Level 3. Trans. Res. Part C: Emerging Technol. **82**, 314–336 (2017). https://doi.org/10.1016/j.trc.2017.07.002
6. Binder, M., Mezhuyev, V., Tschandl, M.: Predictive maintenance for railway domain: a systematic literature review. IEEE Eng. Manage. Rev. **51**(2), 120–140 (2023)
7. Capacity4Rail. http://www.capacity4rail.eu
8. Carnevali, L., Cerboni, S., Montecchi, L., Vicario, E.: Faultflow: an MDE library for dependability evaluation of component-based systems. IEEE Trans. Dependable Sec. Comput., 1–18 (2025).https://doi.org/10.1109/TDSC.2025.3532340
9. Carnevali, L., Ciani, L., Fantechi, A., Gori, G., Papini, M.: An efficient library for reliability block diagram evaluation. Appli. Sci. **11**(9) (2021). https://doi.org/10.3390/app11094026

10. Carnevali, L., Di Giandomenico, F., Fantechi, A., Gnesi, S., Gori, G.: Quantitative dependability evaluation of train control systems in presence of uncertainty: a systematic literature review. IEEE Trans. Intell. Transp. Syst. **26**(4), 4298–4314 (2025). https://doi.org/10.1109/TITS.2025.3530112
11. Carnevali, L., Fantechi, A., Gori, G., Vreshtazi, D., Borselli, A., Cefaloni, M.R., Rota, L.: Data-driven synthesis of stochastic fault trees for proactive maintenance of railway vehicles. In: Remke, A., Steffen, B. (eds.) Formal Methods for Industrial Critical Systems, pp. 162–181. Springer Nature Switzerland, Cham (2026). https://doi.org/10.1007/978-3-032-00942-5_9
12. Chiaradonna, S., Di Giandomenico, F., Masetti, G.: Advanced definition and analysis of anti-icing methods to balance energy usage and dependability in railways. Tech. rep., ISTI-TR-2025/014 (2025)
13. Chiaradonna, S., Di Giandomenico, F., Masetti, G.: Dependability modeling and evaluation of IPS architectures in the railway sector. Tech. rep., ISTI-TR-2025/013 (2025)
14. Chiaradonna, S., Di Giandomenico, F., Masetti, G.: Trading dependability and energy consumption in critical infrastructures: focus on the rail switch heating system. In: 2020 IEEE 25th Pacific Rim Int. Symp. on Dependable Comput. (PRDC), pp. 150–159 (2020)
15. Chiaradonna, S., Di Giandomenico, F., Masetti, G., Basile, D.: A refined framework for model-based assessment of energy consumption in the railway sector. In: ter Beek, M.H., Fantechi, A., Semini, L. (eds.) From Software Engineering to Formal Methods and Tools, and Back. LNCS, vol. 11865, pp. 481–501. Springer, Cham (2019). https://doi.org/10.1007/978-3-030-30985-5_28
16. Chiaradonna, S., Masetti, G., Di Giandomenico, F., Righetti, F., Vallati, C.: Enhancing sustainability of the railway infrastructure: trading energy saving and unavailability through efficient switch heating policies. Elsevier Sustainable Comput. Inform. Syst. **30**, 100519 (2021)
17. Courtney, T., Gaonkar, S., Keefe, K., Rozier, E.W.D., Sanders, W.H.: Möbius 2.3: an extensible tool for dependability, security, and performance evaluation of large and complex system models. In: 39th Annu. IEEE/IFIP Int. Conf. on Dependable Syst. and Netw. (DSN 2009), Estoril, Lisbon, Portugal, pp. 353–358 (2009)
18. Davari, N., Veloso, B., Ribeiro, R.P., Pereira, P.M., Gama, J.: Predictive maintenance based on anomaly detection using deep learning for air production unit in the railway industry. In: 2021 IEEE 8th International Conference on Data Science and Advanced Analytics (DSAA), pp. 1–10 (2021). https://doi.org/10.1109/DSAA53316.2021.9564181
19. EEIG ERTMS User Group: ERTMS/ETCS RAMS System Requirements Specification (1999)
20. EEIG ERTMS User Group: ERTMS/ETCS Systems Requirements Specification (1999)
21. ERTMS/ETCS - System Requirements Specification
22. Europe's Rail. https://rail-research.europa.eu/
23. Fantechi, A., Gnesi, S., Gori, G.: Future Train Control Systems: Challenges for Dependability Assessment. In: Margaria, T., Steffen, B. (eds) ISoLA 2022. LNCS, vol. 13704. Springer, Cham (2022). https://doi.org/10.1007/978-3-031-19762-8_21
24. Flammini, F., Marrone, S., Nardone, R., Vittorini, V.: Compositional modeling of railway virtual coupling with activity networks. Form. Asp. Comput. **33**(6), 989–1007 (2021). https://doi.org/10.1007/s00165-021-00560-5

25. Himrane, O., Beugin, J., Ghazel, M.: Toward formal safety and performance evaluation of gnss-based railway localisation function. IFAC-PapersOnLine **54**(2), 159–166 (2021). https://doi.org/10.1016/j.ifacol.2021.06.049, 16th IFAC Symposium on Control in Transportation Systems CTS, 2021

26. Horváth, A., Paolieri, M., Ridi, L., Vicario, E.: Transient analysis of non-Markovian models using stochastic state classes. Perform. Eval. **69**(7), 315–335 (2012). https://doi.org/10.1016/j.peva.2011.11.002

27. IEEE Vehicular Technology Society: IEEE 1474.1 - Standard for Communications Based Train Control (CBTC) - Performance and Functional Requirements (2004)

28. Kabir, S.: An overview of fault tree analysis and its application in model based dependability analysis. Expert Syst. Appl. **77**, 114–135 (2017)

29. Lindemann, C.: Performance modelling with deterministic and stochastic Petri nets. ACM Sigmetrics Perform. Evaluat. Rev. **26**(2), 3 (1998)

30. Masetti, G., Di Giandomenico, F., Chiaradonna, S.: Dependability analysis of UPS architectures for the italian railway signaling system. In: Springer (ed.) 5th Int. Conf. on Reliab., Saf. and Secur. of Railway Syst. (RSSRail 2023), Berlin, Germany (Oct 2023)

31. Mitchell, I., et al.: ERTMS level 4, train convoys or virtual coupling. IRSE News **219**, 14–15 (2016)

32. Paolieri, M., Biagi, M., Carnevali, L., Vicario, E.: The ORIS tool: quantitative evaluation of non-Markovian systems. IEEE Trans. Software Eng. **47**(6), 1211–1225 (2019)

33. PERFORMINGRAIL. https://www.performingrail.com

34. Ruijters, E., Stoelinga, M.: Fault tree analysis: a survey of the state-of-the-art in modeling, analysis and tools. Comput. Sci. Rev. **15**, 29–62 (2015)

35. Salfner, F., Lenk, M., Malek, M.: A survey of online failure prediction methods. ACM Comput. Surv. **42**(3), 1–42 (2010)

36. Sanders, W.H., Meyer, J.F.: Stochastic activity networks: formal definitions and concepts. In: Brinksma, E., Hermanns, H., Katoen, J.-P. (eds.) EEF School 2000. LNCS, vol. 2090, pp. 315–343. Springer, Heidelberg (2001). https://doi.org/10.1007/3-540-44667-2_9

37. Shift2Rail Joint Undertaking: Multi-annual action plan (2015)

38. da Silva, L.D., Lollini, P., Mongelli, D., Bondavalli, A., Mandò, G.: A stochastic modeling approach for traffic analysis of a tramway system with virtual tags and local positioning. J. Braz. Comput. Soc. **27**(1), 2 (2021). https://doi.org/10.1186/s13173-021-00105-x

39. Song, H., Liu, J., Schnieder, E.: Validation, verification and evaluation of a train to train distance measurement system by means of Colored Petri Nets. Reliability Eng. Syst. Safety **164**, 10–23 (2017). https://doi.org/10.1016/j.ress.2017.03.001

40. Trivedi, K.S., Bobbio, A.: Reliability and Availability Engineering: Modeling, Analysis, and Applications. Cambridge University Press (2017)

41. UIC: Technologies and potential developments for energy efficiency and CO2 reductions in rail systems. Tech. rep., International Union of Railways (UIC) (2016)

42. Zimmermann, A.: Modelling and performance evaluation with TimeNET 4.4. In:
    Bertrand, N., Bortolussi, L. (eds.) QEST 2017. LNCS, vol. 10503, pp. 300–303.
    Springer, Cham (2017). https://doi.org/10.1007/978-3-319-66335-7_19
43. Zimmermann, A., Hommel, G.: Towards modeling and evaluation of ETCS real-
    time communication and operation. J. Syst. Softw. **77**(1), 47–54 (2005)

Opportunities and Risks of Generative AI in Model-Based Engineering of Railway Systems

Francesco Flammini[1,2]([envelope]) [iD], Arianna Nocente[3] [iD], Cinzia Bernardeschi[4] [iD], and Valeria Vittorini[5] [iD]

[1] University of Florence, Florence, Italy
francesco.flammini@unifi.it, francesco.flammini@supsi.ch
[2] University of Applied Sciences and Arts of Southern Switzerland, Lugano, Switzerland
[3] Alstom, Paris, France
a.nocente@studenti.unipi.it
[4] University of Pisa, Pisa, Italy
cinzia.bernardeschi@unipi.it
[5] University of Naples Federico II, Naples, Italy
valeria.vittorini@unina.it

Abstract. The engineering of safety-critical systems demands rigorous assurance while facing growing requirements for automation and resilience. Traditional practices rooted in formal methods and model-based engineering (MBE) have provided the methodological backbone for decades, enabling compliance with international standards. At the same time, the increasing availability of operational data and computational resources has fostered a rapid expansion of artificial intelligence (AI) and machine learning (ML). Recent surveys indicate a paradigm shift from purely deterministic engineering towards hybrid approaches that combine data-driven adaptability with formal rigor. Against this background, the emergence of Generative AI and Large Language Models (LLMs) offers new opportunities to alleviate persistent limitations of MBE, including skill shortages, time-consuming processes, and difficulties in bridging natural language requirements with formal specifications. In this paper we review current research trends on the usage of generative AI and large language models in engineering safety-critical systems with a focus on railway verification and validation. We discuss how those techniques can complement and enhance MBE workflows. Potential applications include automated requirement formalization, model transformation, and test generation; however those applications also raise concerns about transparency and regulatory compliance. By setting such discussion at the intersection of modeling, verification, and emerging AI techniques, the paper highlights opportunities and risks, while honoring the legacy of Prof. Alessandro Fantechi, whose seminal contributions in railway research continue to inspire rigorous and trustworthy innovation.

© The Author(s), under exclusive license to Springer Nature Switzerland AG 2026
M. H. ter Beek et al. (Eds.): Fantechi Festschrift, LNCS 16470, pp. 92–114, 2026.
https://doi.org/10.1007/978-3-032-12484-5_6

Keywords: Railway Engineering · Artificial Intelligence · Machine Learning · Generative AI · Large Language Models · Formal Methods · Model-Based Engineering · Safety-Critical Systems

1   Introduction

Generative Artificial Intelligence (GenAI) and large language models (LLMs) are rapidly emerging as powerful tools to support Model-Based Engineering (MBE) of safety-critical systems. They promise to accelerate activities such as requirements elicitation, model transformation, documentation, and consistency checking, while raising open questions about trustworthiness, explainability, and integration with rigorous engineering processes. These opportunities and challenges cut across domains including health, transportation, energy, and critical infrastructure; transportation—and railway systems in particular—exemplify many of these issues (see, e.g., reference [10]).

The railway domain has long been at the forefront of safety-critical engineering, where the dual imperatives of safety and efficiency must be achieved under increasingly complex operational and regulatory constraints. Over the past decades, research and practice have relied extensively on modeling techniques and formal methods to provide the rigor needed for the specification, verification, and certification of railway control and signaling systems. These approaches have been instrumental in ensuring compliance with standards such as EN 50126, EN 50128, and EN 50129, which formalize the processes for the specification and demonstration of reliability, availability, maintainability, and safety in railway applications. Within this tradition, the contributions of Prof. Alessandro Fantechi have been seminal, particularly in advancing the use of formal methods for the modeling and verification of railway interlocking and control systems, and in shaping the scientific community around dependable railway software engineering [32–35].

At the same time, the digital transformation of railways has opened the door to new opportunities and challenges. Massive amounts of operational data are now collected from infrastructure and rolling stock, enabling novel forms of data-driven analysis. Artificial intelligence (AI) and machine learning (ML) methods are increasingly being deployed for predictive maintenance, anomaly detection, energy optimization, and traffic management. These techniques have demonstrated their potential in improving efficiency, reducing downtime, and supporting more adaptive and resilient operations. For instance, recent surveys and taxonomies of AI in the railway sector have documented the breadth of applications, ranging from condition monitoring of assets to intelligent traffic control, while also emphasizing the regulatory and ethical dimensions that accompany the adoption of such technologies [12, 85].

This growing body of work reflects a shift from purely deterministic engineering towards data-driven approaches that can complement traditional methods.

In recent collaborative work with Prof. Fantechi, the vision of more intelligent train control systems has been articulated, pointing towards architectures where traditional safety logics are enhanced with AI components, yet remain verifiable within a rigorous framework [38]. This interplay highlights a possible future in which generative and learning-based approaches are integrated into model-based engineering workflows, not to replace formal models, but to assist in their construction, validation, and maintenance.

Within this context, this paper first provides a general overview of current research on the use of generative AI in the engineering of safety-critical systems in Sect. 2, with particular emphasis on the verification and validation of AI-based components in cyber-physical systems, which represent a cross-cutting concern across all domains. Building on this foundation, Sect. 3 discusses challenges and opportunities for integrating GenAI into Model-Based Systems Engineering in the railway domain, including application perspectives, transferability concerns, readiness, and risks. Finally, Sect. 4 contains some closing reflections and remarks.

2 Generative AI and Large Language Models in Engineering Critical Systems

2.1 Research Trends

To investigate current research trends in the application of Generative AI (GenAI) techniques and Large Language Models (LLMs) in the engineering of safety-critical systems, we conducted a focused search on the Scopus database. The following query was applied to titles, abstracts, and keywords:

("critical systems" OR "safety-critical" OR "mission-critical" OR "high-assurance") AND ("generative AI" OR "generative artificial intelligence" OR genai OR "large language model" OR llm OR "foundation model" OR chatgpt)

The aim was not a Systematic Literature Review, but rather a structured overview of the main research themes and challenges currently being explored at the intersection of GenAI/LLMs and safety-critical systems.

The search retrieved 204 published articles between 2014 and 2025. Publications before 2023 were negligible, whereas 2024 and 2025 account for over 85% of all results, confirming that research in this area is still in its early stages and is currently undergoing a phase of intense exploration and that many foundational questions are still being addressed. After applying exclusion criteria, removing purely conceptual discussions, editorials, or works not using GenAI / LLM in technical contexts, the final dataset contained 124 papers.

The conceptual map in Fig. 1 summarizes the main research areas and related topics addressed in the literature: i) engineering and assurance activities, including requirements engineering, traceability, formal verification, assurance cases; ii) safety and security, including hazard and risk analysis, anomaly detection for Cyber Physical Systems, testing, simulation; and iii) generation tasks, where GenAI/LLMs produce diverse types of artefacts, such as models, code and data. This topic includes research on retrieval-augmented generation (RAG) to improve LLMs and reduce the need to retrain them with new data. Three methodological, cross-cutting themes span these areas: LLM evaluation, autonomous agents, and AI explainability and verification.

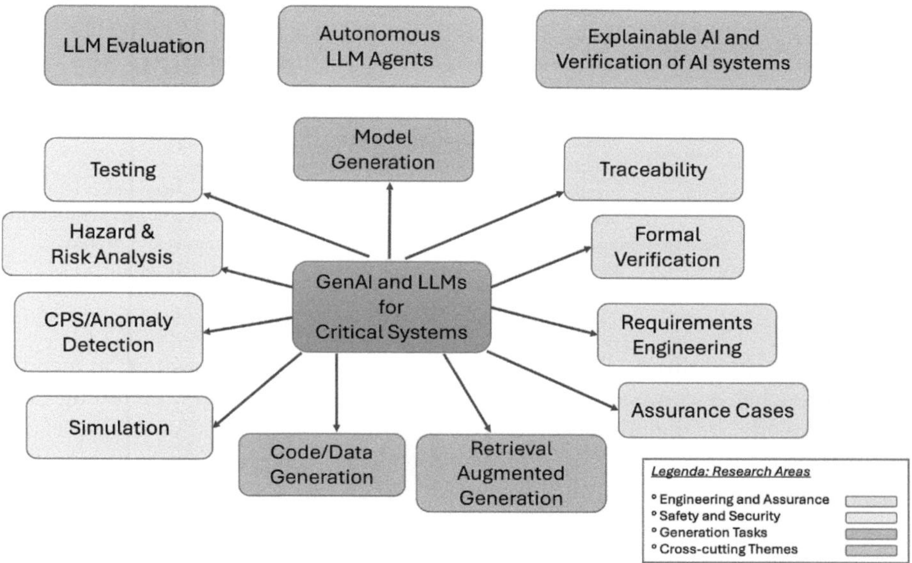

Fig. 1. Main research topics.

Each node of the conceptual map corresponds to one or more of the research topics listed in Table 1, each accompanied by a description of the reason why a paper is considered to address the corresponding topic: this indicates that the paper includes a concrete use of GenAI or LLMs in the context defined by the topic.

The overall distribution of these topics in the reviewed papers is illustrated in Fig. 2, showing the relative frequency of the main research direction. LLM evaluation dominates, reflecting the search focus on generative models; still, a subset of papers focuses on generative applications rather than systematic evaluation. For example, some contributions employ variational autoencoders and temporal fusion transformers to generate latent representations for explainable pattern analysis in time-series data [97], while others explore graph-augmented generation in the healthcare domain [18] or retrieval-augmented pipelines for combining symbolic and textual reasoning [78,89]. In addition, LLMs themselves are sometimes applied in a purely generative role—such as creating traffic scenarios for autonomous driving [6] or producing formally verified code in combination with specification-based verification [79]—without an explicit focus on benchmarking

Table 1. Inclusion criteria for research topics.

Topic	GenAI/LLM role
Code Generation	generate, complete, or suggest source code.
Data Generation	create synthetic data or entire datasets.
Testing	create test cases, inject faults, or support fuzzing.
Traceability	recover or establish links between software artifacts.
Requirements Eng.	extract, classify, refine, validate, or document requirements.
Formal Verification	support formal methods such as model checking.
Model Generation	generate system/software models (e.g., UML, SysML).
Assurance Cases	build or evaluate assurance cases.
Hazard & Risk Analysis	identify, classify, or prioritize hazards and risks.
Anomaly Detection	detect or explain anomalies in CPS.
Simulation	simulate environments, scenarios, or dynamic systems.
Retrieval-Aug. Generation	combined with retrieval for reasoning or generation in safety-critical contexts.
LLM Evaluation	main goal is to evaluate capability or reliability of LLMs in safety-critical tasks.
Explainable AI / AI Verification	approaches/models assessed for explainability, interpretability, or trust.
Autonomous LLM Agents	deployed as agents performing autonomous safety-critical tasks.

their overall capabilities. These examples show that, beyond evaluation, generative approaches encompass a variety of techniques and outputs, including data, scenarios, code, or domain-specific artifacts.

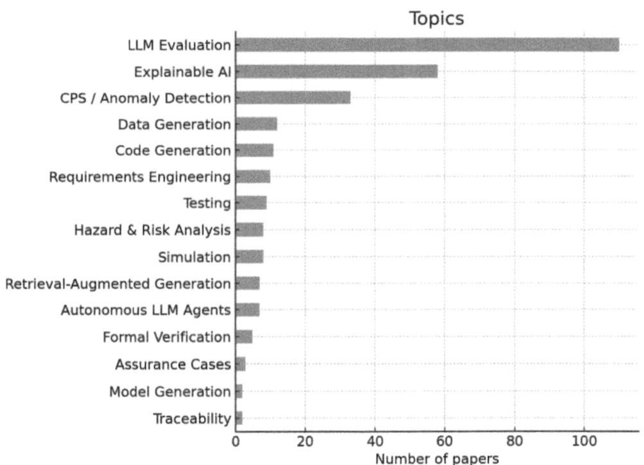

Fig. 2. Distribution of the main research topics across the 124 included papers.

2.2 Main Research Topics by Research Areas

Based on our analysis of the reviewed papers, four macro-areas capture the main directions of current research.

Engineering and Assurance. Several studies explore how GenAI/LLMs can support key phases of the software and system lifecycle. In requirements engineering, LLMs are applied to detecting missing requirements from natural language specifications, or mitigating ambiguities and inconsistencies [14,73,82]. Traceability is another theme, with LLMs used to recover links between requirements, models, and test artifacts [59]. The work on model generation is less frequent but promising, including attempts to derive system or UML diagrams directly from textual descriptions [36], and this aspect is further discussed in Sect. 2.3. In testing and formal verification, LLMs are explored for generating test cases, injecting faults, or supporting fuzzing strategies in automotive and aerospace systems [54,65], as well as for assisting model checking tasks through natural language guidance [56,67] and supporting formal verification [62]. Early research on assurance cases suggests that LLMs could contribute to the construction or evaluation of structured safety arguments [40].

Safety and Security. In the area of safety and security, GenAI and LLMs have been investigated primarily for their potential in safety evaluation [57], risk assessment [72], hazard analysis and assessment [25,49], security and risk analysis [29,30], detection of safety critical events and vulnerability detection [5,17]. A number of works explore how LLMs can assist in detecting or explaining vulnerabilities or anomalies in cyber-physical systems, particularly in the automotive and UAV domain where they have been combined with ensemble learning techniques or benchmarking approaches to assess robustness under diverse operating conditions [50,66,80]. Simulation emerges as a complementary line of research: some papers employ LLMs to generate traffic scenarios and dynamic environments to stress-test autonomous driving systems [16,86]. A discussion of the opportunities and risks that Generative AI introduces for the cybersecurity of cyber-physical systems, including its defensive applications and emerging threat vectors, is provided in [64].

Generation Tasks. LLMs are widely used as generators of code, data, and scenarios. The support of code generation for critical safety software is investigated in the automotive domain (e.g. [51,61]), including the generation of formally verified code [61,79]. Scenario generation is particularly relevant for simulation and testing of autonomous systems, where LLMs are used to design realistic traffic, mission, or emergency scenarios beyond those available in traditional datasets, as already outlined discussing their usage for engineering and assurance activities [6,86,99]. These approaches demonstrate GenAI's versatility in creating valuable inputs and environments, although concerns remain about the reliability and fidelity of generated artifacts.

Cross-cutting Themes. Three transversal themes emerge from the reviewed literature. First, LLM evaluation dominates, with numerous benchmarks assessing their reliability in safety-critical contexts, e.g. [17,26,43], revealing persistent weaknesses in reasoning and robustness. Second, a smaller but growing body of research investigates autonomous LLM agents capable of carrying out tasks such as automated testing or operational monitoring without continuous human supervision [96]. Finally, explainability and verification form a key theme, with efforts to combine natural-language explanations and formal reasoning for interpretable AI systems [97]. These cross-cutting lines point out the importance of systematic evaluation, transparency, and responsible deployment of GenAI in safety-critical domains.

2.3   Model Generation with GenAI/LLMs in MBSE

After analyzing the role of GenAI and LLMs in critical systems engineering, we focus on very recent contributions that address the automatic generation of models through GenAI and LLMs. This topic is of particular relevance for MBSE, since it directly targets the long-standing challenge of bridging natural language requirements with formal and semi-formal system artifacts. The works available in the literature can be broadly grouped into three categories: (i) generation of UML/SysML models, (ii) generation of formal models for verification, and (iii) other model types with potential MBSE relevance.

(i) UML/SysML Models. Several works explore the generation of SysML or UML diagrams from natural language specifications. Recent approaches combine LLMs with retrieval or agent-based loops to produce syntactically valid SysML v2 models [21,92], while others address the automatic derivation of UML sequence diagrams from user stories or textual requirements [36,46]. These studies emphasize both the promise of LLM assistance and the persistence of challenges in completeness and correctness.

(ii) Formal Models. Another relevant category addresses the synthesis of formal models, which are crucial in safety-critical MBSE contexts. Contributions include automatic generation of symbolic protocol models for security verification [63], synthesis of formal abstractions for smart contract verification [23], and co-synthesis of code and its formal representation for model checking [55]. Other works target specific verification tasks, such as invariant generation for hardware design [42] or formal modeling of cryptographic protocols [60]. These studies show that LLMs can accelerate the creation of artifacts traditionally requiring high expertise, though human-in-the-loop validation remains essential.

(iii) Other Model Types. Beyond UML and formal languages, LLMs have been applied to generate business process models (BPMN, Petri nets) [24,53], troubleshooting trees [87,88], and fault trees for safety analysis in nuclear or automotive domains [22,81,95]. While not railway-specific, these contributions illustrate the breadth of generative modeling tasks where LLMs can reduce effort in structuring domain knowledge (Table 2).

This recent research demonstrates that LLM-based model generation can: (1) lower barriers to MBSE adoption by automating initial model creation; (2) complement human expertise in producing verification-ready artifacts; (3)

Table 2. Examples of model generation with GenAI/LLMs

Type of model	Application domain and MBSE relevance
SysML/UML [21,36,46,92]	Systems engineering; bridging NL requirements with SysML/UML artifacts to support semi-formal design workflows.
Formal models [23,42,55,60,63]	Security protocols, smart contracts, hardware design; accelerate verification-ready models for V&V.
Process models [24,53]	Business process management; transform NL into BPMN/Petri nets, extending MBSE with operational views.
FT/troubleshooting trees [22,81,87,88,95]	Safety-critical domains (nuclear, automotive, industrial); provide structured diagnostic models for risk assessment.

extend MBSE practices to a broader range of models (process, safety, diagnostics). However, accuracy, explainability, and integration into toolchains remain open challenges that must be addressed for railway-critical applications.

2.4 Verification and Validation of AI-Generated Models in Safety-Critical Systems

AI-generated models are becoming central to numerous critical applications, from transportation systems to medical diagnostics. These applications require models that are accurate, robust, and reliable under a variety of operating conditions [11]. However, AI models, despite their impressive performance, are often regarded as black boxes because of their complex architectures and high-dimensional parameter spaces. This inherent opacity makes it difficult to guarantee that a model will behave predictably, especially in safety-critical contexts, where failure can lead to severe consequences. Consequently, the development of robust verification methods for AI-models has become an active area of research aimed at assessing and guaranteeing the reliability of these systems against specific operational requirements [37,58].

Traditional verification methods for AI-models have employed a variety of approaches, such as Satisfiability Modulo Theory (SMT) solvers [28,47,48,74], interval analysis [4,8,52], reachability analysis [31,44,94], formal provers [7,77] and hybrid [45]. These techniques offer valuable insight into model behavior by formally analyzing properties such as bounded input-output relationships, stability, and sensitivity to perturbations. For instance, SMT-based tools have been used to verify properties of fully connected neural networks with rectified linear unit (ReLU) activation functions, while other methods, like Monte Carlo simulation, provide empirical reachability analysis for more complex architectures. In [4] neural network inputs are modeled as arithmetic closed intervals and then the bounds are propagated along the network, thus obtaining a bounded output. If the desired safe or required region entirely contains the obtained bound, the desired property is verified. The Coq prover[1] was utilized by the authors of [7] to offer methods for feed-forward neural network verification. The PVS prover[2] was used in [77] to prove neural network properties.

Ensuring the robustness and safety of AI models integrated into safety-critical cyber-physical systems is crucial, and the application of formal methods to AI models remains an open challenge.

The problem is even more complex in the case of GenAI. Generative algorithms process large amounts of sample data and learn from such data. The generative algorithm, that will be used in the model generation process, depends on information computed from the input data during the training phase. Moreover, GenAI not only recognises patterns but also produces new results related to the training data. Often, synthetic data can also be used to improve the accuracy of the results.

In summary, current research on GenAI and LLMs in safety-critical systems is rapidly expanding across requirements engineering, model generation, testing, formal verification, assurance cases, safety and security analyses, and generation tasks. A recurring concern is the need to ensure trustworthiness and rigorous validation of AI-enabled components.

While few works explicitly address the railway sector, many of the identified approaches have potential transferability. Section 3 builds on this by analyzing challenges and opportunities for integrating GenAI into Model-Based Systems Engineering in the railway domain, and outlining transferability and application perspectives.

3　Generative AI and Large Language Models in Railway Model-Based Engineering

While the previous section has outlined general research trends and cross-domain challenges of GenAI in safety-critical engineering, we now turn to the railway sector as a representative case. To understand the specific challenges and opportunities of integrating GenAI into railway engineering, it is necessary to consider the current status of Model-Based Systems Engineering (MBSE) practices, their advances, and their limitations. On this basis, we highlight how generative approaches could complement and enhance MBSE workflows in railways. The discussion then expands to the perspectives and transferability of applications from other safety-critical industries, before addressing requirements processing as a concrete entry point for MBSE adoption, and closing with a critical assessment of readiness, opportunities, and risks.

3.1　Railway MBSE: Advances and Limitations

Modern railway systems are paradigmatic examples of *safety-critical, large-scale systems of systems*. They integrate interdependent subsystems, such as signaling,

---

[1] https://coq.inria.fr/.
[2] https://pvs.csl.sri.com/.

rolling stock, traffic management, communication networks, and human operators, whose interactions must meet stringent dependability and safety requirements. Traditional document-centric engineering has shown severe limitations in this context, including inconsistencies, difficulties in traceability, and limited automation in verification and validation.

Model-Based Systems Engineering (MBSE) has thus emerged as a fundamental approach in the railway domain. MBSE places formal models at the center of engineering workflows, improving requirements traceability, enabling rigorous simulation and analysis, and facilitating compliance with international safety standards such as EN 50126 on Railway Applications - The Specification and Demonstration of Reliability, Availability, Maintainability and Safety (RAMS), EN 50128 concerning Railway applications - Communication, signalling and processing systems - Software for railway control and protection systems, and the broader ISO/IEC 15288 lifecycle processes [1–3]. By providing a unified representation of system structure and behavior, MBSE reduces ambiguity, supports change impact analysis, and allows systematic verification across lifecycle stages. Case studies, such as the New South Wales Digital Systems Program, show that MBSE significantly improves stakeholder communication and architectural clarity in large-scale rail modernization projects [76].

Notable advances have been achieved in railway MBSE practices:

- **SysML-driven architectural modeling**, enabling consistent visualization of requirements, scenarios, and system structures [76].
- **Formal verification integration**, through model transformations between SysML and Event-B, supporting safety property analysis [91].
- **Domain-specific applications**, such as freight logistics terminals, where MBSE supports architectural exploration under variable operational constraints [93].

Despite these successes, several challenges remain:

- **Skill shortage**: Proficiency in modeling languages, formal methods, and toolchains is limited in the railway workforce.
- **Time-consuming and error-prone processes**: Manual synchronization between models and specifications (e.g., SysML–Event-B) is labor-intensive and prone to human error [91].
- **Toolchain fragmentation**: Interoperability across modeling, verification, and documentation environments is still insufficient, hindering seamless workflows.

These barriers restrict scalability and slow the adoption in industrial practice, highlighting the need for innovative support technologies.

As outlined in Sect. 2 GenAI and LLMs have emerged as promising tools to augment MBSE in safety-critical domains. For example, Transformer-based architectures have demonstrated capabilities in natural language understanding, code synthesis, and knowledge retrieval, which are directly relevant to bridging gaps between informal requirements and formal models [15].

We believe potential contributions of GenAI/LLMs to railway MBSE include:

- **Automated requirement formalization**: translating natural-language specifications into formal model elements, reducing ambiguity and improving traceability.
- **Model generation and transformation**: assisting in the creation of SysML or domain-specific models, and supporting semi-automated transformations across languages and tools.
- **Knowledge support and skill augmentation**: serving as intelligent assistants that explain modeling constructs, recommend design alternatives, and guide less-specialized engineers.
- **Consistency and compliance checking**: automatically detecting anomalies and verifying alignment with railway safety standards (EN 5012x).

Rather than replacing rigorous model-based practices, GenAI/LLMs may act as enablers, accelerating processes, mitigating human error, and lowering entry barriers—while preserving the safety assurance foundations of railway system engineering. We will address later in this chapter the implications and acceptability of those approaches within high assurance systems, including possible verification tasks to manage the effects of AI errors.

3.2   Railway Application and Transferability

The railway sector has historically been characterized by high entry barriers, shaped by stringent safety standards, fragmented multi-vendor architectures, and documentation-intensive processes. Standardization and interoperability pose an additional challenge: the European Rail Traffic Management System (ERTMS) was conceived to harmonize signalling and communication across national networks, yet its deployment must still conform to heterogeneous product and operational constraints. This landscape results in a demanding environment where multiple complex subsystems must interact across organizational and technological boundaries. Within this context, generative AI and large language models (LLMs) are redefining opportunities for innovation.

Two dynamics play a central role in this transformation, as they help mitigate structural barriers and broaden the sector's innovation capacity. The first concerns inclusivity: AI-driven pipelines for knowledge extraction and normalization reduce the cognitive and technical burden needed to interpret complex standards and multilingual documentation, enabling smaller enterprises, start-ups, and academic groups to participate in activities traditionally dominated by major industrial players. Modern general-purpose models are progressively improving in their ability to transfer knowledge across domains with limited target-domain data (e.g., via domain adaptation or continual learning) [41], yet large incumbents maintain an advantage through access to extensive proprietary corpora and the capability to generate high-fidelity synthetic data for both natural-language and code-level artefacts (e.g., via LLM-based augmentation) [68]. How far these domain-transfer capabilities will generalize without large domain-specific datasets therefore remains an open and strategically relevant question.

The second dynamic concerns transferability: generative techniques function as a conduit through which practices established in aviation and autonomous driving can be adapted to the railway domain, from model-based assurance and scenario-based testing to predictive maintenance and anomaly detection. In aviation, generative approaches are being explored for scenario-based safety validation and certification support; in the automotive domain, LLMs have been piloted for autonomous driving software development, code synthesis, and safety-case management. These neighbouring sectors demonstrate that generative methods can be integrated into certification-driven workflows and serve as concrete references for railway applications.

A key challenge in applying scenario-based methodologies lies in achieving sufficient coverage of the operational design domain (ODD) and relevant corner cases. Generative models support this by enabling targeted expansion of scenario databases in under-represented conditions and by quantifying how comprehensively test sets span the operational domain [39]. Systematic analysis of generated scenarios helps identify coverage gaps and guides the synthesis of additional test cases to strengthen validation activities. Recent cross-domain surveys and influential reviews from 2023 to 2025 consistently position LLMs as catalysts for sensing, modeling, and lifecycle management in transportation and other safety-critical sectors [27,69], reinforcing the transferability of these techniques to railway applications.

3.3 AI-Enabled Requirements Processing as a Driver for MBSE Adoption

One of the foundational steps in managing complex systems is Requirements Engineering (RE), which constitutes a foundational phase in the lifecycle of safety-critical domains. Before architectural design, verification, or deployment, it is essential to elicit, structure, and validate the functions and behaviors of the intended system under all anticipated operational conditions. In the railway domain, RE remains one of the most critical and challenging activities, given the heterogeneity, scale, and safety constraints of the system specifications.

Railway tenders and specifications are often multilingual, heterogeneous, and unstructured, posing significant barriers to traceability and automation.

Figure 3 summarizes the AI-enabled workflow that converts heterogeneous natural-language specifications into structured model-ready artifacts.

AI-assisted extraction and classification have emerged as pragmatic solutions, as confirmed by recent RE research highlighting hybrid approaches that combine interpretable NLP models with LLM components. In this context, prior work on OCR-aware segmentation pipelines and dual-branch classification (ensemble versus multilingual BERT) has demonstrated that hybridization can balance robustness, interpretability, and linguistic coverage, while preserving human-in-the-loop safeguards essential in safety-critical contexts [9].

Recent investigations indicate that generative AI can support several RE activities, including:

- deduplication of overlapping requirements;
- coverage analysis and assessment of completeness;
- change impact estimation;
- consistency checking across large document sets.

These developments reinforce the role of AI as an enabler rather than a substitute for engineered verification workflows.

Datasets from the railway industry such as multilingual tender documentation and technical specifications released by operators in Europe and Asia—vividly illustrate both the scale of the challenge and the promise of AI-driven pipelines. By progressively reducing the gap between informal natural-language documentation and the formal artifacts required by MBSE, these tools create a structured substrate upon which models can be built and maintained. This capability is particularly valuable in organizations that might otherwise lack the resources or expertise to manage complex, model-driven workflows. Indeed, recent work demonstrates that LLMs can generate initial drafts of SysML or UML models directly from textual requirements for example, producing UML sequence diagrams from natural-language specifications with measurable conformity to standards [36]. Other studies explore how LLMs assist novice users in creating class, use-case, and sequence models from requirements [90], providing empirical support for integrating model generation into early development phases.

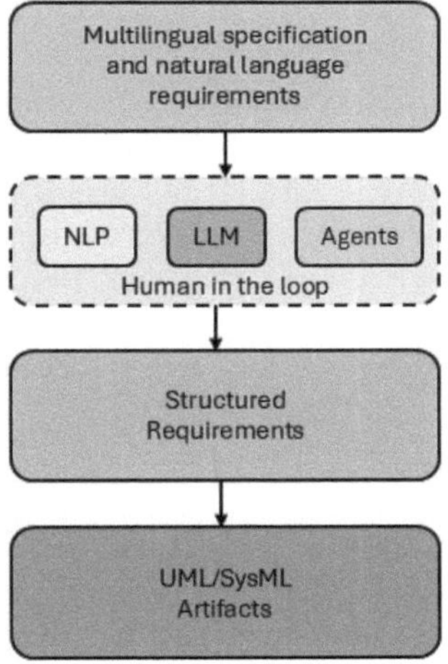

Fig. 3. Pipeline for transforming multilingual and natural-language requirements into structured specifications and UML/SysML artifacts through hybrid NLPLLMAgent processing with human-in-the-loop validation.

To clarify the complementarity of approaches, hybrid pipelines typically combine (i) deterministic NLP components responsible for classification, traceability, and explainability with (ii) LLM-based modules focused on multilingual comprehension and model suggestion.

While performance inevitably depends on data quality and domain specificity, the capacity of LLMs to propose model elements complements the interpretability and precision afforded by classical NLP pipelines. This distinction is particularly relevant in the railway sector, where transparency, safety, and explainability are nonnegotiable prerequisites for certification. Beyond model suggestion, LLM-based conversational agents have been proposed to interact directly with requirement documents, enabling engineers to query large specifications, verify compliance clauses, and monitor document evolution through similarity analysis, traceability links [98] and compliance verification against standards [13]. These assistants illustrate how LLMs can serve as interactive front-ends for navigating complex requirements corpora, provided that deterministic safeguards and validation layers remain in place. Hybrid strategies using LLMs for multilingual comprehension and model suggestion alongside deterministic NLP for classification and traceability are thus emerging as a balanced approach capable of reconciling productivity with certification demands.

In parallel, integration of AI with model-based engineering (MBE) is gaining momentum. The railway signalling domain, and in particular the European Rail Traffic Management System (ERTMS) Radio Block Centre (RBC), offers a compelling exemplar. Multi-agent finite-automata architectures, augmented by AI-assisted requirements processing, have been shown to enhance traceability, explainability, and automated documentation, thereby aligning models more closely with certification practices and facilitating early validation via parametric transition equations [70]. This trajectory illustrates how the rigor of model-based techniques can coexist with AI-driven adaptability, creating engineering workflows that preserve safety while accelerating development cycles, an equilibrium increasingly recognized as essential in safety-critical domains [75].

3.4   Readiness, Opportunities, and Risks

The opportunities outlined above demonstrate clear potential for transforming railway engineering. Achieving widespread adoption, however, requires a rigorous assessment of constraints and risks. Compliance with CENELEC EN 50126, EN 50128, and EN 50129, together with interoperability across heterogeneous vendor toolchains and alignment with emerging regulations such as the EU AI Act, imposes stringent requirements on transparency, auditability, and accountability. Black-box generative models challenge these requirements because their opacity undermines traceability and explainability. Furthermore, reliance on large pretrained models raises concerns about robustness under distributional shift, a particularly critical issue in domains where safety margins are inviolable. These constraints highlight the need for a systematic approach to technological readiness and risk containment.

To mitigate these risks, a combination of strategies is essential. Human-in-the-loop verification ensures expert oversight. Independent and diverse models reduce the likelihood of correlated failures. Explainable AI techniques support the production of auditable evidence that aligns with certification frameworks. In practical terms, mitigation strategies tend to concentrate around three pillars:

- expert-supervised verification and the use of model redundancy;
- explainability methods that generate certifiable and inspectable evidence;
- alignment with formal assurance workflows and sector-specific standards.

Explainability in large language models remains an active and rapidly evolving research frontier. Much of this effort is connected to the structural properties of transformer architectures, including encoder-only, decoder-only, and encoderdecoder configurations [71]. Recent work investigates techniques such as attention attribution, self-explanation, and model auditing to render internal reasoning processes more transparent and suitable for certification in safety-critical engineering domains [100]. Additional contributions from AI safety research, including continuous monitoring, red teaming, and formal risk modeling [83], further strengthen trustworthiness in generative systems [20]. Taken together, these methods are forming a coherent set of tools for evaluating generative AI within realistic operational and regulatory constraints.

A further critical dimension concerns integration and validation. Generative AI solutions must be incorporated into existing engineering toolchains in a way that preserves the integrity and continuity of verification and validation activities. This requires not only synthetic test generation and automated coverage analysis, but also mechanisms for assimilating test results into assurance cases and safety arguments. Continuous validation pipelines are valuable for maintaining the consistency of compliance evidence as requirements evolve and system components are updated, thereby preventing evidence drift or regression. Recent studies in AI assurance emphasize the integration of generative testing, continuous verification, and explainable evidence synthesis within formal certification workflows [84].

A recurring theme is the comparison between specialized NLP approaches and general-purpose large language models. Interpretable and specialized NLP methods, including ensemble linear models, class weighting, and dictionary augmentation, provide controllability, verifiability, and computational efficiency suitable for industrial environments without dedicated GPU infrastructure. Large language models, in contrast, offer advantages in multilingual normalization, cross-domain knowledge transfer, and interactive assistance. They remain more opaque and computationally demanding. For the railway sector, where rigor, traceability, and compliance are essential, a hybrid strategy appears to be the most promising direction. In such an approach, large language models support multilingual ingestion and semantic alignment across heterogeneous technical documents, while specialized NLP components provide deterministic classification, compliance-oriented artifact generation, and integration into model-based workflows. This balance reflects a trend in both research and industrial practice, where hybrid architectures combining symbolic and neural reasoning are increasingly advocated to achieve transparency and efficiency in safety-critical applications [19].

4   Conclusions

The adoption of Generative AI and Large Language Models in safety-critical engineering is still at an early stage, but their potential to complement Model-Based Systems Engineering is clear. By automating requirements formalization, supporting model generation and transformation, and assisting verification activities, these technologies can help reduce skill shortages and accelerate engineering workflows. At the same time, they raise open concerns regarding transparency, explainability, and certification that are particularly stringent in domains such as railways. Focusing on the railway sector, we outlined how GenAI can mitigate long-standing barriers to MBSE adoption, from the complexity of multilingual requirements to fragmented toolchains and interoperability demands. Transferability from adjacent domains such as automotive and aerospace provides encouraging evidence, but careful integration with existing standards and assurance practices remains essential. Overall, the convergence of rigorous modeling traditions and generative AI assistance offers both opportunities and risks. Progress will depend on hybrid strategies that balance productivity with trustworthiness, and on collaborative efforts between AI researchers, railway engineers, and regulators. This direction points toward a cautious but promising evolution of MBSE, where generative techniques act not as replacements, but as enablers of dependable and certifiable engineering.

References

1. En 50128 railway applications - communication, signaling and processing systems - software for railway control and protection systems. European Standard (2011)
2. ISO/IEC/IEEE 15288: Systems and software engineering - system life cycle processes. International Standard (2015)
3. En 50126 railway applications – the specification and demonstration of reliability, availability, maintainability and safety (rams) (2017), European Standard
4. Neural networks in closed-loop systems: verification using interval arithmetic and formal prover. Eng. Appl. Artif. Intell. **137**, 109238 (2024). https://doi.org/10.1016/j.engappai.2024.109238
5. Abu Tami, M., Ashqar, H.I., Elhenawy, M.M., Glaser, S., Rakotonirainy, A.: Using multimodal large language models (mllms) for automated detection of traffic safety-critical events. Vehicles **6**(3), 1571 – 1590 (2024). https://doi.org/10.3390/vehicles6030074, https://www.scopus.com/inward/record.uri?eid=2-s2.0-85205224052
6. Aiersilan, A.: Generating traffic scenarios via in-context learning to learn better motion planner, vol. 39, pp. 14539–14547. Association for the Advancement of Artificial Intelligence (2025)
7. Aleksandrov, A., Völlinger, K.: Formalizing piecewise affine activation functions of neural networks in Coq. In: Rozier, K.Y., Chaudhuri, S. (eds.) NASA Formal Methods, pp. 62–78. Lecture Notes in Computer Science, Springer Nature Switzerland, Cham (2023). https://doi.org/10.1007/978-3-031-33170-1_4
8. Althoff, M.: An introduction to cora 2015. In: Proc. of the 1st and 2nd Workshop on Applied Verification for Continuous and Hybrid Systems, pp. 120–151. EasyChair (2015). https://doi.org/10.29007/zbkv

9. Arianna, N., Riccardo, R., Gabriele, P., Giulio, R.: From unstructured documents to annotated information: an optimized pipeline to process industrial requirements. In: Proceedings of the 2024 8th International Conference on Natural Language Processing and Information Retrieval, pp. 272–278 (2024)

10. ter Beek, M.H., Fantechi, A., Gnesi, S., Lenzini, G., Petrocchi, M.: Can AI help with the formalization of railway cybersecurity requirements? In: Margaria, T., Steffen, B. (eds.) Leveraging Applications of Formal Methods, Verification and Validation. REoCAS Colloquium in Honor of Rocco De Nicola, pp. 186–203. Springer Nature Switzerland, Cham (2025)

11. Bellogín, A., Grau, O., Ryzhyk, L., Schimpf, G., Sengupta, B., Solmaz, G.: The EU AI Act and the wager on trustworthy AI. Commun. ACM **67**(12),(2024). https://doi.org/10.1145/3665322

12. Bešinović, N., De Donato, L., Flammini, F., Goverde, R.M.P., Lin, Z., et al.: Artificial intelligence in railway transport: taxonomy, regulations, and applications. IEEE Trans. Intell. Transp. Syst. **23**(9), 14011–14024 (2022). https://doi.org/10.1109/TITS.2021.3131637

13. Bolton, R., Sheikhfathollahi, M., Parkinson, S., Basher, D., Parkinson, H.: Multi-stage retrieval for operational technology cybersecurity compliance using large language models: a railway casestudy. arXiv preprint arXiv:2504.14044 (2025)

14. Bukhary, N., et al.: Few-shot evaluation of vision language models for detecting visual defects in autonomous vehicle software requirement specifications. IEEE Access **13**, 117914 – 117942 (2025). https://doi.org/10.1109/ACCESS.2025.3586554, https://www.scopus.com/inward/record.uri?eid=2-s2.0-105010211814

15. Cambria, E., Huang, H., Kwok, K., Wang, H.: Neuro-symbolic approaches to artificial intelligence: recent trends and future directions. Inf. Fusion **91**, 1–12 (2023). https://doi.org/10.1016/j.inffus.2022.12.011

16. Cao, Z., Yang, Y., Zhao, H.: Scans: mitigating the exaggerated safety for LLMs via safety-conscious activation steering. vol. 39, pp. 23523 – 23531. Association for the Advancement of Artificial Intelligence (2025). https://doi.org/10.1609/aaai.v39i22.34521, https://www.scopus.com/inward/record.uri?eid=2-s2.0-105004002985

17. Carletti, V., Foggia, P., Mazzocca, C., Parrella, G., Vento, M.: Evaluating large language models for vulnerability detection under realistic conditions. Lecture Notes Comput. Sci. **15999 LNCS**, 135 – 152 (2025). https://doi.org/10.1007/978-3-032-00644-8_8, https://www.scopus.com/inward/record.uri?eid=2-s2.0-105014434153

18. Chen, Y., et al.: Medct: a clinical terminology graph for generative ai applications in healthcare. Lecture Notes Comput. Sci. **15908 LNCS**, 24–38 (2025)

19. Cheng, H., et al.: Generative AI for requirements engineering: a systematic literature review. arXiv preprint arXiv:2409.06741 (2024)

20. Chua, J., Li, Y., Yang, S., Wang, C., Yao, L.: AI safety in generative AI large language models: a survey. arXiv preprint arXiv:2407.18369 (2024)

21. Cibrián, E., Olivert-Iserte, J., Llorens, J.B., Álvarez Rodríguez, J.M.: An agent-based approach for the automatic generation of valid sysmlv2 models in industrial contexts. Comput. Industr. **172** (2025)

22. Clegg, K.D., Habli, I., McDermid, J.A.: Using GPT-4 to generate failure logic. Lecture Notes Comput. Sci. **14989 LNCS**, 148–159 (2024)

23. Corazza, J., Gavran, I., Moreira, G., Neider, D.: Accessible smart contracts verification: synthesizing formal models with tamed LLMs, pp. 542–552. Institute of Electrical and Electronics Engineers Inc. (2025)

24. Daclin, N., Mallek-Daclin, S., Zacharewicz, G.: Generative AI for business model generation (gai4bm): from textual description to business process model, vol. 2024-September. Cal-Tek srl (2024)
25. Diemert, S., Weber-Jahnke, J.H.: Can large language models assist in hazard analysis? Lecture Notes Comput. Sci. **14182 LNCS**, 410–422 (2023)
26. Dona, M.A.M., Cabrero-Daniel, B., Yu, Y., Berger, C.: LLMs can check their own results to mitigate hallucinations in traffic understanding tasks. Lecture Notes Comput. Sci. **15383 LNCS**, 114 – 130 (2025). https://doi.org/10.1007/978-3-031-80889-0_8, https://www.scopus.com/inward/record.uri?eid=2-s2.0-85218460038
27. Du, Y., Li, Y., Zhang, Y., Tian, Z.: A perspective on large language models for transportation systems: opportunities and future directions. Transp. Res. Part C: Emerging Technol. **163**, 104523 (2024). https://doi.org/10.1016/j.trc.2024.104523
28. Ehlers, R.: Formal verification of piece-wise linear feed-forward neural networks. In: D'Souza, D., Narayan Kumar, K. (eds.) Automated Technology for Verification and Analysis, pp. 269–286. Lecture Notes in Computer Science, Springer International Publishing, Cham (2017). https://doi.org/10.1007/978-3-319-68167-2_19
29. Esposito, M., Palagiano, F.: Leveraging large language models for preliminary security risk analysis: a mission-critical case study, pp. 442 – 445. Association for Computing Machinery (2024). https://doi.org/10.1145/3661167.3661226, https://www.scopus.com/inward/record.uri?eid=2-s2.0-85197452753
30. Esposito, M., Palagiano, F., Lenarduzzi, V., Taibi, D.: Beyond words: on large language models actionability in mission-critical risk analysis.. IEEE Comput. Soc., 517 – 527 (2024). https://doi.org/10.1145/3674805.3695401, https://www.scopus.com/inward/record.uri?eid=2-s2.0-85210587760
31. Fan, J., Huang, C., Chen, X., Li, W., Zhu, Q.: ReachNN*: a tool for reachability analysis of neural-network controlled systems. In: Hung, D.V., Sokolsky, O. (eds.) Automated Technology for Verification and Analysis, pp. 537–542. Springer International Publishing, Cham (2020)
32. Fantechi, A.: Connected or autonomous trains? In: Collart-Dutilleul, S., Lecomte, T., Romanovsky, A. (eds.) Reliability, Safety, and Security of Railway Systems. Modelling, Analysis, Verification, and Certification, pp. 3–19. Springer International Publishing, Cham (2019)
33. Fantechi, A., Flammini, F., Gnesi, S.: Formal methods for intelligent transportation systems. In: Margaria, T., Steffen, B. (eds.) Leveraging Applications of Formal Methods, Verification and Validation. Applications and Case Studies, pp. 187–189. Springer Berlin Heidelberg, Berlin, Heidelberg (2012)
34. Fantechi, A., Flammini, F., Gnesi, S.: Formal methods for railway control systems. Int. J. Softw. Tools Technol. Transf. **16**(6), 643–646 (Nov2014)
35. Fantechi, A., Gnesi, S., Haxthausen, A.: Formal methods for distributed computing in future railway systems. In: Margaria, T., Steffen, B. (eds.) Leveraging Applications of Formal Methods, Verification and Validation. Application Areas, pp. 109–111. Springer Nature Switzerland, Cham (2025)
36. Ferrari, A., Abualhaija, S., Arora, C.: In: Model generation with LLMs: from requirements to UML sequence diagrams. In: 2024 IEEE 32nd International Requirements Engineering Conference Workshops (REW), pp. 291–300. IEEE (2024)
37. Ferrari, A., Spoletini, P.: Formal requirements engineering and large language models: a two-way roadmap. Inf. Softw. Technol. **181**, 107697 (2025)

38. Flammini, F., De Donato, L., Fantechi, A., Vittorini, V.: a vision of intelligent train control. In: Reliability, Safety, and Security of Railway Systems. Modelling, Analysis, Verification, and Certification. RSSRail 2022, LNCS 13294, pp. 192–208. Springer, Cham (2022). https://doi.org/10.1007/978-3-031-05814-1_14

39. de Gelder, E., Buermann, M., Den Camp, O.O.: Coverage metrics for a scenario database for the scenario-based assessment of automated driving systems. In: 2024 IEEE International Automated Vehicle Validation Conference (IAVVC), pp. 1–8. IEEE (2024)

40. Gohar, U., Hunter, M.C., Lutz, R.R., Cohen, M.B.: Codefeater: using LLMs to find defeaters in assurance cases, pp. 2262 – 2267. Association for Computing Machinery, Inc (2024). https://doi.org/10.1145/3691620.3695296, https://www.scopus.com/inward/record.uri?eid=2-s2.0-85212392463

41. Guo, X., Yu, H.: On the domain adaptation and generalization of pretrained language models: a survey. arXiv preprint arXiv:2211.03154 (2022)

42. Hassan, M., Ahmadi-Pour, S., Qayyum, K., Jha, C.K., Drechsler, R.: LLM-guided formal verification coupled with mutation testing (2024)

43. Honarvar, S.: Evaluating correct-consistency and robustness in code-generating LLMs, pp. 797 – 800. Institute of Electrical and Electronics Engineers Inc. (2025). https://doi.org/10.1109/ICST62969.2025.10988971, https://www.scopus.com/inward/record.uri?eid=2-s2.0-105007552396

44. Huang, C., Fan, J., Li, W., Chen, X., Zhu, Q.: ReachNN: reachability analysis of neural-network controlled systems. ACM Trans. Embed. Comput. Syst. **18**(5s) (2019). https://doi.org/10.1145/3358228

45. Ivanov, R., Carpenter, T., Weimer, J., Alur, R., Pappas, G., Lee, I.: Verisig 2.0: verification of neural network controllers using taylor model preconditioning. In: Silva, A., Leino, K.R.M. (eds.) Computer Aided Verification, pp. 249–262. Springer International Publishing, Cham (2021). https://doi.org/10.1007/978-3-030-81685-8_11

46. Jahan, M., et al.: Automated derivation of uml sequence diagrams from user stories: unleashing the power of generative AI vs. a rule-based approach, pp. 138–148. Association for Computing Machinery, Inc. (2024)

47. Katz, G., Barrett, C., Dill, D.L., Julian, K., Kochenderfer, M.J.: Reluplex: an efficient SMT solver for verifying deep neural networks. In: Majumdar, R., Kunčak, V. (eds.) Computer Aided Verification, pp. 97–117. Springer International Publishing, Cham (2017)

48. Katz, G., et al.: The marabou framework for verification and analysis of deep neural networks. In: Dillig, I., Tasiran, S. (eds.) Computer Aided Verification, pp. 443–452. Lecture Notes in Computer Science, Springer International Publishing, Cham (2019). https://doi.org/10.1007/978-3-030-25540-4_26

49. Kevvay, M., Gryaznykh, V., Kirovskii, O.M., Korolev, A.S.: Assessing the validity of LLM-driven hazard analysis: an assessor's perspective, pp. 186 – 190. Institute of Electrical and Electronics Engineers Inc. (2025). https://doi.org/10.1109/DSN-S65789.2025.00063, https://www.scopus.com/inward/record.uri?eid=2-s2.0-105011416705

50. Khatiri, S., Di Sorbo, A., Zampetti, F., Visaggio, C.A., Di Penta, M.D., Panichella, S.: Identifying safety–critical concerns in unmanned aerial vehicle software platforms with salient. SoftwareX **27** (2024). https://doi.org/10.1016/j.softx.2024.101748, https://www.scopus.com/inward/record.uri?eid=2-s2.0-85192157664

51. Kirchner, S., Knoll, A.C.: Generating automotive code: large language models for software development and verification in safety-critical systems, pp. 813 – 820. Institute of Electrical and Electronics Engineers Inc. (2025). https://doi.org/10.1109/IV64158.2025.11097503, https://www.scopus.com/inward/record.uri?eid=2-s2.0-105014240620

52. Kochdumper, N., Schilling, C., Althoff, M., Bak, S.: Open- and closed-loop neural network verification using polynomial zonotopes. In: NASA Formal Methods Symposium, pp. 16–36. Springer (2023). https://doi.org/10.1007/978-3-031-33170-1_2, https://link.springer.com/chapter/10.1007/978-3-031-33170-1_2

53. Kourani, H., Berti, A., Schuster, D., van der Aalst, W.M.: Process modeling with large language models. Lecture Notes Bus. Inf. Process. **511 LNBIP**, 229–244 (2024)

54. Kumar, P., Sandeep Abinash, A., Dineshkumar, M.: Llm-based autonomous automotive testing simulation with claude 3.5 sonnet, pp. 25 – 30. Institute of Electrical and Electronics Engineers Inc. (2025). https://doi.org/10.1109/ICCSP64183.2025.11088758, https://www.scopus.com/inward/record.uri?eid=2-s2.0-105013474612

55. Kumar Jha, S.K., Jha, S., Ewetz, R., Velasquez, A.: Co-synthesis of code and formal models using large language models and functors, pp. 215–220. Institute of Electrical and Electronics Engineers Inc. (2024). https://doi.org/10.1109/MILCOM61039.2024.10773930

56. Kumar Jha, S.K., et al.: Counterexample guided inductive synthesis using large language models and satisfiability solving, pp. 944 – 949. Institute of Electrical and Electronics Engineers Inc. (2023). https://doi.org/10.1109/MILCOM58377.2023.10356332, https://www.scopus.com/inward/record.uri?eid=2-s2.0-85182396042

57. Lee, H., Lee, S.h., Yang, H., Kwon, C.: Generative AI-based safety evaluation framework for autonomous racing system via safety-critical scenario generation. J. Inst. Control Robot. Syst. **31**(5), 481 – 489 (2025). https://doi.org/10.5302/J.ICROS.2025.25.0053, https://www.scopus.com/inward/record.uri?eid=2-s2.0-105005228843

58. Li, B., et al.: Trustworthy AI: from principles to practices. ACM Comput. Surv. **55**(9), 1–46 (2023)

59. Li, J., Liu, S., Jin, Z.: Automated formal-specification-to-code trace links recovery using multi-dimensional similarity measures. J. Syst. Softw. **226** (2025). https://doi.org/10.1016/j.jss.2025.112439, https://www.scopus.com/inward/record.uri?eid=2-s2.0-105000552504

60. Li, Q., Han, J., Yuan, L., Li, X., Wang, X.: Constructing formal models of cryptographic protocols from alicebob style specifications via LLM. Sci. Reports **15**(1) (2025)

61. Liu, M., Wang, J., Lin, T., Ma, Q., Fang, Z., Wu, Y.: An empirical study of the code generation of safety-critical software using LLMs. Appl. Sci. (Switzerland) **14**(3) (2024). https://doi.org/10.3390/app14031046, https://www.scopus.com/inward/record.uri?eid=2-s2.0-85186316411

62. Ma, Z., Wen, C., Yu, B., Su, J.: Integrating ensemble learning and large language models for efficient formal verification of IP-based aerospace systems. Inf. Fusion **125** (2026). https://doi.org/10.1016/j.inffus.2025.103466, https://www.scopus.com/inward/record.uri?eid=2-s2.0-105010181912

63. Mao, Z., Wang, J., Sun, J., Qin, S., Xiong, J.: LLM-aided automatic modeling for security protocol verification, pp. 642–654. IEEE Computer Society (2025)

64. Mavikumbure, H.S., Cobilean, V., Wickramasinghe, C.S., Drake, D., Manic, M.: Generative AI in cyber security of cyber physical systems: benefits and threats. IEEE Computer Society (2024). https://doi.org/10.1109/HSI61632.2024.10613562, https://www.scopus.com/inward/record.uri?eid=2-s2.0-85201544602

65. McShane, J., Çelik, L., Aideyan, I.W., Brooks, R.R., Pesé, M.D.: LLM-powered fuzz testing of automotive diagnostic protocols. SAE International (2025). https://doi.org/10.4271/2025-01-8091, https://www.scopus.com/inward/record.uri?eid=2-s2.0-105008181831

66. Mei, Y., Nie, T., Sun, J., Tian, Y.: LLM-attacker: enhancing closed-loop adversarial scenario generation for autonomous driving with large language models. IEEE Trans. Intell. Transp. Syst. (2025). https://doi.org/10.1109/TITS.2025.3578383, https://www.scopus.com/inward/record.uri?eid=2-s2.0-105009484311

67. Moreira, E.J.V.F., Campos, J.C.: On the role of generative AI in explaining model checking counterexamples. Lecture Notes Comput. Sci. **15518 LNCS**, 138 – 158 (2025). https://doi.org/10.1007/978-3-031-91760-8_10, https://www.scopus.com/inward/record.uri?eid=2-s2.0-105007683064

68. Nadăş, M., Dioşan, L., Tomescu, A.: Synthetic data generation using large language models: advances in text and code. IEEE Access (2025)

69. Nie, T., Sun, J., Ma, W.: Exploring the roles of large language models in reshaping transportation systems: a survey, framework, and roadmap. Artif. Intell. Transp. **1**, 100003 (2025)

70. Nocente, A., Pannocchia, G., Rossetti, G.: An integrated AI and model-based approach for railway cyber-physical systems. In: 2025 20th European Dependable Computing Conference Companion Proceedings (EDCC-C), pp. 113–118. IEEE (2025)

71. Palikhe, A., Yu, Z., Wang, Z., Zhang, W.: Towards transparent AI: a survey on explainable large language models. arXiv preprint arXiv:2506.21812 (2025)

72. Papakonstantinou, N., Van Bossuyt, D.L., Bell, R., Naval, R.L., Heikkilä, M.: Privateaidelphi: adopting and adapting private AI for risk assessment of safety critical systems. Institute of Electrical and Electronics Engineers Inc. (2025). https://doi.org/10.1109/RAMS48127.2025.10935226, https://www.scopus.com/inward/record.uri?eid=2-s2.0-105002272287&doi=10.1109

73. Preda, A.R., Mayr-Dorn, C., Mashkoor, A., Egyed, A.J.: Supporting high-level to low-level requirements coverage reviewing with large language models, pp. 242 – 253. Institute of Electrical and Electronics Engineers Inc. (2024). https://doi.org/10.1145/3643991.3644922, https://www.scopus.com/inward/record.uri?eid=2-s2.0-85197388315

74. Pulina, L., Tacchella, A.: An abstraction-refinement approach to verification of artificial neural networks. In: Touili, T., Cook, B., Jackson, P. (eds.) Computer Aided Verification, pp. 243–257. Springer, Berlin Heidelberg (2010)

75. Rädler, S., Berardinelli, L., Winter, K., Rahimi, A., Rinderle-Ma, S.: Bridging mde and AI: a systematic review of domain-specific languages and model-driven practices in ai software systems engineering. Softw. Syst. Model. **24**(2), 445–469 (2025)

76. Roodt, D., Nadeem, M., Vu, L.T.: Managing complexity on digital systems: a model-based systems engineering approach. In: Conference on Railway Excellence (CORE). Shoal Group (2020). case study on MBSE in Sydney rail modernization

77. Rossi, F., Bernardeschi, C., Cococcioni, M., Palmieri, M.: Towards formal verification of neural networks in cyber-physical systems. In: 16th NASA Formal Methods Symposium, Lecture Notes in Computer Science (including subseries Lecture

Notes in Artificial Intelligence and Lecture Notes in Bioinformatics). vol. 14627, pp. 207–222. Springer Nature Switzerland (2024). https://doi.org/10.1007/978-3-031-60698-4_12

78. Schulz, T., Luttermann, M., Möller, R.: Autorag: grounding text and symbols. KI - Kunstliche Intelligenz **38**(3), 203–217 (2024)

79. Sevenhuijsen, M., Etemadi, K., Nyberg, M.: Vecogen: automating generation of formally verified c code with large language models, 101 – 112 (2025)

80. Sezgin, A., Boyaci, A.: Llm-powered UAVs: a rag-based approach for safety-critical operations. Lecture Notes Netw. Syst. **1529 LNNS**, 577 – 584 (2025). https://doi.org/10.1007/978-3-031-97992-7_64, https://www.scopus.com/inward/record.uri?eid=2-s2.0-105013053177

81. Shentu, Y., Trapp, M.: Facilitating fault tree analysis with generative AI. Lecture Notes Computer Sci. **15955 LNCS**, 524–536 (2026)

82. Son, H.: Using large language models in software requirements analysis. Edelweiss Appl. Sci. Technol. **9**(3), 856 – 863 (2025). https://doi.org/10.55214/25768484.v9i3.5357, https://www.scopus.com/inward/record.uri?eid=2-s2.0-105000122709

83. Srivastava, A., Panda, S.: A formal framework for assessing and mitigating emergent security risks in generative AI models. Bridging theory and dynamic risk mitigation. arXiv preprint arXiv:2410.13897 (2024)

84. Tambon, F., et al.: How to certify machine learning based safety-critical systems? a systematic literature review. Automated Softw. Eng. **29**(2), 38 (2022)

85. Tang, R., De Donato, L., Bešinović, N., Flammini, F., Goverde, R.M.P., Lin, Z., et al.: A literature review of artificial intelligence applications in railway systems. Transp. Res. Part C: Emerging Technol. **140**, 103679 (2022). https://doi.org/10.1016/j.trc.2022.103679

86. Tang, S., Zhang, Z., Zhou, J., Lei, L., Zhou, Y., Xue, Y.: Legend: a top-down approach to scenario generation of autonomous driving systems assisted by large language models, pp. 1497 – 1508. Association for Computing Machinery, Inc (2024). https://doi.org/10.1145/3691620.3695520, https://www.scopus.com/inward/record.uri?eid=2-s2.0-85212399727

87. Vidyaratne, L., Lee, X.Y., Kumar, A., Watanabe, T., Farahat, A., Gupta, C.: Generating troubleshooting trees for industrial equipment using large language models (LLM), pp. 116–125. Institute of Electrical and Electronics Engineers Inc. (2024)

88. Vidyaratne, L.S., Shao, H., Watanabe, T., Farahat, A.K., Gupta, C.: Generating troubleshooting trees with fmea using large language models (LLM). Institute of Electrical and Electronics Engineers Inc. (2025)

89. Wan, Y., Chen, Z., Liu, Y., Chen, C., Packianather, M.S.: Empowering llms by hybrid retrieval-augmented generation for domain-centric qa in smart manufacturing. Adv. Eng. Inf. **65** (2025). https://doi.org/10.1016/j.aei.2025.103212, https://www.scopus.com/inward/record.uri?eid=2-s2.0-85218271912

90. Wang, B., Wang, C., Liang, P., Li, B., Zeng, C.: How LLMs aid in UML modeling: an exploratory study with novice analysts. In: 2024 IEEE International Conference on Software Services Engineering (SSE), pp. 249–257. IEEE (2024)

91. Weidmann, N., Salunkhe, S., Anjorin, A., Yigitbas, E., Engels, G.: Automating model transformations for railway systems engineering. J. Object Technol. **20**(3), 1–22 (2021). https://doi.org/10.5381/jot.2021.20.3.a10

92. Wu, R., Wen, G., Zhang, X., Liang, X., Yang, C., Gui, W.: Knowledge-augmented conversational agents for dependency-aware sysml v2 model generation and refinement, 581 – 586 (2025)

93. Wucherpfennig, D., Ehret, M., Schöberl, M., Malzacher, G., Boehm, M., Fottner, J.: Model-based systems engineering for the design of an intermodal high-speed freight train terminal. In: IEEE International Systems Conference (SysCon), pp. 1–8 (2022). https://doi.org/10.1109/SysCon53536.2022.9773867
94. Xiang, W., Tran, H.D., Johnson, T.T.: Output reachable set estimation and verification for multilayer neural networks. IEEE Trans. Neural Netw. Learn. Syst. **29**(11), 5777–5783 (2018). https://doi.org/10.1109/TNNLS.2018.2808470
95. Xiao, X., et al.: A text intelligence-based approach for automatic generation of fault trees in nuclear power plants, vol. 10. American Society of Mechanical Engineers (ASME) (2024)
96. Xu, A., et al.: Agentic AI for enterprise: emerging applications and real-world challenges. vol. 2, pp. 6300 – 6301. Association for Computing Machinery (2025). https://doi.org/10.1145/3711896.3737871, https://www.scopus.com/inward/record.uri?eid=2-s2.0-105014313831
97. Xu, H., Boyaci, A., Lian, J., Wilson, A.J.: Explainable AI for multivariate time series pattern exploration: latent space visual analytics with temporal fusion transformer and variational autoencoders in power grid event diagnosis. IEEE Access (2025)
98. Yan, Y., et al.: Large language models for traffic and transportation research: methodologies, state of the art, and future opportunities. arXiv preprint arXiv:2503.21330 (2025)
99. Zhang, J., Xu, C., Li, B.: Chatscene: knowledge-enabled safety-critical scenario generation for autonomous vehicles. In: Proceedings of the IEEE Computer Society Conference on Computer Vision and Pattern Recognition, pp. 15459 – 15469. IEEE Computer Society (2024). https://doi.org/10.1109/CVPR52733.2024.01464, https://www.scopus.com/inward/record.uri?eid=2-s2.0-85205398410
100. Zhao, H., et al.: Explainability for large language models: a survey. ACM Trans. Intell. Syst. Technol. **15**(2), 1–38 (2024)

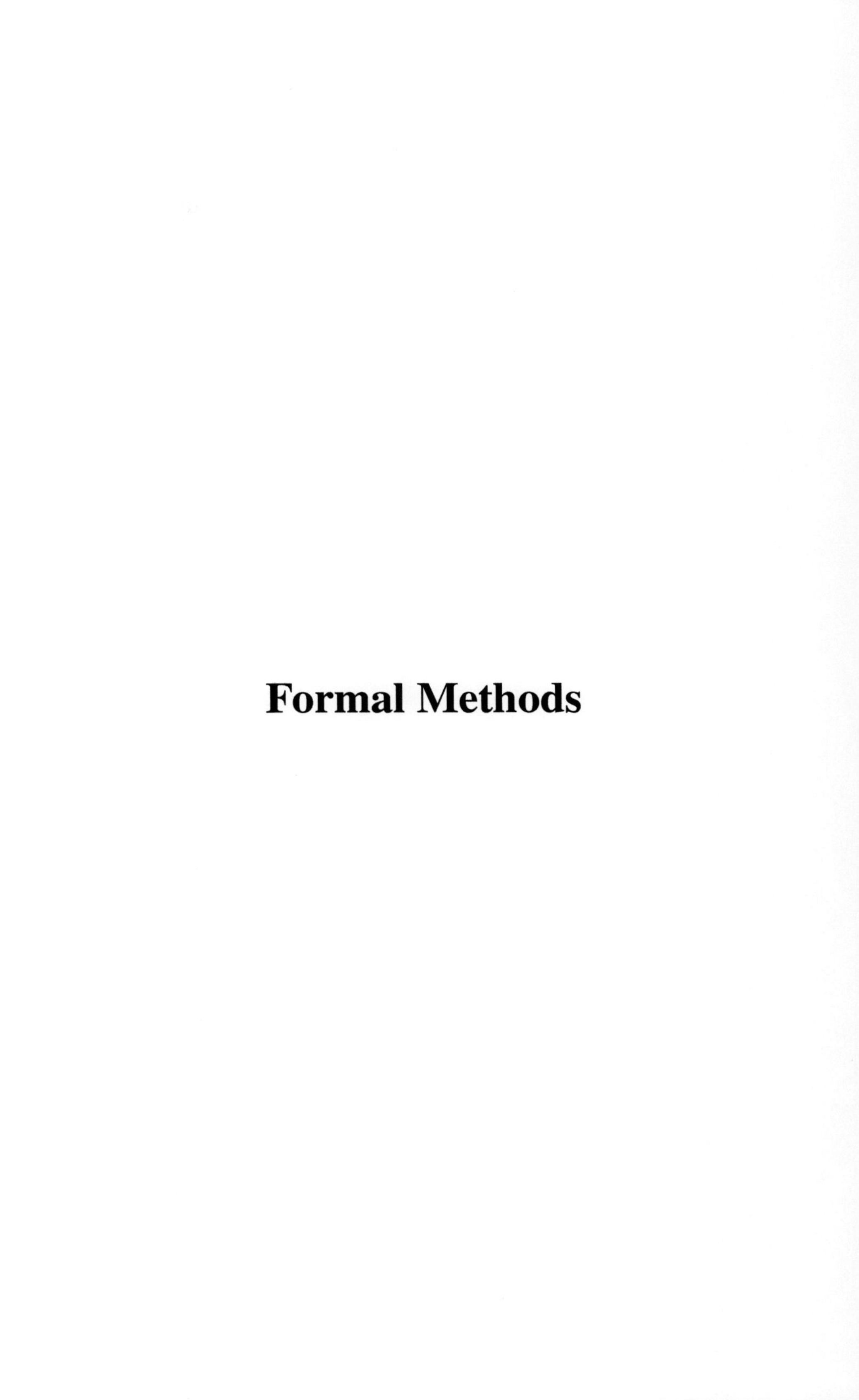

Formal Methods

Formal Methods Meet AI Guidance for Correct Software Development

Marco Krumrey[1,2(✉)] [ID], Tiziana Margaria[1,2] [ID], and Bernhard Steffen[3] [ID]

[1] University of Limerick, Limerick, Ireland
krumrey.marco@ul.ie, tiziana.margaria@ul.ie
[2] CRT-AI, Centre of Research Training in AI, Limerick, Ireland
[3] Lehrstuhl für Programmiersysteme, TU Dortmund, Dortmund, Germany
steffen@cs.tu-dortmund.de

Abstract. Active automata learning is an effective approach for deriving behavioral models in learning-based software testing. A major obstacle, however, is defining the learning alphabet that captures possible user interactions with the system under test. We propose an AI-assisted method that leverages large language models (LLMs) to automate and guide this process. Our approach uses two designed prompts that analyze a web application's source code: the first extracts all possible frontend interactions and presents them as an editable, human-readable list for validation and abstraction refinement; the second uses this refined list and the source code to define concrete alphabet symbols for learning including their implementation. This method lowers the entry barrier to applying active automata learning and improves the quality of resulting models. We demonstrate its effectiveness on a real web application and show how the learned model can serve as behavioral reference for formal analysis and comparison.

Keywords: Active automata learning · High assurance systems · Model driven development · Formal methods · Neurosymbolic design

1 Introduction

Formal methods, encompassing system descriptions, modeling and verification, have established themselves as the quality and quality assurance level of high assurance systems. This is witnessed by standards like DO-178C and more recently DO-333, the formal methods supplement to DO-178-C, where it is clearly stated that while testing is the most common practiced software and system validation technique, for high assurance and (business) critical systems the practice must be elevated to formal proofs, through formal verification.

Alessandro Fantechi has spent an entire career in devising, building and applying methods and tools to make systems, very frequently transportation systems, correct, safe, and provably so. With collaborators, many of them lifelong, he has tackled the problem of understanding requirements usually provided

© The Author(s), under exclusive license to Springer Nature Switzerland AG 2026
M. H. ter Beek et al. (Eds.): Fantechi Festschrift, LNCS 16470, pp. 117–137, 2026.
https://doi.org/10.1007/978-3-032-12484-5_7

as textual formulations by building methods and tools that capture the semantic of Natural Language and transforming them in properties formally expressed in temporal logics [22,26], methods and techniques for describing complex, often embedded systems capturing their structure, operations, and often real-time behaviour [5,10,15,21] frequently also building tools that embody those methods and techniques in a largely automated way [4,18,27,40]. This way, even field engineers, application engineers, and other professional figures who would not be able to produce formal descriptions nor operate theorem provers are powerfully aided through various model checkers and approaches to compositional verification [3,6,32]. Most recently, reflections on the use and usefulness of AI and LLMs extend and complete the technology evolution [13,25].

Beside meeting at many conferences and in other occasions, the two key threads of long term collaboration have been Alessandro's connection with FMICS, the ERCIM Working Group on Formal Methods for Industrial Critical Systems, of which he was President in 2008-2011, and DisCoRail, the track at ISoLA on Formal methods for DIStributed COmputing in future RAILway systems, often co-organized with Stefania Gnesi and Anne Haxthausen. The contribution to the 2012 FMICS book [51] on "Some Trends in Formal Methods Applications to Railway Signaling" [23] is representative of his likely most successful line of research: the specification, modelling and verification of train signalling protocols, according to standards like CENELEC: from technical works like [14] to recent retrospectives from an eagle's point of view like [11]

The key connections to our research are the long standing love for process algebras [24], the adoption of Kripke Transition Systems [55] (that in Alessandro and Stefania's work are called doubly labelled transition systems [12]) as a graph-based system description formalism, the adoption and design of variant of temporal logics to express system properties, and the corresponding model checking or synthesis techniques [44].

In the context of the present work, the following areas of correspondence are notable: the choice of ACTL and NLP translations to modal logica for Alessandro, for us the work on mu-calculus and the Fixpoint Analysis Machine [56] and the GEAR tool [9], as well as the introduction of SLTL for reasoning on ontology-based properties and systems [43]. In particular, the work on the correspondence between automata and temporal logic properties allows to express equivalently an exact characterization of system behaviours. Specifically, the work on characteristic formulas for system behaviours, and how to extract them from an automaton [52], and the use of difference automata to precisely characterize the behavioural difference between sequential systems [42]. The power of these characterization techniques is that, contrary to recent AI based approaches, they are deterministic and complete rather than probabilistic and exploratory. In other words, their "explanations" satisfy the high standard of high assurance system quality. This contrasts with the SHAP and LIME explanations common in today's explainable AI, that do not provide a precise and deterministic justification case by case, for each run of the system or recommendation of the model. In terms of use, as shown in Fig. 1 the combination of these three techniques allows the free choice of preferred formal description technique: an automaton, the set of equivalent characteristic logical formulas, and test suites covering the automaton, in order to describe the abstract behaviour (through properties in logics), the specific system (through an automaton) or operationalize experimental compliance testing through test suites. As there is equivalence between the three, it is possible to change the behavioural description style as needed, depending on the available representation, the appropriate checking technique, or the required format of the evidence of compliance.

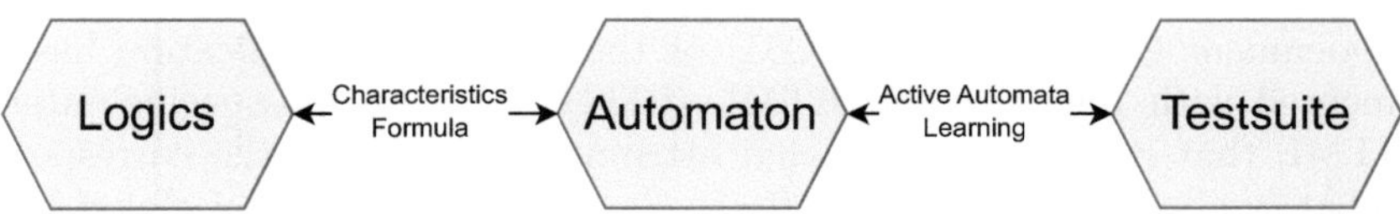

Fig. 1. Styles of behavioural characterization.

In the rest of the paper, we will present our approach to enable high assurance correctness checking of system behaviours in a model driven, no-code paradigm. Specifically, we will enable through AI and automation a competent and high-quality use of AAL techniques in order to produce automata describing a black-box system, so that the automaton can be perused (e.g., for further refinement, system evolution, inspection, compliance verification, application of a wide range of formal and informal verification methods) even when the individual in question is not a programmer, and potentially would not be able to use the current techniques like ALEX and AAL.

2   LLM assisted Active Automata Learning

Model-based software testing is an essential technique for quality assurance and formal verification in software development. One effective method for realizing this approach is active automata learning, which infers a formal behavioral model by interacting with a target application and observing its responses. The outcome of this process is a hypothesis model that approximates the behavior of the system under learning.

However, applying active automata learning requires the learning algorithm to be provided with a learning alphabet, a set of symbols that describe the possible interactions with the application and the expected outcomes. Defining this alphabet poses a significant challenge, as each alphabet symbol must be executable on the target application and must correctly capture the corresponding expected responses.

For the domain of web applications, previous work introduced the Automata Learning EXperience (ALEX) tool [7] to facilitate this process. ALEX provides a wide variety of predefined actions commonly encountered when interacting with web applications, ranging from basic user interactions such as button clicks to the execution of custom JavaScript. Furthermore, ALEX supports the complete setup and execution of learning experiments by leveraging LearnLib [36,46], and it can automatically generate test suites based on the learned behavioral model of a given web application. A previous study demonstrated that ALEX significantly reduces the entry barrier for applying active automata learning to model-based software testing.

Nevertheless, defining the symbols of the learning alphabet remains a largely manual and time-consuming task. To further address this limitation, the Mostly Automated Learning of Web Applications (MALWA) tool [39] was developed. MALWA enables the learning of web applications out of the box, provided that the Document Object Model (DOM) of the target web application has been augmented with Instrumented HTML (iHTML)—a domain-specific extension of HTML that introduces additional attributes to describe the corresponding alphabet symbols. This approach effectively shifts the creation of alphabet symbols to the development phase, embedding them directly into the application's source code.

The approach proposed in this work eliminates the need for direct augmentation of the source code while leveraging ALEX's existing action templates to apply active automata learning with minimal manual intervention. To achieve this, state-of-the-art Large Language Models (LLMs) are employed to analyze the source code of the target web application and identify its possible user interactions. The identified interactions are then presented to the user for verification and, if necessary, refinement. Subsequently, these verified interactions are used to automatically generate the learning alphabet to be utilized by the ALEX tool during the learning process. This approach simplifies the creation of the learning alphabet while maintaining the opportunity for human verification to mitigate the non-deterministic behavior of LLMs.

Related Work Active automata learning has evolved into a well-established and dynamic field of research, encompassing a broad spectrum of theoretical and practical investigations. A considerable body of work has focused on extending learning algorithms to handle richer classes of models, including those that capture timing behavior [47,59,63], infinite input alphabets [20,41], and extended finite-state machines [16,28,58]. Parallel research efforts have concentrated on improving the efficiency and scalability of learning algorithms themselves [33,60].

Beyond methodological advances, a large number of case studies have demonstrated the practical applicability of active automata learning across diverse domains. These include generating formal specifications [1,48,57], verifying communication protocols [29–31], conducting model-based testing [19,50], and even testing autonomous systems such as vehicles [48] or inferring behavioral models of recurrent neural networks [38].

In leveraging the capabilities of large language models (LLMs) for automata learning, recent work has explored using LLMs as natural-language oracles that answer membership queries formulated in textual form. Vazquez-Chanlatte et al. [61] propose L*LM, which integrates an LLM as a membership oracle within the classical active learning framework. Chen et al. [17] treat the LLM as a probabilistic Minimally Adequate Teacher (pMAT) and introduce prompt-based strategies that decompose or verify membership queries to improve reliability.

Among our previous contributions, several works have advanced active automata learning from both theoretical and practical perspectives. For instance, we have provided comprehensive overviews that positioned active learning as a versatile framework for model inference in software and systems engineering [53,54]. We also introduced the redundancy-free TTT algorithm, which improves learning efficiency and scalability through optimized counterexample handling and hypothesis refinement [37]. Further work extended active learning to register automata, enabling the inference of data-dependent behavior and supporting learning over infinite input domains [35]. We further applied active learning to infer behavioral models of legacy systems from observed executions and later extended this idea toward continuous quality control by monitoring and comparing evolving system behavior [34,62].

Outline Section 3 introduces the necessary preliminaries, with a brief overview of active automata learning and the ALEX tool, which forms the foundation of the proposed approach. Section 4 details how Large Language Models (LLMs) are employed to generate the learning alphabet for ALEX and discusses the key challenges involved in this process. Section 5 presents a proof of concept demonstrating the feasibility of the proposed approach. Finally, Section 6 concludes the paper and outlines directions for future work.

3   Background Technologies

Active automata learning is a process that aims to infer a hypothesis model representing the behavior of a given system through systematic interaction and observation of the system's responses. This approach contrasts with passive learning, which relies on pre-existing observations—such as traces or logs—to construct a model based on previously collected data. The active automata learning process alternates between two phases: the learning phase and the testing phase [54]. Figure 2 provides a schematic overview of this process.

At the core of active automata learning is the learner (1), which orchestrates the execution of the underlying learning algorithm. The learner is provided with an input alphabet $\Sigma = \{\sigma_1, \sigma_2, \ldots, \sigma_n\}$, where each alphabet symbol $\sigma \in \Sigma$ represents an abstract definition of an input interaction of the system to be learned.

During the learning phase, the learner issues membership queries (MQs) of the form $MQ = (\sigma_{i_1}, \sigma_{i_2}, \ldots, \sigma_{i_k})$, where $\sigma_{i_j} \in \Sigma$. These queries are executed on the System Under Learning (SUL) (3) via a mapper (2) that translates the abstract symbols σ_{i_j} into concrete instructions. After each symbol execution, the concrete output is captured by the mapper and transformed back into an abstract representation comprehensible to the learner. Using these abstracted input–output pairs, the learner incrementally constructs a hypothesis model (4).

The learning phase concludes when the learner derives a closed and consistent hypothesis model—one that satisfies all executed MQs and their corresponding

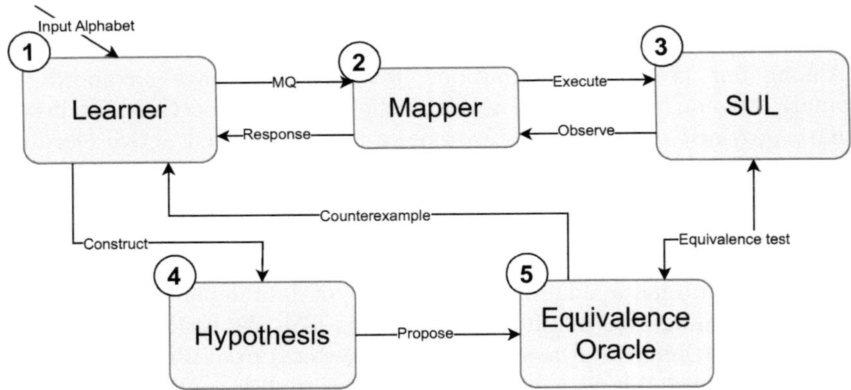

Fig. 2. Overview of the active automata learning process.

outputs. At this point, the testing phase begins. The learner proposes the current hypothesis model as a candidate representation of the SUL's behavior to the equivalence oracle (5). The equivalence oracle evaluates this candidate by comparing its predicted behavior with the actual behavior of the SUL. If a counterexample is found—that is, a query whose observed output diverges from the model's prediction—the learning phase restarts, incorporating the counterexample into the learning process. When no further counterexamples can be identified during testing, the process terminates, and the current hypothesis model is accepted as a suitable approximation of the SUL's behavior.

In this work, active automata learning is applied to the domain of web applications, with the target hypothesis model represented as a Mealy machine capturing the observable behavior of the application. Interactions with web applications occur through the user-facing frontend, which is rendered from the underlying Document Object Model (DOM) that defines the structure of the interface. Since the DOM constitutes the only directly observable state of the web application, it is treated as the output or response of the SUL and is mapped by the mapper to an abstract representation comprehensible to the learner.

To apply active automata learning to a given web application, the learner must be provided with an input alphabet representing the possible user interactions with the frontend. In addition, the process requires an appropriate mapper implementation to generate executable instructions for the interactions, as well as a mechanism to perform these instructions on the web application.

To facilitate the application of active automata learning to web applications, previous work introduced the Automata Learning EXperience (ALEX) tool [7]. ALEX is implemented as a web-based platform built on top of LearnLib and provides collaborative features to support multiple users. It streamlines the process of creating and managing complete learning setups for the application of active automata learning to web applications.

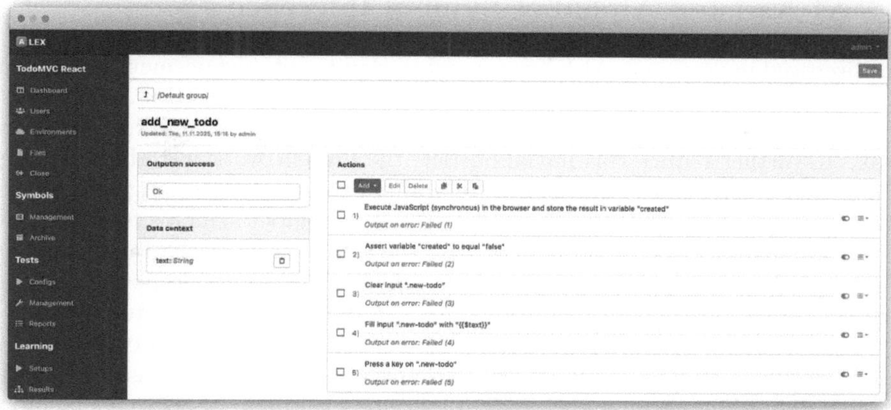

Fig. 3. Symbol creation screen of the ALEX tool.

ALEX offers comprehensive functionality to support the different phases of the learning process. It provides tools for creating and organizing alphabet symbols, generates complete test suites from learned hypothesis models, and includes capabilities for model checking based on Linear Temporal Logic (LTL) formulas. Furthermore, ALEX incorporates its own mapper implementation built on Selenium [49], which serves as the execution component responsible for performing concrete symbol instructions on the web application under learning.

Figure 3 illustrates the ALEX interface, highlighting the process of defining alphabet symbols. Each alphabet symbol is represented as a sequence of actions to be executed in order. To construct these actions, ALEX provides a wide range of predefined interaction templates suitable for web application environments. These templates include simple interactions such as clicking on a specified DOM element and waiting for a defined DOM state change, as well as more complex actions such as executing custom JavaScript snippets.

In a previous study, the impact of ALEX on the practical application of active automata learning for model-based testing of web applications was evaluated through a comparative analysis. The tool was employed by 140 undergraduate students as part of the course "Webtechnologies 2" at the Technical University of Dortmund in 2015, during the development of a practical project in the form of a web application. When compared to the same course project conducted one year earlier in 2014, the results demonstrated a significant increase in functionally correct implementations from 5% to 70% [7]. This outcome highlights ALEX's effectiveness in enabling non-experts to practically apply active automata learning for quality assurance in software development.

4   AI-Assisted Alphabet Symbol Inference

As discussed in Section 3, ALEX represents a significant advancement in assisting the application of active automata learning for web applications. Nevertheless, the initial definition of the symbol alphabet remains a manual and time-intensive task. To further reduce this initial barrier, the present work introduces an approach that leverages the capabilities of state-of-the-art Large Language Models (LLMs) to provide a guided process for defining alphabet symbols for web applications. The approach involves providing the source code of the target application directly to a large language model (LLM) to generate proposed alphabet symbol definitions. These definitions are specific to the ALEX tool, which is used to conduct the learning process and ensures the syntactical correctness of the underlying code executed on the web application, except in cases where the symbol definitions include actions that execute custom JavaScript. To facilitate this process, the LLM is supplied with introductory guidance to address the primary challenges associated with defining a symbol alphabet:

- **Identification of states of quiescence:** Determining when the application has reached a stable state in which external stimuli can be applied is critical in active automata learning. Preemptive execution of alphabet symbols before quiescence can result in incorrectly observed non-deterministic behavior; for example, the same equivalence query may yield different results if one execution occurs before the system reaches a stable state. Correct handling requires precise definition of expected states and verification that these states have been reached.
- **Handling unbounded element collections:** Certain interactions may increase the size of collections without limit, potentially leading to an infinite learning process. Alphabet symbols must therefore incorporate mechanisms to enforce artificial bounds on the number of elements in unbounded collections.
- **Stable element selectors:** Identifying reliable selectors for elements to be manipulated during symbol execution can be challenging, particularly when the structure of the underlying DOM undergoes significant changes during state transitions.
- **Appropriate abstraction level:** Selecting an appropriate level of abstraction for the learning alphabet involves a trade-off between the precision of the resulting behavioral model and the size of its state space, which in turn directly influences the overall learning duration. Moreover, the level of abstraction is inherently situational, as the desired degree of behavioral detail captured by the resulting hypothesis model may vary depending on the specific learning objective. For instance, the learning process may initially focus on a particular subset of a web application's functionality to verify its correctness within a confined scope before extending the learning to capture its interactions with the remaining parts of the application.

The proposed approach addresses these challenges through a two-step process, implemented via sequential LLM prompts that guide the user in defining the final symbol alphabet.

The first prompt instructs the LLM to infer all possible frontend interactions of a given web application by analyzing its source code, while simultaneously identifying predefined characteristics of these interactions relevant to the challenges outlined above. The resulting list of identified interactions is presented to the user in a human-readable format, allowing verification for correctness and adjustment of the proposed level of abstraction.

The second prompt instructs the LLM to use the finalized list of interactions, along with the source code, to generate complete symbol definitions suitable for use by the ALEX tool during the learning process. The instructions for this prompt include concrete strategies for defining symbols based on the characteristics identified in the first step.

```
login:
  action_name: "login"
  description: "Authenticate user with email and password credentials"
  action_details:
    - "Click in the email input field"
    - "Type email address"
    - "Click in the password input field"
    - "Type password"
    - "Click the 'Login' button"
  disambiguation: "Not required - single unique login form on page"
  infinite_expansion: "No - only changes authentication state, does not
      create new structures"
  element_count_change: "No - only changes user session state, does not
      change element count"
  limit: "N/A"
  state_toggle: "No - one-way action that transitions from logged out to
      logged in state"
  validation: "User is redirected to dashboard or home page, login form
      disappears, user profile or logout button becomes visible, and
      authentication token is stored"
```

Listing 1.1. Example of a login interaction definition

Listing 1.1 presents an example of an identified interaction produced by the first prompt, including the analysis of its various predefined characteristics. In this instance, the interaction represents a login process, as commonly found in web applications. The `action_name` field contains a unique identifier for the interaction—in this case, `login`, which is subsequently used as the name of the resulting alphabet symbol. The `description` field provides a concise explanation of the interaction, here indicating that it authenticates the user with an email and password.

The `action_details` field lists the sequential steps required to execute the interaction, describing, in this example, the entry of credentials followed by a press of the Login button. The following fields capture the results of the predefined characteristic analyses necessary for correctly defining the corresponding alphabet symbol:

- **disambiguation** – Specifies how repeated or similar elements can be uniquely identified if involved in the execution of the interaction. For instance, when an interaction modifies specific elements in a collection, identification may be based on the element's position within the collection or on a unique inner text value. The second prompt uses these values to generate appropriate templates for addressing the elements. In the present example, this field states that a specific disambiguation method is not needed, as the login form contains uniquely identifiable elements.

- **element_count_change** – Indicates whether the interaction modifies the size of a collection or repeated elements, such as adding or removing items. This information guides the second prompt in applying verification methods to confirm successful execution and attainment of a state of quiescence. For example, positional disambiguation may require counting elements before and after the main interaction. In this case, the analysis of this aspect concludes that no such interaction is present.
- **infinite_expansion** – Closely related to `element_count_change`, this field identifies whether repeated execution of the interaction could result in unbounded growth of a collection. When applicable, the second prompt ensures that the resulting alphabet symbol enforces an artificial limit on the number of elements, as defined by the `limit` field. Since the `element_count_change` analysis already indicated that no size–modifying interaction regarding a collection is present, the same conclusion naturally applies to this analysis.
- **state_toggle** – Captures whether the interaction switches between two distinct application states. A typical example is marking and unmarking emails in a list. This field instructs the resulting symbol to verify the initial state and perform the corresponding post-interaction validation. However, this does not apply in the present case, as the login process represents a one-way interaction; reapplying it does not result in the user being logged out.
- **verification** – Provides general observations of the effects of the main interaction, which are used to verify the correct execution of the resulting alphabet symbol and to determine whether a state of quiescence has been reached.

A concrete example of the output generated by the second prompt is presented in the following section using a real-world application. Both prompts were developed simultaneously using the Claude Sonnet 4 LLM from Anthropic [2]. The creation process was iterative, beginning with a basic description of each task within the prompts. In each iteration, the prompts were executed on example applications, and the results were evaluated. Identified issues were addressed by instructing the LLM to refine the prompts, after which the revised prompts were tested in a fresh context. If the refinements produced improved results, the updated versions were adopted for subsequent iterations. After approximately every five iterations, the LLM was further prompted to reduce the prompt length and restructure them to maintain a coherent and concise format.

5   Case Study: TodoMVC Application

This section presents the application of the proposed approach to the TodoMVC web application, which was already used in a previous case study [8]. TodoMVC is a minimalistic task management application that enables users to create, modify, and organize a list of todo items.

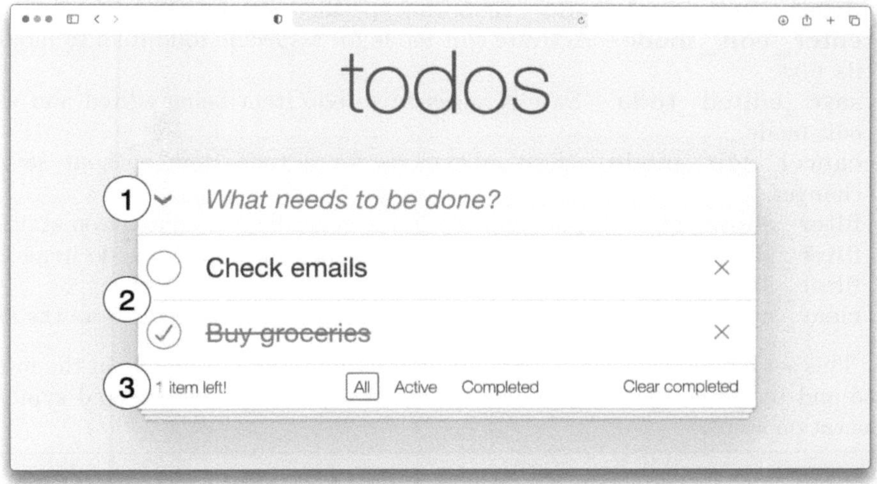

Fig. 4. The TodoMVC application with 2 todo items.

The user interface is depicted in Figure 4. The header section (1) contains an input field where a user can enter the description of a new todo item and press Enter to add it to the list. The chevron-down button located to the left of the input field allows the completion status of all todo items to be toggled simultaneously.

The main section (2) displays the list of existing todo items. Each item can be marked as completed or uncompleted using the checkbox positioned to its left. Completed items are rendered with strikethrough text and a checked checkbox. Hovering over an item reveals an "×" button on its right-hand side, which can be clicked to delete the corresponding todo item. Double-clicking an item's name enables in-place editing; pressing Enter confirms the modification. If the input field is left empty during editing and confirmed, the item is automatically removed from the list. If a click occurs outside the input field during editing, the editing operation is canceled and any changes are discarded.

The footer section (3) provides three filtering options: displaying all todo items, only active (i.e., uncompleted) items, or only completed items. Additionally, a *Clear completed* button is available on the right-hand side of this section, which deletes all completed todo items.

Executing the first prompt with the application's source code included in the context of the language model resulted in the identification of eleven distinct user interactions, described as follows:

- **add_todo_item** – Create a new todo item and add it to the list.
- **toggle_all_todos** – Toggle the completion status of all visible todo items simultaneously.
- **toggle_individual_todo** – Toggle the completion status of a specific todo item.

- **delete_individual_todo** – Remove a specific todo item from the list.
- **enter_edit_mode** – Activate edit mode for a specific todo item to modify its text.
- **save_edited_todo** – Save changes to a todo item being edited and exit edit mode.
- **cancel_edit_mode** – Exit edit mode for a todo item without saving changes.
- **filter_show_all** – Display all todo items, regardless of completion status.
- **filter_show_active** – Display only active (i.e., incomplete) todo items.
- **filter_show_completed** – Display only completed todo items.
- **clear_completed_todos** – Remove all completed todo items from the list.

This set comprehensively covers all interaction types observable in the interface and serves as the foundation for the subsequent abstraction and symbol-generation steps.

```
add_todo_item:
  action_name: "add_todo_item"
  description: "Create a new todo item and add it to the todo list"
  action_details:
    - "Click in the 'What needs to be done?' input field"
    - "Type todo text (minimum 2 characters)"
    - "Press Enter key"
  disambiguation: "Not required - single unique input field in header"
  infinite_expansion: "Yes - each execution creates a new todo item that
      can be added indefinitely to the list"
  element_count_change: "Yes - always adds one new todo item to the list
      when successfully executed"
  limit: "No"
  state_toggle: "No - one-way action that creates new items"
  verification: "New todo item appears in the todo list with the entered
      text, input field clears, and footer becomes visible if it was
      hidden"
```

Listing 1.2. Identified add_todo_item interaction

Code Listing 1.2 presents the complete output corresponding to the identified `add_todo_item` interaction. The generated action detail list correctly consists of three sequential steps: first, clicking within the input field to enable text entry; second, typing the name of the todo item; and third, pressing Enter to confirm and create the new item. Disambiguation is not required in this case, as the input field is unique within the interface. The analysis accurately identifies that this action modifies the size of a collection (`element_count_change: Yes`), since each execution adds a new todo item to the list. Consequently, the process can theoretically result in an unbounded expansion of the list (`infinite_expansion: Yes`), and therefore the `limit` field is set to No at this stage. Furthermore, the action is correctly classified as not representing a state-toggle operation.

The `verification` field specifies that, after execution, the newly created todo item is appended to the end of the existing list, displaying the name provided during input. Additionally, if no other todo items were previously present, the footer section of the application becomes visible, as this section is rendered only when at least one todo item exists.

At this stage, a limit of two concurrent todo items is defined for the subsequent learning process. Accordingly, the value of the `limit` field is set to 2. In addition, the interactions `enter_edit_mode`, `save_edited_todo`, as well as the `cancel_edit_mode` are excluded from the list in order to reduce the resulting state space of the learned hypothesis model.

The second prompt is then executed, incorporating both the finalized list of interactions and the application's source code into the context of the language model. This step yields concrete symbol definitions to be utilized by the ALEX tool for conducting the active automata learning process.

```
add_todo_item:
    actions:
      # STEP 1: Limit check - maximum 2 items allowed
      - name: execute javascript
        args:
          javascript: |
            const currentCount = document.querySelectorAll('.todo-list
                li').length;
            if (currentCount >= 2) {
              throw new Error('Cannot add more items: limit of 2 reached');
            }

      # STEP 2: Count validation BEFORE (element_count_change: Yes)
      - name: execute javascript
        args:
          javascript: |
            window.originalCount = document.querySelectorAll('.todo-list
                li').length;

      # STEP 3: Main interaction - click, type, press Enter
      ....

      # STEP 4: Count validation AFTER
      - name: execute javascript
        args:
          javascript: |
            const TIMEOUT = 5000;
            const check = () => {
              const current = document.querySelectorAll('.todo-list
                  li').length;
              if (current === window.originalCount + 1) return;
              if (Date.now() - window.start > TIMEOUT) throw new
                  Error('Timeout waiting for count change');
              setTimeout(check, 100);
            };
            window.start = Date.now();
            check();
```

Listing 1.3. Symbol definition for the add_todo_item interaction

Code Listing 1.3 presents an excerpt from the generated symbol definition corresponding to the `add_todo_item` symbol. In this definition, the language model correctly includes the specified limit as the first action step within the symbol, implemented via a JavaScript statement that throws an error if the maximum number of concurrent todo items is already present. This behavior ensures that the symbol fails deliberately under these conditions. Furthermore, the definition includes verification steps executed before and after the main interaction (omitted here), which store the number of existing todo items in a global variable within the browser context and subsequently check whether this number has increased by one following execution.

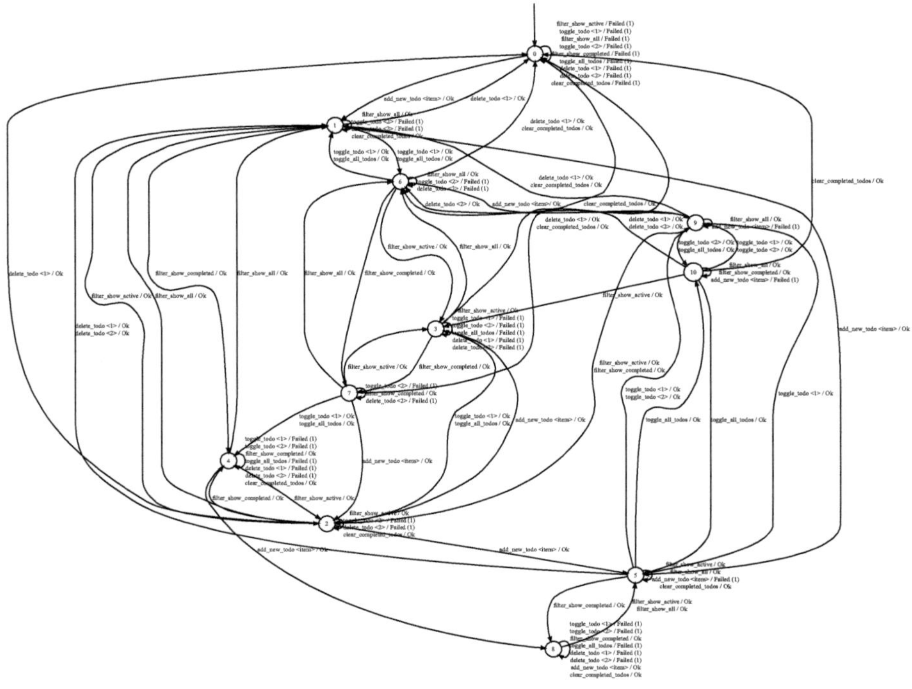

Fig. 5. Learned behaviour model for the TodoMVC app with two todo items.

Executing the actual learning process on the TodoMVC application using these symbol definitions produces the hypothesis model illustrated in Figure 5. It should be noted that the symbols `delete_todo_item` and `toggle_todo_item` are parameterized according to the position of the targeted todo item within the list.

The model can serve as a ground truth for comparison with new versions or variants of the application. To illustrate this, the TodoMVC application was modified to create a variant that is inherently restricted to maintaining only one concurrent todo item at any time. Such artificial limitations are commonly employed for demonstration purposes or to represent free trial versions of a product.

Applying the same learning process to this restricted version of the application results in the hypothesis model depicted in Figure 6. As expected, this model contains fewer states than the previously learned version, seven instead of eleven, reflecting the constraint that only a single concurrent todo item can exist.

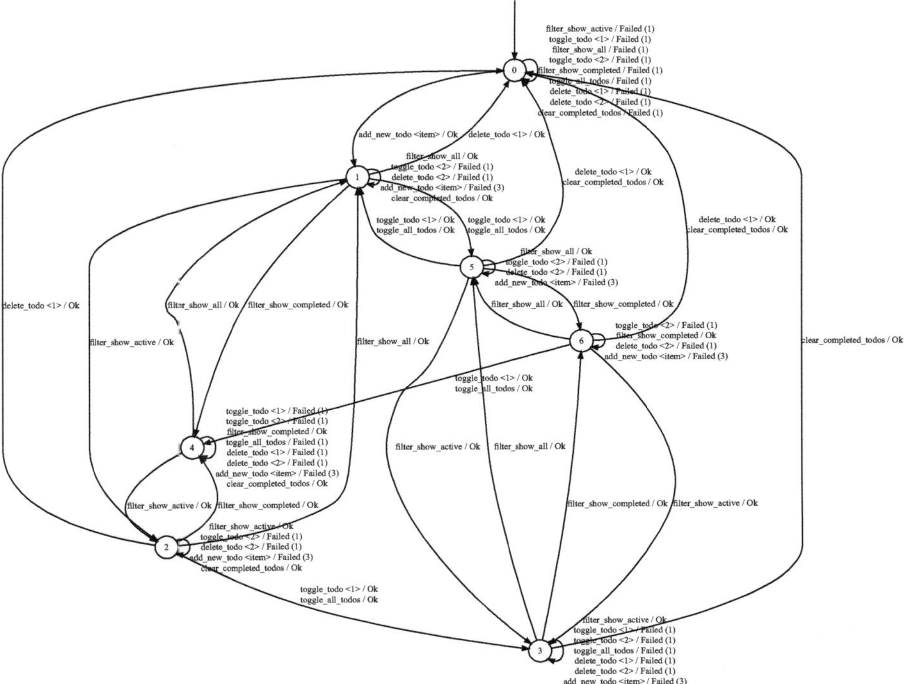

Fig. 6. Learned behaviour model for the TodoMVC app with one todo item.

Having both behavioral models available enables the inference of a difference model, shown in Figure 7, which highlights the exact state-path differences between the two system variants. As shown in the difference model, all executions of the `add_todo_item` symbol fail when a todo item is already present in the list of todo items.

6 Conclusion and Future Work

We have demonstrated how large language models (LLMs) can be applied to automatically infer learning alphabets from the source code of web applications. This addresses one of the major challenges in learning-based testing of web applications. Our approach relies on two generic prompts: one for extracting possible frontend interactions, and another for generating corresponding symbol definitions, including their implementations. We illustrated the essential steps of this process using a to-do-list application as a case study.

Our initial experience with the approach is very encouraging. The first prompt successfully identified all frontend user interactions, failing only to detect a few `element_count_change` and `state_toggle` characteristics. The

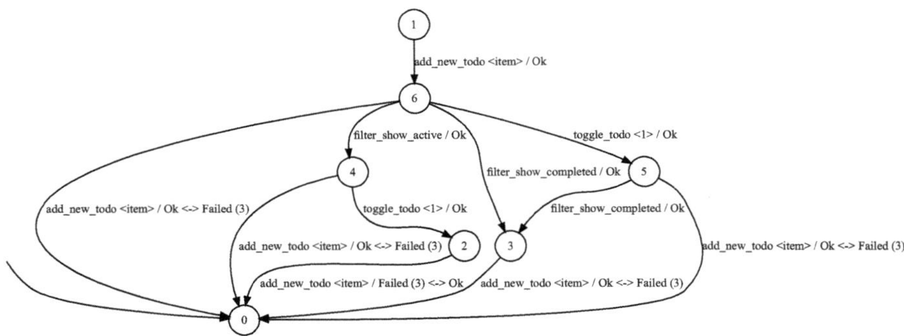

Fig. 7. Difference Model of the learned behaviour models of the TodoMVC application.

few shortcomings of the second prompt were limited to the generation of custom JavaScript snippets.

Naturally, with this low number of alphabet symbols, these findings are still preliminary. We plan to conduct a more systematic analysis to assess both the reliability and scalability of the approach. In particular, we aim to investigate the effectiveness of a compositional method that examines snippets of larger applications piece by piece. We expect this method to capture all local interactions— those that can be inferred from a few connected lines of code. More challenging, however, are global interactions that depend on a broader context, such as user actions that only become available after a specific interaction history. It will be interesting to explore how well such contextual dependencies can be captured within the LLM's context window.

References

1. Fides Aarts et al. "Generating Models of Infinite-state Communication Protocols Using Regular Inference with Abstraction". In: *Form. Methods Syst. Des.* 46.1 (Feb. 2015), pp. 1–41. ISSN: 0925-9856. DOI: https://doi.org/10.1007/s10703-014-0216-x.
2. Anthropic. *Claude 4 System Card*. Tech. rep. Claude Opus 4 & Claude Sonnet 4; 120 pages. Anthropic, May 2025. URL: https://www-cdn.anthropic.com/4263b940cabb546aa0e3283f35b686f4f3b2ff47.pdf.
3. Patrizia Asirelli et al. "A Compositional Framework to Derive Product Line Behavioural Descriptions". In: *Leveraging Applications of Formal Methods, Verification and Validation. Technologies for Mastering Change.* Ed. by Tiziana Margaria and Bernhard Steffen. Berlin, Heidelberg: Springer Berlin Heidelberg, 2012, pp. 146–161. ISBN: 978-3-642-34026-0.
4. Patrizia Asirelli et al. "A Model-Checking Tool for Families of Services". In: *Formal Techniques for Distributed Systems.* Ed. by Roberto Bruni and Juergen Dingel. Berlin, Heidelberg: Springer Berlin Heidelberg, 2011, pp. 44–58. ISBN: 978-3-642-21461-5.
5. Patrizia Asirelli et al. "Formal Description of Variability in Product Families". In: *2011 15th International Software Product Line Conference.* 2011, pp. 130–139. DOI: https://doi.org/10.1109/SPLC.2011.34.

6. Stefano Bacherini et al. "A Story About Formal Methods Adoption by a Railway Signaling Manufacturer". In: *FM 2006: Formal Methods*. Ed. by Jayadev Misra, Tobias Nipkow, and Emil Sekerinski. Berlin, Heidelberg: Springer Berlin Heidelberg, 2006, pp. 179–189. ISBN: 978-3-540-37216-5.

7. Alexander Bainczyk et al. "ALEX: Mixed-Mode Learning of Web Applications at Ease". In: *Leveraging Applications of Formal Methods, Verification and Validation: Discussion, Dissemination, Applications*. Ed. by Tiziana Margaria and Bernhard Steffen. Cham: Springer International Publishing, 2016, pp. 655–671. ISBN: 978-3-319-47169-3.

8. Alexander Bainczyk et al. "Model-Based Testing Without Models: The TodoMVC Case Study". In: *ModelEd, TestEd, TrustEd - Essays Dedicated to Ed Brinksma on the Occasion of His 60th Birthday*. 2017, pp. 125–144.

9. Marco Bakera et al. "Tool-supported enhancement of diagnosis in modeldriven verification". In: *Innovations in Systems and Software Engineering* 5 (3 2009), pp. 211–228. ISSN: 1614-5046. URL: http://dx.doi.org/10.1007/s11334-009-0091-6.

10. Davide Basile et al. "Coherent modal transition systems refinement". In: *Journal of Logical and Algebraic Methods in Programming* 138 (2024), p. 100954. ISSN: 2352-2208. DOI: https://doi.org/10.1016/j.jlamp.2024.100954. URL: https://www.sciencedirect.com/science/article/pii/S2352220824000129.

11. Maurice H. ter Beek, Alessandro Fantechi, and Stefania Gnesi. "Formal Methods for Industrial Critical Systems". In: *The Combined Power of Research, Education, and Dissemination: Essays Dedicated to Tiziana Margaria on the Occasion of Her 60th Birthday*. Ed. by Mike Hinchey and Bernhard Steffen. Cham: Springer Nature Switzerland, 2025, pp. 327–344. ISBN: 978-3-031-73887-6. DOI: https://doi.org/10.1007/978-3-031-73887-6_21. URL: https://doi.org/10.1007/978-3-031-73887-6_21.

12. Maurice H. ter Beek et al. "An Action/State-Based Model-Checking Approach for the Analysis of Communication Protocols for Service-Oriented Applications". In: *Formal Methods for Industrial Critical Systems*. Ed. by Stefan Leue and Pedro Merino. Berlin, Heidelberg: Springer Berlin Heidelberg, 2008, pp. 133–148. ISBN: 978-3-540-79707-4.

13. Maurice H. ter Beek et al. "Can AI Help with the Formalization of Railway Cybersecurity Requirements?" In: *Leveraging Applications of Formal Methods, Verification and Validation. REoCAS Colloquium in Honor of Rocco De Nicola*. Ed. by Tiziana Margaria and Bernhard Steffen. Cham: Springer Nature Switzerland, 2025, pp. 186–203. ISBN: 978-3-031-73709-1.

14. Cinzia Bernardeschi et al. "A Formal Verification Environment for Railway Signaling System Design". In: *Formal Methods in System Design* 12.2 (Mar. 1998), pp. 139–161. ISSN: 1572-8102. DOI: https://doi.org/10.1023/A:1008645826258. URL: https://doi.org/10.1023/A:1008645826258.

15. Cyril Carrez, Alessandro Fantechi, and Elie Najm. "Behavioural Contracts for a Sound Assembly of Components". In: *Formal Techniques for Networked and Distributed Systems - FORTE 2003*. Ed. by Hartmut Konig, Monika Heiner, and Adam Wolisz. Berlin, Heidelberg: Springer Berlin Heidelberg, 2003, pp. 111–126. ISBN: 978-3-540-39979-7.

16. Sofia Cassel et al. "Active learning for extended finite state machines". In: *Formal Aspects Comput.* 28.2 (2016), pp. 233–263.

17. Lekai Chen, Ashutosh Trivedi, and Alvaro Velasquez. *LLMs as Probabilistic Minimally Adequate Teachers for DFA Learning*. 2024. arXiv: 2408. 02999 [cs.FL]. URL: https://arxiv.org/abs/2408.02999.

18. R. De Nicola et al. "An action-based framework for veryfying logical and behavioural properties of concurrent systems". In: *Computer Networks and ISDN Systems* 25.7 (1993). Tools for FDTs, pp. 761–778. ISSN: 0169-7552. DOI: https://doi.org/10.1016/0169-7552(93)90047-8. URL: https://www.sciencedirect.com/science/article/pii/0169755293900478.

19. Ionut Dinca, Florentin Ipate, and Alin Stefanescu. "Model Learning and Test Generation for Event-b Decomposition". In: *Proceedings of the 5th International Conference on Leveraging Applications of Formal Methods, Verification and Validation: Technologies for Mastering Change - Volume Part I*. ISoLA'12. Heraklion, Crete, Greece: Springer-Verlag, 2012, pp. 539–553. ISBN: 978-3-642-34025-3. DOI: https://doi.org/10.1007/978-3-642-34026-0_40.

20. Samuel Drews and Loris D'Antoni. "Learning Symbolic Automata". In: *Tools and Algorithms for the Construction and Analysis of Systems - 23rd International Conference, TACAS 2017, Held as Part of the European Joint Conferences on Theory and Practice of Software, ETAPS 2017, Uppsala, Sweden, April 22-29, 2017, Proceedings, Part I*. Ed. by Axel Legay and Tiziana Margaria. Vol. 10205. Lecture Notes in Computer Science. 2017, pp. 173–189. DOI: https://doi.org/10.1007/978-3-662-54577-5_10. URL: https://doi.org/10.1007/978-3-662-54577-5%5C_10.

21. A. Fantechi et al. "Applications of linguistic techniques for use case analysis". In: *Requirements Engineering* 8.3 (Aug. 2003), pp. 161–170. ISSN: 1432-010X. DOI: https://doi.org/10.1007/s00766-003-0174-0. URL: https://doi.org/10.1007/s00766-003-0174-0.

22. A. Fantechi et al. "Assisting requirement formalization by means of natural language translation". In: *Formal Methods in System Design* 4.3 (May 1994), pp. 243–263. ISSN: 1572-8102. DOI: https://doi.org/10.1007/BF01384048. URL: https://doi.org/10.1007/BF01384048.

23. Alessandro Fantechi, Wan Fokkink, and Angelo Morzenti. "Some Trends in *Formal Methods Applications to Railway Signaling*". In: *Formal Methods for Industrial Critical Systems*. John Wiley & Sons, Ltd, 2012. Chap. 4, pp. 61–84. ISBN: 9781118459898. DOI: https://doi.org/10.1002/9781118459898.ch4. eprint: https://onlinelibrary.wiley.com/doi/pdf/10.1002/9781118459898.ch4. URL: https://onlinelibrary.wiley.com/doi/abs/10.1002/9781118459898.ch4.

24. Alessandro Fantechi, Stefania Gnesi, and Diego Latella. "Towards automatic temporal logic verification of value passing process algebra using abstract interpretation". In: *CONCUR '96: Concurrency Theory*. Ed. by Ugo Montanari and Vladimiro Sassone. Berlin, Heidelberg: Springer Berlin Heidelberg, 1996, pp. 563–578. ISBN: 978-3-540-70625-0.

25. Alessandro Fantechi et al. "Inconsistency Detection in Natural Language Requirements using ChatGPT: a Preliminary Evaluation". In: *2023 IEEE 31st International Requirements Engineering Conference (RE)*. 2023, pp. 335–340. DOI: https://doi.org/10.1109/RE57278.2023.00045.

26. Alessandro Fantechi et al. "Requirement Engineering of Software Product Lines: Extracting Variability Using NLP". In: *2018 IEEE 26th International Requirements Engineering Conference (RE)*. 2018, pp. 418–423. DOI: https://doi.org/10.1109/RE.2018.00053.

27. Alessio Ferrari et al. "Model Checking Interlocking Control Tables". In: *FORMS/FORMAT 2010*. Ed. by Eckehard Schnieder and Geza Tarnai. Berlin, Heidelberg: Springer Berlin Heidelberg, 2011, pp. 107–115. ISBN: 978-3-642-14261-1.

28. Tiago Ferreira et al. "Prognosis: closed-box analysis of network protocol implementations". In: *SIGCOMM*. ACM, 2021, pp. 762–774.

29. Paul Fiterau-Brostean, Ramon Janssen, and Frits W. Vaandrager. "Combining Model Learning and Model Checking to Analyze TCP Implementations". In: *Computer Aided Verification - 28th International Conference, CAV 2016, Toronto, ON, Canada, July 17-23, 2016, Proceedings, Part II*. 2016, pp. 454–471. DOI: https://doi.org/10.1007/978-3-319-41540-6_25.

30. Paul Fiterau-Brostean et al. "Analysis of DTLS Implementations Using Protocol State Fuzzing". In: *USENIX Security Symposium*. USENIX Association, 2020, pp. 2523–2540.

31. Paul Fiterau-Brostean et al. "Model learning and model checking of SSH implementations". In: *Proceedings of the 24th ACM SIGSOFT International SPIN Symposium on Model Checking of Software, Santa Barbara, CA, USA, July 10-14, 2017*. Ed. by Hakan Erdogmus and Klaus Havelund. ACM, 2017, pp. 142–151. DOI: https://doi.org/10.1145/3092282.3092289. URL: https://doi.org/10.1145/3092282.3092289.

32. Anne Elisabeth Haxthausen and Alessandro Fantechi. "Compositional Verification of Railway Interlocking Systems". In: *Form. Asp. Comput.* 35.1 (Jan. 2023). ISSN: 0934-5043. DOI: https://doi.org/10.1145/3549736. URL: https://doi.org/10.1145/3549736.

33. Falk Howar and Bernhard Steffen. "Active Automata Learning as Black- Box Search and Lazy Partition Refinement". In: *A Journey from Process Algebra via Timed Automata to Model Learning*. Vol. 13560. Lecture Notes in Computer Science. Springer, 2022, pp. 321–338.

34. H. Hungar, T. Margaria, and B. Steffen. "Test-based model generation for legacy systems". In: *Test Conference, 2003. Proceedings. ITC 2003. International*. Vol. 1. 30-Oct. 2, 2003, pp. 971–980.

35. Malte Isberner, Falk Howar, and Bernhard Steffen. "Learning register automata: from languages to program structures". In: *Machine Learning* 96.1-2 (2014), pp. 65–98. DOI: https://doi.org/10.1007/s10994-013-5419-7.

36. Malte Isberner, Falk Howar, and Bernhard Steffen. "The Open-Source LearnLib - A Framework for Active Automata Learning". In: *CAV 2015, Part I*. (Best Artifact Award). 2015, pp. 487–495. DOI: https://doi.org/10.1007/978-3-319-21690-4_32.

37. Malte Isberner, Falk Howar, and Bernhard Steffen. "The TTT Algorithm: A Redundancy-Free Approach to Active Automata Learning". In: *RV 2014*. 2014, pp. 307–322. DOI: https://doi.org/10.1007/978-3-319-11164-3_26. URL: http://dx.doi.org/10.1007/978-3-319-11164-3_26.

38. Igor Khmelnitsky et al. "Analysis of recurrent neural networks via propertydirected verification of surrogate models". In: *International Journal on Software Tools for Technology Transfer* 25.3 (June 2023), pp. 341–354. ISSN: 1433-2787. DOI: https://doi.org/10.1007/s10009-022-00684-w. URL: https://doi.org/10.1007/s10009-022-00684-w.

39. Marco Krumrey et al. "Malwa: Learnability by Design". In: *Principles of Verification: Cycling the Probabilistic Landscape : Essays Dedicated to Joost-Pieter Katoen on the Occasion of His 60th Birthday, Part III*. Ed. by Nils Jansen et al. Cham: Springer Nature Switzerland, 2025, pp. 66–88. ISBN: 978-3-031-75778-5. DOI: https://doi.org/10.1007/978-3-031-75778-5_4. URL: https://doi.org/10.1007/978-3-031-75778-5_4.

40. Tommaso Magherini et al. "Using Temporal Logic and Model Checking in Automated Recognition of Human Activities for Ambient-Assisted Living". In: *IEEE Transactions on Human-Machine Systems* 43.6 (2013), pp. 509–521. DOI: https://doi.org/10.1109/TSMC.2013.2283661.

41. Oded Maler and Irini-Eleftheria Mens. "A Generic Algorithm for Learning Symbolic Automata from Membership Queries". In: *Models, Algorithms, Logics and Tools*. Vol. 10460. Lecture Notes in Computer Science. Springer, 2017, pp. 146–169.

42. T. Margaria and B. Steffen. "Distinguishing formulas for free". In: *1993 European Conference on Design Automation with the European Event in ASIC Design*. 1993, pp. 105–110. DOI: https://doi.org/10.1109/EDAC.1993.386492.

43. Tiziana Margaria and Bernhard Steffen. "Backtracking-Free Design Planning by Automatic Synthesis in METAFrame". In: *Proc. of 1st Int. Conf. on Fundamental Approaches to Software Engineering (FASE 1998), Lisbon, Portugal*. 1998, pp. 188–204. URL: http://www.springerlink.com/content/fxtm66d5049hkpt0.

44. Tiziana Margaria et al. "Synthesizing Semantic Web Service Compositions with jMosel and Golog". In: *The Semantic Web - ISWC 2009*. Vol. 5823. LNCS. Springer Berlin / Heidelberg, 2009, pp. 392–407. DOI: https://doi.org/10.1007/978-3-642-04930-9.

45. Karl Meinke. "Active Machine Learning to Test Autonomous Driving". In: *ICST Workshops*. IEEE, 2021, p. 286.

46. Maik Merten et al. "Next Generation LearnLib". In: *Tools and Algorithms for the Construction and Analysis of Systems*. Ed. by Parosh Aziz Abdulla and K. Rustan M. Leino. Berlin, Heidelberg: Springer Berlin Heidelberg, 2011, pp. 220–223. ISBN: 978-3-642-19835-9.

47. Olga Grinchtein and Bengt Jonsson and Martin Leucker. "Inference of Timed Transition Systems". In: *Electronic Notes in Theoretical Computer Science* 138.3 (2005), pp. 87–99.

48. Andrea Pferscher and Bernhard K. Aichernig. "Fingerprinting and analysis of Bluetooth devices with automata learning". In: *Formal Methods Syst. Des.* 61.1 (2022), pp. 35–62.

49. Selenium Project. *Selenium WebDriver*. Accessed: 2025-10-12. 2025. URL: https://www.selenium.dev/.

50. Muzammil Shahbaz and Roland Groz. "Analysis and Testing of Blackbox Component-based Systems by Inferring Partial Models". In: *Softw. Test. Verif. Reliab.* 24.4 (June 2014), pp. 253–288. ISSN: 0960-0833. DOI: https://doi.org/10.1002/stvr.1491.

51. Tiziana Margaria Stefania Gnesi, ed. *Formal Methods for Industrial Critical Systems: A Survey of Applications*. Wiley-IEEE Computer Society Press eBook Series. IEEE Book Number: 6381798. Hoboken, NJ, USA: Wiley-IEEE Press, 2013. ISBN: 9781118459898. DOI: https://doi.org/10.1002/9781118459898. URL: https://ieeexplore.ieee.org/book/6381798.

52. Bernhard Steffen. "Characteristic Formulae". In: *Automata, Languages and Programming*. Ed. by Giorgio Ausiello, Mariangiola Dezani-Ciancaglini, and SimonettaRonchi Rocca. Vol. 372. Lecture Notes in Computer Science. Springer Berlin Heidelberg, 1989, pp. 723–732. ISBN: 978-3-540-51371-1. DOI: https://doi.org/10.1007/BFb0035794. URL: http://dx.doi.org/10.1007/BFb0035794.

53. Bernhard Steffen, Falk Howar, and Malte Isberner. "Active Automata Learning: From DFAs to Interface Programs and Beyond". In: *ICGI 2012*. Vol. 21. JMLR Proceedings. JMLR.org, 2012, pp. 195–209. URL: http://jmlr.csail.mit.edu/proceedings/papers/v21/steffen12a.html.

54. Bernhard Steffen, Falk Howar, and Maik Merten. "Introduction to Active Automata Learning from a Practical Perspective". In: *Formal Methods for Eternal Networked Software Systems: 11th International School on Formal Methods for the Design of Computer, Communication and Software Systems, SFM 2011, Bertinoro, Italy,*

June 13-18, 2011. Advanced Lectures. Ed. by Marco Bernardo and Valerie Issarny. Berlin, Heidelberg: Springer Berlin Heidelberg, 2011, pp. 256–296. ISBN: 978-3-642-21455-4. DOI: https://doi.org/10.1007/978-3-642-21455-4_8. URL: https://doi.org/10.1007/978-3-642-21455-4_8.

55. Bernhard Steffen, Tiziana Margaria, and Andreas Claßen. "Heterogeneous Analysis and Verification for Distributed Systems". In: *Software - Concepts and Tools* 17.1 (1996), pp. 13–25.

56. Bernhard Steffen et al. "The Fixpoint-Analysis Machine". In: CONCUR '95: *Concurrency Theory*. Ed. by Insup Lee and Scott A. Smolka. Vol. 962. Lecture Notes in Computer Science. Springer Berlin Heidelberg, 1995, pp. 72–87. ISBN: 978-3-540-60218-7. DOI: https://doi.org/10.1007/3-540-60218-6_6.

57. Jun Sun et al. "TLV: Abstraction Through Testing, Learning, and Validation". In: *Proceedings of the 2015 10th Joint Meeting on Foundations of Software Engineering*. ESEC/FSE 2015. Bergamo, Italy: ACM, 2015, pp. 698–709. ISBN: 978-1-4503-3675-8. DOI: https://doi.org/10.1145/2786805.2786817.

58. Frits W. Vaandrager. "Active Learning of Extended Finite State Machines". In: *ICTSS*. Vol. 7641. Lecture Notes in Computer Science. Springer, 2012, pp. 5–7.

59. Frits W. Vaandrager, Roderick Bloem, and Masoud Ebrahimi. "Learning Mealy Machines with One Timer". In: *Language and Automata Theory and Applications - 15th International Conference, LATA 2021, Milan, Italy, March 1-5, 2021, Proceedings*. Ed. by Alberto Leporati et al. Vol. 12638. Lecture Notes in Computer Science. Springer, 2021, pp. 157–170. DOI: https://doi.org/10.1007/978-3-030-68195-1_13. URL: https://doi.org/10.1007/978-3-030-68195-1%5C_13.

60. Frits W. Vaandrager et al. "A New Approach for Active Automata Learning Based on Apartness". In: *Tools and Algorithms for the Construction and Analysis of Systems - 28th International Conference, TACAS 2022, Held as Part of the European Joint Conferences on Theory and Practice of Software, ETAPS 2022, Munich, Germany, April 2-7, 2022, Proceedings, Part I*. Ed. by Dana Fisman and Grigore Rosu. Vol. 13243. Lecture Notes in Computer Science. Springer, 2022, pp. 223–243. DOI: https://doi.org/10.1007/978-3-030-99524-9_12. URL: https://doi.org/10.1007/978-3-030-99524-9%5C_12.

61. Marcell Vazquez-Chanlatte et al. *L*LM: Learning Automata from Examples using Natural Language Oracles*. 2025. arXiv: 2402.07051 [cs.LG]. URL: https://arxiv.org/abs/2402.07051.

62. Stephan Windmuller et al. "Active Continuous Quality Control". In: *Proceedings of the 16th International ACM Sigsoft Symposium on Componentbased Software Engineering*. CBSE '13. Vancouver, British Columbia, Canada: ACM, 2013, pp. 111–120. ISBN: 978-1-4503-2122-8. DOI: https://doi.org/10.1145/2465449.2465469.

63. Runqing Xu, Jie An, and Bohua Zhan. "Active Learning of One-Clock Timed Automata Using Constraint Solving". In: *ATVA*. Vol. 13505. Lecture Notes in Computer Science. Springer, 2022, pp. 249–265.

Practical Polyhedral Model Checking
A Gentle Introduction

Yuri Andriaccio[1] , Vincenzo Ciancia[2] , Diego Latella[2] ,
and Mieke Massink[2(✉)]

[1] Scuola Superiore Sant'Anna, Pisa, Italy
`yuri.andriaccio@santannapisa.it`
[2] Istituto di Scienza e Tecnologie dell'Informazione "A. Faedo", Consiglio Nazionale
delle Ricerche, Pisa, Italy
`{Vincenzo.Ciancia,Mieke.Massink}@cnr.it, diego.latella@actiones.eu`

Abstract. We illustrate the potential of spatial model checking of polyhedral models on a number of selected examples. In computer graphics polyhedral models can be commonly found in the form of triangular surface meshes or tetrahedral volume meshes. Polyhedral model checking is used to analyse spatial properties of interest of such models expressed in a suitable spatial logic. For this work we use the recently developed geometric spatial model checker `PolyLogicA`, the visualiser `PolyVisualizer` and the polyhedral semantics of the Spatial Logic for Closure Spaces SLCS.

Keywords: Spatial logics · Polyhedral models · Polyhedral model checking · Logical equivalence · Spatial bisimulation relations

1 Introduction

Polyhedra are an interesting class of spatial models. They form the mathematical basis for the visualisation of objects in *continuous* space. We find such structures in domains that exploit mesh-processing such as in computer graphics. Figure 1 shows an image of a metro carriage and its triangular surface mesh. Such triangular surface meshes and tetrahedral volume meshes can be very large. Spatial model checking for such structures can be used to highlight or identify interesting aspects of such structures.

In [7] we presented the theory we developed for such continuous spaces and related model checking algorithms. We also presented the `PolyLogicA` model checker we developed for polyhedral model checking and an associated visualiser, `PolyVisualizer`, for the graphical presentation of the model checking

The authors are listed in alphabetical order, as they equally contributed to the work presented in this paper.

D. Latella—Formerly with Istituto di Scienza e Tecnologie dell'Informazione "A. Faedo", Consiglio Nazionale delle Ricerche, Pisa, Italy (ret.).

© The Author(s), under exclusive license to Springer Nature Switzerland AG 2026

M. H. ter Beek et al. (Eds.): Fantechi Festschrift, LNCS 16470, pp. 138–159, 2026.
https://doi.org/10.1007/978-3-032-12484-5_8

results. More specifically, we considered *polyhedral models* and SLCS_γ, a variant of the Spatial Logic for Closure Spaces (SLCS) for such models. A polyhedral model is composed of a *polyhedron* and a *valuation function*. A polyhedron $|K|$ is the set union of all the components of a simplicial complex K, which, in turn, is a collection of *simplexes* in $\mathbb{R}^n$, for some dimension n, satisfying certain construction constraints. For our purposes, we set n to 3, so that, by definition, the kind of simplexes we are concerned with are just points, line segments, triangles and tetrahedra. For such simplexes we consider also their relative interior, i.e. the "open" variants of segments, triangles and tetrahedra—the relative interior of the point is the point itself—that form the so called *cells* of the polyhedral model. Polyhedral model checking consists in the automatic verification of a spatial property on a polyhedral model and gives as a result the set of cells in which the property holds. Polyhedral models used for model checking are such that all points in the same cell of the model satisfy the same predicate letters.

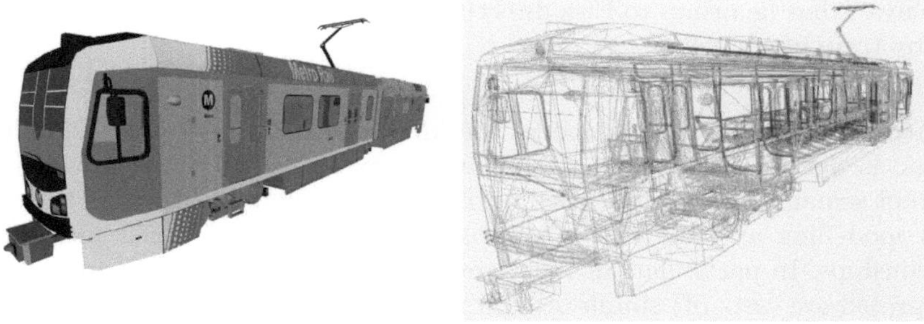

Fig. 1. Image of a metro carriage (left) and its triangular surface mesh (right). Image obtained from **cgtrader** (www.cgtrader.com) on 2025-07-29. Author: **vodolagavaceslav**. Light Rail Train Kinki Sharyo P3010.

Original Contributions. The original contributions of this paper are twofold. As a first contribution, we illustrate how a polyhedral model can be enriched by adding a new predicate letter to those cells of the original model that satisfy the checked property in a previous model checking session. This is useful as it provides a way to reduce the length of formulas to check on such models and to obtain more insightful results when these models are used for graphical visualisation. As a second contribution, we show that this form of enrichment also enables practical model minimisation providing deeper insights in the basic spatial structure of the model in terms of the spatial logic properties it enjoys. The work in this paper is performed using `PolyLogicA`, `PolyVisualizer` and the polyhedral semantics of the Spatial Logic for Closure Spaces SLCS. We first briefly recall an earlier example from [7] to illustrate polyhedral model checking on a synthetic example so that the reader gets acquainted with this novel form of spatial model checking. We then illustrate the contributions using two different case studies originating from the large set of available mesh models in Wavefront .obj format in the field of computer graphics.

This paper is part of the Festschrift in honour of the 70th birthday of Prof. Alessandro Fantechi.Âă We would like to thank Alessandro for his contributions to theÂăFormal Methods and Tools Laboratory at ISTI-CNR, Pisa, Italy. In particular, the work ofÂă Alessandro—together with Stefania Gnesi—on logics and model-checking has been an inspiration for us and for our own recent research on spatial logics and related tools.Âă Some of the authors have started to explore the use of spatial logics and model checking also for applications in the railway domain. See, for example, the work on spatial model checking for smart stations [5] and the work on strategy synthesis for dealing with railway junctions [4]. We hope that the examples on polyhedral model checking, that we describe in the present paper, will spawn new ideas that lead to future applications in the railway domain too. Last, but not least, we want to thank Alessandro for offering us, every autumn, the delicious and authentic specialty "schiacciata con l'uva", that he brings to Pisa directly from a special bakery in Florence! And ...... by train of course!

Related Work. Polyhedral model checking is also addressed in [12]. Therein a logic is defined that shares a similar syntax as SLCS but is provided with different semantics than those used in the present paper. The focus of their work is on modelling and analysis of groups of interactions and their higher-order relationships. In particular, in their work the domain upon which formulas are interpreted are (sets of) simplexes and not (sets of) points in a polyhedra as in the present paper. In [6,8,9] notions of bisimulation for polyhedral models, and for their discrete representation as cell partial order (poset) models, have been proposed. In particular, in [6] an effective model minimisation procedure based on spatial bisimilarity has been presented, as well as its implementation.

From the tools point of view, the python library pymeshlab [14], which is able to programmatically modify 3D meshes based on pre-built operators (mostly traditional 3D imaging filters) is somewhat related to our work. However, a direct comparison of this library and polyhedra model checking would be misleading as the latter uses a declarative language based on SLCS, with automatic parallelisation, and automatic memoization (caching) of intermediate results instead of providing a library of pre-built operators.

Synopsis. Section 2 recalls notation and provides a gentle introduction to relevant concepts concerning polyhedral models, spatial logic, model checking and minimisation. Section 3 presents a selection of examples of surface and volume meshes and illustrates various ways in which spatial polyhedral model checking can be used on such models. Section 4 concludes the paper.

2   Background and Notation

Below we briefly, and mostly informally, recall some basic notions, assuming that the reader has some familiarity with topological spaces, Kripke models, and partially ordered sets (posets). All relevant details can be found in [6]. Intuitively, a *simplex* is the convex hull of a set of affinely independent points. In the context of this paper, a simplex can be a point, or a segment, or a triangle, or a tetrahedron. A simplicial complex is a non-empty collection of simplexes that respect some spatial constraints (see [6] for details). The polyhedron $|K|$ of simplicial complex K is the set union of the points belonging to the components of K.[1]

For the purpose of polyhedral model checking, it is convenient to consider, for each simplex σ, its *relative interior*, or *cell*, $\widetilde{\sigma}$. The cell of a point is just the point itself, whereas the cell of any other kind of simplex coincides with the topological interior of the simplex. For instance, the cell of a line segment is the segment itself without its end-points. Note that, given a simplicial complex K, the set $\widetilde{K}$ of its cells is a partition of the polyhedron $|K|$. Furthermore, it is easy to see that the cells of a simplicial complex K form a partial order $(W, \preccurlyeq)$, where $W = \widetilde{K}$ and $\widetilde{\sigma}_1 \preccurlyeq \widetilde{\sigma}_2$ if and only if $\widetilde{\sigma}_1$ is included in the topological closure of $\widetilde{\sigma}_2$. Finally, for each $x \in |K|$, we let $\mathbb{F}(x) \in \widetilde{K}$ denote the unique cell containing x. Given a set PL of proposition letters, and a simplicial complex K, a *polyhedral model* $\mathcal{P}$ is a pair $(|K|, \mathcal{V}_{\mathcal{P}})$ where $\mathcal{V}_{\mathcal{P}}$ maps proposition letters to sets of points in $|K|$.[2] It is required that the image of any predicate letter be a union of cells. On the basis of the valuation function $\mathcal{V}_{\mathcal{P}}$ of a polyhedral model $(|K|, \mathcal{V}_{\mathcal{P}})$, we can define the valuation function $\mathcal{V}_{\mathcal{F}}$ of its associated poset model[3] $\mathcal{F} = \mathbb{F}(\mathcal{P}) = (W, \preccurlyeq, \mathcal{V}_{\mathcal{F}})$: for each predicate letter p we have that $\widetilde{\sigma} \in \mathcal{V}_{\mathcal{F}}(p)$ if and only if $\widetilde{\sigma} \subseteq \mathcal{V}_{\mathcal{P}}(p)$.

Figure 2 shows a polyhedral model illustrating the various concepts. There are three predicate letters, **red**, **green**, and **gray**, shown by different colours (Fig. 2a). The model is "unpacked" into its cells in Fig. 2b. The latter are collected in the cell poset model, whose Hasse diagram is shown in Fig. 2c.

Besides predicate letters, negation and conjunction, SLCS_γ provides a reachability operator, γ. Informally, a point x in a polyhedral model satisfies the conditional reachability formula $\gamma(\Phi_1, \Phi_2)$ if there is a topological path, i.e. a continuous function from the interval $[0, 1]$ to $|K|$, starting from x, ending in a point y that satisfies Φ_2, and such that all the intermediate points of the path between x and y satisfy Φ_1. Note that neither x nor y is required to satisfy Φ_1. More formally, SLCS_γ can be defined as follows (see also [7]). For $p \in$ PL the

---

[1] Note furthermore that different simplicial complexes can give rise to the same polyhedron.

[2] In the sequel, for the sake of readability, when referring to a polyhedral model, we will often indicate the relevant simplicial complex, say K, only indirectly, via the polyhedron it generates, i.e. $|K|$.

[3] With a little bit of overloading, we let $\mathbb{F}(\mathcal{P})$ denote the poset model associated with polyhedral model $\mathcal{P}$.

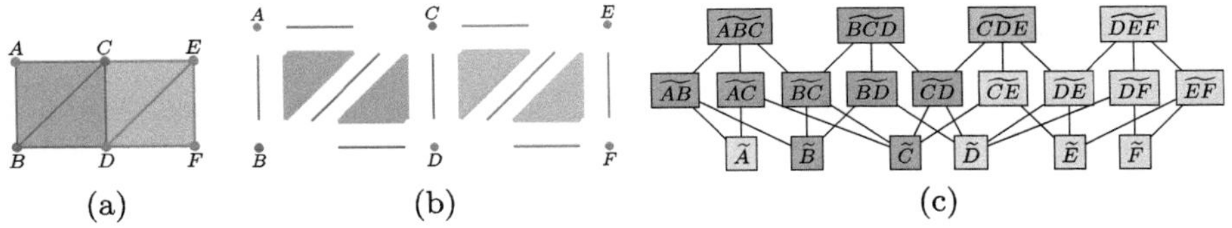

Fig. 2. A polyhedral model $\mathcal{P}$ (a) with its cells (b) and the Hasse diagram of the related cell poset (c).

syntax of the logic is the following:

$$\Phi: = p \mid \neg \Phi \mid \Phi \wedge \Phi \mid \gamma(\Phi, \Phi)$$

The satisfaction relation for $\gamma(\Phi_1, \Phi_2)$, for a polyhedral model $\mathcal{P} = (P, \mathcal{V}_\mathcal{P})$, with $P = |K|$ for some simplicial complex K, and $x \in P$, as defined in [7], is recalled below:

$$\mathcal{P}, x \models \gamma(\Phi_1, \Phi_2) \Leftrightarrow \text{ a topological path } \pi : [0, 1] \rightarrow P \text{ exists such that } \pi(0) = x,$$
$$\mathcal{P}, \pi(1) \models \Phi_2, \text{and } \mathcal{P}, \pi(r) \models \Phi_1 \text{ for all } r \in (0,1).$$

It is worth pointing out that the definition of the satisfaction relation does *not* depend on the specific simplicial complex K that generates the polyhedron $|K|$. In other words: given polyhedral models $\mathcal{P}' = (P, \mathcal{V}_{\mathcal{P}'})$ with $P = |K'|$ and $\mathcal{P}'' = (P, \mathcal{V}_{\mathcal{P}''})$ with $P = |K''| = |K'|$ and $\mathcal{V}_{\mathcal{P}'} = \mathcal{V}_{\mathcal{P}''}$ for all SLCS$_\gamma$ formulas Φ and all $x \in P$ the following holds: $\mathcal{P}', x \models \Phi$ iff $\mathcal{P}'', x \models \Phi$.

Many interesting properties, such as proximity (in the topological sense, i.e. "being in the topological closure of") or "being surrounded by" can be expressed using reachability. In particular, the near operator $\vec{\Diamond}$, corresponding to the classical closure operator, can be defined as a derived operator in this setting: $\vec{\Diamond} \Phi = \gamma(\Phi, \texttt{true})$.

We have also provided an interpretation of SLCS$_\gamma$ on poset models using the notion of $\pm$-path as an image on cell poset models of topological paths in polyhedra. An example of the correspondence between a topological path and its $\pm$-path is shown in Fig. 3. We refer the interested reader to [7] for the relevant formal definitions, here noting only that a $\pm$-path over a poset is a discrete, finite, undirected path $(w_0, w_1, \ldots, w_{n-1}, w_n)$ such that $w_0 \preccurlyeq w_1$ and $w_{n-1} \succcurlyeq w_n$ (see Fig. 3b). The interpretation of γ on a poset model $\mathcal{F} = (W, \preccurlyeq, \mathcal{V}_\mathcal{F})$ is the following: $w \in W$ satisfies $\gamma(\Phi_1, \Phi_2)$ if there is a $\pm$-path starting from w, ending in $w' \in W$ that satisfies Φ_2, and such that all the intermediate elements of the path between w and w' satisfy Φ_1. Note that neither w nor w' is required to satisfy Φ_1. More formally, the satisfaction relation for $\gamma(\Phi_1, \Phi_2)$, for a poset model $\mathcal{F} = (W, \preccurlyeq, \mathcal{V}_\mathcal{F})$ and $w \in W$, is defined as follows:

$$\mathcal{F}, w \models \gamma(\Phi_1, \Phi_2) \Leftrightarrow \text{ a } \pm\text{-path } \pi : [0; \ell] \rightarrow W \text{ exists for some } \ell \geq 2 \text{ s.t. } \pi(0) = w,$$
$$\mathcal{F}, \pi(\ell) \models \Phi_2, \text{and}$$
$$\mathcal{F}, \pi(i) \models \Phi_1 \text{ for all } i \in \{n \in \mathbb{N} \mid 0 < n < \ell\}.$$

In [7] it has been shown that, for all $x \in |K|$ and SLCS_γ formulas Φ, we have: $\mathcal{P}, x \models \Phi$ if and only if $\mathbb{F}(\mathcal{P}), \mathbb{F}(x) \models \Phi$. This result is the theoretical foundation for the model checking algorithm for SLCS_γ on polyhedral models proposed in [7] that actually works on the poset models. The algorithm has been implemented in the tool `PolyLogicA`.[4]

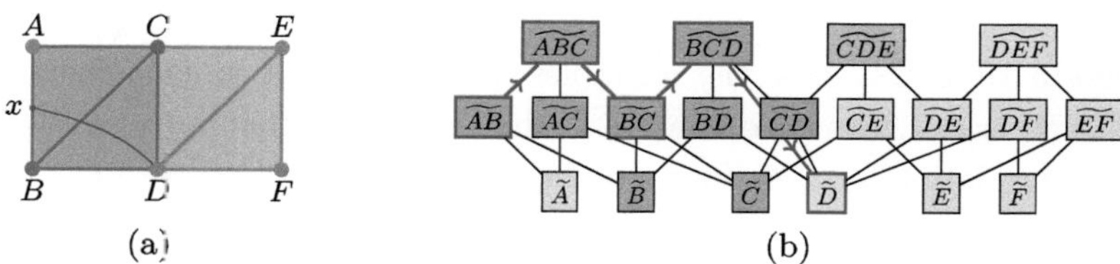

Fig. 3. (a) A topological path from a point x to vertex D in the polyhedral model $\mathcal{P}$ of Fig. 2a. (b) The corresponding $\pm$-path (in blue) in the Hasse diagram of the cell poset model $\mathbb{F}(\mathcal{P})$. (Color figure online)

Finally, note that, in the context of cell poset models, $w \models \vec{\diamond}\, \Phi$ means that there exists a $\pm$-path starting from w leading in one step going up to a cell that satisfies Φ.

Bisimulation-Based Model Minimisation. In [7], *simplicial bisimilarity*, a novel notion of bisimilarity for polyhedral models, has been defined that uses a subclass of topological paths and it has been shown to enjoy the classical Hennessy-Milner property: two points $x_1, x_2 \in |K|$ are simplicial bisimilar, written $x_1 \sim_\triangle^\mathcal{P} x_2$, if and only if they satisfy the same SLCS_γ formulas, i.e. they are equivalent with respect to the logic SLCS_γ, written $x_1 \equiv_\gamma^\mathcal{P} x_2$.

The result has been extended to $\pm$-*bisimilarity* on finite cell poset models, a notion of bisimilarity based on $\pm$-paths: $w_1, w_2 \in W$ are $\pm$-bisimilar, written $w_1 \sim_\pm^\mathcal{F} w_2$, if and only if they satisfy the same SLCS_γ formulas, i.e. $w_1 \equiv_\gamma^\mathcal{F} w_2$ (see [9] for details). In summary, we have:

$$x_1 \sim_\triangle^\mathcal{P} x_2 \text{ iff } x_1 \equiv_\gamma^\mathcal{P} x_2 \text{ iff } \mathbb{F}(x_1) \equiv_\gamma^{\mathbb{F}(\mathcal{P})} \mathbb{F}(x_2) \text{ iff } \mathbb{F}(x_1) \sim_\pm^{\mathbb{F}(\mathcal{P})} \mathbb{F}(x_2).$$

In [8] we showed a similar result for a weaker logic, namely SLCS_η, where $\gamma(\Phi_1, \Phi_2)$ is replaced by $\eta(\Phi_1, \Phi_2)$, which also requires the satisfaction of Φ_1 on the starting point of the path. Intuitively, $\eta(\Phi_1, \Phi_2)$ is the same as $\Phi_1 \wedge \gamma(\Phi_1, \Phi_2)$. Weaker notions of bisimilarity, $\approx_\triangle$ and $\approx_\pm$, have been introduced and the following has been proven:

$$x_1 \approx_\triangle^\mathcal{P} x_2 \text{ iff } x_1 \equiv_\eta^\mathcal{P} x_2 \text{ iff } \mathbb{F}(x_1) \equiv_\eta^{\mathbb{F}(\mathcal{P})} \mathbb{F}(x_2) \text{ iff } \mathbb{F}(x_1) \approx_\pm^{\mathbb{F}(\mathcal{P})} \mathbb{F}(x_2).$$

---

[4] `PolyLogicA` 0.4 and `PolyVisualizer` are available in the branch **polyhedra** of the main **VoxLogicA** repository, see https://github.com/vincenzoml/VoxLogicA.

In [6] we presented an effective toolchain for model minimisation modulo this weaker bisimilarity, and thus also modulo SLCS_η. Let us provide a small example to illustrate spatial bisimulation. With reference to Fig. 2a, we have that no red point, call it y, in the open segment CD is simplicial bisimilar to the red point C. And, in fact, although both y and C satisfy $\gamma(\mathbf{green}, \mathtt{true})$, we have that C satisfies also $\gamma(\mathbf{gray}, \mathtt{true})$, which is not the case for y. Similarly, with reference to Fig. 2c, cell $\widetilde{C}$ satisfies $\gamma(\mathbf{gray}, \mathtt{true})$, which is not satisfied by $\widetilde{CD}$.

Extension of SLCS_γ. For the examples in this work it is convenient to add a further operator, converse near ($\overleftarrow{\diamondsuit}$), that expresses the converse of $\vec{\diamondsuit}$. The satisfaction relation for $\overleftarrow{\diamondsuit}\,\Phi$, for a polyhedral model $\mathcal{P} = (|K|, \mathcal{V}_\mathcal{P})$ and $x \in |K|$, is defined as follows, where for set A, $\mathcal{C}_T(A)$ denotes the topological closure of A:

$$\mathcal{P}, x \models \overleftarrow{\diamondsuit}\,\Phi \Leftrightarrow x' \in \mathcal{C}_T(\mathbb{F}(x)) \text{ exists s.t. } \mathcal{P}, x' \models \Phi.$$

The satisfaction relation for $\overleftarrow{\diamondsuit}$, for a poset model $\mathcal{F} = (W, \preccurlyeq, \mathcal{V}_\mathcal{F})$ and $w \in W$, is defined as:

$$\mathcal{F}, w \models \overleftarrow{\diamondsuit}\,\Phi \Leftrightarrow w' \text{ exists s.t. } w' \preccurlyeq w \text{ and } \mathcal{F}, w' \models \Phi.$$

We leave a more detailed treatment of spatial bisimulation and minimisation for the extended logic for future work.

Polyhedral Model Checking and Visualisation. As we have seen above, SLCS_γ properties of polyhedra can be transformed into equivalent properties on cell poset models. This result is exploited in the polyhedra model checker `PolyLogicA` and in the tool `PolyVisualizer` to visualise the model checking results. `PolyLogicA` is a global model checker that checks a given formula for all cells of the model at once. The algorithm takes as input a finite poset model $\mathbb{F}(\mathcal{P})$ of polyhedron $\mathcal{P}$ and an SLCS_γ formula ϕ. The output is the satisfaction set $\mathsf{Sat}(\phi) = \{\widetilde{\sigma} \in \widetilde{K} \mid \mathbb{F}(\mathcal{P}), \widetilde{\sigma} \models \phi\}$ of nodes in the poset model $\mathbb{F}(\mathcal{P})$ that correspond to the set of cells of $\mathcal{P}$ that satisfy formula ϕ. The satisfaction set Sat is defined recursively on the structure of SLCS_γ formula [7].

The actual input language of `PolyLogicA`, called `ImgQL` (Image Query Language), is an extended set of operations that has SLCS_γ as its core language. The `PolyLogicA` model checker is written in `FSharp`. The model checking results of `PolyLogicA` are generated as a json file. This file contains the name of the property as defined in the `ImgQL` specification, followed by a list of true and false following the order of the definition of the cells in the poset model. Cells for which the corresponding position in the json list is true satisfy the property, cells corresponding to false do not satisfy it. The result file is used by the `PolyVisualizer` tool to present the model checking results for the polyhedron in a graphical way as follows. Cells that satisfy the property are highlighted in their original colour, those that do not satisfy the property are shown in a semi-transparent way. We will see examples of this use in the next section where model checking results are shown as screenshots of the 3D images produced by the `PolyVisualizer` tool. Details on the polyhedra model checking algorithm and the visualiser can be found in [7].

3   Potential of Polyhedral Model Checking

We illustrate the potential of polyhedral model checking for three case studies, each illustrating some different uses. The first is a 3D maze model. The second is a model of a tree-shaped coral. The third is a model of a simple aircraft. The original models of the latter two were provided by a third party in the Wavefront .obj format [15], which is a format widely used in computer graphics. We have developed dedicated python scripts to convert Wavefront .obj images into an input format suitable for polyhedra model checking with `PolyLogicA` and for viewing with the `PolyVisualizer`. An example of such a script can be found in [2].

3.1   Analysing Reachability in a 3D Maze Model

As a first example we consider a volumetric tetrahedral mesh of a 3D maze originally presented in [7]. Its purpose here is to illustrate how `PolyLogicA` can be used to reason about cell colours of an object, where the colours are treated as predicate letters. The maze, shown in Fig. 4a, is a 3D cube structure that is 7 'rooms' wide, 7 'rooms' long and 7 'rooms' high and in which such rooms are connected by 'corridors'. Each room and corridor is itself a polyhedron composed, in turn, by a number of cells such as vertices, segments, triangles and tetrahedra.

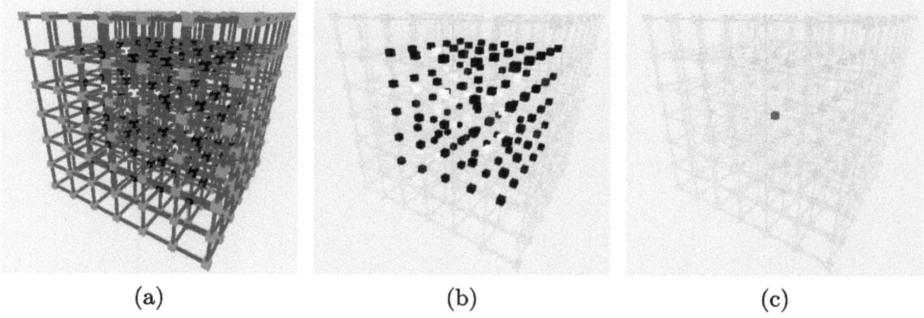

(a)   (b)   (c)

Fig. 4. 3D maze (a), black and white (b) and red rooms (c) in the 3D maze. (Color figure online)

The rooms at the outermost sides of the cube are green. Inside the cube we find black and white rooms (see Fig. 4b) and one red room (see Fig. 4c). The corridors are all dark grey. The images in Fig. 4 have all been obtained by polyhedral model checking with `PolyLogicA`. In particular, Fig. 4b shows all cells that satisfy the formula $B \vee W$, where B is the predicate letter for black cells and W the predicate letter for white cells. The cells that satisfy the formula are shown highlighted in their original colour. The cells that do not satisfy the formula are shown in a pale version of their original colour. The cells satisfying the predicate letter R (red cells) are shown in a similar way in Fig. 4c.

Figure 5 shows SLCS$_\gamma$ formulas that characterise various kinds of corridors, for example, corridors connecting white rooms on both sides are defined using the reachability operator γ, where $\gamma(C, W)$ requires the corridor (C) to connect to a white (W) room and $\neg\gamma(C, G \vee B \vee R)$ makes sure it does not connect to a room of any other colour used in this model.

Formulas Q1, Q2 and Q3 express a few less basic SLCS$_\gamma$ properties. Q1: White rooms and their connecting corridors from which a green room can be reached not passing by black or red rooms, including the green room that is reached; Q2: White rooms and their connecting corridors from which both a red and a green room can be reached not passing by black rooms; Q3: White rooms and their connecting corridors with no path to green rooms. The model checking results of Q1, Q2 and Q3 are shown in Fig. 6, again by highlighting the cells that satisfy the specific formula in their original colour. The full `ImgQL` specification can be found in [2].

$$
\begin{array}{ll}
\text{corridorWW} & \equiv \gamma(C, W) \wedge \neg\gamma(C, G \vee B \vee R) \\
\text{corridorWG} & \equiv \gamma(C, W) \wedge \gamma(C, G) \\
\text{corridorWR} & \equiv \gamma(C, W) \wedge \gamma(C, R) \\
\text{corridorWB} & \equiv \gamma(C, W) \wedge \gamma(C, B) \\
\text{whiteToGreen} & \equiv \gamma((W \vee \text{corridorWW} \vee \text{corridorWG}), G) \\
\text{Q1} & \equiv \text{whiteToGreen} \vee \gamma(G, \text{whiteToGreen}) \\
\text{Q2} & \equiv \gamma((\text{Q1} \vee \text{corridorWR}), R) \vee \gamma((R \vee \text{corridorWR}), \text{Q1}) \\
\text{Q3} & \equiv (W \vee \text{corridorWW}) \wedge \neg\text{whiteToGreen}.
\end{array}
$$

Fig. 5. SLCS$_\gamma$ formulas expressing properties **Q1**, **Q2** and **Q3**; predicate letters G, W, B, R, C are assumed given and their meaning is the obvious one (C for "corridor", G for green and similarly for the other colours). (Color figure online)

3.2 Analysing the Branching Hierarchy of a Coral Model

The second example is used to illustrate a semi-automatic approach to find the various branches in a tree-shape coral (see [1,3]). In this example, `PolyLogicA` is used in combination with the tool MeshLab [10]. MeshLab is a free and open-source software product for the processing and editing of 3D triangular meshes. It provides a wide range of tools for operations such as cleaning, repairing, inspecting, rendering, texturing, and converting meshes. We used MeshLab to perform some initial manual annotations of the model and then to save it in the Wavefront .obj format. We then converted the model, with the help of a dedicated

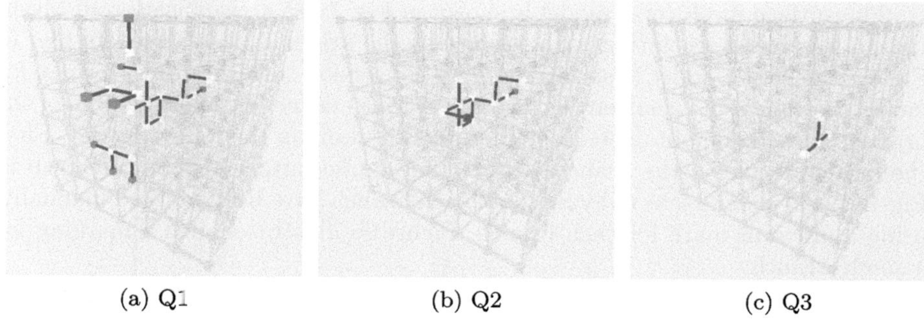

(a) Q1   (b) Q2   (c) Q3

Fig. 6. Spatial model checking results of the properties in Fig. 5 for the 3D maze of Fig. 4.

python script (see [2]), into an input format that is suitable for further analysis using `PolyLogicA`.

In the following, we show that the results of `PolyLogicA` model checking can be used to enrich the model itself with additional predicate letters. The enriched model is then used, in turn, for further model checking or for model minimisation. This novel way of enriching a model with previously obtained spatial model checking results is very interesting and has many advantages. First of all, it can be used to keep the formulas of interest to check in each model checking session much shorter, resulting in reduced model checking times. This is important as models tend to be very large. Second, enriching/changing models this way makes it possible to study their core structure through SLCS_η-property preserving minimisation of the model [6]. Third, such minimised models may, in turn, be used to speed up further model checking.

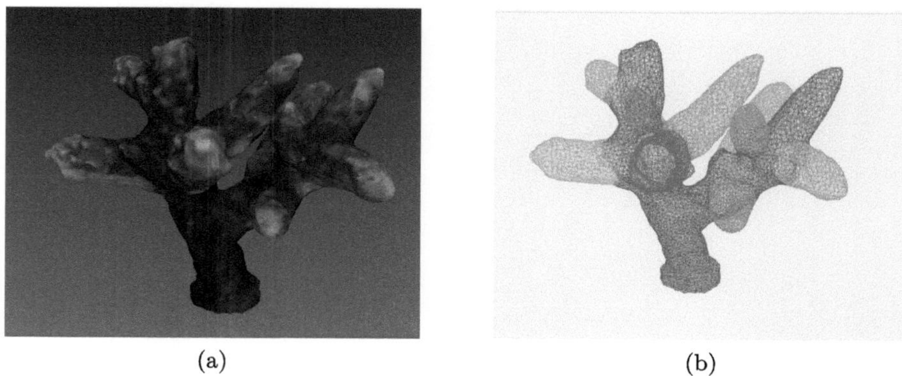

(a)   (b)

Fig. 7. (a) Tree-shape coral in MeshLab; (b) Coral with model checking results for finding branches.

The surface mesh coral model is shown in Fig. 7a as a visualisation in Mesh-Lab in a reduced resolution with respect to the original Wavefront .obj file. In Fig. 7b the same model is shown after its conversion into the input format for model checking and visualisation with `PolyVisualizer`. The identification of the branches have been obtained through model checking in the following way. First the borders between the branches have been marked using MeshLab (shown in Fig. 9a). Then some selected vertices of each branch have been marked manually, using a different mark for each branch. Figure 9b illustrates such a marking for a single branch.

$$
\begin{aligned}
b0 &\equiv \gamma(\neg border, bSel0) \\
b1 &\equiv \gamma(\neg border, bSel1) \\
&\cdots \\
b13 &\equiv \gamma(\neg border, bSel13)
\end{aligned}
$$

Fig. 8. Predicate letters border, bSel0, bSel1, etc. of selected triangular faces for the various branches are assumed given; b0 through b13 characterise the cells belonging to the various branches.

The SLCS_γ formulas to identify the various branches are straightforward and shown in Fig. 8. For example, formula b1 is satisfied by all cells in the model that are not part of a border and through which one can reach a selected cell satisfying bSel1, passing only by such non-border elements (except possibly for the first element of such a path). Providing the visualiser with the model checking results, together with a definition of the colour in which to show the cells satisfying the various properties b0 to b13 and the borders, we obtain the polyhedron shown in Fig. 7b.

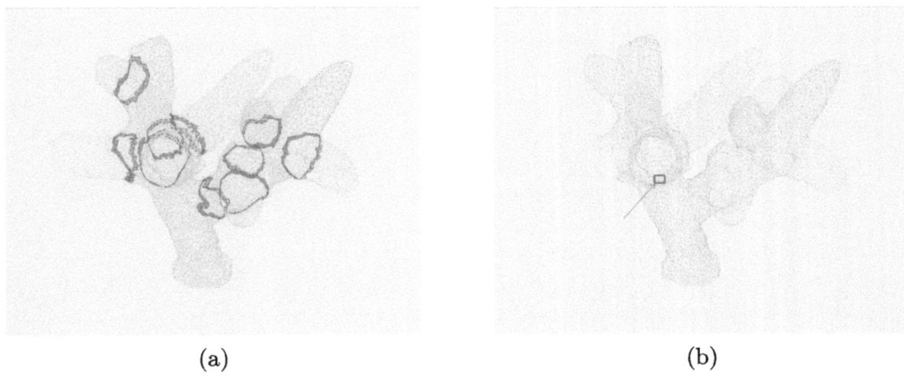

(a)   (b)

Fig. 9. (a) Borders between branches; (b) Example of marked vertex (see arrow) to identify a branch.

Coral Complexity. An interesting aspect of tree-shape corals is to find the branching hierarchy in the coral structure. Such branching hierarchy provides information about the complexity of the corals. It is known from the literature that the covering of the ocean floor with corals, and particularly its covering with branching corals, are positively correlated with the structural complexity of coral reefs. In turn, structural complexity of coral reefs has been shown to positively influence several measures of biodiversity in such reefs. Branching coral cover of the ocean bottom may be particularly likely to contribute fine-scale structural complexity to reefs, which can be important to a range of organisms, such as fish and mobile invertebrates (see e.g. [11] page 322). One way to measure the complexity of a coral is through investigating the parent-child hierarchy of branches. In the following we will use `PolyLogicA` to colour the various groups of branches according to their rank in such a hierarchy. The rank of a branch is its position in an in-order traversal of the tree-shaped coral starting from the root. The root branch of the coral has rank 1, branches attached to the root have rank 2, and so on.

The procedure follows two alternating phases starting from the root of the coral. We define two properties for each rank level n. The first property, indicated by rankPn, defines all the cells that belong to a certain rank level. The root is the first rank level. The second property, indicated by rankAn, defines all the cells that belong to rank level n or lower, including the borders between such branches. We define two derived operators grow(x,y) and throughCom(x,y,z). Informally, the operator grow(x,y)= x $\vee$ (y $\wedge\gamma$(y,x)) extends an area of cells each satisfying x with an adjacent area of cells each satisfying y. The operator throughCom(x, y, z) combines the γ operator with the grow operator. Informally, this formula is satisfied by any cell from which a $\pm$-path starts that passes by cells satisfying x and reaches a cell satisfying grow(z,y). When instantiated as throughCom($\neg$border, border, rank), this operator is used to find cells in the branches, that are not border cells, but via which one can reach border cells passing through cells in branches with a lower rank than that specified in the formula. We also define an auxiliary operator difference(x,y). The latter property is satisfied by cells that satisfy x but not y. The specification in Fig. 10 shows the formulas for identifying three rank levels. Of course, these can be extended in the obvious way to identify the rank of branches in coral with a larger branching structure. The specification assumes that the predicate letters border and rootSel, some selected cells of the root branch, are given. Both were obtained by annotating the model with the tool MeshLab.

The model checking results of the specification in Fig. 10 are shown in Fig. 11a. Rank level rankP1 is shown in purple, rank level rankP2 in green and rank level rankP3 in orange. Borders between branches are shown in brown. The full `ImgQL` specifications for the coral example can be found in [2].

Core Structure of Corals. One might be interested also in the core structure of a branching coral. There are several known computer graphics methods that can be used to obtain such a structure, for instance methods that extract a

$$
\begin{aligned}
\text{grow(x,y)} &\equiv x \vee (y \wedge \gamma(y,x)) \\
\text{throughCom(x,y,z)} &\equiv \gamma(x, \text{grow}(z,y)) \\
\text{difference(x,y)} &\equiv x \wedge \neg y \\
\text{root} &\equiv \gamma(\neg\text{border}, \text{rootSel}) \\
\text{rankP1} &\equiv \text{root} \\
\text{rankA1} &\equiv \text{root} \\
\text{rankP2} &\equiv \vec{\Diamond}\,(\text{difference}(\text{throughCom}(\neg\text{border}, \text{border}, \text{rankP1}), \text{rankA1})) \\
\text{rankA2} &\equiv \text{rankP2} \vee \text{grow}(\text{rankA1}, \text{border}) \\
\text{rankP3} &\equiv \vec{\Diamond}\,(\text{difference}(\text{throughCom}(\neg\text{border}, \text{border}, \text{rankP2}), \text{rankA2})) \\
\text{rankA3} &\equiv \text{rankP3} \vee \text{grow}(\text{rankA2}, \text{border})
\end{aligned}
$$

Fig. 10. Finding the rank of coral branches. Predicate letters border and rootSel are assumed given.

topological 'skeleton' from a triangular surface mesh, i.e. a sort of thin version of the shape that is equidistant to its borders. In our setting we could obtain an abstract version of the structure by minimising the structure w.r.t. $\approx_\pm$, the weaker bisimulation related to SLCS_η (see Sect. 2). The result of minimising the structure in Fig. 11a is shown as a Labelled Transition System (LTS) in Fig. 11b, where the states in the LTS have been given colours that correspond to the rank levels in Fig. 11a. The labels of the self-loops in the LTS, such as ap_clrank1 (denoting the first rank in the hierarchy) and ap_clborder, denote the predicate letters of the states, the other transition labels, chg and dwn, are auxiliary labels used in the minimisation procedure (see [6] for details). This LTS does not give exactly the same information as a topological skeleton, but may reveal other interesting aspects. For example, it shows that there exists at least one branch, attached to the root, from which further branches emanate, leading to a maximum ranking level of 3. This is represented by the longer chain of states in the LTS, starting from the purple state (clrank1) and passing by a brown state (clborder), a green state (clrank2), a brown state again and finally an orange state (clrank2). It also shows that there are branches that emanate from the (purple) root that do not further split into other branches in turn. This is represented by the shorter chain of states in the LTS starting from the purple state.

Let us illustrate how we obtain the minimal LTS model of a coral. First of all, we use PolyLogicA to find the rank levels as described previously. The model checking result for each rank level can be saved in a simple .json format that provides for each cell in the model the value 'true', in case it is part of that rank level, and the value 'false' if it is not. We can use this outcome to add new predicate letters to the original model. For example, in case we have the results for rank level 1, we add the predicate letter "clrank1" to each cell that satisfies the rank1 property in the model file (but not "border"'), replacing the predicate letters that were already there. This is easy to do in an automatic way using a simple python script because in the result file of the model checking session the results are given in exactly the same order as the cells defined in the model file. If we do this for every rank, we get a model with only clrank1, clrank2, clrank3 and

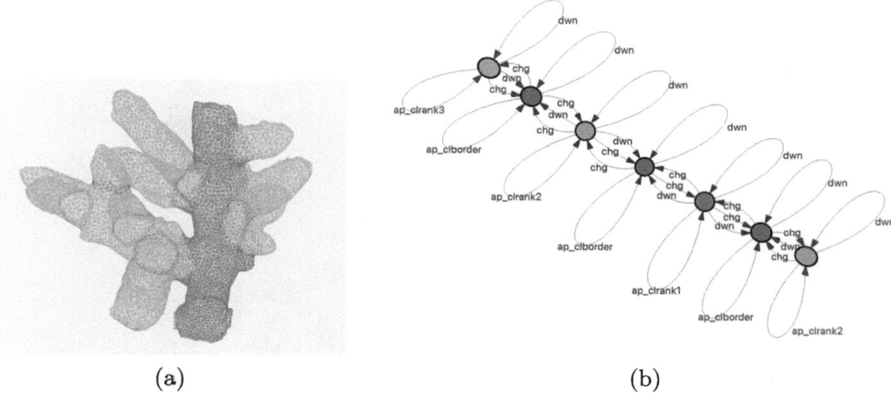

(a)   (b)

Fig. 11. (a) Rank levels in the same coral (turned 180° around its vertical axes w.r.t. Fig. 7); (b) Minimised model as LTS.

clborder as predicate letters, and each cell is labelled by exactly one predicate letter. Applying the toolchain described in [6] for minimising the model modulo $\approx_\pm$, the weaker bisimulation related to SLCS_η, we obtain the minimised LTS as shown in Fig. 11b (apart from colouring the states, which was done manually to facilitate the interpretation of the state labels).

We can perform a similar analysis on the coral model in which all branches were given a different colour as in Fig. 7b. The result of this minimisation is the LTS shown in Fig. 12b. In the latter, the colours of the states representing equivalence classes w.r.t. SLCS_η reflect the colours of the branches of the coral in Fig. 12a. The states representing the border classes are in dark green. This makes it easy to recognise the full structure of the coral reflected in the minimised LTS model. A closer look also reveals an interesting aspect. In the upper right part of the LTS the blue branch and the purple branch are shown to share a border. This was not the case in the minimal model in Fig. 11b, since there these two branches had the same colour because they belonged to the same rank. Furthermore, the orange branch is now a single branch. The ranking procedure had split that branch into two different parts, assigning different ranks.

Note that the above analyses are presenting an interesting and innovative use of model minimisation. Usually model minimisation is applied to increase the efficiency of spatial model checking for large models [8]. Actually, the possibility to add (or replace) predicate letters in a model as we did above can be of great use also in other settings, as it makes it possible to insert intermediate model checking results in the model itself so that further formulas to check can be of much shorter length, saving precious computing resources.

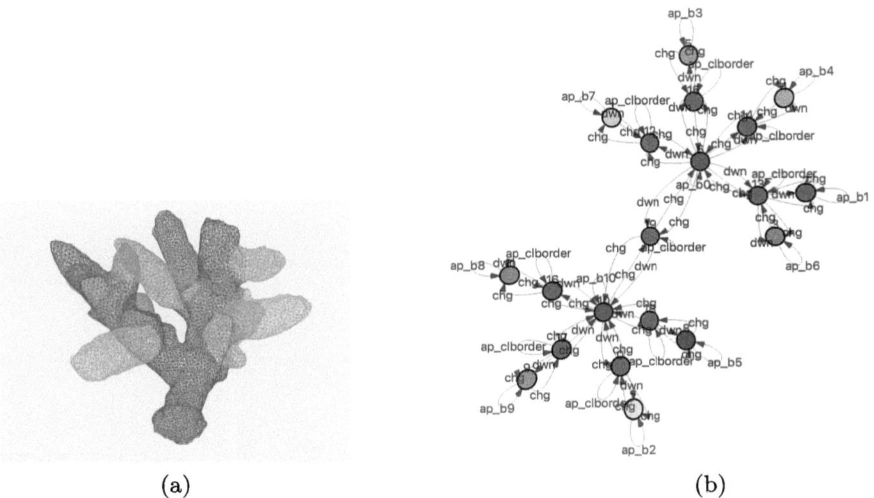

(a)   (b)

Fig. 12. (a) Branches of the coral with individual colours; (b) Minimised model as LTS with state colours reflecting that of corresponding branches in (a), which states representing borders in dark green. (Color figure online)

3.3   Studying Curvature Properties in a Simple Aircraft Model

In this third example we show how `PolyLogicA` can be used to study curvature properties of an object, in this case a simple aircraft model[5] chosen for illustrative purposes. The aircraft is composed of simple surfaces that are connected together. Such connections form angles that can be concave or convex and that can be more or less sharp. The surfaces themselves are mainly flat, but there are some small ridges as well. A view of the aircraft is shown in Fig. 13a and a version in which concave and convex edges are shown in different colours is presented in Fig. 13b.

The image in Fig. 13b has been obtained by computing discrete mean curvature values [13] for each vertex of the triangular mesh with MeshLab [10]. The resulting image was saved as a Wavefront .obj image in which the curvature values are saved as colours for each *vertex*. Blue-coloured vertexes are representing points on a locally highly convex surface (i.e. a high positive mean curvature value). Green vertexes represent points on the surface with a less pronounced convexity (i.e. with a less high but still positive mean curvature value). Red vertexes represent points on a concave surface (i.e. points with a negative mean curvature value). Yellow vertexes represent points where the surface is essentially flat (or, in a few cases, a saddle point).

As described in the previous case study, this .obj image can be converted using a python script into an input format suitable for polyhedra model checking with

---

⁵ Original model downloaded from Free3D at https://free3d.com/3d-model/ufo-triangle-v1--354611.html. Accessed on 21 May 2024.

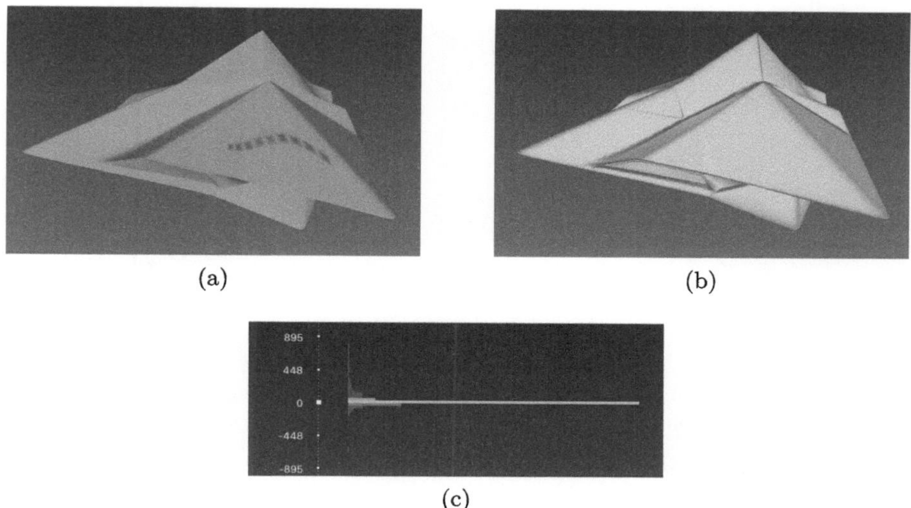

(a)   (b)

(c)

Fig. 13. (a) Aircraft in MeshLab [10]; (b) Discrete Mean Curvature values of the aircraft model as computed by MeshLab [10]: Flat surface in yellow, concave edges in red, convex edges in green and sharp convex edges in blue, as also shown in the histogram of curvature values for vertices (c). (Color figure online)

`PolyLogicA` and for viewing with `PolyVisualizer`. In the python script we can define the relation between the colours of the vertexes and the names of the predicate letters. For example, we defined four predicate letters, with the names 'flat', 'concave', 'convex' and 'convexsharp', corresponding to the four colours used in the histogram in Fig. 13c that was produced with MeshLab by rendering the curvature measure as a vertex quality.

A vertex (or point) satisfies the predicate letter 'concave' if it is red (in rgb terms [255, 0, 0]) within an error margin of 30. Similarly for convex (rgb [0, 255, 0]) and convexsharp (rgb [0, 0, 255]). We gave all remaining vertices the predicate letter 'flat' and all remaining triangles and segments of the aircraft the predicate letter 'ufo' (the original name of this aircraft model). The result of this conversion is shown in the `PolyVisualizer` visualisation of the .json model in Fig. 14a, where we chose to show vertexes satisfying flat in yellow, vertices satisfying concave in red, and so on.

We can now use `PolyLogicA` on the generated .json model to check the predicate letters one by one and generate the associated result files for visualisation with `PolyVisualizer`. For example, in Fig. 14b all vertices satisfying concave are highlighted in red. In Fig. 14b vertices satisfying convex and convexsharp are shown, highlighted in green (Fig. 15a) and highlighted in blue (Fig. 15b), respectively.

More interesting properties are specified in Fig. 16. The formula $\overleftarrow{\diamond}$concave is satisfied by all segments and triangles that are connected to a ver-

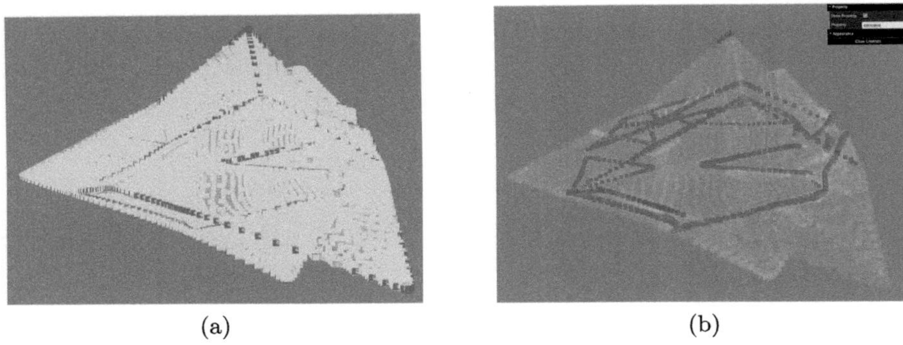

(a)   (b)

Fig. 14. (a) Aircraft in `PolyVisualizer`; (b) Vertices satisfying 'concave' highlighted in red. (Color figure online)

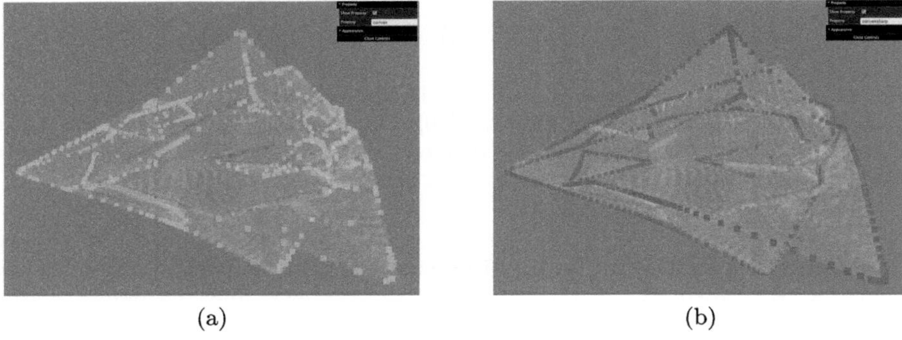

(a)   (b)

Fig. 15. (a) Vertices satisfying 'convex' highlighted in green; (b) Vertices satisfying 'convexsharp' highlighted in blue. (Color figure online)

tex satisfying 'concave'. We can then define convexmeetsconcave = convex $\wedge$ $\gamma(\overleftarrow{\Diamond}$concave,convex). The model checking results are shown in Fig. 17a where the highlighted green vertices satisfy the formula.

Finding Sharp Ridges. A rather subtle property is to find areas that are surrounded by a sharp ridge. We see such an area for example as a triangle shape in the bottom of the aircraft as shown in Fig. 18a. Such ridges are characterised by a thin concave area next to a sharp convex area. One can define such a ridge as ridgeborder = concave $\wedge$ $\gamma(\overleftarrow{\Diamond}$ convexsharp, concave) and then look for an area surrounded by such a ridge defining flatridgearea = $\overleftarrow{\Diamond}$ flat $\wedge$ ($\neg$ grow(ridgeborder), $\overleftarrow{\Diamond}$ flat)), where $\overleftarrow{\Diamond}$ flat are the vertices satisfying flat extended with their directly adjacent segments and triangles. The result of `PolyLogicA` model checking of this formula is shown in Fig. 18b, where the area that satisfies the property is highlighted in yellow. It is easy to see that besides the triangular shape in the bottom of the aircraft there are also other small areas that have this property

$$
\begin{array}{ll}
\mathsf{grow(x,y)} & \equiv x \vee (y \wedge \gamma(y,x)) \\
\mathsf{convexmeetsconcave} & \equiv \mathsf{convex} \wedge \gamma(\overleftarrow{\Diamond}\, \mathsf{concave}, \mathsf{convex}) \\
\mathsf{ridgeborder} & \equiv \mathsf{concave} \wedge \gamma(\overleftarrow{\Diamond}\, \mathsf{convexsharp}, \mathsf{concave}) \\
\mathsf{flatridgearea} & \equiv \overleftarrow{\Diamond}\, \mathsf{flat} \wedge (\neg \mathsf{grow(ridgeborder)}, \overleftarrow{\Diamond}\, \mathsf{flat})).
\end{array}
$$

Fig. 16. Derived SLCS$_\gamma$ operator grow(x,y); SLCS$_\gamma$ formulas expressing the properties convexmeetsconcave, ridgeborder and flatridgearea; predicate letters concave, convex, convexsharp and flat are assumed given.

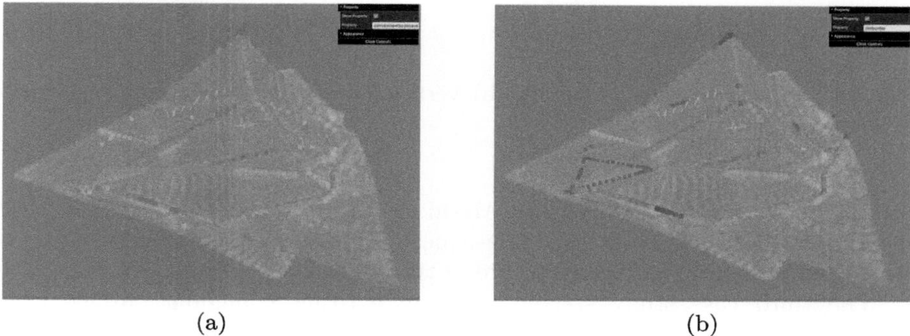

(a) (b)

Fig. 17. (a) convex meeting concave highlighted in green; (b) Vertices satisfying ridgeborder highlighted in red. (Color figure online)

in the rear of the aircraft and along the edges of the wings. This illustrates how PolyLogicA could be used to find aspects of the curvature of an object that are difficult to detect, which might be very useful, for example, when looking for small defects in constructions. The full ImgQL specifications for the aircraft model can be found in [2].

3.4   Preliminary Performance Data and Discussion

We have presented three different case studies to illustrate a variety of ways in which polyhedral model checking can be applied. The first case study concerned a synthetic example, i.e. a 3D polyhedral model that was automatically generated in the format required for the PolyLogicA model checker. This case study served the purpose of illustrating the potential of the conditional spatial reachability operator γ. It also provided a first test case for studying the practical feasibility of polyhedral model checking.

The second case study started from an existing triangular surface mesh of a tree-shaped coral. In this case, the surface mesh still needed to be converted into the format for the PolyLogicA model checker. The converter was developed by one of the authors in such a way that it could be easily adapted to be used to convert other obj surface meshes as well. Furthermore, MeshLab turned out to be a very useful tool set to annotate the original mesh to enable and facilitate

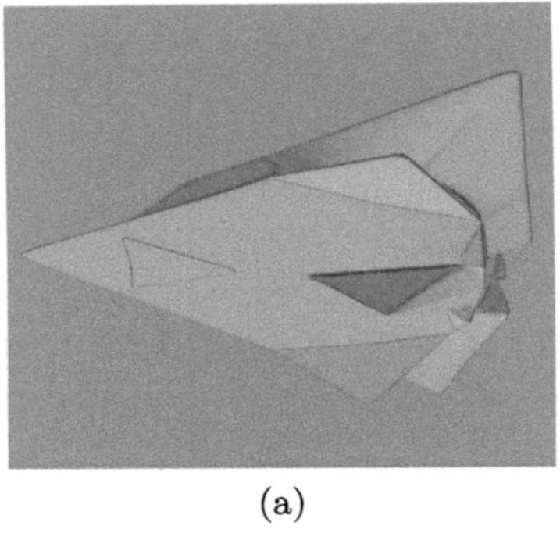
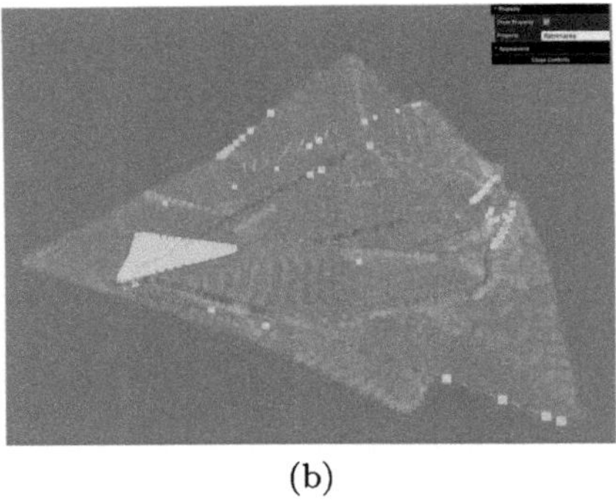

(a)   (b)

Fig. 18. (a) Bottom view of aircraft; (b) Vertices satisfying 'flatridgearea' highlighted in yellow. (Color figure online)

further polyhedral model checking. MeshLab was also used to experiment with rescaling of the coral model and subsequent polyhedral model minimisation to study and visualise the core structure of the coral.

The third case study started from an existing triangular surface mesh obtained from a publicly accessible large repository of such meshes. Also in this case we have successfully converted the obtained model from its original .obj format into the model checking format. Furthermore, in this case MeshLab has been used to apply one of its algorithms to visualise curvature aspects of the model, which have subsequently been investigated using polyhedral model checking. Even if in this paper we illustrated the approach on a simple case study, it should be evident that polyhedral model checking provides interesting potential to analyse such models in more detail than would be possible (or convenient) by pure human visual inspection.

We close this discussion by providing a few preliminary indications on the time performance of `PolyLogicA` model checking on the models introduced in this paper. This work shows only a small part of the potential uses, but it serves as a first step to illustrate ideas and to, hopefully, stimulate others to use `PolyLogicA` in a fruitful way in further case studies.

Preliminary Model Checking Performance Data. Although it is beyond the scope of this paper to study the performance aspects of polyhedral model checking with `PolyLogicA` in detail, we provide some preliminary indications in Table 1 for each of the three examples[6]. Since this is the first polyhedral model checker in its kind, to the best of our knowledge, we have no data to compare our performance results with that of other tools.

The results in Table 1 show that pure model checking times range from 0.38 s for the maze to about 6 s for the analysis of the ranks in the coral model. Con-

---

[6] All experiments in this paper were performed with `PolyLogicA` 0.4 on a Mac M2 pro with 12 cores and 32 GB of memory.

Table 1. For each model the number of vertexes, total number of cells, model checking time including IO (i.e. reading input model and producing result file) and pure model checking time are shown. All times are in seconds. The properties for the maze are the ones shown in Fig. 5, for the coral (branches) those in Fig. 8, for the coral (hierarchy) those in Fig. 10 and for the aircraft those in Fig. 16. The full ImgQL specifications can be found in [2].

model	nr. of vertexes	nr. of cells	MC time incl. IO	pure MC time
maze	11,319	147,245	5.97	0.38
coral (branches)	8,123	48,728	2.7	0.20
coral (hierarchy)	67,573	405,426	22.4	5.94
aircraft	31,810	190,850	10.01	3.35

sidering the number of cells that the models consist of, ranging from several tens of thousands to several hundreds of thousands, these performance times are very encouraging and show the practical feasibility of polyhedral model checking. We note that a significant amount of time is spent performing I/O operations, i.e. the reading and writing of the model and result files, respectively. This is due to the fact that in the current prototype we are using plain text files for models and results. In future work we plan to integrate the various components of the tool chain so that writing and reading intermediate results can be avoided, reducing the time needed for I/O.

The general computational complexity of the polyhedral model checking algorithm (which includes both the translation of the polyhedron into a poset and the model checking algorithm itself), given a fixed maximal dimension of the simplicial complexes in the polyhedral model, is $\mathcal{O}(n \cdot h)$, where n is the number of nodes of the poset and h is the cardinality of the set of different $SLCS_\gamma$ subformulas present in the ImgQL specification that need to be checked. Further details on the model checking algorithm and its complexity can be found in [7].

4   Conclusion

We have shown various ways in which polyhedral model checking can be used to analyse aspects of triangular surface meshes and tetrahedral volume meshes that are abundant in the domain of computer graphics. To this end, we have used our first-in-its-kind spatial polyhedral model checker PolyLogicA in combination with the well-established computer graphics tool MeshLab [10]. The latter provides a huge library of operations on surface and volume meshes, among which manual annotation of objects and operations such as computing the curvature characteristics of objects and many more. The results of such operations can be saved as a mesh object and then converted into the input format of the model checker inserting useful predicate letters in the model. This way models can be formally and automatically analysed from a wide range of perspectives. This paper has only illustrated a small subset of the possibilities.

In future work we plan to address further models from various domains, illustrating also how `PolyLogicA` could be used to check properties from more than one perspective (e.g. curvature, distance, texture) of a model at once. Recent work on geometric analysis through spatial logics to check the consistency of 3D geological models [16] also seems a promising domain of application, besides a continuation of the application of polyhedral model checking in the medical domain [7]. We also plan to investigate its application in the railway domain.

Acknowledgments. Research partially supported by Bilateral project between CNR (Italy) and SRNSFG (Georgia) "Model Checking for Polyhedral Logic" (#CNR-22-010); European Union - Next GenerationEU - National Recovery and Resilience Plan (NRRP), Investment 1.5 Ecosystems of Innovation, Project "Tuscany Health Ecosystem" (THE), CUP: B83C22003930001; European Union - Next-GenerationEU - National Recovery and Resilience Plan (NRRP) – MISSION 4 COMPONENT 2, INVESTMENT N. 1.1, CALL PRIN 2022 D.D. 104 02-02-2022 – (Stendhal) CUP N. B53D23012850006; MUR project PRIN 2020TL3X8X "T-LADIES"; CNR project "Formal Methods in Software Engineering 2.0", CUP B53C24000720005. We thank the anonymous reviewers for their careful review and useful observations.

Disclosure of Interests. The authors have no competing interests to declare that are relevant to the content of this article.

References

1. Andriaccio, Y.: Skeletonization, segmentation and phenotyping of branching corals 3D replicas. B.Sc. thesis, AA 2021/2022, Available from the author (2022)
2. Andriaccio, Y., Ciancia, V., Latella, D., Massink, M.: Practical exploration of polyhedral model checking. CoRR abs/2506.20176 (2025). https://doi.org/10.48550/ARXIV.2506.20176
3. Andriaccio, Y., et al.: Leveraging 3D geometric processing for the phenotyping of branching corals (2024). https://www.reeffutures.com/, oral presentation at Reef Futures
4. Basile, D., ter Beek, M.H., Bussi, L., Ciancia, V.: A toolchain for strategy synthesis with spatial properties. Int. J. Softw. Tools Technol. Transf. **25**(5), 641–658 (2023). https://doi.org/10.1007/S10009-023-00730-1
5. ter Beek, M.H., Ciancia, V., Latella, D., Massink, M., Spagnolo, G.O.: Spatial model checking for smart stations. In: Lluch Lafuente, A., Mavridou, A. (eds.) FMICS 2021. LNCS, vol. 12863, pp. 39–47. Springer, Cham (2021). https://doi.org/10.1007/978-3-030-85248-1_3
6. Bezhanishvili, N., et al.: Weak simplicial bisimilarity and minimisation for polyhedral model checking (2024). https://arxiv.org/abs/2411.11428
7. Bezhanishvili, N., Ciancia, V., Gabelaia, D., Grilletti, G., Latella, D., Massink, M.: Geometric model checking of continuous space. Log. Methods Comput. Sci. **18**(4), 7:1–7:38 (2022). https://doi.org/10.46298/LMCS-18(4:7)2022. https://lmcs.episciences.org/10348. ISSN: 1860-5974. Published on line: 22 Nov 2022
8. Bezhanishvili, N., et al.: Weak simplicial bisimilarity for polyhedral models and SLCS$_\eta$. In: Castiglioni, V., Francalanza, A. (eds.) FORTE 2024. LNCS, vol. 14678, pp. 20–38. Springer, Cham (2024). https://doi.org/10.1007/978-3-031-62645-6_2

9. Ciancia, V., Gabelaia, D., Latella, D., Massink, M., de Vink, E.P.: On bisimilarity for polyhedral models and SLCS. In: Huisman, M., Ravara, A. (eds.) FORTE 2023. LNCS, vol. 13910, pp. 132–151. Springer, Cham (2023). https://doi.org/10.1007/978-3-031-35355-0_9

10. Cignoni, P., Callieri, M., Corsini, M., Dellepiane, M., Ganovelli, F., Ranzuglia, G.: MeshLab: an open-source mesh processing tool. In: Scarano, V., Chiara, R.D., Erra, U. (eds.) Eurographics Italian Chapter Conference. The Eurographics Association (2008). https://doi.org/10.2312/LocalChapterEvents/ItalChap/ItalianChapConf2008/129-136

11. Graham, N.A.J., Nash, K.L.: The importance of structural complexity in coral reef ecosystems. Coral Reefs **32**(2), 315–326 (2013). https://doi.org/10.1007/s00338-012-0984-y

12. Loreti, M., Quadrini, M.: A spatial logic for simplicial models. Log. Methods Comput. Sci. **19**(3) (2023). https://doi.org/10.46298/LMCS-19(3:8)2023

13. Meyer, M., Desbrun, M., Schröder, P., Barr, A.H.: Discrete differential-geometry operators for triangulated 2-manifolds. In: Hege, H.C., Polthier, K. (eds.) Visualization and Mathematics III, pp. 35–57. Springer, New York (2003). https://doi.org/10.1007/978-3-662-05105-4_2

14. Muntoni, A., Cignoni, P.: PyMeshLab. Zenodo (2021). https://doi.org/10.5281/zenodo.4438750

15. Murray, J.D., van Ryper, W.: Encyclopedia of Graphics File Formats, 2nd edn. Springer, Cham (1996). http://oreilly.com/catalog/9781565921610

16. Parquer, M.N., de Kemp, E.A., Brodaric, B., Hillier, M.J.: Checking the consistency of 3D geological models. Geosci. Model Dev. **18**(1), 71–100 (2025). https://doi.org/10.5194/gmd-18-71-2025. https://gmd.copernicus.org/articles/18/71/2025/

The Stipula Platform:
A Workbench for Programming and Analyzing Legal Contracts

Cosimo Laneve[(✉)] [iD]

DISI, University of Bologna, Bologna, Italy
`cosimo.laneve@unibo.it`

Abstract. *Stipula* is a domain-specific programming language specifically designed to model and enforce legal contracts. This paper presents the foundational design principles of *Stipula*, focusing on its ability to express and regulate permissions, obligations, prohibitions, and escrows. We introduce a comprehensive suite of tools developed to support contract development in *Stipula*, including a *visual code editor* for intuitive contract authoring, an interpreter for automatic execution, and a number of analyzers for verifying several legally relevant properties (unreachability of clauses, absence of frozen assets, etc.). These tools are integrated into a unified *workbench*, designed to empower legal practitioners and developers to write, test, debug, and manage legal contracts effectively and efficiently.

1 Introduction

Traditional legal texts are typically expressed in natural language, which is inherently ambiguous and susceptible to multiple interpretations. This linguistic flexibility, while essential for human communication, poses significant challenges for automated processing, analysis, and verification. The digitalization of legal texts offers substantial benefits: it can increase efficiency through faster information retrieval and even enable the automatic execution of well-specified procedures. Moreover, digital representations facilitate improved data organization and promote greater transparency in legal processes. However, the computational treatment of legal texts remains a difficult task. Their complexity, coupled with the expressiveness and ambiguity of natural language, often necessitates human judgment to achieve reliable interpretation.

To address these challenges, several research initiatives have proposed domain-specific programming languages for the specification of legal contracts *e.g.*, [29, 30, 36, 39]. These languages introduce a precise syntax that mitigates some of the ambiguities of natural language, and often provide graphical interfaces to help map normative elements directly to executable code. However, while such efforts advance the expressiveness and accessibility of digital contracts, they typically devote limited attention to the formal verification of correctness.

© The Author(s), under exclusive license to Springer Nature Switzerland AG 2026
M. H. ter Beek et al. (Eds.): Fantechi Festschrift, LNCS 16470, pp. 160–177, 2026.
https://doi.org/10.1007/978-3-032-12484-5_9

This limitation is particularly critical in the legal domain, where ambiguities or unintended execution behaviours may result in severe legal and financial consequences. Although progress has been made in developing methodologies and tools for the formal verification of legal contracts, their adoption in practice remains rare. One major obstacle is the inherent complexity of formal reasoning tools, which discourages their use by legal practitioners and restricts their integration into standard workflows.

To overcome the current lack of automatic verification techniques, in 2021 we introduced *Stipula* [11,12,27], a domain-specific language explicitly designed for the specification of legal contracts. *Stipula* is built around a small set of concise and intelligible primitives that directly capture the distinctive elements of contracts. The language is grounded in a formal operational semantics, ensuring that its behaviour is rigorously defined and thus amenable to automated verification.

The supporting toolchain [13] has been developed to facilitate the entire contract lifecycle. It includes a *visual code editor* that enables intuitive authoring of contracts, an interpreter for automatic execution, a *type inference system* that minimizes the need for explicit annotations, and an *unreachability analyzer* that identifies clauses which can never be executed. Ongoing work extends this suite with a *liquidity analyzer*, which guarantees that no assets remain indefinitely frozen within a contract. While the theoretical framework of liquidity analysis has already been formalized, its implementation is currently under development. All of these tools are integrated into a unified *workbench*, designed to support both legal practitioners and developers in writing, testing, debugging, and managing legal contracts. The workbench provides a seamless environment that promotes efficiency, correctness, and accessibility, thereby bridging the gap between formal verification techniques and their practical use in the legal domain.

The development of the platform began in 2021 with the interpreter and type inference system described in [12]. It was later expanded through two undergraduate theses at the University of Bologna [21,37], which introduced the visual editor and the unreachability analyzer studied in [26]. The environment that integrates and harmonizes these tools was also developed as part of an undergraduate thesis [17]. This paper consolidates these earlier contributions and provides a unified account of the resulting toolchain. Our aim is to present the platform in a way that is both technically rigorous and accessible to practitioners and legal experts, enabling them to experiment with and adopt the system without requiring extensive prior training in formal methods or programming.

The remainder of the paper is organized as follows. Section 2 introduces the *Stipula* language and illustrates its main constructs through an example that demonstrates how obligations, permissions, and events can be naturally expressed. Section 3 presents the execution environment, while Sect. 4 describes the visual editor that supports contract authoring. The integration of type inference within the interpreter is discussed in Sect. 5. Section 6 outlines the analysis technique used to identify unreachable clauses, whereas Sect. 7 is devoted to liquidity analysis, which determines whether contractual assets may remain indefinitely frozen. Section 8 situates our contribution in the context of related research on contract languages and formal verification. Finally, Sect. 9 concludes the paper and discusses avenues for future work.

2   Legal Contracts in **Stipula**

We introduce *Stipula* through a case study modeling a legal contract for bike rentals, structured into three articles:

1. This *Agreement* shall commence when the Borrower takes possession of the Bike and remain in full force and effect until the Bike is returned to Lender. The Borrower shall return the Bike within k hours after the rental and will pay Euro `cost` in advance where half of the amount is of surcharge for late return.
2. *Payment.* Borrower shall pay the amount specified in Article 1 when this agreement commences.
3. *End.* If the Bike is returned within the agreed time specified in Article 1, then half of the `cost` will be returned to Borrower; the other half is given to the Lender. Otherwise the full `cost` is given to the Lender.

These articles are transposed into *Stipula* as follows:

```
1  stipula Bike_Rental {
2    fields cost, k
3    assets wallet, bike
4    agreement (Borrower, Lender){
5        Borrower, Lender : cost, k
6    } ⇒ @Inactive
7    @Inactive Lender : offer[b] {
8        b —o bike // the bike access code is stored in the contract
9    } ⇒ @Payment
10   @Payment Borrower : pay[x]
11     (x == cost) {
12       x —o wallet // the contract keeps the money
13       bike —o Borrower // the Borrower keeps the bike access code
14       now + k ≫ @Using {
15           wallet —o Lender // deadline expired: the whole wallet to Lender
16       } ⇒ @End
17   } ⇒ @Using
18   @Using Borrower : end { // bike returned before the deadline
19     0.5 × wallet —o wallet, Lender // half wallet to Lender
20     wallet —o Borrower // half wallet to Borrower
21   } ⇒ @End
22 }
```

Listing 1. The `Bike_Rental` contract in *Stipula*

The contract named `Bike_Rental` is defined using the `stipula` keyword and distinguishes between two core types of entities: `fields` at line 2, which store scalar values (*e.g.*, integers, booleans), and `assets` at line 3, which represent tangible or transferable items such as currencies, fungible tokens, and non-fungible tokens. The language provides ad-hoc operations for manipulating assets, thereby justifying a clear semantic distinction with fields.

Lines 4–6 define the `agreement` clause, a distinctive feature of a legal contract that models the moment when, after the possible negotiation of the contractual content, the parties, which are listed at line 4, express consent on the values of fields (in this case `cost` and `k`) – the *meeting of the minds*. The contract then starts in the state `Inactive` – line 6 –, thus producing its legal effects.

Stipula adopts a *state-machine programming style* to model *permissions, prohibitions* and *obligations* that usually change over time according to the actions that have been done (or not). For example, in the `Inactive` state, the contract is giving permission to the Lender to send an access code that will be used by the Borrower for unblocking the bike. Once the code has been sent, the contract goes into a state `Payment` where the Lender can no more withdraw from the rental and the unique permitted operation is the payment of the rental by the Borrower. In *Stipula*, permissions are specified in the *function signatures* that define the state, the party that can invoke the function and the arguments.

In the case of `offer`, the argument is an *asset* that represents the code to unblock the bike; for this reason it is in square brackets (on the contrary, standard values are in round brackets). The *move operation* `b ─o bike` at line 8 carries the token in `b` to `bike`, thus *emptying the content of* `b`. In this case the token is *non-fungible*, *i.e.*, indivisible, which means that `bike` is an empty asset that will retain the code `b` after the move.

The function `pay` at lines 10–17 specifies the payment of the rental by the Borrower. In particular, the Borrower has to send an asset `x` that corresponds to the agreed `cost` of the rental. The currency is stored in the `wallet` – line 12 – and, at the same time, the bike code is sent to the Borrower – the operation `bike ─o Borrower` at line 13 –, thus letting Borrower use the bike. The body of `pay` also contains another distinguishing feature of *Stipula*: the *event* clause. In this case, the event is scheduled at time `now + k` – lines 14–16 – and it asserts that, if the bike is not returned within the agreed time of `k` hours (starting from `now`, the time when the function `pay` is invoked), the Borrower has to pay the whole amount in the `wallet` as specified in Article 3. This mechanism is employed in *Stipula* to enforce the Borrower's *obligation* to return the bike within the specified timeframe. Notably, the `wallet` asset functions as an *escrow*, temporarily holding funds as a guarantee of compliance with the contractual terms.

The function at lines 18–21 defines the timely return of the bike by the Borrower (Article 3); the operation `0.5 × wallet ─o wallet, Lender` halves the content of the `wallet` and sends that amount to the Lender; therefore the following operation `wallet ─o Borrower` sends to the Borrower the remaining half. The use of arithmetic operations on the `wallet` asset indicates that it is *fungible*, meaning its units are interchangeable and divisible, as is typical for digital currencies or tokens representing monetary value.

Notably, the foregoing code also reflects an implicit trust placed by both the Lender and the Borrower in the contract itself, which acts as an autonomous intermediary capable of securely storing sensible information and assets. In particular, assets can be temporarily retained by legal contracts and subsequently redistributed when specific conditions are met. To support this, the language treats assets as first-class values, equipped with dedicated operations for explicit and controlled management (the move $\multimap$ and the square brackets in functions' signatures). This contrasts with the traditional rental setting, in which the Borrower typically pays the Lender upfront via credit card, and the transaction is mediated – and guaranteed – by a financial institution acting as a trusted third party, often at a cost. In contrast, *Stipula* enables contracts to directly manage asset transfers, thereby eliminating the need for external intermediaries and enabling more autonomous, cost-efficient agreements. We refer to [12] for the complete definition of the syntax and the semantics of *Stipula*.

It is important to highlight a significant consequence of the digitalization of legal contracts. As illustrated by the code in Listing 2, it is possible for the Borrower to accept the contractual terms without actually completing the payment for the rental. In this scenario, the Lender's bike becomes inaccessible: the access code – stored in the `bike` asset – has been disclosed, but no party can make legitimate use of it thereafter.

This outcome is not a failure of the digitalization process itself, but rather a flaw in the original contract design, specifically within the Articles defined at the beginning of the section. In other words, the contract omits a crucial clause that should state:

2.a If the Borrower does not pay within k/6 h, the contract is deemed invalid and the bike is returned to the Lender.

Translating this provision into *Stipula* entails refining the implementation of the `offer` function as follows:

```
7    @Inactive Lender : offer[b] {
8        b ⊸ bike // the bike access code is stored in the contract
9        now + k/6 ≫ @Payment { bike ⊸ Lender } ⇒ @End
10   } ⇒ @Payment
```

Listing 2. Refinement of the function `offer` in the `Bike_Rental` contract

3   Executing **Stipula**contracts

As a principled high-level language, *Stipula* is designed to be implementation-agnostic and does not assume any specific computing architecture. Nevertheless, given that legal contracts are critical instruments with binding obligations, their digital execution requires strong guarantees from the underlying computing platform. These guarantees are essential to ensure the correctness, security, and legal enforceability of the contract's behaviour. We identify three critical guarantees:

trust: The platform must guarantee that all parties observe a consistent and tamper-proof execution of the contract. This includes providing a reliable notion of time and supporting verifiable asset transfers between parties and contracts, thus ensuring predictable and enforceable contract behaviour.

authentication: Every function invocation must be authenticated using secure identities (*e.g.*, digital signatures or cryptographic credentials), thus ensuring that only authorized parties can interact with the contract and invoke clauses specific to their roles.

auditability: To support accountability and legal enforceability, the platform must produce auditable logs, such as event traces and transaction histories. These records enable post-execution analysis, facilitate dispute resolution, and support compliance verification.

The prototype [13] is implemented in Java and can be executed on a standard computing platform. The notion of trust is grounded in the assumption that the program operates within a secure and trusted environment – such as a bank, court, or notary office – where the integrity of the execution is guaranteed. Authentication is achieved through security credentials issued and managed by the hosting institution, ensuring that only authorized parties can access and interact with the contract. Auditability is supported by systematically recording execution logs, which are archived daily to enable traceability and post-execution verification. (In [12] we also discuss the implementation of the main elements of *Stipula* on top of a distributed system such as a blockchain.)

Let us show the execution flow of Bike_Rental. The process begins with the syntactic analysis of the input code, followed by type inference (see Sect. 5). After these preliminary steps, the interpreter evaluates the contract's agreement clause, which involves generating and displaying a unique code for each party involved. These codes serve as identifiers and access credentials, enabling secure interaction with the contract. In practical deployments, they would correspond to IDs and passwords assigned to the contracting parties. In the case of the Bike_Rental contract, two possible access codes might be:

```
--------------------

Lender: ef6h4
Borrower: MHWBs
--------------------
```

Next, the interpreter prompts the parties to input their assigned access codes, along with the initial values of the fields that require mutual agreement. Once these inputs are provided and their correspondence has been checked, the interpreter identifies and displays the set of functions that are eligible to be invoked at the current stage. For example:

```
# Please, choose which function should run:
Lender.offer()[Asset b]
```

In this scenario, only the Lender is authorized to invoke the offer function. The invocation includes a parameter representing the code used to unlock the bike, typically encoded as a numeric value. In the interpreter, this interaction is simulated by providing the Lender's access code, the name of the function to be invoked, and the corresponding unlock code, as illustrated below:

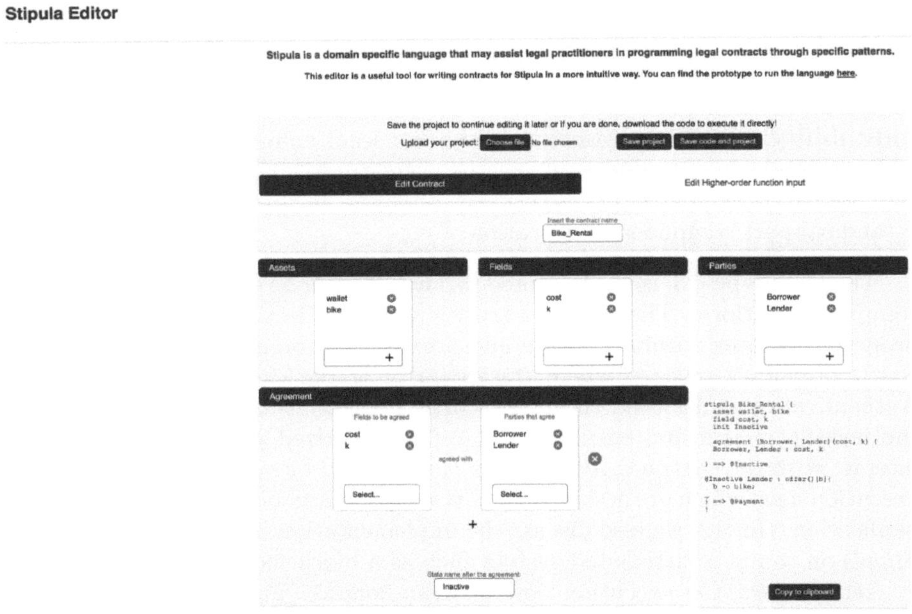

Fig. 1. The Visual Editor Interface: fields, assets, parties and the agreement

```
ef6h4.offer()[1234]
```

Afterward, the prototype interpreter executes the body of the selected function, allowing the contract to progress, by enabling the Borrower to initiate the payment for the rental. The pay function, in turn, schedules an event to be triggered k hours later. For example, if k is set to 0.1, and the Borrower fails to return the bike within 6 minutes, the event is activated automatically. As a consequence, the entire wallet balance is transferred to the Lender.

4   The Visual Code Editor

Stipula is designed to support legal practitioners and individuals with little or no familiarity with programming or formal languages. To enhance accessibility, the language is complemented by a visual interface that facilitates the drafting of contracts through schematic patterns and intuitive graphical representations. This interface lowers the entry barrier for non-technical users, enabling them to express complex contractual logic without writing code directly.

The editor is implemented as a web-based application. Its initial interface is shown in Fig. 1. The interface provides dedicated input fields through which the user can define the fundamental components of a contract, including its name, the involved assets and fields, the parties to the agreement, and the essential elements of the agreement clause. This structured input method simplifies the contract creation process and ensures that the resulting code adheres to the language's syntax and semantics. The bottom-right window contains the code of the contract (in the interface we have inserted the components of the `Bike_Rental` contract).

Following the same visual design, the editor also supports the definition of functions and events. In these cases, the interface provides graphical tools that guide the user in composing valid statements by offering selectable templates for each language construct – for example, update operations such as $x+1 \rightarrow x$ or asset transfers like $x/2 \multimap x$, A. This visual support ensures syntactic correctness and lowers the barrier for non-technical users. Figure 2 shows a snapshot of the editor displaying the implementation of the `offer` function.

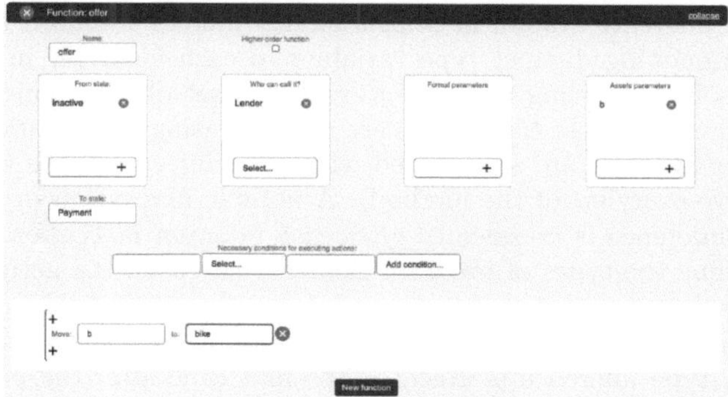

Fig. 2. The Visual Editor Interface: functions

5   Type Inference in *Stipula*

Stipula adopts a type-free surface syntax, deliberately omitting explicit type annotations. This design choice is motivated by the observation that standard legal contracts do not typically involve typed declarations, and such annotations may appear unintuitive or even opaque to non-technical users, particularly legal practitioners. Despite the absence of type annotations, *Stipula* includes a type inference system capable of automatically deriving the types of assets, fields, and function arguments. This system enables early detection of programming errors at compile time, thereby ensuring basic correctness and improving reliability. In this section, we outline the main design principles and technical foundations of the type inference system.

The *Stipula* interpreter has the following *primitive types*

$$T ::= \quad \text{real} \quad | \quad \text{bool} \quad | \quad \text{string} \quad | \quad \text{time} \quad | \quad \text{asset}$$

that mirror the set of values of the language: real numbers, booleans, strings, time values, and assets. In the current prototype a time value is a real number representing hours. For example, the *relative time* expressions `now + 2.0` means two hours later (with respect to the execution of the enclosing function) and `now + 0.5` means 30 minutes. *Stipula* also admits *absolute time* values as the date `"2022/1/1:00:15"T`. With respect to the `asset` type, the current implementation does not yet distinguish between divisible and indivisible assets. Each asset is represented as a sequence of digits, which may encode either a unique identifier or a numerical amount. This simplification reflects the current state of the system, but future releases will refine this model by introducing an explicit distinction between divisible and indivisible assets. For instance, in the `Bike_Rental` contract, the `wallet` asset is considered divisible, as demonstrated by the operation at line 19 of Listing 2.

The type inference system in *Stipula* largely follows standard techniques. It begins by associating distinct type variables to each identifier in the program and proceeds by traversing the code to collect a set of type constraints. Once parsing is complete, these constraints are resolved using a unification algorithm, and the type variables are substituted with their inferred types (see [31] for a comprehensive overview of the method). A notable innovation in our approach is that type inference *is re-executed after each function invocation*, allowing the system to refine the types of program elements based on the actual arguments passed to the function and their subsequent assignment to fields. This dynamic refinement enhances both flexibility and precision in the type system.

As usual, type inference is executed the first time after the parsing. In the case of `Bike_Rental`, the interpreter returns

```
TYPE CHECKING ===
Assets:
    wallet type: Asset
    bike type: Asset
Fields:
    cost type: Real
    k type: Time
Functions:
    Lender.offer()[Asset]
    Borrower.pay()[Asset]
    Borrower.end()[]
==================
```

As the reader may observe, following the initial type inference phase, no type variables remain in the program: the types of all elements – fields, assets, and functions – are fully resolved. While this outcome may appear straightforward for assets and functions in the `Bike_Rental` contract, it is less immediately evident in the case of fields. For example, the field `k` is inferred to have type `Time` due to its occurrence within a time expression. Similarly, the field `cost` is assigned type `Real` because of the equality "`x == cost`" at line 11 of Listing 2. Since `x` is an asset and assets in this context represent real-valued quantities, the unification process infers `cost` to also have type `Real`.

If the equality "`x == cost`" is removed from the contract, the type inference system is no longer able to deduce a concrete primitive type for `cost`. As a result, the system outputs:

```
. . .
    cost type: Type0
```

This is because, in the absence of a usage context that constrains its type, `cost` remains unconstrained and retains its original type variable (`Type0`) that cannot be resolved to a specific primitive type.

The type of `cost` is determined *after the agreement*, once the Lender and the Borrower have decided its initial value. In fact the system, at that point, will return the refined type:

```
. . .
    cost type: Real
```

6   Spotting Unreachable Clauses

A substantial problem in the legal contract domain is spotting normative clauses, either functions or events, that will never be applied. In fact, it is possible, that an unreachable clause is considered too oppressive by one of the parties (take, for instance, the event of the Article 3 in Sect. 2), thus making the legal relationship fail. In [16], we established that the interplay between state evolution, temporal constraints, and non-determinism renders the *unreachability problem* – *i.e.*, determining whether a clause can never be executed – *undecidable*. As a consequence, no complete algorithm can exist for solving this problem in general. Therefore, our analysis must necessarily be conservative: we can aim at a sound analyzer that can safely identify unreachable clauses, though it may not detect all such cases. One such analyzer has been developed in [26], and it is now integrated into the *Stipula* workbench. In the following, we outline the core design principles that guided its development.

The unreachability analyzer determines the set of reachable clauses through a closure operation based on a fixpoint technique. A key challenge in this analysis is the detection of *time anomalies* – clauses whose execution times are incompatible with the overall behaviour of the contract. To address this issue, the analyzer operates over *logical times*, which are symbolic abstractions representing the system clock at runtime, approximated statically. A clause is included in the set of reachable clauses only if its associated logical time is consistent with the logical time of the computation leading to it. If the resulting constraints over logical times are unsatisfiable, the corresponding clauses are deemed unreachable and reported as such. A major complication arises from the presence of *cyclic behaviours*, which induce infinite computations and make direct consistency checks intractable. To circumvent this, we introduce the notion of *linear traces* – finite surrogates of computations in which each clause appears at most once. These traces are well-suited for static time reasoning due to their finiteness, but they lack the expressiveness to fully capture the semantics of cyclic behaviours. To maximize coverage, we adopt a hybrid strategy: the analyzer applies time-based reasoning to acyclic clauses using logical times, while reverting to a standard, untimed analysis for clauses involved in cycles. This combination balances precision and tractability, enabling the detection of many practical cases of unreachability despite the underlying undecidability of the problem.

For instance, applying the analyzer to the `Bike_Rental` contract yields a comprehensive diagnostic trace, which concludes with the following summarized result:

```
"unreachable_code": []
```

The analyzer's output includes a list of the clauses examined, along with the set of linear traces computed – referred to as R in the implementation. A clause is reported under the `unreachable_code` section if it does not appear in any linear trace, indicating that it cannot be executed in any feasible execution path. For example, consider the `Bike_Rental` contract: if a typographical error occurs at line 14, where `@Usng` is written instead of the intended `@Using`, the analyzer will produce the following error message:

```
"unreachable_code": [ "ev('Usng', 'Ev', 14, 'End')" ]
```

where 14 is the line number of the event of `Bike_Rental`.

The unreachability analyzer is also capable of identifying clauses that are conditionally reachable. This situation arises, for example, when the time expressions associated with events depend on contract fields (as illustrated by the `Bike_Rental` contract). In such cases, the continuation of a contract may be possible only under specific conditions on field values?for instance, the analyzer may report a reachability constraint of the form

```
"reachability constraint": [ x >= 5 ]
```

At present, our analyzer incorporates a lightweight constraint-solving mechanism. It performs partial evaluations that exploit the additive structure of time expressions, which suffices to detect straightforward conditions. However, its capabilities are limited: in particular, it does not compute transitive closures of constraints or reason about more complex dependencies. A natural next step in the development of the prototype is to integrate the analyzer with an established, off-the-shelf constraint solver, thereby enhancing its precision and enabling it to capture richer classes of conditional reachability scenarios.

7   Verifying Liquidity

Liquidity is a fundamental security property for any program that manages assets, such as those written in *Stipula*. A *Stipula* contract is said to be *liquid* if no asset remains indefinitely locked within the program – *i.e.*, all resources are ultimately redeemable by at least one of the involved parties [3]. For instance, a contract violates liquidity if the body of a function fails to utilize resources transferred by the caller during invocation. Similarly, liquidity is compromised if the contract terminates with any asset holding a non-zero value – indicating that the resource has not been fully consumed or returned.

The concept of liquidity has been studied extensively, and multiple formalizations exist in the literature. In our previous work [10,25], we adopt the notion of *multiparty strategyless liquidity*, as defined in the taxonomy of [1,3]. This model assumes cooperative behaviour: all parties to the contract invoke the functions made available to them, without adversarial strategies or omissions.

Our liquidity analyzer is based on a type system that symbolically tracks the effects of functions on assets using abstract names. The system ensures a correctness property, which guarantees that the inferred (liquidity) type of the final state of a computation soundly over-approximates the actual runtime state. This allows us to conservatively verify liquidity by checking whether, in all feasible computations, the symbolic asset values at termination are zero – thus ensuring that no residual resources remain trapped within the contract.

We identify two liquidity properties. The first one is h-*separate liquidity*: *if an asset* h *becomes not-empty in a state then there is a continuation where* h *is empty in its final state*. While h-separate liquidity is satisfactory in contracts where assets are separated (no asset field is moved to another asset field, for instance when pairwise different assets have different categories, *e.g.* euros, cars, houses), it is inadequate in unrestricted contracts that move assets between asset fields. In these cases, the following stronger property is more reasonable: *if an asset becomes not-empty in a state then there is a continuation where all the assets are empty in its final state*.

For the two properties, h-separate liquidity and liquidity, we have designed two analysis algorithms with different computational costs and precision accuracies. The computational cost of the less precise algorithm is quadratic with respect to the number of functions. The second algorithm is more precise because, for instance, it accepts contracts that empty assets by means of several function invocations. However, more precision requires more complexity because one has to analyze *computations*. The crucial issue of the analysis is therefore designing a terminating algorithm given that computations may be *infinitely many* because contracts may have cycles. For this reason we restrict to computations whose length is bound by a value (actually we found more reasonable computations where every function can be invoked a bounded number of times). The computational cost of k-separate liquidity and liquidity algorithms is higher than the previous case: it is exponential with respect to the number of functions. It is important to note that the algorithms assume all clauses in the contract are reachable. Consequently, as a preliminary step, they verify the absence of unreachable clauses, as discussed in Sect. 6 (in [10,25] we circumvent this assumption by restricting to the sub-language without events).

We apply our liquidity analysis algorithm to the `Bike_Rental` contract. In this case, both `wallet`-separate and `bike`-separate liquidity analyses are effective, as the two assets are handled independently and are never intermingled. Focusing on `wallet`-separate liquidity, the algorithm proceeds as follows:

- It first checks whether there exists any clause that may render the `wallet` asset non-empty. This condition is satisfied by the pay function, which increases the balance of wallet.
- Next, the algorithm verifies whether, for every possible execution path following this clause, there exists at least one subsequent clause that empties `wallet`. Since the contract is acyclic, the set of continuations is finite. In this case, there are two distinct continuations: (1) the invocation of the `end` function and (2) the execution of the scheduled event at line 14.
- In both cases, the analysis confirms that wallet is correctly emptied, as evidenced by the annotations in the liquidity type system.

With respect to `bike`-separate liquidity, the algorithm proceeds as follows:

- By analyzing the liquidity type system, it identifies that the `offer` function initializes (*i.e.*, fills) the `bike` asset.
- It then computes the set of possible continuations following this action. In this case, the continuations are: (1) `pay; end` and (2) `pay; event_14`.
- Both these execution paths results in the `bike` asset being emptied – *cf.* the move operation at line 13. Therefore, the contract is also `bike`-separate liquid.

While the theoretical framework of the liquidity analysis has been fully developed, the prototype implementation is still under development at the time of writing.

8   Related Work

Dwivedi et al. [19] provide a systematic review of smart contract languages, identifying critical features for drafting legally binding digital agreements. Some of these features are present in existing languages such as Solidity [20], Flint [34], Obsidian [9], and Move [8]. For instance, the representation of contracts as finite state machines, caller-based access restrictions (*e.g.*, Solidity modifiers, Flint's capability blocks, Obsidian's typestates), and the treatment of assets as primitive data types are widely adopted [2,7,14,35]. However, these languages are not designed to model legal obligations explicitly and lack direct support for core legal constructs such as agreement, obligation, prohibition, and judicial enforceability.

In contrast, *Stipula* introduces constructs and patterns that establish a clear correspondence between program logic and legal semantics. Its design enables legal concepts like the meeting of the minds, permissions, and time-bound obligations to be expressed directly and unambiguously in code.

Several efforts have focused on transforming legal norms into formal specifications [15,22,24,33], offering semantic representations of rights and duties. However, these approaches often result in high-level specification languages that are difficult to compile into executable code. *Stipula* fills this gap by acting as an intermediate language – bridging the expressiveness of legal specifications with the executability of programming languages like Java or Solidity. In this respect, it shares motivations with Catala [30] and Orlando [4], which formalize specific legal domains through a core calculus with human-readable syntax. Following the idea of legal calculi [5], *Stipula* offers a minimal but expressive operational model, formalized using concurrency theory.

Unlike declarative legal markup languages such as OpenLaw [39], Lexon [29], and Accord [36], which rely on parameterized templates and external smart contracts, *Stipula* uses explicit programming patterns to capture legal constructs programmatically (see [12]). While Lexon attempts to bridge natural language and code via structured English-like syntax, it lacks formal semantics, leaving the behaviour of its contracts entirely to the generated Solidity code. In contrast, *Stipula* provides built-in primitives – such as agreement and asset transfer – that make the contract's behaviour both explicit and verifiable.

Stipula also differs significantly from financial contract domain specific languages like Marlowe [35] and Findel [7], which are built around algebraic combinators tailored to financial logic. Marlowe ensures liveness through mandatory timeouts and default paths, but this pull-based interaction model often results in indirect and complex control flows. *Stipula* enables a more direct and agent-oriented model, where roles, state transitions, and asset flows are clearly attributed, and timeouts or escape clauses are optional and programmable. While Marlowe executes on the Cardano blockchain using slot-based time, similar mechanisms can be adapted to implement *Stipula*'s timed events on blockchain platforms [12].

We argue that legal contracts are inherently more expressive than financial ones, and require a richer programming model. Unlike Marlowe and Findel, where an interpreter evaluates a fixed combinator structure, *Stipula* defines contracts as programs that are compiled into executable artifacts (e.g., Java applications or smart contracts). Its primitives – such as named states, functions, and events – enable fine-grained control over contract behaviour and lifecycle.

Finally, as regards *Stipula* visual editor, we have been inspired by visual programming tools (*e.g.*, Blockly [38], Babbage [32]) and legal markup languages (*e.g.*, SLCML [13]).

9   Conclusion

We have presented the *Stipula* platform, a comprehensive suite of tools designed to help legal practitioners and developers write, test, debug, and manage legal contracts effectively. The platform currently includes a *visual code editor* for intuitive contract authoring in *Stipula*, an interpreter for automatic execution, and a set of analyzers for verifying legally relevant properties such as clause unreachability and the absence of frozen assets. Together, these components form a unified toolchain that makes formal methods more accessible to non-experts while retaining technical rigor.

This paper has not included an empirical evaluation of the platform. As an immediate step in future work, we plan to provide benchmarks, scalability studies, and case analyses that extend beyond the illustrative examples available in the repository. In parallel, we aim to conduct user studies and collect evidence of adoption among legal practitioners, thereby assessing the usability and practical value of the editor and toolchain. Another priority is to evaluate the scope limitations of the current analyzers: for instance, the unreachability analysis assumes the absence of nested cycles, while the liquidity analysis requires bounded computations. We intend to demonstrate that these restrictions do not significantly limit applicability in practice.

Beyond these analyses, we are pursuing two broader research directions. The first concerns the evolution of the *Stipula* language itself. Recent work has explored mechanisms to support *amendments*, which capture runtime modifications of contractual obligations (*e.g.*, due to force majeure or hardship), and the *integration of norms*, which reflects the fact that contractual obligations are shaped not only by the clauses explicitly stated by the parties but also by implicit legal provisions that ensure validity and regulate legal effects. These extensions have been studied theoretically in [27,28]; prototype support for amendments is already available [13], whereas tooling for norm integration remains an open challenge.

The second direction involves the development of advanced verification tools. We are currently investigating *formal verification mechanisms* to check both partial and total correctness [23]. Our approach translates *Stipula* contracts into JML-annotated Java code, which can then be analyzed using deductive verification tools such as KeY [6]. Counterexamples produced during verification can be mapped back to the contractual level, enabling systematic debugging. At present, our verifier supports contracts with cycles without any state in common (disjoint), and we have developed a prototype for a basic correctness analyzer. Ongoing work aims to lift this restriction, thereby extending verification to contracts with overlapping cycles and richer control flow, potentially through interactive theorem proving or hybrid strategies combining automation with user guidance.

In summary, while the current *Stipula* platform already offers a practical toolchain for authoring and analyzing legal contracts, substantial opportunities remain for empirical validation, language extensions, and advanced verification techniques. These lines of research will further strengthen the platform's applicability and reliability, and ultimately contribute to bridging the gap between formal methods and legal practice.

Sententia Finalis

This paper is dedicated to Alessandro Fantechi on the occasion of the Festschrift celebrating his 70th birthday. Alessandro and Stefania Gnesi were my undergraduate thesis supervisors; they were the ones who introduced me to formal methods and concurrency theory, and who inspired my passion for these fields. After my thesis, we first became friends and then colleagues, and over the years we have always kept in touch. Happy birthday, Alessandro!

References

1. Bartoletti, M., Lande, S., Murgia, M., Zunino, R.: Verifying liquidity of recursive bitcoin contracts. Log. Methods Comput. Sci. **18**(1) (2022)
2. Bartoletti, M., Zunino, R.: BitML: a calculus for bitcoin smart contracts. In: Proceedings of Computer and Communications Security, CCS 2018, pp. 83–100. ACM, New York, NY, USA (2018)
3. Bartoletti, M., Zunino, R.: Verifying liquidity of bitcoin contracts. In: Proceedings of the 8th International Conference on Principles of Security and Trust, pp. 222–247. Springer International Publishing (2019). https://doi.org/10.1007/978-3-030-17138-4_10
4. Basu, S., Foster, N., Grimmelmann, J.: Property conveyances as a programming language. In: Proceedings of the 2019 ACM SIGPLAN International Symposium on New Ideas, New Paradigms, and Reflections on Programming and Software, Onward! 2019, pp. 128–142. Association for Computing Machinery, New York, NY, USA (2019)
5. Basu, S., Mohan, A., Grimmelmann, J., Foster, N.: Legal calculi. Technical report, ProLaLa 2022 ProLaLa Programming Languages and the Law (2022). https://popl22.sigplan.org/details/prolala-2022-papers/6/Legal-Calculi
6. Beckert, B., et al.: The java verification tool key: a tutorial. In: Platzer, A., Rozier, K.Y., Pradella, M., Rossi, M. (eds.) Proceedings of the 26th International Symposium on Formal Methods, Milan, Italy, volume 14934 of LNCS, pp. 597–623. Springer, Cham (2024)
7. Biryukov, A., Khovratovich, D., Tikhomirov, S.: Findel: secure derivative contracts for ethereum. In: Brenner, M., et al. (eds.) FC 2017. LNCS, vol. 10323, pp. 453–467. Springer, Cham (2017). https://doi.org/10.1007/978-3-319-70278-0_28
8. Blackshear, S., et al.: Move: a language with programmable resources (2021). https://developers.diem.com/main/docs/move-paper
9. Coblenz, M., et al.: Obsidian: typestate and assets for safer blockchain programming. ACM Trans. Program. Lang. Syst. **42**(3) (2020)
10. Crafa, S., Laneve, S.: Liquidity analysis in resource-aware programming. In: Proceedings of the 18th International Conference on Formal Aspects of Component Software FACS 2022, volume 13712 of Lecture Notes in Computer Science, pp. 205–221. Springer (2022). https://doi.org/10.1007/978-3-031-20872-0_12
11. Crafa, S., Laneve, C.: Programming legal contracts: a beginners guide to *Stipula*. In: Ahrendt, W., Beckert, B., Bubel, R., Johnsen, E.B. (eds.) The Logic of Software. A Tasting Menu of Formal Methods - Essays Dedicated to Reiner Hähnle on the Occasion of His 60th Birthday, volume 13360 of LNCS, pp. 129–146. Springer, Cham (2022). https://doi.org/10.1007/978-3-031-08166-8_7
12. Crafa, S., Laneve, C., Sartor, G., Veschetti, A.: Pacta sunt servanda: legal contracts in Stipula. Sci. Comput. Program. **225**, 102911 (2023)
13. Crafa, S., Laneve, C., Veschetti, A.: Stipula prototype (2022). github https://github.com/stipula-language
14. Crary, K., Sullivan, M.J.: Peer-to-peer affine commitment using bitcoin. In: Proceedings of the 36th ACM SIGPLAN Conference on Programming Language Design and Implementation, PLDI 2015, pp. 479–488. Association for Computing Machinery, New York, NY, USA (2015)
15. de Kruijff, J.T., Weigand, H.H.: Introducing commitruleml for smart contracts. In: Proceedings of the 13th International Workshop on Value Modeling and Business Ontologies (VMBO), volume 2383. CEUR-WS.org (2019)

16. Delzanno, G., Laneve, C., Sangnier, A., Zavattaro, G.: Decidability problems for micro-stipula. In: Proceedings of the 27th International Conference COORDINATION 2025, volume 15731 of Lecture Notes in Computer Science, pp. 133–152. Springer (2025). https://doi.org/10.1007/978-3-031-95589-1_7

17. Dervishi, E.: Stipula workbench: an integrated environment to design, analyze, and execute stipula code. Bachelor's thesis, University of Bologna (2025)

18. Dwivedi, V., Norta, A., Wulf, A., Leiding, B., Saxena, S., Udokwu, C.: A formal specification smart-contract language for legally binding decentralized autonomous organizations. IEEE Access **9**, 76069–76082 (2021)

19. Dwivedi, V., Pattanaik, V., Deval, V., Dixit, A., Norta, A., Draheim, D.: Legally enforceable smart-contract languages: a systematic literature review. ACM Comput. Surv. **54**(5) (2021)

20. Ethereum: Solidity documentation (2025). https://docs.soliditylang.org/en/v0.8.30/

21. Evangelisti, S.: Analisi di Contratti Legali in Stipula. Bachelor's thesis, University of Bologna (2024)

22. Frantz, C.K., Nowostawski, M.: From institutions to code: towards automated generation of smart contracts. In: Proceedings of the 2016 IEEE 1st International Workshops on Foundations and Applications of Self* Systems (FAS*W), pp. 210–215 (2016)

23. Hähnle, R., Laneve, C., Veschetti, A.: Formal verification of legal contracts: a translation-based approach. In: Proceedings of the 20th International Conference on Integrated Formal Methods (iFM 2025), Lecture Notes in Computer Science. Springer (2025). https://doi.org/10.1007/978-3-032-10794-7_4

24. He, X., Qin, B., Zhu, Y., Chen, X., Liu, Y.: Spesc: a specification language for smart contracts. In: Proceedings of the 2018 IEEE 42nd Annual Computer Software and Applications Conference (COMPSAC), vol. 01, pp. 132–137 (2018)

25. Laneve, C.: Liquidity analysis in resource-aware programming. J. Log. Algebraic Methods Program. **135**(100889), 1–18 (2023)

26. Laneve, C.: Reachability analysis in micro-stipula. In: Proceedings of the 26th International Symposium on Principles and Practice of Declarative Programming, PPDP 2024, pp. 17:1–17:12. ACM (2024)

27. Laneve, C., Parenti, A., Sartor, G.: Legal contracts amending with Stipula. In: Jongmans, S.S., Lopes, A. (eds.) Proceedings of the 25th International Conference COORDINATION, volume 13908 of LNCS, pp. 253–270. Springer, Cham (2023). https://doi.org/10.1007/978-3-031-35361-1_14

28. Laneve, C., Parenti, A., Sartor, G.: Integration of statutory norms in computable contracts. Comput. Law Secur. Rev. (2025)

29. Lexon Foundation: Lexon (2019). http://www.lexon.tech

30. Merigoux, D., Chataing, N., Protzenko, J.: Catala: a programming language for the law. Proc. ACM Program. Lang. **5**(ICFP), 1–29 (2021)

31. Pierce, B.C.: Types and Programming Languages. The MIT Press (2002)

32. Reitwiebner, C.: Babbage - a mechanical smart contract language (2018). https://medium.com/@chriseth/babbage-a-mechanical-smart-contract-language-5c8329ec5a0e

33. Schneider, G.: Specification and Verification of Normative Documents, pp. 307–343. Springer International Publishing (2022). https://doi.org/10.1007/978-3-030-38800-3_6

34. Schrans, F., Eisenbach, S., Drossopoulou, S.: Writing safe smart contracts in flint. In: Proceedings of the 2nd International Conference on Art, Science, and Engi-

neering of Programming, Programming 2018 Companion, pp. 218–219. ACM, New York, USA, (2018)
35. Seijas, P.L., Nemish, A., Smith, D., Thompson, S.: Marlowe: implementing and analysing financial contracts on blockchain. In: Proceedings of the Workshop on Financial Cryptography and Data Security, pp. 496–511. Springer International Publishing (2020). https://doi.org/10.1007/978-3-030-54455-3_35
36. Open Source Contributors: The Accord Project (2018). https://accordproject.org
37. Venturi, E.: Implementazione di un'interfaccia grafica per la scrittura di contratti legali nel linguaggio Stipula. Bachelor's thesis, University of Bologna (2023)
38. Weingaertner, T., Rao, R., Ettlin, J., Suter, P., Dublanc, P.: Smart contracts using blockly: representing a purchase agreement using a graphical programming language. In: Proceedings of the 2018 Crypto Valley Conference on Blockchain Technology (CVCBT), pp. 55–64 (2018)
39. Wright, A., Roon, D., ConsenSys, A.G.: OpenLaw web site (2019). https://www.openlaw.io

User-Friendly Formal Verification
of Protection Systems in Electrical
Networks

Alessandro Nocentini[1], Ahmed Nagy Abdelkhalek Mansour[1],
Samuele Grillo[1], Enrico Ragaini[2], and Matteo Rossi[3]

[1] Dipartimento di Elettronica, Informazione e Bioingegneria, Politecnico di Milano,
20133 Milan, Italy
{alessandro.nocentini,ahmednagy.mansour,samuele.grillo}@polimi.it
[2] ABB S.p.A, SACE, Bergamo, Italy
enrico.ragaini@it.abb.com
[3] Dipartimento di Meccanica, Politecnico di Milano, 20133 Milan, Italy
matteo.rossi@polimi.it

Abstract. Automatic verification processes are increasingly essential in
power systems to enhance productivity and reliability, particularly in the
configuration of protection schemes. These systems disconnect parts of
the electrical network when faults occur, while ensuring selectivity so
that only the minimal portion of load is left unfed. This work presents a
novel, user-friendly tool that supports the formal verification of circuit
breaker configurations in low-voltage distribution grids. Unlike previous
approaches based on the UPPAAL model checker with JSON-based network descriptions, the proposed tool offers a more intuitive interface and
greater control of the verification process.

A custom notation is introduced to graphically represent the target
grids, complemented by the design and implementation of an application that enables seamless modeling and verification. MATLAB was chosen as the development environment, allowing the creation of a custom
Simulink library for the modeling phase and an App Designer interface
for the application. The resulting prototype incorporates various support features and integrates with DOCweb, a software platform used in
industrial practice. Comprehensive testing, including summative usability evaluation, confirmed the tool's effectiveness and demonstrated its
potential to significantly streamline verification workflows in power system protection.

Keywords: Formal verification · User Interface · Protection systems ·
Timed automata · Simulink · Matlab

1   Introduction

Formal methods and formal verification techniques are very useful tools in practice for ensuring the correctness, safety, and reliability of safety-critical systems

© The Author(s), under exclusive license to Springer Nature Switzerland AG 2026

M. H. ter Beek et al. (Eds.): Fantechi Festschrift, LNCS 16470, pp. 178–192, 2026.
https://doi.org/10.1007/978-3-032-12484-5_10

such as those in avionics, railways, and power generation and distribution [2]. In these domains, system failures can have severe or even catastrophic consequences, and mathematical rigor in specifications, verification and validation helps meet demanding safety, performance, and regulatory requirements [19]. Nevertheless, there is a persistent *usability gap*: domain experts (for example, transportation engineers or electrical engineers) typically lack the specialized training required to build formal models from scratch or to carry out formal verification directly. Their day-to-day notations and tools are often semi-formal or informal (e.g., informal diagrams, domain-specific languages, block diagrams), which means that adopting formal verification often involves a steep learning curve or the involvement of external experts [3]. To bridge this gap, tools are needed that allow domain experts to work in the notations they are familiar with, while automatically generating from those notations formal models amenable to rigorous verification. Crucially, such tools must support the *whole workflow*— from the initial model creation, through verification, to the generation of feedback and iterative refinement of the models—so that formal methods become integral, usable, and effective in real engineering practice.

In this paper, we present the user-friendly extension of our Automated Protection system Verification (APV) Tool, which is designed to help and guide power system engineers in creating and verifying models that allow them to check crucial system properties. In particular, the tool focuses on supporting the verification of the *selectivity* of protection systems in electrical distribution networks, a property essential for ensuring both reliability and safety.

In the field of power distribution, low-voltage (LV) distribution grids are the backbone of electricity supply, making their meticulous planning and precise setup essential for seamless power delivery. A critical aspect of these grids is their protection system, which primarily consists of circuit breakers (CBs) designed to safeguard the network from faults and overloads. The correct configuration of these protection systems is paramount, as it directly impacts the reliability and safety of the power supply. A protection system guarantees the selectivity property when it ensures that, in the event of a fault, only the CB nearest to the issue is activated, disconnecting the smallest possible section of the grid. This minimizes power disruption to end consumers. The growing complexity of these grids has increased the need for accurate modeling and verification of these protection systems.

Despite the development of a fully automated verification method using formal models and the UPPAAL model checker [14,15], a significant usability gap remains. This existing approach requires users to have specialized expertise in JSON, MATLAB, and UPPAAL to manually create network descriptions, run verifications, and interpret the raw results. This high barrier to entry limits its accessibility for domain experts who may not specialize in formal verification methods.

To address these limitations, this paper introduces a novel, user-friendly version of our APV Tool designed to make the formal verification of protection systems more accessible. The primary objective is to enable engineers, even those without deep expertise in formal methods, to verify the correctness of CB configurations during the early design stages of distribution grids. The approach involves two main steps: first, the creation of a high-level custom notation for graphically modeling LV distribution grids, and second, the development of a MATLAB application with an intuitive Graphical User Interface (GUI). This application integrates all verification steps, shielding users from the complexities of the underlying processes.

This work makes several new contributions. It introduces a novel workflow that streamlines the entire verification process, from graphical modeling to post-processed results interpretation. The tool leverages a custom Simulink library for intuitive, block-based grid modeling, replacing the cumbersome manual creation of JSON files. Furthermore, it enhances efficiency by integrating with existing industrial software, such as ABB's DOCweb, allowing for the automatic import and conversion of existing grid models. The final prototype, validated through comprehensive usability testing, represents a significant step toward making formal verification methods practical and accessible in an industrial context.

This paper is organized as follows. Section 2 discusses related works. Section 3 provides background information on LV distribution grids, protection systems, and previous work on formal verification. Section 4 describes the methodology, detailing the custom notation, the automated generation of JSON files, and the implementation of the APV Tool. Section 5 presents the results, including the final product, the verification and validation process, and the outcomes of usability testing. Finally, Sect. 6 offers concluding remarks and discusses future work.

2   Related Work

The current landscape of research and practice relevant to this work can be grouped into two main areas. The first focuses on recent advances in graphical interfaces for formal verification, where the emphasis lies in making rigorous methods accessible to non-experts through user-friendly environments. The second concerns international standards and existing tools that support the modeling and graphical representation of LV distribution grids. These efforts establish the technical foundation and interoperability requirements upon which practical applications are built. Together, these perspectives contextualize the development of the APV tool and highlight the broader trend of embedding domain knowledge and verification capabilities within approachable GUI-based frameworks.

2.1   Graphical Interfaces for Formal Verification

Recent research has emphasized the role of graphical interfaces in lowering the entry barrier to formal verification and proof development. For example, Baanen et al. [1] introduced ProofWidgets, a framework for constructing interactive GUIs within the Lean theorem prover. By embedding interface development directly in the prover's metaprogramming environment, ProofWidgets enables dynamic visualization of proof states, discoverable tactics, and interactive exploration of terms, without requiring external tools or specialized coding environments. This approach parallels the objectives of our work, where a MATLAB-based GUI was developed to simplify the modeling and verification of LV distribution grids. Both approaches share the motivation of bridging the gap between powerful formal methods and practical usability.

Similarly, earlier work such as [4] proposed a general-purpose environment for the design and verification of complex hardware and software systems with a strong emphasis on usability. By encapsulating formal methods within a graphical, component-based modeling environment, [4] aimed to make verification accessible to engineers without specialized expertise. While [4] remained a broadly conceived framework, the APV tool can be seen as a domain-specific instantiation of this philosophy, tailored to the needs of electrical engineers working with LV distribution grids.

Taken together, these contributions reflect a broader research trajectory: embedding advanced verification workflows within approachable, domain-specific GUI environments that democratize access to rigorous verification technologies.

2.2 Standards and Tools for LV Grids

International standards play a crucial role in ensuring interoperability and consistency in the modeling of electrical power systems. Among them, the Common Information Model (CIM) [6], maintained by the IEC, provides a unified ontology for describing network models [18]. Of particular interest are IEC 61970 [12], originally intended for transmission systems but extended through CGMES to support distribution networks, and IEC 61968 [11], specifically designed for Distribution Management Systems (DMS), which enables the exchange of network models in both balanced and unbalanced LV grids. Complementary to CIM, the IEEE 315-1975 standard [9] and IEC 60617 [10] offer standardized graphical symbols for representing components, many of which remain widely used despite IEEE 315's deprecation. In practice, large industrial players such as ABB adopt IEC 60617 across their documentation and software (e.g., ABB's DOC and DOCweb[1]), reinforcing its relevance.

Beyond standards, several open-source tools have been developed to graphically represent LV grids. CIMDraw, for example, provides a web-based interface for visualizing and editing CIM-compliant models, including support for CGMES profiles [5,7]. Other general-purpose environments, such as Simulink [16] and OpenModelica [17], offer flexible modeling capabilities across domains, allowing the creation of custom components and libraries suitable for electrical distribution grids. These solutions highlight a consistent demand for graphical, user-friendly environments that abstract away complexity while adhering to established standards.

---

[1] new.abb.com/low-voltage/products/docweb.

3   Background

LV distribution grids form the backbone of electrical networks, delivering power to homes, businesses, and industries. Their complexity and interconnection make them vulnerable to faults, which can compromise reliability and safety. Protection systems are designed to automatically disconnect faulty sections to mitigate hazards, limit equipment damage, and prevent cascading failures. These systems rely on CBs that operate according to timing properties and current thresholds. Ensuring selectivity—where only the breaker closest to the fault trips—is critical to minimize the amount of unfed load. However, configuring such systems is still performed manually by domain experts, making the process error-prone.

Selectivity is typically achieved through time–current coordination, the most widely used method since it can be implemented with conventional CBs without requiring real-time communication. Under this approach, a CB triggers when the current exceeds its pickup threshold and trips after a defined delay, with microcontroller-based devices enabling adjustable curves. Properly coordinated curves ensure a correct tripping sequence, isolating only the faulted section while maintaining service elsewhere.

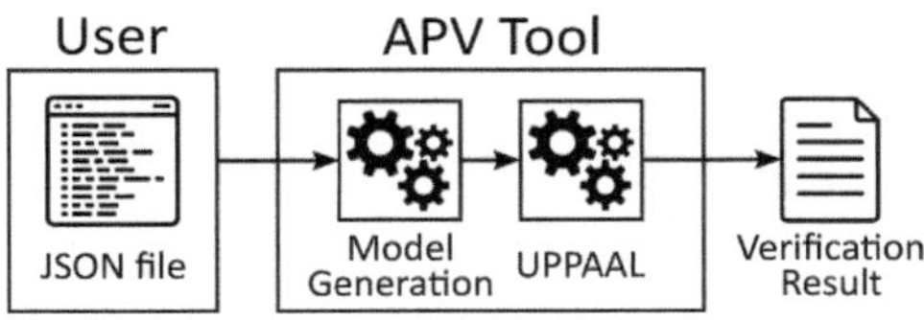

Fig. 1. Original workflow of the APV tool.

Given the importance of accurate configurations, formal methods have been proposed to improve reliability. A previous approach [14,15], introduced a fully automated verification method based on Timed Automata (TA) and implemented in the APV tool. In this previous work, whose workflow is depicted in Fig. 1, JSON-based descriptions of the grid were manually created by users, automatically transformed into TA models, and then checked with the UPPAAL model checker. This allowed selectivity to be formally verified and counterexamples to be generated when the property did not hold. While effective, the approach required users to manually prepare JSON input files and interpret raw verification results, limiting its usability.

To address these limitations, the present work introduces an improved workflow, shown in Fig. 2. The new workflow enhances usability by providing a graphical interface for grid modeling, integrating all verification steps, and including post-processing of results for improved interpretation. This approach streamlines the entire process, making it more accessible to engineers with different levels of expertise.

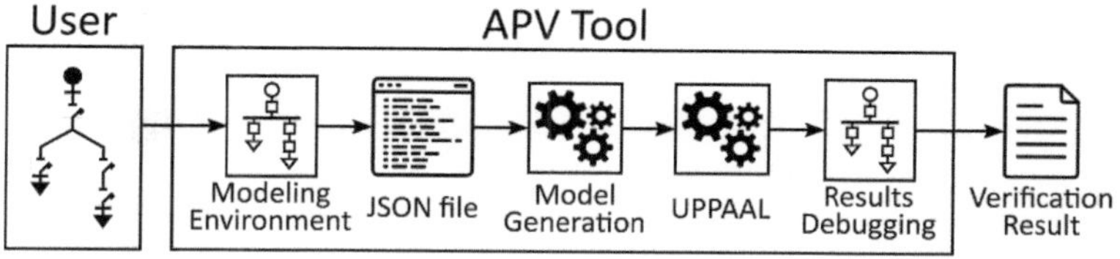

Fig. 2. Proposed workflow with graphical modeling, automated verification, and post-processed results.

4 Methodology

The development of the proposed tool followed a classic software engineering approach, with several stages designed to meet pre-defined goals and requirements, ultimately producing a complete, usable prototype. The core of the methodology involved two primary parts: first, the creation of a custom graphical notation for modeling LV distribution grids and a method to convert these models into the required JSON format; and second, the development of a MATLAB application to consolidate all process steps into a single, intuitive GUI.

4.1 Custom Notation

To facilitate the graphical modeling of electrical grids, a high-level custom notation was developed. The chosen representation aimed to be general and widely recognizable, while also being precise and simple, combining indications from established international standards like CIM, IEEE 315-1975, and IEC 60617. The goal was to ensure that network components are easily identifiable and the overall representation is accurate and intuitive. This was achieved by creating a custom Simulink library of components representing key elements in low-voltage distribution grids (Fig. 3).

Simulink was chosen as the modeling environment due to its flexibility, its block masking feature, and its seamless integration with MATLAB, which was already used to manage the UPPAAL verification process. Each component in the library was created by applying a mask to an existing Simulink block, which allowed for the addition of tunable parameters tailored to the JSON file requirements for the verification process. MATLAB code was used to implement callback functions providing dynamic behavior. These functions include checks for the uniqueness of component IDs, automatic component naming, and adaptive masks for circuit breakers. Furthermore, each block was given a distinctive icon to help users identify components and detect internal errors. The components developed include *load, line, bus, source,* and *circuit breaker.*

A sub-library containing ready-to-use component assemblies was also implemented to further enhance and expedite the modeling phase. This feature was inspired by feedback from ABB engineers, who use a similar function in their proprietary software, DOCweb. Since Simulink does not natively support assemblies within libraries, a novel approach was developed. The solution involved

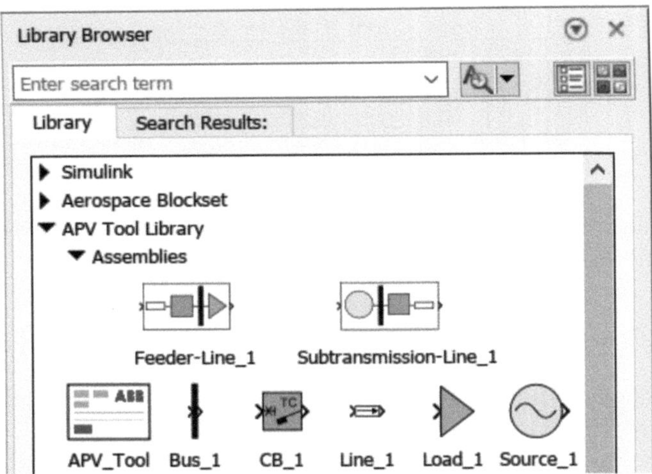

Fig. 3. APV Tool Simulink library.

creating a block that, once dragged into the model, expands into its constituent components, which are then automatically positioned and connected. Figure 4 shows an example of a *feeder line* assembly block and the resulting components once placed in the model (see Fig. 4a for the assembly block and Fig. 4b for the components).

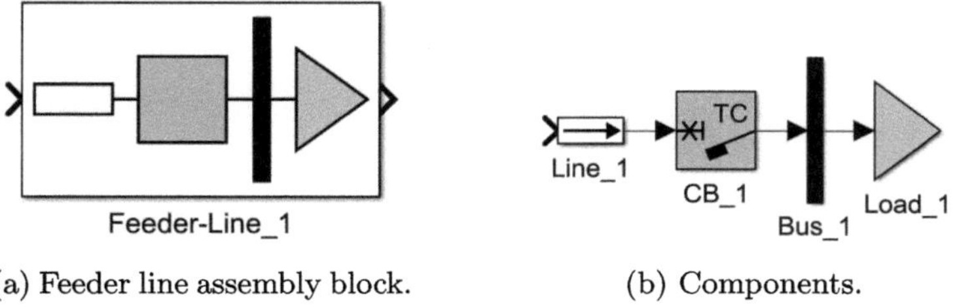

(a) Feeder line assembly block.   (b) Components.

Fig. 4. Feeder line assembly block (a) and its components (b).

4.2   JSON File Generation

To automate the creation of JSON files from the graphical models, a MATLAB script was developed. This script leverages the strong integration between MATLAB and Simulink to extract all block parameters and model connections. The data is first organized into a MATLAB structure that mirrors the final JSON structure. This structure is then converted and saved as a JSON file, ensuring its format is consistent with the requirements of the UPPAAL verification process. Although skipping the JSON intermediate step was considered, retaining it was decided to be the better approach as it keeps the modeling and verification processes decoupled, which simplifies future maintenance and upgrades.

4.3 APV Tool Implementation

A user-friendly application, the APV Tool, was developed using MATLAB App Designer to integrate all tasks into a single graphical interface. App Designer was chosen for its user-friendly interface, which allows for drag-and-drop placement of app components and the ability to program their behavior directly using MATLAB code. The application allows users to model grids, generate JSON files, and run the UPPAAL verification process directly from one environment (Fig. 5). This design shields users from the internal complexities of the UPPAAL functions while providing a simple GUI to control all phases of the process.

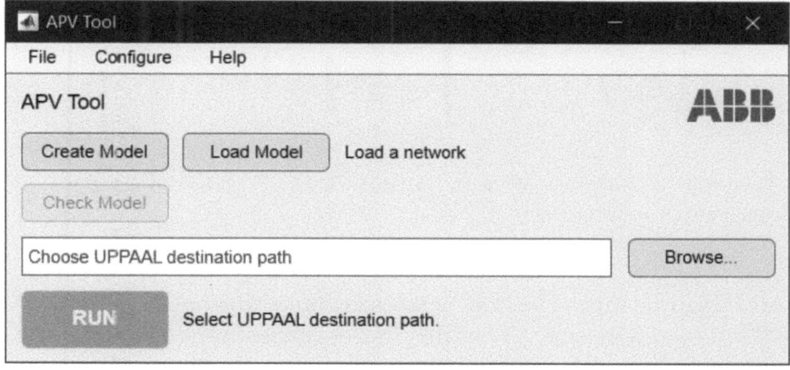

Fig. 5. APV Tool main window.

The GUI provides interactive functionality for verification and results visualization. If verification succeeds, the message `Done. Power system protections achieve selectivity.` is displayed. If verification fails, the tool generates a log file indicating how many misconfigurations were detected, on which lines and for which circuit breakers, as shown in Fig. 6. Furthermore, the tool highlights these blocks in the Simulink model in red so they are easier to locate by the user, as shown in Fig. 7.

4.4 Additional Features

Several additional features were implemented to enhance usability and integration with existing workflows. These include:

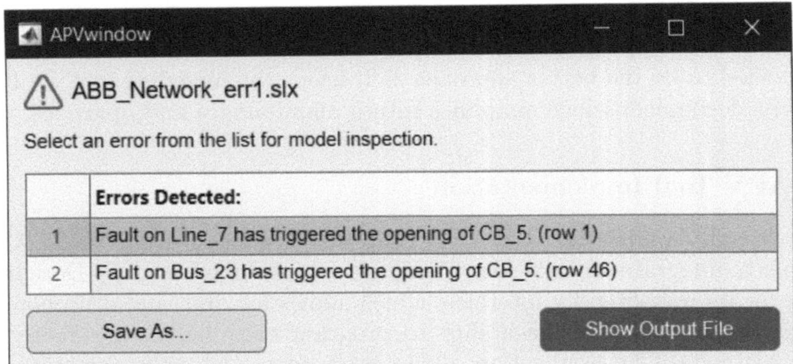

Fig. 6. Verification results window.

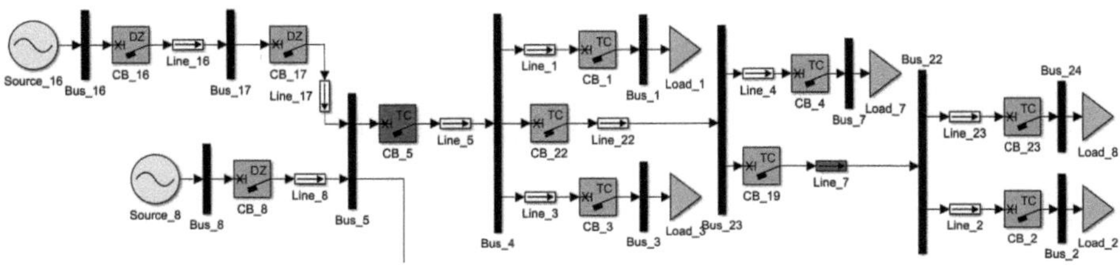

Fig. 7. Example of analyzed grid with blocks related to a detected error highlighted in red. (Color figure online)

- **Model importing:** The tool supports importing models from DOCweb (ABB's design software). This function automatically generates the equivalent Simulink model, placing components, creating connections, and populating parameters extracted from the original file (se Fig. 8). This significantly reduces the time required to create models from scratch, as many users, especially ABB customers, already have their networks represented in DOCweb.
- **Model analysis:** Before verification, the tool performs pre-verification checks on the model's connectivity, parameters, and topology (distinguishing between radial, open-ring, closed-ring, or mesh configurations). Unsupported topologies or incomplete models generate warnings with highlighted errors to guide the user.
- **Deployment support:** An installer script automates the setup of library files and MATLAB paths, simplifying the installation process for users.
- **Documentation and help:** A detailed user guide was prepared to assist users from installation to troubleshooting. Direct links to this guide are embedded in both the GUI and the Simulink component masks for easy access.

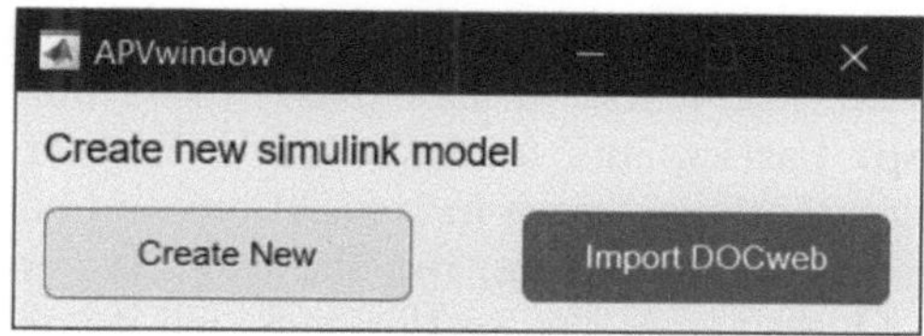

Fig. 8. Secondary window for model import from DOCweb.

5 Tool Functional Validation and Usability Assessment

To ensure the reliability and effectiveness of the proposed tool, its functionality was validated through both internal and external evaluations.

Internally, the tool underwent extensive testing, including detailed verification of individual components and end-to-end assessment of the complete workflow, to confirm its technical robustness and consistency. To further guarantee portability, the application was evaluated across three operating systems—Microsoft Windows, macOS, and Linux—verifying not only functional correctness but also performance consistency and GUI stability across platforms.

Externally, the tool's performance and usability were assessed through a user study involving a group of participants, providing empirical evidence of its practical applicability and user experience. This combined validation approach offers a comprehensive evaluation of the tool's correctness, stability, and usability under realistic conditions.

The remainder of this section presents the design and results of the user study and discusses how the findings informed subsequent improvements and modifications to the tool.

5.1 Usability Testing

Usability testing was carried out through a controlled survey [8] of ten participants with different backgrounds and level of expertise.

The group of participants included both students (Master's and Ph.D. level) and professionals from different engineering disciplines: electrical, mechanical, and automation. Crucially, no participant in the user study was a computer scientist, nor had they a background in formal methods or formal verification. This diversity ensured that the evaluation reflected perspectives beyond specialists in electrical engineering, in line with the tool's aim of being broadly accessible.

Since the tool was subject to a non-disclosure agreement with ABB, participants did not install it directly. Instead, in-person sessions were organized, where each participant used a preconfigured workstation. A Google Form guided the entire test process, structured into three sections:

1. **Simulink library:** Participants were asked to build a Simulink model of a given LV distribution grid using the custom library. They then rated the

difficulty of each step (e.g., *"How difficult was it to build the network using the provided blocks?"*) on a scale from 1 (easy) to 5 (difficult).

2. **MATLAB App:** Participants used the APV Tool to load a pre-defined model containing intentional errors in connections and parameters. They had to identify and correct these errors, run the UPPAAL verification, and interpret the results. Questions in this section included items such as: *"How easy was it to understand the warning messages produced by the tool?"* and *"Did the highlighting feature help you in debugging?"*

3. **Final evaluation:** Participants were asked to provide overall feedback on intuitiveness, efficiency, reliability, and aesthetics, again on a scale of 1 to 5, and to give free-text comments on their experience.

To ensure consistent setup for each participant, a MATLAB script was prepared to duplicate the test model and configure tool settings before each session. This guaranteed that all users faced identical conditions.

The Google Form used for the usability test provided participants with descriptions of the electrical networks to be created and outlined the main steps to follow, such as "model the following network using the tool," "load your model," "check and correct the model," and "run the verification." However, it did not provide detailed, step-by-step instructions for performing each action (for example, it did not specify "click on the RUN button to run the verification"). A user manual was made available to all participants, but they were not required to consult it before performing the tasks; it served as a reference in case they encountered difficulties. In practice, participants primarily learned to use the tool by interacting with it directly rather than by reading the manual, highlighting the intuitive design and the effectiveness of hands-on exploration during the usability test.

The questions included in the Google Form, although not explicitly framed in the terminology of the SQuaRE product quality model of standard ISO/IEC 25010 [13], nevertheless addressed several aspects corresponding to the sub-characteristics of the *Interaction Capability* (formerly *Usability*) quality characteristic of the standard. The following section presents the results of the study and interprets them with reference to these sub-characteristics, highlighting how participant feedback relates to the qualities defined in the standard.

5.2   Results and Threats to Validity

The results indicated that most tasks were rated as easy to moderately easy (average difficulty scores between 1.1 and 2.1). Model building and debugging were considered intuitive, especially by participants with prior Simulink experience, though even those without such background found the workflow manageable.

In the final evaluation, participants gave high ratings for efficiency (4.2), reliability (4.2), performance speed (4.5), and aesthetics (4.4). Intuitiveness (4.2) and simplicity (3.8) were also positively evaluated, while workflow clarity received a slightly lower score (3.4), suggesting room for improvement. Participants highlighted the usefulness of the warning system, the highlighting feature for error identification, and the troubleshooting guide. Some noted difficulties when warning messages were less explicit, though these were mitigated by consulting the guide.

With respect to the usability attributes defined in ISO/IEC 25010, the results of the study indicate that the tool performs well across several key dimensions. *Learnability* appears to be very good: participants reported low difficulty scores (below 2) when interpreting the tool's messages, and in the few cases where clarification was needed, the supplementary documentation provided sufficient support. This also suggests a strong level of *self-descriptiveness*, as users were generally able to understand the system's feedback with minimal external guidance. *Operability* was likewise positively assessed, with users indicating similarly low difficulty in creating electrical networks and resolving errors during the workflow. Finally, regarding *user error protection*, participants expressed particular appreciation for the feature that highlights issues directly within the network model, demonstrating that the tool effectively supports users in identifying and avoiding mistakes.

Overall, the usability test confirmed that the APV Tool is accessible to a wide range of users, effective in supporting modeling and verification tasks, and sufficiently intuitive for first-time users.

The main threat to the validity of the usability test lies in the limited number of participants, as the tool was evaluated by only ten users. Although this group was diverse, including both students and professionals, it did not include ABB customers—the primary target audience—who routinely design LV electrical networks using ABB's existing tools—such as DOCweb—which do not currently support selectivity checking. Furthermore, all participants were under the age of thirty-five and thus likely to have a more flexible and adaptive mindset toward new digital tools. This combination of factors may have led to a more favorable perception of the tool's usability than would be expected from a broader and more representative sample of end users.

5.3   Post-validation Updates

Although the tool was fully developed when provided to participants for usability testing, we incorporated their feedback to implement several improvements in a subsequent version.

One recurring issue concerned the visibility of warning messages: when the tool opened a Simulink model to highlight an error, the warning dialog could be hidden behind the new window. To address this, the application was modified so that its interface automatically regains focus, ensuring that the user immediately sees both the highlighted block and the explanation of the error.

Another refinement concerned the setup window and general interface behavior. Several adjustments were introduced to make interactions more intuitive, such as replacing redundant buttons with clearer actions and adding confirmations where needed. These changes streamlined the workflow and made the overall navigation of the tool more straightforward for new users.

Additionally, a bug affecting the *line* component was identified and corrected. Participants also suggested highlighting missing parameter fields directly during debugging. While this feature could not be implemented due to limitations in Simulink, it remains a useful point for consideration in future versions.

These refinements, together with the overall positive usability scores, confirmed the APV Tool's readiness for practical use. At the same time, the feedback process established a continuous improvement loop, ensuring that future iterations of the tool can be further optimized for clarity, robustness, and user experience.

6   Conclusion

This paper presented a user-friendly tool designed to support the formal modeling and verification of protection systems in LV distribution grids. Building on previous efforts in the formal verification of electrical networks, the work focused on making the process more accessible and intuitive. To this end, a high-level custom notation was introduced for graphically modeling LV distribution grids, accompanied by the design and implementation of a MATLAB application. The application features a simple graphical user interface that manages all stages of the process, abstracting the underlying UPPAAL functions while providing additional capabilities and user support. As a result, users can leverage formal modeling and verification methodologies without requiring specialized expertise.

A central aspect of the project was its user-centric approach, emphasizing continuous testing and the collection of feedback from peers, study participants, and ABB engineers. Looking ahead, the tool could be further enhanced by incorporating new grid components, expanding import compatibility with other software tools, and supporting additional grid topologies and circuit breaker communication logics. Ultimately, this work contributes to simplifying and broadening access to formal modeling and verification in a domain where precision and rigor are paramount.

Acknowledgments. The authors would like to dedicate this contribution to Prof. Alessandro Fantechi in honour of his 70th birthday. Alessandro's contributions to the Italian and international Formal Methods communities are remarkable, and his sustained commitment to promoting their practical applicability in industrial settings has been a lasting source of inspiration.

Disclosure of Interests. The authors have no competing interests to declare that are relevant to the content of this article.

References

1. Ayers, E.W., Jamnik, M., Gowers, W.T.: A Graphical User Interface Framework for Formal Verification. In: Cohen, L., Kaliszyk, C. (eds.) 12th International Conference on Interactive Theorem Proving (ITP 2021). Leibniz International Proceedings in Informatics (LIPIcs), vol. 193, pp. 4:1–4:16. Schloss Dagstuhl – Leibniz-Zentrum für Informatik, Dagstuhl, Germany (2021)
2. ter Beek, M.H., et al.: Formal methods in industry. Form. Asp. Comput. **37**(1), 7:1–7:38 (2025). https://doi.org/10.1145/3689374
3. Bouwman, M., van der Wal, D., Luttik, B., Stoelinga, M., Rensink, A.: A case in point: verification and testing of a EULYNX interface. Form. Asp. Comput. **35**(1) (2023). https://doi.org/10.1145/3528207
4. Cerone, A.: towards a user-friendly design and verification environment. In: 27th Annual NASA Goddard/IEEE Software Engineering Workshop 2002, Proceedings, pp. 199–208 (2002)
5. Daniele Pala: CIMDraw: A WebApp to view IEC CIM (CGMES) files (2021). https://github.com/danielePala/CIMDraw. Accessed 21 Sep 2024
6. Electric Power Research Institute (EPRI): Common information model primer (2022). Accessed 21 Sep 2024
7. ENTSO-E: Common Grid Model Exchange Specification (CGMES) (2018). https://docstore.entsoe.eu/major-projects/common-information-model-cim/cim-for-grid-models-exchange/standards/Pages/default.aspx. Accessed 1 Sep 2024
8. Hass, C.: A practical guide to usability testing, pp. 107–124. Springer International Publishing, Cham (2019). https://doi.org/10.1007/978-3-319-96906-0_6
9. Institute of electrical and electronics engineers: IEEE standard for graphic symbols for electrical and electronics diagrams. Tech. Rep. 315-1975, IEEE (1975)
10. International Electrotechnical Commission: IEC 60617: Graphical symbols for diagrams. Tech. Rep. 60617, IEC (2012)
11. International Electrotechnical Commission: Application Integration at Electric Utilities - System Interfaces for Distribution Management - Part 13: Common distribution power system model profiles. Tech. Rep. 61968-13, IEC (2021)
12. International Electrotechnical Commission: Energy Management System Application Program Interface (EMS-API) - Part 452: CIM Static Transmission Network Model Profiles. Tech. Rep. 61970-452, IEC (2021)
13. International Organization for Standardization: ISO/IEC 25010:2023 – Systems and software engineering: Systems and software Quality Requirements and Evaluation (SQuaRE) – Product quality model. Standard ISO/IEC 25010:2023(E), International Organization for Standardization (ISO) (2023). https://www.iso.org/standard/78176.html
14. Mansour, A.N.A., Grillo, S., Ragaini, E., Rossi, M.: A formal approach to the verification of protection systems in low-voltage distribution grids. In: 2023 IEEE/ACM FormaliSE Conference, pp. 120–129 (2023)
15. Mansour, A.N.A., Grillo, S., Ragaini, R., Rossi, M.: Rigorous automated verification of protection systems in LV distribution grids. In: IEEE EEEIC / I&CPS Europe Conference, pp. 1–6 (2023)
16. MathWorks: Simulink product description - MATLAB & Simulink (2023). https://www.mathworks.com/help/simulink/gs/product-description.html. Accessed 1 Sep 2024
17. Open Source Modelica Consortium (OSMC): OPENMODELICA: an open-source Modelica-based modeling and simulation environment (2023). https://openmodelica.org/. Accessed 1 Sep 2024

18. TopQuadrant, Inc.: IEC CIM Ontology (2024). https://ontology.tno.nl/IEC_CIM/. Accessed 1 Sep 2024
19. Woodcock, J., Larsen, P.G., Bicarregui, J., Fitzgerald, J.: Formal methods: practice and experience. ACM Comput. Surv. (CSUR) 41(4), 1–36 (2009). https://doi.org/10.1145/1592434.1592436

Towards Dynamic Classification in Domain Modeling with Jjodel

Maurice H. ter Beek[1] , Antonio Bucchiarone[2(✉)] , Alfonso Pierantonio[2] , and Bran Selic[3]

[1] FMT Lab, CNR–ISTI, Pisa, Italy
`maurice.terbeek@isti.cnr.it`
[2] SWEN, Università degli Studi dell'Aquila, L'Aquila, Italy
`{antonio.bucchiarone,alfonso.pierantonio}@univaq.it`
[3] Malina Software, Ottawa, ON, Canada
`selic@acm.org`

Abstract. This work addresses the limitations of traditional object-oriented classification in representing evolving systems. Conventional classification enforces rigid hierarchies that hinder dynamic reclassification, concurrent viewpoints, and transient or overlapping states, thus limiting their usefulness for systems that exhibit change, context sensitivity, or adaptation. We propose a modeling notation that extends UML class diagrams with declarative behavioral dynamics directly embedded in structural information. Unlike approaches that separate structure and behavior, our notation unifies them in a framework suitable for both conceptual/domain modeling and evolutionary, context-aware dynamics. The notation is fully defined, including abstract syntax, diagrammatic syntax, semantics, and simulation, within the Jjodel platform, ensuring rigor and tool support. Its structural nature enables the declarative specification of dynamics without imperative constructs. Moreover, the notation can be connected to frameworks for formal verification and model checking, enabling analysis of dynamic properties. Applicability is illustrated through a context-aware scenario in which enriched structural models can be simulated, reasoned about, and eventually verified.

Keywords: Dynamic Classification · Domain Modeling · Evolving Systems · Jjodel

1 Introduction

As software systems continue to evolve toward greater autonomy, adaptivity, and integration with the physical world, the challenges of modeling both their structure and behavior become increasingly pronounced. Within the *domain modeling* realm, the focus has traditionally been on the structural aspects of systems, identifying entities, relationships, and constraints that define the problem domain [10,11]. Behavioral aspects, in contrast, are often introduced only in

© The Author(s), under exclusive license to Springer Nature Switzerland AG 2026
M. H. ter Beek et al. (Eds.): Fantechi Festschrift, LNCS 16470, pp. 193–215, 2026.
https://doi.org/10.1007/978-3-032-12484-5_11

later phases of the modeling process or are expressed through separate, dedicated formalisms such as state machines, statecharts, or activity diagrams [14,32]. Although these behavioral notation has proven effective in many engineering contexts, they offer limited abstraction capabilities and often require cumbersome refinement steps to bridge the conceptual gap between high-level domain understanding and executable specifications [1,19].

Modern cyber-physical and context-aware systems, like autonomous drones, self-organizing sensor networks, or digital twins, expose the shortcomings of this separation between structure and behavior. These systems must dynamically adapt to fluctuating environmental conditions, operational contexts, and user requirements [22]. Their behavior is no longer static or neatly modular, but fluid, overlapping, and continuously evolving. Capturing such dynamics within a coherent, analyzable model remains one of the central challenges of software and systems engineering, particularly when domain models are expected to serve as enduring conceptual anchors throughout system evolution.

The engineering mechanism that has historically enabled abstraction and manageability is the *divide-and-conquer* principle: decomposing complexity into discrete, hierarchically organized components. This approach has long guided domain modeling practices, where systems are conceptualized in terms of entities and their relations, and behavioral specifications are subsequently layered on top [18]. Although effective in traditional, well-bounded domains, this separation falters when systems must continuously interact with—and adapt to—their environment. In nature, modularity exists, yet its boundaries are diffuse and dynamic: a single biological entity may participate simultaneously in multiple overlapping processes. Similarly, in engineered systems, components often assume context-dependent roles whose behavioral facets cannot be captured by rigid statically defined hierarchies [28].

Object-oriented classification, one of the cornerstones of both programming and domain modeling, illustrates this limitation. It supports abstraction and reuse through structural and behavioral encapsulation, but enforces a form of behavioral rigidity: once instantiated, the class membership of an object and associated operations are typically fixed. This assumption clashes with the needs of adaptive systems, where entities evolve, acquire or lose capabilities as contexts change [7]. For example, an autonomous drone can transition from an exploratory to a safety critical operational mode as weather conditions deteriorate, invoking distinct behavioral regimes while maintaining its identity as the same domain entity. Such transitions are continuous and context-sensitive, yet traditional class-based domain models remain bound to static binary notions of membership and state [21].

The motivation for this work is to overcome these long-standing limitations by rethinking domain modeling as an inherently dynamic endeavor, one in which structure and behavior co-evolve and can be expressed uniformly. We argue that classification should not be regarded as a static, structural property of objects but as a *dynamic, viewpoint-dependent construct* capable of evolving with the system it represents. In this view, domain models become living artifacts: they not only describe the ontology of the system, but also encode its potential for behavioral transformation [36].

Contributions. This paper introduces a modeling notation that extends traditional domain modeling formalisms, specifically UML class diagrams, with *declarative behavioral dynamics* embedded directly in structural specifications. Unlike conventional approaches that isolate behavioral descriptions in auxiliary state-based models, our notation unifies structure and behavior within a single declarative framework suitable for both conceptual modeling and context-aware evolution. The notation is formally defined through abstract syntax, diagrammatic conventions, semantics, and executable simulation, and has been implemented within the *Jjodel* platform [6][1] to ensure rigor and tool support. By embedding behavioral variation at the structural level, the approach preserves the expressiveness of domain modeling while enabling the specification and verification of dynamic, context-dependent phenomena without resorting to imperative constructs. The effectiveness of the approach is demonstrated through a context-aware scenario illustrating how enriched domain models can be simulated, reasoned about and verified within an integrated modeling environment.

Outline. The remainder of this paper is organized as follows. Section 2 discusses the background and related work, focusing on the limitations of traditional classification models and previous attempts to introduce dynamic perspectives. Section 3 presents the proposed dynamic classification notation and its metamodel. Section 4 describes the workbench and implementation within the Jjodel environment. Section 6 explores formal bridges to verification frameworks. Finally, Sect. 7 concludes the paper with a discussion and directions for future work.

2   Background and Related Work

The notion of *classification* has long served as a foundational abstraction in both conceptual modeling and programming. It enables software engineers to organize entities into classes according to common properties and behavior, simplifying reasoning about complex systems through modularization and reuse. This abstraction has proved remarkably effective within the divide-and-conquer paradigm that underpins classical software and systems engineering. By encapsulating functionality and structure within well-defined units, traditional classification has contributed to the clarity, maintainability, and reliability of software systems.

However, as modern software becomes increasingly interconnected with the physical world, through cyber-physical systems, Internet-of-Things (IoT) infrastructures, and digital twins, its underlying models must accommodate the fluid and evolving nature of the entities they represents. The crisp modular boundaries of traditional engineering abstractions (cf., e.g., [4]) rarely correspond to

---

[1] https://www.jjodel.io/.

the continuity, overlap, and dynamism found in socio-technical systems. In such contexts, conventional forms of classification appear increasingly restrictive and often misleading.

In most of the main object-oriented languages, including Java, C#, and C++, each object is an instance of a single fixed class throughout its lifetime. Class membership is determined by the static set of structural and behavioral features defined by that class. This rigid binding prevents an accurate representation of the mutable entities whose properties evolve over time. For instance, an autonomous drone may alter its behavior in response to changing environmental conditions, reducing speed and adjusting its flight altitude under strong winds, switching sensors and control modes in low visibility, or returning autonomously to base when battery levels are critical. Each of these operational contexts entails a different configuration of capabilities and constraints, yet the underlying entity remains the same drone. Such *dynamic reconfiguration* cannot easily be modeled if class membership remains immutable, since the system must effectively transition between distinct behavioral states while maintaining a continuous identity.

Existing techniques provide only partial workarounds. Multiple inheritance allows an entity to aggregate features from several parent classes, but it introduces well-known semantic complications such as the *diamond inheritance* problem and the potential propagation of irrelevant or conflicting features (cf., e.g., [23,34]). The *State* design pattern [12] offers another means of representing changing behavior, yet it does so indirectly by externalizing state management and obscuring the intrinsic connection between the entity and its dynamic roles. Both mechanisms highlight a conceptual gap: the inability of current programming languages to treat reclassification as a first-class modeling capability rather than a workaround.

A second, equally fundamental limitation concerns the assumption of a single, dominant classification hierarchy. In practice, the same entity can be viewed from multiple legitimate perspectives, each determined by a particular set of concerns or viewpoints [17]. For example, a person might simultaneously belong to classes defined by employment status, age group, and professional qualification. Each viewpoint focuses on a different subset of features, some relevant in one context and others irrelevant in another. The principle of separation of concerns, a cornerstone of software architecture, suggests that these viewpoints should remain distinct; however, mainstream object-oriented languages enforce a unification that privileges one hierarchy over others. The resulting models lose expressiveness and become difficult to evolve when alternative perspectives are introduced.

A third limitation concerns *transient* and *overlapping* forms. Context-aware systems rarely operate within discrete, mutually exclusive modes; instead, they exhibit continuous adaptations in which capabilities emerge, diminish, or coexist over time. Consider an autonomous drone that gradually transitions between navigation modes as environmental conditions evolve: when facing light turbulence, it may only adjust its stabilization parameters, whereas in severe weather it progressively activates obstacle-avoidance and emergency-landing subsystems.

During such transitions, multiple behavioral configurations can be partially active, resulting in hybrid or *in-between* operational states. Traditional classification models, based on binary feature inclusion, fail to capture these gradual transformations. Likewise, overlapping membership, where an entity validly exhibits characteristics of several operational classes at once, is excluded by design, even though it reflects the behavior of adaptive and cyber-physical systems.

These conceptual inadequacies have practical implications. As software systems increasingly rely on adaptive, context-aware, or self-configuring mechanisms, the ability to represent entities that dynamically change classification or are described from multiple concurrent perspectives becomes crucial. Digital twin systems [20] exemplify this demand: their fidelity depends on maintaining consistent yet adaptive mappings between physical and virtual states, a process that inherently requires dynamic reclassification and viewpoint management. This perspective also aligns with the needs of modern self-adaptive systems [35], where entities must reconfigure not only their control logic, but also their conceptual roles and available features depending on context (cf., e.g., [29–31], which deals with an autonomous underwater robot case study).

Several researchers have recognized these limitations. Initially, Jackson [18] criticized the rigidity of traditional classification hierarchies, arguing that they obscure alternative viewpoints and hinder flexibility. The language *Smalltalk-80* [13] supported a primitive form of dynamic reclassification through its *become* operation, allowing objects to change their class identity at runtime. However, this mechanism was not adopted by later statically typed languages due to its incompatibility with static type checking. The experimental *Fickle* language [9] extended this idea by allowing objects to migrate between classes in a controlled way, but remained largely a research prototype. The concept of *typestates* [8], formalizing object behavior as a set of state-dependent types, provided another influential contribution, anticipating later approaches to dynamic typing and behavioral modeling.

State-based modeling notations such as *Statecharts* [14] have long provided a powerful means to represent dynamic system behavior and context-dependent transitions. By hierarchically structuring states and allowing for concurrency and event-driven transitions, Statecharts extend classical finite state machines to capture complex reactive behavior in embedded and cyber-physical systems. However, despite their expressive power, Statecharts primarily focus on the *control flow* of a system rather than its *classification semantics*. They specify how an entity changes state in response to stimuli, but do not redefine its structural or behavioral features as part of those transitions. In other words, a drone modeled with Statecharts can switch between *Flying*, *Charging*, and *Emergency* states, yet its underlying class membership and associated attributes remain fixed. Integrating the expressive behavioral modeling of Statecharts with a more flexible viewpoint-based classification mechanism would enable richer representations of adaptive systems in which both control logic and conceptual identity evolve consistently over time.

Beyond programming languages, modeling standards such as the *Unified Modeling Language* (UML) introduced the concept of *generalization sets* to support orthogonal classification dimensions. This construct allows modelers to organize generalizations into independent, possibly overlapping, hierarchies, a notion closely aligned with viewpoint-based classification. However, the UML specification explicitly omits details about how such mechanisms should be realized or maintained in executable systems, and the idea has not been incorporated into any formal semantics of UML (cf., e.g., fUML [25]).

Despite these early insights, the prevailing classification model has remained largely unchanged for decades. The resulting gap between the expressive needs of modern software systems and the capabilities of current modeling and programming technologies has become increasingly apparent. As software assumes more dynamic, adaptive, and interdisciplinary roles, mirroring biological, social, or ecological systems, the need arises for frameworks that can represent multiple coexisting viewpoints, transient forms, and dynamic reclassification as intrinsic features of the modeling language itself.

The viewpoint-based approach proposed in this paper seeks to address precisely these challenges. It reframes classification not as an intrinsic property of objects, but as a *subjective construct*, a set of perspectives applied to a collection of entities to serve human reasoning and system comprehension. By allowing classification to evolve dynamically and coexist across multiple schemes, this approach aims to provide a more faithful, flexible, and semantically coherent representation of modern complex, evolving systems.

3   Dynamic Classification

As modern software increasingly operates within complex cyber-physical environments, the need to incorporate accurate models of dynamically evolving real-world phenomena becomes more acute. Traditional modeling languages such as UML [24] and SysML [26,27], while expressive for structural design, are grounded in static type systems derived from classical logic-based programming languages. These formalisms provide limited support for expressing entities whose *classification* changes over time or across contextual boundaries [32,33]. The resulting models tend to separate structural aspects from behavioral dynamics, often relegating the latter to auxiliary state machines or activity diagrams, which restricts abstraction and integration.

In contrast, the Dynamic Classification Notation (DCN) aims to unify structure and behavior by allowing entities to adopt multiple, possibly concurrent, classifications depending on the *viewpoint* applied. This capability reflects the way real-world entities are perceived and organized: classification is not intrinsic to an entity but depends on the modeling perspective and the selected discriminant property. For example, an individual can be simultaneously classified as a *parent*, an *employee*, and a *citizen*, depending on the viewpoint of interest. Similarly, a drone in an adaptive cyber-physical system can be classified as *navigating*, *avoiding collision*, or *returning to base*, depending on its current operational context. A simplified version of the metamodel for DCN is illustrated in Fig. 1. It formalizes the relationships among the core modeling constructs: *StaticClass*, *DynamicClass*, *Viewpoint*, and *Handler*.

The metaclass `StaticClass` represents the enduring structural concept of a phenomenon being modeled. Its instances embody entities that may assume different dynamic classifications over time. Each `StaticClass` aggregates a collection of `Features` (attributes and operations), `Relations`, and one or more `Viewpoints`. A `Viewpoint` denotes a modeling perspective that defines a set of possible `DynamicClasses`, each corresponding to a distinct contextual or temporal state of the same static entity.

A `DynamicClass` encapsulates the properties, invariants, and behavior that are valid when the represented phenomenon occupies a specific classification. Its `invariant` (an `EString` expression) specifies the conditions under which the classification is valid. The `ownedFeatures` and `ownedMonitor` references define the attributes, operations, and behavioral responses that are active within a given classification. The `Monitor` metaclass, in turn, enables the specification of the effects that changes in one aspect of the system have on dependent quantities. For instance, an increase in engine power can influence other performance parameters, such as speed or battery consumption. This mechanism directly integrates behavioral dynamics into the structural representation at the domain level, providing a declarative means to capture interdependencies among evolving features.

The model supports multiple concurrent viewpoints, enabling entities to be classified simultaneously according to different discriminants. For instance, in a biological domain, a `StaticClass` representing a *Frog* may have one `Viewpoint` describing its *life cycle* (*Tadpole*, *Adult*), and another representing its *health state* (*Healthy*, *Infected*). Each `DynamicClass` within these viewpoints activates or deactivates specific `Features` and `Operations` accordingly. For example, a frog in the *Tadpole* classification has a tail but no limbs, while in the *Adult* classification it has limbs but no tail, both modeled as features that dynamically appear or disappear based on the current classification.

Formally, the metamodel integrates declarative behavior for dynamic classification directly into structural models, bridging the gap between traditional domain modeling and behavioral specification. This approach provides a unified foundation for conceptual, executable, and verifiable representations of dynamic, adaptive systems.

4   Workbench and Implementation

The Dynamic Classification Notation (DCN), introduced in the previous section, has been implemented within *Jjodel* [6] (see Footnote 1), a model-driven platform that supports the engineering of domain-specific modeling languages (DSMLs) through the explicit specification of their syntax, semantics, and validation rules. Jjodel integrates these aspects within a unified metamodeling framework, providing both design-time modeling and runtime execution capabilities that pre-

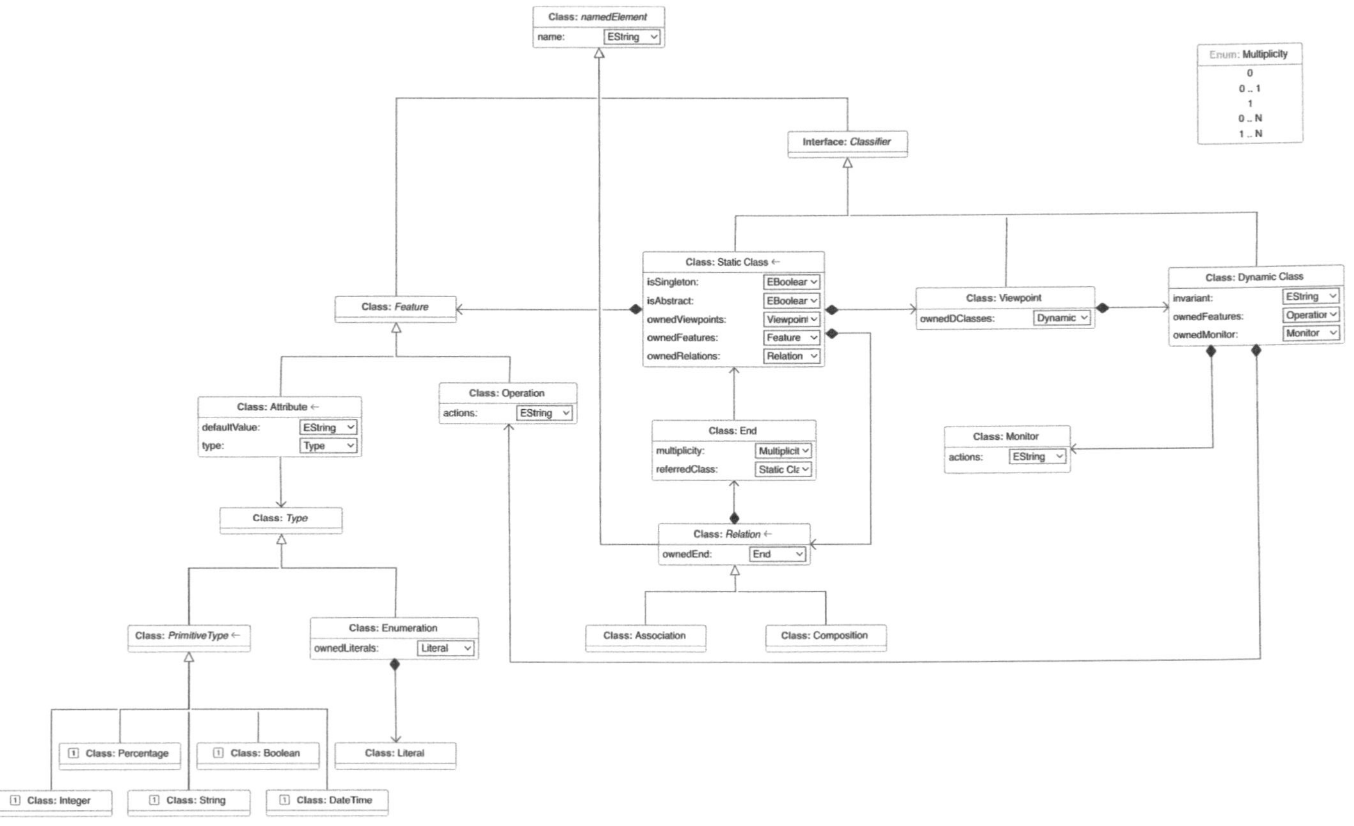

Fig. 1. The metamodel of the Dynamic Classification Notation (DCN).

serve the correspondence between abstract language definitions and executable behavior.

4.1   Defining a Modeling Language in Jjodel

A modeling language in Jjodel is defined by specifying:

- an *abstract syntax*, expressed as a metamodel capturing the domain concepts and their relationships;
- a *concrete syntax*, which defines how those concepts are represented and edited visually or textually; and
- a *semantic mapping*, which provides an interpretation of model elements, enabling simulation or analysis.

Each of these components is defined declaratively within the Jjodel workbench. The platform also integrates constraint checking through OCL-style invariants and offers validation and testing facilities for constraints [5].

For the DCN, the abstract syntax corresponds to the metamodel described in Sect. 3. The metamodel is specified as an `Ecore` model[2] that defines the key metaclasses `StaticClass`, `DynamicClass`, `Viewpoint`, `Feature`, and `Monitor`. These elements define the structural and dynamic aspects of the modeling language. Once defined, the metamodel is registered in the Jjodel repository and linked to a corresponding graphical concrete syntax.

4.2   Concrete Syntax of the Dynamic Classification Notation

The concrete syntax of the DCN employs a diagrammatic representation designed to clearly distinguish structural, contextual, and dynamic dimensions. An example of a DCN model rendered in Jjodel is shown in Fig. 2.

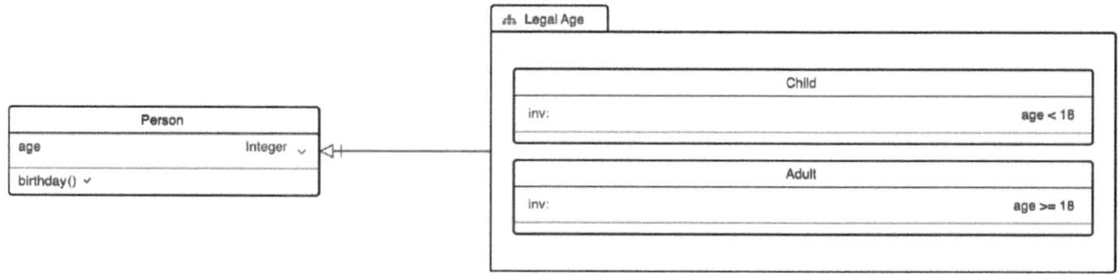

Fig. 2. Example of a DCN model: a `Person` with its `Legal Age` viewpoint specification. Static classes are shown in gray, viewpoints in blue, and dynamic classes in white.

In concrete syntax, static classes represent the enduring structural elements of the system domain (e.g., `Person`). These correspond to instances of the

---

[2] https://eclipse.dev/emf/.

`StaticClass` metaclass. Viewpoints (blue containers) express contextual perspectives from which a static class can be classified dynamically, such as `Legal Age`.

Dynamic classes (white boxes within viewpoints) represent specific classifications under each viewpoint (e.g., `Child`, `Adult`). Each dynamic class specifies its validity condition (`invariant`), active features, and possible behavior through `Monitors`.

4.3   Integration with Object Diagrams

To support simulation and analysis, the DCN metamodel is paired with the object diagram metamodel illustrated in Fig. 3, which defines the structure of runtime configurations.

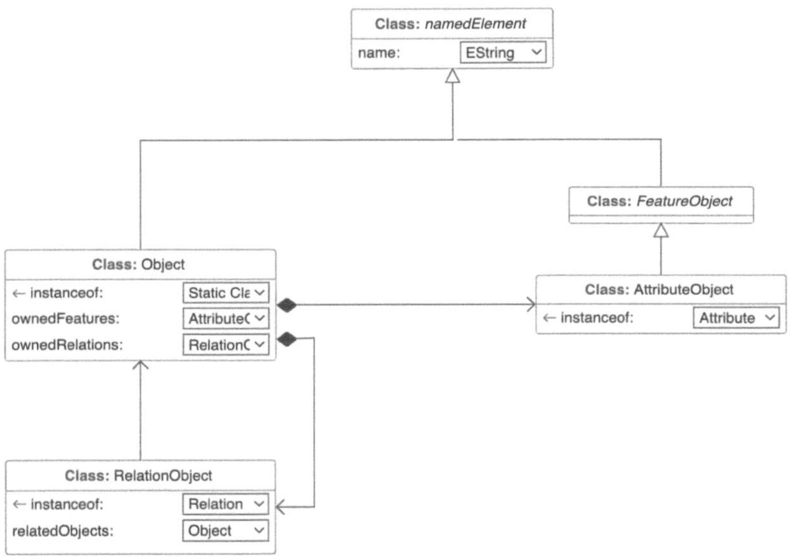

Fig. 3. The metamodel of object diagrams.

This metamodel specifies the structure of instance-level representations that conform to DCN models (i.e., extended class diagrams). To ensure that object instances remain consistent with their corresponding classes in the DCN metamodel, the approach adopts a *multi-view specification*. In this metamodel, the metaclass `Object` denotes an `instanceof` a `StaticClass` and aggregates its `ownedFeatures` (attributes) and `ownedRelations`. The symbol ← preceding the reference name indicates that it is a *cross-link reference*, i.e., a reference targeting a metaclass defined in another metamodel. Accordingly, the `instanceof` references in `Object`, `AttributeObject`, and `RelationObject` point to `StaticClass`,

`Attribute`, and `Relation` in the DCN metamodel, respectively. Together, these elements define runtime configurations that conform to both the object diagram metamodel and the extended class diagram specified by the DCN.

In this setting, each object diagram must conform to:

1. the *object diagram metamodel*, ensuring syntactic correctness (objects, links, and attribute values are well-typed); and
2. a specific *extended class diagram*, which is itself an instance of the DCN metamodel, ensuring semantic consistency with the modeled viewpoints and classification rules, as illustrated in Fig. 4.

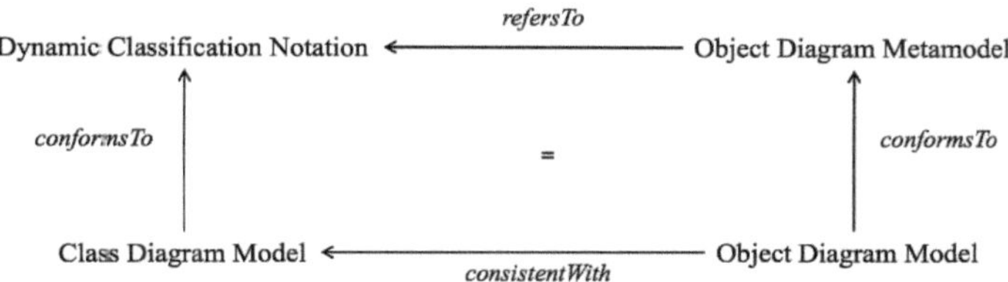

Fig. 4. Conformance and consistency relationships between class and object diagrams.

This dual conformance relation allows object diagrams to represent the dynamic state of a DCN model at runtime. For example, in Fig. 5, a Mario Nintendo instance of `Person` currently satisfies the invariant of the `Adult` dynamic class from the `LegalAge` viewpoint, as his `age` is 20. Conversely, `Luigi Nintendo` is classified as a `Child`, since his `age` is 13. Such configurations are automatically validated within Jjodel, ensuring moreover that runtime instances respect both structural and dynamic constraints. The operation `birthday()` is defined as `age = age + 1` and it can be invoked on each `Person` instance to trigger reclassification when the corresponding invariant condition changes.

This integration between structural modeling (through static and dynamic classes) and instance-level configurations (through object diagrams) provides a seamless workflow: modelers can define, visualize, and simulate dynamic classification behavior directly within the Jjodel workbench, ensuring coherence between conceptual and executable models.

In the next section, we illustrate the method through a more extended case study.

5   Case Study: Specification of an Electric Drone

To demonstrate the applicability of the DCN, we consider a case study based on the specification of an *electric drone*. The system exemplifies a cyber-physical architecture that combines autonomous behavior, adaptive control, and continuous interaction with the physical environment. The specification highlights how the DCN supports multiple viewpoints (structural, contextual, and behavioral) within a unified modeling framework formalized in the Jjodel platform.

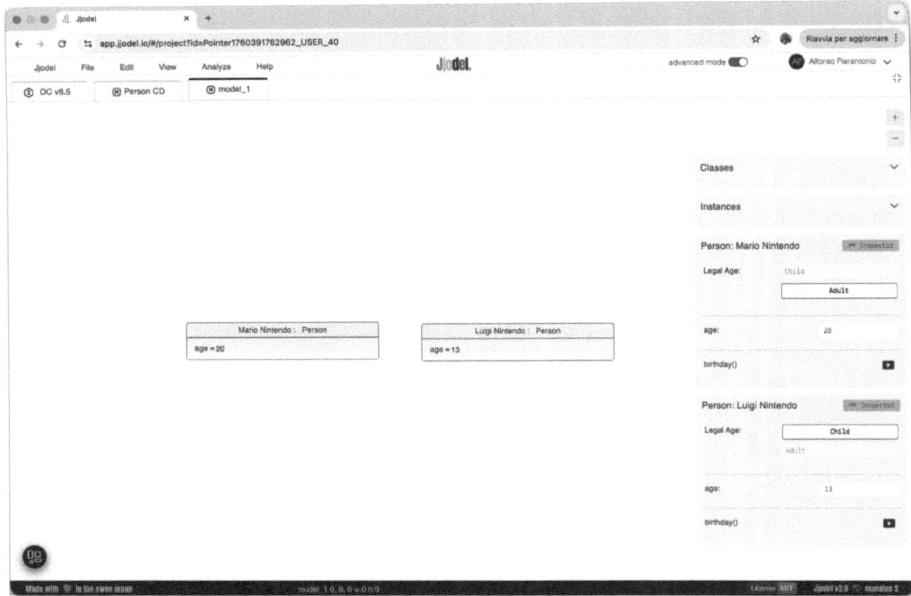

Fig. 5. Simulation of the **Person** domain in Jjodel. The model dynamically updates classifications (**Child** or **Adult**) based on the **LegalAge** viewpoint and current attribute values.

5.1 DCN Class Diagram Specification

The DCN class diagram shown in Fig. 6 models the structural and dynamic features of the drone and its supporting components. The central element is the **Drone** class, which encapsulates measurable physical properties such as **distance**, **speed**, **power**, **battery**, and **vmax**. The following two viewpoints are defined to represent the operational and environmental contexts of the drone.

Mode: describes the operational life cycle of the drone through four dynamic classes: **Charging**, **Ready**, **Flying**, and **Empty**. Each dynamic class specifies the invariants that determine when it is active. For example, the drone is in **Charging** mode when **distance = 0**, **speed = 0**, and **battery < 100**, while the **Flying** mode is maintained when **battery > 0** and **speed > 0**. Behavioral dynamics, such as **rampUp()** or **rampDown()**, are expressed as declarative operations that modify relevant attributes. Please note that while **Charging**, **Ready**, and **Flying** are mutually exclusive, **Empty** overlaps **Charging** to denote that the battery is completely empty.

Alert: defines the environmental classification of the operating context based on the weather conditions detected by the onboard and external sensors. Three dynamic classes (**Safe**, **Moderate**, and **Adverse**) are distinguished by invariant conditions over variables such as wind speed, temperature, humidity, and rain intensity. These classifications support adaptive decisions, e.g., slowing down or returning to base in adverse weather.

The drone interacts with a `WeatherAssessmentUnit` (WAU), which aggregates several types of `Sensor` objects: `WindSensor`, `TempSensor`, `RainSensor`, and `HumiditySensor`. Each sensor provides readings of physical quantities, such as wind speed, temperature, rain, and humidity, modeled by instances of the `PhysicalQuantity` class. The `SensorStatus` enumeration defines possible sensor states (`OK`, `Fault`, `Calibrating`), allowing fault-tolerant behavior to be specified and verified within the DCN framework.

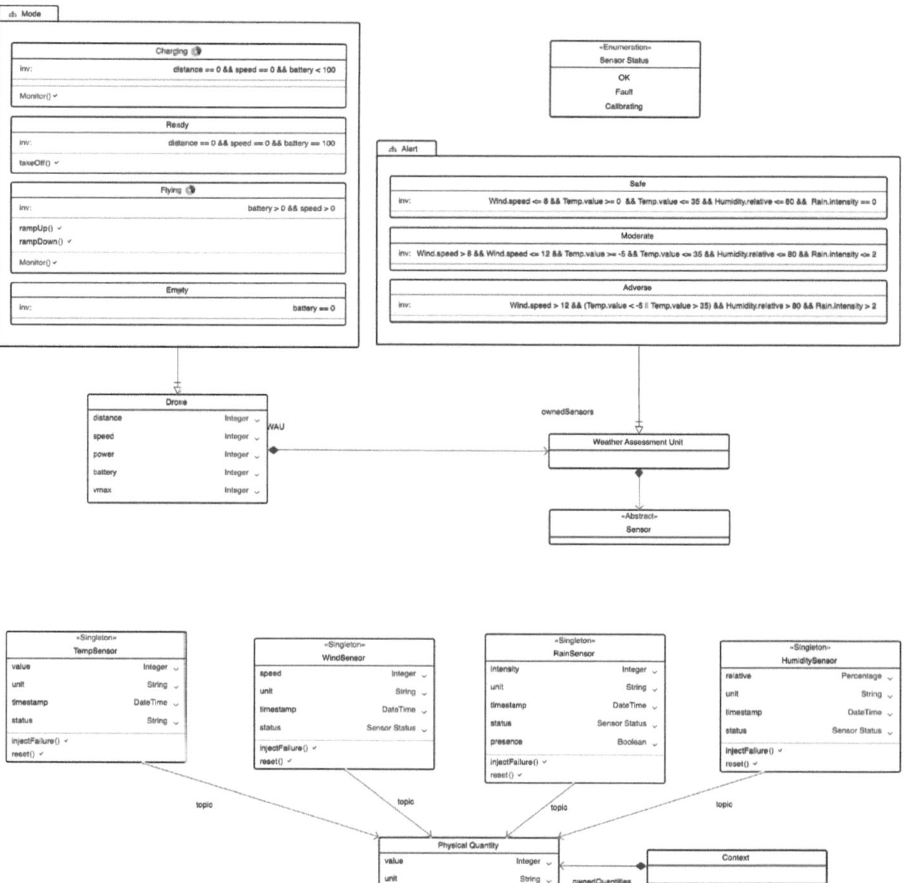

Fig. 6. DCN class diagram of the electric drone system. The model integrates operational (`Mode`) and environmental (`Alert`) viewpoints to describe adaptive behavior.

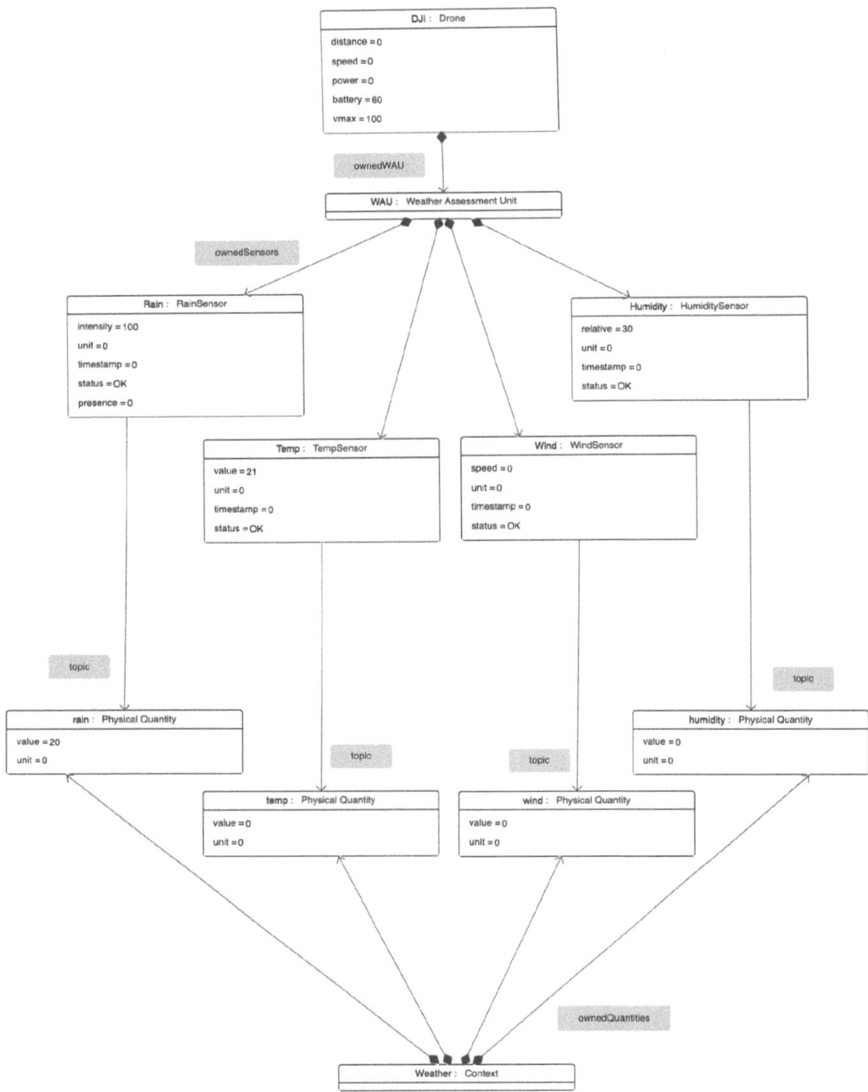

Fig. 7. Object diagram representing a runtime configuration of the electric drone system. The configuration conforms to both the object diagram metamodel and the DCN-based extended class diagram.

5.2   Runtime Configuration and Object Diagram

The corresponding object diagram, depicted in Fig. 7, represents a snapshot of a drone runtime configuration.

In   Fig. 7,   an   instance   `DJI:Drone`   interacts with its associated `WeatherAssess-mentUnit` and sensor instances. The
`TempSensor` records a temperature of 21°C, while the `HumiditySensor` reports
30% relative humidity. The wind and rain sensors indicate nominal conditions
(`speed = 0 m/s, intensity = 0 mm/h`), which collectively satisfy the invariant
of the `Safe` dynamic class under the `Alert` viewpoint. Each object instance in the
diagram conforms simultaneously to (i) the object diagram metamodel, ensuring
that objects, attributes, and relations are well-typed and correctly linked, and
(ii) the extended class diagram (the DCN model), ensuring semantic consistency
with the operational and environmental viewpoints as illustrated in the commu-
tative diagram in Fig. 4. This multi-level conformance enables simulation and
analysis of the adaptive behavior of the drone in Jjodel. For example, when the
`battery` level decreases below the threshold or when environmental conditions
violate the `Safe` invariants, the system may transition dynamically to another
classification (`Charging` or `Adverse`) without requiring re-instantiation. This
runtime adaptability exemplifies how the DCN unifies structure and behavior in
a single declarative framework.

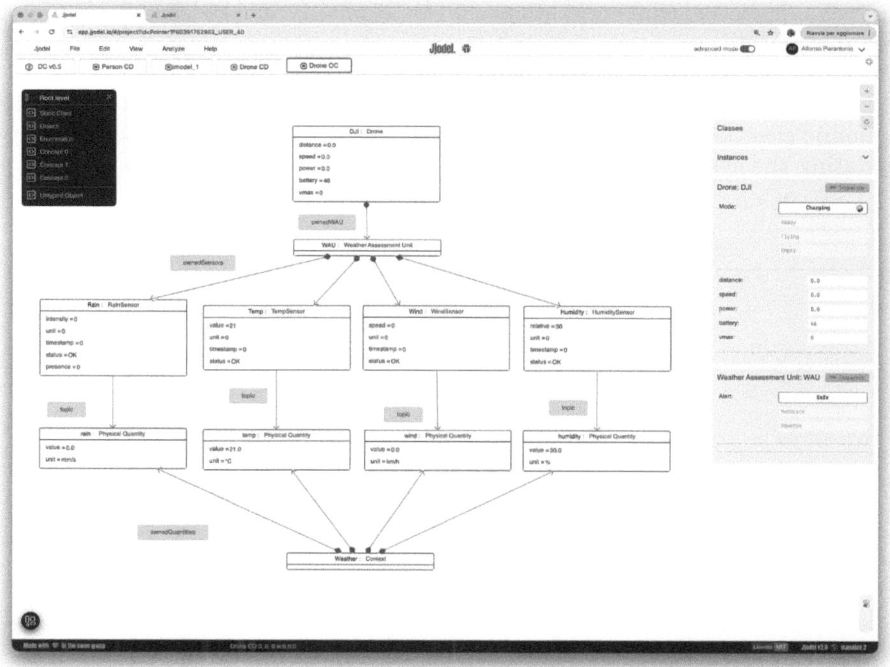

Fig. 8. Runtime execution of the electric drone model in the *Jjodel* platform.

Figure 8 shows the runtime execution environment of the electric drone model within the *Jjodel* platform. The central pane displays the instantiated object diagram corresponding to the previously introduced DCN specification. At the top of the hierarchy, the `DJI:Drone` object represents the drone instance, characterized by its structural attributes such as `distance`, `speed`, `power`, `battery`, and `vmax`, as specified in the corresponding `Drone` static class in Fig. 6. The drone owns a single `WeatherAssessmentUnit` (`WAU`), which in turn aggregates four sensor instances: `WindSensor`, `TempSensor`, `RainSensor`, and `HumiditySensor`. Each sensor reports measured quantities through the corresponding `Physical-Quantity` instances, which are ultimately related to a `Weather:Context` object representing the environmental conditions.

The right-hand inspector panel shows the currently active dynamic classifications for each viewpoint. In this configuration, the drone is in the `Charging` mode under the `Mode` viewpoint, as indicated by the red-highlighted selection. In fact, the associated attributes confirm that the drone is stationary (`distance = 0`, `speed = 0`, `battery = 80`). When the drone is in the `Charging` state, the evolution of the `battery` attribute is governed by the `Monitor` defined in the corresponding dynamic class.

Both `Monitor` and `Operation` elements are specified in a similar way through `actions`; however, while operations can be explicitly invoked by the user or by external events, monitors are continuously evaluated to simulate the ongoing impact of the current state on the attributes of the system.

In the user interface, the presence of a small round icon next to the active dynamic class name indicates that a `Monitor` is currently running, continuously updating the system state according to its declarative specification.

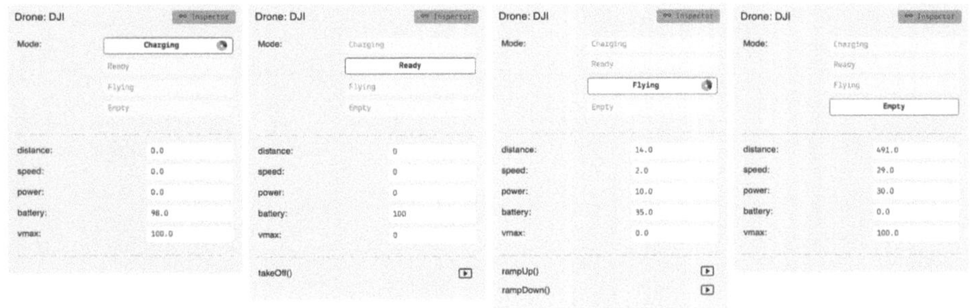

Fig. 9. Different Classifications of `DJI:Drone`.

Figure 9 details the inspector view as the drone transitions through its four operational modes under the `Mode` viewpoint. In the first panel, the drone is in the `Charging` state, with its `battery` gradually increasing under the effect of the running monitor. Once the battery reaches 100%, the invariant of the `Charging` class is no longer satisfied, and the system automatically reclassifies the drone into the `Ready` state. From this configuration, invoking the `takeOff()` operation activates the `Flying` mode, where drone speed and distance progressively increase as power consumption drains the battery. When the `battery` level eventually reaches zero, the invariant of the `Flying` class is violated, and the drone transitions to the `Empty` state, completing its operational cycle.

The user interface supports interactive manipulation of attribute values, allowing modelers to adjust environmental variables or operational parameters and observe in real time how DCN invariants trigger automatic reclassification. This illustrates how Jjodel provides an executable environment for simulating and validating dynamic classification models at runtime.

Overall, this case study illustrates how the DCN supports the modeling and simulation of adaptive cyber-physical systems. Moreover, the Jjodel workbench provides modelers with a means to capture multiple contextual perspectives while preserving formal rigor and executability. The study is preliminary to potential verification, as discussed in the next section.

6   Formal Bridging to Verification Frameworks

The declarative semantics of the DCN lends itself well to formal verification. DCN models capture both structure and dynamics in a uniform constraint-based form, facilitating automatic translation into formal models suitable for model checking. In this section, we sketch how such a mapping could be defined and applied to the case study, relate it to existing approaches from the literature, and outline directions for future work.

6.1   Mapping DCN Models to Formal Models

The DCN notation and models can be connected to state machines to enable the analysis of dynamic properties through formal verification, for instance, by means of model checking. Concretely, state machines should properly reflect the dynamicity of the subclasses of the static class corresponding to the state machine. The behavior (transitions) of the state machines is extracted from the operations that are available in the static class and in its dynamic subclasses, with pre- and postconditions suitably constraining the behavior and allowing state changes based on the validity of feature constraints defined in the form of predicates (logic).

Each DCN model implicitly defines a state space whose states correspond to configurations of dynamic classifications across all viewpoints. More concretely, a state represents a consistent assignment of attribute values, active dynamic classes, and satisfied invariants for all entities in the model. Transitions arise from declarative operations or monitors whose pre- and postconditions describe admissible state changes. Formally, these can be captured as a Kripke structure $\mathcal{K} = (S, s_0, \delta, L)$, in which:

- S is the finite set of reachable DCN configurations;

- $s_0 \subseteq S$ is the set of initial configurations defined by the model initialization;
- $\delta \subseteq S \times S$ is the transition relation induced by operation invocations or monitor evaluations; and
- $L : S \to 2^{AP}$ labels each state with the atomic propositions (AP) that correspond to the satisfied invariants or the viewpoint predicates.

This mapping preserves the semantics of DCN invariants: a transition between two states is permitted only if the target configuration satisfies all invariant predicates of its newly active dynamic classes. The declarative form of DCN operations (expressed as attribute updates and constraints) eliminates the need for explicit control-flow constructs, simplifying the generation of the corresponding transition relation.

We plan to define model transformations that consistently map DCN class diagrams into state machines that represent the behavior of objects according to a given viewpoint. These transformations will establish the foundation for automated analysis, allowing DCN specifications to be systematically connected to verification back ends (in Jjodel). To this aim, we will follow relevant related approaches from the literature.

6.2   Model Checking and Property Specification

Once we have translated the DCN models into Kripke structures, the resulting formal model can be analyzed using well-known temporal logic-based formal verification tools such as mCRL2[3], NuSMV[4], UPPAAL[5], or UMC[6]. UMC is the UML model checker [2] from the KandISTI family of model checkers [3] developed together with Alessandro Fantechi by the FMT Lab at CNR–ISTI. UMC considers UML models defined as a set of concurrently executing UML state machines describing the dynamic aspects of a system component's behavior, considering both its state-based (e.g., values of object attributes) and its event-based (i.e., related to the executed actions) aspects, represented by a doubly-labelled transition system (L^2TS) or Kripke structure whose transitions are labeled with events.

Typical properties that could then be verified for the case study include the following examples.

Safety: *"A drone never flies with `battery = 0`".*
Liveness: *"Whenever the drone is in `Charging` mode and its `battery = 100`, it eventually becomes `Ready`".*
Consistency: *"At any time, exactly one dynamic class per viewpoint is active".*

These properties can be expressed in (action-based) CTL, LTL, or (modal) μ-calculus, depending on the specific target verification framework. The translation of invariants and monitors into logical formulae enables us to directly check these properties over the generated transition system.

---

[3] https://mcrl2.org/.
[4] https://nusmv.fbk.eu/.
[5] https://uppaal.org/.
[6] https://fmt.isti.cnr.it/umc/.

6.3   Relation to Existing Formal Approaches

A promising conceptual correspondence can be drawn with the HELENA approach [15,16], which provides a formal foundation for modeling ensemble-based systems centered on the first-class notion of a *role* that expresses the capabilities that a specific instance of a system component requires when participating in a concrete ensemble. To appreciate the analogy, one can think of a component instance as corresponding to a static class, a role to one of its dynamic classes, and a concrete ensemble to a viewpoint. According to this approach, components can change their roles when needed and participate in multiple ensembles simultaneously by playing different roles, thereby focusing on the capabilities required to collaborate in a particular ensemble composition. The typical component behavior of performing a certain role is modeled in terms of Kripke structures, and dynamic logic is used to specify the properties of the ensembles.

Our vision extends this idea by embedding such role- and viewpoint-based dynamics directly within the structural semantics of the modeling language. Unlike UML/fUML or Statecharts, where behavioral semantics are imperative and often detached from structure, DCN's declarative embedding enables a direct and analyzable correspondence between domain-level constraints and execution semantics. This positions DCN as a bridge between conceptual modeling and formal analysis: high-level structural models can be simulated, validated, and formally verified without rewriting them in a dedicated behavioral formalism.

6.4   Research Agenda

We plan to define a model-to-model transformation from DCN metamodel instances to a formal intermediate representation compatible with model checkers. The transformation should:

1. Identify the set of relevant viewpoints to bound the state space;
2. Encode attribute domains and invariants as logical variables and constraints;
3. Generate transition relations from declarative operations and monitors; and
4. Export the resulting structure to the verification back ends.

This line of research aims to provide bidirectional traceability between the DCN model and its formal counterpart, allowing verification results to be visualized directly within the Jjodel environment. Ultimately, this bridge will support the formal analysis of adaptive and context-aware systems, such as the drone case study, enabling rigorous reasoning about their dynamic reclassification and context-dependent behavior.

7   Conclusion and Future Work

The principal contribution of this work lies in its declarative integration of dynamics into structural models. By embedding behavioral invariants and context-dependent transformations directly within UML-like class diagrams, the

DCN enables modelers to reason about evolution and adaptation without relying on imperative or state-based auxiliary formalisms. This yields three key advantages. First, *expressiveness*: modelers can represent overlapping roles, transient states, and concurrent viewpoints using a single unified formalism. Second, *traceability and analyzability*: since dynamic properties are encoded as logical invariants, models remain suitable for both simulation and formal verification. Third, *tool support and usability*: the Jjodel workbench allows users to define, visualize, and execute DCN models interactively, ensuring consistency between conceptual and runtime representations.

The case study on an adaptive electric drone system demonstrates that the approach naturally supports context-aware systems whose behavior depends on environmental factors. Within Jjodel, these dynamics are simulated declaratively through monitors and operations, allowing entities to reclassify themselves automatically when invariant conditions change. This interactive environment bridges conceptual modeling, simulation, and potential verification, embodying the principles of living models or digital twins for cyber-physical systems.

Although promising, the approach also raises several challenges. Declarative specifications can become complex and computationally intensive when models involve numerous viewpoints, constraints, or dynamically interdependent features. Managing the *scalability of invariant evaluation and reclassification at runtime* will require optimization techniques such as incremental constraint solving and selective evaluation strategies. Moreover, *human comprehensibility* remains crucial: as models grow in size, maintaining readability of overlapping viewpoints and dynamic rules may require novel visualization or abstraction mechanisms. Ongoing work in Jjodel is exploring layered representations and semantic zooming to address these issues.

From a methodological perspective, the integration of the DCN into existing model-driven engineering (MDE) workflows requires guidelines for when and how to apply dynamic classification relative to traditional state machines, fUML behavior, or DSMLs. The relationship between declarative reclassification and more conventional imperative semantics represents a fertile ground for further exploration.

Compared with Statecharts and fUML, the DCN adopts a constraint-based rather than control-based view of behavior. This declarative stance favors analyzability and direct linkage to model checking but sacrifices explicit sequencing semantics. In contrast to viewpoint modeling or role-based frameworks such as HELENA, the DCN integrates these concepts directly within the structural layer, maintaining coherence between roles, invariants, and class features. This synthesis positions the DCN as a bridge between conceptual modeling (concerned with expressing domain knowledge) and formal analysis (concerned with verifying behavioral properties).

Future work will pursue two directions. First, the ongoing formalization of the DCN semantics will define systematic transformations from DCN models to intermediate representations suitable for verification back ends, enabling automated reasoning about safety, liveness, and consistency properties within model-checking tools such as UMC, UPPAAL, NuSMV, or mCRL2. Second, we plan to expand Jjodel's support for hybrid simulation, combining declarative dynamics with real-time data streams to study digital twin scenarios and adaptive systems in operation.

Furthermore, once formal verification is in place, our approach would be particularly well suited for the modeling and analysis of railway systems, the favorite playground of Alessandro Fantechi, since they are cyber-physical, safety-critical, and context-dependent and demand formal verification.

Ultimately, the vision behind Jjodel and the DCN is to enable models that evolve with their systems; not static blueprints but dynamic representations that capture how software and its environment co-adapt over time. This paradigm holds promise for advancing MDE toward the next generation of context-aware, self-adaptive, and verifiable systems.

Acknowledgments. The first two authors are grateful to Alessandro Fantechi for a lasting friendship that began during their years working together in the Formal Methods and Tools (FMT) Lab at CNR–ISTI in Pisa.

This paper, in particular Sect. 6, benefited from discussions with Rolf Hennicker several years ago on viewpoint-based classifications and transient diagrams.

The research presented in this paper is partially funded by the European Union under the Grant Agreement No 101189664. Views and opinions expressed are however those of the author(s) only and do not necessarily reflect those of the European Union or the European Health and Digital Executive Agency (HADEA). Neither the European Union nor the granting authority can be held responsible for them.

Disclosure of Interests. The authors have no competing interests to declare that are relevant to the content of this article.

References

1. acatech – National Academy of Science and Engineering (ed.): Cyber-Physical Systems: Driving force for innovation in mobility, health, energy and production. Springer (2011). https://doi.org/10.1007/978-3-642-29090-9
2. ter Beek, M.H., Fantechi, A., Gnesi, S., Mazzanti, F.: A state/event-based model-checking approach for the analysis of abstract system properties. Sci. Comput. Program. **76**(2), 119–135 (2011). https://doi.org/10.1016/J.SCICO.2010.07.002
3. Margaria, T.: Making sense of complex applications: constructive design, features, and questions. In: Margaria, T., Graf, S., Larsen, K.G. (eds.) Models, Mindsets, Meta: The What, the How, and the Why Not? LNCS, vol. 11200, pp. 129–148. Springer, Cham (2019). https://doi.org/10.1007/978-3-030-22348-9_9
4. Bencomo, N., et al.: Abstraction Engineering. arXiv (2024). https://doi.org/10.48550/ARXIV.2408.14074
5. Bucchiarone, A., Di Rocco, J., Di Vincenzo, D., Pierantonio, A.: From OCL to JSX: declarative constraint modeling in modern SaaS tools. arXiv (2025). https://doi.org/10.48550/ARXIV.2509.17629
6. Bucchiarone, A., Di Rocco, J., Di Vincenzo, D., Pierantonio, A.: Modeling in Jjodel: towards bridging complexity and usability in model-driven engineering. Softw. Syst. Model. 1–25 (2025). https://doi.org/10.1007/s10270-025-01324-y

7. Cardozo, N., Mens, K.: Programming language implementations for context-oriented self-adaptive systems. Inf. Softw. Technol. **143**(C), 106789 (2022). https://doi.org/10.1016/J.INFSOF.2021.106789

8. DeLine, R., Fähndrich, M.: Typestates for objects. In: Odersky, M. (ed.) ECOOP 2004. LNCS, vol. 3086, pp. 465–490. Springer, Heidelberg (2004). https://doi.org/10.1007/978-3-540-24851-4_21

9. Drossopoulou, S., Damiani, F., Dezani-Ciancaglini, M., Giannini, P.: More dynamic object reclassification: *Fickle*$_{||}$. ACM Trans. Program. Lang. Syst. **24**(2), 153–191 (2002). https://doi.org/10.1145/514952.514955

10. Evans, E.: Domain-Driven Design: Tackling Complexity in the Heart of Software. Addison-Wesley (2004)

11. France, R.B., Rumpe, B.: Model-driven development of complex software: a research roadmap. In: Proceedings of the ISCE Workshop on the Future of Software Engineering (FOSE 2007), pp. 37–54. IEEE (2007). https://doi.org/10.1109/FOSE.2007.14

12. Gamma, E., Helm, R., Johnson, R., Vlissides, J.: Design Patterns: Elements of Reusable Object-Oriented Software. Addison-Wesley (1995)

13. Goldberg, A., Robson, D.: Smalltalk-80: The Language and Its Implementation. Addison-Wesley (1983)

14. Harel, D.: Statecharts: a visual formalism for complex systems. Sci. Comput. Program. **8**(3), 231–274 (1987). https://doi.org/10.1016/0167-6423(87)90035-9

15. Hennicker, R.: Role-based development of dynamically evolving esembles. In: Fiadeiro, J.L., et al. (eds.) WADT 2018. LNCS, vol. 11563, pp. 3–24. Springer, Cham (2019). https://doi.org/10.1007/978-3-030-23220-7_1

16. Hennicker, R., Klarl, A.: Foundations for ensemble modeling – the HELENA approach. In: Iida, S., Meseguer, J., Ogata, K. (eds.) Specification, Algebra, and Software. LNCS, vol. 8373, pp. 359–381. Springer, Heidelberg (2014). https://doi.org/10.1007/978-3-642-54624-2_18

17. International Standard ISO/IEC/IEEE 42010: Systems and software engineering—Architecture description (2011). https://doi.org/10.1109/IEEESTD.2011.6129467

18. Jackson, M.: Object-orientation: classification considered harmful. In: Proceedings of NordDATA 1991, pp. 107–121 (1991). https://www.researchgate.net/publication/246987164_Object-Orientation_Classification_Considered_Harmful

19. Jureta, I.J., Borgida, A., Ernst, N.A., Mylopoulos, J.: The requirements problem for adaptive systems. ACM Trans. Manage. Inf. Syst. **5**(3), 17:1–17:33 (2014). https://doi.org/10.1145/2629376

20. Kritzinger, W., Karner, M., Traar, G., Henjes, J., Sihn, W.: Digital twin in manufacturing: a categorical literature review and classification. IFAC-PapersOnLine **51**(11), 1016–1022 (2018). https://doi.org/10.1016/J.IFACOL.2018.08.474, Proceedings of the 16th IFAC Symposium on Information Control Problems in Manufacturing (INCOM'18)

21. Lara, J., Guerra, E., Sánchez Cuadrado, J.: When and how to use multilevel modelling. ACM Trans. Softw. Eng. Methodol. **24**, 1–46 (2014). https://doi.org/10.1145/2685615

22. Lee, E.A.: The past, present and future of cyber-physical systems: a focus on models. Sensors **15**(3), 4837–4869 (2015). https://doi.org/10.3390/s150304837

23. Malayeri, D., Aldrich, J.: CZ: multiple inheritance without diamonds. In: Arora, S., Leavens, G.T. (eds.) Proceedings of the 24th Annual ACM SIGPLAN Conference on Object-Oriented Programming, Systems, Languages, and Applications (OOPSLA 2009), pp. 21–40. ACM (2009). https://doi.org/10.1145/1640089.1640092

24. Object Management Group: OMG Unified Modeling Language (OMG UML) (2017). https://www.omg.org/spec/UML/2.5.1/PDF
25. Object Management Group: Semantics of a Foundational Subset for Executable UML Models (fUML) (2021). https://www.omg.org/spec/FUML/1.5/PDF
26. Object Management Group: OMG Systems Modeling Language (SysML). Part 1: Language Specification (2025). https://www.omg.org/spec/SysML/2.0/Language/PDF
27. Object Management Group: OMG Systems Modeling Language (SysML). Part 2: SysML v1 to SysML v2 Transformation (2025). https://www.omg.org/spec/SysML/2.0/Transformation/PDF
28. Oliver, D., Kelliher, T., Keegan, J.: Engineering Complex Systems with Models and Objects. McGraw-Hill (1997)
29. Päßler, J., ter Beek, M.H., Damiani, F., Dubslaff, C., Johnsen, E.B., Tapia Tarifa, S.L.: Feature-oriented modelling and analysis of a self-adaptive robotic system. Formal Aspects Comput. **37**(4), 32:1–32:39 (2025). https://doi.org/10.1145/3709159
30. Päßler, J., ter Beek, M.H., Damiani, F., Johnsen, E.B., Tapia Tarifa, S.L.: A configurable software model of a self-adaptive robotic system. Sci. Comput. Program. **240**, 103221 (2025). https://doi.org/10.1016/J.SCICO.2024.103221
31. Päßler, J., ter Beek, M.H., Damiani, F., Johnsen, E.B., Tapia Tarifa, S.L.: Analysing self-adaptive systems as software product lines. J. Syst. Softw. **222**, 112324 (2025). https://doi.org/10.1016/J.JSS.2024.112324
32. Rumpe, B.: Modeling with UML: Language, Concepts, Methods. Springer, Cham (2016). https://doi.org/10.1007/978-3-319-33933-7
33. Selić, B., Pierantonio, A.: Fixing classification: a viewpoint-based approach. In: Margaria, T., Steffen, B. (eds.) ISoLA 2021. LNCS, vol. 13036, pp. 346–356. Springer, Cham (2021). https://doi.org/10.1007/978-3-030-89159-6_22
34. Singh, G.B.: Single versus multiple inheritance in object oriented programming. OOPS Messenger **5**(1), 34–43 (1994). https://doi.org/10.1145/182078.182085
35. Weyns, D.: An Introduction to Self-Adaptive Systems: A Contemporary Software Engineering Perspective. Wiley (2020)
36. Whittle, J., Hutchinson, J., Rouncefield, M.: The state of practice in model-driven engineering. IEEE Softw. **31**(3), 79–85 (2014). https://doi.org/10.1109/MS.2013.65

Application of Model-Checking Techniques to Railway Scheduling Problems

Radu Mateescu, Wendelin Serwe$^{(\boxtimes)}$, and Aline Uwimbabazi

Univ. Grenoble Alpes, Inria, CNRS, Grenoble INP, LIG, 38000 Grenoble, France
{radu.mateescu,wendelin.serwe,aline.uwimbabazi}@inria.fr

Abstract. Railway scheduling problems can be formulated as instances of the NP-hard job-shop scheduling problem. In this paper, written in the honour of Alessandro Fantechi, we experiment with various encodings of the job-shop scheduling problem in LNT, a modern formal modelling language with a process calculus flavour. We also report on the computation of solutions with various model checking tools of the CADP toolbox.

1 Introduction

Railway transportation is a complex system of systems, encompassing a variety of control systems (interlocking, traffic management, automatic train control and supervision, etc.) that interact and operate together to ensure safety, availability, and performance of the transport. Railway control systems are developed according to international standards, such as ERTMS/ETCS[1] (European Rail Traffic Management Systems/European Train Control System) and feature embedded, cyber-physical, and distributed heterogeneous architectures. These systems are subject to high safety and availability requirements, which become even more stringent for the advanced (ERTMS/ECTS level 3) train control systems relying on geographically distributed and satellite-based decision-making algorithms. In this context, formal methods and tools are of paramount importance for designing and validating railway control systems, as witnessed by the large number of applications and case-studies carried out over three decades [6,14].

Alessandro Fantechi is one of the foremost scientists promoting the usage of formal methods in the railway domain. He considered the enhancement of the design and development of railway systems with formal methods along various ways: model-based testing and abstract interpretation [15,21], model checking [12,22], as well as quantitative analysis [2,4]. He is also an author of several surveys on the application of formal methods in the railway domain [1,6,13].

Besides his scientific contributions, Alessandro is also deeply involved in dissemination and steering activities. He is one of the originators of the DisCoRail

---

Institute of Engineering Univ. Grenoble Alpes.

[1] https://www.era.europa.eu/domains/infrastructure/european-rail-traffic-management-system-ertms_en.

© The Author(s), under exclusive license to Springer Nature Switzerland AG 2026
M. H. ter Beek et al. (Eds.): Fantechi Festschrift, LNCS 16470, pp. 216–235, 2026.
https://doi.org/10.1007/978-3-032-12484-5_12

workshop, dedicated to formal methods for distributed computing in future railway systems, which became in 2021 a track of the ISOLA conference series [11]. He is regularly leading or participating to research projects aiming at the integration of formal methods in the railway domain, such as ASTRail [5], 4SECU-Rail [7], and ADVENTURE [3]. Alessandro is also active at the European level as a member of the scientific steering group of the Shift2Rail[2] initiative and of the Europe's Rail Joint Undertaking[3].

An important optimisation problem in railway transportation is train scheduling, which consists in producing a schedule for a set of n trains with fixed routes from origin to destination and going through particular sections of m tracks. By considering the trains as jobs, the tracks as machines, and the passings of trains through sections as tasks, the problem of minimising the travel time of all trains can be expressed as an instance of the well-known *job-shop scheduling problem*. Briefly, job-shop scheduling aims at producing a schedule to execute on m machines n jobs, each of which is a sequence of tasks t_i, each characterised by a pair (d_i, m_i) specifying the duration d_i of the task and the required machine m_i. The goal is to finish execution of all tasks as fast as possible, still respecting the order of tasks in each job and the fact that each machine can handle at most one task at a time. This combinatorial problem being NP-hard, an extensive amount of work has been devoted to devising various resolution approaches and heuristics for job-shop scheduling [9,25,31], which has many applications in manufacturing, equipment selection, chemicals, pharmaceutics, healthcare, process planning, and—last, but not least—railway transportation.

Formulations of train scheduling as job-shop scheduling have been proposed for both the single-track case [24,28] and the double-track case [29], and extensive work has been dedicated to solve the corresponding job-shop instances [9,10]. In the context of train scheduling, one needs an additional constraint for the job-shop to represent the fact that a train passes atomically from one section to the next: this means that a free machine (track) must accept any available task (train passing) immediately. Stated otherwise, a machine must only be idle if there is no task requiring it. Alessandro's contributions also encompass the optimisation of railway systems (including timetable improvements for delay minimisation), but using other approaches not related to the job-shop scheduling, such as stochastic models and simulation [20].

In this paper, we investigate the feasibility of tackling job-shop scheduling with the exhaustive state space exploration algorithms implemented in the CADP toolbox[4] [18]. Our work was carried out within the A-IQ Ready project[5], which aims at devising intelligent autonomous electronic control systems based on crucial technologies, such as edge continuum orchestration for artificial intelligence, distributed collaborative intelligence, and quantum sensing. One of the

---

[2] https://rail-research.europa.eu/about-shift2rail/.

[3] https://rail-research.europa.eu/about-europes-rail/europes-rail-structure-of-governance/scientific-steering-group/.

[4] https://cadp.inria.fr.

[5] https://www.aiqready.eu/.

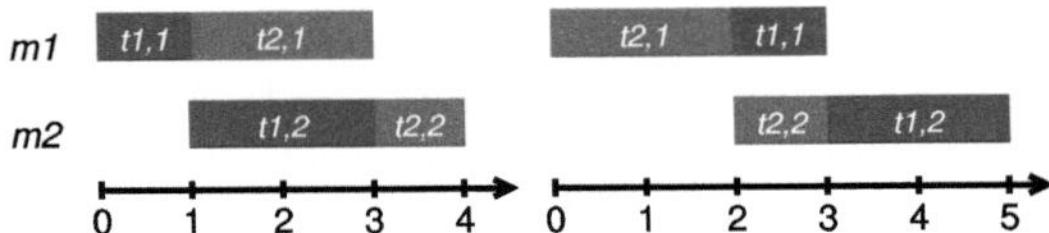

Fig. 1. Schedules for the Job-Shop Instance I2

use cases proposed in A-IQ Ready is related to indoor logistics, namely domestic robots navigating on tracks, for which optimal schedules must be produced. Our state space algorithms being complete, they can provide guarantees for the optimality of a solution, an information sought by project partners to further assess the quality of their application of reinforcement learning to the search of solutions [30]. The idea was to use state space exploration to search for, and possibly prove the absence of, better solutions than those computed by reinforcement learning. We considered a freely available collection of job-shop scheduling instances with solutions[6].

The rest of the paper is organised as follows. Section 2 introduces the common principles adopted for devising our formal models of job-shop scheduling. Sections 3, 4, 5, and 6 are devoted in turn to variants of the formal model, increasingly optimised for reducing the size of the state space. Section 7 describes how the models were exploited for state space generation and verification purposes. Section 8 discusses the heuristics adopted for reducing the state space. Finally, Sect. 9 gives some concluding remarks and directions for future work.

2   Common Modelling Principles

We experimented several encodings in the LNT language [19], a modern language combining the advantages of an imperative syntax with a formally defined semantics taken from process calculi. LNT is supported by the CADP toolbox, which provides tools to compile an LNT model into an LTS (Labelled Transition System). Common to all encodings is the idea to use a separate LNT process for each job and each machine, interacting via actions corresponding to the start and end of tasks. Using this encoding, different interleavings of these actions correspond to different schedules. Execution time of a schedule can be measured in two different ways: either using an offer indicating the current time or using a dedicated TICK action corresponding to a time-step. In any case, the LTS underlying the LNT model contains all possible schedules. Cutting the generation of the LTS at a given maximal time (or a maximal number k of TICKs) enables to search for schedules shorter than k.

To illustrate the various encodings in LNT, consider the following minimalistic instance I2, with two machines m_1 and m_2 and two jobs $j_1 = [(1, m_1); (2, m_2)]$ and $j_2 = [(2, m_1); (1, m_2)]$. Figure 1 shows two possible schedules for this instance: the (optimal) schedule on the left requires four time steps, whereas

---

the one on the right requires five time steps. Notice that both schedules assign a new task to a machine as soon as possible.

A major modelling challenge is to avoid useless, clearly non-optimal schedules, so as not to bloat the LTS pointlessly. For instance, there is absolutely no point to leave all machines idling. A naive modelling, leaving machines and jobs free to interact, would include the case where no job starts executing.

```
type machineID is
   M1, M2
end type

type jobID is
   J0, J1, J2
end type

type task is
      task (duration: nat, machine: machineID)
end type

type task_list is
   list of task
end type
```

Fig. 2. Data Type Definitions

Common to all our encodings is the representation of the available machines and jobs as enumerated data types, and tasks as records with two fields for the duration and the machine, as shown in Fig. 2; a machine executing the particular job J0 is considered to be free.

3   Single-Gate Model

In a first model, a single gate is used for all communications between jobs and machines. This has the advantage of passing all information in a single place, making it easy to enforce ordering constraints at each time step. However, it requires all LNT processes to accept rendezvous on the gate at every time step, and to share the current state of all jobs and machines with all processes. An additional gate finish is used to synchronise all LNT processes at the end when all tasks of all jobs are completed and the machines can stop their execution.

The behaviour of a machine is described by the LNT process shown in Fig. 3, and the behaviour of a job is described by the LNT process shown in Fig. 4. Both processes have a single visible gate current, specified between square brackets and with channel type c specifying that each rendezvous has seven offers: the current time, and for each machine a triple consisting of the currently executed

```
channel c is
   (tick: nat,
     current_job_1: jobID, time_remaining_1: nat, accepted_1: Bool,
     current_job_2: jobID, time_remaining_2: nat, accepted_2: Bool)
end channel

process machine [current: c] (m: machineID) is
   var current_job: jobID, time_remaining: nat, b: bool in
     current_job := J0;
     time_remaining := 0;
     loop
       if current_job != J0 then  -- the machine is executing something
         case m in
           M1 -> current (?any nat, current_job, time_remaining, false,
                            ?any jobID, ?any nat, ?any bool)
         | M2 -> current (?any nat, ?any jobID, ?any nat, ?any bool,
                            current_job, time_remaining, false)
         end case;
         time_remaining := time_remaining - 1
       else  -- the machine is free and ready to accept a new task
         case m in
           M1 -> current (?any nat, ?current_job, ?time_remaining, ?b
                            ?any JobID, ?any nat, ?any bool)
                   where (current_job == J0) =>
                        ((time_remaining == 0) and not (b))
         | M2 -> current (?any nat, ?any JobID, ?any nat, ?any bool,
                            ?current_job, ?time_remaining, ?b)
                   where (current_job == J0) =>
                        ((time_remaining == 0) and not (b))
         end case;
         if time_remaining > 0 then
            time_remaining := time_remaining - 1
         end if
       end if;
       if time_remaining == 0 then
            -- the execution of the current task is terminated and the machine
            -- becomes free
            current_job := J0
       end if
     end loop
   end var
end process
```

Fig. 3. Single-Gate Model: Machine

job, the remaining time, and a Boolean indicating whether the machine has
started the execution of this task in the current time step.

A machine has a variable parameter m corresponding to its identifier and local variables to hold the three values related to the three offers corresponding to machine m.[7] The behaviour of a machine is essentially an infinite loop consisting of a conditional if statement depending whether the machine is free or not. If the machine is executing a task different from J0, it constrains (in the rendezvous on gate current) the three offers (two to four for M1 and five to seven for M2) respectively (a) to the identifier of the job the tasks belongs to, (b) to the time remaining to execute the task, and (c) to the Boolean false indicating that the execution of the task did not start during this time step. Otherwise, the machine is free and ready to accept a new task for execution; if no task is assigned to it, then the remaining time must be 0 and the third offer must be false (enforced by the constraints on the rendezvous). Then, if necessary, the time remaining for the execution of the current task is decremented, and if job execution has finished, the machine is declared to be free by assigned it a task of job J0.

The behaviour of a job is described similarly. Process job has two variable parameters: its identifier j and the initial list of tasks to be executed, each task being a pair consisting of a duration and the identifier of the machine, where the task has to be executed. The body of process job is essentially a sequence of two loops L1 and L2. Loop L1 describes the execution of the tasks of the job, executing the tasks of its task list parameter tasks one by one. Loop L1 thus iterates over the list of tasks, selecting the first task of the list using pattern matching (case statement). For each task, it executes a while loop depending on the duration of the task, trying to start execution as soon as the requested machine becomes free. This is expressed by the nondeterministic choice (alt statement in the then branch of the if) with the two alternatives for a rendezvous on gate current: either the task starts its execution, or a task of another job is running: the job does not accept a rendezvous on current when the machine idles. A task is executed for as many steps as specified by its duration (which is decremented once per iteration of the while loop). When all tasks have been executed, loop L2 permits other jobs to finish the execution of their tasks, enforcing only that no machine executes a task of job j. Using an alt statement permits to detect the situation where all machines are idle and to end the execution of the job.

The complete system is then described by the parallel composition of machines and jobs shown in Fig. 5. Both jobs and machines are grouped together in two separate parallel compositions. When all jobs have ended, their group executes a rendezvous on gate finish, which disrupts the execution of the machines (and the process measure, which simply enforces that the first offer of gate current increases by one each time, indicating elapsed execution time).

Overall, this LNT model has about 200 lines. The corresponding LTS is generated almost instantly and is shown in Fig. 6. Starting from the initial state (numbered 0 at the bottom), the two execution branches correspond to the two schedules shown in Fig. 1. The seven offers of the transitions labelled with a

---

[7] It would also be possible to model each machine as a separate process—removing the need for the parameter m and the repeated case-constructs.

```
process job [current: c] (j: jobID, in var tasks: task_list) is
var k1, k2: jobID in
  loop L1 in
    case tasks var t: task in
      nil -> break L1
    | cons (t, tasks) ->
        var time_remaining: nat, d: nat in
          time_remaining := t.duration;
          while time_remaining > 0 loop
            case t.machine of machineID in
              M1 ->
                if time_remaining == t.duration then
                  alt  -- task t starts its execution
                    current (?any nat, j, time_remaining, true, ?k2,
                            ?any nat, ?any bool) where k2!=j;
                    time_remaining := time_remaining - 1
                  [] -- a task of another job is running
                    current (?any nat, ?k1, ?d, ?any bool, ?k2,
                            ?any nat, ?any bool)
                      where (k1 != J0) and (d != 0) and
                            (k1 != j) and (k2 != j)
                  end alt
                else -- task t is executing
                  assert time_remaining > 0;
                  current (?any nat, j, time_remaining, false, ?k2,
                          ?any nat, ?any bool) where k2 != j;
                  time_remaining := time_remaining - 1
                end if
            | M2 ->
                ... -- symmetric case
            end case
          end loop
        end var
    end case
  end loop;
  loop L2 in
    alt
      -- no more executing jobs
      current (?any nat, J0, 0 of nat, false, J0, 0 of nat, false);
      break L2
    [] -- some jobs still executing
      current (?any nat, ?k1, ?any nat, ?any bool, ?k2, ?any nat,
              ?any bool)
        where (k1 != j) and (k2 != j) and ((k1 != J0) or (k2 != J0))
    end alt
  end loop
end var end process
```

Fig. 4. Single-Gate Model: Job

```
process MAIN [current: c, finish: none] is
   par current, finish in
      par current in
         job [...] (J1, {task(1, M1), task(2, M2)})
      || job [...] (J2, {task(2, M1), task(1, M2)})
      end par;
      finish
   || disrupt
         par current in
            machine [...] (M1)
         || machine [...] (M2)
         || measure [...]
         end par
      by finish
      end disrupt
   end par
end process
```

Fig. 5. Single-Gate Model: Complete System

rendezvous on gate `current` indicate the progress of the execution. For instance, the transition "CURRENT !3 !J0 !0 !FALSE !J1 !2 !TRUE" between states 6 and 8 indicates that in the third time step, machine m_1 is idling, machine m_2 started execution of a task from j_1 that needs two time steps before completion.[8] The transition labelled `exit` between states 11 and 12 indicates successful termination, i.e., that the system finishes (without blocking).

A significant drawback of this modelling style is its lack of modularity: adding a machine or job requires to change all rendezvous in all LNT processes to take into account the additional offers (i.e., parameters describing exchanged data values), which also means changing all the constraints. Furthermore, the state space generation process in CADP uses a Petri net as intermediate format on which to apply optimisations. When constructing this Petri net, all possible rendezvous need to be considered. The many occurrences of gate `current` in the LNT processes `job` and `machine` induce a high number of possible combinations, leading to a large Petri net (and corresponding C code for the state space exploration). This is no difficulty for small instances, but larger instances become difficult to handle. Consider the instance I4 with four machines m_1, m_2, m_3, and m_4 and four jobs (each with four tasks of duration one)[9]. Instance I4 has a single optimal solution requiring four time steps; the corresponding LTS has to be constructed compositionally and the corresponding C code requires almost 50 GB of RAM to be compiled by GCC.

---

[8] When generating the LTS, all characters are converted to upper case.

[9] $j_1 = [(1, m_1); (1, m_2); (1, m_3); (1, m_4)]$, $j_2 = [(1, m_2); (1, m_3); (1, m_4); (1, m_1)]$, $j_3 = [(1, m_4); (1, m_1); (1, m_2); (1, m_3)]$, and $j_4 = [(1, m_3); (1, m_4); (1, m_1); (1, m_2)]$.

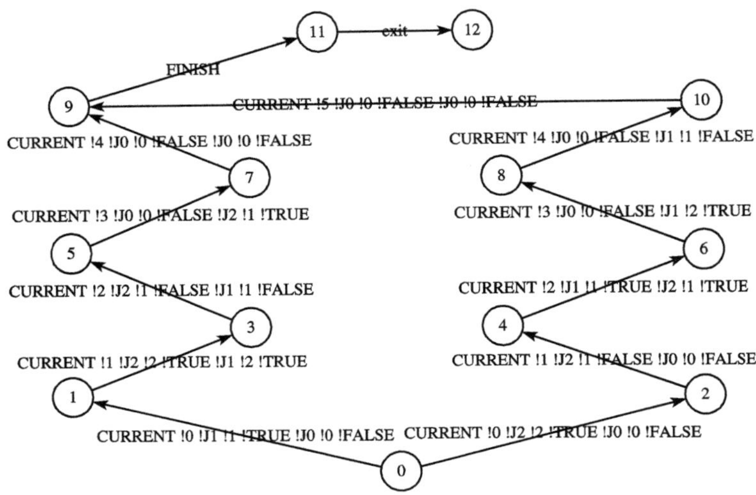

Fig. 6. LTS for the Single-Gate Model

4   Optimised Single-Gate Model

To circumvent some of the problems of the first single-gate model, namely to reduce the number of synchronisations and also avoid the computation of constraints that are provably not required for the next transition, we restructured the single-gate model of the previous section, leading to a second, optimised model. In this second model, a machine is described by the LNT process `machine` shown in Fig. 7, and a job by the LNT process `job` shown in Fig. 8. As before, both processes synchronise (with the same seven offers) on a single gate `current`.

The major difference is that process `machine` in Fig. 7 has a single occurrence of gate `current` (rather than three). For readability, the constraints on the rendezvous are grouped in a predicate (or Boolean function) `m_synchro`, and separated from the update of the local variables, grouped into a procedure (or function without result) `m_update`.

Similarly, the process `job` shown in Fig. 8 has only three occurrences of gate `current` (rather than eight), and groups the constraints into two predicates `job_synchro` (used when the job tries to submit a task for execution) and `j_execution` (used when a task of the job is executed). A third predicate `job_result` encapsulates the test whether job submission was successful. There is no need for a procedure to update the single local variable `d` counting the number of steps a task must still be executed.

The overall parallel composition is the same as before (shown in Fig. 5). Taken altogether, this optimised LNT model has also about 200 lines of LNT and (almost instantly) yields the same LTS (shown in Fig. 6). However, the intermediate Petri net has fewer transitions.

For larger instances, the difference becomes significant. For the instance with four machines, four jobs with four tasks each, the optimised LNT model yields an interme-

```
    process machine [current: c] (m: machineID) is
      var current_job: jobID, time_remaining: nat, k1, k2: jobID,
          d1, d2: nat, b1, b2: bool in
        current_job := J0;
        time_remaining := 0;
        loop
          current (?any nat, ?k1, ?d1, ?b1, ?k2, ?d2, ?b2)
            where m_synchro (m, current_job, k1, k2, d1, d2, b1, b2);
          eval m_update (m, k1, k2, d1, d2, b1, b2, current_job?,
                    time_remaining?);
          if time_remaining == 0 then
            -- nothing more to do for the current task (if any):
            -- the machine becomes free
            current_job := J0
          end if
        end loop
      end var
    end process
```

Fig. 7. Optimised Single-Gate Model: Machine

```
process job [current: c] (j: jobID, in var tasks: task_list) is
var k1, k2: jobID, d, d1, d2: nat, b1, b2: bool in
  loop L1 in
    case tasks var t: task, rest: task_list in
      nil -> break L1
    | cons (t, rest) ->
        current (?any nat, ?k1, ?d1, ?b1, ?k2, ?d2, ?b2)
          where job_synchro (j, t, k1, k2, d1, d2, b1, b2);
        if job_result (j, t.machine, k1, k2, b1, b2) then
          for d := t.duration - 1 while d > 0 by d := d - 1 loop
            current (?any nat, ?k1, ?d1, ?b1, ?k2, ?d2, ?b2)
              where j_execution (j, t.machine, d, k1, k2, d1, d2, b1, b2)
          end loop;
          tasks := rest
        end if
    end case
  end loop;
  loop L2 in
    -- allow other jobs to execute
    current (?any nat, ?k1, ?any nat, ?any bool, ?k2, ?any nat,
            ?any bool) where (k1 != j) and (k2 != j);
    if (k1 == J0) and (k2 == J0) then -- no more running jobs
      break L2
    end if
  end loop
end var end process
```

Fig. 8. Optimised Single-Gate Model: Job

diate Petri net with 137 transitions, which corresponds to a reduction of three orders of magnitude.

Still, the model is not modular: adding machines or jobs is cumbersome because it requires changes in almost all processes and predicates. Furthermore, because each transition synchronises all processes, all conditions need to be checked at each time step, the generation of the LTS is possible, but slow already for slightly larger instances as the one with four machines mentioned above (2.5 min for an LTS with 8 states and 7 transitions).

5   Two-Gate Model

To obtain a modular model, we let jobs and machines interact directly using two gates **assign** (to start execution of a task) and **done** (to indicate termination of the task). Similar to the single-gate models, an additional gate **finish** is used for the final synchronisation. The major advantage of this modelling style is that adding machines and/or jobs requires only changes in the overall parallel composition, because each rendezvous between a job and a machine carries only offers related to the two interacting processes. To measure execution time, all machines also synchronise on a gate **tick** modelling a discrete clock.

```
process machine [assign, done: C, tick, finish: none] (m: machineID) is
var j: jobID, time: Nat in
  loop
    alt
        assign (?j, ?any Nat, ?time, m) where time <= max_job_duration;
        for null while time > 0 by time := time - 1 loop
          tick
        end loop;
        done (j, m)
    [] tick
    [] finish; stop
    end alt
  end loop
end var end process
```

Fig. 9. Two-Gate Model: Machine

In this new model, a machine is described by the much simpler process shown in Fig. 9. It essentially executes a loop containing a nondeterministic choice between accepting a new task to be executed (rendezvous on gate **assign**), letting time progress (rendezvous on gate **tick**) and ending execution (rendezvous on gate **finish**). After accepting a task, the machine participates in as many rendezvous on gate **tick** as the duration of the task before a rendezvous on gate **done** indicating the corresponding job that the task has been executed.

A job is described by the process shown in Fig. 10. It iteratively executes the tasks from its list, each execution consisting in two rendezvous (on gate **assign** to start and

```
    process job [assign, done: C, finish: none]
              (j: jobID, in var tasks: task_list) is
    loop
       case tasks var t: task, next_tasks: task_list in
         cons (t, next_tasks) ->
              assign (j, t.operation, t.duration, t.machine);
              done (j, t.machine);
              tasks := next_tasks
       | nil -> finish; stop
       end case
     end loop
  end process
```

Fig. 10. Two-Gate Model: Job

```
    process MAIN [assign, done: C, tick, finish: none] is
       par assign, done, finish in
          par
             job [...] (J1, job_1)
          || job [...] (J2, job_2)
          end par
       || par tick, finish in
             machine [...] (M1)
          || machine [...] (M2)
          end par
       end par
    end process
```

Fig. 11. Two-Gate Model: Complete System

on gate **done** to end the execution). When all tasks are executed, it synchronises will all other processes on gate **finish**.

The overall parallel composition is shown in Fig. 11. Note that only the machines synchronise on gate **tick** and that there is no need to use the disrupt statement. Also, adding another job or machine is straightforward.

With about 100 lines of LNT, this model is significantly shorter than both single-gate models, but generates (almost instantly) an LTS with 55 states and 84 transitions (when minimised for strong bisimulation), which is significantly larger than the one shown in Fig. 5. Hiding the rendezvous on gate **done** and minimising for branching bisimulation yields an LTS with 28 states and 51 transitions, difficult to reduce further, because the rendezvous on gate **assign** are necessary to extract the scheduling of the task executions, and the rendezvous on gate **tick** are necessary to detect simultaneously started tasks. Besides a shorter source code, this modelling style is better suited to the CADP tools, because it avoids the computation of complex constraints in the data type and favours the selection of choices in the interleavings of the processes. Hence, state space generation is much more efficient: For the instance with four machines and four jobs with four tasks each, the complete LTS (16,550 states and 36,890 transitions) can be generated in about a second.

228   R. Mateescu et al.

Actually, this two-gate model was our first modelling attempt, but was abandoned because it violated the constraint that a (free) machine must execute an available task immediately. Unfortunately, it is impossible to express this constraint in LNT, because LNT has no means to express priorities on alternatives in a choice.[10] Furthermore, in the two-gate model, each state of the LTS corresponding to a state with at least one free machine has a TICK self-loop, introducing a choice between executing a new task immediately or delaying the execution for one TICK. When considering larger instances with more machines, jobs, and tasks, these choices induce a huge number of states and transitions, growing exponentially. The single-gate models were our first try to keep the LTS size under control.

As a second attempt to cope with larger models, we experimented with the compositional state space generation tools available in CADP. The idea is to generate each process separately, minimise it and then compute the overall composition, applying priorities, cutting superfluous execution branches. Due to the high number of possible triples (job, task identifier, duration) to be taken into account every time the machine is free, the naive compositional approach faces the unfortunate situation where a single process is similar in size to the complete state space. However, for each job, the corresponding LTS can be easily generated: thus the exact set of possible assignments emitted by the job is known. Using this set as interface (by means of a chaos automaton with a single state and a self-looping transition for each label in the set), semi-composition [23] enables the generation of the LTSs for the machines. When composing the LTSs for jobs and machines, the application of priority rules further reduces the size of the overall LTS. A first rule enforces that all actions related to job execution have a higher priority than the progression of time; between two TICK transitions, it is sufficient to consider a single ordering of transitions: hence we used priority rules to ensure that DONE is handled before ASSIGN (to have all machines available when choosing the next jobs to execute) and that DONE and ASSIGN are ordered according to increasing machine numbers. We automated these generation, reduction, and composition steps using an SVL [17] script, which takes advantage of the advanced smart reduction heuristics [8] (implemented in the SVL tool) to devise the order of the various steps.

For small instances, there is no gain in execution time, due to the largely increased number of calls to the various CADP tools: for the instance I2 with two machines, two jobs with two tasks each, the generation takes a total of 90 s. However, the resulting LTS is much smaller: 26 states and 26 transitions, which further reduces—after hiding DONE transitions and minimising for branching bisimulation—to 17 states and 17 transitions. Although this is as small as it can get, it is clearly larger than the LTS shown in Fig. 5, because each TICK and each assignment of a task to a machine yields a separate transition rather than merging all assignments of a same time step in a single transition (as in Fig. 5).

For the instance I4 with four machines, direct generation takes less than two seconds, and yields an LTS with 16050 states and 36754 transitions (minimised for strong bisimulation), whereas compositional generation takes 27 s and yields an LTS with 22 states and 21 transitions. Notice that both LTSs correspond to the single optimal solution of I4: the difference is due to the fact that direct generation considers all inter-

---

[10] Notice that a monolithic model, encoding everything using data-types, functions and a single process determining for each time instant the tasks executed by all machines, might have been a solution to express such priorities.

leavings, whereas the priority rules in the compositional approach leave only a single interleaving.

6   Compact Two-Gate Model

To further reduce the number of transitions in the final LTS, we experimented with a compact version of the two-gate model, where sequences of TICK-transitions are combined into a single TICK-transition with an offer corresponding to the length of the sequence. This approach is interesting for instances with long task durations (the durations in the benchmark require most frequently two digits). The corresponding LNT code for a machine is shown in Fig. 12.

```
process machine [assign, done: C, tick: T, finish: none]
                (m: machineID) is
var j: jobID, time, t: Nat in
  loop
    alt
       assign (?j, ?any Nat, ?time, m) where time <= max_job_duration;
       while time > 0 loop
         tick (?t) where (t > 0) and (t <= time);
         time := time - t
       end loop;
       done (j, m)
    [] tick (?t) where (t > 0) and (t <= max_job_duration)
    [] finish; stop
    end alt
  end loop
end var end process
```

Fig. 12. Compact Two-Gate Model: Machine

The condition "time <=max_job_duration" in the rendezvous on gate assign is not necessary when generating the LTS for the complete system, because a single value is provided by the corresponding job; however, the condition helps reducing the size of the LTS of a machine taken separately when computing the overall LTS compositionally.

Direct generation yields (in about 3 s) an LTS with 53 states and 970 transitions (25 states and 934 transitions after hiding DONE and minimising for branching bisimulation). The surprising increase in the number of transitions is due to the $n!$ choices to break up a sequence of n TICK transitions.

When using the compositional generation, an additional priority rule giving priority to the largest time steps avoids this increase. This priority rule specifying the order of all considered values for TICK transitions is generated in the SVL script by ordering all labels of the form "TICK !n" present in all machines. Overall, compositional generation is also improved: As expected, the LTS is smaller, having 23 states and 23 transitions (15 states and 15 transitions after hiding DONE and minimising for branching bisimulation), because the two sequences of two TICK transitions are merged into a single TICK transition. Also, the execution time is divided by more than four (it is reduced to 17 s).

7   Exploitation of the Model(s)

The models presented in the previous sections can be used to study the job-shop scheduling problem using various verification techniques. Generating the complete LTS is interesting to study all possible solutions of a given instance. If the goal is to search for a single solution, it is not necessary to construct the complete LTS, but rather search the solution in the LTS using on-the-fly techniques, e.g., by model checking the following MCL [27] formula:

```
< true*. FINISH > true
```

This formula is necessarily satisfied, because there is always the trivial schedule executing all jobs in sequence. Thus, the diagnostic (here, a witness transition sequence) generated by the model checker describes a possible solution. Another applicable on-the-fly tool is TESTOR [26], which generates conformance test(s) for a test purpose requesting to observe a transition FINISH; depending on the options, this allows to compute a single solution (a test case) or all solutions (the so-called complete test graph).

When the goal is to improve a known solution, it is sufficient to bound the LTS exploration to a given depth, either by modifying the LNT model (e.g., by adding a process limiting the number of TICKs), by using exploration tools limited to a given depth, or by bounding the number of TICKs in the property or test purpose. This on-the-fly exploration can be applied on the complete model, as well as on the compositionally constructed model: the latter has the advantage of enabling the various priority rules to be taken into account.

Table 1. State-Space Generation Statistics for Instance FT10

#jobs	states	transitions
4	1,260	1,281
5	9,234	9,470
6	153,358	159,542
7	4,059,402	4,250,087
8	733,172,821	772,979,502

The generation of small instances of the job-shop benchmarks was successful, with reasonable performance. For example, the LTS for the instance Fisher-Thompson FT06 has 68816 states and 72543 transitions. Unfortunately, larger instances (more than six machines, jobs, and tasks) of the benchmarks could not be handled. Considering the instance Fisher-Thompson FT10 with ten machines and ten jobs with ten tasks each, experiments with compositional state space generation considered adding jobs one by one (because each job assigns tasks to all ten machines, the machines must always be included). Table 1 gives the LTS sizes for four to eight jobs (of the ten jobs of FT10); all LTSs but the one for eight jobs have been minimised for strong bisimulation. Generation of the larger LTSs took advantage of distributed generation tools, using up to sixteen cores. Generation of the LTS for nine jobs was interrupted due to lack of memory (it required more 900 GB of RAM).

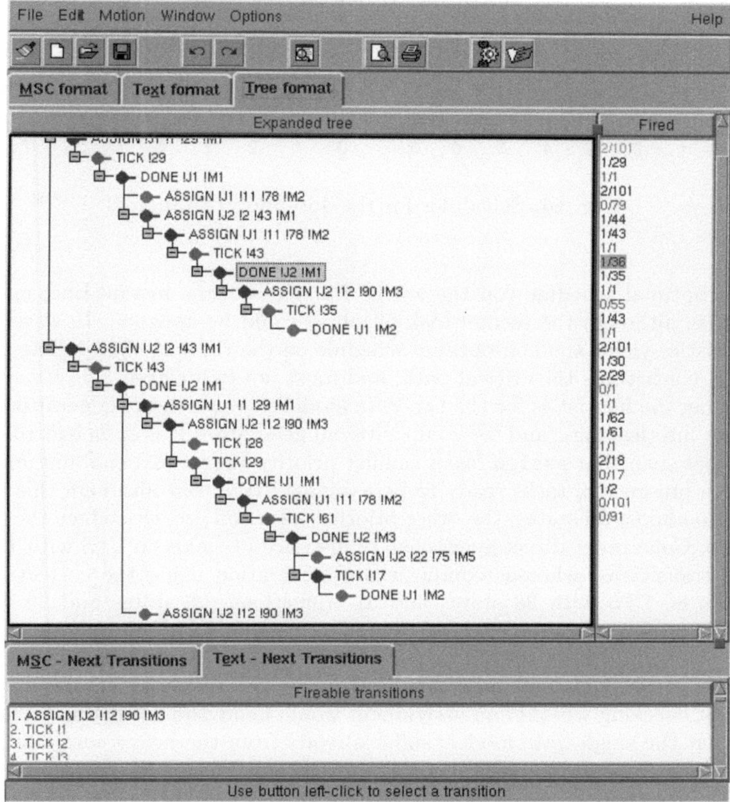

Fig. 13. Interactive Simulation of Instance FT10

Even if generating the complete LTS is out of reach due to the combinatorial explosion inherent to the job-shop scheduling problem, the model is still usable: Fig. 13 is a screenshot of the step-by-step simulator for the instance FT10, running smoothly on a standard laptop.

8   Correction of the Heuristics

The models presented so far were all based on an heuristics, required for the application to railway scheduling, to execute tasks as soon as possible, i.e., if a machine m is free and there is some job searching to execute a task t on m, then t is immediately assigned to m. This heuristics greatly cuts the size of the LTS and was a major reason motivating the switch from the initial two-gate model to the more complex single-gate model. Unfortunately, this heuristics is incorrect for general job-shop scheduling problems, as illustrated by the following instance I3 with three machines m_1, m_2, and m_3, and three jobs $j_1 = [(1, m_1); (3, m_3); (2, m_2)]$, $j_2 = [(2, m_2); (2, m_1); (3, m_3)]$, and $j_3 = [(1, m_3); (2, m_1); (1, m_2)]$.

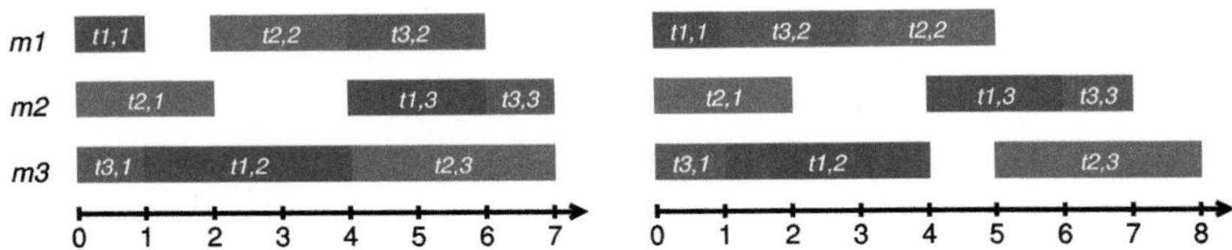

Fig. 14. Schedules for the Job-Shop Instance I3

In the optimal schedule (on the left of Fig. 14) at time instant one, machine m_1 remains free, although the second task of job j_3 could be assigned. However, the previous heuristics yields the non-optimal schedule on the right of Fig. 14. The problem is that job j_2 constitutes the critical path, and must not be delayed.

Changing the heuristics for the two-gate models is easy: direct generation produces all possible interleavings, and for compositional generation it is sufficient to adapt the priority rules such that **assign** has a smaller priority than **tick**, enabling machines to idle even in presence of tasks ready to be assigned. Note that although this adds **tick** self-loops to almost all states, the other priority rules still greatly reduce the size of the state space. Concretely, direct generation of instance I3 yields an LTS with 1219 states and 2082 transitions, whereas compositional generation using the corrected priority rules yields an LTS with 38 states and 51 transitions (26 states and 39 transitions after hiding **done** and minimising for branching bisimulation), containing the optimal schedule.

Correcting the single-gate models is more involved, because it requires one to devise a constraint checking whether an assignment would delay the critical path. Taking into account that the single-gate models suffer already from the heavy computation of the existing constraints, adding such a constraint was not further investigated.

9   Conclusion

We studied how the well-known job-shop scheduling problem can be formulated and solved using modern formal description languages and their associated verification tools. We devised and progressively refined several models of the job-shop problem in LNT, a formal language with user-friendly syntax and process algebraic semantics. The final two-gate model, in which jobs and machines interact via the gates **assign** and **done** (indicating the start and termination of a task, respectively) is modular and compact, allowing one to easily set up new configurations of jobs and machines. The corresponding LTS was made as small as possible by using heuristics (implemented using the priority rules of the SVL language), still being guaranteed to contain the optimal schedules, which can be found using the on-the-fly model checker of the CADP toolbox.

Due to the inherent combinatorial complexity of job-shop scheduling, increasing the number of machines and the size of jobs leads to state-space explosion. However, our two-gate LNT model can be used as basis to implement and experiment various heuristics to guide the search towards optimal schedules, by compositionally adding constraints in the LNT model and exploring the LTS on the fly using the OPEN/CÆSAR environment [16].

Acknowledgments. Part of this work has been supported by the Schlumberger Foundation and by the A-IQ Ready project, which receives funding within the Chips JU (the Public-Private Partnership for research, development and innovation under Horizon Europe) and National Authorities under grant agreement no. 101096658.

References

1. Basile, D., et al.: On the industrial uptake of formal methods in the railway domain. In: Furia, C.A., Winter, K. (eds.) IFM 2018. LNCS, vol. 11023, pp. 20–29. Springer, Cham (2018). https://doi.org/10.1007/978-3-319-98938-9_2

2. Basile, D., ter Beek, M.H., Di Giandomenico, F., Fantechi, A., Gnesi, S., Spagnolo, G.O.: 30 years of simulation-based quantitative analysis tools: a comparison experiment between Möbius and Uppaal SMC. In: Margaria, T., Steffen, B. (eds.) ISoLA 2020. LNCS, vol. 12476, pp. 368–384. Springer, Cham (2020). https://doi.org/10.1007/978-3-030-61362-4_21

3. Basile, D., et al.: An integrated perspective on the evaluation of complex railway systems. In: Margaria, T., Steffen, B. (eds.) ISoLA 2024. LNCS, vol. 15223, pp. 190–207. Springer, Cham (2025). https://doi.org/10.1007/978-3-031-75390-9_13

4. Basile, D., Fantechi, A., Rosadi, I.: Formal analysis of the UNISIG safety application intermediate sub-layer. In: Lluch Lafuente, A., Mavridou, A. (eds.) FMICS 2021. LNCS, vol. 12863, pp. 174–190. Springer, Cham (2021). https://doi.org/10.1007/978-3-030-85248-1_11

5. ter Beek, M.H., et al.: Adopting formal methods in an industrial setting: the railways case. In: ter Beek, M.H., McIver, A., Oliveira, J.N. (eds.) FM 2019. LNCS, vol. 11800, pp. 762–772. Springer, Cham (2019). https://doi.org/10.1007/978-3-030-30942-8_46

6. ter Beek, M.H., Fantechi, A., Gnesi, S.: Formal methods for industrial critical systems. In: Hinchey, M., Steffen, B. (eds.) The Combined Power of Research, Education, and Dissemination. LNCS, vol. 15240, pp. 327–344. Springer, Cham (2025). https://doi.org/10.1007/978-3-031-73887-6_21

7. Belli, D., et al.: The 4SECURail case study on rigorous standard interface specifications. In: Cimatti, A., Titolo, L. (eds.) FMICS 2023. LNCS, vol. 14290, pp. 22–39. Springer, Cham (2023). https://doi.org/10.1007/978-3-031-43681-9_2

8. Crouzen, P., Lang, F.: Smart reduction. In: Giannakopoulou, D., Orejas, F. (eds.) FASE 2011. LNCS, vol. 6603, pp. 111–126. Springer, Heidelberg (2011). https://doi.org/10.1007/978-3-642-19811-3_9

9. Dauzère-Pérès, S., Ding, J., Shen, L., Tamssaouet, K.: The flexible job shop scheduling problem: a review. Eur. J. Oper. Res. **314**(2), 409–432 (2024). https://doi.org/10.1016/j.ejor.2023.05.017

10. Fang, W., Yang, S., Yao, X.: A survey on problem models and solution approaches to rescheduling in railway networks. IEEE Trans. Intell. Transp. Syst. **16**(6), 2997–3016 (2015). https://doi.org/10.1109/TITS.2015.2446985

11. Fantechi, A., Gnesi, S., Haxthausen, A.E.: Formal methods for distributed computing in future railway systems. In: Margaria, T., Steffen, B. (eds.) ISoLA 2020. LNCS, vol. 12478, pp. 389–392. Springer, Cham (2020). https://doi.org/10.1007/978-3-030-61467-6_24

12. Fantechi, A., Haxthausen, A.E., Nielsen, M.B.R.: Model checking geographically distributed interlocking systems using UMC. In: Proceedings of the 25th Euromicro

International Conference on Parallel, Distributed and Network-based Processing (PDP 2017), St. Petersburg, Russia, pp. 278–286. IEEE Computer Society (2017). https://doi.org/10.1109/PDP.2017.66

13. Ferrari, A., et al.: Survey on formal methods and tools in railways: the ASTRail approach. In: Collart-Dutilleul, S., Lecomte, T., Romanovsky, A. (eds.) RSSRail 2019. LNCS, vol. 11495, pp. 226–241. Springer, Cham (2019). https://doi.org/10.1007/978-3-030-18744-6_15

14. Ferrari, A., Beek, M.H.T.: Formal methods in railways: a systematic mapping study. ACM Comput. Surv. **55**(4) (2022). https://doi.org/10.1145/3520480

15. Ferrari, A., Magnani, G., Grasso, D., Fantechi, A., Tempestini, M.: Adoption of model-based testing and abstract interpretation by a railway signalling manufacturer. Int. J. Embed. Real-Time Commun. Syst. **2**(2), 42–61 (2011). https://doi.org/10.4018/JERTCS.2011040103

16. Garavel, H.: OPEN/CÆSAR: an open software architecture for verification, simulation, and testing. In: Steffen, B. (ed.) TACAS 1998. LNCS, vol. 1384, pp. 68–84. Springer, Heidelberg (1998). https://doi.org/10.1007/BFb0054165

17. Garavel, H., Lang, F.: SVL: a scripting language for compositional verification. In: Kim, M., Chin, B., Kang, S., Lee, D. (eds.) Proceedings of the 21st IFIP WG 6.1 International Conference on Formal Techniques for Networked and Distributed Systems (FORTE 2001), Cheju Island, Korea, pp. 377–392. Kluwer Academic Publishers (2001), full version available as INRIA Research Report RR-4223

18. Garavel, H., Lang, F., Mateescu, R., Serwe, W.: CADP 2011: a toolbox for the construction and analysis of distributed processes. Int. J. Softw. Tools Technol. Transfer (STTT) **15**(2), 89–107 (2013)

19. Garavel, H., Lang, F., Serwe, W.: From LOTOS to LNT. In: Katoen, J.-P., Langerak, R., Rensink, A. (eds.) ModelEd, TestEd, TrustEd. LNCS, vol. 10500, pp. 3–26. Springer, Cham (2017). https://doi.org/10.1007/978-3-319-68270-9_1

20. Di Giandomenico, F., Fantechi, A., Gnesi, S., Itria, M.L.: Stochastic model-based analysis of railway operation to support traffic planning. In: Gorbenko, A., Romanovsky, A., Kharchenko, V. (eds.) SERENE 2013. LNCS, vol. 8166, pp. 184–198. Springer, Heidelberg (2013). https://doi.org/10.1007/978-3-642-40894-6_15

21. Grasso, D., Fantechi, A., Ferrari, A., Becheri, C., Bacherini, S.: Model based testing and abstract interpretation in the railway signaling context. In: Proceedings of the 3rd International Conference on Software Testing, Verification and Validation (ICST 2010), Paris, France, pp. 103–106. IEEE Computer Society (2010). https://doi.org/10.1109/ICST.2010.44

22. Haxthausen, A.E., Fantechi, A.: Compositional verification of railway interlocking systems. Formal Aspects Comput. **35**(1), 1–46 (2023). https://doi.org/10.1145/3549736

23. Krimm, J.-P., Mounier, L.: Compositional state space generation from Lotos programs. In: Brinksma, E. (ed.) TACAS 1997. LNCS, vol. 1217, pp. 239–258. Springer, Heidelberg (1997). https://doi.org/10.1007/BFb0035392

24. Lange, J., Werner, F.: Approaches to modeling train scheduling problems as job-shop problems with blocking constraints. J. Sched. **21**(2), 191–207 (2018). https://doi.org/10.1007/S10951-017-0526-0

25. Li, X., et al.: Survey of integrated flexible job shop scheduling problems. Comput. Ind. Eng. **174**(108786) (2022). https://doi.org/10.1016/j.cie.2022.108786

26. Marsso, L., Mateescu, R., Serwe, W.: TESTOR: a modular tool for on-the-fly conformance test case generation. In: Beyer, D., Huisman, M. (eds.) TACAS 2018. LNCS, vol. 10806, pp. 211–228. Springer, Cham (2018). https://doi.org/10.1007/978-3-319-89963-3_13

27. Mateescu, R., Thivolle, D.: A model checking language for concurrent value-passing systems. In: Cuellar, J., Maibaum, T., Sere, K. (eds.) FM 2008. LNCS, vol. 5014, pp. 148–164. Springer, Heidelberg (2008). https://doi.org/10.1007/978-3-540-68237-0_12
28. Oliveira, E., Smith, B.M.: A combined constraint-based search method for single-track railway scheduling problem. In: Brazdil, P., Jorge, A. (eds.) EPIA 2001. LNCS (LNAI), vol. 2258, pp. 371–378. Springer, Heidelberg (2001). https://doi.org/10.1007/3-540-45329-6_36
29. Palgunadi, S., Supraba, D., Harjito, B.: Job-shop scheduling model for optimization of the double track railway scheduling: (case study: Solo-yogyakarta railway network). In: Proceedings of the International Conference on Information & Communication Technology and Systems (ICTS'2016), Surabaya, Indonesia, pp. 90–95. IEEE Computer Society (2016). https://doi.org/10.1109/ICTS.2016.7910279
30. Vivekanandan, D., Wirth, S., Karlbauer, P., Klarmann, N.: A reinforcement learning approach for scheduling problems with improved generalization through order swapping. Mach. Learn. Knowl. Extract. 5, 418–430 (2023). https://doi.org/10.1145/3520480
31. Xiong, H., Shi, S., Ren, D., Hu, J.: A survey of job shop scheduling problem: the types and models. Comput. Oper. Res. 142(105731) (2022). https://doi.org/10.1016/j.cor.2022.105731

Railway Industry

Preliminary Study on 5G Synchronization Signal-Based Positioning for Autonomous Trams

Gianluca Mandò[1]([✉]), Dinesh Tamang[2], Lydia Abady[2], Giulio Bartoli[2], and Andrea Abrardo[2]

[1] Hitachi Rail GTS, Florence, Italy
`gianluca.mando@urbanandmainlines.com`
[2] University of Siena, Siena, Italy
`{dinesh.tamang2,lydia.abady,giulio.bartoli,abrardo}@unisi.it`

Dedicated to Prof. Alessandro Fantechi, whose outstanding contributions to formal methods and software safety have shaped rigorous approaches for dependable systems. His research on modeling and verification has been instrumental in advancing safety-critical applications, inspiring both academia and industry to pursue excellence in reliability and innovation.

Abstract. This paper demonstrates the feasibility of using 5G Synchronization Signal Block (SSB) for tram localization in the context of Autonomous Tram (AT) systems. We develop a comprehensive MATLAB-based Urban Macrocell (UMa) simulation framework that generates synthetic SSB signals under realistic urban channel conditions, enabling systematic evaluation of power-feature-based positioning algorithms. Through extensive experiments, we show that a deep learning approach based on Long Short-Term Memory (LSTM) networks, augmented with cross-attention mechanisms and Kalman Filter (KF), significantly outperforms traditional Round Trip Time (RTT)-based Least Squares (LS) approach, reducing the mean localization error by approximately 87%, from 59.79 m to 7.83 m. The combination of simulation-driven evaluation, comparative analysis against conventional methods, and incorporation of temporal and statistical modeling provides a solid methodological and performance foundation for subsequent experimental and practical deployments.

Keywords: 5G · Autonomous Tram · Localization · Machine Learning · Synchronization Signal

© The Author(s), under exclusive license to Springer Nature Switzerland AG 2026
M. H. ter Beek et al. (Eds.): Fantechi Festschrift, LNCS 16470, pp. 239–258, 2026.
https://doi.org/10.1007/978-3-032-12484-5_13

List of Abbreviations

3GPP	Third Generation Partnership Project
5G	5th Generation
ADAS	Advanced Driver Assistance System
AoD	Angle of Departure
AT	Autonomous Tram
BS	Base Station
CDF	Cumulative Distribution Function
DM-RS	DeModulation-Reference Signal
FPGA	Field-Programmable Gate Array
GLONASS	GLObal NAvigation Satellite System
GNSS	Global Navigation Satellite System
GPS	Global Positioning System
gNB	Next Generation Node B
IMU	Inertial Measurement Unit
INS	Inertial Navigation System
KF	Kalman Filter
kNN	k-Nearest Neighbors
LoS	Line-of-Sight
LS	Least Squares
LSTM	Long Short-Term Memory
MEMS	Micro-Electro-Mechanical Systems
MIB	Master Information Block
ML	Machine Learning
MLP	Multi-Layer Perceptron
mmWave	millimeter Wave
MSE	Mean Squared Error
NGAP	Next-Generation Autonomous Positioning
NLoS	Non Line-of-Sight
NR	New Radio
O2I	Outdoor-to-Indoor
OFDM	Orthogonal Frequency Division Multiplexing
PBCH	Physical Broadcast Channel
PCI	Physical Cell Identity
PRS	Positioning Reference Signal
PSS	Primary Synchronization Signal
RSRP	Reference Signal Received Power
RSRQ	Reference Signal Received Quality
RSSI	Received Signal Strength Indicator
RTT	Round Trip Time
SDR	Software-Defined Radio
SoC	System on Chip
SSB	Synchronization Signal Block
SSS	Secondary Synchronization Signal
STD	Standard Deviation

TDOA	Time Difference of Arrival
TOA	Time of Arrival
TRP	Transmission Reception Point
UE	User Equipment
UMa	Urban Macrocell
USRP	Universal Software Radio Peripheral

1 Introduction

Accurate tramway localization in urban environments is critical for real-time tracking, route optimization, and smart city integration. While systems such as Global Navigation Satellite System (GNSS) and Inertial Navigation System (INS) are widely used, their performance degrades in dense urban areas due to multipath propagation, limited satellite visibility, and susceptibility to jamming or spoofing [1–3]. On-board sensors like tachometers and Doppler radars can improve robustness but suffer from cumulative errors and cannot operate as stand-alone solutions [2].

The emergence of 5G technology offers new opportunities for network-based localization. Third Generation Partnership Project (3GPP) Release 16 specifies sub-meter positioning accuracy using Positioning Reference Signal (PRS) [4]. However, PRS deployment remains limited. As a cost-effective alternative, the use of Synchronization Signal Block (SSB)—primarily used for cell synchronization—deserves detailed investigation for localization purposes. 5G systems operate at higher carrier frequencies and wider bandwidths, requiring precise synchronization between User Equipment (UE) and Next Generation Node B (gNB)s. SSBs facilitate this process during initial cell search. Each SSB consists of the Primary Synchronization Signal (PSS), Secondary Synchronization Signal (SSS), and Physical Broadcast Channel (PBCH). The PSS and SSS enable time and frequency synchronization, while the PBCH carries essential system information. SSBs are transmitted periodically–typically every 5, 10, or 20 ms–and support critical operations such as initial access, handover, and resource coordination. Although SSBs have narrower bandwidth than PRS, several studies have leveraged power features from multiple gNBs for fingerprinting-based positioning.

Unlike conventional fingerprinting methods that use algorithms such as k-Nearest Neighbors (kNN) [5–8], we propose a deep learning approach using Long Short-Term Memory (LSTM) networks. This model captures temporal correlations in sequences of SSB power measurements to estimate the tram's position, improving accuracy by learning the non-linear mapping from signal fingerprints to spatial locations. In particular, this paper assesses the feasibility of using SSB measurements from commercially deployed 5G networks for tram localization in urban environments.

The remainder of the paper is organized as follows. Section 2 reviews related work on 5G positioning using SSB signals. Section 3 outlines positioning requirements for Autonomous Tram (AT)s. Section 4 describes the study on 5G SSB signal acquisition using real hardware, SSB extraction, Physical Cell Identity (PCI) detection, and finally details the development of a MATLAB-based simulator for the considered scenario. Section 7 presents simulation results and discussion. Finally, Sect. 8 concludes the paper summarizing the key findings.

2   Related Work

Existing literature on GNSS/Global Positioning System (GPS)-based localization has consistently highlighted the limitations of conventional satellite positioning in dense urban environments. In so-called urban canyons, tall buildings obstruct direct satellite line-of-sight (Line-of-Sight (LoS)) and introduce strong multipath and non-line-of-sight (Non Line-of-Sight (NLoS)) effects, resulting in large pseudorange biases and non-Gaussian errors [9–11]. Multi-constellation GNSS (GPS+GLObal NAvigation Satellite System (GLONASS)+Galileo+BeiDou) and high-precision carrier-phase techniques can partially improve accuracy but remain unreliable in deep urban canyons due to satellite occlusion, cycle slips, and signal tracking loss [12]. Map- and sensor-aided approaches, including shadow matching and 3D city model integration, reduce cross-street errors but require up-to-date environment models or additional sensors, limiting practicality [9,10]. Recent machine-learning-based techniques attempt to classify LoS/NLoS signals or correct multipath-induced biases, yet their generalization across different urban scenarios and devices is often limited [11].

Building on these observations, 5th Generation (5G)-based positioning has emerged as a promising alternative for urban localization. Existing literature on 5G-based positioning predominantly focuses on static users, employing fingerprinting techniques that utilize signal features such as Reference Signal Received Power (RSRP) or Received Signal Strength Indicator (RSSI), often in conjunction with Machine Learning (ML) models [6–8,13,14]. For instance, Liu et al. [6] achieved high-precision Time of Arrival (TOA) estimation (0.50 m accuracy at 95% Cumulative Distribution Function (CDF)) in an indoor conference room using a software-defined receiver and machine learning under predominantly LoS conditions with a micro-cell. However, outdoor Urban Macrocell (UMa) environments present distinct challenges, including greater Base Station (BS) distances, higher path loss, Outdoor-to-Indoor (O2I) penetration loss, and increased NLoS conditions due to urban obstructions, which significantly degrade TOA accuracy.

Alternative approaches have explored different signal characteristics. Bao et al. [15] utilized the millimeter Wave (mmWave) n257 band for Angle of Departure (AoD) estimation, reporting a horizontal positioning error of 2.5 m at the 80th percentile in outdoor settings. Tedeschini et al. [16] analyzed synchronization errors between BSs in a deployed 5G network, demonstrating that compensating for these errors enables static user localization with an accuracy of 8–10 m in non-obstructed scenarios. A closely related study by Butt et al. [17] employed deep learning for fingerprinting SSB measurements. By constructing fingerprints from power values across multiple beams and Transmission Reception Point (TRP)s, their Multi-Layer Perceptron (MLP) model achieved sub-10 m median error in UMa environments by leveraging multipath characteristics. However, this work was limited to static user localization.

In contrast, our approach addresses the dynamic scenario of a moving UE or a tram. We extend the fingerprinting framework by incorporating LSTM networks to model temporal correlations in sequential SSB measurements and integrate a Kalman Filter (KF) to refine the trajectory, enabling robust positioning in multipath-rich urban macro-cells.

3   Next-Generation Autonomous Positioning (NGAP) for ATs

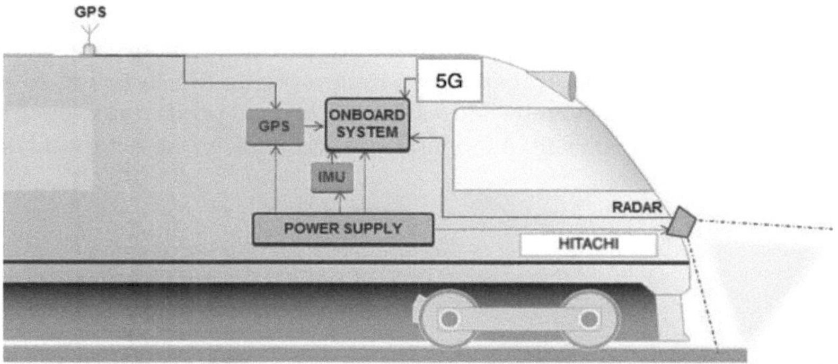

Fig. 1. System architecture of the NGAP framework for AT operations

This work directly supports the development of the NGAP system, a cornerstone technology for an innovative AT pilot program currently being deployed in Florence. The NGAP system represents a critical advancement in urban rail transportation, enabling fully AT operations through robust and precise vehicle localization capabilities. It is a high-precision localization system that enables the tram to continuously determine its position along the route. This system is specifically designed to minimize dependency on fixed ground-based infrastructure, thereby reducing deployment costs while maintaining operational reliability in complex urban environments.

The AT platform integrates two complementary technological systems. First, the NGAP system, as shown in Fig. 1, achieves its precise localization through sophisticated fusion of multiple complementary sensor modalities:

- **Inertial Measurement Unit (IMU)**: A high-performance tactical-grade Micro-Electro-Mechanical Systems (MEMS) inertial system comprising three-axis accelerometers and gyroscopes. This unit provides high-frequency measurements of linear acceleration and angular velocity, enabling dead reckoning capabilities during temporary GNSS outages while characterizing the tram's dynamic motion profile.

- **Ground-facing Doppler Radar**: A downward-oriented radar system that measures the tram's velocity relative to the ground surface with high accuracy. By analyzing the Doppler shift of reflected signals, this sensor provides direct velocity measurements that are immune to wheel slip, making it particularly valuable for precise odometry calculations.
- **Dual-frequency GNSS Receiver**: A multi-constellation satellite positioning system (GPS/European GNSS) capable of receiving both L1 and L2 frequency bands. This configuration enables precise pseudorange and carrier-phase measurements while mitigating ionospheric errors, providing absolute positioning references when satellite visibility is adequate.

Through advanced sensor fusion algorithms, the NGAP system integrates these heterogeneous data streams to generate a continuous, reliable position estimate even in challenging urban scenarios characterized by GNSS signal degradation, multipath effects, and frequent obscuration. Our work specifically focuses on enhancing this localization capability by leveraging 5G signaling to supplement traditional sensors, thereby addressing the critical positioning requirements necessary for safe and efficient AT operations in dense urban environments.

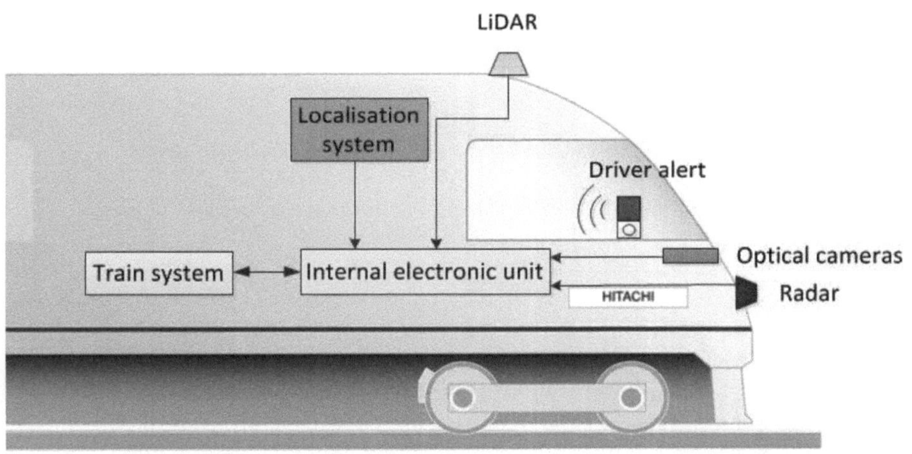

Fig. 2. ADAS System

Next, the AT platform incorporates a comprehensive perception system to ensure safety:

- **Advanced Driver Assistance System (ADAS)**: A comprehensive perception and collision warning system that monitors the tram's surroundings to detect and classify obstacles near the track. This system provides critical safety guarantees by enabling proactive hazard response and enhanced situational awareness, as shown in Fig. 2.

3.1 Main Contribution

This paper presents a foundational investigation into 5G SSB-based localization for urban tramway systems. Our primary contributions are:

- **Development of a MATLAB-based UMa Simulation Framework:** We designed and implemented a comprehensive simulation environment that generates synthetic 5G SSB measurements under controlled urban channel conditions. This framework enables systematic evaluation of power-feature-based positioning algorithms while accounting for realistic propagation effects.
- **Comparative Analysis of Localization Performance:** We conducted extensive experiments comparing our proposed LSTM-based approach with traditional Round Trip Time (RTT)-based Least Squares (LS) methods. We demonstrate that the LSTM architecture effectively captures temporal dependencies in SSB power sequences, achieving sub-10 m positioning accuracy when sufficient feature diversity is available. This establishes a methodological foundation and performance baseline for SSB-based tram localization, providing clear directions for future large-scale validation using real-world measurement data in operational urban environments.

4 SSB Capture and PCI Detection Algorithm

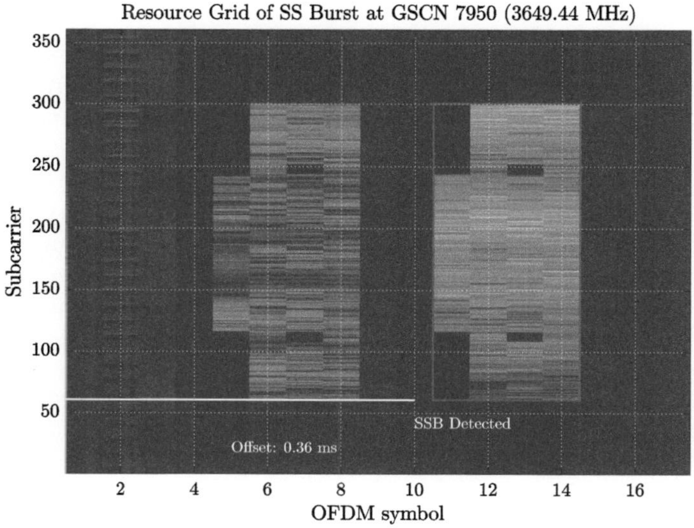

Fig. 3. Resource grid of a captured SSB at GSCN = 7950 and center frequency = 3649.44 MHz, using a Universal Software Radio Peripheral (USRP) SDR E312 [18]. The detected SSB corresponds to the 8-th beam, with $N_{ID}^2 = 2$, $N_{ID}^1 = 16$

To establish the feasibility of using power measurements of SSBs from different PCIs, we first studied the SSB synchronization and PCI detection process using the NI USRP E312 Software-Defined Radio (SDR) [18] in combination with the `MATLAB` 5G Toolbox [19]. The E312 supports a frequency range of 70 MHz to 6 GHz with up to 56 MHz instantaneous bandwidth, making it suitable for sub-6 GHz 5G New Radio (NR). Its embedded Zynq-7000 System on Chip (SoC), combining ARM processors with Field-Programmable Gate Array (FPGA) fabric, enables real-time baseband processing for synchronization and decoding. In our setup, the SDR was configured to operate at the desired 5G NR carrier frequency of 3649.44 MHz, and the received waveforms were processed to detect SSBs by correlating with the known PSS and SSS sequences. This procedure enabled initial cell search and PCI detection under realistic hardware conditions. Once detected, the SSB power levels were quantified in terms of RSRP, Reference Signal Received Quality (RSRQ), and RSSI, which form the primary features for the proposed localization framework.

Figure 3 displays the resource grid of a captured SSB from a commercial 5G NR network operating in band n78 at GSCN = 7950 with a center frequency of 3649.44 MHz, acquired using a USRP SDR E312 [18]. The observed SSB conform to the 3GPP Release 15 specifications, following pattern C with 30 kHz subcarrier spacing, 20 ms periodicity, and occupying 7.2 MHz bandwidth (20 RBs × 12 subcarriers). The identified SSB corresponds to the 8-th beam in the transmission pattern. The SSB detection algorithm consists of several steps. Comprehensive details regarding the SSB extraction procedure and subsequent PCI detection are provided in the following subsections.

4.1 Frequency Offset Evaluation

We begin by performing a PSS search together with coarse frequency offset estimation. The received waveform is frequency-shifted across candidate offsets, spaced at half-subcarrier intervals. Each shifted waveform is correlated with the three possible PSS sequences (indexed by Network Identifier 2 (N_{ID}^2)). The strongest correlation peak reveals the detected PSS sequence, the coarse frequency offset relative to the carrier center, and the time instant of favorable channel conditions. Fine frequency offsets below half a subcarrier are then estimated by correlating the cyclic prefix of each Orthogonal Frequency Division Multiplexing (OFDM) symbol in the SSB with its corresponding useful part, with the phase of this correlation providing the residual frequency error. Figure 4 reports magnitude of the PSS correlation for all the possible frequency offsets and the maximum value obtained for $N_{ID}^2 = 2$.

4.2 Delay Estimation, PCI Detection and PBCH Demodulation

The timing offset to the SSB block is estimated using the reference PSS sequence identified during frequency search as shown in Fig. 5. After applying frequency offset correction, the center frequencies of the received waveform and the reference PSS are aligned. The receiver then performs OFDM demodulation to

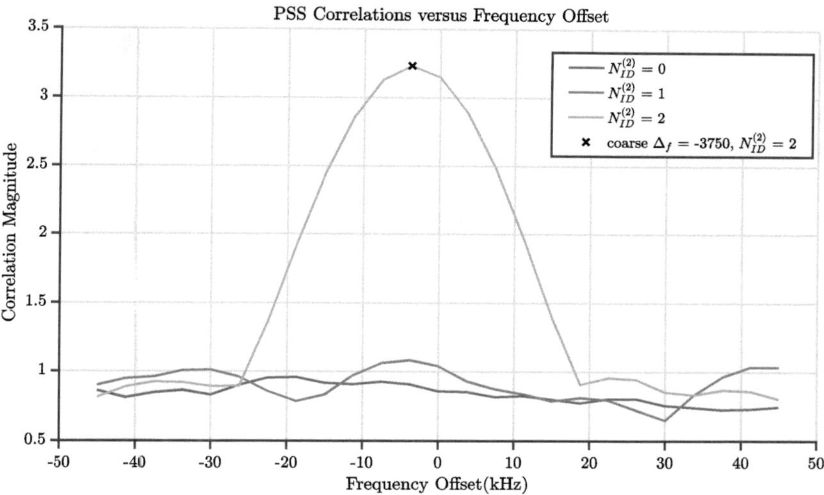

Fig. 4. $N_{ID}^2 = 2$ has the maximum PSS correlation with coarse frequency offset of -3750 Hz

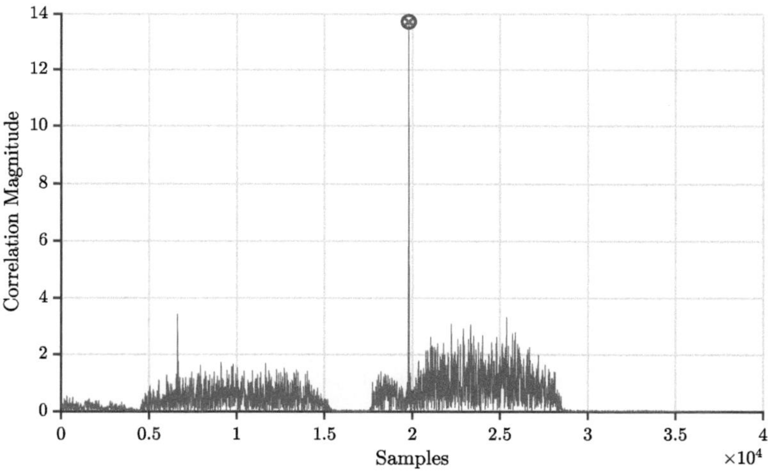

Fig. 5. Timing offset in samples (interpolation $= 4$) where the SSB block is located

extract the full SSB. This timing offset could be utilized in localization to calculate the Time Difference of Arrival (TDOA) for signals from different gNBs, thereby enabling position estimation. In Fig. 3, the detected SSB block has a timing delay of 0.36 ms with respect to the first sample of the captured waveform. This timing offset to the synchronization block also serves as the basis for PCI detection, which is essential for associating each SSB power measurement with its corresponding cell. Then, subsequent steps such as SSS search refinement, PBCH/DeModulation-Reference Signal (DM-RS) decoding, and Master Information Block (MIB) extraction are performed. A practical challenge arises when correlation peaks are ambiguous or weak, which may hinder reliable timing and PCI detection. The implications of these cases, along with potential mitigation strategies, could affect the final localization performance.

5 Development of the 3GPP UMa Downlink SSB Simulator

To complement the hardware-based study and further evaluate the feasibility of using SSB powers for localization, we developed a MATLAB-based simulator that emulates downlink transmissions in a 3GPP UMa scenario. The simulator is designed as a modular and extensible framework, enabling detailed analysis of synchronization signal behavior under realistic channel and mobility conditions. The main objective is to reproduce the acquisition and measurement process of SSBs in controlled yet realistic settings, and to generate reliable features such as RSRP, RSRQ, and RSSI for localization. The simulator incorporates three main components: signal generation, channel modeling, and user mobility described in detail below.

5.1 Signal Generation

The 5G NR waveform is generated in compliance with 3GPP Release 15 specifications using the `MATLAB` 5G Toolbox. The carrier configuration is defined via `nrCarrierConfig`, while the SSB burst is specified through `nrWavegenSSBurstConfig`. PSS, SSS, and the PBCH are mapped onto the resource grid using `nrSSBurst`. Subsequently, OFDM modulation is applied with `nrOFDMModulate` to obtain the time-domain waveform. This process ensures faithful representation of the synchronization signals as transmitted by a gNB. The generated signals can be visualized both in time and frequency domains, enabling validation of their structure and spectral occupancy.

5.2 Propagation Channel Model

The generated waveform is transmitted through a realistic 5G NR propagation channel modeled with the `nrTDLChannel` function. This model accounts for:

- Multipath fading with configurable delay spreads,
- Doppler effects due to UE mobility,
- UMa delay profiles as defined by 3GPP.

These parameters allow the simulator to reproduce challenging channel conditions, including NLoS propagation, shadowing, and fast fading, thereby providing a realistic test environment for synchronization and positioning.

5.3   Received Signal Construction

The downlink signals from multiple gNBs are modeled as delayed and attenuated versions of the transmitted waveforms. Each contribution is affected by path loss, multipath propagation, and the specific channel realization. The signals are then superimposed to form the received composite waveform at the UE. This procedure replicates practical conditions where the UE simultaneously observes multiple SSBs originating from different cells or beams. The resulting waveform serves as input for SSB detection, PCI identification, and feature extraction.

5.4   Mobility Model

User mobility is incorporated to study the impact of dynamic trajectories on localization performance. To realise a realistic tram movement, we adopt a state-space representation that captures position and velocity evolution under stochastic dynamics:

$$S_t = \begin{bmatrix} x_t \\ v_t \end{bmatrix}, \quad S_{t+1} = T \cdot S_t + w_t,$$

where the transition matrix

$$T = \begin{bmatrix} 1 & dt \\ 0 & 1 \end{bmatrix}$$

propagates the state forward in time with step size dt, and $w_t \sim \mathcal{N}(0, P)$ denotes Gaussian process noise with covariance

$$P = \begin{bmatrix} \frac{dt^3}{3}\sigma^2 & \frac{dt^2}{2}\sigma^2 \\ \frac{dt^2}{2}\sigma^2 & dt\sigma^2 \end{bmatrix}.$$

This formulation models trajectories with variable speeds, accelerations, and stop patterns.

6   Deep Learning: Model Architecture

In this section, we describe the proposed deep learning system for positioning an UE using the simulated powers of 5G synchronization signals. The study focuses exclusively on power-domain features and leverages an LSTM network augmented with cross-attention over the tram trajectory. Moreover, the overall methodology is illustrated in Fig. 6.

6.1   Dataset and Preprocessing

For each time instant, three types of power-domain features are considered from five surrounding BSs: RSRQ, RSRP, and RSSI. Each record in the dataset corresponds to one snapshot of the tram's position along a predefined trajectory. The input features are standardized using **StandardScaler**, while the ground-truth positions (the measured positions at the time of acquisition) are normalized

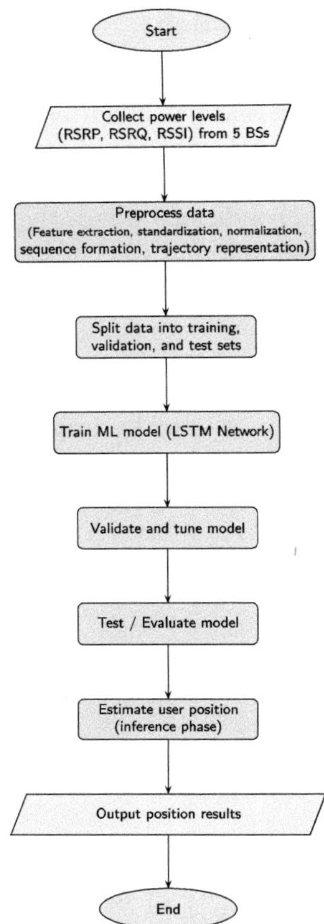

Fig. 6. Overview of the proposed preprocessing, training, and inference pipeline for the localization model.

to the range $[-1, 1]$ using a `MinMaxScaler`. The trajectory is represented as a sequence of two-dimensional coordinates $\mathbf{p}_t = [x_t, y_t]$ of 100,000 records, which serve both as the regression target and as contextual memory for the attention mechanism. The trajectory sequence is normalized with the same scaler of the ground-truth positions. Each set of power level measurements from the five BSs is grouped into one sequence.

6.2   Neural Network Architecture

The proposed neural network architecture combines feature embedding, temporal modeling, and contextual reasoning, as detailed below and represented in Fig. 7.

–   **Power Encoder** The received signal powers (RSRQ, RSRP, and RSSI) are first mapped into a latent feature space using a feed-forward encoder. This component consists of two fully connected layers with ReLU activation and dropout regularization. Such encoders are standard in deep learning for wireless systems [20,21], as they allow the network to extract discriminative representations from raw measurements that are otherwise noisy and highly correlated.

- **Positional Encoding** Since the model processes temporal sequences, sinusoidal positional encodings are added to the embedded features. This technique [22] enables the network to preserve temporal order without relying on explicit indices. In positioning tasks, this ensures that short-term dynamics of the received powers are appropriately contextualized.
- **Cross-Attention with Trajectory Memory** A distinctive feature of the system is the introduction of cross-attention between the input embeddings (queries) and the reference trajectory (keys and values). Here, queries are the instantaneous power feature embeddings, while keys are structured embeddings that encode the global set of possible positions along the tram route. Each key represents a specific coordinate bin. Values carry the trajectory information associated with each key. Through cross-attention [23,24], the network computes similarity scores between instantaneous power feature queries and all keys, normalizes these scores into attention weights, and then aggregates the corresponding values into a context vector. This process allows the model to associate real-time power measurements with the most relevant trajectory segments–effectively anchoring predictions to physically plausible regions. By retrieving value vectors, the mechanism mitigates ambiguities common in urban 5G deployments and ensures that the learned representations remain coherent with the underlying physical map of the tram route.
- **Bi-directional LSTM** Temporal dependencies in received power are modeled using a bi-directional LSTM [25,26]. Unlike feed-forward architectures, LSTMs capture both short-term and long-term temporal correlations in sequential data, making them effective for time-varying wireless channels and trajectory estimation [27,28]. The bi-directional setup leverages both past and future context within each sequence window, thereby improving accuracy and stability of predictions.
- **Output Projection** Finally, a linear projection maps the LSTM hidden states into 2D position estimates $(\hat{x}_t, \hat{y}_t)$. The model is trained end-to-end using the Mean Squared Error (MSE) loss, optimized with Adam [29] and a step-wise learning rate scheduler. Early stopping with patience of 20 epochs prevents overfitting with a total of 300 epochs. Model performance is evaluated in terms of Euclidean error:

$$\mathcal{L} = \frac{1}{T} \sum_{t=1}^{T} \|\hat{\mathbf{p}}_t - \mathbf{p}_t\|_2^2, \tag{1}$$

where $\hat{\mathbf{p}}_t$ denotes the predicted normalized position at time t and $\mathbf{p}_t$ denotes the ground-truth normalized position at time t and T is the batch size. This loss directly penalizes deviations in the predicted coordinates.

7   Performance Test

7.1   Simulation Scenario

We consider a classical 3GPP UMa scenario with a single tram to be localized. The deployment consists of five gNBs placed as shown in Fig. 8, and the detailed simulation parameters are summarized in Table 1. The gNBs transmit SSBs for downlink positioning. We assume an interference-free setting between SSB transmissions, which provides a simple yet realistic framework for modeling SSB-based downlink signals. From these signals, relevant power features can be extracted and later used as input to the machine learning algorithm for tram localization. The tram mobility model has been described in the previous section.

Each gNB transmits SSBs following a specific block pattern with $L_{\mathrm{max}} = 1$, meaning that only one beam per SSB burst is active. The block patterns are defined as follows—BS1: $[1, 0, 0, 0, 0, 0, 0, 0]$, BS2: $[0, 1, 0, 0, 0, 0, 0, 0]$ and so on. This configuration guarantees non-overlapping SSB transmissions across the gNBs, facilitating reliable beam identification and alignment. Furthermore, each gNB is assigned a unique N_{ID}^2 for synchronization. The receiver correlates the incoming waveform with these known PSS sequences, enabling clear distinction between gNBs. Specifically, the assigned N_{ID}^2 values are $[0, 1, 2, 0, 1]$ for gNB1 to gNB5, respectively.

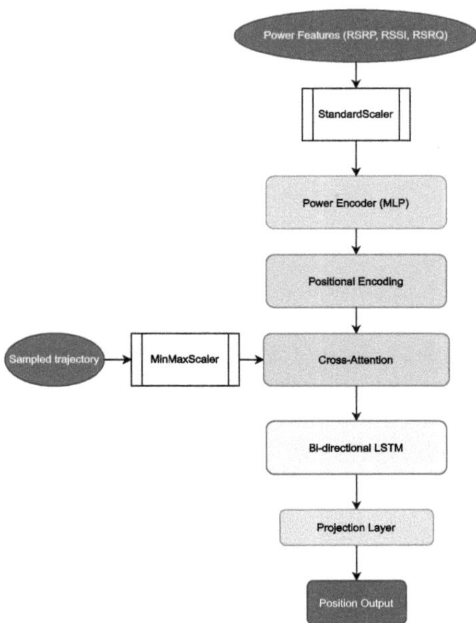

Fig. 7. Proposed LSTM-based positioning system with cross-attention over the tram trajectory.

Table 1. Simulation Parameters

Parameter	Value
Environment	3GPP UMa [30]
Number of Trams	1
Sample Rate	15.36 MHz
Number of gNB	5
SSB Block Pattern	Case C
Center Frequency	3.3 GHz
Channel Model	TDL-A (NLoS), TDL-D (LoS)
SSB Periodicity	20 ms
Numerology	1
Interpolation	4
Tram Height	3 m
gNB Height	25 m
Street Width	5 m
Building Height	5 m

Table 2. Training Parameters

Parameter	Value
Batch Size	16
Epochs	200
Learning Rate	10^{-5}
Sequence Length	5

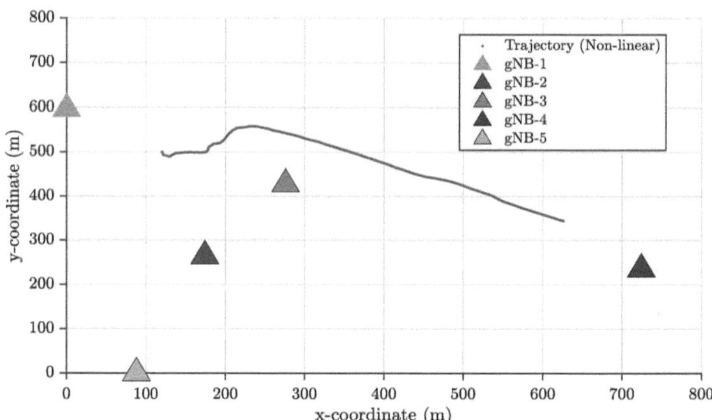

Fig. 8. Network scenario where the triangles represent the gNBs and red curve represents the considered trajectory obtained from the state-space model

7.2   Test Results and Discussion

We compare our solution with traditional RTT based LS approach where the estimated position is obtained by minimizing the squared error between the measured and predicted RTTs from multiple BSs:

$$(\tilde{x}, \tilde{y}) = \underset{(x,y)\in(\mathcal{X},\mathcal{Y})}{\arg\min} \sum_{m=1}^{M} (\alpha_m - \tilde{\alpha}_m(x,y))^2 \tag{2}$$

where:

- M: Total number of BSs
- α_m: Measured RTT for the UE to the m-th BS
- $\tilde{\alpha}_m(x,y)$: Predicted RTT as the Euclidean distance between candidate position (x,y) and the m-th BS
- (x,y): Candidate position of the tram

Neural Network Estimates. To ensure reliability, two datasets of 10,000 samples each were generated: one used for training and the other for testing, and vice versa. The training parameters are reported in Table 2. The averaged results over both train/test splits show that the raw LSTM output achieves a mean error of **11.23 m**, with a Standard Deviation (STD) of **17.08 m** and a 90th percentile error of **22.34 m**, as reported in Table 3.

In the following, the KF operates in the distance domain (1D) rather than directly in cartesian space. This ensures that the filtered trajectory remains constrained to the known tram path while reducing noise, thereby yielding accurate and smooth two-dimensional position estimates.

Post 1D Kalman Filtering. The neural network provides initial position estimates $\hat{x}_k, \hat{y}_k$, which are inherently noisy and not strictly aligned with the known tram trajectory. To improve robustness, we apply a post-processing pipeline consisting of trajectory projection, distance-domain Kalman filtering, and back-projection into Cartesian coordinates.

1. **Projection onto the reference trajectory**: Let the reference tram trajectory be represented as a complex-valued vector

$$\mathcal{T} = x_{\mathrm{t}} + j\, y_{\mathrm{t}},$$

   where x_{t} and y_{t} are the interpolated trajectory coordinates. Each neural network prediction

$$\hat{p}_k = \hat{x}_k + j\, \hat{y}_k$$

   is projected to the closest point on $\mathcal{T}$, yielding projected predictions $(\hat{x}_k^p, \hat{y}_k^p)$ that are constrained to lie on the true path.

2. **Conversion to distance domain:** Each projected point is mapped to a one-dimensional arc-length distance d_k along the trajectory, where $d_k \in \mathbb{R}^+$. The sequence $\{d_k\}$ represents noisy measurements of the tram's progression along the track.
3. **1D Kalman filtering in the distance domain:** We employ a one-dimensional constant-velocity KF to smooth $\{d_k\}$. The state vector is defined as

$$x_k = \begin{bmatrix} p_k \\ v_k \end{bmatrix},$$

where p_k denotes the estimated distance traveled along the trajectory and v_k the velocity. The state evolves according to

$$x_k = Ax_{k-1} + w_k, \quad A = \begin{bmatrix} 1 & \Delta t \\ 0 & 1 \end{bmatrix},$$

with process noise $w_k \sim \mathcal{N}(0, Q)$. Measurements are related to the state by

$$z_k = Hx_k + n_k, \quad H = \begin{bmatrix} 1 & 0 \end{bmatrix},$$

where $n_k \sim \mathcal{N}(0, R)$ models measurement noise. Recursive prediction and correction steps are applied:

$$\text{Prediction:} \quad \hat{x}_{k|k-1} = A\hat{x}_{k-1|k-1}, \tag{3}$$

$$P_{k|k-1} = AP_{k-1|k-1}A^T + Q, \tag{4}$$

$$\text{Update:} \quad K_k = P_{k|k-1}H^T(HP_{k|k-1}H^T + R)^{-1}, \tag{5}$$

$$\hat{x}_{k|k} = \hat{x}_{k|k-1} + K_k\left(z_k - H\hat{x}_{k|k-1}\right), \tag{6}$$

$$P_{k|k} = (I - K_kH)P_{k|k-1}. \tag{7}$$

The output of this step is a smoothed sequence of distances $\{p_k\}$.
4. **Back-projection to Cartesian coordinates:** Finally, each filtered distance p_k is mapped back to the corresponding point on $\mathcal{T}$. This produces the denoised trajectory in cartesian coordinates

$$(\hat{x}_k^f, \hat{y}_k^f), \quad k = 1, \ldots, N,$$

which represents the final position estimates after Kalman smoothing.

When the LSTM predictions are refined using a KF explained above, the performance improves significantly. The hybrid LSTM–KF approach reduces the mean error to **7.83 m**, while also achieving much lower variability, with a standard deviation of **6.01 m** and a 90th percentile error of **13.62 m**. The KF introduces optimal statistical estimation principles that smooth trajectory estimates, mitigate noise, and provide robustness against temporary signal degradations and outliers. By acting as a temporal smoother, it reduces jitter in position estimates and offers a principled framework for optimally fusing predictions with measurements based on their respective confidence levels.

To compare with the traditional benchmark solution without machine learning, the RTT based LS approach results in a much higher mean error of **59.79 m**, a STD of **68.09 m**, and a 90th percentile error of **148.45 m**, clearly highlighting the substantial performance gains achieved by the proposed LSTM–KF hybrid approach.

Table 3. Performance comparison of different localization algorithms.

Algorithm	Mean Error (m)	STD (m)	90th Percentile (m)
RTT based LS Approach (No ML)	59.79	68.09	148.45
ML - LSTM	11.23	17.08	22.34
ML - LSTM (KF)	7.83	6.01	13.62

8   Conclusion and Future Work

This paper has demonstrated the feasibility of using 5G SSBs for accurate tramway localization in urban environments. Through the development of a comprehensive MATLAB-based UMa simulation framework and extensive simulation, we establish that power-based fingerprinting with SSB signals achieves sub-10 m positioning accuracy when enhanced with advanced deep learning architectures. Our proposed LSTM-based approach, augmented with cross-attention mechanisms and Kalman filtering, significantly outperforms conventional LS methods, reducing the mean localization error by approximately **87%**–from **59.79 m** to **7.83 m**.

However, one limitation arises from the projection step following the 1D KF stage. In the current implementation, each network prediction is projected onto the closest point along the tram trajectory, constraining the estimated positions to lie on the true path. While this approach is valid for single-track scenarios, it may lead to incorrect projections in areas where multiple parallel or closely spaced tracks exist (e.g., tram depots or junctions). In such cases, the predicted position could be mistakenly assigned to the wrong track if the spatial separation between tracks is smaller than the positioning uncertainty. Addressing this ambiguity requires incorporating track identification mechanisms or multi-hypothesis projection strategies to ensure consistent trajectory mapping in dense railway configurations.

This study establishes a foundational framework for several promising research directions. Immediate future work will focus on validation using real-world measurement campaigns within operational 5G networks, investigation of multi-operator scenarios for enhanced feature diversity, and exploration of other machine learning techniques like Transformer to address high-dimensional power feature spaces that introduce both opportunities for improved spatial discrimination and computational complexities for model training. In particular, future research must address the challenges associated with extensive data acquisition involving numerous gNBs. The methodology demonstrates significant potential for integration with NGAP systems, enhancing the availability of the positioning solution even in cases where the GNSS signal is absent (e.g. in urban canyons) and avoiding the system switching to dead reckoning mode.

In conclusion, this work confirms that 5G SSB-based positioning, enhanced through sophisticated machine learning architectures, represents a viable and promising approach for advancing AT localization in complex urban environments.

References

1. ETCS system description: railway group guidance note (GE/GN8605). Technical report, Rail Safety and Standards Board Limited (UK) (2010)
2. Kim, K., Seol, S., Kong, S.-H.: High-speed train navigation system based on multi-sensor data fusion and map matching algorithm. Int. J. Control Autom. Syst. **13**(3), 503–512 (2015)
3. Ioannides, R.T., Pany, T., Gibbons, G.: Known vulnerabilities of global navigation satellite systems, status, and potential mitigation techniques. IEEE Proc. **104**(6), 1174–1194 (2016)
4. 3GPP TR 22.862 Technical Specification Group Services and System Aspects. Feasibility Study on New Services and Markets Technology Enablers for Critical Communications, Stage 1 (Release 14). Technical report, September 2016
5. Müürsepp, I., Alam, M.M.: Enhancing fingerprinting-based 5G positioning accuracy with directionally transmitted synchronization signals. In: 2024 19th Biennial Baltic Electronics Conference (BEC), pp. 1–6 (2024)
6. Liu, J.: Indoor fingerprint positioning method based on real 5G signals. Proc. ACM Interact. Mob. Wearable Ubiquit. Technol. **7**(2), 1–20 (2023)
7. Wang, Y., Zhao, K., Zheng, Z., Ji, W., Huang, S., Ma, D.: Indoor positioning with CNN and path-loss model based on multivariable fingerprints in 5G mobile communication system. Sensors **22**(9), 3179 (2022)
8. Huang, S., Zhang, L., Zhang, X.: An optimized fingerprinting-based indoor positioning with Kalman filter for 5G systems. Wirel. Commun. Mob. Comput. **2021**, 9936706 (2021)
9. Groves, P.D.: Shadow matching: a new GNSS positioning technique for urban canyons. J. Navig. **64**(3), 417–430 (2011)
10. Ng, H.-F., Zhang, G., Hsu, L.-T.: Robust GNSS shadow matching for smartphones in urban canyons. IEEE Sens. J. **21**(16), 18307–18317 (2021)
11. Weng, D., Hou, Z., Meng, Y., Cai, M., Chan, Y.: Characterization and mitigation of urban GNSS multipath effects on smartphones. Measurement **223**, 113766 (2023)
12. Wang, L., Groves, P.D., Ziebart, M.K.: Multi-constellation GNSS performance evaluation for urban canyons using large virtual reality city models. J. Navig. **65**(3), 459–474 (2012)
13. Sun, Q.: Wireless communication indoor positioning method in 5G substation. J. Soc. Inform. Display **30**(6), 211–218 (2022)
14. Malmström, M.: 5G positioning using machine learning. DIVA Portal (2018)
15. Bao, J., Akkarakaran, S., Nooraiepour, A., Luo, T.: A 5G NR millimeter-wave-based AoD positioning field experiment. In: Proceedings of the 3rd Workshop on Synergies of Communication, Localization, and Sensing towards 6G (WS05), IEEE International Conference on Communications (ICC), San Diego, CA, USA (2024)

16. Camajori Tedeschini, B., et al.: A feasibility study of 5G positioning with current cellular network deployment. Sci. Rep. **13**(1), 1–11 (2023)
17. Majid Butt, M., Rao, A., Yoon, D.: RF fingerprinting and deep learning assisted UE positioning in 5G. In: 2020 IEEE 91st Vehicular Technology Conference (VTC2020-Spring), pp. 1–7 (2020)
18. USRP E312 Datasheet. https://kb.ettus.com/E310/E312. Accessed 26 May 2025
19. PCI Detection Using SDR. https://www.mathworks.com/help/5g/ug/5g-nr-synchronization-signal-capture-using-software-defined-radio.html. Accessed 26 May 2025
20. Ye, H., Li, G.Y., Juang, B.-H.: Power of deep learning for channel estimation and signal detection in OFDM systems. IEEE Wirel. Commun. Lett. **7**(1), 114–117 (2018)
21. Wang, T., Wen, C.-K., Jin, S., Li, G.Y.: Deep learning for wireless physical layer: opportunities and challenges. China Commun. **16**(1), 92–111 (2019)
22. Vaswani, A., et al.: Attention is all you need. In: Advances in Neural Information Processing Systems, vol. 30 (2017)
23. Bahdanau, D., Cho, K., Bengio, Y.: Neural machine translation by jointly learning to align and translate. In: International Conference on Learning Representations (2015)
24. Chorowski, J.K., Bahdanau, D., Serdyuk, D., Cho, K., Bengio, Y.: Attention-based models for speech recognition. In: Advances in Neural Information Processing Systems, vol. 28 (2015)
25. Hochreiter, S., Schmidhuber, J.: Long short-term memory. Neural Comput. **9**(8), 1735–1780 (1997)
26. Graves, A., Mohamed, A., Hinton, G.: Speech recognition with deep recurrent neural networks. In: 2013 IEEE International Conference on Acoustics, Speech and Signal Processing, pp. 6645–6649. IEEE (2013)
27. Huang, Q., Yang, Z., Xianmin, X.: Indoor localization using LSTM networks: a case study with Wi-Fi fingerprints. Neurocomputing **403**, 128–137 (2020)
28. Mallick, P., Panigrahi, C., Panigrahi, P.K.: LSTM based indoor localization using CSI amplitude. In: 2020 IEEE Wireless Communications and Networking Conference (WCNC), pp. 1–6. IEEE (2020)
29. Kingma, D.P., Ba, J.: Adam: a method for stochastic optimization. arXiv preprint arXiv:1412.6980 (2014)
30. 3GPP. Study on channel model for frequencies from 0.5 to 100 GHz. Technical Report TR 38.901, 3GPP, 2025. Version 18.0.0

Verification of a Novel Interlocking Function for Personnel Protection

Christophe Limbrée$^{(\boxtimes)}$ (iD)

INFRABEL, Place Marcel Broodthaers 2, 1060, Bruxelles, Belgium
`christophe.limbree@infrabel.be`

Abstract. The article discusses the use of formal methods in the context of validating a new system designed to enhance the safety of railway personnel working along the tracks. The Safe Protection Integrator (SPI) is a system designed to enable the Person In Charge Of Possession (PICOP) to control new people protection functions within a Railway Interlocking System (RIS) via a tablet interface. These functions are based on the Elementary Protection Zone (EZE) concept, which allows signals granting access to a track-side work area to be closed. Together with the new RIS functions, the SPI enhances both the efficiency and safety of track-side work operations.

This article presents how formal methods, and more specifically model checking, are applied to model these new principles and support the safety analysis process.

Keywords: Model checking · RIS · SPI · Safety critical system certification

1 Introduction

1.1 Using Formal Verification to Validate a New Concept

This article introduces the new EZE concept and the new SPI system, which aims to enhance the safety of personnel working on railway tracks through a novel function to be implemented within a RIS. We explain how this concept can be formally modelled, enabling the verification of safety properties. Our use case and test scenarios focus on work activities occurring on sections of plain track. The evidence generated through this verification is valuable for the certification of these new safety-critical functions. This is primarily due to three advantages: first, the benefits of formal verification over traditional testing; second, the ability to use the evidence during the certification process with an Independent Safety Assessor (ISA); and third, the possibility to start validation without waiting for a physical RIS implementation.

Model checking - The use case detailed in Sect. 3.1 is relatively simple, involving only one EZE, four signals, four TVPs, and two trains. However, it remains a tedious task for signalling and safety experts to anticipate all possible scenarios

© The Author(s), under exclusive license to Springer Nature Switzerland AG 2026
M. H. ter Beek et al. (Eds.): Fantechi Festschrift, LNCS 16470, pp. 259–278, 2026.
https://doi.org/10.1007/978-3-032-12484-5_14

applicable to this case. In contrast, this exhaustive exploration is precisely what model checkers excel at.

1.2   Structure of the Article

In Sect. 2, we introduce the new concepts related to EZEs, the context of the SPI system, and formal methods used in our research. In Sect. 3, we detail our use case with its formal model. In Sect. 4, we present the results of verification of safety properties applicable to our use case. Finally, we conclude in Sect. 5.

2   Background

This section outlines the current context of personnel protection rules. We introduce a new system, called SPI, and a new concept, called EZE, which aim to reduce the risks faced by track-side workers. Additionally, we provide the background for the formal verification approach proposed in Sect. 4.

2.1   People Protection Today

Track-side personnel are protected either by train approach warnings (announcements) or by exclusive track possession during work periods.

In the first case, lookouts are positioned wisely along the track to announce upcoming trains to working crews. The alert is given early enough so that the crew can reach a safe position before the train arrives. The security of this method relies on the attentiveness of the lookouts and the prompt reaction of the crew.

In the second case, the approach is more conservative and safe. Before starting a work, the area is taken out of operation and no train is allowed to pass. For this, the PICOP communicates with the signalman who blocks the signals leading to the work zone. The PICOP is the person in charge of the application of the protection measures for his work. He is also responsible for the security of his crew members. In modern systems, this blockage is materialized in the RIS or in the route control system. The blockage is controlled by the signalman. Any train that needs to go through the work zone requires the authorization of the PICOP and a temporary removal of the blockage in the systems by the signalman. The track possession approach is, by far, safer than the announcement method. The only drawback of the method is that the signalman cannot always grant possession of a zone as quickly as requested by the PICOP thereby delaying the execution of the work.

The SPI system builds on the track possession method, enabling the work crew to take direct control of their work zone without requiring intervention from the signalman. This is achieved through the addition of the new EZE function in the RIS, which allows safe, autonomous possession management by the crew, enhancing operational efficiency.

2.2   Context of the SPI System

Figure 1 illustrates the complete context of the SPI with its connections to the existing signalling systems (links 1 to 7). The link (1) is a traditional wired connection between the RIS and the field elements like the signals. Link (2) connects the European Train Control System (ETCS) systems to the trains circulating on a railway network. Link (3) shows the mobile network allowing the PICOP to interact with the SPI. Link (4) uses a wired network to connect the SPI to all the RIS. The SPI uses this link to control the EZEs. Link (5) relates to the control of the ETCS by the RIS. It is used to send the status of the signals and the Temporary Speed Restriction (TSR). Link (6) is used by the Elektronische Bedieningspost (EBP) to communicate with the RIS. Link (7) allows for the exchange of train announcements between the EBP and the SPI.

The RIS plays a central role in managing protection zones by directly safeguarding people working on the track and by communicating data to other signalling systems to ensure consistency and coherence among protection measures.

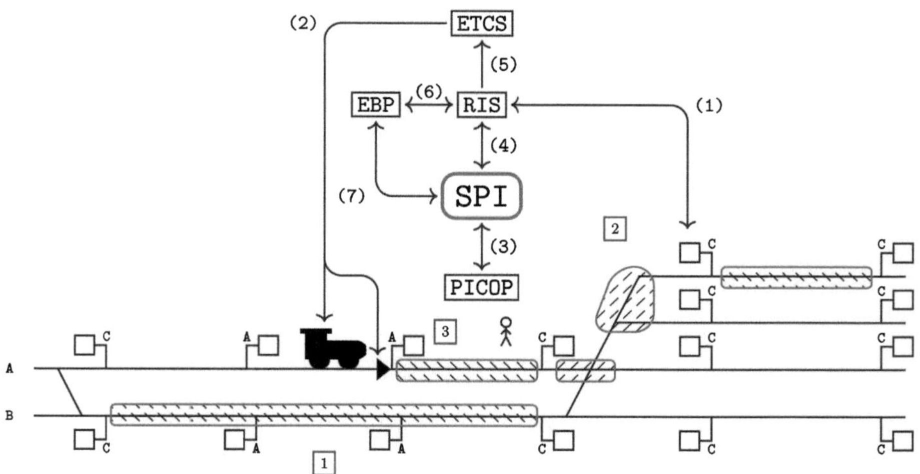

Fig. 1. Signalling systems and EZE context.

2.3   Notion of EZE and Area Safe

Figure 1 also illustrates the concept of EZE. An EZE is a predefined protection zone that is configured in the RIS application data. An EZE can cover a switch or a complete plain track or a single section of a plain track. EZEs do not overlap.

Based on the track-side work to be performed, the PICOP selects one or more EZEs that fully cover the corresponding area. Through his tablet and the SPI, he then initiates their activation in the RIS controlling that section. Activating an EZE modifies the status of the route and railway signals, preventing any train from entering the work zone. Once activation is confirmed by the RIS, the SPI displays "Area Safe" on the PICOP's tablet, allowing the PICOP to begin the work activity.

In certain situations, trains need to pass through the work zone. In such situations, the PICOP receives an announcement–a request to withdraw from the work area–which he must confirm only when both he and his team are in a safe position. This confirmation triggers the Temporary Protection Removal (TPR) function in the RIS. As a result, the corresponding signal clears, and the announced train may proceed. The TPR authorization is then reset following the registration of a specific Track Vacancy Proving (TVP) sequence that involves TVP_n and TVP_n+1 for the TPR of EZE_n.

This article focuses on the formal verification and validation of the individual EZE function applied to a track section and implemented in the RIS. If the PICOP selects multiple EZEs to protect a work zone, the aggregation of the "Area Safe" information or other commands, such as the TPR, is handled by the SPI. The analysis of this aggregation lies beyond the scope of the present document.

2.4   RIS Formal Verification

A RIS is a safety critical system in railway signalling that prevents conflicting train movements through an arrangement of tracks such as junctions, crossings, or stations. It ensures that trains can only proceed when it is safe by controlling and coordinating signals, switches, and other track devices to avoid collisions or derailments. Data preparation for railway interlocking systems is a critical step that involves compiling, validating, and formatting the detailed configuration and application data specific to each railway installation.

Formal verification is the act of proving the correctness of a system with respect to a certain formal property, using formal methods. A more formal definition of model checking is: given a model M of a system, exhaustively and automatically check whether this model meets a property ϕ or more formally: $M \models \phi$. In practice, a Model Checker (MC) allows verifying that a system satisfies a set of properties. The system is encoded as a finite-state transition system and the system behaviour is represented as infinite sequences of states. A common pitfall of the MC approach is the state space explosion problem. It refers to the exponential growth of the number of system states to be analysed as the system's complexity increases.

In our case, we apply model checking [2,3,5] to verify the correctness of the application data implementing the new EZE concept in existing RIS.

2.5   Properties and FAIRNESS Constraints

We will specify the properties with invariant and Linear Temporal Logic (LTL) formulas. Simple properties can be expressed as invariants where an invariant is a condition that must be verified in each state of a system. Hence a property like "the signal must close after a train has passed" requires to be able to specify and reason about time or about an event sequence. In order to specify these properties, we need LTL as introduced in [24].

Safety and Liveness Properties. A safety property states that "bad things" shall not happen. For example: "Area safe" shall not be given when the EZE is Active and TPR is recorded. On the contrary, a liveness property states that "good thing" shall eventually happen. For example : the train shall eventually be shall able to traverse an EZE. Liveness properties are used to validate the model and make sure that all operational scenarios are allowed.

Linear Temporal Logic. In LTL, one can encode formulae about the future of paths (e.g., Something will eventually happen in the future). The logic was introduced by Pnueli et $al.$ [23] in 1977 and the semantics of model checking was defined by Lichtenstein et $al.$ [17] in 1985.

LTL formulas are composed of a finite set of atomic propositions, Boolean connectives ($\neg, \wedge, \vee, and \rightarrow$), and temporal connectives. The different temporal connectives are: **X** ("next time"), **F** ("in the future"), **G** ("globally"), and **U** ("until"). For example, the formula Fp (finally p) states that for each possible execution path of the system, there exists a state where p is $TRUE$. A more complex example is the formula G(alert $\rightarrow$ F halt) where G means that an "alert" will cause a "halt" at some point in the future. G and F are dual operators meaning that $G\phi \equiv \neg F\neg\phi$.

Figure 2 provides a more visual insight of the LTL semantic. Each line show one path where the states are represented by dots. The states where the property p is $TRUE$ are circled in blue. The states where the property q is $TRUE$ are circled in red. For example : the formula **Xp** is true iff p is true in the second state.

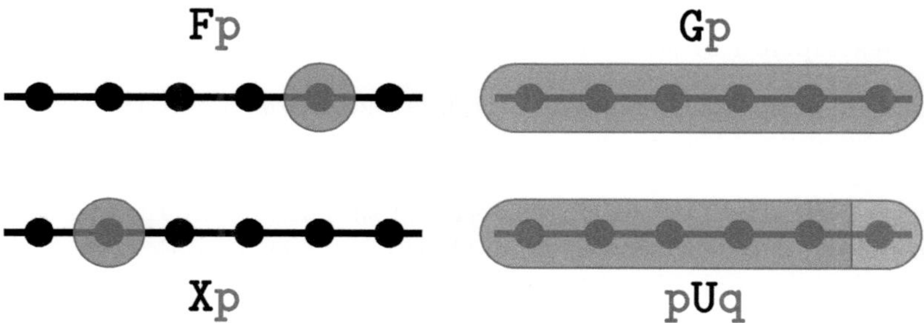

Fig. 2. Visualisation of LTL operators.

FAIRNESS. In NuXMV, fairness refers to constraints that restrict the set of execution paths considered during model checking to those where certain conditions hold infinitely often or certain actions (or events) occur regularly, ensuring more realistic behaviour is analysed. The FAIRNESS constraint is used twice in the RIS model : a first time in the EZE module (List. 3.3) and a second time in the train module (List. 3.4). These two modules are explained in Sect. 3.2.

2.6 Related Work

Formal verification of railway systems has been a hot research topic for over thirty years as stated by Alessandro Fantechi in [7]. Indeed, the use of Formal Methods (FM) is highly recommended by the European standards [1] for the development of railway safety critical systems. Formal Methods were mostly applied to the verification of the application data of the RIS [10,12–14,18,19]. Formal methods were also used to validate new concepts. In [16], Laursen *et al.* propose a model checking approach for the verification of distributed RIS and in [8], Alessandro Fantechi *et al.* apply FM to the verification of a new concept of distributed computing in Future Railway Systems. In the same manner in [11], Haxthausen *et al.* use the UPPAAL model checker to verify Railway Timetables.

As far as I am concerned, I recently had the pleasure to work with Alessandro Fantechi towards the development of a new approach based on compositional verification [9,20,21]. Compositional verification offers an answer to the so-called state space explosion problem. With this method, a large network controlled by several RIS can be decomposed into smaller, less complex, models.

3 Validation of the EZE Principles

This section describes the use case chosen to analyse Safety properties on the new EZE principles. It explains how the new EZE principle was modelled and later used to perform safety analysis.

3.1 Description of the Use Case

Figure 3 illustrates an example of a track layout in which only the behaviour of EZE_n is analysed. The conclusions drawn from this analysis can be extended to the other EZEs (n1 to n3). Four signals and four TVP sections are shown: S_n to S_n3 and TVP_n to TVP_n3. For the sake of simplicity, only the direction from left to right ($\rightarrow$) is represented. Train t1 (t2) occupies Tvp_n1 (Tvp_n). Signals S_n and S_n1 are red. Signal S_n2 is double yellow (YY) to warn that S_n1 is red. The PICOP and his crew are on the area covered by EZE_n.

This layout makes it possible to verify various scenarios involving one or two trains that are safely spaced by the railway signals. It also enables the verification of RIS functions–such as activation, Area Safe, and TPR–associated with the new EZE concept.

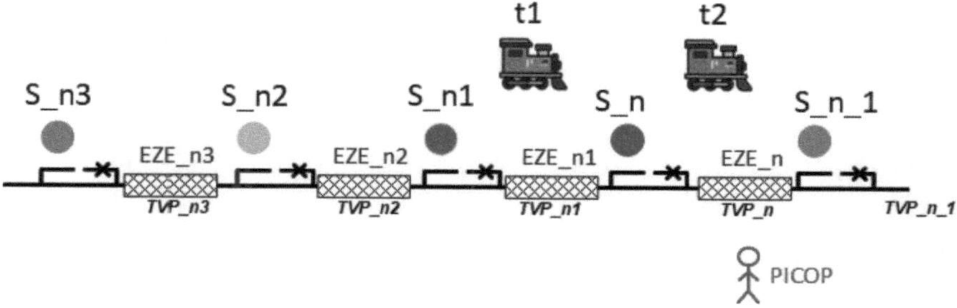

Fig. 3. Use case - an EZE covering a section.

3.2   RIS Model Integrating the EZE Concept

The model formalizing the use case described in Sect. 3.1 is broken down into functional modules. This simplifies the extension of the use to more complex situations. These modules are:

- A TVP module,
- A signal module,
- An EZE module,
- A train module.

The modules are written in SMV language [6] and verified with the NuXMV model checker [4]. A description of these SMV modules is given below.

TVP The TVP module (List. 3.1) hold two states : occupied and clear. The state of each TVP is synchronized with the position of each train formalized in the TRAIN2 module (List. 3.5).

```
1  -- Track-circuit module
2  MODULE TVP
3  VAR
4  st : {o, c};
```

Listing 3.1. TVP module.

Signal. The signal module (List. 3.2) holds three states (aspects) : Red, YY, and Green. The aspect depends on the status of its EZE, home TVP, and the state of the signal ahead (i.e., signal linking). The Control Yellow Green Signal (KYGS) is used to link the signals - if Sn is open with a green or yellow aspect, then Sn_1 can turn green.

```
1    MODULE SIGNAL_AUT(tvp, sigPrec, eze)
2    VAR
3    st : {Red, YY, Green};

5    ASSIGN
6    init(st) := Red;

8    next(st) :=
9      case
10       tvp.st = c & sigPrec.KYGS & eze.perm  : Green;
11       tvp.st = c & !sigPrec.KYGS & eze.perm : YY;
12       tvp.st = o                            : Red;
13       eze.st in {Active}                    : Red;
14       TRUE : st;
15     esac;

17   DEFINE
18   KYGS := st in {YY, Green}; -- Control Yellow Green Signal
```

Listing 3.2. Signal module.

EZE. The EZE module (List. 3.3) holds three states: notActive, Active and ActiveTPR. (not)Active means EZE (not) protected. ActiveTPR means Active but temporarily released (train passage allowed). The EZE modules takes two arguments : tvp1 and tvp2. **tvp1** is the TVP covering the EZE (Tvp_n for EZE_n). **tvp2** (Tvp_n_1 for EZE_n) is used in combination of **tvp1** to trigger the TPR reset as shown in Table 1.

Table 1. TVPs sequence leading to TPR reset.

tvp1	tvp2	TPR status
c	c	set
o	c	set
o	o	set
c	o	reset

The EZE is deemed **safe** if it is in Active state and if tvp1 is clear. It is not safe otherwise. The EZE is permissive (perm) if it is in **notActive** state or **ActiveTPR** state.

The **FAIRNESS** constraint applied to the perm definition guarantees that the EZE is infinitely often permissive.

```
 1   MODULE EZE(tvp1, tvp2)
 2   VAR
 3   st : {Active, ActiveTPR, notActive}; -- ActiveTSR
 4   resetTPRn : resetTPR(tvp1, tvp2);

 6   ASSIGN
 7   init(st) := Active;

 9   next(st) :=
10     case
11       st = notActive & condAct : Active;
12       st = ActiveTPR & resetTPRn.resetTPRtrig  : Active;
13       st = ActiveTPR                           : ActiveTPR;
14       st = Active
     : {Active, ActiveTPR};
15       TRUE : st;
16     esac;

18   DEFINE
19   condAct := TRUE; -- temporarily
20   safe := (st = Active) & (tvp1.st = c);
21   perm := st in {ActiveTPR, notActive};

23   FAIRNESS perm; -- GF perm
```

Listing 3.3. EZE module.

The TRAIN module contains the topology of the track in terms of sequence of
track sections. The train is characterised by a front and a tail that can occupy two
different sections of track. The tail of the train follows its front. The Tprogress
variable enables the train to stop. A FAIRNESS constraint on this variable
ensures that the train will eventually move.

```
 1   MODULE TRAIN2(mainP) -- 2nd version of my TRAIN module

 3   VAR
 4   front : {beg, Tvp_n_1, Tvp_n, Tvp_n1, Tvp_n2, Tvp_n3, end};
 5   tail : {beg, Tvp_n_1, Tvp_n, Tvp_n1, Tvp_n2, Tvp_n3,end};

 7   Tprogress : boolean;

 9   ASSIGN
10   init(front) := beg;
11   init(tail) := beg;
12   init(Tprogress) := FALSE;

14   next(tail) := front;
```

```
16   next(front) :=
17     case
18     front = beg & stepG & Tprogress & mainP.S_n3.KYGS : Tvp_n3;
19     front = Tvp_n3 & stepG & Tprogress & mainP.S_n2.KYGS : Tvp_n2;
20     front = Tvp_n2 & stepG & Tprogress & mainP.S_n1.KYGS : Tvp_n1;
21     front = Tvp_n1 & stepG & Tprogress & mainP.S_n.KYGS : Tvp_n;
22     front = Tvp_n & stepG & Tprogress & mainP.S_n_1.KYGS : Tvp_n_1;
23     front = Tvp_n_1 & stepG & Tprogress : end;
24     front = end :beg;
25     TRUE : {front};
26     esac;

28   DEFINE
29   stepG    := front = tail; -- step granted
30   isStarting := (front = beg & next(front) != beg) ? TRUE : FALSE;

32   Tvpb_n3   := front = Tvp_n3 | tail = Tvp_n3;
33   Tvpb_n2   := front = Tvp_n2 | tail = Tvp_n2;
34   Tvpb_n1   := front = Tvp_n1 | tail = Tvp_n1;
35   Tvpb_n    := front = Tvp_n | tail = Tvp_n;
36   Tvpb_n_1  := front = Tvp_n_1 | tail = Tvp_n_1;

38   FAIRNESS Tprogress;
```

Listing 3.4. SMV train module.

The Frame module shown in List. 3.5 links the train positions to the TVPs.
For example (line 6), when one train moves to the Tvp_n1 position, then Tvp_n1
gets occupied.

```
1    MODULE FrameAXioms(mainP)
2    ASSIGN

4    mainP.Tvp_n3.st  := (mainP.t1.Tb_n3 | mainP.t2.Tb_n3) ? o : c;
5    mainP.Tvp_n2.st  := (mainP.t1.Tb_n2 | mainP.t2.Tb_n2) ? o : c;
6    mainP.Tvp_n1.st  := (mainP.t1.Tb_n1 | mainP.t2.Tb_n1) ? o : c;
7    mainP.Tvp_n.st   := (mainP.t1.Tb_n | mainP.t2.Tb_n) ? o : c;
8    mainP.Tvp_n_1.st := (mainP.t1.Tb_n_1 | mainP.t2.Tb_n_1) ? o : c;
```

Listing 3.5. Linking between train positions and TVP states.

System with Two Trains. The system (main module in SMV) instantiates
the individual modules to create an executable module on which the verification
can be performed. The synchronization between the modules happens by means
of shared variables passed as arguments. The system (List. 3.6) instantiates :

- 5 TVP with TVPn_1 being the track-circuit covered by Sn_1. This TVP is needed to generate the TRP reset of EZE_n.
- 4 EZE. The EZE_n(1 to 3) are always in ActiveTPR state. They are declared for the sake of uniformity but they are no part of the verification.
- 5 signals. S_n_1 is a simplified module with no dependence on TVP or EZE. KYGS is emitted to Sn.
- 2 trains.
- 1 frame axioms - connect the trains with the TVP.

```
1   #include "./genMods.smv"
2   #include "./TRAIN2.smv"

4   MODULE main
5   VAR

7   -- The track-circuits
8   Tvp_n_1 : TVP; -- Down Tvp\_n
9   Tvp_n   : TVP;
10  Tvp_n1  : TVP;
11  Tvp_n2  : TVP;
12  Tvp_n3  : TVP;

14  -- Train announcemnt counter
15  annN : annCNT(annEZE\_n);

17  -- The EZE
18  EZE_n  : EZE(Tvp_n, Tvp_n_1);
19  EZE_n1 : permissiveEZE;
20  EZE_n2 : permissiveEZE;
21  EZE_n3 : permissiveEZE;

23  -- The signals
24  S_n_1 : permissiveSIGNAL_AUT(Tvp_n_1);
25  -- Signal protecting the EZE\_n
26  S_n  : SIGNAL_AUT(Tvp_n, S_n_1, EZE_n);
27  S_n1 : SIGNAL_AUT(Tvp_n1, S_n, EZE_n1);   -- UP Sn
28  S_n2 : SIGNAL_AUT(Tvp_n2, S_n1, EZE_n2);  -- UP Sn
29  S_n3 : SIGNAL_AUT(Tvp_n3, S_n2, EZE_n3);  -- UP Sn

31  t1 : TRAIN2(self); -- Trains
32  t2 : TRAIN2(self);
33  g1 : FrameAXioms(self); -- Linking

35  DEFINE
36  -- Announcement condition for EZE\_n
37  annEZE\_n := (Tvp_n3.st = o)|(Tvp_n2.st = o)|(Tvp_n1.st = o);
38  -- Prevents the two trains to start at the same time.
39  INVAR !(t1.Tvpb_n3 & t2.Tvpb_n3)
```

Listing 3.6. System with two trains in SMV.

4   Verification of the EZE Implementation

The section describes the verification performed on the system introduced in Sect. 3.2. The model comprises 7.03×10^6 reachable states, generated using NuXMV's default Binary Decision Diagram (BDD) algorithm. Our primary objectives are to validate the EZE implementation principles within a RIS and to test various scenarios related to the use cases outlined in Sect. 3.1. When appropriate, we also verify properties known to be FALSE, in order to produce witness traces for illustration purposes (e.g., timing diagrams). We believe these diagrams are valuable assets in the overall certification process of the SPI.

4.1   Verification Method

Figure 4 illustrates the verification and illustration process. First, the model is fed into the MC, which generates the reachable state space. Next, the model checker verifies each property of interest, resulting in one of two possible outcomes: the property is either satisfied (TRUE) or not satisfied. In the latter case, a counterexample trace is produced and passed to a Python script that generates a timing diagram in PlantUML [22], visually depicting the evolution of the variables of interest over time (i.e., states). These variables include, for example, those related to the TVP, signals, EZE, and trains. The variables in the NuXMV model adhere to the naming conventions used in the data preparation rules of the real RIS (Solid State Interlocking (SSI) in Belgium). The script also allows filtering to focus on a specific subset of variables.

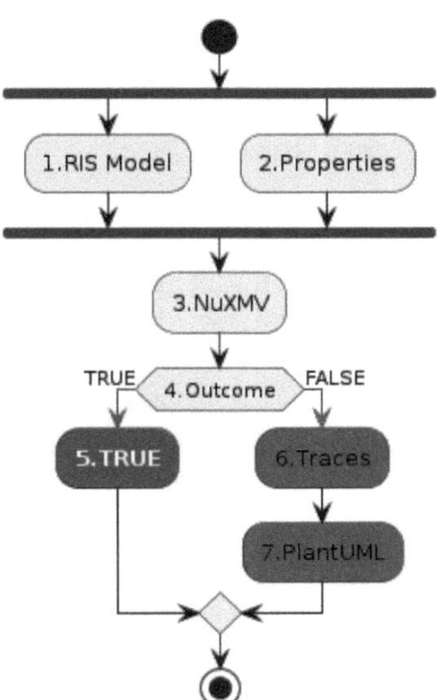

Fig. 4. Verification flow.

List 4.1 presents an example of a trace produced by NuXMV. In this case, the property specifies that Tvp_n3 should never be occupied. As expected, the related trace reveals that Tvp_n3 is in fact eventually occupied (line 20) when train t1 moves to Tvp_n3 (line 21).

```
1   nuXmv > check_invar -p "!(Tvp_n3.st = o)"
2   -- invariant !(Tvp_n3.st = o)  is false
3   -- as demonstrated by the following execution sequence
4   Trace Description: AG alpha Counterexample
5   Trace Type: Counterexample
6     -> State: 1.1 <-
7       Tvp_n3.st = c
8       S_n3.st = Red
9       t1.front = beg
10      t1.Tprogress = FALSE
11      S_n3.KYGS = FALSE
12      t1.isStarting = FALSE
13      t2.isStarting = FALSE
14    -> State: 1.2 <-
15      S_n3.st = YY
16      t1.Tprogress = TRUE
17      S_n3.KYGS = TRUE
18      t1.isStarting = TRUE
19    -> State: 1.3 <-
20      Tvp_n3.st = o
21      t1.front = Tvp_n3
```

Listing 4.1. Trace example (Tvp_n3 gets eventually occupied).

4.2   Verification of the EZE Behaviour

The system and modules detailed in Sect. 3.2 model the use case represented in Fig. 3. This section introduces a few safety properties related to the EZE. Most of them come from the safety requirements defined in the new SPI system. Some are derived from questions asked by the safety engineer evaluating the EZE concept. When a safety property does not hold, a trace and its timing diagram is explained.

Validation of the Model. A specific set of properties (List. 4.2) is used to validate the model in the first place. It must be verified that the system is collision free (lines 1) and that the trains instances run properly from S_n3 to S_n_1 (lines 2, 3, 4, and 7). Lines 5 and 6 formalise the property that the S_n signal shall be at danger when its home TVP is occupied. In its invariant form (line 5), it is FALSE as shown in Fig. 5). The use of the **next** operator in the signal module (List. 3.2) adds a transition between the TVP occupation and the signal replacement. The LTL property at line 6 incorporates this characteristic using the next operator (X), enabling verification of the replacement property. This characteristic of our model is totally in line with that of a real RIS where the inputs are first read before the outputs can be actuated.

```
1   INVARSPEC NAME invP11 := !(t1.front != beg & t1.front =
        t2.front)
2   LTLSPEC NAME ltlP11 := G(Tvp_n1.st = o -> (F Tvp_n.st = o
        ))
3   LTLSPEC NAME ltlP12 := G(Tvp_n2.st = o -> (F Tvp_n1.st =
        o))
4   LTLSPEC NAME ltlP13 := G(Tvp_n3.st = o -> (F Tvp_n2.st =
        o))
5   INVARSPEC NAME invP12 := (Tvp_n.st = o) -> (!S_n.KYGS)
6   LTLSPEC NAME ltlP14 := G((Tvp_n.st = o) -> X(!S_n.KYGS))
7   LTLSPEC NAME ltlP15 := G((t1.front = Tvp_n3) -> F (t1.
        front = end))
```

Listing 4.2. Model validation properties.

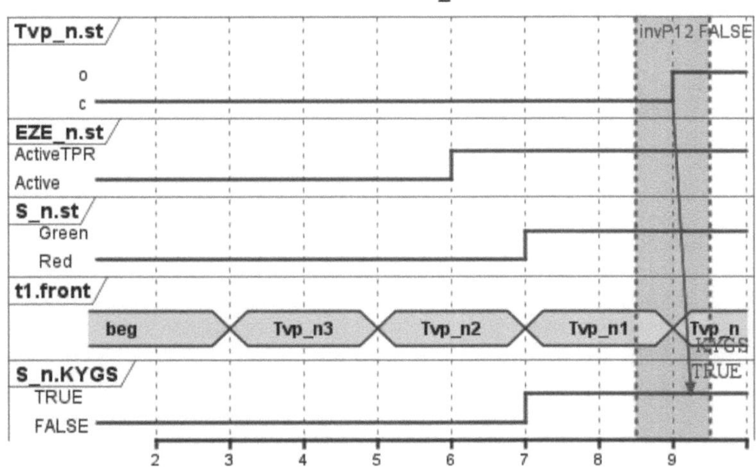

Fig. 5. Timing diagram showing that the property invP12 is FALSE.

Verification of the EZE Protection Capabilities. The EZE is a new function implemented in the RIS. Its role is to allow track worker to take possession of a section by controlling the protecting signals at danger (lines 1 and 2). In

our use case (Fig. 3), the S_n signal protects the EZE_n. The property invP21 is
FALSE as shown in Fig. 6. This is again justified by the use of the next operator
in the signal module (List. 3.2 - line 8). The LTL property at line 2 incorporates this characteristic using the next operator (X), enabling verification of the
replacement property.

```
1  INVARSPEC    NAME invP21  :=  !EZE_n.perm -> !S_n.KYGS
2  LTLSPEC      NAME ltlP21  :=  G(!EZE_n.perm -> X(!S_n.KYGS))
3  INVARSPEC    NAME invP22  :=  !(EZE_n.st in {ActiveTPR,
      notActive}) -> !EZE_n.perm
```

Listing 4.3. Properties related to the EZE.

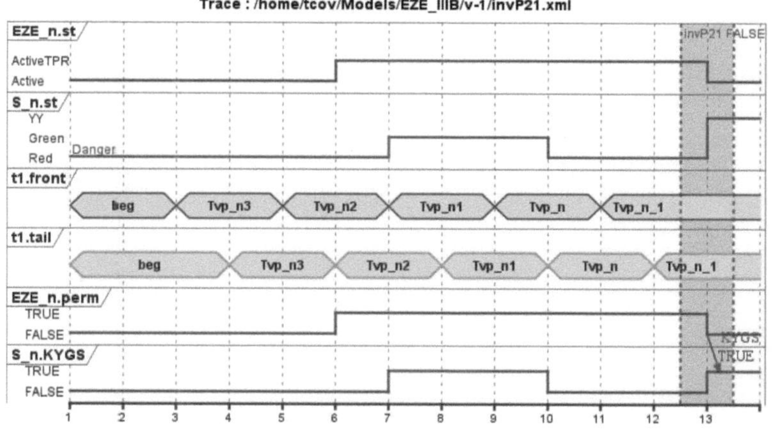

Fig. 6. Timing diagram showing that the property invP21 is FALSE.

Reset of Temporary Authorisation. The TPR function is used to grant
passage to a unique train through an active (protected) EZE. The property in
List. 4.4 allows to verify that the TPR is properly reset (EZE protected again)
after the train passage has been recoded. The reset transition is visible in Fig. 7
- state 13. The figure shows the states of the EZE, the position of the train, and
the status of the two TVP participating in the release sequence of the TPR. It
also proves that EZE_n returns to its Active state after TPR reset.

```
1  INVARSPEC NAME invP31    :=  !EZE_n.resetTPRn.resetTPRtrig
```

Listing 4.4. Property related to the reset of the TPR.

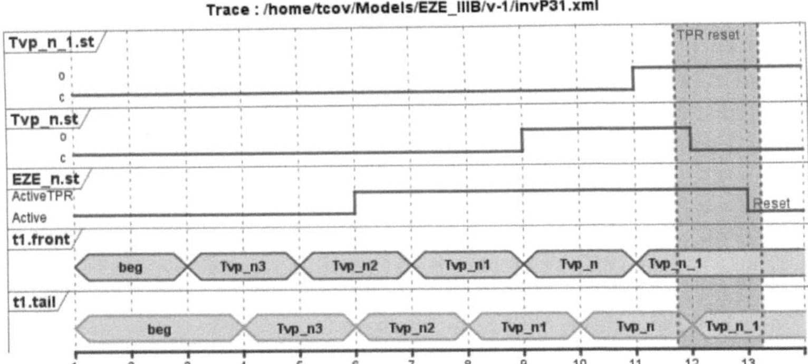

Fig. 7. Timing diagram showing that the reset of the TPR is triggered properly by Tvp_n and TVP_n_1.

Announcement. An announcement is a request sent to the PICOP by the RIS to let a train through an EZE under its possession. A positive acknowledgement of the announcement by the PICOP triggers a TPR. It is crucial to verify that the RIS triggers an announcement for each train approaching an EZE. The verification of the properties in List. 4.5 produces a trace (Fig. 8) proving that the RIS can trigger one announcement for each train heading for the EZE_n.

```
1  -- Just one train is announced
2  INVARSPEC NAME invP41   := !(annN.nb_ann = one_)
3  -- Two trains are announced
4  INVARSPEC NAME invP42   := !(annN.nb_ann = two)
```

Listing 4.5. Properties related to the registration of train announcements towards the EZE_n.

Area Safe. The "Area Safe" information given to the PICOP on its tablet guarantees that the EZE under his possession is protected (by the RIS). The properties in List. 4.6 allow verifying that this information is only given if the home TVP is clear (line 1) and if the EZE is in active state (line 2). Both properties are TRUE.

```
1  INVARSPEC NAME invP51 := !((EZE_n.tvp1 = o) & EZE_n.safe)
2  INVARSPEC NAME invP52 := !(!(EZE_n.st = Active) & EZE_n.
     safe)
```

Listing 4.6. Property related to Area Safe information given to the PICOP.

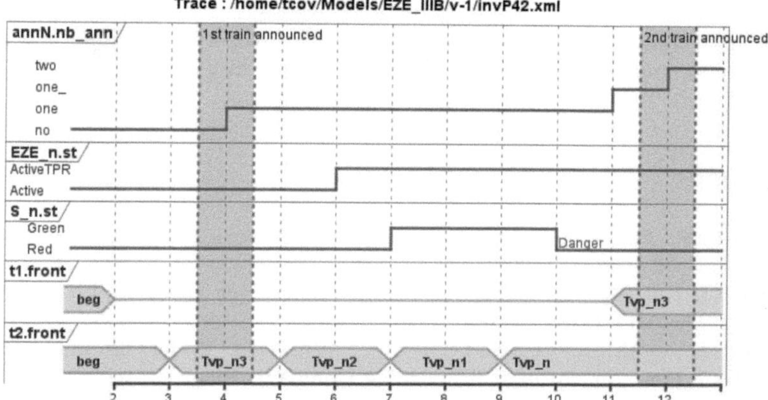

Fig. 8. Timing diagram showing that the RIS can trigger two announcements (one for *t1* and one for *t2*).

5   Conclusions and Future Work

In this article, we applie formal methods to validate a novel people protection concept called EZE. An EZE represents a small, predefined geographic area within the railway infrastructure and is a new type of object implemented in the RIS. This object interacts with signals and routes to prevent train traffic from entering the area covered by the EZEs. The PICOP, responsible for safeguarding the on-site crew, controls these EZEs via a tablet and a newly developed system called SPI. The SPI guarantees that the EZEs requested by the PICOP provide a safe working environment. Additionally, the SPI can request authorization from the PICOP to allow a train to pass through its work area–a process known as TPR, which is integral to the EZE concept.

We developed a comprehensive SMV model representing a real-life use case involving four sections of a plain track. Our model formalizes actual railway signalling components, including signals, TVP, EZE, and trains. Using this model, we verified the behaviour of the new EZE concept under various scenarios by checking relevant safety properties. Additionally, we deliberately verified properties known to be FALSE to generate witness traces illustrating our use case. These traces were rendered as timing diagrams to facilitate interpretation. We argue that our model will significantly facilitate the validation and certification of this new concept by our ISA.

The implementation of the EZE concept in the RIS only partially fulfils our ambition to enhance the safety of track workers. However, our current model does not yet encompass the SPI and its associated safety logic. In future work, we plan to model and verify the SPI functionalities, as well as its interactions with both the RIS and the PICOP. If timing constraints need to be verified, we could adopt a different formalism, such as Timed Automata using UPPAAL [15].

Acknowledgement. I am deeply grateful to Alessandro Fantechi for accepting to serve on my thesis jury. I also sincerely thank Alessandro for providing me with the opportunity to conduct research and publish alongside him.

References

1. IEC 61508: Functional safety of electrical/electronic/programmable electronic safety-related systems (1998)
2. Baier, C., Katoen, J.P.: Principles of Model Checking (Representation and Mind Series). The MIT Press (2008)
3. Berard, B., et al.: Systems and Software Verification: Model-Checking Techniques and Tools, 1st edn. Springer Publishing Company, Incorporated (2010). https://doi.org/10.1007/978-3-662-04558-9
4. Cavada, R., et al.: The NUXMV symbolic model checker. In: Biere, A., Bloem, R. (eds.) Computer Aided Verification - 26th International Conference, CAV 2014, Held as Part of the Vienna Summer of Logic, VSL 2014, Vienna, Austria, 18-22 July 2014. Proceedings. LNCS, vol. 8559, pp. 334–342. Springer (2014). https://doi.org/10.1007/978-3-319-08867-9_22
5. Clarke, E.M.: The Birth of Model Checking, pp. 1–26. Springer, Heidelberg (2008). https://doi.org/10.1007/978-3-540-69850-0_1
6. Clarke, E., McMillan, K., Campos, S., Hartonas-Garmhausen, V.: Symbolic model checking. In: Alur, R., Henzinger, T.A. (eds.) CAV 1996. LNCS, vol. 1102, pp. 419–422. Springer, Heidelberg (1996). https://doi.org/10.1007/3-540-61474-5_93
7. Fantechi, A.: Twenty-five years of formal methods and railways: What next? In: Counsell, S., Núñez, M. (eds.) Software Engineering and Formal Methods - SEFM 2013 Collocated Workshops: BEAT2, WS-FMDS, FM-RAIL-Bok, MoKMaSD, and OpenCert, Madrid, Spain, 23-24 September 2013, Revised Selected Papers. LNCS, vol. 8368, pp. 167–183. Springer (2013). https://doi.org/10.1007/978-3-319-05032-4_13
8. Fantechi, A., Gnesi, S., Haxthausen, A.E.: Formal methods for distributed computing in future railway systems. In: Margaria, T., Steffen, B. (eds.) Leveraging Applications of Formal Methods, Verification and Validation: Applications - 9th International Symposium on Leveraging Applications of Formal Methods, ISoLA 2020, Rhodes, Greece, 20-30 October 2020, Proceedings, Part III. LNCS, vol. 12478, pp. 389–392. Springer (2020). https://doi.org/10.1007/978-3-030-61467-6_24
9. Fantechi, A., Gori, G., Haxthausen, A.E., Limbrée, C.: Compositional verification of railway interlockings: Comparison of two methods. In: Dutilleul, S.C., Haxthausen, A.E., Lecomte, T. (eds.) Reliability, Safety, and Security of Railway Systems. Modelling, Analysis, Verification, and Certification - 4th International Conference, RSSRail 2022, Paris, France, 1-2 June 2022, Proceedings. LNCS, vol. 13294, pp. 3–19. Springer (2022). https://doi.org/10.1007/978-3-031-05814-1_1
10. Ferrari, A., Magnani, G., Grasso, D., Fantechi, A.: Model checking interlocking control tables. In: Schnieder, E., Tarnai, G. (eds.) FORMS/FORMAT 2010 - Formal Methods for Automation and Safety in Railway and Automotive Systems [8th Symposium on Formal Methods for Automation and Safety in Railway and Automotive Systems, Braunschweig, Germany, 2-3 December 2010, pp. 107–115. Springer (2010). https://doi.org/10.1007/978-3-642-14261-1_11

11. Haxthausen, A.E., Hede, K.: Formal verification of railway timetables - using the UPPAAL model checker. In: ter Beek, M.H., Fantechi, A., Semini, L. (eds.) From Software Engineering to Formal Methods and Tools, and Back - Essays Dedicated to Stefania Gnesi on the Occasion of Her 65th Birthday. LNCS, vol. 11865, pp. 433–448. Springer (2019). https://doi.org/10.1007/978-3-030-30985-5_25

12. Hong, L.V., Haxthausen, A.E., Peleska, J.: Formal modeling and verification of interlocking systems featuring sequential release. In: Artho, C., Ölveczky, P.C. (eds.) Formal Techniques for Safety-Critical Systems - Third International Workshop, FTSCS 2014, Luxembourg, 6-7 November 2014. Revised Selected Papers. Communications in Computer and Information Science, vol. 476, pp. 223–238. Springer (2014). https://doi.org/10.1007/978-3-319-17581-2_15

13. Iliasov, A., Taylor, D., Laibinis, L., Romanovsky, A.: Formal verification of signalling programs with SafeCap. In: Gallina, B., Skavhaug, A., Bitsch, F. (eds.) SAFECOMP 2018. LNCS, vol. 11093, pp. 91–106. Springer, Cham (2018). https://doi.org/10.1007/978-3-319-99130-6_7

14. James, P., et al.: Verification of solid state interlocking programs. In: Counsell, S., Núñez, M. (eds.) Software Engineering and Formal Methods - SEFM 2013 Collocated Workshops: BEAT2, WS-FMDS, FM-RAIL-Bok, MoKMaSD, and OpenCert, Madrid, Spain, 23-24 September 2013, Revised Selected Papers. LNCS, vol. 8368, pp. 253–268. Springer (2013). https://doi.org/10.1007/978-3-319-05032-4_19

15. Larsen, K.G., Pettersson, P., Yi, W.: Uppaal in a nutshell. Int. J. Softw. Tools Technol. Transfer 1, 134–152 (1997). https://doi.org/10.1007/s100090050010

16. Laursen, P.L., Trinh, V.A.T., Haxthausen, A.E.: Formal modelling and verification of a distributed railway interlocking system using UPPAAL. In: Margaria, T., Steffen, B. (eds.) Leveraging Applications of Formal Methods, Verification and Validation: Applications - 9th International Symposium on Leveraging Applications of Formal Methods, ISoLA 2020, Rhodes, Greece, 20-30 October 2020, Proceedings, Part III. LNCS, vol. 12478, pp. 415–433. Springer (2020). https://doi.org/10.1007/978-3-030-61467-6_27

17. Lichtenstein, O., Pnueli, A.: Checking that finite state concurrent programs satisfy their linear specification. In: Proceedings of the 12th ACM SIGACT-SIGPLAN Symposium on Principles of Programming Languages - POPL 85. Association for Computing Machinery (ACM) (1985). https://doi.org/10.1145/318593.318622

18. Limbrée, C.: Formal verification of railway interlocking systems. Ph.D. thesis, Catholic University of Louvain, Louvain-la-Neuve, Belgium (2019). http://hdl.handle.net/2078.1/225609

19. Limbrée, C., Cappart, Q., Busard, S., Pecheur, C., Schaus, P.: Verification of railway interlocking systems. In: Pang, J., Liu, Y., Mauw, S. (eds.) Proceedings 4th International Workshop on Engineering Safety and Security Systems, ESSS 2015, Oslo, Norway, 22 June 2015. EPTCS, vol. 184, pp. 19–31 (2015)

20. Limbrée, C., Cappart, Q., Pecheur, C., Tonetta, S.: Verification of railway interlocking - compositional approach with OCRA. In: Lecomte, T., Pinger, R., Romanovsky, A.B. (eds.) Reliability, Safety, and Security of Railway Systems. Modelling, Analysis, Verification, and Certification - First International Conference, RSSRail 2016, Paris, France, 28-30 June 2016, Proceedings. LNCS, vol. 9707, pp. 134–149. Springer (2016). https://doi.org/10.1007/978-3-319-33951-1_10

21. Limbrée, C., Haxthausen, A.E., Gori, G., Fantechi, A.: Formal verification of railway interlockings: a compositional approach based on a library of pre-verified components. In: Margaria, T., Steffen, B. (eds.) Leveraging Applications of Formal Methods, Verification and Validation. Application Areas - 12th International Symposium, ISoLA 2024, Crete, Greece, 27-31 October 2024, Proceedings, Part V. LNCS, vol. 15223, pp. 127–141. Springer (2024).https://doi.org/10.1007/978-3-031-75390-9_9
22. PlantUML team: PlantUML: a tool to generate UML diagrams from plain text. https://plantuml.com/timing-diagram (2025). Accessed 9 Nov 2025
23. Pnueli, A.: The temporal logic of programs. In: 18th Annual Symposium on Foundations of Computer Science, Providence, Rhode Island, USA, 31 October - 1 November 1977, pp. 46–57 (1977). https://doi.org/10.1109/SFCS.1977.32
24. Rozier, K.Y.: Linear temporal logic symbolic model checking. Comput. Sci. Rev. 5(2), 163–203 (2011). https://doi.org/10.1016/j.cosrev.2010.06.002

Digital Twins and Railway Networks Maintenance: A Partnership for Efficiency and Safety

Anis Mhalla[1]([✉]) [iD] and Simon Collart-Dutilleul[2] [iD]

[1] Laboratory of Automation, Electrical Systems Environment (LAESE), National Engineering School of Monastir (ENIM), Monastir, Tunisia
anis.mhalla@enim.rnu.tn
[2] COSYS Department, ESTAS Laboratory, Gustave Eiffel University, Lille, France

Abstract. This paper investigates the concept of Digital Twin (DT) applied to the maintenance of railway transport networks, a revolutionary approach that exploits advanced technologies to improve reliability, safety and efficiency of these critical infrastructures. A digital twin is a dynamic virtual replica of a physical asset (a train, a track section, a station, etc.) or an entire system, constantly updated with real-time data from sensors. This replica allows the simulation, analysis, visualization, and optimization of the asset or system's behavior in the real world. DT and predictive maintenance (PM) are two closely related concepts in Maintenance 4.0; DT is the advanced environment for performing PM in an optimum and comprehensive manner. Subsequently, PM is a major DT feature as it is fueled by DT data and context.

Traditional maintenance, often reactive or preventive at fixed intervals, is restricted in its ability to proactively predict and prevent failures. Intelligent maintenance, conversely, integrates IoT sensors, Big Data analysis, Artificial Intelligence (AI) and machine learning to monitor the state of railway assets (track, rolling stock, signaling, etc.) in real time.

This approach enables a shift from corrective maintenance to predictive maintenance, where abnormalities and failure warning signs are detected and assessed in order to schedule appropriate interventions before a breakdown occurs. The benefits are manifold: lower maintenance costs thanks to optimized interventions and fewer unplanned shutdowns, improved safety by preventing accidents due to equipment failures, and increased network availability and improved passenger and freight service quality.

This report will cover the different technologies and methods involved in the DT maintenance of rail networks, such as remote condition monitoring, vibration analysis, infrared thermography, natural language processing for the analysis of maintenance reports, and failure prediction algorithms. It will also highlight the challenges involved in deploying these systems, including managing and integrating massive data, cybersecurity, and training staff in the new technologies.

The findings in this paper have been derived from Alessandro Fantechi's research on railway networks, focusing mainly on the application of formal methods for ensuring the safety, dependability and security of critical systems.

Keywords: DT · Railway maintenance · Predictive Maintenance · safety

© The Author(s), under exclusive license to Springer Nature Switzerland AG 2026
M. H. ter Beek et al. (Eds.): Fantechi Festschrift, LNCS 16470, pp. 279–291, 2026.
https://doi.org/10.1007/978-3-032-12484-5_15

1   Introduction

Digital twins provide revolutionary applications for rail transport network maintenance, enabling more efficiently, proactively, and safely managed infrastructures and rolling stock. These Digital Twins (DT) can be applied to Predictive and conditional maintenance of railway infrastructure is structured on real-time asset monitoring using sensors embedded in tracks, bridges, overhead lines and other equipment, which continuously gather data on their condition (vibrations, temperature, wear, stress, etc.). The Digital Twin aggregates and analyzes this data in real time [1–3].

Another application of DT is fault prediction: Through data analysis (often aided by AI and machine learning), the DT can spot early warning signs of potential failures [4, 5]. This allows a shift from reactive maintenance or preventive maintenance to predictive maintenance, where interventions are only initiated when required [6].

The third mission of the DT is to optimize maintenance schedules, by knowing the accurate status of each component, operators can optimally schedule maintenance interventions [7], minimizing service disruptions and extending the useful life of assets [8].

Another key benefit of DTs is reduced costs, in fact predictive maintenance reduces costs associated with emergency repairs, unplanned downtime, and premature part replacements.

These DTs can also be leveraged for rolling stock management (Trains) by monitoring the status of trains, the performance of locomotives, braking systems, and automatic doors, and fleet optimization, as DT can help manage entire train fleets by predicting the maintenance requirements of each railcar and optimizing their allocation to ensure maximum availability [9, 10].

The digital twin can be used for decision support by integrating data from a variety of sources [11], giving decision-makers an overview of network status and operations [12].

Digital twins technology is also revolutionizing the management of the overall rail transport network lifecycle through predictive maintenance. Powered by IoT sensors, digital twins monitor the state of assets (track, catenaries, signaling, trains, etc.) in real time in order to detect anomalies and signs of premature wear. By analyzing these data and incorporating machine learning algorithms, the Digital Twins can accurately predict when a failure might occur. This enables timely intervention, avoiding unexpected breakdowns and extending equipment service life by performing maintenance only when required [13, 14].

The authors in [15] comprehensively introduce cutting-edge papers covering DT applications in Railway Engineering systems. In contrast to existing research, the presented work addresses the research papers holistically from the DT and railway systems perspective, spanning a large range of DT domains and four Railway Systems: tracks, structures, railcars and overhead contact lines. It provides a stepping stone to the adoption of DT in railway systems by providing a thorough overview of current research areas, enabling technologies and tools for DT in railway systems. In addiction, the paper reviews current case studies and frameworks, illustrating how DT is a critical enabler for upgrading rail infrastructures, increasing operational efficiency, raising maintenance levels and improving rail system safety. Other works presenting a state-of-the-art on the

DT application in railway transport networks and examining the latest advances in DT technology in the railway sector are presented in [16].

Overall, Digital Twins are transforming railway maintenance by making it smarter, more predictive, and enabling optimized resource management and significant improvements in network safety and reliability.

2 State of Art: DT and Railway Transport Network

In [17], the authors introduce a prototype for a simulation-based DT that allows railway station managers to provide capabilities such as predicting pedestrian flow, congestion early warning, evacuation response planning and intelligent gate management. The simulation-based DT functions as a highly complex mirror of a station's crowd dynamics, extracting data from its physical counterpart at a specific frequency, simulating the evolution of the system over a given time horizon, sending warning messages and assessing various corrective solutions.

The studied framework, based on specific cases, confirms the efficiency of the methods and engineering solutions designed on an ad hoc basis to reach an acceptable trade-off between accuracy, performance and scalability. In particular, it involves tackling the challenges of synchronisation between the physical and virtual worlds, data integration and the interoperability with existing systems, as well as the human-system interaction.

A study on the use of various scientific databases enabled by a multiple search tool is presented in [3]. In addition, a literature review was performed, highlighting DT applications evolution over the past decade and pinpointing key fields as predictive maintenance, condition monitoring and process decision making. The paper highlights the different levels of adoption in different transport sectors and highlights promising new areas for future development, especially in underrepresented fields such as supply chains and waterborne transport.

Future research directions are suggested, with an emphasis on improving predictive diagnostics, automated maintenance processes and improved inventory management. The research also presents a DT framework for transportation systems, outlining the key components and functionality needed for effective maintenance management. The findings provide a blueprint for future DT application innovation and improvement in the transportation sector.

In [18], the authors aimed to provide an understanding of the current state of DT for Railways (DTR). In addition, this research provides clarity on how DT can benefit twin rail system designers and developers. As DTR is currently in its early adoption stage, little clear guidance exists for identifying technologies for specific DTR applications. Therefore, based on the results, a DTR taxonomy for designers and developers is provided. Finally, a depiction of the potential challenges, traps and opportunities of DTR for prospective researchers is presented.

The work presented in [19] describes a conceptual architecture to build a DT platform to transparently incorporate and connect automatically numerical models and datasets from different subsystems into a large-scale holistic railway system. Frameworks for model cooperation, communications strategies and a visualisation toolkit are introduced in this study. A specific use-case of the platform is also implemented and extensively discussed. This research aims to bring new insight into sustainable large-scale holistic rail infrastructure system development.

The literature on DT in rail and road networks is reviewed in [20]. The findings reveal that DT research in this discipline is rare and that few use cases have received the scientific community's attention. The research results also suggest that most DT applications in rail and road networks are focused on their operational and maintenance aspects, and there is considerable unexplored potential for DT applications in this sector.

The study in [21] focused on specific research findings of each key technology and outlined the RT-based high-performance wireless network optimization and scheduling system developed. This paper outlines a framework for the realisation of intelligent railways wireless, providing direction for future research. Relevant key technologies for solving life-cycle management problems of wireless railway networks are also outlined and presented, including the physical Electromagnetic (EM) environment properties of materials and the 3D autonomous environment model reconstruction.

In [22], the project authors describe an Augmented Digital Twin (ADT) for railway applications that provides real-time risk of derailment in railway operations. A case study of a heavy haul iron Ore wagon with three-section trucks was performed to test the ADT. A numerical multi-body simulation program consisting of 2100 simulation cases was created. The substitution model was developed with linear regression, polynomial regression and decision tree. A longitudinal rail simulator was employed to compute the velocity and lateral force of the coupling throughout a train journey.

This article [23] describes an approach with a successful implementation of an initial version of an infrastructure Digital Twin, complemented by services designed to meet the diverse expectations of users. This milestone underscores commitment to leveraging cutting-edge technology and collaborative frameworks to enhance railway management, promote sustainable transportation practices, and contribute significantly to the reduction of GHG (Greenhouse Gas) emissions. Whilst continuing to refine and develop our digital twin capabilities, remain committed to advancing the future of intelligent and environmentally friendly transport systems.

Digital twin modeling approach is demonstrated in [24] on an operating rail transit structure with two years of vibration data under normal operational circumstances. By training the allowable vibration pattern ranges, the numerical twin identifies abnormal spectrum peaks indicating a potential shift in the structural stability of the bridge. The longer-term trial demonstrates that this inexpensive Structural Health Monitoring (SHM) system provides real-time automated alerts of bridge damage, and also supports less expensive, in-house-engineered transducers featuring state-of-the-art computing capacity, such as the ones involved in the pilot project.

3   Intelligent Maintenance of Railway Transport Networks

Intelligent maintenance of rail transport networks draws on a set of advanced techniques and technologies to increase the infrastructure's reliability, safety and efficiency. Here are some of these techniques, illustrated by concepts and applications.

These techniques, combined and adapted to the specific characteristics of rail transport networks, form the basis of intelligent maintenance, enabling higher levels of performance and safety to be achieved while optimising operating costs.

3.1 IoT Condition Monitoring

Intelligent sensors (temperature, vibrations, acoustics, stress, humidity, etc.) are fitted to trains' critical components (wheels, motors, brakes, etc.) and infrastructure (rails, switches, catenaries, etc.). These sensors provide real-time data on the state of health of these assets [25].

The aim of this monitoring process is to detect any significant changes in a machine's parameters that might point to an imminent fault or a performance drop (Fig. 1).

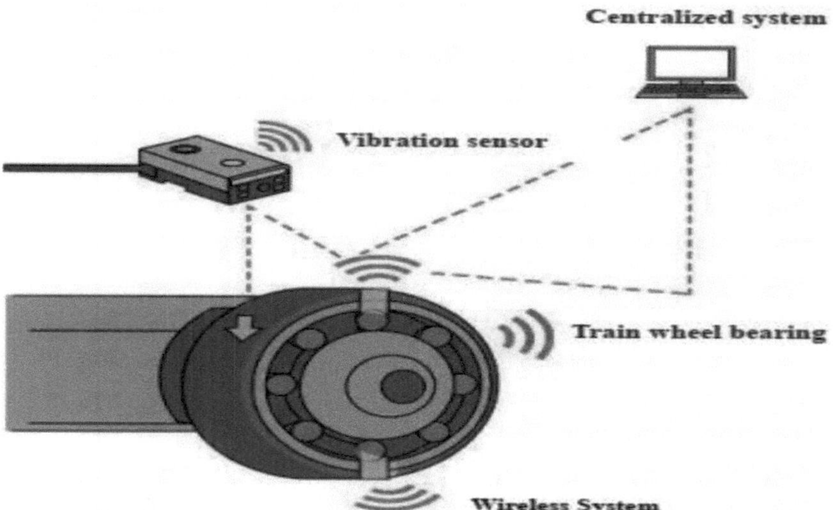

Fig. 1. A drawing illustrating a vibration sensor fitted to a train wheel bearing, transmitting data to a centralised system wirelessly

3.2 Big Data Analysis and Artificial Intelligence (AI)

The large quantities of data gathered by sensors and other sources (maintenance history, operating data, environmental conditions) are analyzed using AI and machine learning algorithms. These analyses enable anomalies to be detected, trends to be identified and potential failures to be predicted. Figure 2 shows a diagram illustrating the flow of data: sensors in the rail line transmitting data to a Big Data cloud platform, where AI algorithms carry out analysis and generate alerts or predictions [26].

In substance, the Big Data is the resource, and AI is the enabling technology unlocking the resource's value, allowing previously unimaginable automation, intelligence, and predictive ability.

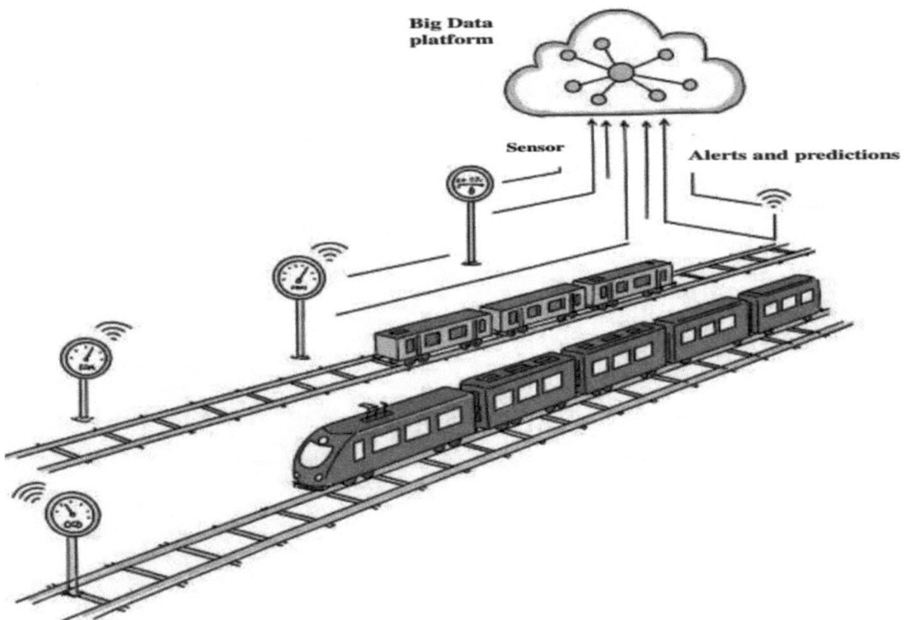

Fig. 2. Data transmission from rail sensors to the Big Data cloud platform

3.3 Predictive Maintenance

Based on data analysis, predictive maintenance seeks to anticipate when a maintenance intervention will be required before failure occurs. This enables maintenance to be planned proactively, optimising costs and minimising downtime. Figure 3 presents a graph illustrating the evolution of a parameter (vibratory amplitude) over time. An alert threshold and a failure threshold are defined. This plot represents the discrepancy between estimated (yellow curve) and measured (blue curve) vibration amplitude parameter values. Predictive maintenance intervenes when the parameter approaches the alert threshold.

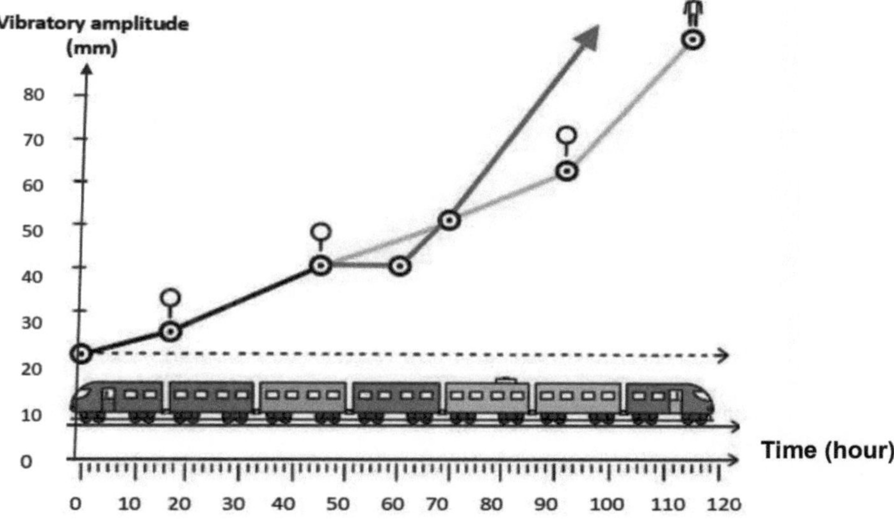

Fig. 3. Predictive maintenance principle in railway transport networks

3.4 Remote Diagnostics and Remote Maintenance

Remote diagnostics and remote maintenance are fundamentally transforming rail system operation and maintenance, enabling a shift from planned or reactive maintenance to predictive (or proactive) and condition based maintenance. This is often called RDPMS (Remote Diagnostic and Predictive Maintenance System) and uses IoT and AI to keep track of rail systems in real time [27].

Experts can monitor equipment status remotely and diagnose problems without requiring a physical presence on site. In some cases, maintenance actions or software updates can even be carried out remotely. Figure 4 illustrates a user interface displaying data from several sensors on a screen in real time, with a visual alert for anomalies in railway networks. A remote technician can view this data and take the appropriate actions.

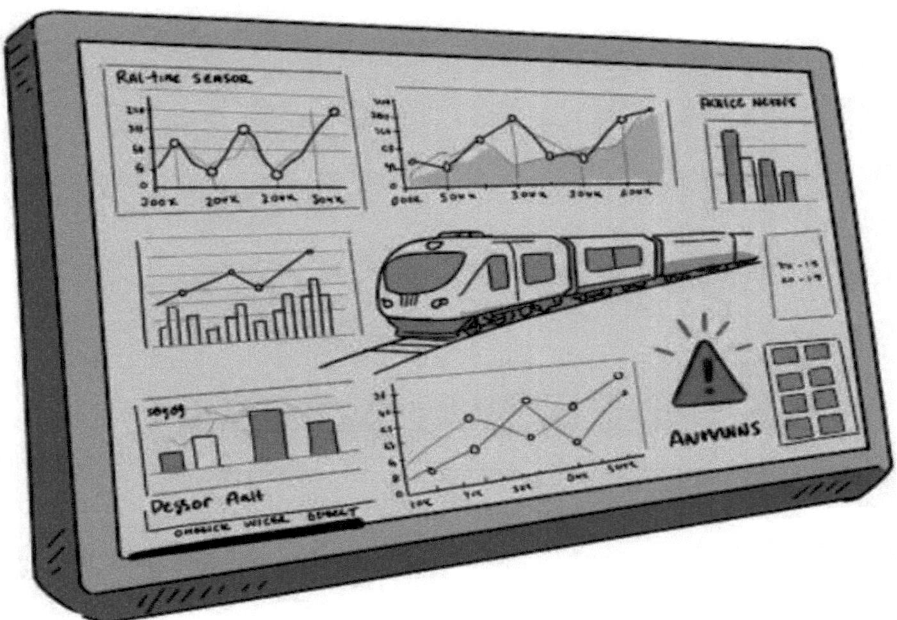

Fig. 4. Transport network supervision via an interface

3.5   Drones and Robotics for Inspection

Drones and robotics are critical technologies that are revolutionizing railway network inspection and monitoring, improving safety, data quality, and operational efficiency. They allow a shift from lengthy and dangerous manual inspections to automated and accurate processes [28].

Drones equipped with high-resolution cameras and specific sensors (thermal, etc.) can survey large sections of track, bridge and tunnel faster and safer than manual inspections. Robots can also carry out dangerous or repetitive maintenance tasks, as illustrated on Fig. 5.

Fig. 5. A drone flies over a railway track, capturing high-definition images which are then analyzed to detect defects (cracks, wear, etc.).

3.6 Augmented Reality (AR) for Maintenance Assistance

Augmented Reality (AR) is a 4.0 Maintenance technology that overlays digital information (instructions, diagrams, real-time data) on the railway maintenance technician's actual visual field, usually via smart glasses or a tablet.

It serves as a digital assistant that enables operatives to perform complex or critical tasks more swiftly, accurately, and safely.AR can overlay digital information (maintenance manuals, schematics, instructions) onto a technician's real-world view using smart glasses or tablets. This facilitates maintenance procedures and reduces errors (Fig. 6).

Fig. 6. A technician wearing AR glasses and viewing repair instructions superimposed on a real train component

3.7   Digital Twins

The Digital Twin concept in the railway sector is a virtual real-time physical replica of an asset (train, track section, signalling subsystem) or an overall system. This virtual replica uses data gathered by IoT for supervision, simulation, optimization and decision-making. DT is fed with real-time data and can be used to simulate different scenarios, predict future performance and optimize maintenance strategies [29] (Fig. 7).

Fig. 7. A virtual 3D model of a train displayed on a screen, with real-time data superimposed showing the state of each component.

The successful implementation of Predictive Maintenance (PM) in rail transport networks raises several Complex challenges, from data collection (failure history, data quality and reliability, etc.) to the validation of Artificial Intelligence models, as well as technological and integration challenges (connectivity and sensor deployment, cybersecurity, etc.)

4 Conclusion

Predictive maintenance and digital twins are pillar technologies in railway digitalization, enabling more intelligent, safer, and more efficient transport network management. Predictive maintenance for rail transport networks offers a significant advance in the management of infrastructure and rolling stock. Drawing on real-time analysis of data and Artificial Intelligence, it overcomes the constraints of traditional approaches (corrective and preventive).

The main benefits of predictive maintenance include

- Safety optimization: By detecting potential anomalies before they become critical, predictive maintenance significantly reduces the accident risk and guarantees the passenger's and staff's safety.
- Improved availability, scheduling maintenance interventions at the optimal time minimizes unplanned stoppages and prolongs equipment life, thus increasing network and traffic availability.
- Reduced costs: By accurately identifying the components that require maintenance, and avoiding unnecessary replacement or servicing, maintenance costs can be reduced significantly.

However, implementing predictive maintenance is not without its challenges:

- Data collection and analysis: The reliability of predictions hinges on the data collected, both in quality and quantity. High-performance sensors and robust analysis platforms are therefore indispensable.
- Expertise and training, indeed data interpretation and maintenance strategy implementation require specific skills in data analysis, artificial intelligence and railway maintenance.
- Existing systems integration, in fact predictive maintenance solutions can be a complex task to incorporate into existing information and management systems.

In conclusion, predictive maintenance represents a major investment in rail networks, allowing operators to improve their safety, reliability and cost-effectiveness. Although some challenges remain, the benefits in risk reduction, improved availability and optimized costs make it an extremely important strategic direction for the railways of the future. Investing in this approach, along with careful data management and staff training, is liable to yield a significant return and contribute to a more efficient and more sustainable rail system.

References

1. Dirnfeld, R., et al.: Integrating AI and DTs: challenges and opportunities in railway maintenance application and beyond. SIMULATION **100**(9), 903–917 (2024)

2. Sarp, S., Kuzlu, M., Jovanovic, V., Polat, Z., Guler, O.: Digitalization of railway transportation through AI-powered services: digital twin trains. Eur. Transp. Res. Rev. **16**(1), 58 (2024)

3. Werbińska-Wojciechowska, S., Giel, R., Winiarska, K.: Digital twin approach for operation and maintenance of transportation system—Systematic review. Sensors **24**(18), 6069 (2024)

4. Zhang, X., Ru, Y.: Fault prediction of railway track circuit based on machine learning. Int. J. Sensor Netw. **45**(4), 216–228 (2024)

5. Zhu, L., Chen, C., Wang, H., Yu, F.R., Tang, T.: Machine learning in urban rail transit systems: a survey. IEEE Trans. Intell. Transp. Syst. **25**(3), 2182–2207 (2023)

6. Nwamekwe, C.O., Chikwendu, O.C.: Machine learning-augmented digital twin systems for predictive maintenance in highspeed rail networks. Int. J. Multidiscip. Res. Growth Evaluat. **6**(01), 1783–1795 (2025)

7. Tang, R., et al.: A literature review of Artificial Intelligence applications in railway systems. Transp. Res. Part C Emerg. Technol. **140**, 103679 (2022)

8. Pappaterra, M.J., Flammini, F., Vittorini, V., Bešinović, N.: A systematic review of artificial intelligence public datasets for railway applications. Infrastructures **6**(10), 136 (2021)

9. Crespo Márquez, A., Leturiondo, U., Marcos, J.A., Guillén, A.J., Candón, E.: On the definition of requirements for a digital twin. A case study of rolling stock assets. In: Crespo Márquez, A., Gómez Fernández, J.F., González-Prida Díaz, V., Amadi-Echendu, J. (eds.) World Congress on Engineering Asset Management. LNME, October 2022, pp. 76–86. Springer, Cham (2022). https://doi.org/10.1007/978-3-031-25448-2_8

10. Guillén, A.J., Candón, E.: On the definition of requirements for a digital twin. A case study of rolling stock assets. In: 16th WCEAM Proceedings, vol. 76 (2023)

11. Krmac, E., Djordjevic, B.: Digital twins for railway sector: current state and future directions. IEEE Access (2024)

12. Dirnfeld, R., De Donato, L., Flammini, F., Azari, M.S., Vittorini, V.: Railway digital twins and artificial intelligence: challenges and design guidelines. In: Marrone, S., et al. (eds.) European Dependable Computing Conference, September 2022, pp. 102–113. Springer, Cham (2022). https://doi.org/10.1007/978-3-031-16245-9_8

13. Aewunruen, S., Sresakoolchai, J., Lin, Y.H.: Digital twins for managing railway maintenance and resilience. Open Res. Eur. **1**, 91 (2021)

14. Gao, Y., Qian, S., Li, Z., Wang, P., Wang, F., He, Q.: Digital twin and its application in transportation infrastructure. In: 2021 IEEE 1st International Conference on Digital Twins and Parallel Intelligence (DTPI), July 2021, pp. 298–301. IEEE (2021)

15. Anu, T.E., Lu, P., Alimo, P.K., Atuobi, H.B., Akoto, E.T., Abbew, C.K.: Revolutionizing railway systems: a systematic review of digital twin technologies. High-Speed Rail. (2025)

16. Kushwaha, D., Kumar, A., Harsha, S.P.: Advancements and applications of digital twin in the railway industry: a literature review. Int. J. Rail Transp., 1–26 (2024)

17. Padovano, A., Longo, F., Manca, L., Grugni, R.: Improving safety management in railway stations through a simulation-based digital twin approach. Comput. Ind. Eng. **187**, 109839 (2024)

18. Ghaboura, S., Ferdousi, R., Laamarti, F., Yang, C., Saddik, A.E.: Digital twin for railway: a comprehensive survey. IEEE Access **11**, 120237–120257 (2023). https://doi.org/10.1109/ACCESS.2023.3327042

19. Zhou, S., et al.: A conceptual model-based digital twin platform for holistic large-scale railway infrastructure systems. Procedia CIRP **109**, 362–367 (2022)

20. Vieira, J., Poças Martins, J., Marques de Almeida, N., Patrício, H., Gomes Morgado, J.: Towards resilient and sustainable rail and road networks: a systematic literature review on digital twins. Sustainability **14**(12), 7060 (2022)

21. Guan, K., et al.: Key technologies for wireless network digital twin towards smart railways. High-Speed Rail. **2**(1), 1–10 (2024)

22. Bernal, E., Wu, Q., Spiryagin, M., Cole, C.: Augmented digital twin for railway systems. Veh. Syst. Dyn. **62**(1), 67–83 (2024)
23. Issa, M., et al.: Railway system Digital Twin: a tool for extended enterprises to perform multimodal transportation in a decarbonization context. In: Transport Research Arena 2024, TRA'24, April 2024 (2024)
24. Armijo, A., Zamora-Sánchez, D.: Integration of railway bridge structural health monitoring into the internet of things with a digital twin: a case study. Sensors **24**(7), 2115 (2024)
25. Padhi, S., Subhedar, M., Behra, S., Patil, T.: IoT based condition monitoring for railway track fault detection in smart cities. IETE J. Res. **69**(9), 5794–5803 (2023)
26. Okrepilov, V.V., Kovalenko, B.B., Getmanova, G.V., Turovskaj, M.S.: Modern trends in artificial intelligence in the transport system. Transp. Res. Procedia **61**, 229–233 (2022)
27. Giani, M.: Remote diagnostics to support maintenance activities in railway industry (2023)
28. Mortezaei, A., Mirahmadi, S.S., Derakhshan, F.: A new era in railway track inspection: drone based image processing integrated with IoT. In: 2024 10th International Conference on Artificial Intelligence and Robotics (QICAR), February 2024, pp. 311–315. IEEE (2024)
29. Kaewunruen, S., AbdelHadi, M., Kongpuang, M., Pansuk, W., Remennikov, A.M.: Digital twins for managing railway bridge maintenance, resilience, and climate change adaptation. Sensors **23**(1), 252 (2022)

Type-Safe Validation of XML Railway
Data in B

Jan Gruteser[1]([✉]) [iD], Michael Leuschel[1] [iD], and Susanne Wunsch[2] [iD]

[1] Faculty of Mathematics and Natural Science, Institute of Computer Science,
Heinrich Heine University Düsseldorf, Universitätsstr. 1, 40225 Düsseldorf, Germany
`jan.gruteser@hhu.de`, `leuschel@hhu.de`
[2] Chair of Traffic Process Automation, "Friedrich List" Faculty of Transport and
Traffic Sciences, TUD Dresden University of Technology, 01062 Dresden, Germany
`susanne.wunsch@tu-dresden.de`

Abstract. We present a typed translation of XML data to the B method, to enable processing data in a principled and safe fashion. Indeed, data validation for railways is a success story of formal methods in general and B and PRoB in particular. Data formats range from custom Excel to the railML standard, with many data sources being in XML.

The new typed translation has been integrated into the PRoB toolset, and enables automated import of XML data in B machines. We implemented various features and performance improvements in PRoB, notably to process large XML files. We evaluated our approach on an industrial railway design case study from Deutsche Bahn. We compare the performance with existing tooling based on the XML-specific Schematron framework. The PRoB based solution offers similar performance, and adds new features like visualisation of rule violations.

Keywords: Data Validation · B Method · XML · Schematron · Railways

1   Introduction

Formal methods play an important role in industry in general [5] and for railways in particular [4,6,18]. The formal B method [1,2] is popular in the railway sector, see, e.g., the surveys [4] or [6]. One particular success story of the B method in the railway sector is data validation [9]. Automated validation of design data is a key challenge in the digitization of large-scale railway infrastructure projects. While some infrastructure managers still rely on manually verified Excel sheets, many have adopted XML-based formats such as railML [33] or custom solutions like PlanPro [32].

In this paper, we investigate the applicability of the formal B method to the validation of data in XML in general and for a particular case study from the railway domain, comparing it to an existing validation chain based on Schema-

© The Author(s), under exclusive license to Springer Nature Switzerland AG 2026
M. H. ter Beek et al. (Eds.): Fantechi Festschrift, LNCS 16470, pp. 292–313, 2026.
https://doi.org/10.1007/978-3-032-12484-5_16

tron [23] (a constraint description language for XML data). As such, we address the relevant quality aspect "import/export vs. external tools" identified in [4]. The general procedure of our toolchain based on PROB is illustrated in Fig. 1. First, we implemented a new translation (called "XML2B") for the *typed* reading of XML data (`.xml`) in accordance with an XML Schema (`.xsd`). This provides us with a B representation of the static input data. Part of this work was also the development of a new file format for the efficient loading of large B data structures (`.probdata`). The static input data can be referenced by rules machines, which are special B machines using a domain-specific language (DSL) for describing validation rules. Finally, the validation rules are checked by PROB and the validation results can be output in newly developed output formats, such as a human-readable HTML file, a machine-readable XML file, or an SVG-based VISB visualisation highlighting error locations.

Along with this, we present the following contributions:

- A generic, XSD-based, and typed translation of XML data to the formal B method, with tooling usable via command line;
- An illustration of how XPath expressions can be formulated with the B language;
- A translation of selected Schematron rules to B and comparison of the two approaches in terms of performance, complexity and readability;
- General improvements and extensions to the B-Rules DSL and PROB, e.g. rule validation reports, performance, and a new mechanism for fast loading of data;
- Discussion/comparison with Schematron-based case study in terms of performance, readability, cost;
- VISB visualisation of the geographical track layout indicating erroneous locations.

Note that our translation from XML to B, as well as the approach in general, is *generic* and not limited to railway data. In the following, the structure closely follows the process described above, after first introducing the motivation and background in Sect. 2.

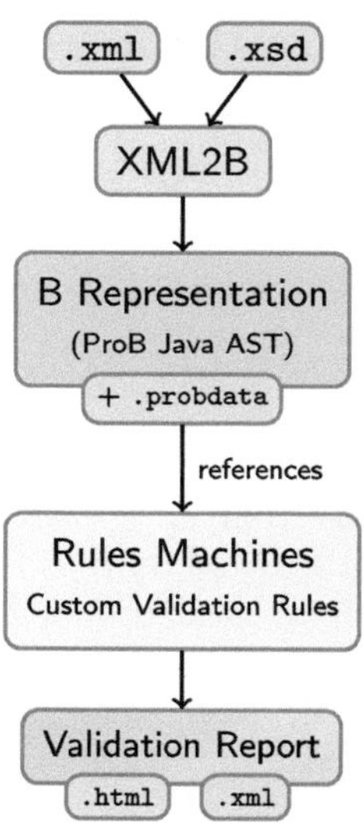

Fig. 1. XML2B Validation Toolchain

2 Motivation and Background

Railway infrastructure managers (IMs) face several challenges in fulfilling their responsibility to provide reliable and safe services. A significant issue documented across European railway networks lies in the outdated and deteriorating state of many current Control-Command and Signaling systems (CCS), with a comprehensive 2022 study [11] analyzing data from 15 European countries representing over two-thirds of the EU railway network and reflecting the state around 2020 showing that legacy interlocking technologies still represent 73% of all systems (relay 38%, mechanical 25%, other 10%) compared to only 27% electronic systems, indicating widespread infrastructure that urgently requires modernization. To address this demand for designing modern CCS, the entire process chain is being re-evaluated to enable digitization and automation.

However, the number of experts in CCS – both design engineers and authorized inspectors – is decreasing due to an aging workforce and a lack of interest among younger generations to pursue careers in this field. Consequently, railway IMs must adopt digital solutions that integrate user-friendly, automated, and quality-assured processes to ensure a reliable and safe railway network in the future. As CCS design falls within a safety-critical domain, the ultimate goal is to provide certified tools. Certification criteria could potentially include the validation of results by two independent tools producing identical outcomes.

In this paper, we therefore explore an approach with PROB to support certification efforts. More specifically, we investigate the applicability of the formal B method to the validation of data in XML format, in particular applied to a case study from the railway domain, and compare it to an existing validation chain based on Schematron.

B Method, ProB, B-Rules DSL. The B method [1] is a state-based formal method based on first-order logic and set theory for specifying and verifying software systems. It has been used industrially for more than 25 years [9] to generate software that is "correct by construction" [16] and certification at the system level [14,37,38], but also for data validation [21,27,29]. Formal methods in general are of great interest in the railway sector [17] and are recommended by the norm EN 50128 [12]. Here, we apply the B method for data validation.

PROB [28][1] is an animator, model checker, and constraint solver for the B method and other high-level formal specification languages. Companies such as Siemens, Alstom, CLEARSY and Thales have used PROB to validate the safe configuration of train systems throughout the world (e.g., Paris, São Paulo, Barcelona) [9]. In this setting PROB has been certified according to the European norm EN 50128. The surveys [4] and [18] demonstrate considerable usage of PROB in the railway domain.

In prior work, we have extended PROB with capabilities to read and validate railML data [20] using a domain-specific language for rule validation integrated in PROB [21,36]. It facilitates the formulation and validation of comprehensible static *rules* and the pre-*computation* of necessary data structures. In this article, we use PROB and its integrated rules DSL in a similar way to validate the static input parameters of PlanPro files.

---

[1] PROB is available for download at https://prob.hhu.de.

PlanPro, PlaZ, Schematron. In 2012, the large German IM, DB InfraGO, began developing a digitized and partially automated design process for CCS, in collaboration with industry partners and universities. This initiative resulted in *PlanPro*, an XML-based data format for CCS design data, and *PlaZ*, a validation framework for plausibility and admissibility checking for these data [32].

PlanPro's data structure and types are modeled in UML (Unified Modeling Language), which is then automatically converted into XML Schema. This approach enables software tools to validate them against the XML Schema, identifying mismatched structures or incorrect data types. Both the UML model and the XML Schema are provided as open-source resources[2]. Additionally, a sample file, known as P-Hausen, is included to demonstrate the application of the PlanPro format. In this paper, we use it as a case study for the evaluation of our B validation approach compared to the existing PlaZ approach.

The PlaZ framework complements PlanPro by validating CCS design data against predefined rules. Developed by TU Dresden since 2016, PlaZ relies on the *Schematron* language, which specializes in rule definitions for XML files [24,25][3]. The entire validation process is described by Wunsch et al. [44]. As Schematron is specified in the ISO/IEC 19757-3 standard [23], it has undergone rigorous review processes, which enhances confidence in its reliability and effectiveness.

As the size of the PlanPro files for large-scale projects increases significantly, the existing approach has to cope with longer processing times. Another obstacle is the limited availability of programmers with expertise in Schematron and an understanding of railway-specific requirements. This motivates this work, where PROB is used as a second chain to investigate how these problems can be tackled.

3   Translating XML to B

PROB already provides external functions to import data from files, such as `READ_CSV`, `READ_JSON`, or `READ_XML`, which are used in practice [20,40]. These functions are implemented in Prolog and provide generic ways to load data into B machines. `READ_XML` represents XML elements as classical B records [13] and attribute values as strings and can load arbitrary XML data. For example, the XML element `<edge from="A" to= "B" length="70.5" active="true''/>` is translated by `READ_XML` into the following B record:

```
rec(attributes: {("from","A"), ("to","B"), ("length","70.5"),
     ("active",'true")}, element: "edge", meta: [...], pId: 0, recId: 1).
```

As you can see, all attributes are stored in a single relation from strings (names of attributes) to strings (values). While this is very generic, it has no information about the data types of the values and does not use the B type system to more faithfully represent and more safely process the values. Moreover,

---

[2] https://www.dbinfrago.com/web/schienennetz/dienstleistende/planpro.
[3] https://github.com/susi-wunsch/schematron.

the interpretation of numbers as strings can cause problems, e.g. in simple arithmetic operations: "1.0" /= "1". When validating data, it is essential to take into account the appropriate data types for accurate data interpretation [40].

Consequently, part of this work involves creating a similarly generic translation from XML to B, called "XML2B"[4], incorporating the derivation of attribute types, which is not provided by PROB's external function READ_XML. Our implementation allows the user to import an XML file, which gets automatically translated to a "virtual" fully typed B machine.[5] The type derivation can be executed with or without using XSD schema files. XML2B can either be integrated directly into Java applications via its API or used standalone via a command line interface. A graphical user interface is available through integration in PROB2-UI.

3.1 Using Free Types for Data Values

B is a strongly typed language, which means that all elements of a set must be of the same B type. Obviously, this leads to a problem when converting XML elements with attributes that can have different types. In the above-mentioned function READ_XML, this is handled by converting all data values to strings. To represent the data in a type-safe way in B, while using similar record structures, we use the "free types", originating from Z (see Sect. 3.10 of [39]). These describe inductive data types and are also supported by PROB [35] (for Z but also for inductive data types of Event-B theories [10]). In PROB, free types can be defined in classical B machines within the FREETYPES section[6]. We use a free type to encapsulate all possible XML attribute values in a type-safe way.

Listing 1. Free Type Declaration for XML Attribute Values in PROB

```
FREETYPES XML_ATTRIBUTE_TYPES =
    XmlBool(BOOL), XmlString(STRING), XmlInteger(INTEGER),
    XmlReal(REAL), XmlEnumSet(EnumSet)
```

For this, we declare the free type as shown in Listing 1, where we have a constructor for each base type and one constructor per enumerated set (which are extracted from the XSD schema, as described in Sect. 3.2). This allows us to wrap attribute values using the constructors of the free type, e.g. XmlReal(70.5) for the decimal value 70.5 or XmlEnumSet(EnumValue), where EnumValue is an element of the enumerated set EnumSet (enumerated sets form new types in B). In particular, we can now group our four attributes from above in a typed-fashion in a single relation mapping strings to XML values:

```
rec(attributes: {("from",XmlString("A")), ("to",XmlString("B")),
             ("length",XmlReal(70.5)),("active",XmlBool(TRUE))}.
```

---

[4] XML2B is available as open source at https://github.com/hhu-stups/xml2b.

[5] The conversion is implemented in Java using existing libraries, as to our knowledge there is no library for traversing XSD schemas in SICStus Prolog (there is work for SWI Prolog [34]).

[6] Further documentation at: https://prob.hhu.de/w/index.php?title=Free_Types.

Listing 2. A XSD Simple Type Restriction

```
<xs:simpleType name="aType">
   <xs:restriction base="xs:string">
     <xs:enumeration value="foo"/>
     <xs:enumeration value="bar"/>
     <xs:enumeration value="baz"/>
   </xs:restriction>
</xs:simpleType>
```

Listing 3. B Translation of Listing 2

```
SETS
   aType = {aType_foo,
            aType_bar,
            aType_baz}
```

This enables the attributes to be stored in the same way as with `READ_XML`, except that the range consists of free type values rather than string values. To access the value of an attribute, the destructor of the corresponding free type can be used, e.g. `70.5 = XmlReal~(XmlReal(70.5))`. Note that the ~operator in B stands for relational inverse, i.e., the destructor is the inverse of the constructor.

Listing 4. B Type of the Translated XML Data

```
seq(struct(Element: STRING, ns: STRING,
    recId: INTEGER, pIds: seq(INTEGER), maxCId: INTEGER,
    content: POW(XML_ATTRIBUTE_TYPES),
    attributes: STRING +-> XML_ATTRIBUTE_TYPES,
    xmlLocation: INTEGER*INTEGER*(INTEGER*INTEGER)))
```

3.2 Determination of B Types

Our translation has two modes: if an XSD schema file is provided along with the XML file, a schema-based translation is performed, extracting all data types from the XSD schema. Otherwise, we try to derive the data types automatically by just inspecting the XML file.

Schema-based Types. If the XML file is provided with an XSD schema file, we first perform an XSD schema validation when reading the XML file to ensure its syntactical correctness. This also provides useful assumptions that we can rely on later in our custom rules (e.g. the guaranteed existence of a child element). Next, the XSD schema is read to obtain the required type information. For this, we use the XML Schema Object Model (XSOM) Java library[7].

Before gathering the type information of the elements, we iterate over all `xs:simpleTypes` (which define the allowed values of attributes[8]) to determine which of them are to be translated as enumerated sets in B. For translation, we consider all simple types with a restriction on the base type `xs:string` consisting only of `xs:enumeration` elements as an enumerated set. Listing 2 shows an example of such a simple type with only enumerated valid values. These are translated into the B enumerated set shown in Listing 3. As the identifiers of the enumerated set elements have to be unique in B, the permitted values are prefixed with the type's name. In XSD schemas, however, simple types can also

---

[7] https://central.sonatype.com/artifact/org.glassfish.jaxb/xsom.

[8] For further details, we refer to https://www.w3schools.com/xml/schema_intro.asp for a tutorial on XSD schemas and XSD data types.

Table 1. Type Conversions with Provided XSD Types

B Type	XSD Base Types (`xs:`)
BOOL	boolean
INTEGER	int, integer, negativeInteger, nonNegativeInteger, nonPositiveInteger, positiveInteger, unsignedInt, long, unsignedLong, short, unsignedShort, byte, unsignedByte
FLOAT	float
REAL	decimal, double, duration, dayTimeDuration, yearMonthDuration
Enum. Set	string with explicitly enumerated value restrictions
STRING	anything else, e.g. string, ID, Name, language

be composed of several simple types (`xs:union`). In this case, we unify all enumerated elements of the individual subtypes and assign them to the supertype. In the special case that subtypes are defined via an `xs:pattern` with base type `xs:string` (e.g. `<xs:pattern value="[a-z]"/>`), the enumerated set is created as *extensible* during the translation, so that the values that are not given by the schema are added to the enumerated set during translation from the XML file (the value is valid by XSD schema validation). The other `xs:restriction` types that are not enumerations only provide upper/lower bounds on the value lengths, which are already checked by schema validation, and are therefore not relevant for the translation and ignored.

To extract the remaining types from the schema, we search for all element declarations (`xs:element`) within the schema and collect their base *content* type (e.g. integer in `<xs:element name="age" type="xs:integer"/>`). If the element type is given by a complex or simple type declared in the schema and not a base type from Table 1, the types are explored recursively until such a base type is reached (this is because a type can extend another type). Then these XSD base types are assigned to their corresponding B types, as shown in Table 1. In addition, during the recursive search, all attribute declarations of the traversed types are collected, e.g. `<xs:attribute name="attr" type="xs:string"/>`. Their types themselves are reduced again to the base types of Table 1 and translated into B types in the same way, taking the previously derived enumerated sets into account. The valid attribute values and their respective types are then linked to the element currently being considered. The mapping between the extracted element types and the elements of the read XML data is determined by the unique sequence of parent elements of each element, as well as its namespace. If elements appear in the XML file that do not have a type assigned by the XSD schema, we apply the translation rules for string values (see the next paragraph; cf. Table 2). Note that we only do a *type* conversion, which means, for example, that the XSD type `nonNegativeInteger` is translated to a B integer instead of `NATURAL` (which is not a pure B type).

Table 2. Type Conversions for String Values

Type of String	B Type	Example	B Value
duration	REAL (converted duration in ms)	"PT6S"	6000.0
number	REAL	"-1"	-1.0
		"27.5"	27.5
boolean	BOOL	"true"	TRUE
anything else	STRING	"data"	"data"

Types without Schema. If no XSD schema is provided with the XML file, we perform a conversion of the input strings based on the rules specified in Table 2. Attributes with inconsistent types (e.g. "true" and then "n/a" elsewhere), are treated as strings to avoid type conflicts in B.

3.3   Translation of Typed XML Data Into B

Reading the actual data from an XML file is the same for both approaches. We use an SAX parser (Simple API for XML) that collects all XML elements sequentially together with their attribute values and text content. In addition, each element is assigned a record ID, as in READ_XML, that specifies its position in the sequence of elements in the document (the root has ID 0). The IDs of its ancestors and last descendant element are also recorded.

The final translation step is the generation of the ProB Java AST (Abstract Syntax Tree) consisting of the following steps:

1. Create free type XML_ATTRIBUTE_TYPES with a free type constructor for each *occurring* B data type T of the form XmlT(T) (cf. Listing 1).
2. Create constant XML_DATA and its properties:
   (a) Type predicate, see Listing 4
   (b) Value assignment (using READ_PROB_DATA_FILE, cf. Section 5)
3. Create sets clause using *all* enumerated sets extracted from the XSD schema and containing values added during translation in step 2b for extensible sets.

A record of a translated XML element (cf. Listing 4) consists of:

- Element: the tag of the element as string;
- ns: the namespace of the element, if available (empty string otherwise)
- recId: the internal record ID assigned to this record, this is the index of this record in the sequence of elements. Useful for quick access to a data record;
- pIds: sequence of *all* record IDs of the ancestors of this element (parents), in ascending order. Useful for path semantics;
- maxCId: largest child record ID. Can be used to obtain all descendants of the element with the B interval recId+1..maxCId;
- content: content within the element, empty set if the element has no content;
- attributes: attributes of the element, map of attribute names to their values for *present* attributes (cf. Sect. 3.1);

Table 3. Translation of Selected XPath Operators to B

XPath	Translation
$//e$	`elements("e")`
e/c	`childs_of_type[elements[{"e"}] * {"c"}]`
$e/*$	`childs[elements[{"e"}]`
$e//d$	`descendants_of_type[elements[{"e"}] * {"d"}]`
$//e/ancestor::a$	`ancestors_of_type[elements[{"e"}] * {"a"}]`
$e1/e2/e3$	`xpath[elements[{"e1"}] * {["e2","e3"]}]`

– `xmlLocation`: location of the element in the XML file (number of start and end line/column). Useful for error messages during validation.

If an attribute or content is not specified but the XSD schema provides a `default` or `fixed` value for it, this value is used for the B translation.

In addition to having the XML data in B, an efficient selection of the elements of interest is required. The following subsection outlines how the semantics of the XPath language can be transferred to corresponding expressions in B.

3.4   Formulate XPath Expressions in B

An important concept for XML validation, especially with Schematron, is XPath (XML Path Language) expressions[9]. With XPath, one can select elements or attributes from an XML document. Furthermore, predicates can be used to constrain the selected elements.

To formulate such constructs in B, we need similar logic to query XML elements conveniently. It is evident that, in contrast to XPath and Schematron, B is not orientated towards XML structures. Hence, we do not provide full support for XPath logic and focus on important concepts such as querying all elements of a certain type or restrictions regarding ancestors or descendants of an element. These concepts can be implemented as *abstract constants* in the B model so that we can make use of *memoization* (cf. Section 5). Table 3 illustrates our B translation for some basic tree functions[10]. As the purpose is to make it easier to get started with B, their functionality should be self-explanatory. Each of them returns a set of indices that refer to the selected elements in the B sequence of all translated XML elements. For example, Listing 5 shows the recursive definition of an unrestricted XPath expression that collects all XML elements that match the hierarchy. The hierarchy is provided as a sequence of element types encoded as strings, which is a compact way to express the paths in B, e.g. `xpath(recId,["City","ID_City","Value"])` for the XPath `City/ID_City/Value` evaluated in the context of the element with index `recId`.

---

[9] https://www.w3.org/TR/xpath.

[10] Details on the XPath operators can be found at https://www.data2type.de/en/xml-xslt-xslfo/xpath/xpath-introduction.

Listing 5. Unrestricted XPath Function in B

```
xpath = %(curr,path).(curr : dom(XML_DATA) & path : seq(STRING) |
    IF path = {} THEN {curr} ELSE union(xpath[childs_of_type(curr,
        first(path)) * {tail(path)}]) END )
```

Although this is straightforward for XPath expressions without constraints, we cannot apply the above functions directly for XPath expressions with predicates. Instead, we have to express the (element-wise) restrictions as B predicates within set comprehensions that describe the elements to be selected. Consider, for example, the XPath expression `City[ID_City = $ID_Destination]/Name`. This can be written in B as shown in Listing 6, assuming that a variable $ID_{Destination}$ is defined, where `getId` is a special function that returns the string value of a unique child element (here `ID_City`).

Listing 6. XPath with Predicates in B

```
{ t . t : elements("City") & ID_Destination : getId(t,"ID_City")
        | XmlString~(XML_DATA(t)'attributes("Name")) }
```

Observe that we use the free type destructor `XmlString~`, as described in Sect. 3.1, to obtain the actual string value of the attribute. In this example, we assume that the well-definedness of both function applications is provided by means of the XSD schema validation carried out beforehand, which ensures the existence and uniqueness of the requested elements.

In Sect. 4, we apply these generic functions in the context of the case study, showing their use in realistic application.

3.5   Example: Data Validation with PROB

Before presenting the application to a real-world case study in the following Sect. 4, we illustrate the validation process with PROB using a simple example. For this, consider again the example from the beginning of this section. Suppose that another edge is defined in the same way and a path connecting two nodes:

```
<example> <edge from="A" to="B" length="70.5" active="true" />
          <edge from="B" to="C" length="49.1" active="false"/>
          <path id="p1"  start="A" end="C"/>                    </example>
```

We now want to validate that all paths are fully connected by active edges no longer than 50 units.

For validation of this rule with PROB, the XML file is translated using XML2B, as described above. Together with the set of attributes, as discussed in Sect. 3.1, the generated record of the second edge is the following (the entries for the other elements are similar):

```
rec(Element:"edge",attributes:{("from",XmlString("B")),("to",XmlString("C")),
    ("length",XmlReal(49.1)),("active",XmlBool(FALSE))}, content:{}, ns:"",
    maxCId:2, pIds:[1], recId:2, xmlLocation: <omitted>)
```

Note that the generic translation from XML to B is standalone and can in principle be included in any classical B machine. To validate the aforementioned rule, we include the data in a "rules machine", where we can use PROB's DSL for rule validation. The implementation is shown in Listing 7.

Listing 7. Example of a Machine in ProB's Rules DSL

```
1   RULES_MACHINE demo_rules REFERENCES demo_data
2   DEFINITIONS element(T) == {e | e:ran(XML_DATA) & e'Element=T}
3   OPERATIONS
4     COMPUTATION comp_edge BODY DEFINE EDGE VALUE
5       {r,a. r:element("edge") & a=r'attributes | rec(edge: a("from")|->a(
            "to"),
6               length: XmlReal~(a("length")), active: XmlBool~(a("active")
                  )) }
7     END END;
8     RULE route BODY
9       RULE_FORALL p WHERE p : element("path")
10        EXPECT p'attributes("start") |-> p'attributes("end") :
11               closure1({e. e:EDGE & e'active=TRUE & e'length<=50.0 | e'
                     edge })
12        ON_SUCCESS/COUNTEREXAMPLE XmlString~(p'attributes("id"))
13    END END END
```

There are a few things that can be observed here. First, the definitions provide an implementation for the **elements** operator to ease access to element types (see Table 3). Furthermore, a computation is used to collect all relevant edge data in a record format. We apply free type destructors to retrieve the correctly typed attribute values. Note that this is not necessary for the node IDs, as their free type values of the form **XmlString("ID")** can be used in the relation. In the actual rule, we use a comprehension set to filter for the edges fulfilling the requirements and then compute their transitive closure. The expression of such relational connections is a particular strength of the B method. Finally, it is checked that the start and end of the path are connected by the transitive closure.

Validation of this rule would obviously fail because the first edge is too long and the second edge is not active. Hence, the counter-example message (i.e. the ID of the path) is provided to the user.

Listing 8. Example of a PlanPro Schematron Rule (Excerpt)
(Fstr_DWeg – overlap, Fstr_Fahrweg – route path)

```
1   <iso:rule role="error" context="Fstr_DWeg[ancestor::$Group]">
2     <iso:let name="ID_Route_Path" value="ID_Fstr_Fahrweg/Wert"/>
3     <iso:let name="Nominal_Overlap_Length" value="f:number(Fstr_DWeg_Allg
          /Laenge_Soll/Wert)"/>
4     <iso:let name="segment" value="key('Fstr_Fahrweg', $ID_Route_Path, ./
          ancestor::$Group)/Bereich_Objekt_Teilbereich"/>
5     <iso:let name="Limit_A" value="sum($segment/Begrenzung_A/f:number(
          Wert))"/>
6     <iso:let name="Limit_B" value="sum($segment/Begrenzung_B/f:number(
          Wert))"/>
7     <iso:let name="Diff" value="abs($Limit_A - $Limit_B)"/>
8     <iso:let name="Tolerance" value="0.1"/>
9     <iso:assert test="$Diff + $Tolerance ge $Nominal_Overlap_Length">
10      The actual length of the overlap is not equal to or greater than
            the nominal length.
11    </iso:assert>
12  </iso:rule>
```

4   Comparison with Schematron-Based Validation

Our use case for the translation from XML to B is the formal data validation of the existing rule set mentioned in Sect. 2. These rules are currently implemented using Schematron and applied to XML data in PlanPro format. In this section, we describe how we encode a selection of these rules in PROB. We discuss the readability and cost of writing a rule in B compared to the existing Schematron-based tooling.

4.1   Encode Schematron Rules in B

For this study, we consider three rules of varying complexity from the interlocking domain of railways, which are implemented in Schematron and deal with the overlap of a route, that is the track section beyond a target signal that must stay clear when a train approaches for the rare case of overrunning a stop signal due to bad braking. For each rule, we analyse a semi-formal specification and corresponding sample files provided by DB InfraGO[11]. Note that most of the XML element names are in German (due to the PlanPro schema). We try to provide translations for better understanding in the comments.

An excerpt of a rather simple Schematron rule is shown in Listing 8. It checks whether the actual length of an overlap is greater than (or equals to) its nominal length. The rule is structured so that the required values are first assigned to variables using `iso:let`, which can then be used in subsequent expressions. The values can be determined using functions, e.g. `key` to obtain an XML element with a specific ID value. Finally, the actual assertion is stated by `iso:assert` with a message in natural language.

To express Schematron rules we use PROB's B-Rules DSL [21]. This domain specific language built on top of B provides a convenient syntax for precomputing static values and defining validation rules, similar to Schematron rules. For language details, we refer to the documentation [36].

In the following, we describe our B translation of the rule in Listing 8. Since all three investigated rules have common parts for the computation of the overlap elements (`Fstr_DWeg`) and elements corresponding to their uniquely related route path (`Fstr_Fahrweg`), we can benefit from this by performing only one `COMPUTATION` in B. This is shown in Listing 9, where a set of records is constructed, each record containing the required information for exactly one `Fstr_DWeg`. The result of the computation corresponds to lines 1, 2 and 4 of Listing 8. Observe that the structure is quite similar to the Schematron formulation in that we also collect the required values and assign them to identifiers. Of course, some similarities are due to the given structure of the XML file.

In Listing 10, the actual implementation of the rule is shown, corresponding to the remaining lines of Listing 8. The general structure of a Schematron rule maps quite well to a rule written in B-Rules DSL. For instance, the rule name can be used as its identifier in B. Moreover, rule descriptions in natural language can be added in PROB using the `@desc` pragma attached to a rule, additional rule IDs can be added as rule tags, and the grouping can be maintained by using rule classifications (this is used, e.g., to group all rules for route paths).

---

[11] Sources are available at https://stups.hhu-hosting.de/models/schematron.

Listing 9. Precomputing Values in B (Shortened)

```
1   COMPUTATION set_Overlap_Route BODY
2       DEFINE Overlap_Routes /* all overlap elements with their route path
            */
3       TYPE POW(struct(Group: INTEGER, Overlap: INTEGER, Overlap_ID: STRING
            , Route: INTEGER, Segments: POW(INTEGER)))
4       VALUE { (G, FDW, OvID, FID, FF) .
5               G : union(elements[{"LST_Zustand","LST_Zustand_Ziel"}])
6               & FDW : descendants_of_type(G,"Fstr_DWeg")
7               & OvID : keys(FDW)
8               & FID = getId(FDW, "ID_Fstr_Fahrweg")
9               & FF : descendants_of_type(G,"Fstr_Fahrweg")
10              & FID : keys(FF)
11              | rec(Group: G, Overlap: FDW, Overlap_ID: OvID, Route: FF,
                    Segments: childs_of_type(FF, "Bereich_Objekt_Teilbereich"))
                }
12      END END
```

Listing 10. B Translation of Listing 8

```
1   RULE Route_ID7 CLASSIFICATION ROUTE BODY
2     FOR OR_rec IN Overlap_Routes DO
3     RULE_FORALL Nominal_Overlap_Length, Diff, Tolerance WHERE
4         Nominal_Overlap_Length : number_or_zero[get_wert[
5                   xpath(OR_rec'Overlap,["Fstr_DWeg_Allg","Laenge_Soll"])
                    ]]
6       & Diff = RABS(SIGMA(seg).(seg : OR_rec'Segments |
7                   getReal(seg,"Begrenzung_B") - getReal(seg,"Begrenzung_A
                    ")))
8       & Tolerance = 0.1
9       EXPECT Diff + Tolerance >= Nominal_Overlap_Length
10      ON_SUCCESS '''<success message, analogue to counterexample>'''
11      UNCHECKED OR_rec'Overlap_ID
12      COUNTEREXAMPLE '''${OR_rec'Overlap_ID}: The actual length of the
            overlap (${Diff} + ${Tolerance}) is not equal to or greater
            than the nominal length (${Nominal_Overlap_Length}).'''
13    END END END /*@desc <textual rule description>*/
```

We also observe similarities between the two approaches in the formulation of the actual rules. It first contains the computation of rule-specific data based on the previously computed data using the computation, and then asserts that the requirement is fulfilled in the EXPECTS clause. We use a FOR loop to iterate over all overlap elements to ensure that the validation is performed for all relevant elements. If the predicate in the WHERE clause of the rule is not fulfilled for an element, this means that the assertion is not evaluated and the element is thus unchecked (the element is caught by the newly added UNCHECKED clause). If the predicate is true, the expectation will be checked and return either the ON_SUCCESS (which we added as a new keyword) message if the rule succeeds or the COUNTEREXAMPLE in case the assertion fails.

The existing rules can have additional preconditions that specify the elements in more detail for which the rule is to be applied. In Schematron, this may be managed with custom functions before evaluating the assertion, which select the relevant elements as the rule context. In B, we achieve the same by integrating the preconditions into the predicate of the rule. If this cannot be fulfilled, the rule is considered as unchecked, which corresponds to the same logic.

The mapping of built-in functions from Schematron to B is often straightforward; for instance, we use SIGMA for the sum over all elements and the external function RABS for abs (the absolute value of a real number). Custom functions can be implemented in B using abstract constants, as for the XPath functions, or using FUNCTIONs provided by the B-Rules DSL.

After a rule is executed, there are three sets containing the collected success, counterexample, and unchecked messages. These can be used to present the results in a more comprehensible way to domain experts.

4.2   Representation of Validation Results

Typically, domain experts applying a validation toolchain do not (want to) understand B or Schematron. For this reason, it is important to export the validation results in a way that clearly shows problems and successful rules without requiring any knowledge of the internal data structures. Currently, the results of the Schematron-based process are exported as PDF or HTML file, comprising all validation results along with a textual description. This includes feedback for each rule, indicating for which elements the check was successful, failed, or was not applied. As described in Sect. 4.1, we have added these descriptions as success messages or counterexamples according to the B-Rules DSL, which allows us to present the results visually and textually.

Validation Report. Similarly to the existing PlaZ exports, PROB has now been extended by an HTML rule validation report. It provides a convenient, standalone summary of the validation results. It lists the results for each rule, grouped according to the provided classifications, along with general statistics, e.g. run time of each rule. Figure 2a shows an excerpt from an example report. Three rules with the classification "ROUTE" have been checked, whereby the rule "Route_ID622" failed for *at least* one element and is thus highlighted in red together with the keyword FAIL. By clicking on a rule in the HTML, further details such as the found counterexamples or success messages become visible and can be inspected. The other two rules were successful for all checked elements and are coloured green together with the keyword SUCCESS. In addition, the blue labels contain the rule TAGS, and the rule ID is shown in square brackets.

If the results are to be output in machine-readable form, for instance, because the validation is integrated into a chain of different tools, the rule report can also be created as an XML file. It contains the same information as the HTML report, as can be seen in Listing 11 (with shortened IDs), with the advantage that the data can be further processed automatically.

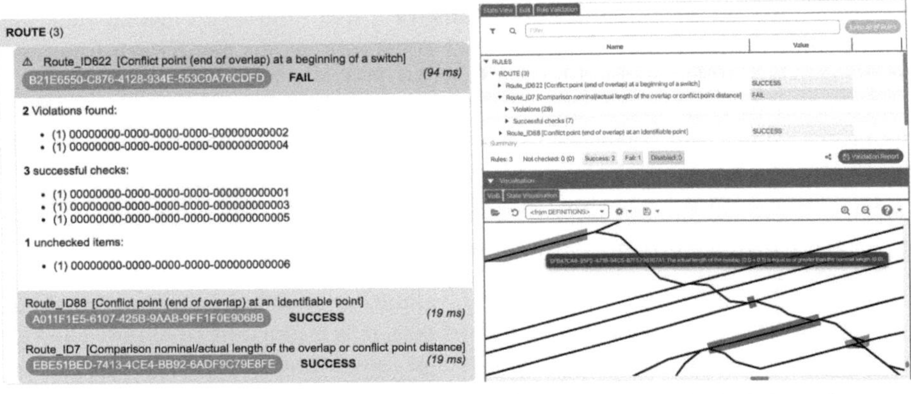

(a) HTML Rule Validation Report   (b) PROB2-UI and VISB Visualisation

Fig. 2. Export and Visualisation of Validation Results

Listing 11. Excerpt of an XML Validation Report created by PROB

```
<classification name="ROUTE" nrRules="3">
  <rule name="Route_ID622" status="FAIL" id="Conflict point (end of overlap)
      at a beginning of a switch">
    <tag>B21E6550-C876-4128-934E-553C0A76CDFD</tag>
    <counterExample   errorType="1">[...]-000000000002</counterExample>
    <counterExample   errorType="1">[...]-000000000004</counterExample>
    <successMessage   ruleBody="1">[...]-000000000001</successMessage>
    <successMessage   ruleBody="1">[...]-000000000003</successMessage>
    <successMessage   ruleBody="1">[...]-000000000005</successMessage>
    <uncheckedMessage ruleBody="1">[...]-000000000006</uncheckedMessage>
    <walltime>110</walltime>
  </rule>
<rule name="Route_ID88" status="SUCCESS" id="Conflict point (end of overlap)
    at an identifiable point">[...]</rule>
<rule name="Route_ID7" status="SUCCESS" id="Comparison nominal/actual length
    of the overlap or conflict point distance">[...]</rule></classification>
```

Visualisation of Counterexamples. The validation results can also be explored interactively in PROB2-UI [7] (cf. Fig. 2b). In the upper section, the validation results can be inspected as in the HTML report. Below, using VISB [43], an integrated SVG-based visualisation technique in PROB, we can provide a visual indication of the locations of validation errors in a schematic track plan. In the case of PlanPro, geographical positions of each edge (`TOP_Kante`) are provided (we leave out the details here). Together with VISB definitions, which allow the direct creation of SVG objects from B code, this gives a graphical view of the track plan. Since we have a mapping of the objects to the corresponding edges we can highlight the matching part of the topology where one of the rules is fulfilled or violated. Additionally, success messages and counterexamples are added as hovers, allowing users to access them directly when inspecting a highlighted element. With PROB's HTML export for VISB, it is possible to make the graphical representation available to domain experts as a standalone file.

4.3   Readability and Cost

Schematron is an approach tailored to XML, which keeps the rules comprehensible as long as the validator is familiar with the underlying XML modelling and XPath. The syntax of XPath is particularly advantageous here as it provides a more compact representation of XML structures. In addition, the path expressions used to query specific XML elements are certainly easier for XML experts to understand. B, on the other hand, as a mathematical language based on set theory, requires the definition of special functions to query the XML elements. This has the disadvantage that queries of XML elements along paths may not be as readable as in XPath expressions. However, this is also due to the special structure of PlanPro, where properties of the elements are specified in (child) elements that must be referenced separately. For XML structures, where properties are expressed using attributes within the corresponding elements, such as railML, we achieve better readability [20].

Regarding costs for developing rules, our approach is at first to translate a Schematron rule to B naively for better understanding of the rule's structure. In a second step, simplifications and optimizations for B can be easily made. During implementation, we identified ambiguities in the natural language formulation, which led to a slightly different implementation in B. This was evident, for example, in the fact that elements were marked as *unchecked* in PROB for some rules, even though Schematron returned that the rule had been *success*fully checked. This is because the Schematron approach pre-filters the elements that are fed into the actual rule (cf. Section 4.1). In B, however, the rule is not checked at all because the rule predicate evaluates to *false*. This demonstrates the usefulness of reimplementing validation rules for a second chain based on the same semiformal description, as this can reveal room for interpretation or even errors in the implementation.

In summary, both approaches require an advanced understanding of syntax and semantics. However, we expect that those with expertise in the XML model to be checked should be able to perform equivalent validations with PROB and the B method after a brief training period.

5   Performance

During the work on this study, several improvements were made to the PROB core and its tooling environment. These were motivated by performance and usability, as well as adding necessary new features. We describe the main new changes and features and compare the performance of the Schematron-based approach with our implementation.

The file size of PlanPro data may increase significantly for large-scale projects. This growth leads to longer processing times, compounded by additional validation rules that aim to cover more PlanPro objects.[12] Despite several implemented mitigations, improving performance remains an ongoing objective

---

[12] The PlaZ framework enables the implementation of any desired rule.

for the Schematron-based approach. A key objective of this work was to investigate whether similar performance can be achieved with the B approach.

Efficient Loading of Translated Data. A major challenge was to efficiently load a complex XML model into PROB (an XML file with 200,000 elements yields a huge B relation with 200,000 record entries) and to achieve reasonable performance during rule execution. Initially, the data was translated directly into the ProB Java AST, meaning that it is stored directly in the generated machine file. This resulted in a significant overhead due to the B parser, which had to parse the entire data again each time the machine is loaded. In addition, the type checker is applied to the parsed machine each time, although the B type of the data is always the same and is ensured by the translation. As a consequence, it was almost impossible to load the P-Hausen example into PROB.

We addressed this by using PROB's mechanism for external functions. That is, rather than encoding the XML data in a large B text file, we load an XML file and convert it into the B internal typed AST representation used by PROB. To achieve this, we write the AST of the translated XML data values in a separate Prolog file, which we call a PROB data file (`.probdata`). Using the new external function `READ_PROB_DATA_FILE`, it is then possible to load the XML data in a regular B machine by providing the B type and the path to a PROB data file.

While this approach avoids parsing and type checking the B encoding, we still have the issue that the Prolog term representing the XML data can become very large. Luckily, SICStus Prolog (SICStus is the default Prolog dialect of PROB) offers a binary file format called *fastrw* (fast read-write), which aims to improve performance when reading large terms.[13] Combining both approaches using a PROB data file in SICStus fastrw format, we are able to load the translated XML data in less than 2 s, compared to unreasonable loading times at the beginning of the study. The only disadvantage is that the converted Prolog data, especially in fastrw format, requires more memory (cf. Table 4).

Memoization. Memoization is a technique integrated in PROB to store values of function applications. We use this to memoize recurring queries to XML elements, which in our implementation corresponds to repeated function applications on abstract constants. In particular, we use the record IDs of the elements instead of the full record to achieve a fast lookup. This is supported by *fast record indexing*, using `Element` (upper case, cf. Listing 4) as the first entry of XML data records.

Evaluation. For comparison, we use the P-Hausen example, which represents an existing medium-sized railway station on a double-track main line, consisting of seven main tracks and further secondary tracks. The example includes 874 routes, 66 flank protection definitions and 86 switches and derailers. We also examined two (confidential) real-world data samples provided by DB InfraGO (named C1 and C2 in Table 4), where C1 is a smaller data set than P-Hausen (approx.

---

[13] This work improved support for writing files in fastrw format from PROB.

Table 4. Performance Results

Tool	Representation	Model	File Size	Run Time	Wall Time
Schematron	XML	P-Hausen	13.3 MB	2.1 s	4.6 s
	XML	C1	4.8 MB	1.6 s	4.5 s
	XML	C2	51.5 MB	3.7 s	8.7 s
PROB	.probdata (text)	P-Hausen	93.1 MB	13.3 s	16.1 s
	.probdata (fastrw)	P-Hausen	105.9 MB	5.8 s	7.5 s
	.probdata (fastrw)	C1	42.6 MB	2.6 s	4.0 s
	.probdata (fastrw)	C2	473.7 MB	21.2 s	27.7 s

130,000 vs. 340.000 XML lines), and C2 is a larger data set with 1.4 million
XML lines. For evaluation, we performed the validation 10 times on a MacBook
Air M2 with 16 GB RAM and computed the median of all run times.

The conversion with XML2B is only required once and takes about 1 s. Note
that with Schematron, the XML file is accessed with every validation run. In
Table 4 we compare the processing times for execution of all three rules with
Schematron and PROB. A significant improvement can be observed for the fastrw format compared to the plain text Prolog data representation. Note that
increasing the global stack size for SICStus also increases performance, as it
then requires fewer garbage collections[14].

In particular, precomputing the values used by multiple rules has significantly reduced computation times and increased readability of subsequent rules
by compactness (cf. Listing 10). The measurements for PROB also include the
startup time to instantiate the B model, which is not affected by the number
of rules. Unfortunately, reading the data from a .probdata file can still be a
bottleneck for large data sets (such as C2). However, ignoring loading time, the
validation time with PROB is almost the same as with Schematron. For the
execution of the analysed rules in an already loaded machine, this gives good
results, with approximately 0.1–0.2 s compared to 0.5-0.6 s with Schematron (for
P-Hausen).

Overall, the results show that our approach can achieve performance of a
similar order of magnitude to that of the existing Schematron-based toolchain.

6   Related Work

Koren et al. [26] propose a Schematron-based validation process to ensure compliance with healthcare standards. In [41], Tutcher et al. showcase a proof-of-
concept for semantic data modeling for the railway domain incorporating on the
one hand the data model itself and on the other hand rules for reasoning. Simple
synthetic rules are provided applying ontology-based techniques. In [30], Malý
and Nečaský provide an approach as part of dealing with integrity constraints in

---

[14] All benchmarks for PROB were run with the SICStus variable `GLOBALSTKSIZE=8G`.

conceptual XML data modeling, which translates Object Constraint Language expressions at the platform-independent level to Schematron expressions. For the domain of aviation there seems to be another relevant approach analyzed by Wang et al. in [42] applying Semantics of Business Vocabulary and Business Rules to the AIXM data. Häußler et al. focused in [22] on code compliance checking of railway related Building Information Modeling data facilitating rules in Business Process Model and Notation and Decision Model and Notation for real-world design guidelines. Banerjee et al. investigated in [3] the design validation for ETCS based on legal rules resulting from a customized tool-chain for this specific problem based on an attributed graph and logical constraints over that graph.

An SMT-based approach for PlanPro has recently been presented in [15]. In [8], a toolchain has been developed that processes PlanPro files to generate Prolog facts that represent an interlocking logic, which could be interesting for dynamic validation with PROB (PROB allows the animation of Prolog specifications). There are several other validation tools based on B and PROB, cf. [9]. For example, [45] also uses PROB underneath and provides visualisations. But none thus far provide a systematic support for XML data. There are also SAT-based approaches [46], based on Prover iLock, or Everest [31] inspired by Alloy.

7   Conclusion and Outlook

In this work, we developed a typed translation from XML data to B that extracts type information from the XSD schema. It enables to use the formal B method to process XML data in a principled and safe fashion. We showed how this generic translation can be used for a specific case study for formal data validation. Our approach demonstrates that validation rules for XML data can be easily written and efficiently validated using the B-Rules DSL based on the formal B method. We compared this with an existing (XML specific) Schematron-based approach for validating PlanPro design data.

The requirements of this study led to several extensions and improvements to the PROB tool in general, but in particular also to PROB's Rules DSL. We have added free type support, two new keywords (ON_SUCCESS and UNCHECKED) and have improved the UI and performance for the Rules DSL in PROB2-UI [7]. We were able to demonstrate that the B approach performs similarly well to Schematron when applied to a large data set. While the Schematron approach has clear advantages in the formulation of XML queries, the B approach is more generic, provides visualisation features, and enables efficient precomputation of reusable data, and the conversion of XML data is only required once, instead of at each validation run. The reimplementation of the rules in B helped to analyse the existing Schematron formulation and to find optimisations there as well. We are able to show that we achieve the same validation results with PROB, and that these can be exported to formats that are understandable to domain experts without knowledge of PROB (human-/machine-readable HTML/XML report).

For the future, the translation to B opens up the possibility of proving properties using the B tooling and enables T3 certification (by using two independent tool chains; see, e.g., Sect. 3.1 of [19]). Future directions also include using PROB's constraint solver for data generation based on given rules, e.g. for the placement of a minimum number of balises in a given topology. It could also serve for data correction with support of a rule dependency graph that can already be generated by PROB. We also plan to use caching of operations across multiple runs of the tool, using SHA hashes of data and rule files to avoid double checking of unchanged data.

Acknowledgments. We kindly thank DB InfraGO, in particular Christoph Klaus, for providing access to the PlanPro schema files, the P-Hausen example, and real-world PlanPro data. We thank Miles Vella for integrating the output of Prolog data in fastrw format into the PROB parser and the documentation of free types.

Dedication. It is with pleasure that we dedicate this article to the Festschrift in honour of Alessandro Fantechi. His works promote the use of formal methods for railways and his surveys [4,6,18] gave us valuable insights and feedback into the use of B and of our PROB tool for industrial applications.

References

1. Abrial, J.R.: The B-Book: Assigning Programs to Meanings. Cambridge University Press (2005)
2. Abrial, J.R.: Modeling in Event-B: System and Software Engineering. Cambridge University Press (2010)
3. Banerjee, M., et al.: A tool-chain for the verification of geographic scheme data. In: Proceedings RSSRail. LNCS, vol. 14784, pp. 211–224. Springer (2023)
4. ter Beek, M.H., et al.: Adopting formal methods in an industrial setting: the railways case. In: Proceedings FM. LNCS, vol. 11800, pp. 762–772. Springer (2019), https://doi.org/10.1007/978-3-030-30942-8_46
5. ter Beek, M.H., et al.: Formal methods in industry. Form. Asp. Comput. (2024). https://doi.org/10.1145/3689374
6. ter Beek, M.H., Fantechi, A., Gnesi, S.: Formal methods for industrial critical systems - 30 years of railway applications. In: The Combined Power of Research, Education, and Dissemination - Essays Dedicated to Tiziana Margaria on the Occasion of Her 60th Birthday. LNCS, vol. 15240, pp. 327–344. Springer (2025). https://doi.org/10.1007/978-3-031-73887-6_21
7. Bendisposto, J., et al.: ProB2-UI: a Java-based user interface for ProB. In: Proceedings FMICS. LNCS, vol. 12863, pp. 193–201. Springer (2021)
8. Boockmeyer, A., et al.: From CCS-Planning to Testautomation: The Digital Testfield of Deutsche Bahn in Scheibenberg - a case study. In: Proceedings IC2E, pp. 258–263 (2021)
9. Butler, M., et al.: The first twenty-five years of industrial use of the B-method. In: Proceedings FMICS. LNCS, vol. 12327, pp. 189–209. Springer (2020)
10. Butler, M.J., Maamria, I.: Practical theory extension in event-B. In: Theories of Programming and Formal Methods - Essays Dedicated to Jifeng He on the Occasion of His 70th Birthday, pp. 67–81 (2013). https://doi.org/10.1007/978-3-642-39698-4_5

11. Bădău, F.: Railway interlockings – a review of the current state of railway safety technology in Europe. Promet - Traffic Transport. **34**(3), 443–454 (2022). https://doi.org/10.7307/ptt.v34i3.3992
12. CENELEC: Railway Applications – Communication, signalling and processing systems – Software for railway control and protection systems. Tech. Rep. EN50128, European Standard (2011)
13. ClearSy: Atelier B, User and Reference Manuals. Aix-en-Provence, France (2009), available at http://www.atelierb.eu/
14. Comptier, M., Déharbe, D., Perez, J.M., Mussat, L., Thibaut, P., Sabatier, D.: Safety analysis of a CBTC system: a rigorous approach with event-B. In: Proceedings RSSRail. LNCS, vol. 10598, pp. 148–159. Springer (2017)
15. Dillmann, S., Hähnle, R.: SMT-based Verification of Railway Plannings. In: Proceedings RSSRail (2025), to appear
16. Essamé, D., Dollé, D.: B in large scale projects: the canarsie line CBTC experience. In: Proceedings B Conference (B2007). LNCS, vol. 4355, pp. 252–254. Springer (2007)
17. Ferrari, A., ter Beek, M.H.: Formal methods in railways: a systematic mapping study. ACM Comput. Surv. **55**(4), 1–37 (2023). https://doi.org/10.1145/3520480
18. Ferrari, A., et al.: Survey on formal methods and tools in railways: the ASTRail approach. In: Proceedings RSSRail. LNCS, vol. 11495, pp. 226–241. Springer (2019). https://doi.org/10.1007/978-3-030-18744-6_15
19. Gleirscher, M., Sachtleben, R., Peleska, J.: Qualification of proof assistants, checkers, and generators: where are we and what next? Sci. Comput. Program. **226**, 102930 (2023). https://doi.org/10.1016/j.scico.2023.102930
20. Gruteser, J., Leuschel, M.: Validation of railML Using ProB. In: Proceedings ICECCS. LNCS, vol. 14784, pp. 245–256. Springer (2024)
21. Hansen, D., Schneider, D., Leuschel, M.: Using B and ProB for data validation projects. In: Proceedings ABZ. LNCS, vol. 9675, pp. 167–182. Springer (2016)
22. Häußler, M., Esser, S., Borrmann, A.: Code compliance checking of railway designs by integrating BIM, BPMN and DMN. Automation in Construction (Jan 2021)
23. ISO/IEC 19757-3:2020, Information technology - Document Schema Definition Languages (DSDL) - Part 3: Rule-based validation using Schematron
24. Klaus, C.: Specification of a test tool for the automated testing of CCS engineering data in XML format. Ph.D. thesis, Dresden University of Technology (2024). https://nbn-resolving.org/urn:nbn:de:bsz:14-qucosa2-906663
25. Klaus, C., Jaekel, B., Wunsch, S., Lehnert, M.: The automated semantic validation of planning data for signalling systems using Schematron. SIGNALLING & DATACOMMUNICATION pp. 14–22 (03 2018). https://eurailpress-archiv.de/SingleView.aspx?show=143849
26. Koren, A., Jurcevic, M., Prasad, R.: Semantic constraints specification and Schematron-based validation for internet of medical things' data. IEEE Access **10**, 65658–65670 (2022)
27. Lecomte, T., Mottin, E.: Formal data validation in the railways. In: Safety-critical Systems Symposium 2016 (2016)
28. Leuschel, M., Butler, M.: ProB: an automated analysis toolset for the B method. Int. J. Softw. Tools Technol. Transfer **10**(2), 185–203 (2008)
29. Leuschel, M., Falampin, J., Fritz, F., Plagge, D.: Automated property verification for large scale B models with ProB. Formal Aspects Comput. **23**, 683–709 (2011)
30. Malý, J., Necaský, M.: Model-driven approach to modeling and validating integrity constraints for XML with OCL and Schematron. Inf. Syst. Frontiers **17**(4), 917–946 (2015)

31. Martins, J., et al.: Verification of railway network models with EVEREST. In: Proceedings MODELS 2022, pp. 345–355 (2022). https://doi.org/10.1145/3550355.3552439

32. Maschek, U., Klaus, C., Gerke, C., Uminski, V., Girke, K.J.: PlanPro – Durchgängige elektronische Datenhaltung im ESTW-Planungsprozess. SIGNALLING & DATACOMMUNICATION, pp. 22–26 (09 2012). https://fis.tu-dresden.de/portal/files/34533917/S_D_PlanPro_final.pdf

33. Nash, A., Hürlimann, D., Schütte, J., Krauß, V.P.: Railml - a standard data interface for railroad applications. In: Computers in Railways, vol. IX, pp. 233 – 242. WIT Press, Southampton (2004)

34. Nogatz, F., Kalkus, J.: Declarative XML schema validation with SWI–prolog: system description. In: International Workshop on Functional and Constraint Logic Programming. LNCS, vol. 10997, pp. 187–197. Springer (2017)

35. Plagge, D., Leuschel, M.: Validating Z specifications using the ProB animator and model checker. In: Proceedings iFM. LNCS, vol. 4591, pp. 480–500. Springer (2007)

36. ProB-Documentation: Rules DSL. https://prob.hhu.de/w/index.php?title=Rules-DSL. Accessed 28 Apr 2025

37. Sabatier, D.: Using formal proof and B method at system level for industrial projects. In: Proceedings RSSRail. LNCS, vol. 9707, pp. 20–31. Springer (2016)

38. Sabatier, D., Burdy, L., Requet, A., Guéry, J.: Formal proofs for the NYCT Line 7 (Flushing) modernization project. In: Proceedings ABZ. LNCS, vol. 7316, pp. 369–372. Springer (2012)

39. Spivey, J.M.: The Z Notation: a reference manual. Prentice-Hall (1992). available at https://github.com/Spivoxity/zrm

40. St-Denis, R.: A comparison of three solver-aided programming languages: αRby, ProB, and Rosette. J. Comput. Lang. **77** (2023)

41. Tutcher, J., Easton, J.M., Roberts, C.: Enabling data integration in the rail industry using RDF and OWL: The RaCoOn Ontology. ASCE-ASME J. Risk Uncertainty Eng. Syst., Part A: Civ. Eng. (Jun 2017)

42. Wang, X., Tian, Y., Fu, S., Musila, C.M.: Research on semantic verification method of AIXM data based on SBVR. In: Artificial Intelligence in China, pp. 260–271. Springer (2023)

43. Werth, M., Leuschel, M.: VisB: A lightweight tool to visualize formal models with SVG graphics. In: Proceedings ABZ. LNCS, vol. 12071, pp. 260–265. Springer (2020)

44. Wunsch, S., Jaekel, B., Lehnert, M., Klaus, C., Gruteser, J., Leuschel, M.: Automated semantic validation of railway signaling data on the basis of Schematron. In: Proceedings RSSRail (2025), to appear

45. Yar, A., Idani, A., Ledru, Y., Dutilleul, S.C., Mammar, A., Vega, G.: An iterative formal model-driven approach to railway systems validation. In: Proceedings ICECCS. LNCS, vol. 14784, pp. 272–289. Springer (2024)

46. Zickert, G., Stathatos, N.: Halfway generic verification of railway control systems. In: Proceedings RSSRail. LNCS, vol. 14198, pp. 178–189. Springer (2023)

Action-Based Security Rules for Railway Control Systems

Rocco De Nicola[1,3] and Simone Soderi[2,3(✉)]

[1] IIT CNR, Pisa, Italy
[2] IMT School for Advanced Studies Lucca, Lucca, Italy
`simone.soderi@imtlucca.it`
[3] Cybersecurity National Laboratory, CINI, Roma, Italy
`rocco.denicola@iit.cnr.it`

Abstract. This paper presents an *action-based* methodology for securing railway signalling systems, building upon the TS 50701 framework. In TS 50701, zones represent groups of assets that share common security requirements, while conduits denote controlled communication channels that interconnect zones and enforce defined security policies. Railway systems described within this framework comprise wayside and onboard components, interconnected by a Data Communication System (DCS). We propose an attacker model centred on inter-zone conduits that specifies enforceable rule templates for each conduit. These templates define requirements for source authentication, integrity, freshness, and semantic consistency, thereby constraining permissible behaviours that can be implemented at boundary monitors. Through qualitative security analysis, we demonstrate how these rules address specific threats and trace how security degradations may propagate to safety-critical effects. By formalising zones and conduits as terms in a process description language, system properties can be expressed as sequences of observable actions. This formalisation enables the use of Action-Based Temporal Logic (ACTL) to verify whether security properties are guaranteed, which constitutes our long-term research goal.

Keywords: Railway signalling · TS 50701 · Process Description Languages · Temporal Logic · Cybersecurity Assessment · Safety

1 Introduction

Railway signalling has evolved into a distributed, software-intensive system in which control logic and traffic management exchange critical information across heterogeneous networks.

The progressive digitalisation of railway signalling has increased exposure to cyber threats across operational technology domains. IXL, RBC, ATS/OCCs, and lineside equipment exchange information over heterogeneous networks and

© The Author(s), under exclusive license to Springer Nature Switzerland AG 2026
M. H. ter Beek et al. (Eds.): Fantechi Festschrift, LNCS 16470, pp. 314–332, 2026.
https://doi.org/10.1007/978-3-032-12484-5_17

protocols; misconfiguration or malicious manipulation of these systems can degrade availability or integrity and, in extreme cases, create conditions that stress safety margins [8,26].

In this setting, cybersecurity measures must be implemented to enable operators to monitor and intervene at both the interfaces between *zones* and along the *conduits* that connect them, as prescribed by TS 50701:2021 (which will be replaced in mid-2026 by the IEC 63452 standard) and related guidance [3,10]. While modelling systems in terms of zones and channels is important, it is equally crucial to examine whether a gap exists between these architectural artifacts and the cybersecurity requirements applicable to safety-critical railway systems.

The industry guidelines defined by TS 50701 structure System under Consideration (SuC) cybersecurity by creating logical elements called *zones* and *ducts*. Meanwhile, ENISA details a zoning/ducting methodology for the railway sector, providing concrete architectural models and risk management practices [3,10].

In the reference architecture of the European Rail Traffic Management System/European Train Control System (ERTMS/ETCS), the functions are partitioned between subsystems *trackside* and *onboard*. Trackside comprises the *Interlocking* (IXL) with train detection, the *Lineside Electronics Units* (LEU) driving balises, the *Radio Block Centre* (RBC), and the *Global System for Mobile CommunicationsRailway* (GSM-R). Onboard, the *European Train Control System* (ETCS) equipment supervises train movement using odometry and balise updates via the Driver Machine Interface (DMI); Automatic Train Operation (ATO) over ETCS can be added to execute driving profiles under ETCS supervision. At Level 2^1, the RBC issues Movement Authorities (MAs) over the radio link while eurobalises provide position reference; at Level 1, movement authorities are conveyed at fixed points through eurobalises/loops. The Operations Control Centre (OCC) hosts Automatic Train Supervision (ATS), which plans traffic and interfaces with IXL and RBC to coordinate routing and movement authority delivery across the corridor [9].

Accordingly, this paper adopts an *action-based* perspective, defining abstract zones and exposing observable actions, namely commands, indications, and authority updates. Security requirements are then expressed over admissible action traces using Action-Based Temporal Logic (ACTL) [6]. We propose enforceable action-based rules on the conduits among railway systems to prevent malicious manipulation of commands, indications, and movement authorities, aligning these controls with TS 50701. The choice is pragmatic: action-level properties align with how rail operators monitor and gate traffic on conduits, and compose with established formal results for signalling (e.g., interlocking verification and model-based environments) without imposing heavyweight verification on the entire system [12,19].

---

[1] ETCS levels define the supervision/authority mechanism: Level 0 means no ETCS; Level 1 means intermittent balise/loop-based with lineside signals; Level 2 means continuous radio via an RBC with balise position reference; Level 3 implements radio-only moving block with train-integrity supervision.

Grounded in this zoning-and-conduits view, the objective here is to model *possible attacks* as *action-based* behaviours and to express enforceable security requirements in a logic like ACTL. On the verification side, formal analyses have matured for signalling safety, e.g., compositional verification of interlockings and dedicated verification environments, but there remains a gap between architectural zoning and enforceable *behavioural* security constraints [12,19].

Our contribution is an *action-based* security specification that (i) models, as LTS, the TS 50701 zones and conduits of the SuC comprising wayside, onboard, and the DCS; (ii) defines a three-tier attacker model centred on inter-zone conduits (with explicit consideration of compromised endpoints) and aligned with railway threat catalogues; and (iii) derives a compact set of ACTL-style rules that constrain admissible behaviours on critical conduits. The proposed rules are phrased in terms of observable actions and can be enforced at gateways; a brief analysis discusses how security degradations may propagate into safety concerns.

The rest of the paper is organised as follows. Section 2 positions this work within the context of railway cybersecurity, zoning/conduits practice, and action-based reasoning while stressing the role of TS 50701 in coordinating security and safety and the use of formal methods for specification and verification. Section 3 defines the SuC and its zoning/conduits. Section 4 introduces the attacker model. Section 5 presents the action-based modelling of an abstract railway system using a simple process description language. Section 6 reports on security analysis. Section 7 offers concluding remarks.

2   Related Works and Background

The cybersecurity literature for railways spans signalling systems, onboard communications, and enterprise interfaces. Comprehensive surveys document threats, assets, and defence-in-depth strategies across both operational and information-technology domains [8,26]. In the rest of this paper, the term *asset* refers to any equipment that constitutes a railway system, whether installed on the ground or on board, or the communication system between them. Sector guidance codifies security engineering via *zones* and *conduits* in CENELEC TS 50701 [3] (from now onward we refer to it simply as TS 50701) complemented by ENISA's zoning-and-conduits security architecture specific to railways [10]. Within Communication-Based Train Control (CBTC), the security of DCS has been analysed with emphasis on wireless jamming and integrity risks [25], while intra-vehicular architectures have been evaluated with respect to performance and security [21]. Model-based development of ATO for CBTC illustrates how engineering choices shape the attack surface of control loops [7]. Broader infrastructure-focused overviews situate cybersecurity controls across wayside and enterprise networks [22]. Recent studies examine risks and mitigations in DCS [13], availability of Industrial Control Systems (ICS) attack datasets from railway cyber ranges [27], and threats to Federated Learning (FL) pipelines used in railway AI workloads [28].

On the assurance front, Formal Methods (FM) have a long tradition in the railway domain. In this context, the contributions by Alessandro Fantechi and collaborators have been particularly significant. A position paper by Alessandro reflects on twenty-five years of FM adoption and open challenges [12]; a systematic mapping study covering 1989–2020 quantifies techniques, tools, and targets (with Interlocking, IXL, as the core system) [14]; and an empirical evaluation assesses the usability of mainstream FM tools for signalling-system design [15]. At the level of concrete verification results, compositional verification has been advanced for large interlocking systems [19]. At the same time, prior milestones include verified modelling of signalling rules [20], model-driven development and verification for train control [23], and formal development and verification of distributed railway control in [18].

Table 1 summarises representative contributions by *study focus* and *methodology*, covering: CBTC/DCS analyses [21, 25], surveys and guidance [3, 8, 10, 24, 26], FM perspectives, mappings, and tool evaluations [12, 14, 15], compositional verification and verified modelling [18–20], model-driven control [23], infrastructure overviews and DCS risk studies [13, 22], ICS datasets and covert-channel evidence [27], and FL attack/defence work for rail AI [28]. This synthesis motivates the paper's contribution: action-based security rules stated over PA/LTS at zone/conduit interfaces, aligned with TS 50701 and informed by CBTC/DCS realities.

Table 1: Representative related works: study focus and methodology.

Citation	Study focus	Methodology
[26]	Rail threats, assets, defence-in-depth	Survey; taxonomy
[25]	CBTC DCS security (jamming, integrity)	Analysis; security considerations
[12]	FM in railways; challenges	Position/survey
[19]	Compositional verification of IXL	Compositional model checking
[14]	Mapping of FM in rail (1989–2020)	Systematic mapping study
[15]	FM tools for signalling	Empirical tool evaluation
[22]	Railway infrastructure cybersecurity overview	Practitioner/standards overview
[1]	Cybersecurity–safety co-engineering	Conceptual framework
[27]	ICS attack dataset (rail cyber-range)	Dataset; attack simulation
[13]	DCS risks, vulnerabilities, mitigations	Risk review; mitigation map
[28]	FL poisoning threats and defences in railway AI	Analytical & experimental study

Up to now, safety aspects and cybersecurity for railway systems have been considered mainly as separate concerns. TS 50701 provides a common framework to unify safety and security in railway systems. By structuring cybersecurity around zones and conduits, it enables the separation of concerns, the precise placement of controls, and the reuse of the same artefacts for both risk assessment and safety assurance. These structures serve as anchors to link security rules with operational safety objectives—for example, enforcing restrictive behaviours under uncertainty or attack. Adopting TS 50701 terminology ensures traceability from architecture to enforceable rules, while ENISA's complementary guidance adds patterns and documentation practices. Together, they support the co-engineering of safety and security as integral elements of resilient railway systems [3,10].

Building on this, we adopt a process-algebraic approach that enables compositional descriptions of components interacting through observable actions. This enables the compositional description of components that interact through *observable actions*. We take TS 50701 as the starting point for specifying the behaviour and expressing security properties of railway systems. Signalling subsystems and zones (e.g., interlocking, RBC, ATS/OCC, lineside equipment) can be modelled as interacting labelled transition systems that emit or consume domain actions (e.g., commands, indications, authority updates). Conduits are modelled as channels and used to synchronise selected actions and impose policy constraints. This perspective permits us to describe

- *Behavioural specifications*: Behaviours are phrased over sequences of observable actions (e.g., only authenticated, fresh commands affect an interlocking state; movement authority application requires corroboration under disturbance)
- *Required properties*: Properties are specified in terms of ACTL [4], an action-based temporal logics that provide a natural language for expressing security rules over the labelled transition system induced by the composed processes, and tools for verifying correctness of the behavioural specification with respect to the envisaged property [11].

In this way, security requirements can be articulated and possibly verified where they can be observed and enforced, i.e., at zone and conduit boundaries, while remaining compatible with established FM practice on IXL and related subsystems.

3   System Model: Architecture, Zones and Conduits

The SuC is the *entire railway signalling system architecture*, comprising wayside, onboard, and the DCS that interconnect them. Wayside includes IXL, RBC (where applicable), ATS/OCC, LEU, and balises, as well as train detection (e.g., axle counters or track circuits). Onboard comprises ETCS/ATP/ATO, including odometry and the DMI. The DCS covers wired operational backbones, radio bearers for trainground communication (e.g., GSM–R/FRMCS), time distribution, segmentation and filtering devices, security gateways, central logging and monitoring, and controlled maintenance access. Figure 1 sketches this architectural context. In particular, the figure shows how the local railway signalling networks at each station, which control the various train movement systems, exchange information via a WAN network[2]. Our terminology for routes, sig-

---

[2] In WAN architecture, Multiprotocol Label Switching (MPLS) connects sites, Open Shortest Path First (OSPF) handles internal routing, and Border Gateway Protocol (BGP) exchanges routes between WAN domains and providers.

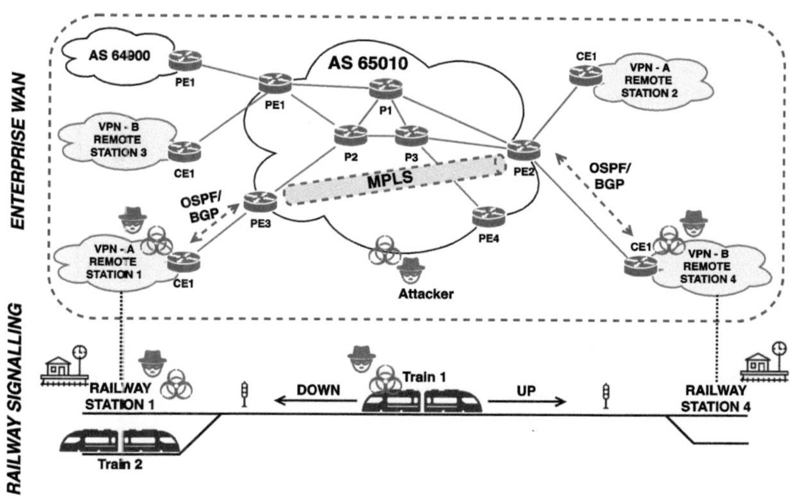

Fig. 1: SuC: railway signalling system architecture with potential attack points.

nals, track segments, and points is aligned with that used in the IXL literature [12,19,26].

Zoning and conduits are the architectural primitives used to place and enforce
cybersecurity controls in railway signalling, as defined in TS 50701 and aligned
with ENISA guidance [3,10]. A *zone* is a set of assets with shared security
requirements, exposure, trust level, and function; boundaries enumerate assets,
interfaces, assumptions, and required controls. A *conduit* is the controlled communication path between zones that carries specified information flows and
enforces policy (identification, authentication, filtering, monitoring). In practice,
conduits are realised in three recurring patterns:

- *transparent* (segmentation/forwarding only, no content inspection),
- *filtered* (boundary enforcement via stateful allow-listing, protocol mediation,
  or proxy/inspection in a DMZ), and
- *unidirectional* (data diode to prevent backflow).

Independent add-on controls, such as VPN/IPsec/TLS tunnelling, time-sync
constraints, logging, and bandwidth or rate-limit guarantees, may be applied to
any conduit pattern to fulfil confidentiality, integrity, availability, and forensic
objectives [3,10].

For the SuC, typical zones include ATS/OCC, IXL, RBC, lineside I/O (LEU,
balises, train detection), onboard ETCS/ATP/ATO, DCS/telecommunications,
and support services (e.g., time and logging). Critical conduits include ATSIXL,
ATSRBC, RBConboard ETCS, IXLLEU/balises, IXLtrain detection, and controlled maintenance/monitoring paths. Each conduit is documented with permitted flows (direction, endpoints, protocols), trust assumptions (identities, credentials), enforcement points (filters, proxies, diodes), and performance envelopes

(latency, availability); these artefacts serve as anchors for the action-based rules developed later in the paper [3,10].

Figure 2 illustrates a zoning and conduits model for the SuC, highlighting critical conduits (e.g., Zone WAN to Zone Wayside, Zone RBC to Zone Wayside, Zone onboard to Zone Trackside, etc.) where action-based rules will be applied.

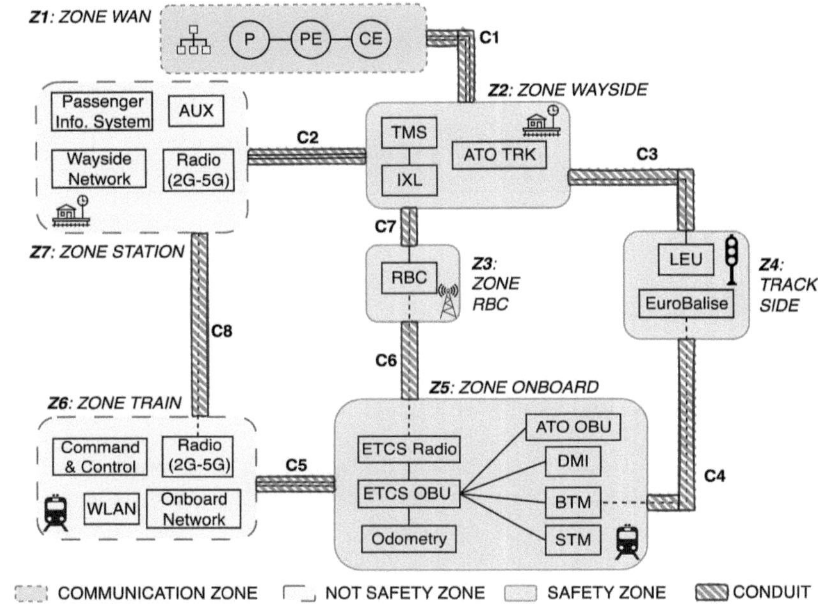

Fig. 2: Zoning and conduits of the SuC.

Table 2 clarifies which interzone exchanges are architecturally permitted and how they are controlled. In this table, each cell shows (Conduit ID, Type) with Type $\in$ {F = filtered, T = transparent, U = unidirectional}. A dash (–) denotes that inter-zone communication is *not permitted*. Thus, in the cells:

- (Cx, F) denotes *filtered* conduits (policy enforcement at the boundary);
- (Cx, T) denotes *transparent* conduits (segmentation/forwarding only);
- (Cx, U) denotes *unidirectional* conduits (datadiode pattern).

A dash (–) indicates that interzone communication is not allowed, and the diagonal is intentionally empty to denote intrazone traffic. This representation follows the zoningandconduits approach in TS 50701 and the ENISA rail security architecture, where security requirements are apportioned to zones and enforced along the conduits that connect them [3,10].

The matrix highlights a small number of securityrelevant exchanges. Between Z1 (WAN) and Z2 (wayside), C1 is filtered to constrain exposure at the perimeter. Z2Z7 (waysidestation) is likewise filtered (C2), reflecting the heterogeneity

Table 2: Zone-to-zone conduits.

Zone ID	Z1	Z2	Z3	Z4	Z5	Z6	Z7
Z1		(C1, F)	–	–	–	–	–
Z2	(C1, F)		(C7, F)	(C3, T)	–	–	(C2, F)
Z3	–	(C7, F)		–	(C6, F)	–	–
Z4	–	(C3, T)	–		(C4, U)	–	–
Z5	–	–	(C6, F)	(C4, U)		(C5, T)	–
Z6	–	–	–	–	(C5, T)		(C8, F)
Z7	–	(C2, F)	–	–	–	(C8, F)	

of station assets. Z2Z4 (waysidetrackside) includes a transparent conduit (C3) used for deterministic lineside I/O, while Z4Z5 (tracksideonboard) is unidirectional (C4), reflecting that balise/BTM flows are oneway by design. RBConboard (Z3Z5) is filtered (C6) to protect the radioborne movement authority exchange, and Z2Z3 (waysideRBC) is filtered (C7) to restrict control and configuration paths. The onboardtrain backbone (Z5Z6) is transparent (C5) to preserve performance within the vehicle, whereas Z6Z7 (trainstation) is filtered (C8) to control platform WLAN/maintenance connectivity. All other pairs are explicitly disallowed (–) to reduce lateral movement opportunities and to simplify assurance arguments.

This structure prepares the ground for the attacker model in the next section. Each conduit class implies distinct threats and feasible controls: transparent conduits prioritise determinism and thus are more exposed to eavesdropping, replay, or injection unless endpoints authenticate and protect their traffic; filtered conduits can be targeted via credential abuse, policy gaps, or device misconfiguration; unidirectional conduits block backflow but may still be susceptible to spoofed lowside inputs or timing/availability manipulation. By enumerating *which* interzone exchanges exist (C1–C8), *how* they are mediated (F/T/U), and *which* pairs are prohibited, Table 2 provides the precise scope of attacker capabilities and the actionbased rules (Sect. 5) to be enforced.

4   Attacker Model and Threats

The SuC is the *entire railway signalling system architecture* (wayside, onboard, and the DCS interconnecting them). By adopting the zoneconduit perspective from TS 50701, we assume the adversary primarily targets inter-zone conduits to influence behaviour across zones; endpoint exposures are considered whenever they provide leverage over conduit traffic.

The attacker is modelled in three tiers to capture plausible attacks while keeping mitigations implementable at zone/conduit enforcement points.

Tier A (conduit-only): The attacker can manipulate traffic only on the conduits in Table 2, e.g., by eavesdropping, injecting, replaying, reordering, or selectively dropping packets; flooding or jamming radio bearers; or disturbing time synchronisation used for correlation and gating.

Tier B (endpoint-assisted): The attacker may additionally compromise selected wayside or onboard assets to originate seemingly legitimate traffic or to modify boundary configurations, e.g., by exploiting remote maintenance channels or misusing credentials.

Tier C (privileged): The attacker can leverage insider knowledge or supply-chain access to alter policies or credentials, potentially gaining broader access to the system.

In Sect. 5, we instantiate formal rules for Tier A. The same ACTL properties can be extended to Tiers BC by modelling endpoint compromise as the capability to perform authenticated yet policy-inconsistent actions or to alter enforcement. Such deviations are detected through source validation, freshness checks, corroboration (i.e., independent consistency checks), and change-control constraints. This approach keeps the rules concise and enforceable at conduits while remaining sensitive to endpoint compromise, as recommended in TS 50701 and ENISA guidance [3,10].

Without assuming broken cryptography, the attacker can eavesdrop on mis-segmented or transparent paths, inject, replay, reorder, or selectively drop packets; flood or jam radio bearers; tamper with boundary devices through credential abuse or misconfiguration; disrupt time synchronisation used for correlation and gating; and misuse remote maintenance channels. These capabilities are bound to the permitted conduits in Table 2: filtered conduits (e.g., C1, C2, C6, C7, C8) are exposed to policy bypass and misconfiguration; transparent conduits (e.g., C3, C5) favour determinism but admit observation and injection unless endpoints protect their exchanges; unidirectional conduits (e.g., C4) block backflow yet remain susceptible to spoofed low-side inputs or timing/availability manipulation.

The following threat classes refine attacker capabilities by mapping them to the specific inter-zone conduits of the SuC (Table 2). Next, we outline representative ways in which an adversary may alter control or indication flows, or degrade their timeliness, to create unsafe preconditions during degraded operation. Each item identifies the affected conduit(s) (C1C8) and, where relevant, provides a possible compromised-endpoint to highlight that authenticated yet policy-inconsistent traffic remains a realistic vector [8,26].

Perimeter control paths (C1, C2). Manipulation of TMS–IXL directives or IXL–TMS indications on filtered conduits (e.g., injection, replay, reordering). *Example (C2, Z7–Z2):* a compromised station Human Machine Interface in Z7 emits valid-looking directives into Z2 over the filtered path C2.

Train–ground movement authorities (C6) and RBC integration (C7). Spoofing or replay in the RBC–onboard exchange and misconfiguration of wayside–RBC interfaces. *Example (C7, Z2–Z3):* a wayside engineering workstation in Z2 is reused to push configuration to RBC in Z3 using stolen session material.

Trackside indications and lineside I/O (C4, C3). Interference with balise/BTM one-way flows or deterministic lineside signals, causing false position/occupancy cues. *Example (C3, Z2–Z4):* firmware-modified lineside I/O in Z4 emits plausible but false indications accepted into Z2 across the transparent conduit C3.

Onboard backbones and controllers (C5). Exploitation of transparent onboard networks to influence trainborne decisions via control-frame injection or replay. *Example (C5, Z6–Z5):* malware on the onboard backbone in Z6 injects frames toward ETCS/ATP/ATO in Z5.

Maintenance and station connectivity (C8, Z6–Z7). Lateral movement by means of filtered maintenance links toward operational zones. *Example (C8, Z6–Z7):* abuse of temporary maintenance connectivity from Z7 to Z6 to produce data or pivot toward operational assets.

On-path Denial of Service (DoS) via intentional interference. forcing the underlying radio connection to drop and re-establish (e.g., via jamming or network-induced release) *Example (C6, Z2–Z3):* targeted RF interference against GSM–R/FRMCS drops the EuroRadio session, delaying MAs until the onboard times out into a restrictive profile.

These scenarios are consistent with prior studies and with good-practice threat catalogues [8,26]. Since these attacks can potentially produce *authenticated* traffic, additional safeguards are necessary. The rules presented in the following section address this challenge by requiring freshness, corroboration, and approved change-control witnesses before any action can modify the zone state.

5 Action-Based Security Rules for Railway Systems

Building on the threat model established above, this section presents our approach to specifying security-aware operational rules using process description languages. First, we provide a set of enforceable rules, and then we discuss how process description languages can be used to describe railway systems by modelling them as sets of interacting processes performing conditioned actions. These descriptions are expressed as terms that model systems exposing *typed, observable actions*, representing commands and configuration requests, indications and status reports, movement-authority updates, authentication and freshness outcomes, as well as error or timeout signals.

Conduits control selected actions and apply policy according to their classification: filtered, transparent, or unidirectional. The formal rules are defined over process descriptions (*behaviour*), allowing only actions that satisfy *source, integrity, freshness, semantic consistency* to affect zone state. Let us remark that by *semantic consistent* systems we refer to systems exchanging *content- and context-based* validated messages; i.e., messages with admissible temporal ordering and rates, topology and route compatibility, and with value ranges consistent with the operational context.

Examples of *semantically consistent* behaviour include: (i) only authenticated and fresh TMS directives are allowed to change IXL state on perimeter conduits; (ii) RBC messages are applied only if they conform to the authorised route model and current topology; and (iii) when a lineside device (e.g., noisy balise/track-circuit events), do not act on consistently with the rest of the system; hold the update unless an independent source (e.g., onboard odometry or a redundant sensor) confirms it within the allowed time window. These requirements are constraints on admissible sequences of observable actions (action traces) and can be directly formalised in ACTL. For readability, we present them textually here and omit the explicit formulae. It is worth noting that transforming the following textual descriptions into ACTL formulas remains a non-trivial task that warrants further investigation. Interested readers are encouraged to consult relevant literature on formal methods and temporal logic verification, starting from [4, 12, 19].

5.1   Rules For Securing Railway Signalling Systems

A concise set of enforceable rules is associated with the conduits identified in Table 2; each rule names the conduit and its corresponding control points. The rules align with TS 50701 and ENISA guidance on zoning and conduit enforcement [3, 8, 10]; they are organised according to the main operational contexts within the SuC: perimeter and wayside control paths, lineside interfaces, onboard networks, trainground radio and RBC integration, and maintenance and station connectivity.

Perimeter and Wayside Control Paths:

- **C1 (filtered, Z1Z2):** TMS-to-IXL directives are applied only if the session is authenticated by both peers, messages are fresh, and the requested route change is *semantically consistent* with current topology and locking state. Otherwise, messages are discarded, and the last safe state is recovered from the log.
- **C2 (filtered, Z7Z2):** Station-to-wayside exchanges (e.g., operator consoles, auxiliary services) are restricted by an allow-list of endpoints and protocols; write operations are authorised after dual control.

Lineside Interfaces:

- **C3 (transparent, Z2Z4):** Deterministic lineside I/O is accepted only from provisioned endpoints and within *contextual validation windows* (e.g., temporal ordering/rate limits and route context). Out-of-window sequences are quarantined and require secondary confirmation.
- **C4 (unidirectional, Z4Z5):** Trackside to onboard flows (e.g., balise/BTM) are one-way. Onboard processing performs the balise's messages' integrity checks and kinematic/model consistency checks against odometry data. In

the presence of interferences, the expected telegram cannot be received (the onboard system has a database with all the balises for each track), authority updates are suspended until validation succeeds or a restrictive fallback is entered.

Onboard Networks:

- **C5 (transparent, Z6Z5):** The onboard backbone carries ETCS/AT-P/ATO control and telemetry. Only authenticated channels are accepted; *semantic/temporal consistency* constraints are enforced on control sequences; anomalies (replay, reordering) trigger degraded mode (i.e., restricted, fail-safe operation with conservative speed supervision and reduced automation) and local logging.

Trainground radio and RBC integration:

- **C6 (filtered, Z3Z5):** RBC-to-onboard exchanges must satisfy origin, integrity, and freshness; movement authority changes are applied only if reconciled with the current track-occupancy model and the route authorised by IXL; inconsistent or stale items are rejected and logged.
- **C7 (filtered, Z2Z3):** Wayside-to-RBC control/configuration paths are restricted to authenticated sessions, with protocol allow-listing and rate limits; configuration changes require signed artefacts and out-of-band approval; failure to validate reverts the SuC to the last approved configuration.

Maintenance and Station Connectivity:

- **C8 (filtered, Z6Z7):** Trainstation connectivity (e.g., WLAN, maintenance uplinks) denies write paths into safety-related zones by default; temporary enablement follows a break-glass procedure with time-bound access, session recording, and post-hoc verification.

Across all conduits, the *restrictive-under-uncertainty* principle applies: if origin, freshness, or semantic consistency cannot be established within specified budgets, affected actions are ignored and the system transitions to a safe degraded mode; alarms and evidence are recorded for forensic analysis.

5.2   Modelling a Simple Railway System

In this subsection, we begin an initial abstract formalisation of railway systems by modelling zones and conduits as interacting processes. Zones, representing trains, tracks, and stations, are rendered as processes that expose typed actions (e.g., commands, indications, authority updates). Conduits, on the other hand, are rendered as processes that control message exchange between zones and enforce the appropriate policy (filtered, transparent, or unidirectional). The overall system is described as the parallel composition of these processes. A distinct component is the MA, which models the electronically issued permissions by the control system (e.g., RBC/IXL) and determines how far a train may proceed and under which constraints. Such constraints may include limits on authority, permitted speeds/gradients, and timing or conditional data, to ensure onboard protection.

In the following, we describe the main steps to define the operational model:

1. **Define zones and conduits (TS 50701):** Identify the SuC and partition it into functional zones (e.g., Z1 WAN, Z2 wayside with IXL/TMS, Z3 RBC, Z4 trackside, Z5 onboard, Z6 train, Z7 station). Enumerate conduits (C1C8) and classify them as filtered, transparent, or unidirectional; record permitted flows, identities, and performance budgets.
2. **Translate operations into a set of process terms:** Model each zone as a process with typed actions (command, indication, authority, auth_ok, fresh_ok, error/timeout). Model each conduit as a synchronisation/middleware process that enforces the conduit's policy and exposes the resulting observable actions.
3. **Compose processes and restrict action visibility:** Compose zone and conduit processes in parallel, while taking into account their interaction with MA and possibly restricting internal actions to reflect policy scoping and configuration, following the zoning artefacts of TS 50701.

The terms listed in Example 1 illustrate simplified process definitions for key zones and conduits, as well as the overall system composition. In this initial modelling, we use only three basic process algebra operators, namely the one for action sequentialization, and those for nondeterministic and parallel composition:

Action Prefixing `Act --> P` for indicating a process performing action Act and then behaving like P.
Nondeterministic Choice `P + Q` for indicating alternative behaviour of a process, possibly based on some conditions.
Parallel Composition `P || Q` for indicating the parallel composition of processes.

Most of the process description languages proposed contain additional operators, such as those for hiding or relabeling actions, enforcing synchronisation, and others. Here, for the sake of simplicity, we limit ourselves to this basic set of operators that are present in essentially all proposed languages. We refer the reader to [5] for a bird's-eye overview of these languages and for detailed references.

We concentrate on five zones (`TMS`, `IXL`, `RBC`, `ONB`, `TRKS`) and on four conduits connecting them (`C_TI`, `C_IR`, `C_RO`, `C_CO`) where the two letters after `C_` are the initials of the two connected zones. The behaviour of the five zones is the following:

- TMS plans traffic and requests route settings,
- IXL enforces the establishment of safe routes and reports the track status.
- RBC computes and transmits MAs consistently with the IXL topology and occupancy, as well as the TMS plan, over EuroRadio.

- ONB (the onboard ETCS) collects information from MA, supervises speed and braking against its constraints, and reports train status upstream to support subsequent TMS/IXL/RBC decisions;
- TRKS models trackside equipments, such as Eurobalise, that send encoded messages (typically referred to as telegrams) to the onboard train signalling system.

Below, we provide two simple models of railway systems using a basic process description language.

Example 1:

```
TMS    = send_TI --> TMS + error --> TMS )
IXL    = recv_TI --> (policy_tt --> apply_route --> send_IR
         --> IXL) + (policy_ff --> reject --> IXL)

RBC    = (recv_IR --> MA_update --> RBC) +  (send_RO --> RBC)
ONB    = MA_read --> (consistency_TT --> apply_ma --> ONBOARD)
         + (consistency_FF --> ONBOARD)

C_XY   = authenticate --> freshness --> filter_cmd --> C_XY

SYS    = (TMS || IXL || RBC || ONBOARD || C_TI || C_IR || C_RO
         || MA)
```

In this system, TMS issues a traffic instruction (send_TI); IXL receives it (recv_TI), checks whether the required policies are respected. If compliant, it applies the route (apply_route) and sends a report (send_IR); otherwise it rejects the request. Subsequently, RBC consumes the interlocking report (recv_IR) to update the movement authority (MA_update). Finally, ONB reads the MA (MA_read) and applies it only if the consistency check is successful. All communication conduits (C_TI, C_IR, C_RO) enforce authenticate, freshness, and filter_cmd. The main system SYS composes all processes in parallel and synchronises on matching send/recv actions.

As a further example, we focus on three zones—RBC, ONB, and TRKS—and on the baliseBTM conduit C4 (modelled as C_BTM, unidirectional TRKS→ONB). RBC updates and issues MAs from interlocking reports; TRKS emits balise telegrams; ONB receives both inputs (radio for MA, C_BTM for telegrams), checks consistency, and applies the MA if the checks are successful, otherwise it holds the state or enters a fail-safe fallback on timeout.

Example 2:

```
RBC    = (recv_IR--> MA_update --> RBC) + (send_RO --> RBC)
ONB    = MA_read --> ( consistency_TT --> apply_ma--> ONB)
         + (consistency_FF -->  ONB)
         + timeout --> fallback --> ONB
TRKS   = send_EB --> TRKS
C_BTM  = recv_EB --> send_CO --> C_BTM
ONB    = recv_CO --> (consistency_TT --> apply_ma
```

```
              --> ONBOARD) + (consistency_FF --> ONBOARD)
SYS    = (RBC || ONB || Trackside || C_BTM)
```

According to the above description, RBC performs MA_update after recv_IR (or send_RO). ONB then reads the MA (MA_read) and applies it only if consistency_TT holds, otherwise it idles, and a timeout will trigger a fallback. Separately, TRKS produces an Eurobalise messages event that is received by C_BTM on the unidirectional C_BTM path (recv_EB) and forwarded to ONB. C_BTM abstracts conduit C4. After receipt, ONB uses a consistency predicate to decide whether to apply_ma. As in Example 1, SYS composes all processes in parallel and synchronises on matching action names at conduit boundaries.

6 Security Analysis

The analysis maps the rule catalogue to the threat classes and enforcement points established by zoning and conduits (C1C8). Enforcement is placed at zone boundaries so that only actions satisfying *source, integrity, freshness, semantic consistency,* and *corroboration* can affect zone state; violations trigger restrictive behaviour, alarms, and evidence capture, in line with TS 50701 and ENISA guidance.

Perimeter and Wayside Control Paths

C1: bind signalling information to enumerated TMS identities, enforce mutual authentication and freshness, and require topology consistency before any route is affected; on mismatch or timeout, take no action and log the event.

C2: enforce default-deny for writes toward Z2. Segregate read/write paths, require dual control and time-limited sessions for any write to safety-related functions, and allowlist protocols; block any non-allowlisted ingress.

Lineside Interfaces

C3 (transparent): boundary monitors enforce contextual validation windows (ordering, rate limits) and dual-sensing policies (e.g., axle counter vs. track circuit) before indications can influence IXL logic; out-of-window sequences are quarantined pending confirmation.

C4 (unidirectional): onboard processing accepts trackside telegrams only after performing integrity checks and cross-checks with odometry. If a disturbance is detected, authority updates are blocked, or a restrictive fallback is entered.

Onboard Networks

C5: Only authenticated channels are accepted on the transparent onboard backbone; sequencing and timing guards detect replay/reordering. When anomalies are observed, trainborne logic shifts to degraded mode and records local evidence, limiting the impact of injections originating from a compromised train network segment.

TrainGround Radio and RBC Integration

C6: EuroRadio authentication and integrity-bound content-level attacks to cryptographic compromise; feasible on-path effects are availability losses (delay/-drop/jam). In this case, the rules budget timeouts and enforce restrictive-under-uncertainty, requiring any Movement Authority to be reconciled with the route/occupancy model before application.

C7 (waysideRBC management): Strict change control (signed artefacts, out-of-band approval, rollback to last-known-good) prevents unauthorised configuration drifts that could yield authenticated yet policy-inconsistent behaviour.

Maintenance and Station Connectivity

C8: Write paths into safety-related zones are denied by default. Temporary enablement follows a time-bound, dual-control "break-glass" procedure with full session recording and post-hoc verification, limiting lateral movement opportunities through service conduits. Break-glass grants tightly scoped emergency access that two authorised operators must co-approve and that is fully recorded and reviewed.

Monitoring, Evidence, and Time Coherence. All enforcement points produce structured logs (including identities, sequence numbers, policy decisions, and timing) to support incident response and assurance. Time synchronisation bounds (used for freshness and correlation) are monitored; exceeding them triggers conservative treatment of affected actions. These practices are consistent with TS 50701 artefacts and ENISA good practices.

SecuritySafety Propagation. Security degradations primarily manifest as loss, delay, or manipulation of control/indication flows. If unmitigated, these degradations can increase headways, create route-setting inconsistencies, or stress braking margins. By biasing behaviour toward restrictive modes under uncertainty, requiring corroboration before effectual actions, and reconciling authorities with the interlocking model, the proposed rules reduce exposure time and limit unsafe preconditions, complementing established safety verification and operational procedures.

7 Conclusions

This paper presents an *action-based* methodology that aligns TS 50701 zoning and conduits with process algebraic modelling to derive conduit-specific, enforceable security rules at the observable interfaces of the railway signalling architecture (wayside, onboard, and the Data Communication System). An attacker model grounded the rule design in realistic exposure. At the same time, the *restrictive-under-uncertainty* principle and *semantic consistency* requirements addressed the residual risk of authenticated-but-policy-inconsistent traffic. The result is a set of deployable controls implementable at zone boundaries that complements established safety-oriented verification by constraining admissible behaviours before they influence safety logic.

The approach assumes correct time synchronisation and uncompromised trust anchors for authentication and integrity, and does not quantify operational performance under sustained denial-of-service attacks. Despite these limitations, the methodology is portable across ETCS/CBTC deployments and amenable to incremental adoption because rules bind to existing zoning artefacts and boundary devices.

This work is just an initial step towards providing a formal modelling of railway systems specified according to TS 50701 specification style. Much remains to be done, and should be seen as an invitation to other researchers to join forces with us to:

1. provides a complete algebraic model of zones and conduits using the full expressive power of process algebras;
2. instantiate ACTL properties over the action alphabet and verify them with LTS-based toolchains like KandISTI [2] CADP/MCL [16] or mCRL2 [17];
3. validate the rules against configuration baselines and operational logs;
4. align the rule set to evolving standardisation (e.g., the transition from TS 50701 toward IEC 63452), while integrating runtime monitors with SOC/SIEM workflows for continuous assurance.

We hope this research helps the ongoing effort to bring formal methods and safetysecurity co-engineering together in the railway field. We also hope it encourages young researchers to explore these topics, ideally working with us and with Alessandro. This goal honours the legacy of Alessandro, whose work showed how careful and precise modeling and checking can ensure that complex, critical systems work correctly.

References

1. Bajan, P.M., et al.: Proposal of cybersecurity and safety co-engineering approaches on cyber-physical systems. In: Computer Safety, Reliability, and Security: 41st International Conference, SAFECOMP 2022, Munich, Germany, September 6–9, 2022, Proceedings, pp. 175–188. Springer-Verlag, Berlin, Heidelberg (2022). https://doi.org/10.1007/978-3-031-14835-4_12
2. ter Beek, M.H., Gnesi, S., Mazzanti, F.: From EU projects to a family of model checkers - from kandinsky to kandisti. In: Nicola, R.D., Hennicker, R. (eds.) Software, Services, and Systems - Essays Dedicated to Martin Wirsing on the Occasion of His Retirement from the Chair of Programming and Software Engineering. Lecture Notes in Computer Science, vol. 8950, pp. 312–328. Springer (2015). https://doi.org/10.1007/978-3-319-15545-6_20
3. CENELEC: TS 50701:2021 Railway applications – Cybersecurity. Technical specification, European Committee for Electrotechnical Standardization (Jul 2021)
4. De Nicola, R., Fantechi, A., Gnesi, S., Ristori, G.: An action-based framework for veryfying logical and behavioural properties of concurrent systems. Comput. Netw. ISDN Syst. **25**(7), 761–778 (1993). https://doi.org/10.1016/0169-7552(93)90047-8
5. De Nicola, R.: Process Algebras. In: Padua, D.A. (ed.) Encyclopedia of Parallel Computing, pp. 1624–1636. Springer (2011). https://doi.org/10.1007/978-0-387-09766-4_450

6. De Nicola, R., Vaandrager, F.W.: Action versus state based logics for transition systems. In: Guessarian, I. (ed.) Semantics of Systems of Concurrent Processes, LITP. Lecture Notes in Computer Science, vol. 469, pp. 407–419. Springer (1990). https://doi.org/10.1007/3-540-53479-2_17

7. Di Claudio, M., Fantechi, A., Martelli, G., Menabeni, S., Nesi, P.: Model-based development of an automatic train operation component for communication based train control. In: Intelligent Transportation Systems Conference (ITSC), pp. 1015–1020. IEEE (2014). https://doi.org/10.1109/ITSC.2014.6957821

8. ENISA: Railway Cybersecurity - Good Practices in Cyber Risk Management. European Union Agency for Cybersecurity (Nov 2021)

9. European Commission, DG MOVE, M., Transport: Subsystems and constituents of the ertms. European Commission, DG MOVE, Mobility and Transport - Accessed Sep. 19, 2025. https://transport.ec.europa.eu/transport-modes/rail/ertms/what-ertms-and-how-does-it-work/subsystems-and-constituents-ertms_en

10. European Union Agency for Cybersecurity, Helmut, K., Schlehuber, C., Ooms, K., Theocharidou, M., Naydenov, R.: Zoning and conduits for railways. European Union Agency for Cybersecurity (2022). https://doi.org/10.2824/761090

11. Fantechi, A., Gnesi, S., Mazzanti, F., Pugliese, R., Tronci, E.: A symbolic model checker for actl. In: Hutter, D., Stephan, W., Traverso, P., Ullmann, M. (eds.) Applied Formal Methods — FM-Trends 98. pp. 228–242. Springer Berlin Heidelberg, Berlin, Heidelberg (1999). https://doi.org/10.1007/3-540-48257-1_14

12. Fantechi, A.: Twenty-five years of formal methods and railways: What next? In: Counsell, S., Núñez, M. (eds.) Software Engineering and Formal Methods, pp. 167–183. Springer International Publishing, Cham (2014). https://doi.org/10.1007/978-3-319-05032-4_13

13. Fernandes, T., Magalhães, J.P., Alves, W.: Cybersecurity in smart railways: exploring risks, vulnerabilities and mitigation in the data communication services. Green Energy Intell. Transport. 4(4), 100305 (2025). https://doi.org/10.1016/j.geits.2025.100305

14. Ferrari, A., ter Beek, M.H.: Formal methods in railways: A systematic mapping study. ACM Comput. Surv. 55(4) (Nov 2022). https://doi.org/10.1145/3520480

15. Ferrari, A., Mazzanti, F., Basile, D., ter Beek, M.H.: Systematic evaluation and usability analysis of formal methods tools for railway signaling system design. IEEE Trans. Software Eng. 48(11), 4675–4691 (2022). https://doi.org/10.1109/TSE.2021.3124677

16. Garavel, H., Lang, F., Mateescu, R.: Compositional verification of asynchronous concurrent systems using CADP. Acta Informatica 52(4-5), 337–392 (2015). https://doi.org/10.1007/S00236-015-0226-1

17. Groote, J.F., Mousavi, M.R.: Modeling and Analysis of Communicating Systems. MIT Press (2014). https://mitpress.mit.edu/books/modeling-and-analysis-communicating-systems

18. Haxthausen, A., Peleska, J.: Formal development and verification of a distributed railway control system. IEEE Trans. Software Eng. 26(8), 687–701 (2000). https://doi.org/10.1109/32.879808

19. Haxthausen, A.E., Fantechi, A.: Compositional verification of railway interlocking systems. Form. Asp. Comput. 35(1) (Jan 2023). https://doi.org/10.1145/3549736

20. Ledru, Y., Idani, A., Ben Ayed, R., Ait Wakrime, A., Bon, P.: A separation of concerns approach for the verified modelling of railway signalling rules. In: Collart-Dutilleul, S., Lecomte, T., Romanovsky, A. (eds.) Reliability, Safety, and Security of Railway Systems. Modelling, Analysis, Verification, and Certification, pp. 173–190.

Springer International Publishing, Cham (2019). https://doi.org/10.1007/978-3-030-18744-6_11

21. Liyanage, M., Kumar, P., Soderi, S., Ylianttila, M., Gurtov, A.: Performance and security evaluation of intra-vehicular communication architecture. In: 2016 IEEE International Conference on Communications Workshops (ICC), pp. 302–308 (2016). https://doi.org/10.1109/ICCW.2016.7503804

22. Nunes, J., Cruz, T., Simões, P.: Railway infrastructure cybersecurity: an overview. In: European Conference on Cyber Warfare and Security, vol. 23, pp. 331–340 (06 2024). https://doi.org/10.34190/eccws.23.1.2296

23. Peleska, J., Feuser, J., Haxthausen, A.E.: The model-driven openetcs paradigm for secure, safe and certifiable train control systems. In: Railway Safety, Reliability, and Security: Technologies and Systems Engineering, pp. 22–52. IGI Global Scientific Publishing (2012). https://doi.org/10.4018/978-1-4666-1643-1.ch002

24. Schlehuber, C., Benoliel, S.: CENELEC prTS 50701 (Railway applications – Cyber-Security). In: Cybersecurity in Railways, pp. 1–18. ENISA-ERA (2021)

25. Soderi, S., Masti, D., Hämäläinen, M., Iinatti, J.: Cybersecurity considerations for communication based train control. IEEE Access **11**, 92312–92321 (2023). https://doi.org/10.1109/ACCESS.2023.3309005

26. Soderi, S., Masti, D., Zacchia Lun, Y.: Railway cyber-security in the era of inter-connected systems: a survey. Trans. Intell. Transport. Syst. (2023). https://doi.org/10.1109/TITS.2023.3254442

27. Yusof, A., Liu, Y., Kang, N., Seah, C.M., Liang, Z., Chang, E.C.: Signals and symptoms: ICS attack dataset from railway cyber range (2025). https://arxiv.org/abs/2507.01768

28. Zhu, Y., et al.: Privacy-preserving large-scale ai models for intelligent railway transportation systems: Hierarchical poisoning attacks and defenses in federated learning. Comput. Model. Eng. Sci. **141**(2), 1305–1325 (2024). https://doi.org/10.32604/cmes.2024.054820

Safety Monitoring for Future Train Control Systems

Jan Peleska[1]([✉])[iD] and Anne E. Haxthausen[2][iD]

[1] Department of Mathematics and Computer Science, University of Bremen,
Bremen, Germany
`peleska@uni-bremen.de`
[2] DTU Compute, Technical University of Denmark, Kongens Lyngby, Denmark
`aeha@dtu.dk`

Abstract. In this paper, we present and discuss the advantages of cloud-based safety monitoring for railway control systems, using digital twin technology. It is explained why additional safety supervision techniques will become necessary in the near future, to counter increasingly threatening security attacks and to cope with the complexity of ETCS Level 3 systems or even fully automated driverless systems according to GoA 4 and beyond. The presentation is informal but structured: we show how existing technologies and theoretical results can be used today to prepare for the safety-related challenges of tomorrow's railway control systems.

Keywords: Railway control systems · Runtime verification · Digital twins · ETCS Level 3

1 Introduction

1.1 Motivation

The paper [15] by Alessandro Fantechi et al. presents a vision for the future of intelligent and autonomous train control systems. For such systems they advocate the use of digital twins for predicting safety risks. In the line of these ideas, in this paper, we consider the utilisation of digital twins for safety monitoring of future railway control systems. We elaborate on how the ideas in [15] can be met in practice to predict and also to mitigate safety risks.

Today's signalling and interlocking architectures already achieve a very high safety assurance level, verified and validated according to safety integrity level SIL-4 [8]. Nevertheless, we expect that several emerging challenges will require an additional, redundant level of safety supervision in the near future:

- **Countering increasingly complex security attacks.** The number of security attacks against railway infrastructure is currently increasing, and we must expect coordinated attacks on physical infrastructure and in

© The Author(s), under exclusive license to Springer Nature Switzerland AG 2026
M. H. ter Beek et al. (Eds.): Fantechi Festschrift, LNCS 16470, pp. 333–352, 2026.
https://doi.org/10.1007/978-3-032-12484-5_18

cyberspace [12].[1] Consequently, failures in railway control systems can no longer be attributed solely to hardware faults and rarely occurring software bugs. Instead, *any* erroneous – even malicious – behaviour must be taken into account.

- **Higher network density under moving-block operation.** The moving-block technique foreseen for ETCS Level 3 [31] benefits from scalable computing in the cloud: safety-relevant train-trajectory predictions can be computed with higher precision, allowing denser traffic on the network.
- **Network-wide situational awareness.** Cloud-based safety monitoring enables supervision of complete networks (e.g. the railway network of a whole country), whereas conventional interlocking systems only control smaller regions of the network, using handover protocols for trains crossing region boundaries.
- **Heterogeneous and legacy integration.** During the long transition to full digitalisation, legacy and unequipped trains will continue to operate alongside modern ETCS L3 vehicles. DT supervision offers a uniform safety monitoring layer bridging these heterogeneous systems.
- **Predictive and resilience-oriented safety.** By correlating real-time data with historical patterns, DTs can identify early indicators of degraded braking performance, communication anomalies, or environmental disruptions, thus enhancing resilience beyond traditional fail-safe logic.
- **Fleet learning for GoA 4 trains.** For driverless trains according to *Grade of Automation GoA 4*[2], functions based on machine learning (ML) will become necessary, for example, for obstacle detection [17] or passenger-door operation. These ML-based functions benefit from *fleet learning*, which is best deployed in the cloud.
- **Safety monitoring for autonomous trains.** In the long run, we expect train-control technology beyond GoA 4; this will introduce *true autonomy*, for example, by negotiating route changes with interlockings to circumvent network sections that have become unavailable. This higher degree of autonomy requires another level of safety supervision that is currently not available. Again, cloud-based safety monitors benefit from the bird's-eye view of the complete railway network.

1.2 Background

The core idea of digital-twin (DT) technology is that real-world objects – the *physical twins (PT)* – are associated with digital counterparts that can be used to explore their behaviour without harmful interference. Digital twins have become an accepted technology that is widely used for a multitude of different purposes.

---

[1] see also https://www.helpnetsecurity.com/2025/09/09/railway-systems-cybersecurity/?utm_source=chatgpt.com.

[2] Grade of Automation 4 (GoA 4) corresponds to Unattended Train Operation (UTO), in which trains operate fully automatically at all times, including start-up, running, stopping, and door operation, without any staff on board.

The capabilities of digital twins and the design prerequisites for exploiting them are comprehensively described by Fitzgerald et al. [14]. In this paper, we focus on their utilisation for monitoring the safe execution of the *physical* twin. This is a specific aspect of the more general *runtime verification* methodology [3,20].

Though not mandatory, the use of DTs is closely linked to *cloud computing* [21,30]: in-depth analyses of DTs paired with complex physical twins requires considerable computing power. Flexible cloud mechanisms to scale CPU and memory usage are helpful to cope with dynamically changing complex object configurations representing, for example, systems-of-systems [22].

The approach to increase the safety of future railway control systems using digital twins and cloud computing is currently an active research field: German Railways, for example, has initiated a general investigation about the benefits to be expected from using cloud infrastructure for safety-critical aspects of railway control [10]. Potential use cases for DTs in railways are manifold [16][3] – from railway maintenance [2,4] to the improvement of railway operations and railway safety [11,29]: industrial suppliers already advocate the use of DTs[4], so this is no longer a pure research topic. In particular, the objective to enable GoA 4 trains in the future, will make use of DT technology to enhance the safety of driverless trains; for example, by performing image-based obstacle detection in a cloud-based DT.[5]

1.3   Main Contributions

Based on existing insights about DTs and cloud computing in the railway domain and additional ideas elaborated by the authors, we propose a comprehensive approach to augment railway interlockings with safety monitors using DT technology deployed across geographically distributed cloud infrastructures. Our premise is that wide-area, redundant supervision complements certified interlocking and onboard functions, particularly under (i) rising cyberâĂŞphysical threat levels and (ii) the operational complexity introduced by high-speed services and ETCS Level 3 with mixed traffic and heterogeneous equipment.

This paper makes the following contributions:

1. **Principled allocation of safety functions.** We delineate which safety checks can be reliably offloaded to cloud-hosted DT monitors and which *must* remain on board (e.g., ceiling-speed enforcement, braking-curve adherence, and emergency-brake initiation). The result is a clear, auditable onboard/cloud split that preserves SIL 4 responsibilities while exploiting DT situational awareness. (Section 3)

---

[3] https://www.smartspatial.com/post/18-use-cases-of-operational-digital-twins-in-railways.

[4] See, for example, https://www.prover.com/modeling/the-need-for-digital-twins-in-rail-control-projects/.

[5] https://digitale-schiene-deutschland.de/en/news/2022/digital-twin.

2. **Mixed-traffic treatment, including unequipped trains.** Our analysis explicitly covers heterogeneous fleets: ETCS Level 3-capable trains with continuous trainborne positioning, as well as "vintage" trains that provide only block-occupancy information (no radio link, no speed/location telemetry). We define conservative protection envelopes and monitoring logic that remain valid across this spectrum, relying on track-side vacancy detection where necessary. (Section 2.5)

3. **Train-centric safety monitoring.** We shift from a purely network-centric viewpoint to a *train-centric* one. For each moving train, the DT evaluates (i) hazards *to others* induced by that train's potential motion and (ii) hazards *to the train itself* arising from infrastructure states (e.g., point positions) or movement-authority (MA) inconsistencies. This decomposition yields modular runtime monitors with clear responsibility boundaries. (Section 2.3)

4. **Revisiting classical interlocking constraints under DT supervision.** We explain how "classical" constructs (flank protection, overlaps, partial route release) can be *safely* parameterised and, where appropriate, conservatively relaxed under DT oversight. We identify the invariants that must continue to hold and show how additional DT checks can maintain safety while enabling higher throughput and denser traffic. (Section 2.8)

To the best of our knowledge, these signalling-oriented monitoring details are not treated comprehensively in prior railway publications investigating DTs; we provide the first integrated treatment at this operational level that also covers software architectural considerations.

1.4   Overview

In Sect. 2, the key concepts of redundant safety monitoring by DTs are described. We explain the benefits of a train-centric monitoring approach and outline a set of interactions to be provided for communication between the DT, the trains, and the interlockings it supervises. The fundamental monitoring functions are described, as well as the support of mixed traffic allowing to monitor "vintage" trains without positioning or communication equipment. We briefly touch on additional monitoring support for GoA 4 trains and for truly autonomous trains of the future. While Sect. 2 explains safety monitoring on a level that abstracts from concrete execution platforms, the crucial features of a DT architecture deployed in the cloud are explained in Sect. 3. Section 4 contains a conclusion.

Throughout the paper, we refer to related work where appropriate.

2   Safety Monitoring

2.1   Certification Considerations and Functional Implications

As pointed out in Sect. 1, DTs monitoring railway networks could not only be used to detect safety issues, but also to *improve* traffic flow by detecting and predicting when certain protections (flank protection, locked track elements) are no longer required and by enforcing the release of these protections. From a certification perspective, however, such optimisations constitute safety-critical functionality that must be verified and validated according to SIL-4.

For railway applications in the cloud, this is not impossible: Siemens' DS3 centralises interlocking logic in data centres while maintaining SIL-4 by means of a safety-platform architecture on standardised (COTS) servers – redundant and diverse instances with safe voting and a safety OS layer – rather than relying on bespoke hardware. This architecture is publicly described in Siemens materials and was approved in operation at ÖBB Achau[6], see also [23]. This, however, implies that the interlocking logic cannot be deployed on *general-purpose* cloud server farms, since their platforms do not implement such a safety architecture; achieving SIL-4 for general cloud software stacks (e.g. Linux variants with a Kubernetes[7] orchestration layer) is, in practice, infeasible given complexity, change rates, and cost.

In this paper, we focus on safety monitoring and intervention mechanisms that, even in the presence of DT malfunctions, cannot introduce additional safety hazards, but at most impair availability (e.g., unnecessary braking or stops). A failure to detect a hazardous situation merely fails to *improve* the safety level, so that the conventional SIL-4 safety logic of interlockings and train controllers (*onboard units (OBU)*) remains solely effective. Hence, deploying monitoring and intervention mechanisms in the cloud is uncritical. Consequently, DTs can be hosted on *any* cloud platform, and the advantages of cloud service layers can be fully exploited without incurring certification issues. This facilitates investment in DTs that provide monitoring and intervention only.

Should safety-critical optimisation functions be required in the future, two design options are available:

- If critical DT proposals (like forgoing flank protection in a specific situation) can be independently verified and, if necessary, rendered ineffectual by small *vital enforcers* deployed within the interlocking, the DT can still run on any cloud platform. The safety-critical, fail-safe function is then allocated to the enforcer, which blocks any unsafe proposal.
- If such enforcers cannot be made sufficiently complete, the vital part of the DT must be deployed in a railway-specific data centre on a SIL-4 safety platform, with the non-vital DT functions remaining on general cloud platforms. This entails a DT software design that differs significantly from purely non-vital cloud deployments.

In the light of these considerations, the DT monitors proposed here are intentionally non-vital: any malfunction can at most cause unnecessary braking or a refusal to set routes and thus reduces availability without compromising safety. The top-level assurance claim is therefore that *DT monitors do not introduce unsafe actuation*. This is supported by (i) design isolation – the IXL/OBU remain

---

[6] https://press.siemens.com/global/en/pressrelease/first-signalling-cloud-operation.
[7] https://kubernetes.io.

the sole safety authorities and accept only the pre-defined safe interventions from DTs, (ii) bounded interventions – DTs only advise or request pre-defined fail-safe actions, and (iii) secure train (PT) $\leftrightarrow$ trackside communication per EN 50159 with diverse, timestamped evidence sources for cross-checks.

For future safety-critical optimisations, we advocate the railway-specific data centres as described above, since the alternative (vital enforcers at the IXL boundary) would become ineffective in situations where attacks to infrastructure could "hijack" (i.e. take control of) a local IXL. Non-vital DT services (forecasting, what-if analysis, user interfaces, etc.) can remain on general cloud platforms, preserving scalability without diluting safety.

2.2 Digital Twin Structure

We propose to deploy digital twins on cloud server farms with communication links to all track elements in the railway network, to the IXLs or their associated radio block centres (RBC), and to all trains equipped with modern communication technology. While the railway network may be partitioned into smaller regions, each region controlled by its own IXL, the cloud server farm has a bird's eye view on *all* track elements, IXLs, and trains in the whole network. The DTs are structured into two types of sub-DTs.

1. **Network DT.** One sub-DT representing the topology of the railway network and the actual state of each track element, including its association with current movement authorities.
2. **Train DT.** One sub-digital twin $DT(T)$ for each train T residing in (and traversing) the network.

Each train digital twin $DT(T)$ is aware of the current protection envelope of its physical twin T. Following the *publish-subscribe paradigm* [6], $DT(T)$ subscribes at the network DT to the track elements on the route it is travelling on and a suitable portion of track elements beyond the end of movement authority (EOA) to take safety overlaps into account. The subscriptions to track elements it has already passed on its route are released.

Moreover, $DT(T)$ subscribes at the digital twin $DT(T')$ of the train T' in front (if any) traversing the same route as T according to the moving block paradigm. This subscription is to receive all protection envelope changes of T'. Information about such a train (if it exists) can be obtained from the track element states provided by the network DT as will be explained below. The PE subscription at $DT(T')$ is released as soon as T' departs from T's route.

More details about the DT software architecture are discussed in Sect. 3.

2.3 Train-Centric Approach

Classical interlocking is network-centric: safety is ensured by global route-setting rules and mutual exclusions. The related checks to ensure that only non-conflicting routes are assigned to trains are performed by analysing the railway network structure and the track element states (vacancy, point positions, signal states). In contrast, we organise the digital-twin (DT) safety checks *train-centrically* [33]. In the variant we advocate, a DT instance is created for each train T and projects T's authorised path and associated protection envelope along a path coordinate s and continuously verifies (i) its own safety regarding track element states along the authorised route and (ii) the safety of other trains that might be threatened by T. This is discussed in more detail in Sect. 2.6 below.

Note that train-centric monitoring is not a novelty: it exists, for example, in ETCS onboard controllers responsible for *automated train protection (ATP)* and checking ceiling speed, target speed, and adherence to movement authority [31].

2.4   Interactions Between Physical and Digital Twin

Modern track elements (points, track vacancy detectors, and signals, where still required) can be remotely controlled from cloud data centres and report their status over wide-area networks. Communication can be assumed to be safe and secure, using redundancy and encryption according to EN 50129 and EN 50159 [7,8]. This enables solutions where interlocking logic is relocated from trackside to global data centres. Interlockings communicate established movement authorities (MAs) and route-specific speed profiles to trains via radio block centres; conversely, modern trains provide status information (position, speed) upstream to interlockings.

For our purposes, physical twins (PT) are assumed to exchange the following messages with their DT counterparts.

Message direction PT $\rightarrow$ DT (Observations)

1. **Track elements $\rightarrow$ network sub-DT.** Current status per element: *type, id, commanded state, proved state, occupancy* (free/occupied/unknown), *position report* for points (Plus/Minus/Unknown), *lock status* (locked/unlocked), and *health* (diagnostics).
2. **IXL $\rightarrow$ network sub-DT.** Movement authorities

$$\text{MA} = (T, \text{routeid}, \langle e_1, \ldots, e_k \rangle, \text{speed profile}, t_{\text{issue}}),$$

   where T is the train id; $\langle e_i \rangle$ is the sequence of locked elements in the route-aligned coordinate frame.
3. **Train (OBU) $\rightarrow$ train sub-DT.** *Protection envelope (PE)* [13,19,32]

$$\text{PE} = (T, \overline{x}, x_F, x_R, v; t)$$

   with T the train id; x_R the estimated rear-end position, x_F the estimated front position, and $\overline{x}$ the emergency-brake standstill position, all expressed in along-track curvilinear coordinates on the train's (planned or allocated) route. Parameter v is a velocity estimate, and t the OBU computation time.[8]

---

[8] In the detailed PE design, each parameter value $\overline{x}, x_F, x_R, v$ is expressed by intervals indicating lower and upper parameter bounds, and each interval is paired with a

Message direction DT $\rightarrow$ PT (Intervention Requests)

1. **DT $\rightarrow$ IXL.** Requests to *depower* track sections, *set signal aspect* to HALT or to REDUCED SPEED, *refuse MA* to routes traversing certain track elements,
2. **DT $\rightarrow$ Trains.** Request to *reduce speed* to a specified profile, *trigger service brakes, trigger emergency brakes, hold short* (i.e. do not accept MA) on specified route.

2.5   Mixed-Traffic Treatment

For trains without communication or onboard positioning, the interlocking provides *approximated protection envelopes* inferred from occupied *track vacancy detection (TVD)* blocks, configurable maximal assumed train length, the maximal permissible speed on the current and forthcoming sections, and conservative braking models. Front/rear bounds are aligned to TVD block limits with conservative offsets to cover undetected overhang. These envelopes are flagged as *inferred (lower trust)* and carry the underlying assumptions. Uncertainty grows monotonically without fresh observations and is reset or reduced when TVD state changes occur (e.g. block cleared/occupied). The interlocking that issued the train's MA transmits the approximated PE to the DT; any subsequent interventions for such trains are executed via the interlocking, since no direct DT$\rightarrow$train commands can be transmitted.

The intervention options of an IXL to stop or slow down these trains are limited, since the IXL can only act via lineside signalling and infrastructure. Available options are: (i) *replacement to STOP* of all protecting signals on the train's path and *hold approach locking* so aspects do not restore automatically; (ii) enforce *restrictive approach sequences* (e.g. caution/double-yellow, approach control) to compel braking before the protecting STOP; (iii) *cancel routes ahead* of the train and *inhibit new route setting* so no conflicting movement is formed; (iv) *extend overlaps* and *lock points/switchable crossings* in protective positions (flank protection) to contain the movement; (v) where fitted, *set trap points/derailers* to the protective position; (vi) on electrified lines, *de-power* the relevant traction sections to prevent further movement (note: ineffective for non-electrified traction); (vii) apply *blocking/artificial-occupation facilities* at the IXL so protecting signals are forced to remain at STOP and sections remain unavailable.

These measures are executed solely by the IXL; no RBC/ETCS emergency-stop requests are assumed.

2.6   Monitoring Safety Along Train Routes

---

confidence value expressing the probability that the true parameter value will reside inside the interval. Additionally, the PE tuple will be associated with a validity horizon indicating how long the current value can be safely used. For the high-level description of this paper, we abstract from these details, as they would only clutter the presentation.

Invariant Checking in the Network DT. Despite the train-centric monitoring strategy described next, certain invariant safety conditions are best – indeed, necessarily – checked by the network DT. Railway safety requires continuous supervision of assets even when not in current use: latent failures must be detected and mitigated *before* a route needs them. Examples of invariants include (i) no route formation over track elements with failed or unproven states; (ii) points and switchable crossings proved in the commanded position prior to and during route holding; (iii) signals not exhibiting dark/invalid aspects; and (iv) consistent track vacancy detection (e.g., axle-counter section states without contradictions).

In normal operation, these checks are performed by the interlocking (IXL). However, the IXL can be unavailable, degraded, or compromised; therefore, the network DT provides an *independent* line of defence based on proved states and timestamps received via diverse channels. The DT classifies anomalies (suspected vs. confirmed with hysteresis), stores their status, and (a) notifies affected train DTs and traffic management, and (b) issues failure reports to maintenance (including asset id, fault code, time, and evidence). Operational authority remains with the IXL; the DT may request protective actions (e.g., route inhibition over the failed asset), but the IXL arbitrates and executes as long as the IXL itself has not been detected to be compromised (see below). When track elements recover and remain stable over a configured dwell time, the DT automatically clears the anomaly.

Detection Support for Conflicting Movement Authorities. Conflicting MAs can be classified as follows: (i) A straight track segment with ends a and b is allocated for MAs with different directions ab and ba. This illegal double-allocation would lead to a front-to-front collision if not detected. (ii) A point with ends a, b, c has multiple MA allocations with at least two different directions out of the four possible ones (ab, ba, ac, ca). Here, illegal double allocations could lead to front-to-front and front-to-flank collisions. (iii) A crossing with ends a, b, c, d has multiple MA allocations with at least two different directions out of the possible ones (for a switched diamond crossing, this would be ac, ad, bc, bd, ca, cb, da, db).

For each element, the admissible direction set (e.g., $\{ab, ba\}$ for a straight, $\{ab, ba, ac, ca\}$ for a point, and $\{ac, ad, bc, bd, ca, cb, da, db\}$ for a switched diamond) is fixed by the topology; an MA induces the corresponding element/direction pairs by following the route's topological path.

To detect illegal multiple allocations, each network DT component representing a straight segment, point, or crossing manages FIFO lists L_{wz} of tokens τ for every possible direction $wz \in \{ab, ba, \dots\}$. A token τ either carries a real train identifier (modern trains) or is an anonymous placeholder ("vintage trains" without onboard id). When an MA affecting (element, wz) is issued, we append a token to L_{wz}. Upon proven sectional release provided by a *train detection sys-*

tem (TDS)[9] that is consistent with the end position x_R contained in the train's PE, the train id is popped again from this list.

Following the moving-block paradigm of ETCS Level 3, the lists L_{wz} may contain more than one entry, since consecutive trains traversing the same route in the direction wz are allowed, as long as their protection envelopes don't overlap. If L_{wz} is non-empty, however, the other lists $L_{w'z'}$, $w'z' \neq wz$ must be empty; otherwise this indicates that conflicting, illegal MAs have been issued. Below we explain how this is checked by the train DTs.

Safety Monitoring and Interventions by Train DTs. The train DTs have two objectives:

– **Protect the own train** against track element failures and conflicting (therefore illegal) MAs.
– **Protect other trains** against front-to-rear, front-to-front, and front-to-flank collisions that could be caused by the own train.

As with the network DT, train DTs execute cyclic checks. In each cycle, checks cover the track partition from the train's rear end x_R (from the protection envelope PE $= (T, \overline{x}, x_F, x_R, v, t)$) up to a downstream *safety overlap* beyond the *End of Authority (EOA)*. The overlap length depends on the current PE estimates for the standstill position $\overline{x}$ after emergency braking and the velocity bound v.

Protection of the own train. Using their actual protection envelope PE, train DTs perform the following checks:

1. **Own MA coverage and no conflicts.** For every element from the train T's rear x_R to the EOA, the element's list L_{wz} for the direction wz associated with the T's path must satisfy $T \in L_{wz}$. All other $L_{w'z'}$ must be empty.
2. **No MA in the safety overlap.** All elements within the current overlap have empty lists $L_{w'z'}$ for all conflicting directions. (In train T's direction wz, a preceding train may already have obtained MA to traverse the element, so L_{wz} may be non-empty.)
3. **No track element failures.** No element between the rear and the end of the overlap end is flagged failed or unproven (e.g. all points are locked in the correct position for the route).
4. **Vacancy up to the standstill point.** Track sections from immediately ahead of the train's front to the PE standstill point $\overline{x}$ are vacant. Preceding trains on the same route may exist beyond $\overline{x}$, consistent with moving-block operation.

---

[9] This is EULYNX terminology for a group of one or more track elements associated with an OCCUPIED/VACANT detection technology, such as several axle counters monitoring whether trains enter or leave this section. See https://eulynx.eu/ resource-hub-deliverables/.

5. **Consistent point positions.** From the rear x_R to the EOA, points and switchable crossings are in the correct position for the issued route variant, *proved* to match the command, and *locked*. In the safety overlap, all points and switchable crossings are in positions that would not cause de-railing.

Interventions (own-train protection). If one of the 5 failure situations listed above is detected, the train DT triggers the following interventions.

- If still at route start: do not commence movement (hold).
- If traversing: apply service brake when the PE shows a stop can be achieved before the first unsafe element; otherwise request to trigger emergency brake.
- Report detected element failures to the responsible interlocking and maintenance; request inhibition of routes over the failed track elements until cleared.
- If illegal MA allocation is detected with corroborating evidence (e.g., non-empty conflicting list $L_{wz}, L_{w'z'}$ and TVD/point proofs), escalate: notify the network DT and mark the interlocking that issued the MAs as degraded; request inhibition of new MAs and hold protecting signals at STOP for the affected sub-network. Trains already within the sub-network stop and await IXL recovery or manual routing procedures.

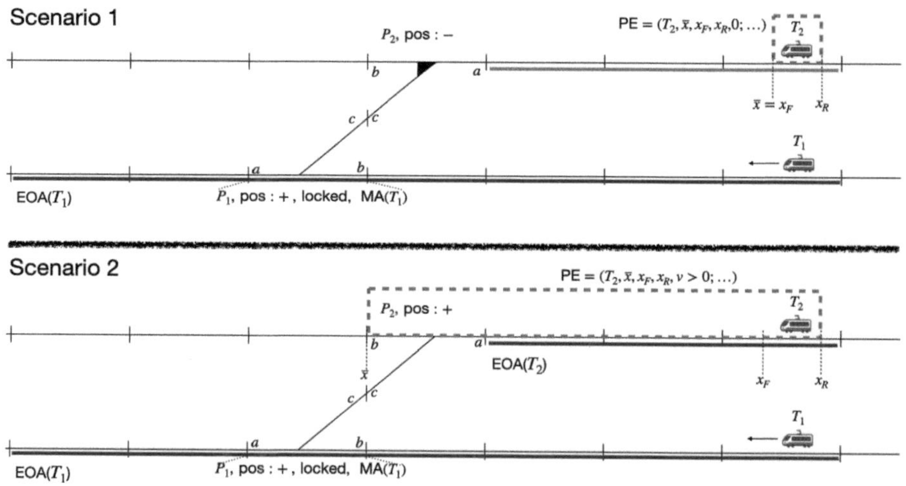

Fig. 1. Two scenarios involving flank protection.

Example 1. Consider train T_2 in Fig. 1, Scenario 1. The train T_2 is still standing, but has received an MA up to (excluding) P_2 (so EOA $= P_2$). Point P_2 is part of the safety overlap and in position "$-$". Since a single point is too short to span the overlap, the other point P_1 will also become part of it. Now DT(T_2) will detect violations of protection rules 2 and 5 listed above since

344   J. Peleska and A. E. Haxthausen

- (P_1, L_{ba}) has list content $L_{ba} = \langle T_1 \rangle$, and
- Point P_1 is in position "+" which could cause de-railing of T_2.

Therefore, $\mathtt{DT}(T_2)$ triggers a *"hold"* intervention at train T_2 and an intervention *"hold train T_2 until P_2 is in position "+" (this would ensure flank protection for train T_1) or until P_1 is in position "−" and no longer associated with an MA"* at the responsible IXL.

Protection of other Trains. Once an MA has been issued for a train, its digital twin $\mathtt{DT}(T)$ supervises whether T could endanger other trains by performing:[10]

1. **No PE overlaps in moving block.** Let wz be the element-specific direction on T's path. Inspect the FIFO lists L_{wz} of the elements ahead of T; if for some element e_i we have $L_{wz}(e_i) = \langle \ldots, T', T, \ldots \rangle$, then T' is immediately ahead of T on the same route. Every train/token T' has a twin $\mathtt{DT}(T')$:
   - for modern trains, $\mathtt{DT}(T')$ maintains $\mathtt{PE}(T')$ from onboard reports;
   - for vintage trains, $\mathtt{DT}(T')$ maintains an over-approximation of the true PE from occupied/free element states along the route plus conservative braking/length assumptions, as explained in Sect. 2.5.

   $\mathtt{DT}(T)$ subscribes to updates from $\mathtt{DT}(T')$ and continuously checks whether $\mathtt{PE}(T)$ and $\mathtt{PE}(T')$ overlap.
2. **No PE overlap with the EOA (target-speed supervision).** Continuously check whether $\bar{x}(T) \geq \mathtt{EOA}(T)$ (optionally with a safety margin), i.e. whether the current standstill point from the PE would overrun the EOA. Equivalently, detect whether $\mathtt{PE}(T)$ overlaps the EOA.

Interventions (protection of other Trains). If any of the above conditions is violated, $\mathtt{DT}(T)$ triggers:

- *On-train braking:* if the illegal overlap can be removed with service braking, command service brake; otherwise trigger the emergency brake.
- *IXL-mediated measures (when T does not respond or is associated with a vintage train):*
  - Set/hold protecting signals to restrictive aspects or STOP to reduce speed and/or contain T.[11]
  - De-energise traction sections on T's path (for electric traction, where available).
  - Reserve additional protection ahead of T: extend the protected zone beyond $\mathtt{EOA}(T)$ (no route formation / no MA issuance into that zone). If containment is required, the IXL may divert T onto a safe low-speed path or into a siding with sand drag, and set trap/catch points to their protective positions to prevent fouling of protected tracks.

---

[10] For "vintage trains" without means of communication, T is the auxilary token introduced above.

[11] In the sense of *fault containment*: limiting the effects of a suspected malfunction of T, so these malfunctions cannot propagate to other trains or infrastructure.

Example 2. Consider again train T_2 in Fig. 1, now in Scenario 2. Flank protection for T_1 is ensured, since point P_2 is in position + (proved and locked). However, the current protection envelope of T_2 indicates a potential EOA overrun, since $\overline{x}(T_2) > \text{EOA}(T_2)$. Therefore, $\text{DT}(T_2)$ intervenes to slow down T_2, either by using the service brake or the emergency brake, depending on the current velocity estimate $v(T_2)$ and the length $\overline{x}(T_2) - \text{EOA}(T_2)$ of the EOA-overshoot to avoid.

2.7 Monitoring Support for GoA 4 and Beyond

For driverless trains at grade of automation GoA 4, safety-critical monitoring duties formerly performed by drivers (obstacle detection, signal aspect recognition, passenger-door supervision, etc.) move to onboard systems. These topics have been widely studied, see [17,25].

As advocated by Fantechi et al. [15], such functions benefit from digital twins that *predict* and *cross-check* safety risks. Beyond the DT tasks identified above (useful for any GoA level), we highlight GoA-4âĂŞspecific monitoring that becomes effective when *allocated to the cloud*:

Example: Obstacle Detection Cross-Checks. Onboard detection uses sensor fusion (radar, LiDAR, cameras, ...) with CNN-based vision [24,27]. The train streams selected frames, redacted video snippets, or compact feature embeddings to its DT; the DT runs redundant, higher-capacity models and performs contextual checks (map priors, work-zones, schedule conflicts) that may be useful to avoid false positives. If the DT detects an obstacle missed on board, it issues a *time-bounded advisory*: the OBU remains the safety authority. Loss of connectivity leads to graceful degradation (OBU continues autonomously; DT resumes when connected).

Fleet Learning and Model Governance. Images and features from many GoA-4 trains are aggregated to *train and validate* improved DT-side models (fleet learning [18]). New models first run in *shadow mode* within DTs with statistical acceptance criteria; only after meeting predefined performance thresholds and updating the safety case are frozen versions rolled out to OBUs with versioning and rollback.

Beyond GoA 4. For truly autonomous functions (e.g. onboard negotiation of alternative routes with IXL agents [26]), DTs provide the network-wide "bird's-eye" monitor that validates proposals against safety invariants (flank protection, overlaps) before execution.

2.8 Relaxation of "Classical" Safety Restrictions

As discussed in Sect. 2.1, DTs could perform safety-critical tasks when hosted on certified platforms (SIL 4). In that setting, DTs can enable *conditional* relaxations of conservative rules while preserving safety invariants, as follows.

1. **Earlier sectional route release via trajectory prediction.** DTs maintain filtered trajectory estimates from protection envelopes and predict when elements behind a train have been fully cleared. The IXL remains responsible for *proof of release* (e.g. based on TVDs); the DT provides an *early, high-confidence prediction* to arm a conditional release so that, once proof arrives, conflicting routes can be set without additional delay.
2. **Time-separated conflict resolution (dynamic flank/route protection).** Collision risk on a conflict element e exists only if two trains can *co-occupy* it within the same time window. Using the PEs (with confidence levels) for two trains on conflicting paths, the DT estimates:

$$t_{\mathrm{arr}}^{\min}(T_2, e) \quad \text{and} \quad t_{\mathrm{clr}}^{\max}(T_1, e).$$

If $t_{\mathrm{arr}}^{\min}(T_2, e) \geq t_{\mathrm{clr}}^{\max}(T_1, e) + \Delta t_{\mathrm{guard}}$ (with spatial margin $\Delta x_{\mathrm{guard}}$ and probability $\geq 1 - \alpha$), the conflict is *time-separated*. The IXL may then *condition* route setting to this predicate instead of requiring static flank protection, reverting to classical constraints immediately if inputs become stale or inconsistent, or if α is too large to ensure sufficient confidence.

Example 3. Consider train T_2 in Fig. 1, Scenario 1. Based on $\mathrm{PE}(T_1)$, the DT predicts that T_1 will clear point P_1 well before T_2 could reach P_1 even under a worst-case EOA overshoot. Formally,

$$t_{\mathrm{arr}}^{\min}(T_2, P_1) \ \geq \ t_{\mathrm{clr}}^{\max}(T_1, P_1) + \Delta t_{\mathrm{guard}},$$

where $t_{\mathrm{arr}}^{\min}$ denotes earliest arrival time, $t_{\mathrm{clr}}^{\max}$ latest clearance time, and $\Delta t_{\mathrm{guard}}$ a time safety margin; confidence and spatial margins have not be shown in this formula, but would be present in the detailed design. In this case, the IXL may issue *an* MA to T_2 immediately as a *conditional route*: either (i) P_2 proved in position + (*static* flank protection), or (ii) the *time-separation predicate* above holds at execution time. If (ii) ceases to hold or proofs become stale, the condition fails and the IXL blocks movement (reverting to classical protection).

3   Monitor Design Using Digital Twins and Cloud Support

3.1   Conceptual Model and Boundary Conditions

Model Layers. Independently of the concrete cloud operating system and orchestration support, the *conceptual model* of the cloud-based DTs described above has a layered structure (see Fig. 2).

Operational Data Flow. Train OBUs publish protection envelopes $\mathrm{PE}(T)$ to their Train-DT via a secure bearer. The Train-DT subscribes to movement-authority and track-state streams for the train's planned path via the Network-DT discovery. On each update, the Train-DT evaluates the route-local rules in Sect. 2.6 (coverage and conflicts, overlap clearance, point proofs, vacancy to

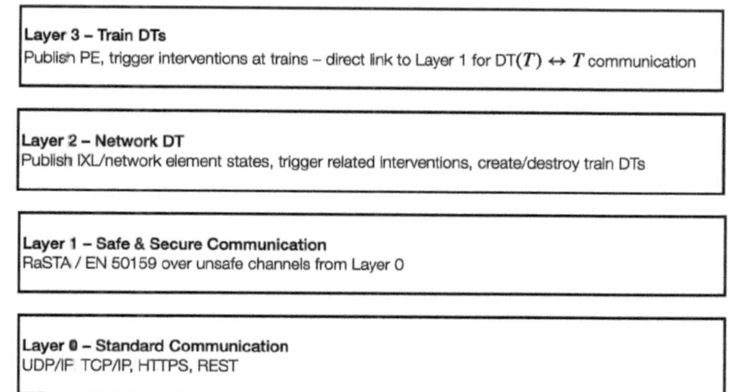

Fig. 2. Layered structure of the conceptual models of DTs in the cloud.

standstill) and, if a predicted violation occurs within the radio latency horizon, issues a time-bounded advisory/intervention to the OBU; if the OBU is unresponsive or the train is unequipped, IXL-mediated measures are requested. The Network-DT runs in activeâĂŞactive replica mode; status changes are event-sourced and replayed to newly joined nodes, and Train-DT subscriptions are idempotent so failover remains transparent.

Timing Considerations. For enabling effective interventions by network DT or train DTs, the following execution-time considerations are important.

- High-speed trains may travel with a maximum speed of 350 km/h (97.22 m/s).
- When triggering the emergency brakes at maximum speed, a train will need a distance of about 5,100 m to come to a standstill [9, 13].
- We therefore allocate a maximal end-to-end decision time of 200 ms for processing in the cloud, during which the train travels up to 20 m.

We regard 20 m as acceptable, since typical safety overlaps are *considerably* longer. In addition, human train drivers' perceptionâĂŞresponse times exceed 200 ms in realistic operating conditions, so a DT-triggered intervention remains faster than a manual one. Finally, the protection envelopes are calculated conservatively ("on the safe side"), so an additional 20 m of run-on does not immediately imply an unsafe state. (Note that 20 m is $\approx 0.4\%$ of the worst-case emergency-braking distance above.)

Predictive DT Interventions Under Bearer Latency. Over today's GSM-R, small ETCS-class transactions exhibit roundâĂŞtrip delays on the order of seconds. Consequently, a conservative budget of about 1 s one-way for train→DT or DT→train messages is appropriate. Hence, train DTs must operate *predictively*: an intervention (e.g. to avoid an EOA overshoot) is issued *before* the protection envelope actually violates a limit, using forecasted states and braking curves with a look-ahead at least equal to the bearer latency plus a safety margin.

As railway communication migrates to FRMCS (4G/5G), substantially tighter latencies become feasible in practice: recent field trials measured one-way user-plane transmission around 20 ms (mean) on the network path and end-to-end application round-trip times of 90âĂŞ110 ms (i.e. $\approx$ 40âĂŞ55 ms one-way) under dynamic conditions with handovers [1]. This supports DT control loops with total budgets in the 60âĂŞ200 ms range, depending on deployment.

Further Consequences of Timing Considerations. A further consequence is that functions requiring tight, continuous feedback (e.g. ceiling-speed supervision and virtual coupling control) are better performed in the OBU, where reaction is immediate and independent of radio bearer jitter.

Implications for Intra-Cloud Communication. Given these timing considerations, general-purpose Layer 0 interfaces such as HTTPS/REST are not ideal for communication between DT components, due to higher per-message overhead and jitter. We retain orchestration tooling (e.g. Kubernetes) for deployment and lifecycle, but bypass Service/Ingress paths for live DT traffic. Instead, the intra-cloud data plane should provide:

1. *Local IPC* on the same node (shared-memory or equivalent) for single-digit to low-tens of microseconds hop latency;
2. *Fast UDP-based transport* across nodes with loss detection and selective retransmission to keep latency flat under rare loss;
3. Efficient *one-publisherâĂŞmany-subscribers* delivery with no per-subscriber duplication at the publisher application, and minimal duplication in the I/O path.
4. Explicit *backpressure*[12] to prevent slow consumers from stalling producers.

These features are provided, for example by Aeron Transport[13] communication services.

Intra-cloud security and diagnostics/logging (including replay) are out of scope for this paper. Since DT interventions discussed here can at most impair availability, the intra-cloud exchanges are not safety-relevant in the sense of EN 50159; safety-layer allocation remains at Layer 1 on the trainâĂŞtrackside path.

3.2 DT Design

Both network and train DTs run as containerised applications [5, 28] in the cloud. This facilitates creation, distribution across the server farm, load balancing, and destruction when no longer needed (in the case of train DTs).

---

[12] Backpressure is a core concept in reactive programming to ensure consumers don't get overloaded by a high volume of incoming messages.

[13] https://aeron.io/aeron-open-source/.

With contemporary cloud servers offering main memory capacities on the order of terabytes, a complete railway network – together with its dynamically changing element states – can be represented in memory on a single node. Consequently, the network DT may be deployed on one node. However, re-instating the network status after a node crash can be time-consuming. We therefore recommend a replicated, activeâĂŞactive configuration: three server nodes operate simultaneously, each mirroring the current network state. While all nodes are healthy, redundancy can be exploited to balance train-DT subscriptions. If one node fails, the remaining nodes continue without interruption. Repaired nodes are reintegrated asynchronously by being progressively updated from the active nodes and from status messages received from Layer 2.

The network DT also activates train DTs when physical trains first appear in the network. To this end, a tiny *control plane* is used: on each compute node, a control *daemon* runs permanently. When instructed by the network DT via message passing, the daemon launches a train-DT container *on the local node* using standard container commands, passing the communication endpoints to use (e.g., for a fast intra-cloud transport). Train DTs terminate automatically when they no longer occupy any network element from which routes can be allocated (e.g., after coming to a standstill at a maintenance site).

4   Conclusion

We presented a DT framework for railway safety monitoring that augments certified onboard and interlocking functions with wide-area, predictive supervision in the cloud. The core ingredients are: (i) network-centric checks of track element states for continued supervision of assets, (ii) train-centric supervision of movement authorities and associated conditions for track element states, (iii) train-centric supervision of protection envelopes to prevent overshooting end-of-authority or front-to-back collisions in moving-block traffic. Moreover, software design aspects for effective processing of DTs in the cloud were discussed.

Dedication. This paper is dedicated to Alessandro Fantechi on the occasion of his 70th birthday. Alessandro is one of the foremost scientists in the development and promotion of formal methods for railways. We thank him for inspiration, fruitful collaboration, and for the friendship that he has shown us.

Disclosure of Interests. The authors have no competing interests to declare that are relevant to the content of this article.

References

1. 5GRAIL Consortium: Conclusion report on 5g frmcs field trials. Deliverable D5.3, 5GRAIL Project (H2020, GA No. 951725) (Jan 2024). https://5grail.eu/wp-content/uploads/2024/05/D5.3-Conclusion-Report-on-5G-FRMCS-Field-Trials.pdf, leader: DB Netz; Due: 2023-11-30; Submitted: 2024-01-25

2. Ariyachandra, M.M.F., Wen, Y., Yu, J.: Advancing rail infrastructure: integrating digita twins and cyber-physical systems for predictive maintenance. In: Proceedings of the 2025 European Conference on Computing in Construction. Computing in Construction, vol. 6. European Council on Computing in Construction, Porto, Portugal (July 2025). https://doi.org/10.35490/EC3.2025.272, https://ec-3.org/publications/conference/paper/?id=EC32025_272
3. Bartocci, E., Falcone, Y., Francalanza, A., Reger, G.: Introduction to Runtime Verification, pp. 1–33. Springer International Publishing, Cham (2018). https://doi.org/10.1007/978-3-319-75632-5_1
4. ter Beek, M.H.: Models for formal methods and tools: the case of railway systems. Softw Syst Model (Feb 2025). https://doi.org/10.1007/s10270-025-01276-3
5. Bernstein, D.: Containers and cloud: From LXC to docker to kubernetes. IEEE Cloud Comput. **1**(3), 81–84 (2014). https://doi.org/10.1109/MCC.2014.51
6. Buschmann, F., Meunier, R., Rohnert, H., Sommerlad, P., Stal, M.: Pattern-Oriented Software Architecture, Volume 1: A System of Patterns. John Wiley & Sons, Chichester, UK (2001)
7. CENELEC: EN 50159 Railway applications - Communication, signalling and processing systems - Safety-related communication in transmission systems (2010)
8. CENELEC: EN 50129 Railway applications - Communication, signalling and processing systems - Safety related electronic systems for signalling (2019)
9. CRRC Corporation Limited: 350 km/h High-Speed Train — Product Specification (Apr 2017). https://www.crrcgc.cc/Portals/73/Uploads/Files/2017/4-26/636288008989396590.pdf, spec sheet: includes "Maximum emergency braking distance is 5100 m at the initial speed of 350 km/h"
10. Deutsche Bahn / DSD (SIL4 CLOUD project): SIL4 CLOUD — cloud infrastructure for safety-relevant subsystems including future ETCS level 3 (2022). https://digitale-schiene-deutschland.de/Downloads/Report%20-%20SIL4%20Cloud.pdf, internal / project report
11. Djordjević, B., Krmac, E., Lin, C.Y., Fröidh, O., Kordnejad, B.: An optimisation-based digital twin for automated operation of rail level crossings. Expert Systems with Applications **239**, 122422 (2024). https://doi.org/10.1016/j.eswa.2023.122422, https://www.sciencedirect.com/science/article/pii/S095741742302924X
12. Erriadi, W., Renukappa, S., Suresh, S., Georgakis, P., Almohammad, A., Seabright, L.: Adapting railway sector to repel cyber threats: A critical analysis. High-speed Railway **3**(3), 229–237 (2025). https://doi.org/10.1016/j.hspr.2025.05.002, https://www.sciencedirect.com/science/article/pii/S2949867825000248
13. European Union Agency for Railways (ERA): Introduction to etcs braking curves. Technical Report ERA_ERTMS_040026, ERA, ERTMS Unit (Aug 2020). https://www.era.europa.eu/system/files/2022-11/Introduction%20to%20ETCS%20braking%20curves.pdf, 28 pp
14. Fitzgerald, J., Gomes, C., Larsen, P.G. (eds.): The Engineering of Digital Twins. Springer, Cham (2024). https://doi.org/10.1007/978-3-031-66719-0, https://link.springer.com/book/10.1007/978-3-031-66719-0
15. Flammini, F., De Donato, L., Fantechi, A., Vittorini, V.: A vision of intelligent train control. In: Collart-Dutilleul, S., Haxthausen, A.E., Lecomte, T. (eds.) Reliability, Safety, and Security of Railway Systems. Modelling, Analysis, Verification, and Certification. Lecture Notes in Computer Science, vol. 13294, pp. 192–208. Springer International Publishing, Cham (2022)
16. Ghaboura, S., Ferdousi, R., Laamarti, F., Yang, C., Saddik, A.E.: Digital twin for railway: a comprehensive survey. IEEE Access **11**, 120237–120257 (2023). https://doi.org/10.1109/ACCESS.2023.3327042

17. Gleirscher, M., Haxthausen, A.E., Peleska, J.: Probabilistic risk assessment of an obstacle detection system for goa 4 freight trains. In: Proceedings of the 9th ACM SIGPLAN International Workshop on Formal Techniques for Safety-Critical Systems, pp. 26–36. FTSCS 2023, Association for Computing Machinery, New York, NY, USA (2023). https://doi.org/10.1145/3623503.3623533

18. Hoque, R., et al.: Fleet-dagger: Interactive robot fleet learning with scalable human supervision. In: Liu, K., Kulic, D., Ichnowski, J. (eds.) Proceedings of The 6th Conference on Robot Learning. Proceedings of Machine Learning Research, vol. 205, pp. 368–380. PMLR (14–18 Dec 2023), https://proceedings.mlr.press/v205/hoque23a.html

19. IEEE: IEEE Std 1474.1-2004: IEEE Standard for Communications-Based Train Control (CBTC) Performance and Functional Requirements. Standard (Sep 2004). https://doi.org/10.1109/IEEESTD.2004.95746

20. Leucker, M., Schallhart, C.: A brief account of runtime verification. J. Logic Algebraic Programm. **78**(5), 293–303 (May/June 2009). http://dx.doi.org/10.1016/j.jlap.2008.08.004

21. Mell, P., Grance, T.: The NIST definition of cloud computing. Tech. Rep. Special Publication 800-145, National Institute of Standards and Technology (2011). https://doi.org/10.6028/NIST.SP.800-145, https://csrc.nist.gov/pubs/sp/800/145/final

22. Nielsen, C.B., Larsen, P.G., Fitzgerald, J.S., Woodcock, J., Peleska, J.: Systems of systems engineering: Basic concepts, model-based techniques, and research directions. ACM Comput. Surv. **48**(2), 18:1–18:41 (2015). https://doi.org/10.1145/2794381

23. Peleska, J.: New distribution paradigms for railway interlocking. In: Margaria, T., Steffen, B. (eds.) Leveraging Applications of Formal Methods, Verification and Validation: Applications - 9th International Symposium on Leveraging Applications of Formal Methods, ISoLA 2020, Rhodes, Greece, October 20-30, 2020, Proceedings, Part III. Lecture Notes in Computer Science, vol. 12478, pp. 434–448. Springer (2020). https://doi.org/10.1007/978-3-030-61467-6_28

24. Peleska, J., Brüning, F., Gleirscher, M., Huang, W.: A stochastic approach to classification error estimates in convolutional neural networks. CoRR **abs/2401.06156** (2024). https://doi.org/10.48550/ARXIV.2401.06156

25. Peleska, J., Brüning, F., Gleirscher, M., Huang, W.l.: Hidyve: Ultra complex and autonomous cyber- physical systems — state-of-the-art analysis (Jun 2025). https://doi.org/10.5281/zenodo.15745068

26. Peleska, J., Haxthausen, A.E., Lecomte, T.: Standardisation considerations for autonomous train control. In: Margaria, T., Steffen, B. (eds.) Leveraging Applications of Formal Methods, Verification and Validation. Practice - 11th International Symposium, IScLA 2022, Rhodes, Greece, October 22-30, 2022, Proceedings, Part IV. Lecture Notes in Computer Science, vol. 13704, pp. 286–307. Springer (2022). https://doi.org/10.1007/978-3-031-19762-8_22

27. Rajabli, N., Flammini, F., Nardone, R., Vittorini, V.: Software verification and validation of safe autonomous cars: a systematic literature review. IEEE Access **9**, 4797–4819 (2021). https://doi.org/10.1109/ACCESS.2020.3048047

28. Red Hat Documentation: Introduction to Linux Containers (2023). https://docs.redhat.com/en/documentation/red_hat_enterprise_linux_atomic_host/7/html/overview_of_containers_in_red_hat_systems/introduction_to_linux_containers

29. Seisenberger, M., et al.: Safe and secure future AI-driven railway technologies: challenges for formal methods in railway. In: Margaria, T., Steffen, B. (eds.) Leveraging Applications of Formal Methods, Verification and Validation. Practice - 11th International Symposium, ISoLA 2022, Rhodes, Greece, October 22-30, 2022, Proceedings, Part IV. Lecture Notes in Computer Science, vol. 13704, pp. 246–268. Springer (2022). https://doi.org/10.1007/978-3-031-19762-8_20
30. Tanenbaum, A.S., Bos, H.: Modern Operating Systems. Pearson, 5 edn. (2022)
31. UNISIG: Ertms/etcs system requirements specification (srs), chapter 2: Basic system description. Specification SUBSET-026-2, v3.6.0, UNISIG, https://www.era.europa.eu/era-folder/archived-set-specifications-3-etcs-b3-r2-gsm-r-b1, eRTMS/ETCS Baseline 3 Release 2
32. UNISIG: Ertms/etcs system requirements specification (srs), chapter 3: Principles. Specification SUBSET-026-3, v3.6.0, UNISIG, https://www.era.europa.eu/era-folder/archived-set-specifications-3-etcs-b3-r2-gsm-r-b1, eRTMS/ETCS Baseline 3 Release 2
33. Wang, H., Zhao, N., Ning, B., Tang, T., Chai, M.: Safety monitor for train-centric CBTC system. IET Intell. Transp. Syst. **12**(8), 931–938 (2018). https://doi.org/10.1049/iet-its.2018.5231, https://ietresearch.onlinelibrary.wiley.com/doi/abs/10.1049/iet-its.2018.5231

Author Index

© The Editor(s) (if applicable) and The Author(s), under exclusive license
to Springer Nature Switzerland AG 2026
M. H. ter Beek et al. (Eds.): Fantechi Festschrift, LNCS 16470, pp. 353–354, 2026.
https://doi.org/10.1007/978-3-032-12484-5

MIX
Papier aus verantwortungsvollen Quellen
Paper from responsible sources
FSC® C105338

If you have any concerns about our products,
you can contact us on
ProductSafety@springernature.com

In case Publisher is established outside the EU,
the EU authorized representative is:
Springer Nature Customer Service Center GmbH
Europaplatz 3, 69115 Heidelberg, Germany

Printed by Libri Plureos GmbH
in Hamburg, Germany

MIX
Papier aus verantwortungsvollen Quellen
Paper from responsible sources
FSC® C105338

If you have any concerns about our products,
you can contact us on
ProductSafety@springernature.com

In case Publisher is established outside the EU,
the EU authorized representative is:
Springer Nature Customer Service Center GmbH
Europaplatz 3, 69115 Heidelberg, Germany

Printed by Libri Plureos GmbH
in Hamburg, Germany